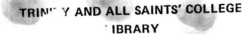
Symbolic Interaction

SYMBOLIC INTERACTION:
A Reader in Social Psychology

THIRD EDITION

Jerome G. Manis
Western Michigan University

Bernard N. Meltzer
Central Michigan University

ALLYN AND BACON, INC.
Boston, London, Sydney, Toronto

For Laura Glance Manis and Ida Wasserman Meltzer

LIBRARY OF CONGRESS CATALOGING IN PUBLICATION DATA

Manis, Jerome G   comp.
  Symbolic interaction.

  Includes bibliographies and index.
    1. Symbolic interactionism—Addresses, essays,
lectures. 2. Social psychology—Addresses,
essays, lectures. I. Meltzer, Bernard N.,
joint comp. II. Title.
HM291.M37 1978   301.1   77-25080

ISBN 0-205-06062-5

Contents

Preface
to the Third Edition

The third edition of this book, we believe, reflects an important phase in the development of symbolic interactionism—a period of assessment of the perspective as well as progress in applying it to new topics (see especially the new selections in Part Two). In the first edition, we sought to bring together some of the most significant contributions to this social psychological perspective. A second edition incorporated more current theoretical and empirical materials, including several from the related viewpoints of ethnomethodology, labeling theory, and the dramaturgical approach. Our present goal has been to clarify the present status of symbolic interactionism by reviewing its origins, stating its basic propositions, adding recent contributions, and presenting criticisms of the perspective. Our task has been both aided and complicated by the large volume of published work relevant to this goal.[1]

Much of the third edition involves major changes from the earlier ones. As in the second edition, more than a third of the readings are new. We have added a general introduction, which briefly presents a review of the intellectual antecedents of symbolic interactionism and an overview of its key ideas. The introductions to the various parts of the book have been revised, as has the Conclusion. The Selected References following each Part have been updated. Finally, we have made an important organizational change in the book by including a new Part containing appraisals of symbolic interactionism from several theoretical, methodological, and ideological standpoints. This material, in our judgment, offers the student a balanced understanding of the subject.

We herewith acknowledge our indebtedness to colleagues who carefully reviewed our prospectus for this edition: Charles Bolton, Portland State University; Dennis Brissett, University of Minnesota at Duluth; Clyde W. Franklin, Ohio State University; John P. Hewitt, University of Massachusetts; Sheldon Stryker, Indiana University; and William C. Yoels, Indiana University Northwest. We are also deeply indebeted to Susan Shott for her invaluable assistance in almost every phase of our work, and to William J. Meltzer, who helped us to evaluate several of the new reading selections. And, finally, we are grateful to Gary L. Folven, Senior Editor of Allyn and Bacon, Inc., for his numerous useful recommendations and his amiable perseverance, and to Cynthia Hartnett, Production Editor, for her proficiency in handling the production of this book.

JGM

BNM

NOTES

1. Illustrative of recent textbooks, collections of readings, and monographs falling within the symbolic interactionism tradition or related traditions are: Arnold Birenbaum and Edward Sagarin (eds.), *People in Places: The Sociology of the Familiar* (New York: Praeger Publishers, 1973); Niels Winther Braroe, *Indian and White: Self-Image and Interaction in a Canadian Plains Community* (Stanford: Stanford University Press, 1974); Dennis Brisset and Charles Edgley (eds.), *Life as Theater: A Dramaturgical Source Book* (Chicago: Aldine Publishing Company, 1975); Arthur Brittan, *Meanings and Situations* (London: Routledge and Kegan Paul, 1973); James B. Cowie and Julian B. Roebuck, *An Ethnography of a Chiropractic Clinic: Definitions of a Deviant Situation* (New York: The Free Press, 1975); Irwin Deutscher, *What We Say/ What We Do: Sentiments and Acts* (Glenview, Illinois: Scott, Foresman and Company, 1973); John P. Hewitt, *Self and Society: A Symbolic Interactionist Social Psychology* (Boston: Allyn and Bacon, Inc., 1976); Robert H. Lauer and Warren H. Handel, *Social Psychology: The Theory and Application of Symbolic Interactionism* (Boston: Houghton Mifflin Company, 1977); Wilfred B. W. Martin, *The Negotiated Order of the School* (Canada: Macmillan, 1976); Hugh Mehan and Houston Wood, *The Reality of Ethnomethodology* (New York: John Wiley and Sons, 1975); Bernard N. Meltzer, John W. Petras, and Larry T. Reynolds, *Symbolic Interactionism: Genesis, Varieties and Criticism* (London: Routledge and Kegan Paul, 1975); Monica B. Morris, *An Excursion into Creative Sociology* (New York: Columbia University Press, 1977); George Psathas (ed.), *Phenomenological Sociology: Issues and Applications* (New York: John Wiley and Sons, 1973); Robert A. Stebbins, *Teachers and Meaning: Definitions of Classroom Situations* (Leiden: E. J. Brill, 1975); and Roy Turner (ed.), *Ethnomethodology* (Middlesex, England: Penguin Education, 1974).

Preface
to the Second Edition

Since the appearance in 1967 of the first edition of this book, we have been gratified by the publication of several other textbooks, monographs, and anthologies with similar orientations.[1] A growing research literature in books and professional journals also attests to the significance and viability of symbolic interactionism, as does the diffusion of this perspective within the disciplines of sociology and social psychology.

Currently, symbolic interactionism can no longer be identified with a few individuals at a few major universities. The articles in this book are representative of the work of a great number of contributors to theory and research. Their efforts, as well as the many more cited in the Selected Bibliography at the close of each Part of the book, are evidence of the widespread prevalence of the symbolic interactionism perspective in American social psychology.

The present edition embodies some important changes from the earlier one. More than a third of the selections are new, and the total number of selections has been increased, along with the total number of pages in the book. We have retained, however, our emphasis on current, significant, and readable materials—both theoretical and empirical. Of greater significance is the inclusion of recent selections from the social psychologies spawned or strongly influenced by symbolic interactionism: ethnomethodology, labeling theory, dramaturgical sociology, and the "sociology of the absurd."[2] These orientations emphasize the active, self-aware nature of human conduct and enjoin those who wish to understand that conduct, whether for scientific or "everyday" reasons, to take the standpoint of the actor. Drawing inspiration from existentialism and phenomenology, as well as from symbolic interactionism, they number among their major progenitors such diverse names as Edmund Husserl and his interpreters, Alfred Schutz and Maurice Merleau-Ponty; Jean-Paul Sartre and Edward A. Tiryakian; Erving Goffman; and Edwin M. Lemert, along with George Herbert Mead and other classical symbolic interactionists. Representative of the newer orientations are the selections in this book by Arlene Kaplan

Daniels (selection 46), Harold Garfinkel (selections 17 and 32), Erving Goffman (selections 20 and 45), George Psathas (selection 9), and Marvin B. Scott and Stanford M. Lyman (selection 36).

The editors herewith acknowledge their special indebtedness to Carl J. Couch, University of Iowa, and John W. Petras, Central Michigan University, who prepared intensive evaluations of the first edition. Their critical comments and suggestions, while as frequently rejected as accepted by us, informed the present edition. We also thank our many other colleagues in the field who appraised the earlier edition for us and who made numerous suggestions for the revised edition. And, finally, we offer our gratitude to Gary L. Folven and Nancy L. Murphy of Allyn and Bacon, Inc., who gave us their painstaking and invaluable assistance in various phases of the production of this book.

JGM
BNM

NOTES

1. Among these are Herbert Blumer, *Symbolic Interactionism: Perspective and Method* (Englewood Cliffs: Prentice-Hall, Inc., 1969); Alfred R. Lindesmith and Anselm L. Strauss (eds.), *Readings in Social Psychology* (New York: Holt, Rinehart & Winston, Inc., 1969); Peter McHugh, *Defining the Situation: The Organization of Meaning in Social Interaction* (Indianapolis: The Bobbs-Merrill Co., Inc., 1968); Tamotsu Shibutani (ed.), *Human Nature and Collective Behavior: Papers in Honor of Herbert Blumer* (Englewood Cliffs: Prentice-Hall, Inc., 1970); Gregory P. Stone and Harvey A. Farberman (eds.), *Social Psychology Through Symbolic Interaction* (Waltham: Ginn/Blaisdell, 1970).

2. The following books are representative of these approaches: Hans Peter Dreitzel (ed.), *Recent Sociology, No. 2: Patterns of Communicative Behavior* (London: Collier-Macmillan, Ltd., 1970); Jack D. Douglas (ed.), *Understanding Everyday Life: Toward the Reconstruction of Sociological Knowledge* (Chicago: Aldine Publishing Company, 1970); Harold Garfinkel, *Studies in Ethnomethodology* (Englewood Cliffs: Prentice-Hall, Inc., 1967); Erving Goffman, *Interaction Ritual: Essays on Face-to-Face Behavior* (Chicago: Aldine Publishing Company, 1967); Stanford M. Lyman and Marvin B. Scott, *A Sociology of the Absurd* (New York: Appleton-Century-Crofts, 1970); George J. McCall and J. L. Simmons, *Identities and Interactions: An Examination of Human Associations in Everyday Life* (New York: The Free Press, 1966).

Preface

to the First Edition

This book is, we believe, the *first* attempt to bring together a sizable number of previously published contributions to symbolic interactionist theory,[1] a theory, or orientation, which has influenced most American sociologists specializing in social psychology.[2]

The historical development of symbolic interactionism has been traced by several writers.[3] Its roots are to be found in the rationalism of John Locke, the foreshadowing of the role-taking process by such "Scottish Moralists" as David Hume and Adam Smith, the idealist epistemology of Kant, and other diverse sources. Its emergence as a distinct perspective in social psychology occurred in the work of John Dewey, Charles Horton Cooley, James Mark Baldwin, William I. Thomas, Florian Znaniecki, and, most notably, George Herbert Mead. Mead, the chief architect of symbolic interactionism, lectured at the University of Chicago between 1893 and 1931, and books based upon lecture-notes taken by students in his classes were published after his death in 1931.[4]

Since then, the two foremost exponents of the orientation have been Herbert G. Blumer and the late Manford H. Kuhn. At the University of Chicago and, currently, the University of California at Berkeley, Blumer has continued to lead what can properly be called the "Chicago school" of symbolic interactionism. Stressing the *processual* character of human behavior and the need for "sympathetic introspection" in the study of human behavior, the school includes most of the writers represented in this book. Kuhn's "self theory," based at the State University of Iowa, has sought to "operationalize" symbolic interactionism by reconceptualizing the self in structural terms, by abandoning such "nonempirical" concepts as Mead's "I," and by developing paper-and-pencil measures of the self.

The organization of the readings in this book is quite simple. Part I introduces the reader to the fundamental concepts, propositions and methods of symbolic interactionism; Parts II, III, and IV organize readings under rubrics corresponding to the words in the title of Mead's vastly influential book. Our transposition of the order of these words more accurately reflects the Meadian emphasis upon the priority of society to the rise of individual selves and minds. Part V gives attention to readings which are less concerned with the explication of concepts than with their applications in exploring a wide range of topics. Following each part is a briefly annotated Selected Bibliography which suggests additional readings for the interested reader.

The introductory comments for each part have been kept brief. By selecting material that would, largely, speak for itself, we have reduced to a minimum the need for editorial comment.

In selecting material for the collection, we were confronted by an embarrassment of riches. Only a small portion of the works we considered worthwhile is included, because of limitations of space. Conspicuous omissions are the writings of Ernst Cassirer, Kurt Riezler, Walter Coutu, and Arnold Rose. What we present to the reader, therefore, aims at representativeness, not comprehensiveness. The criteria guiding our selection of items are several. We have sought a judicious blend of "classics" and more recent works, of speculative and research products. We have given preference to items not readily available to students in multiple copies, to items that would be readable by undergraduate students in multiple copies, to items by a number of different authors rather than by a few "name" people. In addition, we have tried to avoid fragmentation of selections; articles appear in their entirety, and excerpts from books are self-sufficient units of thought.

A word of explanation is needed about our omission of readings from Mead's works. We considered such readings superfluous for the following reasons: the extensive citations of his thinking in various other selections, the inclusion of a summary of his ideas, and the accessibility of his major ideas in college libraries and bookstores.[5]

This collection is designed, primarily, for use as supplementary reading in courses in social psychology, especially those in which intensive attention is given to symbolic interactionism. Our hopes for the book stress its stimulation, not of doctrinaire devotion, but of critical assessment of that perspective.

We are indebted to the various authors, journals, and publishers out of whose materials we constructed this compilation. In a very real sense, the book is the product of their labors. Both of us also acknowledge the important role played by Herbert Blumer's courses at the University of Chicago in directing our attention and interest to the subject of this book.

NOTES

1. A book by Rose compiles thirty-four articles written from the standpoint of symbolic interactionism; however, all but nine of these were written specifically for his book. See Arnold M. Rose (ed.), *Human Behavior and Social Processes* (Boston: Houghton Mifflin Company, 1962).

2. The more widely used social psychology textbooks incorporating symbolic interaction theory have been: E. T. Krueger and Walter C. Reckless, *Social Psychology* (New York: Longmans, Green and Company, 1930); Walter Coutu, *Emergent Human Nature* (New York: Alfred A. Knopf, 1949); Alfred R. Lindesmith and Anselm L. Strauss, *Social Psychology* (New York: The Dryden Press, 1949, revised, 1956); Robert E. L. Faris, *Social Psychology* (New York: The Ronald Press Company, 1952); Hubert Bonner, *Social Psychology* (New York: American Book Company, 1953); Hans Gerth and C. Wright Mills, *Character and Social Structure* (New York: Harcourt, Brace & World, Inc., 1953); Tamotsu Shibutani, *Society and Personality* (Englewood Cliffs: Prentice-Hall, Inc., 1961).

3. See, for example, Fay Berger Karpf, *American Social Psychology* (New York: McGraw-

Hill Book Company, 1932), *passim;* Floyd Nelson House, *The Development of Sociology* (McGraw-Hill Book Company, 1936), Chapter 27; Don Martindale, *The Nature and Types of Sociological Theory* (Boston: Houghton Mifflin Company, 1960), Chapter 14.

4. Of most relevance is *Mind, Self and Society* (Chicago: The University of Chicago Press, 1934), edited by Charles W. Morris.

5. Books summarizing Mead's position or including selections from his work abound. See, for example: Grace Chin Lee, *George Herbert Mead* (New York: King's Crown Press, 1945); Paul E. Pfuetze, *The Social Self* (New York: Bookman Associates, 1954); Anselm Strauss (ed.), *George Herbert Mead on Social Psychology* (Chicago: The University of Chicago Press, 1964); Andrew J. Reck (ed), *Selected Writings: George Herbert Mead* (Indianapolis: The Bobbs-Merrill Co., Inc., 1964).

Symbolic Interaction

introduction ═══════

Intellectual Antecedents and Basic Propositions of Symbolic Interactionism

Our purpose in this introduction is to present, in a brief form, an exposition of two important topics: (1) the major intellectual antecedents of present-day symbolic interactionism, and (2) the basic propositions this perspective puts forward about human behavior. A knowledge of these topics will prepare the way for a better understanding of the remaining material of this book. As our immediate concern is a preliminary discussion of the principles of symbolic interactionism, we have chosen to sacrifice both depth of treatment and documentation in the interest of brevity and readability. At the same time, however, we have sought to avoid a superficial or elliptical presentation.

INTELLECTUAL ANTECEDENTS OF SYMBOLIC INTERACTIONISM

A brief exposition cannot trace every source of symbolic interactionism, nor can it fully describe each of the cited sources. Instead, we shall deal only with the most important precursors, confining our comments to those ideas that relate most closely to symbolic interactionism. The intellectual antecedents with which we shall be concerned are European (German idealism, the Scottish Moralists, and the theory of evolution), American (functional psychology and pragmatism), and the early symbolic interactionists (Baldwin, James, Cooley, Dewey, and Thomas).

European Roots

Emerging as a distinct perspective around the turn of the present century, symbolic interactionism drew inspiration from several influential intellectual movements of the time, as well as some earlier sources. Among the latter, we must acknowledge the influence of eighteenth-century German idealism as represented by Johann Fichte, Immanuel Kant, and Friedrich von Schelling. The most important idea symbolic interactionism draws from this source is that human beings "construct" their worlds, their realities. While eschewing a thoroughgoing subjective idealism, symbolic interactionists hold that whatever may actually be "out there," individuals will structure their worlds of reality by what they perceive and conceive them to be.

The Scottish Moralists of the eighteenth century—Adam Ferguson, David Hume, Francis Hutcheson, Lord Kames (Henry Homes), John Millar, Thomas Reid, and, most notably, Adam Smith—comprise a second source of influence. In the writings of this school of philosophers, the concepts of sympathy and the impartial spectator anticipated the symbolic-interactionist concepts of "role-taking" (adopting the standpoint of another) and the "generalized other" (the standpoint of others in general), respectively. In addition, Adam Smith developed views foreshadowing the concepts of "the I" (the spontaneous aspect of self) and "the Me" (the internalized standpoint of others). Other influential ideas developed by the Scottish Moralists anticipated the symbolic-interactionist conception of mind and self as *social* products.

In the nineteenth century, Charles Darwin's theory of evolution emphasized the view that all behavior, human and otherwise, is performed in adaptation to the environment. Denying the occurrence of what sometimes seemed to be random activity, evolutionists considered the behavior of organisms as efforts to cope with their individual environments. Moreover, evolutionary theory conveyed the idea that each organism and its environment fit together in a dialectical relationship, each influencing the nature and impact of the other. That is, the way the environment impinges on an organism is shaped, in part, by the nature, past experience, and current activity of the organism itself. Environments differ for different organisms, and at times even for the same organism depending upon its activity. The converse of this relationship is also true: Organisms can affect their environment, thereby altering its influence upon them. A final important idea drawn from evolutionism comes from Henri Bergson's theory of emergent or creative evolution. The idea states that, in addition to gradual or step-by-step evolution, abrupt departures from earlier life forms or behavior patterns can and do occur as a result of new combinations of biological or behavioral components. Many symbolic interactionists employ the concept of emergence in describing the presumed unpredictability of much human conduct.

American Antecedents

Two currents of thought influential to symbolic interactionism were developed in the United States. One of them was the school of functional psychology, the chief adherents of which were James R. Angell, John Dewey, William James, and Charles Judd. Drawing upon evolutionism, functionalists held that thought is adaptive behavior; i.e., that mind is not a structure or organ, but a *function* of the organism serving as a means of adaptation. Equally significant in its influence was the functional school's conception of all life as active, not merely reactive. By this they meant that organisms do not simply respond to their environments, but rather select stimuli in terms of their ongoing activity. Activity is always present in the organism, and stimuli do not cause activity, but instead are used by the organism in furthering its activity.

The philosophical system of pragmatism, formulated by John Dewey, William James, Charles Peirce, and Josiah Royce, provided another major source for the symbolic-interactionist perspective. That Dewey and James are both functional psychologists and pragmatists underscores the affinities between these orientations, which hold in common the view that all organisms play a part in shaping the environments with which they must cope. This is one of the fundamental ideas of symbolic interactionism. One important idea deriving from pragmatism is that the meanings of objects reside in the behavior directed toward them and not in the objects themselves. Thus, the meaning of "chair" refers to the way this object is to be used. If, as the pragmatists held, the criterion of truth is practical experience, we can readily understand their insistence upon such an empirical, practical, adaptation-serving conception of meaning. Building upon evolutionary doctrine and functional psychology, pragmatism also put forward a conception of humans as active, creative beings. As such, human beings can play a role in directing their own destinies. A corollary to this idea is the pragmatist view of society as subject to deliberate change by human effort.

Early Symbolic Interactionists

In the remaining paragraphs of this survey of symbolic interactionism's intellectual ancestors, we shall consider the contributions of five early exponents of this perspective: James Mark Baldwin, William James, Charles Horton Cooley, John Dewey, and W. I. Thomas.[1] We shall not deal with

[1] For an expanded version of these paragraphs, see Chapter 1 of Bernard N. Meltzer, John W. Petras, and Larry T. Reynolds, *Symbolic Interactionism: Genesis, Varieties and Criticisms* (London and Boston: Routledge & Kegan Paul, 1975).

George Herbert Mead, a contemporary of most of these men, who is the most significant contributor to the new perspective. His omission from the following treatment is justified by our inclusion in Part I of a reading that expounds his seminal ideas.

At a time when instinctivist explanations of human behavior held sway, William James maintained the view that instincts are modified and inhibited by social learning. This view helped pave the way for the symbolic-interactionist concept of impulse as a replacement for the instinctivist orientation. James also recognized the crucial importance of other persons in forming the individual self. For him, the self was a multiple entity, comprising four component selves: a material self, a social self, a spiritual self, and pure ego. As for the social self, he held that a human being has as many different social selves as there are distinct groups of persons about whose opinion the individual cares.

James Mark Baldwin modified the Jamesian view of the social self as simply one segment of a larger self, claiming that the total self is an undifferentiated *social* self. This view rejected James's fragmentation of the self and proved more compatible with the observed unity and continuity of the self-conceptions of individuals. Baldwin's writings also provided the foundation for both Cooley's concept of "the looking-glass self"—where individuals derive feelings about themselves from imagining the reactions of others to them—and Cooley's method of "sympathetic introspection," which emphasizes adopting the standpoints of social actors as the basis for empathetically understanding their behavior in a given situation.

In John Dewey's works, several elements of symbolic interactionism make explicit appearance. He repeatedly emphasized that a stimulus has no fixed quality of its own, that the nature of a sensation will depend upon the activity underway at the time. Along with Mead, Dewey specified language as the element differentiating humans from other species on the phylogenetic continuum. For him, linguistic communication constituted the process making human society possible. Dewey's other contributions to symbolic interactionism have been mentioned in our comments on functional psychology and pragmatism, both of which number him among their exponents.

Having studied under Dewey, Charles Horton Cooley carried forward Dewey's important ideas, as well as originating many of his own. Cooley perceived his major contribution to social-psychological theory to be the theory of the mental nature of human society, which regarded society as existing in the minds of the individuals constituting a social unit. Putting it another way: The essential nature of society is found in the social bonds that exist between human beings through ideas and feelings. Laying the foundation for some of Mead's ideas, Cooley concluded from studying his own children that the child develops an awareness of other selves before it develops an awareness of its own self. Writing on the protean concept of human nature, Cooley made some important breakthroughs; rejecting the long-extant view that human nature is inborn and nonsocial, he stressed the importance of life in groups, particularly primary groups, in the formation of human nature. Further, he described the intrinsic components of this universal and distinctive human nature as sympathy (role-taking) and the sentiments involving sympathy. Equally influential was his emphasis on the pronounced plasticity, or teachability, of human nature. In a sense, Cooley was also symbolic interactionism's first methodologist. His insistence on the necessity for sympathetic introspection contended that students of human conduct must not settle for observations of external behavior but must endeavor to tap the meanings and definitions held by the participants.

Two major ideas constitute W. I. Thomas' contribution to symbolic interactionism. The first is his concept of the "definition of the situation," which builds upon Dewey's view that the stimuli confronting a person have no fixed quality, and also points out that self-aware conduct entails prior interpretation and deliberation by the actor. Thomas' second influence upon symbolic interactionism lies in the fact that he was one of the first social psychologists to extend the principles of that perspective (developed with reference to the socialization of children) to the adult level, directing attention to social conditions that lead individuals to reconceptualize their developed selves. This extension represents the first major demonstration of symbolic interactionism's relevance to behavior in the everyday world.

BASIC PROPOSITIONS OF SYMBOLIC INTERACTIONISM

The following paragraphs briefly present seven basic propositions that summarize the main features of modern symbolic interactionism. Given the diversity of orientations within this perspective, not all of these propositions will be acceptable to every symbolic interactionist. Moreover, we make no claim for the exhaustiveness of the summary. Our intent here is to indicate in broad outline the major substantive and methodological elements constituting the symbolic-interactionist perspective. To specify the full range of symbolic-interactionist concepts and propositions would take us beyond the scope of this preliminary exposition. The introductions and readings in the various Parts of this book fill in conceptual and propositional details omitted from this discussion and thereby clarify all of the propositions.

Each of the following propositions identifies a fundamental element of symbolic interactionism. These elements are listed below.

1. the meaning component in human conduct
2. the social sources of humanness
3. society as process
4. the voluntaristic component in human conduct
5. a dialectical conception of mind
6. the constructive, emergent nature of human conduct
7. the necessity of sympathetic introspection

1. *Distinctively human behavior and interaction are carried on through the medium of symbols and their meanings.* This is the central idea in symbolic interactionism. It entails the recognition that human beings do not typically respond directly to stimuli, but assign meanings to the stimuli and act on the basis of the meanings. Thus, while sharing with nonhuman organisms certain kinds of behavior (such as the direct stimulus-response activities called reflexes), humans usually engage in a unique form of behavior involving their interpretation of stimuli and act on the basis of that interpretation. By bringing meaning into the picture, symbolic interactionists add a unique dimension to human behavior.

The meanings of stimuli are socially derived through interaction with others rather than inherent in the stimuli themselves or idiosyncratically assigned by the individual. Such terms as symbols and objects (which will appear frequently in this book) imply the social character of meaning, each involving shared group definitions which comprise the social world of given actors.

2. *The individual becomes humanized through interaction with other persons.* Human beings become capable of distinctively human conduct only through association with others. By distinctively human conduct, we mean the ability to imagine how other persons feel in given situations (what Cooley calls human nature), the use of symbols (thinking, or mind), and the ability to behave toward oneself as toward others (self). We are not born human, then, but become human. Human nature, mind, and self are not biological givens; rather, they emerge out of the processes of human interaction. True, a certain kind of organism is necessary for humanization to occur, one marked by, among other things, a highly complex central nervous system and a very high degree of plasticity. But our key point is that society is indispensable to the formation of humanness.

This proposition expands the conventional view of socialization from the individual's social learning of culture, statuses, and roles, to the symbolic interactionist conception of socialization as comprising humanization, enculturation, and personality formation. Thus, interaction with others is seen as giving rise to the acquisition of human nature, thinking, self-direction, and all other attributes that distinguish the behavior of humans from that of other forms of life.

3. *Human society is most usefully conceived as consisting of people in interaction.* This proposition emphasizes the processual nature of human society in preference to the more common metaphors of social structure, social organization, and social system. These latter terms tend to reify society, thereby implying certain unacceptable views about the relationships between society and the individual. For example, many sociologists and social psychologists shift their assumptions radically when they move from studying human conduct on the individual or interpersonal level to studying it at the group, institutional, or societal level. Commonly, they grant humans some modicum of free will on the former level and deny that modicum

on the latter level. That is, they may assume that individuals define situations and act in accordance with those definitions in interpersonal relationships, but they convert these same individuals into mindless robots on the societal or aggregate level. They ignore the fact that the features (structures) of society are maintained and changed by the *actions* of people, and are not autonomous, or self-regulating.

Symbolic interactionists recognize that individuals act and interact within larger networks of other individuals and groups. Some of the networks are far removed from given individuals in time and space, and yet have an appreciable impact on them. Nonetheless, the organization of any society is a *framework* within which social action takes place, not a set of complete determinants of the action. Such structural features as social roles, social classes, and the like set conditions for human behavior and interaction, but do not cause or fully determine the behavior and interaction.

4. *Human beings are active in shaping their own behavior.* This proposition was implied in the preceding one. Conventional views of human behavior tend to assume a deterministic, nonvoluntary character. The individual, according to such views, passively reacts in accordance with the inexorable dictates of specific internal and external stimuli or impersonal forces. These views, prevalent today, can be found to have been held by the first two textbooks published (in 1908) under the title *Social Psychology,* divergent as the books were on many other matters. Edward A. Ross, a sociologist, viewed the individual as coerced by social processes, while William H. McDougall, a psychologist, traced social behavior and institutions to individual "instincts." By contrast, symbolic interactionists generally allow humans some degree of choice in their behavior. Given the ability to select and interpret stimuli—rather than to respond immediately and directly to whatever stimuli are present—and the ability to interact with themselves (i.e., to engage in thought), humans are capable of forming new meanings and new lines of action. This does not mean that human beings transcend all influences; however, it does draw attention to their activity in modifying these influences and in creating and changing their own behavior.

This proposition points to the fact that the socialization of human beings both enmeshes them in society and frees them from society. Individuals with selves are not passive, but can employ their selves in an interaction which may result in behavior divergent from group definitions.

5. *Consciousness, or thinking, involves interaction with oneself.* When one thinks, or engages in "minded" behavior, one necessarily carries on an internal conversation. One makes indications of things to oneself, sometimes rehearsing alternative lines of action. This dialectical process involves two components of the self: the I, a spontaneous and impulsive aspect, and the Me, a set of internalized social definitions. In the interplay between these aspects of the self, individuals import into their behavior the same processes that take place during a dialogue.

Clearly, the human being is, in the most profound sense, a social being.

Only through the use of socially derived symbols in intrapersonal activity duplicating interpersonal activity can the individual perform such uniquely human functions as abstract and reflective thinking. These modes of thought allow the individual to designate objects and events remote in time and space, create imaginary phenomena and other abstractions, and thereby learn without having direct experience of the things to be learned.

6. *Human beings construct their behavior in the course of its execution.* Earlier (proposition 4), we pointed to the active shaping of behavior by humans. That proposition implies, but does not make explicit, the present point. Human behavior is an elaborate process of interpreting, choosing, and rejecting possible lines of action. This process cannot be understood in terms of mechanical responses to external stimuli. Nor can it be fully understood in terms of the mere expression of pre-established inclinations or meanings held by the individual. The behavior that emerges from the interactions within an individual, according to many symbolic interactionists, is not necessarily a product of past events or experiences. That is, the behavior may be an unpredictable emergent constructed in the thought processes of the actor, or in the course of interaction with others.

This proposition directs attention to an important tenet of most humanistic views of conduct: Human beings are, at least in part, participants in creating their own destinies. It would be a mistake to construe this idea as synonymous with the notion that humans have completely free will. That notion is as unpalatable to symbolic interactionists as the notion of thoroughgoing determinism. Much more acceptable is a soft determinism, a view of human conduct as *influenced*—but not entirely determined—by antecedent events.

7. *An understanding of human conduct requires study of the actors' covert behavior.* This proposition states the chief methodological implication of symbolic interactionism. Perhaps we can begin to clarify the nature of this implication by briefly contrasting the antithetical views of George Herbert Mead, exemplar of symbolic interactionism, with those of John B. Watson, founder of the school of behaviorism in psychology. Like Watson's radical behaviorism, Mead's approach included the study of the observable actions of individuals; but, unlike the former, it conceived behavior in terms broad enough to include unobservable activity. Mead felt the study of unobservable human behavior was necessary to understand the distinctive character of human conduct, which Mead considered to be a qualitatively different emergent behavior from nonhuman behavior. Watson's behaviorism, on the other hand, reduced human behavior to the mechanisms found on the nonhuman level. Thus, while Watson insisted upon a strictly "scientific" study of overt behavior, Mead allowed for an intuitive, *verstehende* investigation of aspects of human behavior excluded from Watson's purview.

If human beings act on the basis of their interpretations or meanings, it becomes essential to get at actors' meanings in order to understand and explain their conduct. As we pointed out in proposition 6, the inner phase of human acts is marked by the richest development of the acts. If follows, then, that no amount of simply observing behavior from the outside will provide an understanding of actors' views of their social world, and hence, an understanding of their conduct. The use of procedures allowing sympathetic introspection is part of the methodology of most symbolic interactionists.

Taken collectively, the foregoing set of propositions presents images of human behavior, the social setting within which such behavior occurs, and the relationship between human behavior and its social setting. These images, however, are set forth in such broad terms as to represent only the irreducible minimum of symbolic interactionist ideas. Both the breadth and high level of abstraction of the propositions make it exceedingly difficult to test the propositions empirically. Nevertheless, as various readings in this book will make abundantly clear, many specific propositions compatible with those presented here have been investigated and verified.

PART one

Theory and Methods

From our exposition of its basic propositions, it should be clear that symbolic interactionism constitutes both a theoretical perspective within social psychology and a methodological orientation. Its concern with the inner, or phenomenological aspects of human behavior has both substantive and research implications. The term symbolic interactionism directs our attention to the most fundamental proposition of this perspective: Distinctively human behavior and interaction is carried out through the medium of symbols and their meaning. This proposition guides the theoretical and research focus of symbolic interactionism, while differentiating it from other perspectives in social psychology. A brief consideration of two opposing frames of reference in the study of human behavior can be of help in clarifying the symbolic-interactionist position.

Some social psychologists, impressed with the dramatic achievements of the natural sciences, have sought to apply similar concepts and techniques to the study of human beings. A notable example is the reinforcement theorists, who emphasize operant conditioning and behavior modification. Their focus is on observables, the overt responses of organisms. From the study of rats, chickens, and other animals, they have shown the efficacy of rewards, or positive reinforcers, in shaping behavior. Aiming at "objective" knowledge, operant-oriented researchers contend that such terms as thinking, or mind, are subjective, and therefore inappropriate for science. They insist that the behavior of the human animal can be studied with the same concepts, the same techniques, and the same degree of success as in the study of other animals.

The reinforcement (or behaviorist) approach to human behavior is based upon a positivist conception of science. A basic premise of the positivist viewpoint in social psychology is monism—the contention that the behavior of all organisms is essentially similar, and that conclusions obtained from the study of animal behavior can also explain human conduct. A second premise is elementarism, the assumption that complex actions can be understood by analyzing their various components, such as stimuli, responses, operants, etc. Third is associationism, the idea that the identifiable elements of complex behavior are mechanistically, or automatically, linked together—as in stimulus-response couplets. Closely related is a fourth premise, determinism, which views these elements of animal and human action as sequential and invariable. An example of this premise is the assertion that responses are the automatic and universal consequence of reinforcing stimuli.

Rejecting such premises are the various cognitive approaches to behavior (i.e., those stressing mental processes). In the gestalt perspective, for example, cognition is viewed as a unitary experience that cannot be explained by an analysis of its constituent parts. What humans perceive is organized wholes, not sets of separate stimuli. Moreover, our perceptions, gestaltists hold, are inextricably interwoven with our thoughts and feelings. We may, accordingly, interpret an action by a friend very differently from the same action by a complete stranger.

Phenomenologists stress the distinctive character of human actions and relationships. While positivists are most concerned with the objectivity of their methods and data, phenomenologists focus on the subjective experiences of people as the necessary component of social-psychological knowledge. A propos of this point is the seventh basic proposition of symbolic interactionism: An understanding of human conduct requires study of the actors' covert behavior.

As can be seen, phenomenological approaches to human behavior are in direct conflict with behaviorist approaches—human behavior is considered to be qualitatively different from nonhuman behavior and, therefore, requires its own specialized concepts, theories, and research methods. A second premise of phenomenological theory, similar to the gestalt perspective, is that human behavior is best conceived in holistic terms, i.e., that human thoughts, feelings, and actions are meaningfully interrelated into wholes that are more than the sum of their parts. The third phenomenological premise is voluntarism, i.e., that human conduct is guided by interpretation and intention rather than mechanical, automatic reactions to stimuli. As human action and interaction are voluntaristic, or intentional, they are held to be, to some extent, emergent and unpredictable.

The following selections present some of the fundamental concepts and propositions held in common by symbolic interactionists. In addition, they indicate some of the divergent views on how the validity of such theoretical materials can be tested. These views range from a demand for a phenomenological methodology that stresses "feeling one's way inside the experience of the actor" to one that comes somewhat closer to the positivist method.

George Herbert Mead is responsible for laying the foundation of the symbolic-interactionist perspective. During nearly four decades as a philosopher at the University of Chicago, Mead formulated and taught his theory. His approach, which he called social behaviorism, is summarized in the article by Bernard N. Meltzer. We hope that this résumé of Mead's assumptions and concepts will encourage the reader to delve into his major work, *Mind, Self and Society*.

The contributions of self-defined symbolic interactionists, as well as nonadherents to symbolic interactionism, serve as the basis for Manford H. Kuhn's excellent, detailed article integrating their achievements. Unfortunately, his efforts to bridge the gap between these differing camps has not been followed up by his successors—one of the major shortcomings of symbolic interactionism.

Underscoring the diversity of viewpoints within symbolic interactionism, the selection by Bernard N. Meltzer, John W. Petras, and Larry T. Reynolds analyzes the ideas of two leading symbolic interactionists and of two leaders of closely related offshoots. At the University of Chicago, Herbert Blumer became the Chicago school's foremost spokesman, elaborating a strong phenomenological view of human and group activity. Meanwhile, Manford Kuhn at the University of Iowa adopted a somewhat more positivist position, one which provides a major share of the research selections in this book. The offshoots, the dramaturgical approach developed by Erving Goffman, and ethnomethodology initiated by Harold Garfinkel, are amplified in later articles by themselves and by their adherents and critics. All four of these orientations share the substantive view that human beings construct their realities in a process of interaction with other human beings. And each accepts, to some degree, the methodological necessity of "getting inside" the actors in order to understand their realities.

Although the first three articles focus primarily on substantive theory, the following readings were selected for their methodological emphasis. A central feature of symbolic interactionism is its implication for empirical inquiry. On the premise that "each theory demands a special view of methods," Norman K. Denzin formulates seven methodological principles congruent with the theory.

Blumer's article questions the applicability of conventional methods of variable analysis. His criticisms need to be viewed in conjunction with both his theoretical and broader methodological contributions, such as the leading article in Part II and the first chapter of his recent book, *Symbolic Interaction*. Taken together, the two writings suggest that the nature of humans both requires and provides certain essential tools for the study of themselves and their society.

Two articles exemplify the research techniques of Chicago and Iowa researchers. Howard S. Becker and Blanche Geer discuss the distinctive features of participant observation, while Manford H. Kuhn and Thomas S. McPartland introduce the Twenty Statements Test. Later sections, particularly Part V, illustrate the research methods of contemporary symbolic interactionists. Currently, symbolic interactionism can no longer be identified with a few individuals at a few major universities. The articles in this and later sections represent the work of a great number of theorists and researchers. Their efforts, as well as the many more cited in the bibliographies at the close of each part, evidence the widespread prevalence of the symbolic-interactionist perspective in American social psychology.

The selections in Part I tend to be of broader scope and higher abstraction than those in other Parts of this book, where the selections will focus more sharply on the explication and empirical testing of important concepts in symbolic-interactionist theory. The reader is advised to refer back to Part I from time to time to place the later materials in context.

Mead's Social Psychology

A. PRELIMINARY REMARKS

While Mead's system of Social Psychology is given its fullest exposition in *Mind, Self and Society*, each of three other books (as well as a few articles) round out the complete picture.

It should be pointed out at this juncture that Mead himself published no full-length systematic statement of his theory. All four of the books bearing his authorship are posthumously collected and edited works. They comprise a loose accumulation of his lecture notes, fragmentary manuscripts, and tentative drafts of unpublished essays. Since the chief aim of his editors has been completeness—rather than organization—the books consist, in considerable part, of alternative formulations, highly repetitive materials, and sketchily developed ideas.

Nevertheless, a brief description of these volumes is in order, since they constitute the major source-materials concerning Mead's social psychology.

Philosophy of the Present (1932) contains the Paul Carus Foundation lectures delivered by Mead in 1930, a year before his death. These lectures present a philosophy of history from the pragmatist's point of view. Moreover, this volume presents his ideas on the analogous developments of social experience and of scientific hypotheses.

Mind, Self and Society (1934) is chiefly a collection of lectures delivered to his classes in Social Psychology at the University of Chicago.

Bernard N. Meltzer, "Mead's Social Psychology." From *The Social Psychology of George Herbert Mead*, pp. 10–31, 1964, Center for Sociological Research, Western Michigan University.

Movements of Thought in the 19th Century (1936) is largely a collection of lectures delivered to his classes in the History of Ideas.

Philosophy of the Act (1938), according to Paul Schilpp, represents a fairly *systematic* statement of the philosophy of pragmatism. This "systematic" statement I found (as did G. S. Lee) to be made up of essays and miscellaneous fragments, which are technical and repetitious, obscure and difficult.

A final observation regarding the content of these books should be made: Mead's orientation is generally *philosophical*. Rather than marshaling his own empirical evidence, he uses the findings of various sciences and employs frequent apt and insightful illustrations from everyday life. These illustrations usually are not used to prove points, but rather to serve as data to be analyzed in terms of his scheme.

Before launching upon a presentation of Mead's social-psychological theories, it might be wise to explain his designation of his viewpoint as that of "Social Behaviorism." By this term Mead means to refer to the description of behavior at the distinctively human level. Thus, for social behaviorism, the basic datum is the social act. As we shall later see, the study of social acts entails concern with the covert aspects of behavior. Further, the concept of the "social act" implies that human conduct and experience has a fundamental social dimension—that the social context is an inescapable element in distinctively human actions.

Like Watsonian radical behaviorism, Mead's social behaviorism starts with the observable ac-

; but *unlike* the former, social [?] [?]ives behavior in broad enough [?]*overt* activity. This inclusion is [?] to understanding the distinc- [?] human conduct, which Mead [?]atively different emergent from [?]avior. Watson's behaviorism, on the other hand, reduces human behavior to the very same mechanisms as are found on the infra-human level. As a corollary, Watson sees the social dimension of human behavior as merely a sort of external influence upon the individual. Mead, by contrast, views generically human behavior as *social* behavior, human acts as *social* acts. For Mead, both the content and the very existence of distinctively human behavior are account-able only on a social basis. (These distinctions should become more clear in the course of this report.)

It can readily be inferred from this brief ex-planation of Mead's usage of the term "social be-haviorism" that, before we can explore the nature and function of the mind—which Mead considers a uniquely human attribute—supporting theories of society, and self—another uniquely human at-tribute—require elaboration. Hence, the natural, logical order of Mead's thinking seems to have been society, self, and mind—rather than "Mind, Self, and Society."

B. CONTENT OF MEAD'S SOCIAL PSYCHOLOGY

1. Society

According to Mead, all group life is essentially a matter of cooperative behavior. Mead makes a distinction, however, between infrahuman soci-ety and human society. Insects—whose society most closely approximates the complexity of human social life—act together in certain ways be-cause of their biological make-up. Thus, their co-operative behavior is physiologically determined. This is shown by many facts, among which is the fact of the fixity, the stability, of the relationships of insect-society members to one another. Insects, according to the evidence, go on for countless generations without any difference in their pat-terns of association. This picture of infrahuman

society remains essentially valid as one ascends the scale of animal life, until we arrive at the human level.

In the case of human association, the situation is fundamentally different. Human cooperation is not brought about by mere physiological fac-tors. The very diversity of the patterns of human group life makes it quite clear that human cooper-ative life cannot be explained in the same terms as the cooperative life of insects and the lower animals. The fact that human patterns are not stabilized and cannot be explained in biological terms led Mead to seek another basis of explana-tion of human association. Such cooperation can only be brought about by some process wherein: (a) each acting individual ascertains the *intention* of the acts of others, and then (b) makes his own response on the basis of that intention. What this means is that, in order for human beings to coop-erate, there must be present some sort of mecha-nism whereby each acting individual: (a) can come to understand the lines of action of others, and (b) can guide his own behavior to fit in with those lines of action. Human behavior is not a matter of responding directly to the activities of others. Rather, it involves responding to the *intentions* of others, *i.e.*, to the future, intended behavior of others—not merely to their present actions.

We can better understand the character of this distinctively human mode of interaction be-tween individuals by contrasting it with the infra-human "conversation of gestures." For example when a mother hen clucks, her chicks will re-spond by running to her. This does not imply how-ever, that the hen clucks *in order* to guide the chicks, *i.e.*, with the *intention* of guiding them. Clucking is a natural sign or signal—rather than a significant (meaningful) symbol—as it is not meaningful to the hen. That is, the hen (according to Mead) does not take the role, or viewpoint, of the chicks toward its own gesture and respond to it, in imagination, as they do. The hen does not envision the response of the chicks to her clucking. Thus, hens and chicks do not share the same experience.

Let us take another illustration by Mead: Two hostile dogs, in the pre-fight stage, may go through an elaborate conversation of gestures (snarling, growling, baring fangs, walking stiff-leggedly around one another, etc.). The dogs are adjusting themselves to one another by responding to one another's gestures. (A gesture is that portion of an act which represents the entire act; it is the initial, overt phase of the act, which epitomizes it, *e.g.,* shaking one's fist at someone.) Now, in the case of the dogs the response to a gesture is dictated by pre-established tendencies to respond in certain ways. Each gesture leads to a direct, immediate, automatic, and unreflecting response by the recipient of the gesture (the other dog). Neither dog responds to the *intention* of the gestures. Further, each dog does not make his gestures with the intent of eliciting certain responses in the other dog. Thus, animal interaction is devoid of conscious, deliberate meaning.

To summarize: Gestures, at the non-human or non-linguistic level, do not carry the connotation of conscious meaning or intent, but serve merely as cues for the appropriate responses of others. Gestural communication takes place immediately, without any interruption of the act, without the mediation of a definition or meaning. Each organism adjusts "instinctively" to the other; it does not stop and figure out which response it will give. Its behavior is, largely, a series of direct automatic responses to stimuli.

Human beings, on the other hand, respond to one another on the basis of the intentions or meanings of gestures. This renders the gesture *symbolic, i.e.,* the gesture becomes a symbol to be interpreted; it become something which, in the imaginations of the participants, stands for the entire act.

Thus, individual A begins to act, *i.e.,* makes a gesture: for example, he draws back an arm. Individual B (who perceives the gesture) completes, or fills in, the act in his imagination; *i.e.,* B imaginatively projects the gesture into the future: "He will strike me." In other words, B perceives what the gesture stands for, thus getting its meaning. In contrast to the direct responses of the chicks and the dogs, the human being inserts an interpretation between the gesture of another and his response to it. Human behavior involves responses to *interpreted* stimuli.[1]

We see, then, that people respond to one another on the basis of imaginative activity. In order to engage in concerted behavior, however, each participating individual must be able to attach the same meaning to the same gesture. Unless interacting individuals interpret gestures similarly, unless they fill out the imagined portion in the same way, there can be no cooperative action. This is another way of saying what has by now become a truism in sociology and social psychology: Human society rests upon a basis of *consensus, i.e.,* the sharing of meanings in the form of common understandings and expectations.

In the case of the human being, each person has the ability to respond to his own gestures; and thus, it is possible to have the same meaning for the gestures as other persons. (For example: As I say "chair," I present to myself the same image as to my hearer; moreover, the same image as when someone else says "chair.") This ability to stimulate oneself as one stimulates another, and to respond to oneself as another does, Mead ascribes largely to man's vocal-auditory mechanism. (The ability to hear oneself implies at least the potentiality for responding to oneself.) When a gesture has a shared, common meaning, when it is—in other words—a *linguistic* element, we can designate it as a "significant symbol." (Take the words, "Open the window": the pattern of action symbolized by these words must be in the mind of the speaker as well as the listener. Each must respond, in imagination, to the words in the same way. The speaker must have an image of the listener responding to his words by opening the window, and the listener must have an image of his opening the window.)

The imaginative completion of an act—which Mead calls "meaning" and which represents mental activity—necessarily takes place through *role-taking*. To complete imaginatively the total act

---

[1] The foregoing distinctions can also be expressed in terms of the differences between "signs," or "signals," and symbols. A

sign stands for something else because of the fact that it is present at approximately the same time and place with that "something else." A symbol, on the other hand, stands for something else because its users have agreed to let it stand for that "something else." Thus, signs are directly and intrinsically linked with present or proximate situations; while symbols, having arbitrary and conventional, rather than intrinsic, meanings, transcend the immediate situation. (We shall return to this important point in our discussion of "mind.") Only symbols, of course, involve interpretation, self-stimulation and shared meaning.

which a gesture stands for, the individual must put himself in the position of the other person, must identify with him. The earliest beginnings of role-taking occur when an already established act of another individual is stopped short of completion, thereby requiring the observing individual to fill in, or complete, the activity imaginatively. (For example, a crying infant may have an image of its mother coming to stop its crying.)

As Mead points out, then, the relation of human beings to one another arises from the developed ability of the human being to respond to his own gestures. This ability enables different human beings to respond in the same way to the same gesture, thereby sharing one another's experience.

This latter point is of great importance. Behavior is viewed as "social" not simply when it is a response to others, but rather when it has incorporated in it the behavior of others. The human being responds to himself as other persons respond to him, and in so doing he imaginatively shares the conduct of others. That is, in imagining their response he shares that response.[2]

2. Self

To state that the human being can respond to his own gestures necessarily implies that he possesses a *self*. In referring to the human being as having a self, Mead simply means that such an individual may act socially toward himself, just as toward others. He may praise, blame, or encourage himself; he may become disgusted with himself, may seek to punish himself, and so forth. Thus, the human being may become the object of his own actions. The self is formed in the same way as other objects—through the "definitions" made by others.

The mechanism whereby the individual becomes able to view himself as an object is that of role-taking, involving the process of communication, especially by vocal gestures or speech.

(Such communication necessarily involves role-taking.) It is only by taking the role of others that the individual can come to see himself as an object. The standpoint of others provides a platform for getting outside oneself and thus viewing oneself. The development of the self is concurrent with the development of the ability to take roles.

The crucial importance of language in this process must be underscored. It is through language (significant symbols) that the child acquires the meanings and definitions of those around him. By learning the symbols of his groups, he comes to internalize their definitions of events or things, including their definitions of his own conduct.

It is quite evident that, rather than assuming the existence of selves and explaining society thereby, Mead starts out from the prior existence of society as the context within which selves arise. This view contrasts with the nominalistic position of the Social Contract theorists and of various individualistic psychologies.

Genesis of the Self. The relationship between role-playing and various stages in the development of the self is described below:

1. *Preparatory Stage* (not explicitly named by Mead, but inferable from various fragmentary essays). This stage is one of meaningless imitation by the infant (for example, "reading" the newspaper). The child does certain things that others near it do without any understanding of what he is doing. Such imitation, however, implies that the child is incipiently taking the roles of those around it, *i.e.*, is on the verge of putting itself in the position of others and acting like them.
2. *Play Stage.* In this stage the actual playing of roles occurs. The child plays mother, teacher, storekeeper, postman, streetcar conductor, Mr. Jones, etc. What is of central importance in such play-acting is that it places the child in the position where it is able to act back toward itself in such roles as "mother" or "teacher." In this stage, then, the child first begins to form a self, that is, to direct activity toward itself— and it does so by taking the roles of others. This is clearly indicated by use of the third person in referring to oneself instead of the first person: "John wants . . . ," "John is a bad boy."

---

[2] To anyone who has taken even one course in sociology it is probably superfluous to stress the importance of symbols, particularly language, in the acquisition of all other elements of culture. The process of socialization is essentially a process of symbolic interaction.

However, in this stage the young child's configuration of roles is unstable; the child passes from one role to another in unorganized, inconsistent fashion. He has, as yet, no unitary standpoint from which to view himself, and hence, he has no unified conception of himself. In other words, the child forms a number of separate and discrete object of itself, depending on the roles in which it acts toward itself.

3. *Game Stage.* This is the "completing" stage of the self. In time, the child finds himself in situations wherein he must take a number of roles simultaneously. That is, he must respond to the expectations of several people at the same time. This sort of situation is exemplified by the game of baseball—to use Mead's own illustration. Each player must visualize the intentions and expectations of several other players. In such situations the child must take the roles of groups of individuals as over against particular roles. The child becomes enabled to do this by abstracting a "composite" role out of the concrete roles of particular persons. In the course of his association with others, then, he builds up a *generalized other*, a generalized role or standpoint from which he views himself and his behavior. This generalized other represents, then, the set of standpoints which are common to the group.

Having achieved this generalized standpoint, the individual can conduct himself in an organized, consistent manner. He can view himself from a consistent standpoint. This means, then, that the individual can transcend the local and present expectations and definitions with which he comes in contact. An illustration of this point would be the Englishman who "dresses for dinner" in the wilds of Africa. Thus, through having a generalized other, the individual becomes emancipated from the pressures of the peculiarities of the immediate situation. He can act with a certain amount of consistency in a variety of situations because he acts in accordance with a generalized set of expectations and definitions that he has internalized.

The "I" and the "Me." The self is essentially a social process within the individual involving two analytically distinguishable phases: The "I" and the "Me."

The "I" is the impulsive tendency of the individual. It is the initial, spontaneous, unorganized aspect of human experience. Thus, it represents the undirected tendencies of the individual.

The "Me" represents the incorporated other within the individual. Thus, it comprises the organized set of attitudes and definitions, understandings and expectations—or simply meanings—common to the group. In any given situation, the "Me" comprises the generalized other and, often, some particular other.

Every act begins in the form of an "I" and usually ends in the form of the "Me." For the "I" represents the initiation of the act prior to its coming under control of the definitions or expectations of others (the "Me"). The "I" thus gives *propulsion* while the "Me" gives *direction* to the act. Human behavior, then, can be viewed as a perpetual series of initiations of acts by the "I" and of acting-back-upon the act (that is, guidance of the act) by the "Me." The act is a resultant of this interplay.

The "I," being spontaneous and propulsive, offers the potentiality for new, creative activity. The "Me," being regulatory, disposes the individual to both goal-directed activity and conformity. In the operation of these aspects of the self, we have the basis for, on the one hand, social control and, on the other, novelty and innovation. We are thus provided with a basis for understanding the mutuality of the relationship between the individual and society.[3]

---

[3] At first glance, Mead's "I" and "Me" may appear to bear a close affinity with Freud's concepts of Id, Ego, and Superego. The resemblance is, for the most part, more apparent than real. While the Superego is held to be harshly frustrating and repressive of the instinctual, libidinous, and aggressive Id, the "Me" is held to provide necessary direction—often of a *gratifying* nature—to the otherwise undirected impulses constituting the "I." Putting the matter in figurative terms: Freud views the Id and the Superego as locked in combat upon the battleground of the Ego; Mead sees the "I" and "Me" engaged in close collaboration. This difference in perspective may derive from different preoccupations: Freud was primarily concerned with tension, anxiety, and "abnormal" behavior; Mead was primarily concerned with behavior generically.

It is true, on the other hand, that the Id, Ego, and Superego—particularly as modified by such neo-Freudians as Karen Horney, Erich Fromm, and H. S. Sullivan—converge at a few points with the "I" and "Me." This is especially evident in the emphasis of both the Superego and "Me" concepts upon the internalization of the norms of significant others through the process of identification, or role-taking.

Incidentally, it should be noted that both sets of concepts refer to processes of behavior, *not* to concrete entities or structures. See, also, the discussion of "mind" which follows.

Implications of Selfhood. Some of the major implications of selfhood in human behavior are as follows:

1. The possession of a self makes of the individual a society in miniature. That is, he may engage in interaction with himself just as two or more different individuals might. In the course of this interaction, he can come to view himself in a new way, thereby bringing about changes in himself.
2. The ability to act toward oneself makes possible an inner experience which need not reach overt expression. That is, the individual, by virtue of having a self, is thereby endowed with the possibility of having a mental life: He can make indications to himself—which constitutes *mind.*
3. The individual with a self is thereby enabled to direct and control his behavior. Instead of being subject to all impulses and stimuli directly playing upon him, the individual can check, guide, and organize his behavior. He is, then, *not* a mere passive agent.

All three of these implications of selfhood may be summarized by the statement that the self and the mind (mental activity) are twin emergents in the social process.

3. Mind

Development of Mind. As in the instance of his consideration of the self, Mead rejects individualistic psychologies, in which the social process (society, social interaction) is viewed as presupposing, and being a product of, mind. In direct contrast is his view that mind presupposes, and is a product of, the social process. Mind is seen by Mead as developing correlatively with the self, constituting (in a very important sense) the self in action.

Mead's hypothesis regarding mind (as regarding the self) is that the mental emerges out of the organic life of man through communication. The mind is present only at certain points in human behavior, *viz.,* when significant symbols are being used by the individual. This view dispenses with the substantive notion of mind as existing as a box-like container in the head, or as some kind of fixed, ever-present entity. Mind is seen as a *process,* which manifests itself whenever the individual is interacting with himself by using significant symbols.

Mead begins his discussion of the mind with a consideration of the relation of the organism to its environment. He points out that the central principle in all organic behavior is that of continuous adjustment, or adaptation, to an environing field. We cannot regard the environment as having a fixed character for all organisms, as being the same for all organisms. All behavior involves selective attention and perception. The organism accepts certain events in its field, or vicinity, as stimuli and rejects or overlooks certain others as irrelevant to its needs. (For example, an animal battling for life ignores food.) Bombarded constantly by stimuli, the organism selects those stimuli or aspects of its field which pertain to, are functional to, the acts in which the organism is engaged. Thus, the organism has a hand in determining the nature of its environment. What this means, then, is that Mead, along with Dewey, regards all life as ongoing activity, and views stimuli—not as initiators of activity—but as elements selected by the organism in the furtherance of that activity.

Perception is thus an activity that involves selective attention to certain aspects of a situation, rather than a mere matter of something coming into the individual's nervous system and leaving an impression. Visual perception, *e.g.,* is more than a matter of just opening one's eyes and responding to what falls on the retina.

The determination of the environment by the biologic individual (infrahumans and the unsocialized infant) is not a cognitive relationship. It is selective, but does not involve consciousness, in the sense of reflective intelligence. At the distinctively human level, on the other hand, there is a hesitancy, an inhibition of overt conduct, which is *not* involved in the selective attention of animal behavior. In this period of inhibition, mind is present.

Human behavior involves inhibiting an act and trying out the varying approaches in imagination. In contrast, as we have seen, the acts of the biologic individual are relatively immediate, direct, and made up of innate or habitual ways of reacting. In other words, the unsocialized organism lacks consciousness of meaning. This being the case, the organism has no means for the abstract analysis of its field when new situations are met, and hence no means for the reorganization of action-tendencies in the light of that analysis.[4]

Minded behavior (in Mead's sense) arises around problems. It represents, to repeat an important point, a temporary inhibition of action wherein the individual is attempting to prevision the future. It consists of presenting to oneself, tentatively and in advance of overt behavior, the different possibilities or alternatives of future action with reference to a given situation. The future is, thus, present in terms of images of prospective lines of action from which the individual can make a selection. The mental process is, then, one of delaying, organizing, and selecting a response to the stimuli of the environment. This implies that the individual *constructs* his act, rather than responding in predetermined ways. Mind makes it possible for the individual purposively to control and organize his responses. Needless to say, this view contradicts the stimulus-response conception of human behavior.

When the act of an animal is checked, it may engage in overt trial and error or random activity. In the case of blocked human acts, the trial and error may be carried on covertly, implicitly. Consequences can be imaginatively "tried out" in advance. This is what is primarily meant by "mind," "reflective thinking," or "abstract thinking."

What this involves is the ability to indicate elements of the field or situation, abstract them from the situation, and recombine them so that procedures can be considered in advance of their execution. Thus, to quote a well-known example, the intelligence of the detective as over against the intelligence of the bloodhound lies in the capacity of the former to isolate and indicate (to himself and to others) what the particular characters are which will call out the response of apprehending the fugitive criminal.

The mind is social in both origin and function. It arises in the social process of communication. Through association with the members of his groups, the individual comes to internalize the definitions transmitted to him through linguistic symbols, learns to assume the perspectives of others, and thereby acquires the ability to think. When the mind has risen in this process, it operates to maintain and adjust the individual in his society; and it enables the society to persist. The persistence of a human society depends, as we have seen, upon consensus; and consensus necessarily entails minded behavior.

The mind is social in function in the sense that the individual continually indicates to himself in the role of others and controls his activity with reference to the definitions provided by others. In order to carry on thought, he must have some standpoint from which to converse with himself. He gets this standpoint by importing into himself the roles of others.

By "taking the role of the other," as I earlier pointed out, we can see ourselves as others see us, and arouse in ourselves the responses that we call out in others. It is this conversation with ourselves, between the representation of the other (in the form of the "Me") and our impulses (in the form of the "I") that constitutes the mind. Thus, what the individual actually does in minded behavior is to carry on an internal conversation. By addressing himself from the standpoint of the generalized other, the individual has a universe of discourse, a system of common symbols and meanings, with which to address himself. These are presupposed as the context for minded behavior.

Mead holds, then, that mental activity is a peculiar type of activity that goes on in the experience of the person. The activity is that of the person responding to himself, of indicating things to himself.

---

[4] The reader should recognize here, in a new guise, our earlier distinction between signs and symbols. Signs have "intrinsic" meanings which induce direct reactions; symbols have arbitrary meanings which require interpretations by the actor prior to his response or action. The former, it will be recalled, are "tied to" the immediate situation, while the latter "transcend" the immediate situation. Thus, symbols may refer to past or future events, to hypothetical situations, to nonexistent or imaginary objects, and so forth.

To repeat, mind originates in the social process, in association with others. There is little doubt that human beings lived together in groups before mind ever evolved. But there emerged, because of certain biological developments, the point where human beings were able to respond to their own acts and gestures. It was at this point that mind, or minded behavior, emerged. Similarly, mind comes into existence for the individual at the point where the individual is capable of responding to his own behavior, *i.e.*, where he can designate things to himself.

Summarizing this brief treatment of mind, mental activity, or reflective thinking, we may say that it is a matter of making indications of meanings to oneself as to others. This is another way of saying that mind is the process of using significant symbols. For thinking goes on when an individual uses a symbol to call out in himself the responses which others would make. Mind, then, is symbolic behavior.[5] As such, mind is an emergent from non-symbolic behavior and is fundamentally irreducible to the stimulus-response mechanisms which characterize the latter form of behavior.

It should be evident that Mead avoids both the behavioristic fallacy of reduction and the individualistic fallacy of taking for granted the phenomenon that is to be explained.

Objects.   Returning to Mead's discussion of the organism-in-environment, we can now give more explicit attention to his treatment of *objects*. As we have seen, we cannot regard the environment as having a fixed character for all organisms. The environment is a function of the animal's own character, being greatly determined by the make-up of the animal. Each animal largely selects its own environment. It selects out the stimuli to-

ward which it acts, its make-up and on-going activity determining the kinds of stimuli it will select. Further, the qualities which are possessed by the objects toward which the animal acts arise from the kind of experiences that the animal has with the objects. (To illustrate, grass is not the same phenomenon for a cat and for a cow.) The environment and its qualities, then, are always functional to the structure of the animal.

As one passes on to the human level, the relation of the individual to the world becomes markedly more complicated. This is so because the human being is capable of forming objects. Animals, lacking symbols, see stimuli, such as patches of color—not objects. An object has to be detached, pointed out, "imaged" to oneself. The human being's environment is constituted largely by objects.

Now, let us look at the relation of the individual to objects. An object represents a plan of action. That is, an object doesn't exist for the individual in some pre-established form. Perception of any object has telescoped in it a series of experiences which one would have if he carried out the plan of action toward that object. The object has no qualities for the individual, aside from those which would result from his carrying out a plan of action. In this respect, the object is constituted by one's activities with reference to it. (For example, chalk is the sum of qualities which are perceived as a result of one's actions: a hard, smooth, white writing implement.)

The objects which constitute the "effective environment," the individual's experienced environment, are established by the individual's activities. To the extent that his activity varies, his environment varies. In other words, objects change as activities toward them change. (Chalk, for instance, may become a missile.)

Objects, which are constituted by the activities of the human individual, are largely *shared* objects. They stand for common patterns of activity of individuals. This is true, Mead points out, by virtue of the fact that objects arise, and are present in experience, only in the process of being indicated to oneself (and, hence, explicitly or implicitly, to others). In other words, the perspective from which one indicates an object implicates def-

---

[5] A growing number of linguists, semanticists, and students of speech disorders are becoming aware of the central role of symbols in the *content*, as well as the process of thought. Edward Sapir and Benjamin Whorf have formulated "the principle of linguistic relativity," which holds that the structure of a language influences the manner in which the users of the language will perceive, comprehend, and act toward reality. Wendell Johnson, in the field of semantics, and Kurt Goldstein, in the study of aphasia, are representative investigators who have recognized the way in which symbols structure perception and thought. Mead's theory clearly foreshadows these developments.

initions by others. Needless to say, these definitions involve language, or significant symbols. The
individual acquires a commonality of perspective
with others by learning the symbols by which they
designate aspects of the world.[6]

4. The Act

All human activity other than reflex and habitual action is built up in the process of its execution; *i.e.*, behavior is constructed as it goes along,
for decisions must be made at several points. The
significance of this fact is that people act—rather
than merely react.

For Mead, the unit of study is "the act,"
which comprises both overt and covert aspects
of human action. Within the act, all the separated
categories of the traditional, orthodox psychologies find a place. Attention, perception, imagination, reasoning, emotion, and so forth, are seen
as parts of the act—rather than as more or less
extrinsic influences upon it. Human behavior
presents itself in the form of acts, rather than
of concatenations of minute responses.

The act, then, encompasses the total process
involved in human activity. It is viewed as a complete span of action: Its initial point is an impulse
and its terminal point some objective which gives
release to the impulse. In between, the individual
is in the process of constructing, organizing his
behavior. It is during this period that the act undergoes its most significant phase of development.
In the case of human behavior, this period is
marked by the play of images of possible goals
or lines of action upon the impulse, thus directing
the activity to its consummation.

In pointing out that the act begins with an
impulse, Mead means that organisms experience

disturbances of equilibrium. In the case of the
lower animals, their biological make-up channel-
izes the impulse toward appropriate goals. In the
case of the human being, the mere presence of
an impulse leads to nothing but mere random,
unorganized activity. This is most clearly—but
definitely not exclusively—seen in the instance
of the behavior of infants. Until the defining actions of others set up goals for it, the human infant's behavior is unchannelized. It is the function
of images to direct, organize and construct this
activity. The presence in behavior of images implies, of course, a process of indicating to oneself,
or mind.

The act may have a short span (*e.g.*, attending
a particular class meeting, or starting a new page
of notes) or may involve the major portion of a
person's life (*e.g.*, trying to achieve a successful
career). Moreover, acts are parts of an interlacing
of previous acts, and are built up, one upon another. This is in contradistinction to the view that
behavior is a series of discrete stimulus-response
bonds. Conceiving human behavior in terms of
acts, we become aware of the necessity for viewing any particular act within its psychosocial
context.[7]

Using the concept of the act, Mead sets up
classes of acts—the automatic act, the blocked act,
the incomplete act, and the retrospective act—
and analyzes them in terms of his frame of reference. Space does not permit presentation of these
intriguing analyses.

---

[6] The contrast between this view of learning and the neo-behav-
ioristic "learning theory" of Clark Hull and other psychologists
should be clearly evident. Basically, learning theorists attempt
to reduce human learning to the mechanisms found in infrahuman learning. This is reflected in their tendency to ignore the
role of linguistic symbols in human behavior, their conceptualization of human activity in terms of stimulus-response couplets,
and their view of learning as equivalent with conditioning. (For
an excellent critique of learning theory from the symbolic interactionist standpoint, see: Manford H. Kuhn, "Kinsey's View of
Human Behavior," *Social Problems*, 1 (April 1954), pp. 119–
125.

[7] The reader may have noted that this discussion makes no explicit reference to the problem of motivation. Mead had little
to say regarding motives. Adherents to his general orientation
have tended either to regard motives as implicit in the concept
of *object* ("a plan of action") or to consider them "mere" verbal
labels offered in supposed explanation of the actions of oneself
or of others.

In my judgment, a conception of motivation can be formulated that is both useful and consistent with Mead's theories.
Motivation can refer to "a process of defining (symbolically,
of course) the goal of an act." Thus, while both human and
infrahuman behavior may be viewed as goal-directed, only human behavior would be considered "motivated." Just as "motive" would be restricted to the human level, "drive" might
serve a comparable function on the infrahuman level.

This would not imply that motives lie back of, or "cause,"
human acts. Rather, human acts are in constant process of construction, and the goal-definitions by individuals undergo constant reformulation. I mean to designate by "motive," however,
the definition the individual makes, *at any given time,* of the
objectives of his own specific acts. Such definitions, obviously,
would be socially derived.

C. SUMMARY

At several points in this report the reader must have been aware of the extremely closely interwoven character of Mead's various concepts. In the discussions of society, of self, and of mind, certain ideas seemed to require frequent (and, perhaps, repetitious) statement. A brief summary of Mead's position may help to reveal more meaningfully the way in which his key concepts interlock and logically imply one another.

The human individual is born into a society characterized by *symbolic interaction.* The use of *significant symbols* by those around him enables him to pass from the conversation of gestures—which involves direct, unmeaningful response to the overt acts of others—to the occasional *taking of the roles* of others. This role-taking enables him to share the perspectives of others. Concurrent with role-taking, the *self* develops, *i.e.,* the capacity to act toward oneself. Action toward oneself comes to take the form of viewing oneself from the standpoint, or perspective, of the *generalized other* (the composite representative of others, of society, within the individual), which implies defining one's behavior in terms of the expectations of others. In the process of such viewing of oneself, the individual must carry on symbolic interaction with himself, involving an internal conversation between his impulsive aspect (the "I") and the incorporated perspectives of others (the "Me"). The *mind,* or mental activity, is present in behavior whenever such symbolic interaction goes on—whether the individual is merely "thinking" (in the everyday sense of the word) or is also interacting with another individual. (In both cases the individual must indicate things to himself.) Mental activity necessarily involves *meanings,* which usually attach to, and define, *objects.* The meaning of an object or event is simply an image of the pattern of action which defines the object or event. That is, the completion in one's imagination of an act, or the mental picture of the actions and experiences symbolized by an object, defines the act or the object. In the unit of study that Mead calls "the *act,* "all of the foregoing processes are usually entailed. The concluding point to be made in this summary is the same as the point with which I began: Mead's concepts intertwine and mutually

imply one another. To drive home this important point, I must emphasize that human society (characterized by symbolic interaction) both precedes the rise of individual selves and minds, and is maintained by the rise of individual selves and minds. This means, then, that symbolic interaction is both the medium for the development of human beings and the process by which human beings associate as human beings.

Finally, it should be clearly evident by now that any distinctively human act necessarily involves: symbolic interaction, role-taking, meaning, mind, and self. Where one of these concepts is involved, the others are, also, necessarily involved. Here we see, unmistakably, the organic unity of Mead's position.

D. CRITIQUE

In criticizing Mead's social psychology, it should be borne in mind that he gave his position no extended systematic write-up; that most of the published material which forms the basis of our knowledge of that position was not originally intended for publication, at least not in the form in which it has been printed; and that the various alternative statements of that position that appear in his posthumous works sometimes carry conflicting particulars. Still, we can evaluate only on the basis of the available, published materials.

1. Many of Mead's major concepts are somewhat vague and "fuzzy," necessitating an "intuitive" grasp of their meaning. This vagueness stems, I believe, primarily from two sources: (1) the fragmentary and alternative formulations of his ideas; and (2) his emergent view of human conduct, which inescapably entangles him in the necessity of striking a balance between the continuity of infrahuman and human behavior, on the one hand, and the novelty of human behavior, on the other.

(a) For example, the exact nature of "impulses" is not clearly specified. Whether impulses are biological in character, or can also be socially derived, is not clear from Mead's exposition. However, the contexts in which the term sometimes appears suggest that the latter interpretation would be more valid and useful.

(b) Similarly, the intertwined concepts of "meaning" and of "mind" are not consistently employed. At times, these terms are used generically, applying to both infrahuman and human levels of behavior, and at times specifically, applying only at the level of self-conscious human conduct. Fortunately, the context of each usage usually provides a key to Mead's intended meanings.

(c) Coincident with Mead's varying referents of "mind" and of "meaning," we find his vacillation between a restriction of role-taking ability to the human level (in symbolic interaction) and his granting of that ability to infrahuman animals (in the conversation of gestures). Again, we are fortunate in having his distinction between self-conscious role-playing and unwitting role-playing. The reader of Mead must bear in mind that the latter type of "role-playing" is *not* what Mead usually has in mind when he employs the concept.

(d) The concept of the "I," as William Kolb indicates, represents a vaguely defined residual category. Mead clearly specifies the nature of the "Me," but in effect, labels the "I" as simply the not-Me aspect of the self. As in the case of the very closely related concept of "impulse," Mead does not indicate the limits of the "I." From his discussion, the "I" would seem, however—and this is an inference—to include everything from biological urges to the effects of individual variations in life-history patterns. Still, as Barnes and Becker point out, the "I" serves the very useful purpose of evading a complete collective, or sociological, determinism of human conduct.

The ambiguity of the concept of the "I" also reveals itself in the various discussions in the secondary literature on Mead's treatment of habitual behavior. For some writers, habitual acts represent manifestations of the operation of the "I" alone; for others, of the "Me" alone; and for still others, a fusion of the "I" and the "Me."

(e) The concept of "self" also lacks clear, unambiguous definition in Mead's work. A certain amount of confusion enters the picture when the self is defined in terms of "the individual's viewing himself as an object." This confusion is not at all dissipated by Mead's tendency to vary between, on the one hand, synonymous usages of "self" and "self-consciousness" and on the other hand, slightly different usages of these two terms.

(f) Mead's concept of the "generalized other" needs sharpening. He oversimplifies the concept by assuming, apparently, a single, universal generalized other for the members of each society—rather than a variety of generalized others (even for the same individuals), at different levels of generality.[8] The inadequacy of this concept is clearly shown in his characterization of the criminal as one who "has not taken on the attitude of the generalized other toward property, (and who therefore) lacks a completely developed self." Such a characterization overlooks, of course, the sociogenic elements in crime causation.

(g) A final case of vagueness of conceptualization that we shall consider relates to Mead's usages of "object" and "image." Both of these are described as "telescoped acts," and both are used at times interchangeably and at times slightly differently. It is probably safe to infer that images are the mental representations of objects, *i.e.*, that images are the imaginative projections of the acts which define objects.

Other sources of ambiguity lie in Mead's varying uses of the concepts of "attitude," "gesture," and "symbol"; his vacillation between, on the one hand, ascribing objects and images to the infrahuman level of behavior and, on the other hand, denying them to that level; etc. All of these ambiguities and inconsistencies reflect chiefly the confusion engendered by publication of all the alternative formulations of Mead's ideas—the early formulations along with the later. The thoughtful and assiduous reader of Mead, however, should be able to abstract out some single, fairly consistent statement of Mead's position.

2. A second series of adverse criticisms centers around certain broad substantive omissions in Mead's theory.

(a) Mead's position, as Blumer states, constitutes a purely analytical scheme, which lacks content. That is, he presents an analysis of human conduct in terms of the mechanisms of development of such conduct, but indicates few ingredi-

[8] Current work on "reference groups" has served to remedy this deficiency. True, several competing definitions of this concept are extant. I have in mind, however, the conception of reference groups as collections of "significant others," that is, of persons with whom a given individual identifies and who, therefore, have a significant influence upon his personality.

ents of that conduct. In concerning himself wholly with process but not content, with the "how" but not the "why" of conduct, he provides no basis for explaining specific behaviors. For example, he gives no clues as to why one object rather than another will be formed by an individual or group. Thus, his scheme, as it stands, has no explanatory value with reference to such matters as the rise of particular popular heroes, or the high valuation of money, or the myth of Santa Claus.

(b) Related to this "error" of omission is Mead's virtual ignoring of the role of affective elements in the rise of the self and in social interaction generally. The importance of the sentiments and emotions manifested in personal relationships are given no recognition in Mead's position. This lack is supplied—perhaps, oversupplied—in Cooley's work.

(c) Nothing in Mead's theory enables a clear stand on the matter of the nature (or even existence) of the unconscious, or subconscious, and the related mechanisms of adjustment.

3. Mead's position can also be criticized from a third and final general standpoint, that of methodology.

(a) First of all, Mead's theory, for the most part, does not seem to be highly researchable. As yet, little truly significant research has been conducted chiefly in terms of his frame of reference. Recent efforts to measure self-conceptions may help to remedy this deficiency.

(b) Mead, himself, gives no explicit formulation as to how his analytical scheme can be used in research. He makes no specific recommendations as to the techniques appropriate to the study of human behavior.

(c) As I indicated earlier in this report, Mead presents no systematic evidence for his position. Nevertheless, many social psychologists find his theory highly congruent with the experiences of everyday life—something which cannot be as readily said for a number of competing positions.

E. POSITIVE CONTRIBUTION

The extent of Mead's contribution to social psychology can be only roughly gauged by refer-

ence to the work of other adherents of the Symbolic Interactionist approach. Among the more eminent sociologists and social psychologists influenced by his viewpoint are: Cooley, Thomas, Park, Burgess, E. Faris, and Blumer. Some of the textbooks which incorporate his position are: in sociology, those by Park and Burgess, Dawson and Gettys, Francis Merrill, Kingsley Davis; in social psychology, Lindesmith and Strauss, M. Sherif, T. Newcomb, Walter Coutu, and Hubert Bonner. In addition, the recent interests in "role theory," "reference-group theory," and "self-theory" represent, basically, derivatives of Symbolic Interactionism.

Mead's substantive contribution has converged with, or at least has found some parallels in, certain methodological positions in modern sociology and social psychology. Such positions are those in which study of the inner, subjective part of the act is deemed indispensable. Methodologies of this sort are indicated by (1) Thomas's concept of "definition of the situation," (2) Cooley's "sympathetic introspection," (3) Weber's *Verstehen*," (4) Znaniecki's "humanistic coefficient," (5) MacIver's "dynamic assessment," (6) Sorokin's "logico-meaningful analysis," and other references to the covert aspects of human conduct.

Mead's more specific contributions can be only briefly listed in this report:

1. He contributed to the increasing acceptance of the view that human conduct is carried on primarily by the defining of situations in which one acts; that is, the view that distinctively human behavior is behavior in terms of what situations *symbolize*. This is the essence of the Symbolic Interactionist viewpoint.
2. Adopting a distinctly sociological perspective, he helped direct attention to the fact that mind and self are not biologically given, but are social emergents.
3. He delineated the way in which language serves as a mechanism for the appearance of mind and self.
4. His concept of the "self" explains how the development, or socialization, of the human being both enmeshes the individual in society and frees him from society. For the individual with a self is not passive, but can employ his self in an interaction which may result in selections divergent from group definitions.
5. An extremely provocative conception of the

nature of the human mind is provided by him: He views mind, or the mental, as an importation within the individual of the social process, *i.e.*, of the process of social interaction.

6. His concept of the "act" points out the tendency for individuals to construct their behavior in the course of activity and, thus, to "carve out" their objects, their environments. What this means is that human beings are not passive puppets who respond mechanically to stimuli. They are, rather, active participants in a highly organized society, and what they perceive is functional in their ongoing activity. This theoretical position implies the importance of acquired predispositions (interests, values, etc.) and of the social context of behavior. It points to the influential significance of the group settings in which perceptions occur, and also places the meaning of what is perceived in the

context of the ongoing activities of persons. This leads directly into the next contribution by Mead.

7. He described how the members of a human group develop and form a common world, *i.e.*, common objects, common understandings and expectations.

8. He illuminated the character of social interaction by showing that human beings *share* one another's behavior instead of merely responding to each other's overt, external behavior as do infrahuman organisms.

As a concluding and overall evaluation of Mead as a contributor to social psychology, I can do no better than to repeat Dewey's oft-quoted appraisal: "His was a seminal mind of the first order."

Manford H. Kuhn **2**

Major Trends in Symbolic Interaction Theory in the Past Twenty-Five Years

The year 1937 lies virtually in the middle of a four-year period which saw the publication of *Mind, Self, and Society; Movements of Thought in the Nineteenth Century;* and *The Philosophy*

Manford H. Kuhn, "Major Trends in Symbolic Interactionist Theory in the Past Twenty-five Years," *The Sociological Quarterly*, vol. 5 (Winter 1964), pp. 61–84. Reprinted by permission.

Paper read before the Midwest Sociological Society at its twenty-fifth anniversary meetings, Des Moines, Iowa, April 12–14, 1962. (The paper was prepared for oral presentation. Footnotes have been added. Where additional information is given which was not implied or suggested in the original text, this has been clearly indicated—The Editor.)

of the Act.[1] It would represent the greatest naiveté to suggest that thus the year 1937 represented the introduction of symbolic interactionism. We are all aware of the long development: from James, Baldwin, and Cooley to Thomas, Faris, Dewey, Blumer, and Young. Even the Tardean imitation and suggestion which underlay

[1] George H. Mead, *Mind, Self and Society;* ed. with an Introduction by Charles W. Morris (Chicago: Univ. of Chicago Press, 1934); *Movements of Thought in the Nineteenth Century;* ed. by Merritt H. Moore (Chicago: Univ. of Chicago Press, 1936); *The Philosophy of the Act,* ed. by Charles W. Morris (Chicago: Univ. of Chicago Press, 1938).

Ross's *Social Psychology*[2] contributed a good deal ordinarily not credited to him in the development of interaction theory. Nor is it the fact that Mead represents the fullest development of the orientation that makes so significant the posthumous publication of his works (for which we may conveniently take 1937 as an anchoring point). Mead's ideas had been known for a very long time. He had taught University of Chicago students from 1893 to 1931. His notions were bruited about in classes and seminars wherever there were professors conducting them who had studied at the University of Chicago—not least in the great heartland included in the Midwest of our society. Some of Mead's students had published their versions of his ideas or quotations from some of his philosophical papers—Kimball Young's *Source Book in Social Psychology* of a decade earlier contained a paper by Mead, and his *Social Psychology* bore the strong imprint of Meadian interactionism.[3]

No, the significance of the publication of Mead's books is that it ended what must be termed the long era of the "oral tradition," the era in which most of the germinating ideas had been passed about by word of mouth. (It should be noted parenthetically that Mead had published earlier a considerable number of papers, but they were mainly in journals devoted to philosophy and ethics, journals not likely to be read by sociologists or social psychologists. His only paper in a sociological journal—of which I am aware—was his assessment of Cooley's theories.)[4]

The oral tradition, it must be noted, has some generic peculiarities which are evidenced equally by primitive myth and by unpublished intellectual orientation: there tends to be much (almost ritual) repetition; there is a strain to "get it right,"

that is, to be correct; there is much debate over orthodoxy, and whatever intellectual powers there may be, are more devoted to casuistry and criticism than to inquiry and creativity. The mnemic effort freed from its task of remembering "how it goes" is somehow transformed into energy for imagination on the one hand and for the drudgery of testing and justification on the other. This is what was made possible by the belated publication of the three books by Mead.

Mead had not been the only one of the symbolic interactionists who had failed to publish. The year 1937 was the one in which some of the papers of Ellsworth Faris appeared under the title, *The Nature of Human Nature.*[5] Here, too, was a belated publication which, in its sprinkling and scatter, speaks more for what Faris never published—a rounded theoretical conception of his social psychology. Thomas's *theoretical* formulations were similarly scarce, scattered and incomplete—however influential. While Dewey published voluminously, his chief formulation of symbolic interaction theory is, in my view, his *Experience and Nature* which did not appear until late and which is written in such a forbidding Germanic version of the English language that many sociologists and social psychologists have not read it even yet.[6] Blumer, the young and promising heir apparent, has published relatively little and has nowhere gathered together a rounded version of his point of view.

But even though the oral tradition has some tendency to continue in symbolic interactionism, the past twenty-five years have seen a marked increase in all kinds of activity involving the published symbol: three textbooks on "our side of the social psychological fence"—that by R. E. L. Faris, that by Lindesmith and Strauss (now in its second edition) and the very recent one by Shibutani;[7]

[2] Edward Alsworth Ross, *Social Psychology* (New York, 1908).

[3] George H. Mead, "Thought, Symbols, and Language," in Kimball Young (ed.), *Source Book for Social Psychology* (New York: Alfred A. Knopf, 1928), pp. 341–46, reprinted from "The Behavioristic Account of the Significant Symbol," *Journal of Philosophy*, 19:159–63 (1922). Kimball Young, *Social Psychology: An Analysis of Social Behavior* (New York: F. S. Crofts, 1930).

[4] [Kuhn is referring to George H. Mead, "Cooley's Contribution to American Social Thought," *American Journal of Sociology*, 35:693–706 (Mar., 1930). The same journal did in fact publish two earlier papers by Mead: "The Working Hypothesis in Social Reform," *American Journal of Sociology*, 5:367–71 (Nov., 1899); "The Psychology of Primitive Justice," *ibid.*, 23:577–602 (Mar. 1918).—The Editor.]

[5] Ellsworth Faris, *The Nature of Human Nature and Other Essays in Social Psychology* (New York and London: McGraw-Hill, 1937).

[6] John Dewey, *Experience and Nature* (Chicago: Open Court Publishing Company, 1925).

[7] Robert E. L. Faris, *Social Psychology* (New York: The Ronald Press, 1953); Alfred R. Lindesmith and Anselm L. Strauss, *Social Psychology* (New York: The Dryden Press, 1949: rev. ed., 1956); Tamotsu Shibutani, *Society and Personality: An Interactionist Approach to Social Psychology* (Englewood Cliffs, N.J.: Prentice-Hall, 1961).

a sizable fraction of Newcomb's text[8] and lesser amounts of others on the "other side"; a considerable number of monographs, and into the hundreds of journal articles.

Basically the past twenty-five years have constituted, in contrast to the preceding era, the *age of inquiry* in symbolic interactionism.

But while it has been an era of inquiry, the inquiry has been directed at the testing and developing of what amounts almost to a welter of subtheories going by a variety of names other than symbolic interactionism. This spawning of smaller, less inclusive theories has been due, in my opinion, neither to the propensity of scholars to attempt to make names for themselves by renaming what has already been proposed, nor to their having modified or augmented symbolic interaction in significant measure. This development of sub- or related orientations has stemmed from the essential ambiguities and contradictions in the Meadian statement—ambiguities and contradictions which were generally interpreted to be dark, inscrutable complexities too difficult to understand as long as the orientation remained largely in the oral tradition. Much of this confusion and contradiction may be summed up—but only in a vastly oversimplifying way and for purposes limited to immediate ones I hope here to expound—as a contradiction between [*determinacy*] and [*indeterminacy*] in Mead's overall point of view.

It is apparent that Mead took the view that the individual is initially dependent on the antecedent existence of a social system, specifically as it exists in the ongoing process of a functioning language, for the means wherewith to engage in experience or to take any kind of self-conscious and self-directed action. This internalization of language and the concomitant internalization of the role of the other has, in the Meadian description, nothing in it inconsistent with strict regularity or determinism.[9] Yet, as Mead proposed the *I* and the *Me* as the internal conversationalists constituting in their conversation the self, he indicated that the *I* is impulsive and essentially unpredictable—and furthermore that the *I* is the initiating, acting aspect of the self. It is never completely clear whether he meant only that the *I* is *subjectively* unpredictable or that it is indeterminate in a scientific sense.

Furthermore, it seems apparent that there was a basic initiative attributed to the self in the whole process of role-taking, at any rate after the early learning of language and probably even during that process as well. Mead, after all, insisted that the self constitutes its own environment, its own reality. Furthermore, there is the implicit possibility of indeterminacy in the whole conversation between the *I* and the *Me*. And, finally, it is possible to see in Mead's notion of the self such an antithesis to structure, such a dynamically volatile process of shifting self-indications that, whatever the *theoretical* view of determinacy vs. indeterminacy in any of the attributes of the self, the whole matter is so evanescent and shifting that it is obviously a practical impossibility to obtain access to any—possibly determinate—antecedents in time to make usable or testable predictions.

We may sum up this set of ambiguities about determinism as follows: The notion that the *I* is indeterminate but the *Me's* are determinate; the notion that both the *I* and the *Me's* are indeterminate; the notion that whereas both the *I* and *Me's* are determinate results of identifiable events, the interaction (conversation) between the two is somehow itself indeterminate or emergent.

But this is a preliminary view and does not cover the varieties of ways in which symbolic interactionism may be structured and, for that matter, has been structured by those proposing inquiry under its aegis. The two most frequently complicating considerations are: (1) the question whether the self is conceived, for research purposes, as the antecedent variable with criterion events (especially behaviors) as consequent variables, or conversely whether antecedent variables (ascribed identities, affiliations, associations, or communication variables and other events) are conceived to predict—that is, to exist in regularity with—consequent self variations; and (2) the question whether the relevant antecedent variables

[8] Theodore M. Newcomb, *Social Psychology* (New York: The Dryden Press, 1950).

[9] "Mead's account of conduct . . . is not opposed, in principle, to a deterministic view of behavior."—Guy E. Swanson, "Mead and Freud, Their Relevance for Social Psychology." *Sociometry* 24:327 (Dec., 1961).

are conceived to be *immediate* or *remote* in time with respect to the events thought of as consequent.

This set of questions and ambiguities in symbolic interaction theory has led to a variety of answers. One answer structures human behavior deterministically by conceiving antecedent, causal variables to be contemporaneous social ones with the consequent ones having to do with the nature or structure of the self (either as a whole or of the elements seen to constitute the whole).

A second answer conceives the antecedent variables to be historical or developmental, thus possibly quite temporally remote from the consequent variables which are, as in the first answer, taken to be the nature or structure of the self, either holistically or elementally constituted.

A third answer conceives the antecedent variables to be the self, either as a whole or elementally, and the consequent variables to be those of overt behavior.

A fourth answer conceives the antecedent variables to be self variables which among themselves produce consequent, novel, but determinate self-attributes.

A similar variety of *indeterminate* answers has been given to the questions raised by ambiguities and inconsistencies in symbolic interaction orientation.

One answer appears to see virtually all significant attributes of behavior to be internal choices and other self-indications, all of which are conceived to be emergent, with no observable, regular antecedent.

Another is similar to this view but sees antecedents to these internal events in experiences lost, or partially lost, in the antiquity of the individual's early biography, and without too close a dependence on, or regularity with, such early happenings.

A third sees the significant variables as external behaviors which are either unrelated to the self, or deviously related, or only loosely related to the self. Such is often the kind of orientation held by those who see a sharp disjunction between public and private selves, where the private self is the true self with unresearchable antecedents, and where the public self is the so-

cial self, both in that it relates to observable behaviors and in that it has social antecedents.

A fourth conceives external events to be shaped more or less unpredictably by self-activities which in turn are "self-developed," *i.e.*, indeterminate in any testable way.

If one were to arrogate to oneself the privilege of deciding these issues and others raised essentially by the ambiguities in symbolic interaction orientation, one could narrow sharply the task of surveying the major trends in this theory in the past twenty-five years. This, however, I deem to be neither proper nor useful. Similarly, if symbolic interactionists had their own professional organization, their own journal or journals, their own pontifical leader or tight-knit little clique of leaders clearly assigned the role of determining the "correct" view among competing doctrinal differences, the survey of the fruits of orthodoxy might be simple. Instead, however, we have none of these things, and for the most part we wish none of them. But the consequences are that there is a welter of partial orientations which bear varying relationships to the general point of view.

There is, for example, *role theory*. Role theory has many intellectual antecedents other than those in Cooley, Dewey, Thomas, Faris, and Mead. There are debts, for instance, to Linton, to Moreno, to Parsons; there are often overtones of one or another of the learning theories. These are but a few of the strands of thought in role theory. Yet role theory is not sharply distinguishable—if at all—from symbolic interactionism. The *emphasis* in role theory is on overt role playing and on the researchable relation between role expectations and role performances; the emphasis is either less, or altogether lacking, on role-taking, on the interior processes of the self, and what Shibutani calls the sentiments are often ignored. Thus role theory tends toward what Turner wishes to call the processes of conformity.[10]

Yet I must underscore the word *emphasis*,

[10] [Cp. Shibutani, *op. cit.*, pp. 323 ff., 548 ff. *et passim;* Ralph H. Turner, "Role-Taking: Process Versus Conformity," in *Human Behavior and Social Processes: An Interactionist Approach,* Arnold M. Rose, ed. (Boston: Houghton Mifflin, 1962), pp. 20–40.—The Editor].

for in Sarbin's useful chapter in the *Handbook of Social Psychology*, there is no ignoring of self nor of empathy, nor is there in his own research (of which there is a fine example indicating a positive relation between role-taking ability on the one hand and degree of malleability of self-conception on the other).[11] But on the whole, role theory has implied [determinacy] of Type I.

Among the important contributions of the quarter-century under the general aegis of role theory have been the preliminary systematization provided in the early part of Gross, Mason, and McEachern's *Explorations in Role Analysis,* and Turner's paper in Rose's *Human Behavior and Social Processes,* in which issues of determinacy vs. indeterminacy of the sort here proposed for all of symbolic interactionism are made with respect specifically to role theory.[12] Role theory has engendered a great deal of research; in fact, it is as much to role theory as to any other development that I point when I have designated this period under scrutiny as the era of inquiry. This is no place in which to attempt to summarize this research. By and large we can say it has underscored Thomas's dictum that "people tend to play the roles assigned to them." There is by no means any strong evidence that there is a completely determinate relation between role expectations or recipes on the one hand and role performance on the other. On the other hand, there is a growing mountain of evidence that with "known" or public role recipes in hand we can make very useful probabilistic predictions with respect to subsequent behaviors, not alone those representing the answering role performances but even those which are but logically related and ancillary behaviors.

Much of the utility of role theory has been demonstrated thus far in the study of internalized role conflicts and contradictions. This study has ranged from the imaginative employment of personal documents and interviews by Mirra Komarovsky in her study of the conflicts surrounding the role of young women in college[13] to the construction of fairly precise and rigorous scales in the measure of such role conflict in the work of Stouffer and Toby. Even in such studies which imply internalization and thus the interposition of intermediate or intervening variables into our Type I determinacy pattern, such intervening variables are basically unnecessary even in the operations by Komarovsky; for although they involved reports of subjective valuations, these reports could have been replaced by direct observations of communications applying the opposing pressures—it was simply inconvenient to do so.

Another equally salient development has been that of *reference group* theory, so-named, of course, by Hyman[14] but getting much of the attention it has received from the concept of relative deprivation as employed by Stouffer in *The American Soldier* and as reworked in the well-known chapter on reference group theory by Merton and Kitt.[15] There have been a number of useful theoretical critiques as well as creative employments of reference group theory, notable among them those of Kelley, Shibutani, Turner, Newcomb, and Sherif. The notion of reference group is obviously closely related to the whole problem of the other as dealt with by Mead and Sullivan on the one hand, and to that of the primary group as described by Cooley and Faris on the other. Much of the employment of this new theory has been so far to provide *ex post* or circular explanation (explanation by naming). Controversy abounds, to be sure, over the meaning of the term *reference group* itself—whether it refers

[11] Theodore R. Sarbin, "Role Theory," in *Handbook of Social Psychology,* ed. by Gardner Lindzey (Cambridge, Mass.: Addison-Wesley Publishing Company, 1954), 1:223–58. [The example of Sarbin's own research that Kuhn probably had in mind is Theodore R. Sarbin and Norman L. Farberow, "Contributions to Role-Taking Theory: A Clinical Study of Self and Role," *Journal of Abnormal and Social Psychology,* 47:117–25 (Jan., 1952).—The Editor.]

[12] Neal Gross, Ward S. Mason, and Alexander W. McEachern, *Explorations in Role Analysis: Studies of the School Superintendency Role* (New York: John Wiley, 1958); Ralph H. Turner, "Role-Taking: Process Versus Conformity," *op. cit.*

[13] Mirra Komarovsky, *Women in the Modern World: Their Education and Their Dilemmas* (Boston: Little, Brown, 1953).

[14] H. Hyman, *The Psychology of Status* (Archives of Psychology, Vol. 38, no. 269, June, 1942).

[15] Robert K. Merton and Alice S. Kitt, "Contributions to the Theory of Reference Group Behavior," in *Continuities in Social Research: Studies in the Scope and Method of "The American Soldier,"* ed. by Robert K. Merton and Paul F. Lazarsfeld (Glencoe, Illinois: The Free Press, 1950): reprinted in Robert K. Merton, *Social Theory and Social Structure,* revised and enlarged edition (Glencoe, Ill.: Free Press, 1957), pp. 225–80.

to a normative or to an evaluative function; whether it must point to groups, to categories or both; whether it may best refer to relationships, as Rose suggests, or whether we may better use it to refer to derivative orientations, as Shibutani indicates. May we use the term to refer to empirically identifiable attitudes, expectations, and norms of existent *others,* or must we limit ourselves to such matters only after they have been transmuted to the images in the imagination of the *actors* themselves, to which Cooley referred as the "solid facts" of social life?

The classification of reference group theory is difficult, for in the theoretical statements of it, indeterminate model 7 fits, but in the actual application of the theory, determinate models 1 through 4 have been variously employed. The contradictions between theoretical statements and operational implications in reference group theory are one of the most unhappy aspects of symbolic interactionism today, in this author's opinion.

Next consider the related development of points of view known as *social perception* and *person perception.* If we regard the ancient dicta: "We see things not as they are but as we are," and "We do not first see and then define; we define first and then see," as intimately involved in the point of view of symbolic interactionism, we may properly claim at least a strong interest in the development of these interrelated schools. The researches contained in the volume edited by Petrullo and Tagiuri, for example, bear in many instances on hypotheses generated by symbolic interactionism.[16] On the other hand, this research movement is led by men relatively unacquainted with "our" literature. Consequently our own reaction to any one piece of research such as is contained in Petrullo and Tagiuri's volume is that it is in one or more respects naive: in its lack of sophistication about the function of language in interaction, in its failure to employ a concept equivalent to social act or social object or significant other, etc., etc.

Jerome Bruner, whose own experimental

work on the differential perception of the size of coins by subjects of different income levels is a classic study in the field of social perception, has admirably stated in summary form the general position of these schools in "Social Psychology and Perception," in the third edition of *Readings in Social Psychology* edited by Maccoby, Newcomb, and Hartley.[17] His summary is such that the symbolic interactionist can easily deduce for himself the common ground this position shares with symbolic interaction theory; I am therefore spared this task by citing this article. I would only object that the Bruner paper misleads somewhat in failing to indicate the degree to which "perceptual set" as a key concept central to this school has come to serve as umbrella for Freudian rather than symbolic interaction variables, and for implying, on the other hand, that social perception treats what people are doing as central to the nature of what they perceive (for this is not borne out by their experimental designs).

The models on which social and person perception theory rests appear to be types 1 and 4. That is, they are determinate and tend to designate either immediate or temporally distal antecedent social variables and consequent behavioral variables. Had symbolic interactionists initiated the exploration of this field, they would have emphasized the ways in which the individual conceives himself as antecedent and the manner he perceives other objects including persons as consequent, with probably some attention to designs in which these types of variables are reversed in time.

So far, we have dealt with subtheories which have had very ambiguous boundaries. The same thing is certainly true of *self* theory with which I have identified my own research activities. It was my intention in 1946 or 1947 to employ a term which would not so much differentiate an emerging point of view from the more or less orthodox ideas of symbolic interaction as it would enable, on the other hand, a distinction between a body of conjectural and deductive orientation—

---

[16] *Person Perception and Interpersonal Behavior,* ed. by Renato Tagiuri and Luigi Petrullo (Stanford, Calif.: Stanford University Press, 1958).

[17] Jerome Bruner, "Social Psychology and Perception," in *Readings in Social Psychology,* 3rd ed., Editorial Committee: Eleanor E. Maccoby, Theodore M. Newcomb, Eugene L. Hartley (New York: Henry Holt, 1958), pp. 85–94.

TABLE 2.1. Types of symbolic interaction theory

Presupposing Determinacy	*Presupposing Indeterminacy*

(1) Soc $A_1 \longrightarrow$ Beh C

(6)   A $\overset{*}{Ch}$
                  Ind

(2) Soc $A_1 \longrightarrow$ Self C

(7) $A_2 \overset{*}{\dashrightarrow} \overset{*}{Ch}$
                  Ind

(3) Soc $A_2 \longrightarrow$ Self C

(8) $Self_{pr}$ $A \overset{*}{\dashrightarrow} \overset{*}{Self_{pub}}$

(4) Self A $\longrightarrow$ Beh C
(5) Self A $\longrightarrow$ Self C

(9) $Self_{pr}$ $\overset{*}{A} \overset{*}{\dashrightarrow}$ Beh C

Where Soc refers to social variable
  Self refers to self variable, either holistic or elementalistic
  $Self_{pr}$ refers to "private self"
  $Self_{pub}$ refers to "public self"
  A indicates antecedent variable
  A_1 indicates immediately antecedent variable
  A_2 indicates antecedent but temporarily distal variable
  C indicates consequent variable
  Beh indicates overt behavioral variable
  Ch indicates internal choice-making
  Ind indicates internal (self) indications
  Em indicates an emergent (I or Me)
  Det indicates a determinate (I or Me)
  Solid arrow indicates a determinate, causal process
  Broken arrow indicates an indeterminate, emergent process
  Asterisk (*) indicates the locus of indeterminacy; this may lie
    in the nexus between antecedent and consequent variables
    as well as in any of the following internal aspects of the self:
      (a) $A \longrightarrow (I_{Em} \dashrightarrow Me_{Det}) \dashrightarrow$ Beh C
      (b) $A \longrightarrow (I_{Em} \dashrightarrow Me_{Em}) \dashrightarrow$ Beh C
      (c) $A \longrightarrow (I_{Det} \dashrightarrow Me_{Det}) \dashrightarrow$ Beh C

as represented by Cooley, Dewey, and Mead—and a derivative but developing set of generalizations, tested by empirical research. I found later that, at about the same time, Carl Rogers had also termed as self theory his notions in clinical psychology having to do with the varying discrepancies between the actual or perceived self and the ideal self. Since then the term has been variously employed, often as an umbrella word, to cover several or all of the subtheories here under consideration.

The work undertaken by students of symbolic interaction at the State University of Iowa followed in several respects the programmatic proposals of the summary monograph on social psychology in the 1930s by Leonard Cottrell and Ruth Gallagher and of Cottrell's later presidential address before the American Sociological Society; that is to say, there has been considerable attention to the self itself and to role-taking.[18]

[18] Leonard S. Cottrell, Jr., and Ruth Gallagher, *Developments in Social Psychology, 1930–1940* (New York: Beacon Press, 1941); Leonard S. Cottrell, Jr., "Some Neglected Problems in Social Psychology," *American Sociological Review*, 15:705–12 (Dec., 1950).

McPartland[19] pioneered in his study relating differential nexi-to-social-structure to the differential characteristics of the self. Later he has studied the relations among self, social strata, and the differential syndromes of mental-emotional disturbance. Fred Waisanen[20] explored relations between self characteristics and prejudice. Stewart[21] demonstrated the often alleged relation of the self to a system of objects, as did Carl Waisanen[22] and Wynona Garretson[23] in other ways. Maranell[24] studied relations between self and role-taking and began the exploration of transparency, the obverse of empathy. Rogler[25] established that there is a direct relation between role-taking and access to a communication system. The validation and extension of symbolic interaction ideas represented in these researches is for the most part preliminary and one must assess it as modest. Perhaps the most significant contribution of the Iowa research is simply that in which it joins the research of Miyamoto and Dornbusch, Deutsch and Solomon, Dick, Dinitz and Mangus, McKee and Sheriffs, Stryker, Videbeck and Bates, and many others in demonstrating to some degree at least that the key ideas of symbolic interactionism could be operationalized and utilized successfully in empirical research.[26]

[19] Thomas S. McPartland, "The Self and Social Structure," unpublished doctoral dissertation, State University of Iowa, 1953; "Self Conception, Social Class, and Mental Health," *Human Organization*, 17:24–29 (1958); T. S. McPartland, John H. Cumming and Wynona S. Garretson, "Self Conception and Ward Behavior in Two Psychiatric Hospitals," *Sociometry*, 24:11–24 (June, 1961).

[20] F. B. Waisanen, "The Prejudice Variable: A Social Psychological and Methodological Study," unpublished doctoral dissertation, State University of Iowa, 1954.

[21] Robert L. Stewart, "The Self and Other Objects: Their Measurement and Interrelationship," unpublished doctoral dissertation, State University of Iowa, 1955.

[22] Carl E. Waisanen, "Preference Aspects of Self-Attitudes," unpublished doctoral dissertation, State University of Iowa, 1957.

[23] Wynona Smutz Garretson, "College as Social Object: A Study in Consensus," unpublished doctoral dissertation, State University of Iowa, 1961; "The Consensual Definition of Social Objects," *Sociological Quarterly*, 3:107–13 (Apr., 1962).

[24] Gary M. Maranell, "Role-Taking: Empathy and Transparency," unpublished doctoral dissertation, State University of Iowa, 1959.

[25] Lloyd H. Rogler, "An Experimental Study of the Relationship between Structured Behavior Patterns and Accuracy of Social Sensitivity," unpublished doctoral dissertation, State University of Iowa, 1957.

[26] See the appended bibliography.

Self theory of this variety has implied one or another of the five determinate models in our diagram, although this point is implicit rather than explicit, and never a salient issue. The general attempt rests on the notion that there is among the several important matters a process considered nomothetic or genotypical by the symbolic interaction orientation.

Among the subtheories that seem to imply indeterminacy—phenomenological theory, the study of careers, language, and culture of Sapir and Whorf, the interpersonal theory of H. S. Sullivan, the self-constancy and self-actualizing theories of such men as Stegner and Maslow—one seems to stand out as just a shade more radical and eye-catching than the rest: the *dramaturgical* school of Kenneth Burke, Erving Goffman, and possibly Nelson Foote and Gregory Stone. The most significant alteration made by this school is the general transmutation of the social act from what in traditional symbolic interactionism had continued to be paradoxically an individual model (triggered by organic tensions and impulses and following through the course of the action with reference to the single—almost feral—man to equilibrium, restitution of tensionlessness in the organism) to the team-of-players model which implies that social agenda rather than tissue conditions serve to initiate the act and to cue its end as well. This, of course, is but one of the extremely provocative aspects of dramaturgical theory, especially as initiated by Burke and developed by Goffman.

The difficulties with this subtheory are, in the main, those of deriving from it any testable generalizations. One must be tentative about this, it seems to me, for this was exactly the complaint lodged against the whole of symbolic interaction orientation in its early years. It may well be that ingenious solutions will be found to the problems of operationalizing the basic conceptions of this orientation.

Of the models we suggest diagrammatically, numbers 8 and 9 seem to be the ones most frequently implied in dramaturgical theory, although the team characteristics of Goffman's units appear to imply models indicating team rather than individual conduct.

The longitudinal study of socialization and

especially of career trajectories, best indicated in the work of E. C. Hughes and Howard S. Becker, seems also to lie on the indeterminacy side. The work of these two men is virtually as imaginative and as creative as that of Burke and of Goffman. There is, in the literature, no more insightful account of the relation of the actor to a social object through the processes of communication and of self-definition, than Becker's account of becoming a marijuana user.[27] Hughes's sensitivity to lingual indicators of status is wonderfully revealed in his well-known and fundamental essay, "Work and the Self."[28] In it he presents a modern-age social psychological interpretation of "what the social classes owe to each other."

Again, the difficulties with this approach seem to lie in operationalization. It is most difficult to establish generalizations valid for human behavior without methods wherewith to make precise checks on intersubjective perceptions of events such as are involved in witnessing transitional stages in a socialization process or rites of passage in the trajectory of a career.

The indeterminate model on which this approach seems to rest is our type no. 7; that is, the antecedent variables, temporarily distal, are loosely (indeterminately) related to the processes of choice and self-indication which constitute the self.

The *interpersonal theory* of psychiatry proposed by Harry Stack Sullivan was constructed early in this quarter-century period.[29] It has been almost ubiquitously incorporated into the general body of symbolic interaction orientation, or perhaps the verb should be "reincorporated" since Sullivan had been well introduced to Meadian theory in the 1920s and had built the interpersonal theory in significant part out of elements provided by Mead on the one hand and by Freud on the other. The theory is distinctive for the unique way in which it manages a synthesis of Meadian and Freudian viewpoints without admitting any of the Freudian nonsense about phylogenetic inheritance of unconscious sense of guilt, the early Oedipus notion, the nature of man pitted against society, etc., while utilizing to the full the power of Freudian explanation of interpersonal rivalry and of distortions in communication—down to the utilization of the concept of self-derogation and self-rejection and repression (the not-me)—concepts hinging on interpersonal relations (reflected appraisals by others) rather than on thwarted instincts and biological drives as Freud had it.

Unfortunately the Sullivan interpersonal theory is quite disjoined from ideas of culture and of formal social organization. This has led Shibutani to set up disjunctive self components: Those derived from conventional role-playing and those derived as sentiments from the kinds of interpersonal processes Sullivan described, completely divorced from culture and organized systems. It is also unfortunate that the interpersonal theory suffers from the same difficulties as the other indeterminate theories: inability to apply the usual scientific methods in order to build increasingly supported, dependable generalizations. The Sullivan model appears to rest on a combination of models, 7, 8, and 9, thus indicating looseness between antecedent, intervening and consequent variables, plus the possibility for further emergence in the interior processes of the self. The specific, temporally distal, antecedent variables on which the theory rests are those having to do with what Sullivan calls the *parataxic* and *prototaxic* stages in what is essentially the preverbal period. In these, there is no real opportunity conceived for direct empirical observation, and thus there is further indeterminacy beyond the posited looseness between these stages and later self-attributes.

One more indeterminate subtheory is the Sapir-Whorf-Cassirer *language and culture orientation*.[30] This is truly a theory behind a the-

---

[27] Howard S. Becker, "Becoming a Marihuana User," *American Journal of Sociology* 59:235–42 (Nov., 1953) [reprinted in Part V of this book—The Editor]. [Cp. Howard S. Becker, *Outsiders: Studies in the Sociology of Deviance* (New York: Free Press of Glencoe, 1963)—The Editor.]

[28] Everett C. Hughes, "Work and the Self," in *Social Psychology at the Crossroads: The University of Oklahoma Lectures in Social Psychology*, ed. by John H. Rohrer and Muzafer Sherif (New York: Harper and Brothers, 1951), pp. 313–23.

[29] See the appended bibliography.

[30] [See, *e.g.* Edward Sapir, *Language: An Introduction to the Study of Speech* (New York: Harcourt, Brace, 1921): Benjamin L. Whorf, *Language, Thought and Reality: Selected Writings*, ed. by John B. Carroll (Technology Press of Massachusetts Institute of Technology, 1956); Ernst Cassirer, *The Philosophy of Symbolic Forms*, 2 vols. (New Haven: Yale Univ. Press, 1953–1955)—The Editor.]

ory, for it tends to be presumed by symbolic inter-actionists as being preliminary even to a consideration of the basic assumptions of the theory under review. The language and culture point of view is surely so familiar as not to need much description. It points to the basic proposition that a language consists of a very finite and limited number of concepts out of an unlimited set of possibilities. Furthermore it underscores the fact that even the ultimate and basic concepts—which we in our society think of as those dealing with time, motion, matter and space—are themselves lingually variable and relative. And, perhaps even more important, it takes the position that the very grammar of a language is based on an unspoken, taken-for-granted logic which determines how people in that society think about anything. Thus it must follow that the categorization of one's self and his attributes, as well as of his others, and of the significant nonhuman objects in his system of objects is entirely dependent on the language of his group. He cannot think of himself or his experiences, or of his relationships, except in the arbitrary conceptualizations provided him in his language.

This is an indeterminate theory in so far as the individual person's behavior is concerned, for the language only sets the basic framework for his thought and the outer limits, beyond which he cannot conceive of things. Within these limits, and around this framework, there is a looseness of connection. No determinate statements are suggested. However, attached as a preliminary set of assumptions to any of the previously examined determinant subtheories, this point of view removes it from determinacy only in the sense that, as is pointed out posthumously in the *American Anthropologist* by the late Clyde Kluckhohn, the Whorf-Sapir-Cassirer notions are basically untestable.[31]

There are a number of other subtheories which have had their development during these past twenty-five years and which are related in one or several respects to symbolic interactionism, and which serve, if nothing else, to suggest

extensions or amendments to the orientation. These include such points of view as cognitive theory, field theory, phenomenology, the developmental notions of Piaget, the current scrutiny of identity which bears strong overtones of ego psychology, the self-constancy theory of Stager and others, and the self-actualizing theory of Maslow, in addition to which there is the self theory of Carl Rogers, already mentioned. Many of those theories were developed by students in the field of psychology. Few indicate acquaintance with the intellectual stream to which symbolic interactionism belongs. The line I have drawn, excluding these from consideration but including the ones I have discussed, is highly arbitrary and may not be defensible in any other sense than that time places limitations even upon the most condensed of discussions.

APPLICATIONS

So far we have considered the development of amplifications, subtheories, and operationalizations of symbolic interaction theory. We cannot conclude without considering the promising starts made in applying the orientation to problem areas. There is the much neglected book by Lemert, *Social Pathology*,[32] which should have been called *A Social Psychology of Deviants*, in which the author makes the interesting proposal that a fundamental distinction exists in the behaviors of those whose deviation is accompanied by no corresponding self-definition and those whose deviation is so accompanied— he refers to the difference as secondary differentiation.

Much of the application of symbolic interaction theory has been made by students of crime and delinquency—notably Crossey, Glaser and Reckless. Of the Iowa students, Nardini in the field of the criminal,[33] Mulford in the area of the

[31] Clyde Kluckhohn, "Notes on Some Anthropological Aspects of Communication," *American Anthropologist* 63:895–910 (Oct., 1961).

[32] Edwin M. Lemert, *Social Pathology: Approach to the Theory of Sociopathic Behavior* (New York: McGraw-Hill, 1951).

[33] William Nardini, "Criminal Self-Conceptions in the Penal Community: An Empirical Study," unpublished doctoral dissertation, State University of Iowa, 1959.

alcoholic,[34] Hurlburt in the area of family adjustment,[35] and Nass in the field of driver safety records,[36] have made application of self-dimensions as antecedent variables in promising endeavors to understand consequent variable behavior in problem fields. The new compilation edited by Rose already referred to, *Human Behavior and Social Processes*, contains as its third and final section a set of papers on the relation of interaction theory to social problem areas. Notable is Rose's own paper presenting his social-psychological theory of neurosis, which has a number of parallels with Sullivan's theory, but is distinctive in most respects for its general application of the symbolic interaction orientation.[37]

NEGLECTED PROBLEMS

I cannot leave the consideration of the development of symbolic interactionism in the past twenty-five years without reconsidering the title of Cottrell's presidential address—the question of "neglected problems." Many of the problems which he found to be neglected are still neglected, while others—such as role-taking, on which his own student, R. F. Dymond, made such a notable start[38]—are beginning to

be studied with more and more sophistication.

There is no time here to make a thorough canvass of neglected problems, but I should like to mention two. One is the failure to make appropriate conceptualization of the varieties of functional relations that regularly occur between self and other. At present we appear to be in that rather foolish and useless situation in which we debate what a reference group really is. Most of the suggestions point to varieties of functional relations between self and groups or categories of others. The question ought not to be which of these is really a reference group, but rather, what special term shall we agree to use for each particular relation?[39] Having reached a consensus on a constructed vocabulary with which to refer to these functional relationships between self and other, we need then to consider the serious questions of operationalization. What kinds of questions must be asked to discover the nature of the particular relationship under inquiry?

A second pressing question implied in much of this paper has to do with the process by which self-conceptions change. Some theorists, notably those who lean toward the indeterminate side, discuss self-change as if it were most volatile and evanescent; the self shifts with each new indication one makes to himself, and these indications are the constant accompaniments of experience. Others see in the self the more or less stable, continuous, organizing principle for the personality, offering the only constant, non-shifting anchorage for the perception of other objects. We have arrived at the point in sharpening of the tools by which we may identify self-attributes and measure them and compare them with those of others, where we may treat this issue as a researchable question. As we attempt to measure the relative stability of the self, we need to study the concomitants of self-attitude change. It may be argued that the self, like any attitude, may be usefully treated as an hypothesis which the individual holds about himself, and with respect to which he holds certain notions about testing for validity. We need to study in short what corre-

[34] Harold A. Mulford, Jr., "Toward an Instrument to Identify and Measure the Self, Significant Others, and Alcohol in the Symbolic Environment: An Empirical Study," unpublished doctoral dissertation, State University of Iowa, 1955.

[35] Julia Knaff Hurlburt, "Role Expectations and the Self: An Empirical Study of Their Relationship to Marital Adjustment," unpublished doctoral dissertation, State University of Iowa, 1960.

[36] Gilbert D. Nass, "A Study of the Teen-Age Driver, His Self-Definition, and Definition of the Driving Situation," unpublished Master's thesis, State University of Iowa, 1958.

[37] Arnold M. Rose, "A Systematic Summary of Symbolic Interaction Theory," in *Human Behavior and Social Processes*.

[38] [See Rosalind F. Dymond, "A Preliminary Investigation of the Relation of Insight and Empathy," *Journal of Consulting Psychology*, 12:228–33 (1948); "A Scale for the Measurement of Empathic Ability," *Journal of Consulting Psychology*, 13:127–33 (1949), reprinted in *Small Groups: Studies in Social Interaction*, ed. by A. Paul Hare, Edgar F. Borgatta, and Robert F. Bales (New York: Alfred A. Knopf, 1955), pp. 226–35. See also Rosalind F. Dymond, Anne S. Hughes, and Virginia L. Raabe, "Measurable Changes in Empathy with Age," *Journal of Consulting Psychology*, 16:202–6 (1952); Rosalind Dymond Cartwright, Julius Seeman, and Donald L. Grummon, "Patterns of Perceived Interpersonal Relations," *Sociometry* 19:166–77 (Sept., 1965)—The Editor.]

[39] [Cf. Manford H. Kuhn, "The Reference Group Reconsidered" (in this issue of *The Sociological Quarterly*), which was written shortly after the present essay.—The Editor.]

lates of self-attitude stability are phenomenal and which are non-conscious and outside self-directed control.

If I may be permitted a brief look at the crystal ball, I would see in it for the next twenty-five years of symbolic interaction theory an accelerated development of research techniques on the one hand, and a coalescing of most of the separate subtheories under consideration in this paper on the other. I have a basic confidence that symbolic interactionism will hold its own and gain against the competition of such major theories as psychoanalysis, the learning theories, and field theory. The reason I am confident is that I believe that of these major theories only symbolic interactionism is logically consistent with the basic propositions of the social sciences: the psychic unit of man (Boas); the extreme cultural variability of man; the creativity of man; the continual socializability and modifiability of man; the ability of man to feed back complex correctives to his behavior without engaging in trial and error, or conditioning, learning.

REFERENCES

Apple, D. "Learning Theory and Socialization," *American Sociological Review,* 16:23–27 (Feb., 1951). Comment by J. Gillin, *American Sociological Review,* 16:384 (June, 1951).

Argyris, C. "The Fusion of an Individual with the Organization," *American Sociological Review,* 19:267–72 (June, 1954).

Becker, Ernest. "Socialization, Command of Performance, and Mental Illness," *American Journal of Sociology,* 67:484–501 (Mar., 1962).

Becker, Howard S. "Problems of Inference and Proof in Participant Observation," *American Sociological Review,* 23:652–60 (Dec., 1958).

Becker, Howard S., and Carper, James. "The Elements of Identification with an Occupation," *American Sociological Review,* 21:341–48 (June, 1956).

Becker, Howard S., and Geer, Blanche. "The Fate of Idealism in Medical School," *American Sociological Review,* 23:50–56 (Feb., 1958).

Blau, Zena Smith. "Changes in Status and Age Identification," *American Sociological Review,* 21:198–203 (Apr., 1956).

Blumer, Herbert. "Sociological Analysis and the Variable," *American Sociological Review,* 21:683–90 (Dec., 1956).

Boggs, Stephen T. "An Interactional Study of Ojibwa Socialization," *American Sociological Review,* 21:191–98 (Apr., 1956).

Bordua, David J. "Authoritarianism and Intolerance of Nonconformists," *Sociometry,* 24:198–216 (June, 1961).

Brim, Orville, J., Jr. "Family Structure and Sex Role Learning by Children: A Further Analysis of Helen Koch's Data," *Sociometry,* 21:1–16 (Mar., 1958).

Brown, J. C. "An Experiment in Role-Taking," *American Sociological Review,* 17:587–97 (Oct., 1952).

Bucher, Rue, and Strauss, Anselm. "Professions in Process," *American Journal of Sociology,* 66:325–34 (Jan., 1961).

Burke, Kenneth. *A Grammar of Motives.* New York: Prentice-Hall, 1945.

———. *A Rhetoric of Motives.* New York: Prentice-Hall, 1950.

Cameron, Norman. *The Psychology of Behavior Disorders.* Boston: Houghton Mifflin Co., 1947.

Cartwright, Rosalind Dymond, Seeman, Julius, and Grummon, Donald L. "Patterns of Perceived Interpersonal Relations," *Sociometry,* 19:166–77 (Sept., 1956).

Clark, John P. "Measuring Alienation Within a Social System," *American Sociological Review,* 24:849–52 (Dec., 1959).

Coates, Chas. H., and Pellegrin, Roland J. "Executives and Supervisors: Contrasting Self-Conceptions and Conceptions of Each Other." *American Sociological Review,* 22:217–20 (Apr., 1957).

Corwin, Ronald G. "A Study of Identity in Nursing," *Sociological Quarterly,* 2:69–86 (Apr., 1961).

Couch, Carl J. "Self-Attitudes and Degree of Agreement with Immediate Others," *American Journal of Sociology,* 63:491–96 (Mar., 1958).

———. "Family Role Specialization and Self-Attitudes in Children," *Sociological Quarterly,* 3:115–21 (Apr., 1962).

Cottrell, L. A., Jr. "The Adjustment of the Individual to His Age and Sex Roles," *American Sociological Review,* 7:617–20 (Oct., 1942).

———. "The Analysis of Situational Fields in Social Psychology," *American Sociological Review,* 7:370–82 (June, 1942).

———. "Some Neglected Problems in Social Psychology," *American Sociological Review*, 15:705–12 (Dec., 1950).

Coutu, Walter, *Emergent Human Nature*. New York: Knopf, 1949.

———. "Role-Playing *vs.* Role-Taking: An Appeal for Clarification," *American Sociological Review*, 16: 180–87 (Apr., 1951). Comment by J. L. Moreno, *ibid.*, 16:550–51 (Aug., 1951).

Dai, B. "A Socio-Psychiatric Approach to Personality Organization," *American Sociological Review*, 17:44–49 (Feb., 1952).

———. "Personality Problems in Chinese Culture," *American Sociological Review*, 6:688–96 (Oct., 1941).

Davis, James A. "A Formal Interpretation of the Theory of Relative Deprivation," *Sociometry*, 22:280–96 (Dec., 1959).

Deutsch, Morton, and Solomon, Leonard. "Reactions to Evaluations by Others as Influenced by Self-Evaluations," *Sociometry*, 22:93–112 (June, 1959).

Dick, Harry R. "The Office Worker: Attitudes toward Self, Labor and Management," *Sociological Quarterly*, 3:45–56 (Jan., 1962).

Dinitz, Simon, Mangus, A. R., and Passamanick, Benjamin. "Integration and Conflict in Self-Other Conceptions as Factors in Mental Illness," *Sociometry*, 22:44–55 (Mar., 1959).

Faris, R. E. L. *Social Psychology*. New York: Ronald Press, 1952.

———. "Sociological Causes of Genius," *American Sociological Review*, 5:689–99 (Oct., 1940).

Foote, Nelson N. "Anachronism and Synchronism in Sociology," *Sociometry*, 21:17–29 (Mar., 1958).

———. "Identification as a Basis for a Theory of Motivation," *American Sociological Review*, 16:14–21 (Feb., 1951). Comment by R. Bendix, *ibid.*, 16:22 (Feb., 1951).

Garretson, Wynona Smutz. "The Consensual Definition of Social Objects," *Sociological Quarterly*, 3:107–13 (Apr., 1962).

Gerth, Hans, and Mills, C. Wright. *Character and Social Structure*. New York: Harcourt Brace and Co., 1953.

Getzels, J. W., and Guba, E. G. "Role, Role Conflict and Effectiveness: An Empirical Study," *American Sociological Review*, 19:164–75 (Apr., 1954).

Glaser, Daniel. "Criminality Theories and Behavioral Images," *American Journal of Sociology*, 61:433–44 (Mar., 1956).

Goffman, Erving. *The Presentation of Self in Everyday Life*. Garden City, N.Y.: Doubleday Anchor, 1959.

Goldhamer, H. "Recent Developments in Personality Studies," *American Sociological Review*, 13:555–65 (Oct., 1948).

Gough, H. G. "A New Dimension of Status: I. Development of a Personality Scale," *American Sociological Review*, 13:401–9 (Aug., 1948).

Gross, Neal, Mason, Ward S., and McEachern, Alexander W. *Explorations in Role Analysis: Studies of the School Superintendent Role*. New York: Wiley, 1958.

Halbwachs, M. "Individual Psychology and Collective Psychology," *American Sociological Review*, 3:615–23 (Oct., 1938).

Heider, Fritz. *The Psychology of Interpersonal Relations*. New York: Wiley, 1958.

Hyman, H. *The Psychology of Status* (Archives of Psychology, vol. 38, no. 269, 1942).

Ichheiser, G. "Structure and Dynamics of Interpersonal Relations," *American Sociological Review*, 8:302–5 (June, 1943).

Jackson, Jay. "Reference Group Processes in a Formal Organization," *Sociometry*, 22:307–27 (Dec., 1959).

Kohn, Melvin L. "Social Class and the Exercise of Parental Authority," *American Sociological Review*, 24:352–66 (June, 1959).

Kohn, A. Robert, and Fiedler, Fred E. "Age and Sex Differences in the Perceptions of Persons," *Sociometry*, 24:157–64 (June, 1961).

Kuenzli, Alfred E. (ed.) *The Phenomenological Problem*. New York: Harper, 1959. Papers by Combs, Snygg, McLeod, Smith, Jessor, *et al.*

Lemert, Edwin M. *Social Pathology*. New York: McGraw-Hill, 1951.

Lindesmith, A. R. "The Drug Addict as a Psychopath," *American Sociological Review*, 5:914–20 (Dec., 1940).

Littman, Richard A., Moore, Robert C. A., and Jones, John Pierce. "Social Class Differences in Child Rearing: A Third Community for Comparison with Chicago and Newton," *American Sociological Review*, 22:694–704 (Dec., 1957).

Lundy, Richard M. "Self Perceptions and Descriptions of Opposite Sex Sociometric Choices," *Sociometry*, 19:272–77 (Dec., 1956).

———. "Self Perceptions Regarding M–F and Descriptions Same and Opposite Sex Sociometric Choices," *Sociometry*, 21:238–46 (Sept., 1958).

McKee, John P., and Sherriffs, Alex C. "Men's and Women's Beliefs, Ideals, and Self-Concepts," *American Journal of Sociology*, 64:356–63 (Jan., 1959).

McPartland, T. S., Cumming, John H., and Garretson, Wynona S. "Self-Conception and Ward Behavior in Two Psychiatric Hospitals," *Sociometry*, 24:111–24 (June, 1961).

Mead, George Herbert. *Mind, Self and Society.* Chicago: University of Chicago Press, 1934.

———. *Movements of Thought in the Nineteenth Century.* Chicago: University of Chicago Press, 1936.

———. *The Philosophy of the Act.* Chicago: University of Chicago Press, 1938.

Merrill, Francis, "Stendhal and the Self: A Study in the Sociology of Literature," *American Journal of Sociology*, 66:446–53 (Mar., 1961).

Merton, Robert K., and Kitt, Alice S. "Contributions to the Theory of Reference Group Behavior," in R. K. Merton and P. F. Lazarsfeld (eds.), *Continuities in Social Research: Studies in the Scope and Method of "The American Soldier."* Glencoe, Ill.: Free Press, 1950.

Mills, C. Wright. "Language, Logic and Culture," *American Sociological Review*, 4:670–80 (Oct., 1939).

———. "Situated Actions and Vocabularies of Motive," *American Sociological Review*, 5:904–13 (Dec., 1940).

Miyamoto, S. Frank, and Dornbusch, Sanford M. "A Test of Interactionist Hypotheses of Self-Conception," *American Journal of Sociology*, 61:399–403 (Mar., 1956).

Motz, A. B. "The Role Conception Inventory: A Tool for Research in Social Psychology," *American Sociological Review*, 17:465–71 (Aug., 1952).

Mullahy, Patrick. *The Contributions of Harry Stack Sullivan.* New York: Hermitage House, 1952.

Natanson, Maurice. *The Social Dynamics of George H. Mead.* Washington, D.C.: Public Affairs Press, 1956.

Pfuetze, Paul E. *The Social Self.* New York: Bookman Associates, 1954.

Phillips, Bernard S. "A Role Theory Approach to Adjustment in Old Age," *American Sociological Review*, 22:212–17 (Apr., 1957).

Reckless, Walter C., Dinitz, Simon, and Murray, Ellen. "Self Concept as an Insulator Against Delinquency," *American Sociological Review*, 21:744–46 (Dec., 1956).

Reckless, Walter C., Dinitz, Simon, and Kay, Barbara. "The Self Component in Potential Delinquency and Potential Non-Delinquency," *American Sociological Review*, 22:566–70 (Oct., 1957).

Rose, Arnold (ed.) *Human Behavior and Social Processes.* Boston: Houghton Mifflin Co., 1962.

Rosengren, William R. "The Self in the Emotionally Disturbed," *American Journal of Sociology*, 66:454–62 (Mar., 1961).

Sarbin, Theodore, "Role Theory," in Gardner Lindzey (ed.), *Handbook of Social Psychology* (Cambridge, Mass.: Addison-Wesley Publ. Co., 1945), vol. 1, ch. 6, pp. 223–58.

Schuessler, K. F., and Strauss, A. "A Study of Concept Learning by Scale Analysis," *American Sociological Review*, 15:752–62 (Dec., 1950).

Shibutani, Tamotsu. *Society and Personality.* Englewood Cliffs, N.J.: Prentice-Hall, 1961.

Simpson, Richard L., and Simpson, Ida Harper. "The Psychiatric Attendant: Development of an Occupational Self-Image in a Low-Status Occupation," *American Sociological Review*, 24:389–92 (June, 1959).

Slater, Philip E. "Parental Role Differentiation," *American Journal of Sociology*, 67:296–311 (Nov., 1961).

Strauss, Anselm. *Mirrors and Masks: The Search for Identity.* Glencoe, Ill.: The Free Press, 1959.

Stryker, Sheldon. "Role-Taking Accuracy and Adjustment," *Sociometry*, 20:286–96 (Dec., 1957).

Sullivan, Harry Stack. "A Note on the Implications of Psychiatry. The Study of Interpersonal Relations for Investigations in the Social Sciences," *American Journal of Sociology*, 42:846–61 (May, 1937).

———. "Conceptions of Modern Psychiatry," *Psychiatry*, 3:1–117 (1940).

———. *Conceptions of Modern Psychiatry.* Washington: Wm. A. White Psychiatric Foundation, 1947.

———. *The Interpersonal Theory of Psychiatry.* New York: Norton, 1953.

Swanson, Guy E. "Mead and Freud: Their Relevance for Social Psychology," *Sociometry*, 24:319–39 (Dec., 1961).

Tagiuri, Renato, and Petrullo, Luigi (eds.) *Person Perception and Interpersonal Behavior.* Stanford, Calif.: Stanford University Press, 1958.

Tremmel, Wm. C. *The Social Concepts of George Herbert Mead.* Emporia State Research Studies, Kansas State Teachers College, vol. 5, no. 4 (June, 1957).

Troyer, W. L. "Mead's Social and Functional Theory of Mind," *American Sociological Review*, 11:198–202 (Apr., 1946).

Turner, R. H. "Moral Judgment: A Study in Roles," *American Sociological Review,* 17:70–77 (Feb., 1952).

———. "Self and Other in Moral Judgment," *American Sociological Review,* 19:249–59 (June, 1954).

Videbeck, Richard. "Self-Conception and the Reactions of Others," *Sociometry,* 23:351–59 (Dec., 1960).

Videbeck, Richard, and Bates, Alan P. "An Experimental Study of Conformity to Role Expectations," *Sociometry,* 22:1–11 (Mar., 1959).

Watson, Jeanne, "A Formal Analysis of Sociable Interaction," *Sociometry,* 21:269–80 (Dec., 1958).

White, L. A. "Culturological vs. Psychological Interpretations of Human Behavior," *American Sociological Review,* 12:686–98 (Dec., 1947).

Whorf, Benjamin Lee. *Language, Thought and Reality.* New York: Wiley and the Technology Press of MIT, 1956.

Wylie, Ruth. *The Self Concept: A Critical Survey of Pertinent Research Literature.* Lincoln: University of Nebraska Press, 1961.

Bernard N. Meltzer,
John W. Petras, &
Larry T. Reynolds   3

Varieties of Symbolic Interactionism

THE CHICAGO AND IOWA SCHOOLS[1]

During the major portion of the past generation, the two leading progenitors of the symbolic interactionist perspective have been H. G. Blumer and the late M. H. Kuhn. Through his writings and his students at the University of Chicago and the University of California (Berkeley), Blumer has elaborated the best-known variety of interactionism—an approach we call the Chicago school. This approach continues the classical, Meadian tradition. The Iowa school developed through the work of Kuhn and his students at the State University of Iowa. This orientation, sustained almost exclusively, until quite recently, by articles published in the *Sociological Quarterly,* represents a more eclectic form of interactionism.

Bernard N. Meltzer, John W. Petras, and Larry T. Reynolds, *Symbolic Interactionism: Genesis, Varieties, and Criticism,* (London: Routledge and Kegan Paul Ltd., 1975), pp. 55–82. Reprinted by permission.
[1] This section draws heavily upon Meltzer and Petras (1970).

The two schools differ in important substantive and methodological matters, which can be delineated and illustrated from the writings of the chief progenitor of each school. These matters reflect broader controversies throughout the behavior disciplines.

Most influential of the interactionists we shall be considering, Blumer has had a career that requires only brief exposition here. His doctoral work at the University of Chicago brought him into close association with Mead and E. Faris (an early interactionist), as well as with R. E. Park (whose work in collective behavior Blumer later expounded). Beginning in 1925, three years prior to his receipt of the doctorate, he held a position in the Department of Sociology at Chicago, where he established himself as the inheritor of Mead's mantle in symbolic interactionism. In 1952 he joined the faculty of the Department at Berkeley.

A brief examination of Kuhn's intellectual background may assist an effort to understand his modifications of symbolic interactionism. While earning his Master's and Doctor's degrees at the

University of Wisconsin, Kuhn studied with K. Young, an eclectic proponent of the Meadian perspective. Following brief periods in the faculties of the University of Wisconsin, Whittier College, and Mount Holyoke College, Kuhn established himself at the State University of Iowa in 1946, remaining there until his death in 1963. In this latter post, he taught graduate students who were also being exposed to the logical positivism of G. Bergman and to K. Spence's positivistic works in psychology and in the philosophy of science. That these briefly sketched currents of thought influenced Kuhn's work is readily apparent.

Before launching upon the differences between the Chicago and Iowa schools, we shall venture, briefly, to relate these schools to their respective social backgrounds. Taken as a general orientation, symbolic interactionism has been described as an almost predictable product of American society and culture. One writer comments (Shaskolsky, 1970:16):

It is doubtful whether a theory such as symbolic interactionism could have arisen in any social and political context other than a society such as America's with its egalitarian ethos and its mobile class structure. The basic thesis on which it rests is clearly inapplicable to a class-structured society steeped in the formalistic, often fossilized, modes of behavior handed down from previous generations.

And more specifically (1970:20):

symbolic interaction theory is a worthy attempt to create a unique philosophic rationale for the finer aspects of American society—for what is known at the more colloquial level as the American way of life, characterized as it is by respect for the individual and a belief in gradual change to meet society's fluctuating needs. Intrinsic to the theory is the sense of fluidity and its accent . . . on flexible interpersonal relationships as a basis for an understanding of the working of society.

While the foregoing comments may suggest the social sources of the general orientation, we must look elsewhere for clues to the differentiation of the Chicago and Iowa schools. In a series of pertinent articles, Reynolds offers empirical support for one plausible source (see Reynolds *et al.*, 1970; Reynolds and McCart, 1972; Reynolds and Meltzer, 1973; Vaughan and Reynolds, 1968).

It is his contention that certain associational patterns are conducive to the development and/or perpetuation of particular types of sociological work. Focusing upon patterns of institutional affiliation (fellow doctoral-level students, professors and students, and departmental colleagues), his studies indicate that representatives of the two schools exhibit different patterns. His data suggest that a relatively strong, multi-bonded network of supportive associations may account for the persistence of such unconventional approaches as the Chicago school's. On the other hand, the absence of a network of this kind may foster the development and persistence of an approach more harmonious with the prevailing perspectives in the discipline, as appears to be the case with the Iowa school.

It can be argued plausibly that the most fundamental point of divergence between the Chicago and Iowa schools is that of methodology. We find here, as in various disciplines studying human behavior, the opposition between "humanistic" and "scientific" viewpoints. Blumer argues the case for a distinctive methodology in the study of such behavior, while Kuhn stresses the unity of method in all scientific disciplines. Continuing the nineteenth-century distinction between *Geisteswissenschaften* and *Naturwissenschaften*, one position proposes an idiographic (or non-generalizing) function for behavioral studies, and the other a nomothetic (or generalizing) function. Thus, while Blumer strives simply "to make modern society intelligible," Kuhn seeks universal predictions of social conduct. Three intertwined topics represent the basic specifics of this methodological divergence: (1) the relative merits of phenomenological and operational approaches; (2) the appropriate techniques of observation; and (3) the nature of the concepts best suited for the analysis of human behavior.

Although both Blumer and Kuhn claim to be interested in what goes on "inside the heads" of humans, their approaches to this subject matter differ significantly. Blumer's advocacy of a special methodology lays heavy stress upon the need for insightfully "feeling one's way inside the experience of the actor." The student of human conduct, he contends, must get inside the actor's world and must see the world as the actor sees it, for the actor's behavior takes place on the basis of his/her own particular meanings. Through some form of sympathetic introspection, the student must take the standpoint of the acting unit (person or group) whose behavior he/she is studying and must attempt to use each actor's own categories in capturing that actor's world of meaning. This intuitive, *verstehende* approach emphasizes intimate understanding more than inter-subjective agreement among investigators.

In a posthumously published article, Kuhn (1964:72) describes as "perhaps the most significant contribution of the Iowa research" its demonstration "that the key ideas of symbolic interactionism could be operationalized and utilized successfully in empirical research." Continuing in this vein, he refers to self theory (his designation of what we have labeled the "Iowa school") as an effort to develop a set of generalizations tested by empirical research—in contrast with the earlier "body of conjectural and deductive orientations" constituting symbolic interactionism. It is with this effort in mind that Kuhn sought to "empiricize" Mead's ideas, reconceptualizing or abandoning those he deemed "non-empirical" and developing observational techniques that were consistent with this aim. His writings repeatedly sounded the call for the operational definition of concepts, for methods that would meet "the usual scientific criteria," and for a "standardized, objective, and dependable process of measurement . . . of significant variables" (Hickman and Kuhn, 1956:224–5). Kuhn and the Iowa school do not however, reject the study of the covert aspects of human behavior. Rather, they urge the utilization of objective overt-behavioral indices (chiefly verbal protocols by the actor) of the covert aspects.

In the light of Blumer's insistence upon sympathetic introspection, it is entirely expectable that he advocates the use of such observational techniques as life histories, autobiographies, case studies, diaries, letters, interviews (especially of the free, or non-directive, type), and, most importantly, participant observation. Only through intimate association with those who are being studied, he maintains, can the investigator enter their inner worlds. His basic criticism of the experimental, instrumental, and quantitative methodology, in the form of questionnaires, schedules, tests, laboratory procedures, and detached observation "from the outside," is that they completely fail to catch the "meanings" that crucially mediate, and determine how individuals respond to, objects and situations. Apparently untroubled by critics of the "soft science" techniques, Blumer shrugs off such strictures against these techniques as the following: these techniques are subjective and, hence, unsuited to the development of scientific knowledge; information gathered through their use is too variable and unique for comparison and generalization; they tend to be too time-consuming for convenient use; it is not known how we can teach the subtle skills required in their use; and they do not, typically, lend themselves to the conventional testing of explicitly formulated theories by procedures subject to independent validation. Striking back against the methods that characterize mainstream American sociology, Blumer (1969:26–7) writes:

> The overwhelming bulk of what passes today as methodology is made up of such preoccupations as the following: the devising and use of sophisticated research techniques, usually of advanced statistical character; the construction of logical and mathematical models, all too frequently guided by a criterion of elegance; the elaboration of formal schemes on how to construct concepts and theories; valiant application of imported schemes, such as input-output analysis, systems analysis, and stochastic analysis; studious conformity to the canons of research design; and the promotion of a particular procedure, such as survey research, as *the* method of scientific study. I marvel at the supreme confidence with which these preoccupations are advanced as the stuff of methodology.

A case can plausibly be made for equating Kuhn's methodology with the technique of the twenty statements test (TST), as C. Tucker (1966) does. Known also as the "Who Am I?" test, the TST was developed by Kuhn, in 1950, as part of his endeavor to transform the concepts of symbolic interactionism into variables that might be employable in generating and testing empirical propositions. In his concern with the construction of an instrument for eliciting attributes of the self, Kuhn explicitly rejected as unfeasible all attempts to "get inside the individual and observe these interior plans of action directly" or to infer them from overt behavior. He concluded, rather, that such devices as questionnaires and attitude scales could be adapted to identify and measure self-attributes. The resultant instrument, based upon an open-response model, requires a content analysis of the responses and can be subjected to Guttman-scale analysis. Today, the TST is the most widely used technique for studying self-conceptions, has had a section (entitled "Iowa Studies in Self-Attitudes") devoted to it at the 1958 meetings of the American Sociological Association, has been utilized in over 100 reported researches, and achieved a measure of national popular attention when it was administered to the early astronauts (Spitzer *et al.*, no date).

To study "the natural social world of our experience"—a phrase that recurs in his writings—Blumer urges the employment of "sensitizing concepts." As Sjoberg and Nett (1968:59) comment: "That Blumer objects to operational definitions of concepts and advocates the use of 'sensitizing concepts' is consistent with his image of social reality." The image includes both societal fluidity and a humanistic view of the actor's ability to shape and reshape his/her environment. Contrasting conventional scientific concepts ("definitive concepts") with sensitizing concepts, Blumer asserts that the former provide prescriptions of what to see, while the latter merely suggest directions along which to look. A concept should, he adds, sensitize one to the task of "working with and through the distinctive nature of the empirical instance, instead of casting the unique nature aside . . ." (Blumer, 1954:8). In Blumer's view, the student of human conduct moves from the abstract concept to the concrete distinctiveness of the instance; for, he/she must use the distinctive expression in order to discern the common. Putting it more fully:

> Because of the varying nature of the concrete expression from instance to instance we have to rely, apparently, on general guides and not on fixed objective traits or modes of expression. To invert the matter, since what we infer does not express itself in the same fixed way, we are not able to rely on fixed objective expressions to make the inference.

We can be quite brief in presenting the viewpoint of Kuhn and the Iowa school on the nature and function of concepts, for theirs is the conventional viewpoint within present-day sociology. In Kuhn's effort to convert the imprecise Meadian concepts into researchable "variables," he has formulated explicitly operational definitions of "self," "social act," "social obect," "reference group," and other concepts. An instructive example is the following excerpt from his discussion of the self: "Operationally the self may be defined . . . as answers which an individual gives to the question which he directs to himself, 'Who am I?' or the question another directs to him, such as 'What kind of a person are you?,' 'Who are you?' etc." (no date: 4). These proposed questions, of course, are the basis of the TST.

A final issue in the methodological divergences between the two schools relates to Blumer's attack on the use in social inquiry of "variables"—with their mechanistic implications of a static, stimulus-response image of human behavior. Despite Kuhn's rejection of psychological behaviorism, his quest for variables commits him to some of its favored methodological orientations, as we have already seen. Thus, it is evident that our two protagonists assign different priorities to relevant understanding versus precise analysis, as well as to the discovery of ideas versus the testing of propositional knowledge. We can plausibly argue, further, that Blumer's image of humans led him to a particular methodology, while Kuhn's methodological predilections led him to a particular image of humans. We now turn to these somewhat contrasting images.

A second salient difference beween the two schools raises the ancient question of whether human behavior is free or determined. Conceiving such behavior in terms of an interplay between the spontaneous and the socially derived aspects of the self, Blumer builds into the behavior an unpredictable, indeterminate dimension. For him, this interplay is the fundamental source of innovation in human society. By contrast, exponents of the Iowa school reject both indeterminism in human conduct and the explanation of social innovation in terms of the emergent, creative element in human acts. The key issue is the place of impulse in conduct.

In order to facilitate presentation of this issue, we shall briefly touch on the ideas below. Following Mead's treatment quite closely, Blumer views the self as involving two analytically distinguishable phases, the I and the Me. The first of these analytical entities is the impulsive tendency of the individual. It is the initial, spontaneous, unorganized aspect of human experience. It represents, then, the undisciplined, unrestrained, and undirected tendencies of the individual, which take the form of diffuse and undifferentiated activity. An example would be one's immediate impulse of anger upon being struck by another. The Me, on the other hand, represents the incorporated other within the individual. Hence, it comprises the organized set of attitudes and definitions prevailing within the group. In any given situation, the Me constitutes the generalized other and, often, some particular other. Every act begins in the form of an I and, generally, ends in the form of a Me. For the I constitutes the initiation of the act prior to its coming under the control of the definitions of expectations of others (the Me). The I, thus, provides propulsion, while the Me provides direction, to the act. Human behavior, then, is viewed as an ongoing series of initiations of incipient acts by impulses (the I) and of guidance of the acts by the Me. The act is a resultant of this dialectical interplay and "cannot be accounted for by factors which precede the act" (Blumer, 1962:183).

It is not entirely clear from Blumer's work whether the indeterminacy that characterizes human conduct is the product simply of the exploratory, improvising, and impulsive I or is a more complex emergent from the interaction between the I and the Me. Contrasting the symbolic-interactionist view with stimulus-response approaches and other conventional views, he points out that the former is interested in *action,* and the latter in *reaction.* More specifically, he contends that activity begins with an inner impulse rather than with an external stimulus, and that this activity may undergo a significant course of development before coming to overt expression. This development may bring the emergence of new definitions and new arrangements of definitions. In any case, Blumer expresses skepticism of social-scientific theories that purport to embody determinate, precisely predictive propositions.

In Kuhn's self theory we find no explicit cognizance of either impulses or the I and Me composition of the self. For him, as for conventional role theory, behavior is socially determined—by the actor's definitions, particularly self-definitions. Thus, the self becomes a Me exclusively, and conduct is held to be wholly predictable (in principle) on the basis of internalized prescriptions and proscriptions. If we know the actor's reference groups, according to Kuhn, we can predict his/her self-attitudes; and, if we know these, we can predict his/her behavior. In short, antecedent conditions determine the human being's self; and his/her self determines his/her conduct. This view, of course, conveniently disposes of such "non-empirical" concepts as the I and impulses. At the same time, it preserves a premise that many consider indispensable to the scientific enterprise, that of determinism. In so doing, however, it sacrifices the processual character of the self and the negotiated character of behavior, points to which we shall soon devote attention.

If the preceding few paragraphs were exhaustive of the determinacy-indeterminacy controversy as it is manifested in the two schools, the matter might find a relatively easy resolution. Both standpoints might compromise simply by accepting a *probabilistic* frame of reference for human behavior. As the next several paragraphs will demonstrate, however, the controversy holds important implications for other substantive elements in the viewpoints of the two schools.

We have made passing reference, in the course of the preceding discussion, to related fundamental divergences in imagery. We now turn our attention to a more direct and fuller presentation of these divergences, placing them in the clarifying context of a process–structure distinction. The Chicago school tends to conceive of both self and society in processual terms, while the Iowa school stresses structural conceptions of both phenomena. These opposing views are clearly discernible in two very intimately related topics: (1) images of behavior as "constructed" or as "released," and (2) images of role performance as "role-making" or as "role-playing."

Blumer states his predilection for a processual image of human conduct and his repudiation of the structuralist image in the following terms (1953:199):

the likening of human group life to the operation of a mechanical structure, or to the functioning of a system seeking equilibrium, seems to me to face grave difficulties in view of the formative and explorative character of interaction as the participants judge each other and guide their own acts by that judgment.

Similarly, as we have noted previously, he refers to the self as a flowing process of interaction between the I and the Me, and not merely a summation of the two aspects nor an organization of attitudes. This reflexive process is one in which the actor makes indications to himself/herself, that is to say, takes note of things and ascertains their import for his/her line of action. Action is seen to be built up, or constructed, in the course of its execution, rather than "merely being released from a pre-existing psychological structure by factors playing on the structure" (Blumer, 1966:536). The conditions accounting for the action are not present at its beginning; for, "with the mechanism of self-interaction the human being ceases to be a responding organism whose behavior is a product of what plays upon him from the outside, the inside, or both" (1966:535). Rather, he/she rehearses his/her behavior, summoning up plans of action, assessing them, changing them, and forming new ones, while indicating to himself/herself what his/her action will be. This tentative, exploratory process gives rise, we have suggested, to the possibility of novelty in behavior.

Although Kuhn has maintained that "the individual is not merely a passive agent automatically responding to the group-assigned meanings of objects" (Hickman and Kuhn, 1956:26), he and his adherents are compelled by their methodological and deterministic commitments to deviate a bit from this disavowal. Conceiving the self as a structure of attitudes derived from the individual's internalized statuses and roles, they assign causal significance in behavior to these somewhat fixed attributes. That these elements are considered stable "traits," at least during a given time-period, is reflected in the use of the TST as a predictor of behavior without specification of the situations in which the test is administered or to which the predictions will be applied.[2] This

same assumption of relative stability, or fixity, is found in Kuhn's implied notion of a "core" self, as expressed in his assertion that: "Central to an individual's conception of himself is his identity, that is, his generalized position in society . . ." (no date: 6). Omitting the I, impulses, or the spontaneous component of the self from his consideration, Kuhn is constrained to overlook the important process of interplay between the different aspects of the self.

The foregoing discussion implies divergent conceptions of the nature of role-behavior. These conceptions can be summarized as "role-making," which designates a tentative, dynamic, and creative process, and "role-playing" (occasionally termed "role-taking" by some writers), which designates behavior in response to the role expectations of others. Both D. Wrong (1961) and R. Turner (1962) have remarked upon the changing character of role theory. Originally, such theory depicted an exploratory and emergent interaction process, one marked by fluidity and, often, some degree of innovation. Increasingly, however, this theory has come to be linked with the concepts of "status" and "role-playing" and employed as a refinement of theories of conformity, or social control. Blumer resists this movement toward a collective determinism, describing human group life as a process of formative transactions. He sees cultural norms, status positions, and role relationships as only the frameworks within which social action takes place and not the crucial and coercive determinants of that action. With other members of the Chicago school, he conceives of the human being as creating or remaking his/her environment, as "carving out" his/her world of objects, in the course of action—rather than simply responding to normative expectations.

As we have seen, Kuhn, in sharp contrast, conceives of personality as an organization of attitudes, which are, in effect, internalizations of the individual's role recipes. He describes the individual's roles as the norm in terms of which he/she structures objects and situations. Putting the matter quite succinctly, Kuhn writes (Hickman and Kuhn, 1956:45):

---

[2] C. Tucker (1966:354–5). Tucker also points out that the TST contradicts its own purported assumptions by requiring the investigator to impose his own meanings on the subject's responses.

As self theory views the individual, he derives his plans of action from the roles he plays and the statuses he occupies in the groups with which he feels identified—his reference groups. His attitudes toward himself as an object are the best indexes to these plans of action, and hence to the action itself, in that they are the anchoring points from which self-evaluations and other evaluations are made.

Anyone familiar with the TST, in which the assumption of conformity is implicit, will find no surprise in the foregoing statement. This assumption is foreshadowed, also, in an early (pre-TST) essay by Kuhn, in which he claims: "Social and cultural factors become determinants of personality factors only as the individual comes to internalize the roles he plays and the statuses he occupies. He asks 'Who am I?' and can answer this question of identity only in terms of his social position . . ." (1954:60). Even idiosyncratic elements in role-performance are fully explainable, for Kuhn, in terms of composites or resultants of the role-expectations held by the actor's various reference groups.

We see, then, that Blumer and Kuhn attribute different properties to the self, the former emphasizing the deliberate element, out of which a "new" image may emerge, and the latter emphasizing more or less preset attitudes and responses. According to Blumer, the self is a process of internal conversation, in the course of which the actor can come to view himself/herself in a new way, thereby bringing about chances in himself/herself. Moreover, in his/her transactions with others, there occurs a continuing sequence of interpretation of the conduct of others, during which the actor may subject his/her attributes to highly variable use—or disuse. As Blumer puts it: "The vital dependency of the attitude on the nature of the on-going interaction suggests how fallacious it is to use the attitude to construct the scheme of that interaction" (1953:193). Kuhn, on the other hand, characterizes both the self and human interaction as structured. The organized set of self-attitudes serves as a system of pre-established plans of action. And human association takes the form of fairly stable, ready-made patterns of role and counter-role prescriptions. For him, then, prescriptions of behavior and descrip-

tions of behavior tend to coincide. Thus is social order maintained. The implications of these opposing conceptions, the processual and structural models of human social life, extend to such topics as the nature of socialization, social order, social control, social change, social disorganization, and social action generally.

Of the many other, relatively minor, points of differentiation between the schools, we shall select only one for consideration—that of the basic forms of human interaction. Although the disagreement is a clear-cut one, its implications are not very far-reaching. Hence, our discussion will be brief.

Following Mead, Blumer distinguishes two forms, or levels, of human interaction: symbolic interaction (which is uniquely and distinctively human) and non-symbolic interaction (which is shared with infrahuman organisms). The latter is a conversation of gestures, essentially of a stimulus-response nature, in which each organism responds to the perceived actions, or gestures, of the other without making efforts to ascertain the standpoint of the other. An example is provided by the vague feelings of uneasiness two persons may experience in one another's presence, feelings that may spiral in intensity even in the absence of symbolic behavior. Such interaction may arise from sources of which the actors are unaware and may involve either unwitting and unintended responses or responses to unindicated attributes of the other.

It is true that this level of interaction has received little theoretical attention and even less research attention from members of the Chicago school. But, it appears to have been completely ignored by the Iowa school. By focusing its concern upon the conduct of socialized persons, and viewing such conduct as responsive only to shared meanings, the latter school leaves no room for non-symbolic behavior. In view of this school's negation of the I concept, this omission is, of course, to be expected. What emerges, then, is a conception of human behavior and interaction as highly cognitive, non-affective phenomena. For all practical purposes, however, the divergence on this matter between the two schools is one of small degree rather than of kind.

Summarizing the issues dividing the Chicago

and Iowa schools, we find them, upon close examination, to have an organic, systematic character. In making this point, it is useful to recall an argument we presented earlier: while Blumer's image of humans dictates his methodology, Kuhn's methodology dictates his image of humans. Thus, Blumer commences with a depiction of human behavior and interaction as emergent, processual, and voluntaristic, entailing a dialogue between impulses and social definitions, in the course of which acts are constructed. He pauses, however, to recognize a level of human interaction devoid of social definitions and reflecting sheerly spontaneous behavior. Holding these two preceding ideas, he exhibits skepticism regarding the extent to which human behavior is predictable. And, finally, in the light of the foregoing components of his imagery, he must insist upon a methodology that "respects the nature of the empirical world," relying upon a phenomenological approach, participant observation, and sensitizing concepts—all linked with a research "logic of discovery."

Oppositely, Kuhn begins with a scientific concern, stressing operationalism, the TST (a paperand-pencil instrument), and definitive concepts—all linked with a "logic of verification." Although conjoined with his symbolic-interactionist orientation, this concern brings him to an acceptance of a basically deterministic image of human behavior. Bound to the service of scientism and determinism, he must deny to the I any role whatsoever in conduct, thereby dismissing the possibilities of both emergence and true voluntarism, on the one hand, and non-symbolic human interaction, on the other. In recognition of the magnitude of these modifications of symbolic interactionism, Kuhn relinquishes the customary name of that orientation in favor of "self theory."

It appears quite likely that these two schools of thought may continue their present tendency of taking little cognizance of one another and going their separate ways. This tendency is evidenced by the rarity with which representatives of each school cite the work of the other school. Fostering such parochialism and militating against the reconvergence of the Chicago and Iowa schools, is their fundamental and irreconcilable divergence on the methodological level.

THE DRAMATURGICAL APPROACH[3]

The major exponent of the dramaturgical approach in symbolic interactionism has been E. Goffman. While obtaining two graduate degrees from the University of Chicago, he gained exposure to Blumer, E. C. Hughes, and W. L. Warner (as well as other mentors) and, through them, to the influential ideas of Mead, Durkheim, and Simmel. It is from these latter that he appears to have derived the inspiration for his views on the reality-constructing behavior of humans, the persuasive significance of ceremony and ritual in human social life, and the utility of a "formal" orientation that overlooks historical specificities in a quest for universal generalizations. His approach shows greater affinity, both substantively and methodologically, for the Chicago than for the Iowa school. Commenting upon a related matter, Lofland (1970:38) refers to Goffman's prolific invention of "mini-concepts" and credits (or blames) the "conceptually impoverished symbolic interactionist tradition at the University of Chicago in the later forties and early fifties."

The point of departure for Goffman's dramaturgical metaphor, derived partly from the influential ideas of the philosopher-critic K. Burke (especially 1945 and 1950), is the premise that when human beings interact each desires to "manage" the impressions the others receive of him/her. In effect, each puts on a "show" for the others. The preface of Goffman's first monograph in the "life as theater" vein puts the matter as follows (1959:xi):

> The perspective employed in this report is that of the theatrical performance; the principles derived are dramaturgical ones. I shall consider the way in which the individual . . . presents himself and his activity to others, the ways in which he guides and controls the impressions they form of him, and the kinds of things he may and may not do while sustaining his performance before them.

Thus, interactants, singly or in "teams," give "performances," during which they enact "parts," or "routines," which make use of a "setting" and "props," as well as both the "front re-

---

[3] This section, as well as the two subsequent ones, draws upon Petras and Meltzer (1973).

gion" of the "scene" and the "back-stage" (hidden from the "audience"). The outcome of each performance is an imputation by the audience of a particular kind of self to the performed character(s). This imputation is as much, or more, a product of the expressive, ritualistic, or ceremonial elements in the actor's behavior as of the instrumental, practical, or substantive elements.

The core aspect of the actor's histrionics is presented in another statement by Goffman (1959:15):

> I assume that when an individual appears before others he will have many motives for trying to control the impressions they receive of the situation. This report is concerned with some of the common techniques that persons employ to sustain such impressions and with some of the common contingencies associated with the employment of these techniques . . . I shall be concerned only with the participant's dramaturgical problems of presenting the activity before others.

As Goffman points out, "Information about the individual helps to define the situation, enabling others to know in advance what he will expect of them and what they expect of him" (1959:1). It is to the individual's advantage, of course, to present himself/herself in ways that will best serve his/her ends. In Goffman's analysis, then, the self becomes an object about which the actor wishes to foster an impression.

If we even cursorily scan the essays in one of Goffman's numerous books, we can give some further impressions of his orientation. *Interaction Ritual: Essays in Face-to-Face Behavior* (1967) furnishes a representative set of ideas. The first essay, "On Face Work," presents the keynote idea that human beings strive to interact with others in ways that maintain both their own "face" and that of other interactants. Such management of impressions is the fundamental principle of the tacit norms governing such brief encounters as conversations, track meets, banquets, jury trials, street loitering, and the like. "The Nature of Deference and Demeanor" draws upon Goffman's observations of mental patients to illustrate how deference represents the conveyance of regard or respect, and demeanor provides the means through which the actor creates an image of himself/herself for others. In "Embarrassment and

Social Organization," Goffman describes situations in which some event threatens, challenges, or discredits the claims an actor has projected about himself/herself. The social function of embarrassment is shown to reside in the demonstration that the face-losing actor is at least disturbed by it and may prove more worthy another time. "Alienation from Interaction" describes ways in which an actor may lose his/her involvement in a conversational encounter. Such "misinvolvements" (e.g., external preoccupation, self-consciousness, etc.) violate the social requirement that interactants must elicit and sustain spontaneous involvement in a shared focus of attention. Challenging the view that psychotic behavior is a defect in information transmitting or in interpersonal relating, "Mental Symptoms and Public Order" presents the view that symptomatic behavior may well been seen as a failure to conform to the tacit rules of decorum and demeanor that regulate interpersonal "occasions." "Where the Action Is" employs the vocabulary of gambling in analyzing activities in which actors knowingly take avoidable risks. These activities provide special opportunities to establish and maintain face.

In common with the ethnomethodologists, whom we shall consider in a later section, Goffman recognizes that the norms regulating social conduct tend to escape notice, because they are taken for granted, and he stresses instances in which norms are violated in order to disclose what they are and how they are maintained. Collins and Makowsky describe this concern as "the sociology of the common man," often concentrating upon "embarrassment, uneasiness, self-consciousness, awkward situations, *faux pas,* scandals, mental illness" (1972:202). Despite such concentration, however, Goffman's actors play their roles with minimal manifestations of love, hate, or other emotions.

Among the many commonalities of dramaturgy and the Chicago school, is their shared corrective to the conventional assumption that roles determine the behavior of interactants. Stressing the calculative and situational behavior of actors, both approaches remind us that norms, positions, and roles are simply the frameworks within which human interaction occurs. As we shall soon see, however, important differences obtain between these approaches as to how they portray role-performances. Goffman's concept of "role distance" —the hiatus between the actor's role prescriptions and role performance—captures, in its overtones of cynicism, a significant component of this difference.

In his pursuit of the intricacies of impression-management in face-to-face situations, Goffman has relied upon sympathetic introspection as his method of observation and upon a felicitous style of presentation. Reactions to these aspects of his work have frequently employed such encomiums as "insightful, sensitive observer," "stylistic elegance," "brilliant, provocative," "witty and graceful writing," and so on. Other critical responses have been less favorable. His work has been criticized on theoretical, methodological, and ideological grounds. The emotive language comprising his style of presentation is quite compatible with his "literary" methodology and its substantive products. We find in his work no explicit theory, but a plausible and loosely organized frame of reference; little interest in explanatory schemes, but masterful descriptive analysis; virtually no accumulated evidence, but illuminating allusions, impressions, anecdotes, and illustrations; few formulations of empirically testable propositions, but innumerable provocative insights. In addition, we find an insufficiency of qualifications and reservations, so that the limits of generalization are not indicated. Duncan (1968) essays a heroic exercise in remedying the latter deficiency, presenting an inventory of 12 "axiomatic propositions," 24 "theoretical propositions," and 35 "methodological propositions."

To many commentators, Goffman's scheme of imagery suggests a sordid, disenchanting view of humans and their society, one marked by both duplicity and despair. It is contended that this view celebrates the subordination of reality to appearance, of *Gemeinschaft* to pseudo-*Gemeinschaft*, of morality to opportunism. Thus, commentators refer to Goffman's views of the human being as "an amoral merchant of morality," or as a "detached, rational impression-manager," and of the self "as pure commodity." Cuzzort, for example, scores the conceptions of "humanity as the big con," the "reduction of humanity to

an act or performance," "the 'phony' element" in all social performances, and "man as role player and manipulator of props, costumes, gestures, and words" (1969:175–92).

This conception of Goffman's imagery is clearly described by Lyman and Scott, employing the titles of several of Goffman's published works (1970:20):

> Goffman's social actor, like Machiavelli's prince, lives externally. He engages in a daily round of impression management, presenting himself to advantage when he is able, rescuing what he can from a bad show. His everyday life consists of interaction rituals, employing deference and demeanor, saving his own and someone else's face, inhibiting actions that would spoil the fun in games, being intimate when occasion demands, maintaining his distance when proximity would be unwise, and in general being continuously alive to the requirements of behavior in public places.

Goffman's predecessors in the symbolic interactionist perspective (Mead, Dewey, Cooley, Thomas and others) gave no extensive consideration to impression management, insincerity, hypocrisy, or inauthentic self-presentations. His analysis advances, in effect, a significant reconstruction of the image of human beings offered in symbolic interactionism. In later paragraphs, we shall essay a possible explanation of this reconstruction. First, however, we shall touch upon a demurrer from the pejorative commentaries upon Goffman's metaphor and shall, also, describe a few more unfavorable criticisms of his views.

Messinger *et al.* (1962), challenge the foregoing interpretation of Goffman's imagery, arguing that the dramaturgic analyst does not consider the theatrical model as representing his subjects' view of the world. The dramaturgical frame of reference is, rather, a device used by the analyst to focus attention upon the effects of the actor's behavior upon the perceptions of him/her by others. Whatever the actor's beliefs may be about what he/she is doing, the dramaturgist attends to the *impression* the actor has upon others. The analyst's frame of reference, then, may or may not comport with that used by the actor in viewing his/her own conduct. As a matter of fact, according to these defenders of Goffman, the very strength of dramaturgical analysis may reside in the discrepancy between the two frames of reference. For such discrepancy may enable the analyst to elucidate matters of which his/her subjects are unaware. Specifically, he/she may then reveal the way in which interactants construct, through their own acts, the "reality" that they take for granted is "out there."

Some critics have attacked Goffman from another quarter, questioning his notion of the functional necessity of "performances" in the maintenance of social order (Collins and Makowsky, 1972:212). In their view, the increasing informality of modern interpersonal relationships and the erosion of rank in contemporary American society raise doubts about the degree to which such rituals are essential to social life. In any event, there appears to be good reason for doubting the ubiquity of cool, calculating impression management in human affairs.

An intensive critique of Goffman's approach appears in a review, by Blumer, of one of the former's recent books. Blumer, while commending both the book and Goffman's work in general, discusses certain important weaknesses in the approach. These weaknesses (Blumer, 1972:52):

> stem from the narrowly constructed area of human group life that he has staked out for study. He has limited the area to face-to-face association with a corresponding exclusion of the vast mass of human activity falling outside of such association. Further, he has confined his study of face-to-face association to the interplay of personal positioning at the cost of ignoring what the participants are doing.

In other words, the dramaturgical approach ignores the macrocosm within which its micro-level concerns are imbedded. Similarly, the approach overlooks the actual substantive content of human encounters in its concern exclusively with the expressive forms of the encounters. The resultant image of the human condition is a partial, truncated one. This defect is exacerbated by an assumption that human interaction is always organized and stable, an assumption that excludes dynamic, unstructured, and problematic interpersonal situations. Still, this assumption is occasionally bent (but not violated) by the analysis of

such pathological incidents as social miscues and lapses.

How does Goffman come by his image of humans in society? One can make a good case for linking the genesis and popular appeal of the dramaturgical approach to the changing character of American society. We can point to mass society, with its mass production, mass marketing, and mass manipulation of tastes, as directing sociological attention to social appearances. As D. Martindale expresses it (1960:79):

> Since the days of James, Cooley, and Mead, the full implications of mass society have gradually become clear. . . . The old intimacy of small town image and incident disappears as the elaborate complexities of the mass societies are presupposed. The analysis shifts to social appearances and takes place in terms of roles, acts, scenes, and incidents. Man as an opportunist rather than moral agent is visualized operating at the center of his web. Both the religious and the humanistic view of man are excluded from the new theory.

A. Gouldner (1970a), in much the same vein, elaborates upon several interrelated societal sources of the dramaturgical metaphor. He points out that modern men and women are likely to be functionaries or clients of large-scale bureaucratic organizations over which they have little influence. This being the case, Goffman pays little attention to the efforts of people to alter the structure of such organizations. Further, in such organizations individuals tend to become readily interchangeable units whose sense of worth and power is, consequently, impaired. Lacking impact on the organizational structure and its functioning, they bend their efforts to the management of impressions that will maintain or enhance status. These efforts, Gouldner asserts plausibly, are more likely to be made by persons who retain individualistic and competitive orientations to life, but who are dependent for their livings upon large-scale organizations.

The newer, salaried middle classes are those most directly vulnerable to the conditions just described. Gouldner characterizes Goffman's dramaturgy as "a revealing symptom of the latest phase in the long-term tension between the middle class's orientation to morality and its concern with utility" (1970a:386). Constrained by the new exigencies, their faith in both utility and morality seriously undermined, the new middle class endeavors to "fix its perspective in aesthetic standards, in the appearance of things" (390).

Gouldner suggests still another way in which the social situation described above impinges upon the dramaturgical view. Mirroring today's society, Goffman (as we have seen) focuses upon the episodic, or situational, upon micro-analysis of brief encounters, without reference to historical circumstances or institutional frameworks (390). This feature of Goffman's imagery is, of course, common to the varieties of contemporary symbolic interactionism.

The foregoing ideas about the social framework of dramaturgical analysis are not universally held. Brittan (1973:121–6) considers these ideas to be in error, for dramatic performances are, for him, a feature of all interaction, whether in preliterate or contemporary society. Humans, he contends, offer their audiences what they believe the audiences expect, trying to maximize the efficacy and power of their performances in order to maximize the social cohesion. The Durkheimian roots of this defense are readily evident.

We have seen that dramaturgical analysis has its detractors, chiefly on the basis of its ideologically unpalatable imagery and, to a lesser extent, its "soft" methodology. This variety of interactionism, however, also has its equally ardent admirers. Among these, R. Collins and M. Makowsky are specially laudatory, perhaps extravagantly so. They applaud the dramaturgical perspective for making social behavior "the central focus of attention, not in unrealistic laboratory situations, but in real-life encounters that make up the substance of society," and they claim that for the first time there opens up a real possibility of sociology's becoming a science—a precise and rigorous body of knowledge . . ." (1972:213). To those who agree with this appraisal, Goffman's dramaturgical stance only partially accounts for it. Equally important are his contributions to the labeling perspective ("the dramatization of evil") on deviance, in *Stigma: Notes on the Management of Spoiled Identity* (1963), and his scintillating depiction of "total institutions," in *Asylums: Essays on the Social Situation of Mental Patients and Other Inmates* (1961).

ETHNOMETHODOLOGY

Several writers have discussed the affinities (for example: Denzin, 1969, 1970; Dreitzel, 1970; Petras and Meltzer, 1973; Wallace, 1969; Warshay, 1971) and the differences (for example: Deutscher, 1973; Douglas, 1970c; Heap and Roth, 1973; Hinkle, 1972; Zimmerman and Wieder, 1970) between ethnomethodology and symbolic interactionism. We agree with Wallace, who writes: "Insofar as ethnomethodology embraces a theoretic (rather than methodologic) viewpoint, it is clearly symbolic interactionist" (1969:35). Hence, we shall examine ethnomethodology as a variation of the general interactionist perspective.

H. Garfinkel, leading progenitor of ethnomethodology, has been on the faculty of the University of California (Los Angeles) since 1954. From this post he has developed and led a group of thinkers (several now at the Santa Barbara branch of the University of California) who have felt themselves to be adherents of an embattled, "encapsulated" specialty, targets of contemptuous rejection by mainstream American sociology. His intellectual precursors have included, most notably, A. Schutz, E. Husserl, M. Merleau-Ponty, A. Gurwitsch, and other phenomenologists, as well as various linguistic philosophers. Of these former, Schutz has been most influential in Garfinkel's thinking; but, T. Parsons, one of Garfinkel's mentors at Harvard during his doctoral studies, has also exerted important influence.[4]

Any attempt to grasp the nature of ethnomethodology must come to grips with Garfinkel's convoluted, opaque prose. Additionally, one must acquire a degree of facility with a large array of esoteric concepts, such as the following: "bracketing," "deep rules," "documentation," "epoche," "et cetera clause," "glossing," "idealization," "reduction," "reflexivity," "second order conceptions," "typification," etc. With this caution in mind, we shall follow the lead of P. Filmer (1972:206–7) and present some of the many "definitions," or delimitations of ethnomethodology's scope offered by Garfinkel:

---

[4] See Mullins (1973:183–92) for a more complete discussion of Garfinkel's intellectual antecedents, co-workers, and students.

Ethnomethodological studies analyze everyday activities as members' methods for making those same activities visibly-rational-and-reportable-for-all-practical-purposes, i.e. "accountable," as organizations of commonplace everyday activities. The reflexivity of that phenomenon is a singular feature of practical actions, of practical circumstances, of common sense knowledge of social structures, and of practical sociological reasoning. By permitting us to locate and examine their occurrence the reflexity of that phenomenon establishes their study.

Their study is directed to the tasks of learning how members' actual, ordinary activities consist of methods to make practical actions, practical circumstances, common sense knowledge of social structures, and practical sociological reasoning analyzable; and of discovering the formal properties of commonplace, practical common sense actions, "from within" actual settings, as ongoing accomplishments of those settings. The formal properties obtain their guarantees from no other source, and in no other way (1967:vii–viii).

The following studies seek to treat practical activities, practical circumstances, and practical sociological reasoning as topics of empirical study, and by paying to the most commonplace activities of daily life the attention usually accorded extraordinary events, seek to learn about them as phenomena in their own right. Their central recommendation is that the activities whereby members produce and manage settings of organized everyday affairs are identical with members' procedures for making these settings "account-able." The "reflexive," or incarnate character of accounting practices and accounts make up the crux of that recommendation (1967:1).

I use the term "ethnomethodology" to refer to the investigation of the rational properties of indexical expressions and other practical actions as contingent ongoing accomplishments or organized artful practices of everyday life (1967:11).

Given the ponderous and difficult character of Garfinkel's writing, we shall limit further quotations from his works. Much of the following material will expatiate upon the implications of the foregoing definitions. As the first step towards such expatiation, we shall briefly summarize the book from which the definitions are quoted, Garfinkel's sole published book to date (1967).

An introductory chapter "What Is Ethnomethodology?" illustrates the approach by examining the contingencies and practices that shape decisions in coding cases of suspected suicide. We learn that, despite definite and elaborate rules, in each case "et cetera," "unless," "let it pass," and "factum valet" understandings come into play in the actual coding. The seven following essays (three of them published previously) provide further illustrations. "Studies of the Routine Grounds of Everyday Activities" describes observations and experiments, by students in Garfinkel's classes, whereby the background understandings that are taken for granted in commonplace conversations and incidents are disclosed. The chief technique of experimentation is that of disrupting the smooth flow of routine events. In "Common Sense Knowledge of Social Structures: the Documentary Method of Interpretation in Lay and Professional Fact Finding," we see how persons who are led to believe that they are receiving counseling on personal problems manage to make sense of random "yes" and "no" responses to their questions by pseudo-counselors. "Some Rules of Correct Decisions that Jurors Respect" reports on the methods used by jury members to negotiate resolutions of differences between legal rules and everyday rules. One of Garfinkel's more notorious studies is reported in "Passing and the Managed Achievement of Sex Status in an Intersexed Person." Based upon interviews with a male transvestite, the paper describes the techniques by which the subject adapted to the development of female secondary sex characteristics. In an appendix to the paper, Garfinkel confesses to having been duped by the subject into believing that these characteristics developed spontaneously, whereas later information revealed that the subject had been taking estrogens surreptitiously. "Good Organizational Reasons for 'Bad' Clinic Records" clarifies how case records (of the outpatient Psychiatric Clinic at the U.C.L.A. Medical Center) may be quite useful only for staff-members (who have the necessary background understandings) while being virtually useless for actuarial or research purposes. What appears to be Garfinkel's most ambitious essay, replete with interesting diagrams and statistical tables, is "Methodological Adequacy in the Quantitative Study of Selection Criteria and Selection Activities in Psychiatric Outpatient Clinics." Here we find an analysis of the actual decision-making process in selecting outpatients for treatment and for discharge. The final paper, "The Rational Properties of Scientific and Common Sense Activities," challenges the applicability of the conventional scientific method to an understanding of the banalities of everyday life.

What each of these essays accomplishes on a small scale, Cicourel's *The Social Organization of Juvenile Justice* (1968) does more fully in an intensive, thorough study. Cicourel succeeds in revealing, more fully than previous investigators using different theoretical frameworks and methods, the artifactual character of juvenile delinquency. Examining the everyday routines of discretionary behavior by police, probation officers, court officials, and school personnel, he minutely documents the "creation" of delinquency. Additional ethnomethodological investigations are those by Sudnow (1967), McHugh (1968), and MacAndrew and Edgerton (1969).

In his comments on this variant of symbolic interactionism, L. Churchill (1971:183) notes that "the ethnomethodologist continually asks the technical question 'How is that social activity done?" Ethnomethodology, thus, concerns itself with the process by which we understand the world; hence, it examines human behavior on both the conscious and, more importantly, taken-for-granted levels. An excellent summary of the position by P. Filmer (1972:203–34) stresses the following ideas. Commonplace (everyday, taken-for-granted) activities are characterized by an implicit order that emerges in the course of interaction and the activity itself. This order functions to make situations "accountable," that is, explainable or understandable. Much of our daily activity, for example, assumes the existence of an "et cetera clause," whereby our expressions (verbal and non-verbal) imply a continued directive towards a given type of social activity that is not explicitly stated. Filmer (1972:210) makes it clear that

> according to ethnomethodology, sociology is the study of all aspects of everyday social life, however trivial they may seem, just as much as it is the study of extraordinary events; and . . . sociology is, in an important sense, itself an everyday activity.

We have noted the debt owed to the earlier work of the phenomenologists, especially A. Schutz. However, ethnomethodology attempts to move beyond the understanding of human behav-

ior in terms of the meanings constructed by each individual in social interaction, to a systematic search (documentary interpretation) for the ways in which shared meanings ("indexical expressions") come to be taken for granted in human society (see Psathas, 1968). The basic position of this approach entails, of course, a processual view of human society. Everyday reality continually undergoes construction; for, although humans act in terms of a naïve realism, they must actively negotiate each social situation in terms of problematic subjective interpretations.

We should like to point out two significant departures of ethnomethodology from the general interactionist tradition. Dreitzel indicates one of these, noting that ethnomethodologists, unlike most other interactionists, maintain that: "the social order, including all its symbols and meanings, exists not only precariously but has no existence at all independent of the members' accounting and describing practices" (1970:xv). The implied thorough-going idealism and solipsism are suggested in Cooley's views but vigorously denied in Mead's. In any case, the focus of ethnomethodology "is not on activity but rather on the process by which members manage to produce and sustain a sense of social structure" (Mullins, 1973:195).

Secondly, ethnomethodology has established itself as an important force in the rise, or resurgence, over the past few years, of the sociology of sociology. In works by Cicourel (1964) and Douglas (1970a; 1970b) we find depictions of the flimsy nature of social reality in general society, as well as indications of the ways in which sociologists construct with each other an equally flimsy social reality. This latter enterprise often gives rise to the assumption by sociologists of certain givens that hinder efforts to understand social conduct from the perspective of the actor.

Thus, to assume the existence of a social reality actually "out there" appears to be universal. As "social realities" emerge relative to our particular position in social and cultural matrixes, exactly *what* system of reality is defined as warranting our trust varies. This assumed reality, in turn, defines the ways in which the relationships themselves are interpreted and carried out during interaction. Ethnomethodologists are interested in the "methods" used by the observed and the observer alike for dealing with their everyday life realities (see, for example, Collins and Makowsky, 1972:209).

So, ethnomethodology closely approximates to the Chicago school in methodological preferences, with emphasis upon sympathetic introspection and participant-observer research. The ethnomethodologists, however, have shown, in many instances, a greater cognizance of the role of history in behavior, as well as such traditional interactionist concerns as time, place, and situation (see, for example, Warshay, 1971:25). Needless to say, such cognizance has its defects as well as its virtues, rendering trans-situational generalization problematic. Generally speaking, however, interactionism has been notably ahistorical, with little follow-up of the types of analyses appearing in Mead's *Movements of Thought in the Nineteenth Century* (1936). We shall conclude our consideration of ethnomethodology by briefly examining the image of humans portrayed in the writings of that variety of interactionism.

Much of the criticism leveled against ethnomethodology is directed at it as both a sociological theory and a methodological approach. For example, ethnomethodology has been castigated for ignoring relationships between individuals and larger social units, for offering no clear demonstration of how taken-for-granted assumptions operate in interaction, and for a lack of precision in explicating the documentary method (Denzin, 1969:929). One attempt to rebut the first of these criticisms, a criticism launched against the interactionist framework generally, is described by Dreitzel (1970). He contends that ethnomethodology "tends to cut off all macrosociological considerations *for the time being* in order to concentrate on the basic rules of everyday communication and interaction" (x, our emphasis). Ethnomethodologists claim, he writes: "Until we have understood how we . . . understand each other, all further sociological inquiry will be useless" (1970:x).

Gouldner, however, touches upon what seems to us to be an even more serious criticism, one that involves ideological considerations,

rather than the traditional problems of theory and research. In *The Coming Crisis in Western Sociology* (1970a:395), Gouldner puts forward the view that, "Garfinkel's is a sociology more congenial to the activistic 1960s and particularly to the more politically rebellious campuses of the present period." Warshay, too, opines (1971:25) that ethnomethodology is a sociology of involvement at all levels. More than that, however, it is often a sociology of instigation. Whereas Goffman appears content merely to study the drama of coping with the depersonalization and alienation prevalent in modern society, Garfinkel and his cohorts often deliberately inflict these conditions upon others. Demonstrations of the acquisition of power by disrupting taken-for-granted assumptions, e.g., not accepting statements at their face value, bargaining for fixed-value items in a store, and falsely purporting to help individuals with personal problems (Garfinkel, 1967:62–71 and Chapter Three), all position the investigator as a superordinate manipulator and his subjects as mystified dupes. Thus, Goffman's opportunist becomes Garfinkel's blundering fool, trusting in something that isn't there, willfully destroyed by those pretending to share his/her trust.

SUMMARY

We have presented a brief overview of four of the most prominent varieties of contemporary symbolic interactionism. These approaches have been shown to differ not only in terms of what they consider to be the appropriate theoretical stance of interactionism but also in terms of the image of humans that results from, and interacts with, that particular stance.

In the Chicago school's orientation we find a conception of human beings as active agents in creating the social environment which, in turn, influences their behavior. The school's preferred methodology for understanding human behavior remains an unattained ideal in sociology. At present, research techniques are not adequately attuned to in-depth analysis of this unique feature of human conduct. The Iowa school, on the other hand, by insisting upon faithful adherence to posi-

tivism, has imaged relatively passive "human beings as internalizers," studying verbally expressed
products of internalization. The dramaturgical approach has added a new dimension to the interactionist tradition—the manipulative penchant of
humans. This focus has drawn attention to the
taken-for-granted world in which the rituals of
impression management are enacted. In doing
so, the approach has laid a foundation for study
of the "world of everyday life" that provides the
subject matter of ethnomethodology.

We must note, albeit belatedly, that our application of the label "schools" to these varieties is
not intended to imply that theorists and researchers working within each perspective necessarily
define themselves as adherents to the given perspective. Parenthetically, it should be clear that
the Chicago and Iowa schools refer to intellectual
perspectives, not to geographical locations. Two
"deviant cases" that illustrate this point are A.
Rose, who studied with Blumer at Chicago, and
N. Denzin, who received his doctorate from the
State University of Iowa. In general, it seems to
us that members of the Iowa school share little
in the nature of a consciousness of kind. We conjecture that this is due primarily to the circumstance that the major thrust of this approach
incorporates, rather than differentiates it from,
the mainstream of American sociological theory
and research. Members of the Chicago school, in
contrast, appear to be much more conscious of
their distinctive theoretical and methodological
position. Similarly, Goffman and his disciples
stand forth as clearly identifiable. Among the ethnomethodologists, defined by themselves and by
others as most at variance with current American
sociology, self-identification is most highly salient;
for, as Deutscher expresses it, "They see themselves as a new discipline—a radical perspective
on human behavior and its study" (1973:357).

Having surveyed these different orientations
within modern interactionism, we are in a position to indicate one common element that has
been connoted by much of our discussion but now
merits explicit mention. We have in mind the
important point that human interaction is a process of sharing one another's behavior rather than
of merely responding to each other's words and
actions. Such sharing is indispensable to, part and

parcel of, the formation of a common world by
members of any human group.

REFERENCES

Blumer, H. "Psychological Import of the Human
Group," in M. Sherif and M. D. Wilson (eds.), *Group
Relations at the Crossroads*. New York: Harper &
Brothers, 1953 pp. 185–202.

———. "What Is Wrong with Social Theory?" *American
Sociological Review*, vol. 19 (February 1954) pp.
3–10.

———. "Society as Symbolic Interaction," in A. M. Rose
(ed.), *Human Behavior and Social Processes*. Boston:
Houghton Mifflin, 1962, pp. 179–192.

———. "Sociological Implications of the Thought of
G. H. Mead." *American Journal of Sociology*, vol.
71 (March 1966), pp. 535–544.

———. *Symbolic Interactionism*. Englewood Cliffs,
N. J.: Prentice-Hall, 1969.

———. "Action vs. Interaction," review of *Relations in
Public*, by E. Goffman, *Society*, vol. 9 (April 1972);
pp. 50–3.

Brittan, A. *Meanings and Situations*. London: Routledge & Kegan Paul, 1973.

Burke, K. *A Grammar of Motives*. New York: Prentice-
Hall, 1945.

———. *A Rhetoric of Motives*. New York: Prentice-Hall,
1950.

Churchill, L. "Ethnomethodology and Measurement."
Social Forces, vol. 50 (December 1971); pp. 182–
91.

Cicourel, A. V. *Method and Measurement in Sociology*.
New York: Free Press, 1964.

———. *The Social Organization of Juvenile Justice*. New
York: Wiley, 1968.

Collins, R., and M. Makowsky. *The Discovery of Society*.
New York: Random House, 1972.

Cuzzort, R. P. *Humanity and Modern Sociological
Thought*. New York: Holt, Rinehart & Winston,
1969.

Denzin, N. K. "Symbolic Interactionism and Ethnomethodology: A Proposed Synthesis." *American Sociological Review*, vol. 34 (December 1969); pp.
922–34.

———. "Symbolic Interactionism and Ethnomethodology," in J. D. Douglas (ed.), *Understanding Everyday Life.* Chicago: Aldine, 1970, pp. 261–284.

Deutscher, I. *What We Say/What We Do.* Glenview: Scott, Foresman & Company, 1973.

Douglas, J. D. (ed.) *The Impact of Sociology.* New York: Appleton-Century-Crofts, 1970a.

———. (ed.), *The Relevance of Sociology.* New York: Appleton-Century-Crofts, 1970b.

———. (ed.), *Understanding Everyday Life.* Chicago: Aldine; London: Routledge & Kegan Paul, 1970c.

Dreitzel, H. P. (ed.) *Recent Sociology,* no. 2, London: Macmillan, 1970.

Duncan, H. D. *Symbols in Society.* New York: Oxford University Press, 1968.

Filmer, P. "On Harold Garfinkel's Ethnomethodology," in P. Filmer, M. Phillipson, D. Silverman, and D. Walsh (eds.), *New Directions in Sociological Theory.* London: Collier-Macmillan, 1972, pp. 203–234.

Garfinkel, H. *Studies in Ethnomethodology.* Englewood Cliffs, N.J.: Prentice-Hall, 1967.

Goffman, E. *The Presentation of Self in Everyday Life.* Garden City, N.Y.: Doubleday, 1959.

———. *Asylums.* Garden City, N.Y.: Doubleday, 1961.

———. *Stigma.* Englewood Cliffs, N.J.: Prentice-Hall, 1963.

———. *Interaction Ritual.* Garden City, N.Y.: Doubleday, 1967.

Gouldner, A. W. *The Coming Crisis in Western Sociology.* New York: Basic Books, 1970.

Heap, J. L., and P. A. Roth. "On Phenomenological Sociology." *American Sociological Review,* vol. 38 (June 1973); pp. 354–67.

Hickman, C. A. and M. H. Kuhn. *Individuals, Groups, and Economic Behavior.* New York: Dryden, 1956.

Hinkle, G. J. " 'Forms' and 'Types' in the Study of Human Behavior: An Examination of the Generalizing Concepts of Mead and Schutz." *Kansas Journal of Sociology,* vol. VIII (Fall 1972), pp. 91–110.

Kuhn, M. H. "Lectures on the Self," mimeographed (no date).

———. "Factors in Personality: Socio-cultural Determinants as seen through the Amish," in F. L. K. Hsu (ed.), *Aspects of Culture and Personality.* New York: Abelard-Schuman, 1954, pp. 34–60.

———. "Major Trends in Symbolic Interaction Theory in the Past Twenty-Five Years." *Sociological Quarterly,* vol. 5 (Winter 1964), pp. 61–84.

Lofland, J. "Interactionist Imagery and Analytic Inter-

ruptus," in T. Shibutani (ed.), *Human Nature and Collective Behavior.* Englewood Cliffs, N.J.: Prentice-Hall, 1970, pp. 35–45.

Lyman, S. M., and M. B. Scott. *A Sociology of the Absurd.* New York: Appleton-Century-Crofts, 1970.

MacAndrew, C., and R. Edgerton. *Drunken Comportment: A Social Explanation.* Chicago: Aldine, 1969.

McHugh, P. *Defining the Situation.* Indianapolis: Bobbs-Merrill, 1968.

Martindale, D. *American Society.* Princeton: Van Nostrand, 1960.

Mead, G. H. *Movements of Thought in the Nineteenth Century,* ed. by M. H. Moore. Chicago: University of Chicago Press, 1936.

Meltzer, B. N., and J. W. Petras. "The Chicago and Iowa Schools of Symbolic Interactionism," in T. Shibutani (ed.), *Human Nature and Collective Behavior.* Englewood Cliffs, N.J.: Prentice-Hall, 1970, pp. 3–17.

Messinger, S. E., with H. Sampson, and R. D. Towne. "Life as Theatre: Some Notes on the Dramaturgic Approach to Social Reality." *Sociometry,* vol. 25 (September 1962), pp. 98–110.

Mullins, N. C., with the assistance of C. J. Mullins. *Theories and Theory Groups in Contemporary American Sociology,* New York: Harper & Row, 1973.

Petras, J. W., and B. N. Meltzer. "Theoretical and Ideological Variations in Contemporary Interactionism," *Catalyst,* 7 (Winter 1973), pp. 1–8.

Psathas, G. "Ethnomethods and Phenomenology," *Social Research,* vol. 35 (September 1968), pp. 500–20.

Reynolds, L. T., Vaughan, T. R., Reynolds, J. M., and Warshay, L. H. "The Self in Symbolic Interaction Theory," in L. T. Reynolds and J. M. Reynolds (eds.), *The Sociology of Sociology.* New York: McKay, 1970, pp. 422–439.

Reynolds, L. T., and C. McCart, "The Institutional Basis of Theoretical Diversity," *Sociological Focus,* vol. 5 (Spring 1972), pp. 16–39.

Reynolds, L. T., and B. N. Meltzer, "The Origins of Divergent Methodological Stances in Symbolic Interactionism." *Sociological Quarterly,* vol. 14 (Spring 1973), pp. 189–99.

Reynolds, J. M., and L. T. Reynolds, "Interactionism, Complicity and the Astructural Bias," *Catalyst,* vol. 7 (Winter, 1973), pp. 76–85.

Shaskolsky, L. "The Development of Sociological Theory in America—A Sociology of Knowledge Interpretation," in L. T. and J. M. Reynolds (eds.), *The*

Sociology of Sociology. New York: McKay, 1970, pp. 6–30.

Sjoberg, G., and R. Nett. *A Methodology for Social Research.* New York: Harper & Row, 1968.

Spitzer, S., C. Couch, and J. Stratton. *The Assessment of Self.* Iowa City: Escort-Sernoll (no date).

Sudnow, D. *Passing On: The Social Organization of Dying.* Englewood Cliffs, N.J.: Prentice-Hall, 1967.

Tucker, C. W. "Some Methodological Problems of Kuhn's Self Theory." *Sociological Quarterly,* vol. 7 (Summer 1966), pp. 345–358.

Turner, R. H. "Role-Taking: Process versus Conformity," in A. M. Rose (ed.), *Human Behavior and Social Processes.* Boston: Houghton Mifflin, 1962, pp. 20–40.

Vaughan, T. R., and L. T. Reynolds. "The Sociology of Symbolic Interactionism." *American Sociologist,* vol. 3 (August 1968), pp. 208–214.

Wallace, W. L. (ed.) *Sociological Theory,* Chicago: Aldine, 1969.

Warshay, L. "The Current State of Sociological Theory: Diversity, Polarity, Empiricism, and Small Theories." *Sociological Quarterly,* vol. 12 (Winter 1971), pp. 23–45.

Wrong, D. H. "The Over-Socialized Conception of Man." *American Sociological Review,* vol. 26 (April 1961), pp. 185–93.

Zimmerman, D. H., and D. L. Wieder. "Ethnomethodology and the Problem of Order: Comments on Denzin," in J. D. Douglas (ed.), *Understanding Everyday Life.* Chicago: Aldine, 1970, pp. 287–295.

Norman K. Denzin   **4**

The Research Act

THE INTERRELATIONSHIP OF THEORY AND METHOD

The sociological enterprise may be said to rest on these elements: theory, methodology, research activity, and the sociological imagination. The function of *theory,* which I define as an intergrated body of propositions, the derivation of which leads to explanation of some social phenomenon, is to give order and insight to research activities. *Methodology,* on the other hand, represents the principal ways the sociologist acts on his environment; his methods, be they experiments, surveys, or life histories, lead to different features of this reality, and it is through his methods that he makes his research public and reproducible

by others. As the sociologist moves from his theories to the selection of methods, the emergence of that vague process called *research activity* can be seen. In this process the personal preferences of a scientist for one theory or method emerge. Furthermore, his selection of a given problem area (e.g., delinquency, the family, etc.) often represents a highly personal decision.

Order is given to theory, methodology, and research activity through the use of what Mills termed the *sociological imagination.*

The sociological imagination, I remind you, in considerable part consists of the capacity to shift from one perspective to another, and in the process to build up an adequate view of a total society and its components. It is this imagination, of course, that sets off the social scientist from the mere technician. Adequate technicians can be trained in a few years. The sociological imagination can also be cultivated;

certainly it seldom occurs without a great deal of routine work. Yet there is an unexpected quality about it. . . . There is a playfulness of mind back of such combining as well as a truly fierce drive to make sense of the world, which the technician as such usually lacks. Perhaps he is too well trained, too precisely trained. Since one can be *trained* only in what is already known, training sometimes incapacitates one from learning new ways; it makes one rebel against what is bound to be at first loose and even sloppy. But you cling to such vague images and notions, if they are yours, and you must work them out. For it is in such forms that original ideas, if any, almost always first appear [1959, pp. 211–12].

The sociological imagination demands variability in the research process. The processes by which sociology is done should not be made too rigorous; an open mind is required. What some regard as doctrinaire will be challenged by others and, therefore, methodological and theoretical principles must always be evaluated in terms of the sociological imagination. Rather than applying just a set of methodological principles to research strategies—which leads to an even greater gap between theory and method—I combine a theoretical perspective with a series of methodological rules, with symbolic interactionism as the theoretical framework and taking certain key principles from the scientific method and applying them to both theory and method. My aim is first to show that each method takes on a different meaning when analyzed in the interactionist framework—and hence can be shown to have different relevance for that theory—and second, by employing notions from the scientific method, I indicate how these methods can best be put to use to fit the demands of interaction theory. Third, and returning to the central thesis, I will suggest that methods are not atheoretical tools, but rather means of acting on the environment and making that environment meaningful. This point of view will, I hope, permit sociologists to overcome what I view as errors of the past, and reduce the gap that presently exists between theory and method. It should also lead sociologists to cease using methods in rote and ritualistic fashion, and enable us to move away from middle-range and small-scope theories to what I will term formal theory (see Simmel, 1950). Finally, I hope

that this perspective will assist sociology toward the goal of a mature science of human interaction.

THE INTERACTIONIST PERSPECTIVE

The interactionist's conception of human behavior assumes that behavior is self-directed and observable at two distinct levels—the symbolic and the interactional (or behavioral). By "self-directed," I mean that humans can act toward themselves as they would toward any other object. As Blumer (1966) says, the human may "perceive himself, have conceptions of himself, communicate with himself, and act toward himself [p. 535]." This behavior, which Blumer calls "self-interaction," permits humans to plan and to align their actions with others. Integral to this position is the proposition that man's social world is not constituted of objects that have intrinsic meaning, but that the meaning of objects lies in man's plans of action. Human experience is such that the process of defining objects is ever changing, subject to redefinitions, relocations, and realignments, and for conduct toward any object to be meaningful, the definition of the object must be consensual. That is, if I cannot persuade another sociologist to accept my definition of what a particular research method means, I shall be incapable of discussing my actions with him.

The interactionist assumes that humans are able to act because they have agreed on the meanings they will attach to the relevant objects in their environment. But before such consensus can occur, common symbolic languages must be present, and in sociology it is mandatory that agreement over basic terms be established before serious activity can begin. Consequently it will be necessary to give precise definitions to the terms *theory, method, experiment, social survey, participant observation* and *validity.* The interactionist additionally assumes that man learns his basic symbols, his conceptions of self, and the definitions he attaches to his social objects through interaction with others. Man simultaneously carries on conversations with himself and with his significant others.

METHODOLOGICAL CONSIDERATION FROM INTERACTION THEORY

Given these basics of the interactionist perspective, I can now propose a series of principles that this perspective demands of its methodologies. If human behavior is observable at two levels—the symbolic and the behavioral—then central to understanding such behavior are the range and variety of symbols and symbolic meanings shared, communicated, and manipulated by interacting selves in social situations. Society contributes two essential elements that reflect directly on concrete interactions: the symbols, or various languages provided and communicated through the socialization process; and the concrete behavioral settings in which behavior occurs.

An interactionist assumes that a complete analysis of human conduct will capture the symbolic meanings that emerge over time in interaction. But the sociologist must also capture variations in ongoing patterns of behavior that reflect these symbols, images, and conceptions of self. These symbols are manifold and complex, verbal and nonverbal, intended and unintended. Verbal utterance, nonverbal gesture, mode and style of dress, and manner of speech all provide clues to the symbolic meanings that become translated into and emerge out of interaction.

The *first methodological principle* is that symbols and interaction must be brought together before an investigation is complete. To focus only on symbols, as an attitude questionnaire might, fails to record the emergent and novel relationships these symbols have with observable behavior. If I am studying the relationship between marijuana use and the strategies of concealing the drug in the presence of nonusers I will want to show that a marijuana user's attitude toward outsiders is reflected in his behavior in their presence. It would be insufficient to document only the fact that users do not like to get "high" when an outsider is present. Committed to the interactionist position, I must go further and demonstrate how this attitude is influenced by contact with nonusers.

Becker (1953, 1955, 1962) has provided such an analysis. In his interviews (1962, p. 597) it was discovered that among nonregular smokers fear of discovery took two forms: that nonusers would discover marijuana in one's possession; and that one would "be unable to hide the effects of the drug when he is 'high' with nonusers." This type of user adopts deliberate strategies to conceal the effects and presence of marijuana; he may even smoke infrequently because he cannot find a "safe" setting. Among regular users such fears are not present, although Becker indicated that as their interactional contacts change regular users may find it necessary to revert to only occasional use. One regular user who had married a nonuser eventually turned to irregular use. The following excerpt from Becker describes this pattern and demonstrates how the meanings attached to the social object (marijuana) actually emerged in patterns of interaction:

(This man had used marihuana quite intensively but his wife objected to it.) Of course, largely the reason I cut off was my wife. There were a few times when I'd feel like . . . didn't actually crave for it but would just like to have had some. (He was unable to continue using the drug except irregularly on those occasions when he was away from his wife's presence and control [1962, p. 598].)

A *second methodological principle* suggests that because symbols, meanings, and definitions are forged into self-definitions and attitudes, the reflective nature of selfhood must be captured. That is, the investigator must indicate how shifting definitions of self are reflected in ongoing patterns of behavior. He must, therefore, view human conduct from the point of view of those he is studying—"take the role of the acting other in concrete situations"—and this may range from learning the other's language to capturing his salient views of self. Returning to the example of the marijuana user, it would be necessary to learn the language of marijuana subcultures, which, as Becker shows, includes special words for getting "high" and has various categorizations for "outsiders."

Taking the role of the acting other permits the sociologist to escape the *fallacy of objectivism;* that is, the substitution of his own perspective for that of those he is studying. Too often the sociologist enters the field with preconceptions that prevent him from allowing those studies to tell it "as they see it." A student of marijuana use, for example, may incorrectly generalize from his own experiences with it to the group of users he is studying. Often the investigator will find that the meanings he has learned to attach to an object have no relevance for the people he is observing. This error occurs frequently in areas of conduct undergoing rapid change; studies of racial interaction, political activity, fads and fashions, and even analyses of stratification hierarchies in bureaucracies may provide cases where the definitions of the sociologist bear only slight resemblances to the actual situation.

EVERYDAY AND SCIENTIFIC CONCEPTIONS OF REALITY

I wish to maintain a distinction between the sociologist's conceptions of his subject's behavior and the motives and definitions that subjects ascribe to their own conduct. The way a subject explains his behavior is likely to differ from the way a sociologist would. Marijuana users, for example, do not employ such terms as "morality," "rationalization," "collusion," "social control," "subculture," "socialization," or "role behavior." Commenting on this fact Becker notes that the sociological view of the world is "abstract, relativistic and generalizing [1964, p. 273]." On the other hand, the everyday conception of reality that guides our subject's conduct is specific, tends not to be generalizing, and is based on special concepts that often lack any scientific validity.

These points suggest that it is insufficient merely to state that the sociologist must take the role of the acting other in his investigations, and that a distinction must be made between everyday conceptions of reality and scientific conceptions of that reality. An adherence to my second principle suggests that the sociologist first learns the everyday conceptions of this reality and then interprets that reality from the stance of his sociological theory. This is the strategy Becker employed in his analysis of the marijuana user. He began with a symbolic interactionist conception of human conduct, and applied it to behavior in the marijuana subculture. His concepts were shaped by the meanings given them by the user,

but he retained their sociological meaning. The sociologist must operate between two worlds when he engages in research—the everyday world of his subjects and the world of his own sociological perspective. Sociological explanations ultimately given for a set of behaviors are not likely to be completely understood by those studied; even if they prove understandable, subjects may not agree with or accept them, perhaps because they have been placed in a category they do not like or because elements of their behavior they prefer hidden have been made public. An irreducible conflict will always exist between the sociological perspective and the perspective of everyday life (Becker, 1964). This is a fact the sociologist must recognize. I raise this problem at this point to indicate that a commitment to my second principle goes further than merely taking the role of the other; sociologists must also place their interpretations within a sociological perspective.

Taking the role of the acting other leads to the *third methodological principle:* The investigator must simultaneously link man's symbols and conceptions of self with the social circles and relationships that furnish him with those symbols and conceptions. Too frequently failure to achieve this link leaves studies of human conduct at an individualistic level, and as a consequence the impact of broader social structures on subjects' conduct can be only indirectly inferred. This principle is not unique to the interactionist perspective, but derives ultimately from a conception of sociology that holds that the impact of social structure on groups and individuals must be examined.

Applying this principle to the study of marijuana use suggests that the investigator must demonstrate how an individual user's definitions of the object are related to his group's conceptions. The following excerpt from Becker's interview with a regular user satisfies this principle.

(You don't dig [like] alcohol then?) No, I don't dig it at all. (Why not?) I don't know. I just don't. Well, see, here's the thing. Before I was at the age where kids start drinking I was already getting on (using marihuana) and I saw the advantages of getting on, you know, I mean there was no sickness and it was much cheaper. That was one of the first things I learned, man. Why do you want to drink? Drinking is dumb, you know. It's so much cheaper to get on and you don't get sick, and it's not sloppy and takes less time. And it just grew to be the thing you know. So I got on before I drank, you know. . . .

(What do you mean that's one of the first things you learned?) Well, I mean, as I say, I was just starting to play jobs as a musician when I got on and I was also in a position to drink on the jobs, you know. And these guys just told me it was silly to drink. They didn't drink either [1962, p. 603].

This interview offers an excellent instance of how a person's attitude toward a social object represents a combination of his own attitudes and those of his social groups. My third principle is satisfied when personal and social perspectives are blended in a fashion similar to Becker's analysis.[1]

The *fourth methodological principle* derives from the statement that any society provides its members with a variety of behavior settings within which interaction can occur. Research methods must therefore consider the "situated aspects" of human conduct—that is, whenever sociologists engage in observation, they must record the dynamics of their specific observational situations. Situations vary widely in terms of the norms governing conduct within them, and participants in any behavioral setting both create and interpret the rules that influence normal conduct within that situation. Recording the situationality of human interaction would be less important if it were not that symbols, meanings, conceptions of self, and actions toward social objects all vary because of the situation. As shown by Becker's study of marijuana users, in "safe" situations among regular users, the marijuana smoker is likely to get "high" and feel no restraints in discussing the effects of the object on his conduct; in "unsafe" situations he will go to extremes of secrecy and concealment.

"Situating" an observation or a respondent may require no more than asking the respondent to answer questions in terms of the situations where he normally engages in the behavior under study. Stone (1954) achieved this goal in his study of female shoppers in a large urban locale; he

explicitly situated his respondents by symbolically placing them within their favored shopping locale, thus permitting a designation and description of relevant activities on the basis.

Social selves, I am suggesting, are situated objects that reflect ongoing definitions of social situations. For this reason both the meanings attached to these situations and the types of selves and interactions that emerge within them must be examined. Stone's investigation treats the meanings attached to shopping situations and indirectly infers the types of selves that flow from them. Becker's study achieves both goals: the meaning or definitions of the situation and the self-attitudes of marijuana users in varying situations.

Implicit thus far has been the assumption that the forms and processes of interaction must be reflected in sociological methodologies. Since the emergent relationship between self-conceptions, definitions of social objects, and ongoing patterns of interaction must be recorded, analyzed, and explained, the *fifth methodological principle* is that research methods must be capable of reflecting both stable and processual behavioral forms. Speaking of models of causation, Becker makes the following argument for processual analyses of human behavior.

All causes do not operate at the same time, and we need a model which takes into account the fact that patterns of behavior *develop* in orderly sequence. In accounting for an individual's use of marijuana, as we shall see later, we must deal with a sequence of steps, of changes in the individual's behavior and perspectives, in order to understand the phenomenon. Each step requires explanation, and what may operate as a cause at one step in the sequence may be of negligible importance at another step. We need, for example, one kind of explanation of how a person comes to be in a situation where marijuana is easily available to him, and another kind of explanation of why, given the fact of its availability, he is willing to experiment with it in the first place. And we need still another explanation of why, having experimented with it, he continues to use it. In a sense, each explanation constitutes a necessary cause of the behavior. That is, no one could become a confirmed marijuana user without going through each step. He must have the drug available, experiment with it, and continue to use it. The explanation of each step is thus part of the explanation of the resulting behavior [1963, p. 23].

---

[1] In chapters 7 through 11 of his *The Research Act,* Denzin shows that the major methods of the sociologist meet this requirement in different ways.

As I turn to the individual methods of the sociologist it will become apparent that some are better suited than others for the above kinds of analyses, that surveys better measure static and stable forms of behavior while life histories and participant observation more adequately lend themselves to processual analyses.

THE ROLE OF METHODS

The *sixth methodological principle* necessarily becomes more abstract and reflects directly on the role of methods in the entire sociological enterprise. It states that the very act of engaging in social research must be seen as a process of symbolic interaction, that being a scientist reflects a continual attempt to lift one's own idiosyncratic experiences to the level of the consensual and the shared meaning. It is in this context that the research method becomes the major means of acting on the symbolic environment and making those actions consensual in the broader community of sociologists.

When a sociologist adopts the surveys as a method of research he does so with the belief that when he reports his results other investigators will understand how he proceeded to gather his observations. The word *survey* designates a social object that has some degree of consensus among other sociologists. But more than this the word implies a vast variety of actions in which one will engage after he has adopted the method. Persons will be sampled, questionnaires will be constructed, responses will be coded, computers will be employed, and some form of statistical analysis will be presented. If, on the other hand, participant observation is chosen as a method, smaller samples will be selected, documents will be collected, informants will be selected, unstructured interviewing will be done, and descriptive statistical analyses will be presented.

If a situation can be imagined in which two sociologists adopt different methods of study, the impact of symbolic interaction on their conduct can be vividly seen. Suppose that the same empirical situation is selected—for example, a mental hospital. The first investigator adopts the survey as his method; the second, participant observation. Each will make different kinds of observations, engage in different analyses, ask different questions, and—as a result—may reach different conclusions. (Of course the fact that they adopted different methods is not the only reason they will reach different conclusions. Their personalities, their values, and their choices of different theories will also contribute to this result.)

Ultimately the sociologist's actions on the empirical world are achieved by the adoption of specific methodologies. His actions are translated into specific methods through lines of action that reflect his definitions of those methods. At the heart of this interaction is the concept. The concept, in conjunction with the research method, enables the sociologist to carry on an interaction with his environment. Observers indicate to themselves what a concept and a method mean and symbolically act toward the designation of those meanings. Sociologists are continually reassessing their imputed object meanings—assessing them against their relationships to theories, their ability to be observed by others, and their ability to generate understanding and explanation of empirical reality.

This point can be illustrated by again turning to Becker's study of the marijuana user. Beginning with an interactionist conception of human conduct, Becker applied the generic principles from that perspective to the problem of how occupancy of a role in a subculture shapes a person's perceptions and activities. His theory suggested that an intimate knowledge of the subject's perspective must be learned, and to this end he adopted the open-ended interview and participant observation as methodological strategies. Beginning with this conception, Becker's main line of action was to approach marijuana users and to have them present their experiences as they saw them. The final result of his analysis was a series of research findings that modified a role theory and subcultural theory of deviant behavior. In formulating his research observations and conclusions, Becker continually assessed his findings against his conceptual framework; his methods and concepts continuously interacted with observations and theory—that is, symbolic interaction guided the process of his research and theory construction.

The scientist, then, designates units of reality

to act upon, formulates definitions of those objects, adopts research methods to implement these lines of action, and assesses the fruitfulness of his activity by his ability to develop, test, or modify existing social theory. Thus, both his concept and his research methodology act as empirical *sensitizers* of scientific observation. Concepts and methods open new realms of observation, but concomitantly close others. Two important consequences follow: If each method leads to different features of empirical reality, then no single method can ever completely capture all the relevant features of that reality; consequently, sociologists must learn to employ multiple methods in the analysis of the same empirical events.

It can of course be argued that all research methods stand in an instrumental relationship to the scientific process. Methods become plans of action employed as sociologists move from theory to reality. They are the major means of organizing creative energy and operational activities toward concepts and theories and, as such, they at once release and direct activity, the success of which is assessed by the ability to satisfy the normal criteria of validity while establishing fruitful ties with theory.

Research methods serve to provide the scientist with data that later may be placed in deductive schemes of thought. By observing several discrete instances of a concept or a series of concepts, scientists are able to move above the single instance to the more common problems that transcend immediate perceptions and observations. A failure to move beyond particularistic observations leaves the sociologist at the level of descriptive empiricism. He must establish articulations between his observations and some variety of theory. To the extent that Becker's investigation was related to a theoretical framework, he satisfied this demand. I can now claim another important role for methods in the scientific process: Methods are one of the major ways by which sociologists gather observations to test, modify, and develop theory.

In this sense, methods go hand in hand with the following less rigorous techniques of theory-work. It is reasonable to argue, I believe, that methods do not do all the relevant work for the sociologist. As stated earlier, underlying the use

of methods must be a sociological imagination. It is necessary to recognize that such techniques as introspection, the use of imagined experiments, and the playful combination of contradictory concepts also serve as aids in the development of theory. Methods, because of their more public nature are too frequently given greater attention than these other techniques that are of equal relevance. (In Chapter 2 I will develop further the use of introspection and imagined experiments in the construction of social theory.)

The *seventh methodological principle* indicates that from the interactionist's perspective the proper use of concepts is at first sensitizing and only later operational; further, the proper theory becomes formal; and last, the proper causal proposition becomes universal and not statistical. By *sensitizing concepts* I refer to concepts that are not transformed immediately into *operational definitions* through an attitude scale or check list. An operational definition defines a concept by stating how it will be observed. Thus if I offer an *operational definition* for "intelligence," I might state that intelligence is the score received on an I.Q. test. But if I choose a *sensitizing approach* to measuring intelligence, I will leave it nonoperationalized until I enter the field and learn the processes representing it and the specific meanings attached to it by the persons observed. It might be found, for example, that in some settings intelligence is not measured by scores on a test but rather by knowledge and skills pertaining to important processes in the group under analysis. Among marijuana users intelligence might well be represented by an ability to conceal the effects of the drug in the presence of nonusers. Once I have established the meanings of a concept, I can then employ multiple research methods to measure its characteristics. Thus, closed-ended questions, direct participation in the group being studied, and analysis of written documents might be the main strategies of operationalizing a concept. Ultimately, all concepts must be operationalized—must be measured and observed. The sensitizing approach merely delays the point at which operationalization occurs.

Goffman's treatment of stigma provides an excellent example of what I mean by "sensitizing a concept." He began with a rather vague and loose definition of stigma that he claimed was "an attribute that is deeply discrediting." Three types of this attribute were designated: abominations of the body or physical deformities, blemishes on character (mental disorder, homosexuality, addiction, alcoholism), and last, tribal stigma of race, nation, and religion. Moving beyond classification, he analyzed data collected in such traditional sociological specialties as social problems, ethnic relations, social disorganization, criminology, and deviance. From these areas, relevant commonalities were organized around the stigma theme. In summarizing this analysis he states:

> I have argued that stigmatized persons have enough of their situations in life in common to warrant classifying all these persons together for purposes of analysis. An extraction has thus been made from the traditional fields of social problems. . . . These commonalities can be organized on the basis of a very few assumptions regarding human nature. What remains in each one of the traditional fields could then be reexamined for whatever is really special to it, thereby bringing analytical coherence to what is now purely historic and fortuitous unity. Knowing what fields like race relations, aging and mental health share, one could then go on to see, analytically, how they differ. Perhaps in each case the choice would be to retain the old substantive areas, but at least it would be clear that each is merely an area to which one should apply several perspectives, and that the development of any one of these coherent analytic perspectives is not likely to come from those who restrict their interest exclusively to one substantive area [1963, pp. 146–47].

Sensitizing a concept permits the sociologist to discover what is unique about each empirical instance of the concept while he uncovers what it displays in common across many different settings. Such a conception allows, indeed forces, the sociologist to pursue his interactionist view of reality to the empirical extreme.

The notion of formal as opposed to other types of theory will be further developed in chapters 2 and 3. At this point it is only necessary to indicate that such a stance relates directly to the assumption that universal explanations of human behavior can be developed. With Simmel (1950, pp. 3–25), I argue that human conduct presents itself in behavioral forms that differ only in content. The job of sociology is to discover the forms that universally display themselves in slightly dif-

ferent contexts. Simmel termed this the strategy of "formal sociology," an attempt to abstract from generically different phenomenon commonalities or similarities. The synthesis of these common threads into a coherent theoretical framework represents the development of "formal theory."

Society, for Simmel, existed only in forms of interaction:

> More specifically, the interactions we have in mind when we talk of "society" are crystallized as definable, consistent structures such as the state and the family, the guild and the church, social classes and organizations based on common interests.
>
> But in addition to these, there exists an immeasurable number of less conscious forms of relationship and kinds of interaction. Taken singly, they may appear negligible. But since in actuality they are inserted into the comprehensive and, as it were, official social formations, they alone produce society as we know it. . . . Without the interspersed effects of countless minor syntheses, society would break up into a multitude of discontinuous systems. Sociation continuously emerges and ceases, emerges again. . . . That people look at one another and are jealous of one another; that they exchange letters or dine together; that irrespective of all tangible interests they strike one another as pleasant or unpleasant; that gratitude for altruistic acts makes for inseparable union; that one asks another man after a certain street, and that people dress and adorn themselves for one another—the whole gamut of relations that play from one person to another and that may be momentary or permanent, conscious or unconscious, ephemeral or of grave consequence (and from which these illustrations are quite causally drawn), all these incessantly tie men together. Here are the interactions among the atoms of society [1950, pp. 9–10].

The sociological task, for Simmel, became the isolation of these forms of interaction.

> In its very generality, this method is apt to form a common basis for problem areas that previously, in the absence of their mutual contact, lacked a certain clarity. The universality of sociation, which makes for the reciprocal shaping of the individuals, has its correspondence in the singleness of the sociological way of cognition. The sociological approach yields possibilities of solution or of deeper study which may be derived from fields of knowledge continually quite different (perhaps) from the field of particular problem under investigation [1950, p. 14].

As examples of this strategy Simmel suggests that the student of mass crimes might profitably investigate the psychology of theater audiences. Similarly, the student of religion might examine labor unions for what they reveal about religious devotion, the student of political history, the history of art. The argument, I believe, is clear: A series of concepts and propositions from the interactionist perspective are thought to be sufficient to explain the wide ranges of human behavior—whatever the social or cultural context.

More contemporary spokesmen of this position include Goffman and Homans. Goffman proposes a "formal sociological" stance for the analysis of fact-to-face interaction.

Throughout this paper it has been implied that underneath their differences in culture, people everywhere are the same. If persons have a universal human nature, they themselves are not to be looked to for an explanation of it. One must look rather to the fact that societies everywhere, if they are to be societies, must mobilize their members as self-regulating participants in social encounters. One way of mobilizing the individual for this purpose is through ritual; he is taught to be perceptive, to have feelings attached to self and a self expressed through face, to have pride, honor and dignity, to have considerateness, to have tact and a certain amount of poise. . . . If a particular person or group or society seems to have a unique character of its own, it is because its standard set of human-nature elements is pitched and combined in a particular way. Instead of much pride, there may be little. Instead of abiding by rules, there may be much effort to break them safely. But if an encounter or undertaking is to be sustained as a viable system of interaction organized on ritual practices, then these variations must be held within certain bounds and nicely counterbalanced by corresponding modifications in some of the other rules and understandings. Similarly, the human nature of a particular set of persons may be specially designed for the special kind of undertakings in which they participate, but still each of these persons must have within him something of the balance of characteristics required of a usable participant in any ritually organized system of social activity [1967, pp. 44–45].

While the reader need not accept Goffman's theoretical perspective, its thrust is apparent—a small set of very abstract and general principles can explain all human behavior. Statements similar to Goffman's have been made by Homans, who has suggested that principles from economics and behavioral psychology can be employed to explain all of human conduct.

I believe that, in view of the deficiencies of functional theory, the only type of theory in sociology that stands any chance of becoming a general one is a psychological theory, in the sense that the deductive systems by which we explain social behavior would, if completed, contain among their highest-order propositions one or more of those I call psychological. The time may come when they will lose their place at the top, when they in turn will be shown to be derivable from still more general propositions such as those of physiology. But the time has not come yet, and psychological propositions remain our most general ones [1964, p. 968].

In the statements of Simmel, Goffman, and Homans there is an explicit commitment to formal sociological theory. Homans' theory would be based on propositions from psychology, Goffman's from functional theory and certain portions of symbolic interaction. In this context I can now *define* formal theory as any set of interrelated propositions based on a small set of concepts. Furthermore, these concepts will be ordered in such a way that some are more specific than others and hence capable of being derived from higher-order statements. Once this feature is achieved, *explanation* of the behavior indicated by those propositions shall be said to have occurred. A last feature of the formal theory, which distinguishes it from other types of theory, is the fact that it explicitly rests on empirical referents. Goffman's formulations are based on the observation that wherever face-to-face interaction occurs, participants will be observed employing strategies of tact, pride, defense, honor, and dignity. His highest-order proposition holds that all societies train their member-participants in the rituals of face-to-work because to do otherwise would leave that society without participants who could routinely engage in interaction. His lower-order propositions then include predictions concerning the balance between various types of rituals and their enactment in daily encounters.

While I have not extensively quoted from Homans, his highest-order proposition holds that "The more rewarding men find the results of an action, the more likely they are to take this action" [1964, p. 968]. It is Homans' belief that variations on this proposition will explain historical revolutions, daily interactions in work groups, and conduct within social organizations.

The work of these two spokesmen illustrates the use of formal theory as I have defined it. Contrast their perspective with that of Merton (1967, pp. 39–72), who believes that sociologists should develop middle-range theories of specific problem areas. Merton's formulation is too restrictive for our purposes; it leads to the endless proliferation of small-scope theories. (I shall develop this point in greater detail in the next chapter.) Grand theory represents the other alternative; it suggests that one very abstract and general theory can be developed to explain all of human behavior. Unfortunately, as it is currently practiced, grand theory has few, empirical referents. Formal theory, empirically grounded at all points, is preferable to a grand theory with a few empirical referents, or a series of middle-range theories, each of which have their own methods and specific domains.

Basic to formal theory will be universal interactive propositions that are assumed to apply to all instances of the phenomenon studied—at least until a negative case is discovered. By stating that these propositions will be interactive, I suggest that they will describe interrelationships between processes that mutually influence one another. In Becker's analysis of the marijuana user, an explicit reliance on interactive propositions of universal relevance can be seen.

> The analysis is based on fifty intensive interviews with marijuana users from a variety of social backgrounds and present positions in society. The interviews focused on the history of the person's experience with the durg, seeking major changes in his attitude toward it and in his actual use of it and the reasons for these changes. Generalizations stating necessary conditions for the maintenance of use at each level were developed in initial interviews, and tested and revised in the light of each succeeding one. The stated conclusions hold true for all the cases collected and may tentatively be considered as true of all marijuana users in this society, at least until further evidence forces their revisions [1962, p. 592].

Becker's generalizations rest on the assumption that they apply to all persons who have ever used marijuana. More abstractly, his formulations bear a relationship to a formal theory concerning symbolic interaction and the development of self-

attitudes in a group setting. The earlier quoted passage describing the marijuana user who altered his using patterns after marrying a non-user represents a description of an instance of interaction. The user's attitudes toward the object shifted and changed as he was forced to interact daily with a person who did not hold his definitions.

If the fact of human behavior is interaction, then sociological propositions must take an interactional form. In this sense Becker's analysis fits the criterion. The seventh principle, to summarize, is that methods must be constructed so that they contribute to formal theory while at the same time permitting sensitizing concept analysis and the discovery and verification of universal interactive propositions.

THE INTERACTIONIST PRINCIPLES IN REVIEW

I have shown that interaction theory suggests seven principles against which methods and sociological activity may be evaluated. These principles state:

1. Symbols and interactions must be combined before an investigation is complete.
2. The investigator must take the perspective or "role of the acting other" and view the world from his subjects' point of view—but in so doing he must maintain the distinction between everyday and scientific conceptions of reality.
3. The investigator must link his subjects' symbols and definitions with the social relationships and groups that provide those conceptions.
4. The behavior settings of interaction and scientific observation must be recorded.
5. Research methods must be capable of reflecting process or change as well as static behavioral forms.
6. Conducting research and being a sociologist is best viewed as an act of symbolic interaction. The personal preferences of the sociologist (e.g., his definitions of methods, his values and ideologies, etc.) serve to shape fundamentally his activity as an investigator, and the major way in which he acts on his environment is through his research methods.

7. The proper use of concepts becomes sensitizing and not operational; the proper theory becomes formal and not grand or middle-range; and the causal proposition more properly becomes interactional and universal in application.

REFERENCES

Becker, Howard S., 1953. "Becoming a Marihuana User." *American Journal of Sociology* 59 (November): 235–42.

———. 1955. "Marihuana Use and Social Control." *Social Problems* 3 (July): 35–44. Reprinted in *Human Behavior and Social Processes,* Arnold M. Rose, ed., pp. 589–607. Boston: Houghton Mifflin.

———. 1963. *Outsiders: Studies in the Sociology of Deviance.* New York: Free Press.

———. 1964. "Problems in the Publication of Field Studies." In *Reflections on Community Studies,* Arthur J. Vidich, Jospeh Bensman, Maurice R. Stein, eds. pp. 267–84. New York: John Wiley.

Blumer, Herbert, 1966. "Sociological Implications of the Thought of George Herbert Mead." *American Journal of Sociology* 71 (March): 535–44.

Goffman, Erving, 1963. *Stigma.* Englewood Cliffs, New Jersey: Prentice-Hall.

———. 1967. *Interaction Ritual.* Chicago: Aldine Publishing Company.

Homans, George Caspar, 1964. "Contemporary Theory in Sociology." In *Handbook of Modern Sociology,* R. E. L. Faris, ed., pp. 951–77. Chicago: Rand McNally.

Merton, Robert K., 1967. *On Theoretical Sociology.* New York: The Free Press.

Mills, C. Wright, 1959. *The Sociological Imagination.* New York: Oxford University Press.

Simmel, Georg, 1950. *The Sociology of Georg Simmel,* Kurt Wolff, tran. New York: Free Press.

Stone, Gregory P., 1954. "City Shoppers and Urban Identification: Observations of the Social Psychology of City Life." *American Journal of Sociology* 60 (July): 36–45.

Herbert Blumer　　5

Sociological Analysis and the "Variable"

My aim in this paper is to examine critically the scheme of sociological analysis which seeks to reduce human group life to variables and their

Herbert Blumer, "Sociological Analysis and the 'Variable,'" *American Sociological Review,* vol. 21 (December 1956), pp. 683–690. Reprinted by permission.

Presidential address read at the annual meeting of the American Sociological Society, September 1956.

relations. I shall refer to this scheme, henceforth, as "variable analysis." This scheme is widespread and is growing in acceptance. It seems to be becoming the norm of proper sociological analysis. Its sophisticated forms are becoming the model of correct research procedure. Because of the influence which it is exercising in our discipline, I think that it is desirable to note the more serious of its shortcomings in actual use and to consider certain limits to its effective application. The first part of my paper will deal with the current shortcomings that I have in mind and the second part with the more serious question of the limits to its adequacy.

SHORTCOMINGS IN CONTEMPORARY VARIABLE ANALYSIS

The first shortcoming I wish to note in current variable analysis in our field is the rather chaotic condition that prevails in the selection of variables. There seems to be little limit to what may be chosen or designated as a variable. One may select something as simple as a sex distribution or as complex as depression; something as specific as a birth rate or as vague as social cohesion; something as evident as residential change or as imputed as a collective unconscious; something as generally recognized as hatred or as doctrinaire as the Oedipus complex; something as immediately given as a rate of newspaper circulation to something as elaborately fabricated as an index of anomie. Variables may be selected on the basis of a specious impression of what is important, on the basis of conventional usage, on the basis of what can be secured through a given instrument or technique, on the basis of the demands of some doctrine, or on the basis of an imaginative ingenuity in devising a new term. Obviously the study of human group life calls for a wide range of variables. However, there is a conspicuous absence of rules, guides, limitations and prohibitions to govern the choice of variables. Relevant rules are not provided even in the thoughtful regulations that accompany sophisticated schemes of variable analysis. For example, the rule that variables should be quantitative does not help, because with ingenuity one can impart a quantitative dimension to almost any qualitative item. One can usually construct some kind of a measure or index of it or develop a rating scheme for judges. The proper insistence that a variable have a quantitative dimension does little to lessen the range or variety of items that may be set up as variables. In a comparable manner, the use of experimental design does not seemingly exer-

cise much restriction on the number and kind of variables which may be brought within the framework of the design. Nor, finally, does careful work with variables, such as establishing tests of reliability, or inserting "test variables," exercise much restraint on what may be put into the pool of sociological variables.

In short, there is a great deal of laxity in choosing variables in our field. This laxity is due chiefly to a neglect of the careful reduction of problems that should properly precede the application of the techniques of variable analysis. This prior task requires thorough and careful reflection on the problem to make reasonably sure that one has identified its genuine parts. It requires intensive and extensive familiarity with the empirical area to which the problem refers. It requires a careful and thoughtful assessment of the theoretical schemes that might apply to the problem. Current variable analysis in our field is inclined to slight these requirements both in practice and in the training of students for that practice. The scheme of variable analysis has become for too many just a handy tool to be put to immediate use.

A second shortcoming in variable analysis in our field is the disconcerting absence of generic variables, that is, variables that stand for abstract categories. Generic variables are essential, of course, to an empirical science—they become the key points of its analytical structure. Without generic variables, variable analysis yields only separate and disconnected findings.

There are three kinds of variables in our discipline which are generally regarded as generic variables. None of them, in my judgment, is generic. The first kind is the typical and frequent variable which stands for a class of objects that is tied down to a given historical and cultural situation. Convenient examples are: attitudes toward the Supreme Court, intention to vote Republican, interest in the United Nations, a college education, army draftees and factory unemployment. Each of these variables, even though a class term, has substance only in a given historical context. The variables do not stand directly for items of abstract human group life; their application to human groups around the world, to human groups in the past, and to conceivable human groups in the future is definitely restricted. While their use may yield propositions that hold in given culture settings, they do not yield the abstract knowledge that is the core of an empirical science.

The second apparent kind of generic variable in current use in our discipline is represented by unquestionably abstract sociological categories, such as "social cohesion," "social integration," "assimilation," "authority," and "group morale." In actual use these do not turn out to be the generic variables that their labels would suggest. The difficulty is that such terms, as I sought to point out in an earlier article on sensitizing concepts,[1] have no fixed or uniform indicators. Instead, indicators are constructed to fit the particular problem on which one is working. Thus, certain features are chosen to represent the social integration of cities, but other features are used to represent the social integration of boys' gangs. The indicators chosen to represent morale in a small group of school children are very different from those used to stand for morale in a labor movement. The indicators used in studying attitudes of prejudice show a wide range of variation. It seems clear that indicators are tailored and used to meet the peculiar character of the local problem under study. In my judgment, the abstract categories used as variables in our work turn out with rare exception to be something other than generic categories. They are localized in terms of their content. Some measure of support is given to this assertion by the fact that the use of such abstract categories in variable research adds little to generic knowledge of them. The thousands of "variable" studies of attitudes, for instance, have not contributed to our knowledge of the abstract nature of an attitude; in a similar way the studies of "social cohesion," "social integration," "authority," or "group morale" have done nothing, so far as I can detect, to clarify or augment generic knowledge of these categories.

The third form of apparent generic variable in our work is represented by a special set of class terms like "sex," "age," "birth rate," and "time period." These would seem to be unquestionably generic. Each can be applied universally to hu-

man group life; each has the same clear and common meaning in its application. Yet, it appears that in their use in our field they do not function as generic variables. Each has a content that is given by its particular instance of application, e.g., the birth rate in Ceylon, or the sex distribution in the State of Nebraska, or the age distribution in the City of St. Louis. The kind of variable relations that result from their use will be found to be localized and non-generic.

These observations on these three specious kinds of generic variables point, of course, to the fact that variables in sociological research are predominantly disparate and localized in nature. Rarely do they refer satisfactorily to a dimension or property of abstract human group life. With little exception they are bound temporally, spatially, and culturally and are inadequately cast to serve as clear instances of generic sociological categories. Many would contend that this is because variable research and analysis are in a beginning state in our discipline. They believe that with the benefit of wider coverage, replication, and the co-ordination of separate studies disparate variable relations may be welded into generic relations. So far there has been little achievement along these lines. Although we already have appreciable accumulations of findings from variable studies, little has been done to convert the findings into generic relations. Such conversion is not an easy task. The difficulty should serve both as a challenge to the effort and an occasion to reflect on the use and limitations of variable analyses.

As a background for noting a third major shortcoming I wish to dwell on the fact that current variable analysis in our field is operating predominantly with disparate and not generic variables and yielding predominantly disparate and not generic relations. With little exception its data and its findings are "here and now," wherever the "here" be located and whenever the "now" be timed. Its analyses, accordingly, are of localized and concrete matters. Yet, as I think logicians would agree, to understand adequately a "here and now" relation it is necessary to understand the "here and now" context. This latter understanding is not provided by variable analysis. The variable relation is a single relation, necessarily stripped bare of the complex of things that sustain

[1] "What Is Wrong with Social Theory?" *American Sociological Review,* 19 (February 1954), pp. 3–10.

it in a "here and now" context. Accordingly, our understanding of it as a "here and now" matter suffers. Let me give one example. A variable relation states that reasonably staunch Erie County Republicans become confirmed in their attachment to their candidate as a result of listening to the campaign materials of the rival party. This bare and interesting finding gives us no picture of them as human beings in their particular world. We do not know the run of their experiences which induced an organization of their sentiments and views, nor do we know what this organization is; we do not know the social atmosphere or codes in their social circles; we do not know the reinforcements and rationalizations that come from their fellows; we do not know the defining process in their circles; we do not know the pressures, the incitants, and the models that came from their niches in the social structure; we do not know how their ethical sensitivities are organized and so what they would tolerate in the way of shocking behavior on the part of their candidate. In short, we do not have the picture to size up and understand what their confirmed attachment to a political candidate means in terms of their experience and their social context. This fuller picture of the "here and now" context is not given by variable relations. This, I believe, is a major shortcoming in variable analysis, insofar as variable analysis seeks to explain meaningfully the disparate and local situations with which it seems to be primarily concerned.

The three shortcomings which I have noted in current variable research in our field are serious but perhaps not crucial. With increasing experience and maturity they will probably be successfully overcome. They suggest, however, the advisability of inquiring more deeply into the interesting and important question of how well variable analysis is suited to the study of human group life in its fuller dimensions.

LIMITS OF VARIABLE ANALYSIS

In my judgment, the crucial limit to the successful application of variable analysis to human group life is set by the process of interpretation or definition that goes on in human groups. This

process, which I believe to be the core of human action, gives a character to human group life that seems to be at variance with the logical premises of variable analysis. I wish to explain at some length what I have in mind.

All sociologists—unless I presume too much —recognize that human group activity is carried on, in the main, through a process of interpretation or definition. As human beings we act singly, collectively, and societally on the basis of the meanings which things have for us. Our world consists of innumerable objects—home, church, job, college education, a political election, a friend, an enemy nation, a tooth brush, or what not—each of which has a meaning on the basis of which we act toward it. In our activities we wend our way by recognizing an object to be such and such, by defining the situations with which we are presented, by attaching a meaning to this or that event, and where need be, by devising a new meaning to cover something new or different. This is done by the individual in his personal action, it is done by a group of individuals acting together in concert, it is done in each of the manifold activities which together constitute an institution in operation, and it is done in each of the diversified acts which fit into and make up the patterned activity of a social structure or a society. We can and, I think, must look upon human group life as chiefly a vast interpretative process in which people, singly and collectively, guide themselves by defining the objects, events, and situations which they encounter. Regularized activity inside this process results from the application of stabilized definitions. Thus, an institution carries on its complicated activity through an articulated complex of such stabilized meanings. In the face of new situations or new experiences individuals, groups, institutions and societies find it necessary to form new definitions. These new definitions may enter into the repertoire of stable meanings. This seems to be the characteristic way in which new activities, new relations, and new social structures are formed. The process of interpretation may be viewed as a vast digestive process through which the confrontations of experience are transformed into activity. While the process of interpretation does not embrace everything that leads to the formation of human group activity and structure, it is, I think, the chief means through which human group life goes on and takes shape.

Any scheme designed to analyze human group life in its general character has to fit this process of interpretation. This is the test that I propose to apply to variable analysis. The variables which designate matters which either directly or indirectly confront people and thus enter into human group life would have to operate through this process of interpretation. The variables which designate the results or effects of the happenings which play upon the experience of people would be the outcome of the process of interpretation. Present-day variable analysis in our field is dealing predominantly with such kinds of variables.

There can be no doubt that, when current variable analysis deals with matters or areas of human group life which involve the process of interpretation, it is markedly disposed to ignore the process. The conventional procedure is to identify something which is presumed to operate on group life and treat it as an independent variable, and then to select some form of group activity as the dependent variable. The independent variable is put at the beginning part of the process of interpretation and the dependent variable at the terminal part of the process. The intervening process is ignored or, what amounts to the same thing, taken for granted as something that need not be considered. Let me cite a few typical examples: the presentation of political programs on the radio and the resulting expression of intention to vote; the entrance of Negro residents into a white neighborhood and the resulting attitudes of the white inhabitants toward Negroes; the occurrence of a business depression and the resulting rate of divorce. In such instances—so common to variable analysis in our field—one's concern is with the two variables and not with what lies between them. If one has neutralized other factors which are regarded as possibly exercising influence on the dependent variable, one is content with the conclusion that the observed change in the dependent variable is the necessary result of the independent variable.

This idea that in such areas of group life the independent variable automatically exercises its influence on the dependent variable is, it seems to me, a basic fallacy. There is a process of definition intervening between the events of experience presupposed by the independent variable and the formed behavior represented by the dependent variable. The political programs on the radio are interpreted by the listeners; the Negro invasion into the white neighborhood must be defined by the whites to have any effect on their attitudes; the many events and happenings which together constitute the business depression must be interpreted at their many points by husbands and wives to have any influence on marital relations. This intervening interpretation is essential to the outcome. It gives the meaning to the presentation that sets the response. Because of the integral position of the defining process between the two variables, it becomes necessary, it seems to me, to incorporate the process in the account of the relationship. Little effort is made in variable analysis to do this. Usually the process is completely ignored. Where the process is recognized, its study is regarded as a problem that is independent of the relation between the variables.

The indifference of variable analysis to the process of interpretation is based apparently on the tacit assumption that the independent variable predetermines its interpretation. This assumption has no foundation. The interpretation is not predetermined by the variable as if the variable emanated its own meaning. If there is anything we do know, it is that an object, event or situation in human experience does not carry its own meaning; the meaning is conferred on it.

Now, it is true that in many instances the interpretation of the object, event or situation may be fixed, since the person or people may have an already constructed meaning which is immediately applied to the item. Where such stabilized interpretation occurs and recurs, variable analysis would have no need to consider the interpretation. One could merely say that as a matter of fact under given conditions the independent variable is followed by such and such a change in the dependent variable. The only necessary precaution would be not to assume that the stated relation between the variables was necessarily intrinsic and universal. Since anything that is defined may be redefined, the relation has no intrinsic fixity.

Alongside the instances where interpretation is made by merely applying stabilized meanings there are the many instances where the interpretation has to be constructed. These instances are obviously increasing in our changing society. It is imperative in the case of such instances for variable analysis to include the act of interpretation in its analytic scheme. As far as I can see, variable analysis shuns such inclusion.

Now the question arises, how can variable analysis include the process of interpretation? Presumably the answer would be to treat the act of interpretation as an "intervening variable." But, what does this mean? If it means that interpretation is merely an intervening neutral medium through which the independent variable exercises its influence, then, of course, this would be no answer. Interpretation is a formative or creative process in its own right. It constructs meanings which, as I have said, are not predetermined or determined by the independent variable.

If one accepts this fact and proposes to treat the act of interpretation as a formative process, then the question arises how one is to characterize it as a variable. What quality is one to assign to it, what property or set of properties? One cannot, with any sense, characterize this act of interpretation in terms of the interpretation which it constructs; one cannot take the product to stand for the process. Nor can one characterize the act of interpretation in terms of what enters into it— the objects perceived, the evaluations and assessments made of them, the cues that are suggested, the possible definitions proposed by oneself or by others. These vary from one instance of interpretation to another and, further, shift from point to point in the development of the act. This varying and shifting content offers no basis for making the act of interpretation into a variable.

Nor, it seems to me, is the problem met by proposing to reduce the act of interpretation into component parts and work with these parts as variables. These parts would presumably have to be processual parts—such as perception, cognition, analysis, evaluation, and decision-making in the individual; and discussion, definition of one another's responses and other forms of social interaction in the group. The same difficulty exists in making any of the processual parts into variables that exists in the case of the complete act of interpretation.

The question of how the act of interpretation can be given the qualitative constancy that is logically required in a variable has so far not been answered. While one can devise some kind of a "more or less" dimension for it, the need is to catch it as a variable, or set of variables, in a manner which reflects its functioning in transforming experience into activity. This is the problem, indeed dilemma, which confronts variable analysis in our field. I see no answer to it inside the logical framework of variable analysis. The process of interpretation is not inconsequential or pedantic. It operates too centrally in group and individual experience to be put aside as being of incidental interest.

In addition to the by-passing of the process of interpretation there is, in my judgment, another profound deficiency in variable analysis as a scheme for analyzing human group life. The deficiency stems from the inevitable tendency to work with truncated factors and, as a result, to conceal or misrepresent the actual operations in human group life. The deficiency stems from the logical need of variable analysis to work with discrete, clean-cut and unitary variables. Let me spell this out.

As a working procedure variable analysis seeks necessarily to achieve a clean identification of the relation between two variables. Irrespective of how one may subsequently combine a number of such identified relations—in an additive manner, a clustering, a chain-like arrangement, or a "feedback" scheme—the objective of variable research is initially to isolate a simple and fixed relation between two variables. For this to be done each of the two variables must be set up as a distinct item with a unitary qualitative make-up. This is accomplished first by giving each variable, where needed, a simple quality or dimension, and second by separating the variable from its connection with other variables through their exclusion or neutralization.

A difficulty with this scheme is that the empirical reference of a true sociological variable is not unitary or distinct. When caught in its actual social character, it turns out to be an intricate and inner-moving complex. To illustrate, let me take what seems ostensibly to be a fairly clean-cut variable relation, namely between a birth control program and the birth rate of a given people. Each of these two variables—the program of birth control and the birth rate—can be given a simple discrete and unitary character. For the program of birth control one may choose merely its time period, or select some reasonable measure such as the number of people visiting birth control clinics. For the birth rate, one merely takes it as it is. Apparently, these indications are sufficient to enable the investigator to ascertain the relations between the two variables.

Yet, a scrutiny of what the two variables stand for in the life of the group gives us a different picture. Thus, viewing the program of birth control in terms of *how it enters into the lives of the people,* we need to note many things such as the literacy of the people, the clarity of the printed information, the manner and extent of its distribution, the social position of the directors of the program and of the personnel, how the personnel act, the character of their instructional talks, the way in which people define attendance at birth control clinics, the expressed views of influential personages with reference to the program, how such personages are regarded, and the nature of the discussions among people with regard to the clinics. These are only a few of the matters which relate to how the birth control program might enter into the experience of the people. The number is sufficient, however, to show the complex and inner-moving character of what otherwise might seem to be a simple variable.

A similar picture is given in the case of the other variable—the birth rate. A birth rate of a people seems to be a very simple and unitary matter. Yet, in terms of what it expresses and stands for in group activity it is exceedingly complex and diversified. We need consider only the variety of social factors that impinge on and affect the sex act, even though the sex act is only one of the activities that set the birth rate. The self-conceptions held by men and by women, the conceptions of family life, the values placed on chil-

dren, accessibility of men and women to each other, physical arrangements in the home, the sanctions given by established institutions, the code of manliness, the pressures from relatives and neighbors, and ideas of what is proper, convenient and tolerable in the sex act—these are a few of the operating factors in the experience of the group that play upon the sex act. They suffice to indicate something of the complex body of actual experience and practice that is represented in and expressed by the birth rate of a human group.

I think it will be found that, when converted into the actual group activity for which it stands, a sociological variable turns out to be an intricate and inner-moving complex. There are, of course, wide ranges of difference between sociological variables in terms of the extent of such complexity. Still, I believe one will generally find that the discrete and unitary character which the labeling of the variable suggests vanishes.

The failure to recognize this is a source of trouble. In variable analysis one is likely to accept the two variables as the simple and unitary items that they seem to be, and to believe that the relation found between them is a realistic analysis of the given area of group life. Actually, in group life the relation is far more likely to be between complex, diversified and moving bodies of activity. The operation of one of these complexes on the other, or the interaction between them, is both concealed and misrepresented by the statement of the relation between the two variables. The statement of the variable relation merely asserts a connection between abbreviated terms of reference. It leaves out the actual complexes of activity and the actual processes of interaction in which human group life has its being. We are here faced, it seems to me, by the fact that the very features which give variable analysis its high merit—the qualitative constancy of the variables, their clean-cut simplicity, their ease of manipulation as a sort of free counter, their ability to be brought into decisive relation—are the features that lead variable analysis to gloss over the character of the real operating factors in group life, and the real interaction and relations between such factors.

The two major difficulties faced by variable

analysis point clearly to the need for a markedly different scheme of sociological analysis for the areas in which these difficulties arise. This is not the occasion to spell out the nature of this scheme. I shall merely mention a few of its rudiments to suggest how its character differs fundamentally from that of variable analysis. The scheme would be based on the premise that the chief means through which human group life operates and is formed is a vast, diversified process of definition. The scheme respects the empirical existence of this process. It devotes itself to the analysis of the operation and formation of human group life as these occur through this process. In doing so it seeks to trace the lines of defining experience through which ways of living, patterns of relations, and social forms are developed, rather than to relate these formations to a set of selected items. It views items of social life as articulated inside moving structures and believes that they have to be understood in terms of this articulation. Thus, it handles these items not as discrete things disengaged from their connections but instead, as signs of a supporting context which gives them their social character. In its effort to ferret out lines of definition and networks of moving relation, it relies on a distinctive form of procedure. This procedure is to approach the study of group activity through the eyes and experience of the people who have developed the activity. Hence, it necessarily requires an intimate familiarity with this experience and with the scenes of its opera-

tion. It uses broad and interlacing observations and not narrow and disjunctive observations. And, may I add, that like variable analysis, it yields empirical findings and "here-and-now" propositions, although in a different form. Finally, it is no worse off than variable analysis in developing generic knowledge out of its findings and propositions.

In closing, I express a hope that my critical remarks about variable analysis are not misinterpreted to mean that variable analysis is useless or makes no contribution to sociological analysis. The contrary is true. Variable analysis is a fit procedure for those areas of social life and formation that are not mediated by an interpretative process. Such areas exist and are important. Further, in the area of interpretative life variable analysis can be an effective means of unearthing stabilized patterns of interpretation which are not likely to be detected through the direct study of the experience of people. Knowledge of such patterns, or rather of the relations between variables which reflect such patterns, is of great value for understanding group life in its "here-and-now" character and indeed may have significant practical value. All of these appropriate uses give variable analysis a worthy status in our field.

In view, however, of the current tendency of variable analysis to become the norm and model for sociological analysis, I believe it important to recognize its shortcomings and its limitations.

Participant Observation and Interviewing: A Comparison

The most complete form of the sociological datum, after all, is the form in which the participant observer gathers it: an observation of some social event, the events which precede and follow it, and explanations of its meaning by participants and spectators, before, during, and after its occurrence. Such a datum gives us more information about the event under study than data gathered by any other sociological method. Participant observation can thus provide us with a yardstick against which to measure the completeness of data gathered in other ways, a model which can serve to let us know what orders of information escape us when we use other methods.[1]

By participant observation we mean that method in which the observer participates in the daily life of the people under study, either openly in the role of researcher or covertly in some disguised role, observing things that happen, listening to what is said, and questioning people, over some length of time.[2] We want, in this paper,

to compare the results of such intensive field work with what might be regarded as the first step in the other direction along this continuum: the detailed and conversational interview (often referred to as the unstructured or undirected interview).[3] In this kind of interview, the interviewer explores many facets of his interviewee's concerns, treating subjects as they come up in conversation, pursuing interesting leads, allowing his imagination and ingenuity full rein as he tries to develop new hypotheses and test them in the course of the interview.

In the course of our current participant observation among medical students,[4] we have thought a good deal about the kinds of things we were discovering which might ordinarily be missed or misunderstood in such an interview. We have no intention of denigrating the interview or even such less precise modes of data gathering as the questionnaire, for there can always be good reasons of practicality, economy, or research design for their use. We simply wish to

Howard S. Becker and Blanche Geer, "Participant Observation and Interviewing: A Comparison." Reproduced by permission of the Society for Applied Anthropology. From *Human Organization*, 16(3), 1957.

[1] We wish to thank R. Richard Wohl and Thomas S. McPartland for their critical reading of an earlier version of this paper.

[2] Cf. Florence R. Kluckhohn, "The Participant Observer Technique in Small Communities," *American Journal of Sociology,* 45 (Nov., 1940), 331–43; Arthur Vidich, "Participant Observation and the Collection and Interpretation of Data," *ibid.,* 60 (Jan., 1955), 354–60; William Foote Whyte, "Observational Field-Work Methods," in Marie Jahoda, Morton Deutsch, and Stuart W. Cook (eds.), *Research Methods in the Social Sciences* (New York: Dryden Press, 1951), II, 393–514, and *Street Corner*

Society (Enlarged Edition) (Chicago: University of Chicago Press, 1955), 279–358.

[3] Two provisos are in order. In the first place, we assume in our comparison that the hypothetical interviewer and participant observer we discuss are equally skilled and sensitive. We assume further that both began their research with equally well formulated problems, so that they are indeed looking for equivalent kinds of data.

[4] This study is sponsored by Community Studies., Inc., of Kansas City, Missouri, and is being carried out at the University of Kansas Medical Center, to whose dean and staff we are indebted for their wholehearted cooperation. Professor Everett C. Hughes of the University of Chicago is director of the project.

make explicit the difference in data gathered by one or the other method and to suggest the differing uses to which they can legitimately be put. In general, the shortcomings we attribute to the interview exist when it is used as a source of information about events that have occurred elsewhere and are described to us by informants. Our criticisms are not relevant when analysis is restricted to interpretation of the interviewee's conduct *during the interview*, in which case the researcher has in fact observed the behavior he is talking about.[5]

The differences we consider between the two methods involve two interacting factors: the kinds of words and acts of the people under study that the researcher has access to, and the kind of sensitivity to problems and data produced in him. Our comparison may prove useful by suggesting areas in which interviewing (the more widely used method at present and likely to continue so) can improve its accuracy by taking account of suggestions made from the perspective of the participant observer. We begin by considering some concrete problems: learning the native language, or the problem of the degree to which the interviewer really understands what is said to him; matters interviewees are unable or unwilling to talk about; and getting information on matters people see through distorting lenses. We then consider some more general differences between the two methods.

LEARNING THE NATIVE LANGUAGE

Any social group, to the extent that it is a distinctive unit, will have to some degree a culture differing from that of other groups, a somewhat different set of common understandings around which action is organized, and these differences will find expression in a language whose nuances are peculiar to that group and fully understood only by its members. Members of churches speak differently from members of informal tavern groups; more importantly, members of any particular church or tavern group

have cultures, and languages in which they are expressed, which differ somewhat from those of other groups of the same general type. So, although we speak one language and share in many ways in one culture, we cannot assume that we understand precisely what another person, speaking as a member of such a group, means by any particular word. In interviewing members of groups other than our own, then, we are in somewhat the same position as the anthropologist who must learn a primitive language,[6] with the important difference that, as Icheiser has put it, we often do not understand that we do not understand and are thus likely to make errors in interpreting what is said to us. In the case of gross misunderstandings the give and take of conversation may quickly reveal our mistakes, so that the interviewee can correct us; this presumably is one of the chief mechanisms through which the anthropologist acquires a new tongue. But in speaking American English with an interviewee who is, after all, much like us, we may mistakenly assume that we have understood him and the error be small enough that it will not disrupt communication to the point where a correction will be in order.

The interview provides little opportunity of rectifying errors of this kind where they go unrecognized. In contrast, participant observation provides a situation in which the meaning of words can be learned with great precision through study of their use in context, exploration through continuous interviewing of their implications and nuances, and the use of them oneself under the scrutiny of capable speakers of the language. Beyond simply clarifying matters so that the researcher may understand better what people say to each other and to him, such a linguistic exercise may provide research hypotheses of great usefulness. The way in which one of us learned the meaning of the word "crock," as medical students use it, illustrates these points.

> I first heard the word "crock" applied to a patient shortly after I began my field work. The patient in question, a fat, middle-aged woman, complained

[5] For discussion of this point, see Thomas S. McPartland, *Formal Education and the Process of Professionalization: A Study of Student Nurses* (Kansas City, Missouri: Community Studies, Inc., 1957), 2–3.

[6] See the discussion in Bronislaw Malinowski, *Magic, Science, and Religion and Other Essays* (Glencoe: The Free Press, 1948), 232–8.

bitterly of pains in a number of widely separated locations. When I asked the student who had so described her what the word meant, he said that it was used to refer to any patient who had psychosomatic complaints. I asked if that meant that Mr. X——, a young man on the ward whose stomach ulcer had been discussed by a staff physician as typically psychosomatic, was a crock. The student said that that would not be correct usage, but was not able to say why.

Over a period of several weeks, through discussion of many cases seen during morning rounds with the students, I finally arrived at an understanding of the term, realizing that it referred to a patient who complained of many symptoms but had no discoverable organic pathology. I had noticed from the beginning that the term was used in a derogatory way and had also been inquiring into this, asking students why they disliked having crocks assigned to them for examination and diagnosis. At first students denied the derogatory connotations, but repeated observations of their disgust with such assignments soon made such denials unrealistic. Several students eventually explained their dislike in ways of which the following example is typical: "The true crock is a person who you do a great big workup for and who has all of these vague symptoms, and *you really can't find anything the matter with them.*"

Further discussion made it clear that the students regarded patients primarily as objects from which they could learn those aspects of clinical medicine not easily acquired from textbooks and lectures; the crock took a great deal of their time, of which they felt they had little enough, and did not exhibit any interesting disease state from which something might be learned, so that the time invested was wasted. This discovery in turn suggested that I might profitably investigate the general perspective toward medical school which led to such a basis for judgment of patients, and also suggested hypotheses regarding the value system of the hospital hierarchy at whose bottom the student stood.

At the risk of being repetitious, let us point out in this example both the errors avoided and the advantages gained because of the use of participant observation. The term might never have been used by students in an ordinary interview; if it had, the interviewer might easily have assumed that the scatological term from which it in fact is descended provided a complete definition. Because the observer saw students on their daily rounds and heard them discussing everyday problems, he heard the word and was able to pursue it until he arrived at a meaningful definition. Moreover, the knowledge so gained led to further

and more general discoveries about the group under study.

This is not to say that all of these things might not be discovered by a program of skillful interviewing, for this might well be possible. But we do suggest that an interviewer may misunderstand common English words when interviewees use them in some more or less esoteric way and not know that he is misunderstanding them, because there will be little chance to check his understanding against either further examples of their use in conversation or instances of the object to which they are applied. This leaves him open to errors of misinterpretation and errors of failing to see connections between items of information he has available, and may prevent him from seeing and exploring important research leads. In dealing with interview data, then, experience with participant observation indicates that both care and imagination must be used in making sure of meanings, for the cultural esoterica of a group may hide behind ordinary language used in special ways.

MATTERS INTERVIEWEES ARE UNABLE OR UNWILLING TO TALK ABOUT

Frequently, people do not tell an interviewer all the things he might want to know. This may be because they do not want to, feeling that to speak of some particular subject would be impolitic, impolite, or insensitive, because they do not think to and because the interviewer does not have enough information to inquire into the matter, or because they are not able to. The first case—the problem of "resistance"—is well known and a considerable lore has developed about how to cope with it.[7] It is more difficult to deal with the last two possibilities for the interviewee is not likely to reveal, or the interviewer to become aware, that significant omissions are being made. Many events occur in the life of a social group and the experience of an individual so regularly

---

[7] See, for example, Arnold M. Rose, "A Research Note on Interviewing," *American Journal of Sociology*, 51 (Sept., 1945), 143–4; and Howard S. Becker, "A Note on Interviewing Tactics," *Human Organization*, 12:4 (Winter, 1954), 31–2.

and uninterruptedly, or so quietly and unnoticed, that people are hardly aware of them, and do not think to comment on them to an interviewer; or they may never have become aware of them at all and be unable to answer even direct questions. Other events may be so unfamiliar that people find it difficult to put into words their vague feelings about what has happened. If an interviewee, for any of these reasons, cannot or will not discuss a certain topic, the researcher will find gaps in his information on matters about which he wants to know and will perhaps fail to become aware of other problems and areas of interest that such discussion might have opened up for him.

This is much less likely to happen when the researcher spends much time with the people he studies as they go about their daily activities, for he can see the very things which might not be reported in an interview. Further, should he desire to question people about matters they cannot or prefer not to talk about, he is able to point to specific incidents which either force them to face the issue (in the case of resistance) or make clear what he means (in the case of unfamiliarity). Finally, he can become aware of the full meaning of such hints as are given on subjects people are unwilling to speak openly about and of such inarticulate statements as people are able to make about subjects they cannot clearly formulate, because he frequently knows of these things through his observation and can connect his knowledge with these half-communications.

Researchers working with interview materials, while they are often conscious of these problems, cannot cope with them so well. If they are to deal with matters of this kind it must be by inference. They can only make an educated guess about the things which go unspoken in the interview; it may be a very good guess, but it must be a guess. They can employ various tactics to explore for material they feel is there but unspoken, but even when these are fruitful they do not create sensitivity to those problems of which even the interviewer is not aware. The following example indicates how participant observation aids the researcher in getting material, and making the most of the little he gets, on topics lying within this range of restricted communication.

A few months after the beginning of school, I went to dinner at one of the freshman medical fraternities. It was the night nonresident members came, married ones with their wives. An unmarried student who lived in the house looked around at the visitors and said to me, "We are so much in transition. I have never been in this situation before of meeting fellows and their wives."

This was just the sort of thing we were looking for—change in student relationships arising from group interaction—but I failed in every attempt to make the student describe the "transition" more clearly.

From previous observation, though, I knew there were differences (other than marriage) between the nonresidents and their hosts. The former had all been elected to the fraternity recently, after house officers had gotten to know them through working together (usually on the same cadaver in anatomy lab). They were older than the average original member; instead of coming directly from college, several had had jobs or Army experience before medical school. As a group they were somewhat lower in social position.

These points indicated that the fraternity was bringing together in relative intimacy students different from each other in background and experience. They suggested a search for other instances in which dissimilar groups of students were joining forces, and pointed to a need for hypotheses as to what was behind this process of drawing together on the part of the freshman and its significance for their medical education.

An interviewer, hearing this statement about "transition," would know that the interviewee felt himself in the midst of some kind of change but might not be able to discover anything further about the nature of that change. The participant observer cannot find out, any more than the interviewer can, what the student had in mind, presumably because the student had nothing more in mind than this vague feeling of change. (Interviewees are not sociologists and we ought not to assume that their fumbling statements are attempts, crippled by their lack of technical vocabulary, to express what a sociologist might put in more formal analytic terms.) But he can search for those things in the interviewee's situation which might lead to such a feeling of transition.

While the participant observer can make immediate use of such vague statements as clues to an objective situation, the interviewer is often bothered by the question of whether an interviewee is not simply referring to quite private experiences. As a result, the interviewer will place less reliance on whatever inferences about the facts of the situation he makes, and is less likely to be sure enough of his ground to use them as a basis for further hypotheses. Immediate observation of the scene itself and data from previous observation enable the participant observer to make direct use of whatever hints the informant supplies.

THINGS PEOPLE SEE THROUGH DISTORTING LENSES

In many of the social relationships we observe, the parties to the relation will have differing ideas as to what ought to go on in it, and frequently as to what does in fact go on in it. These differences in perception will naturally affect what they report in an interview. A man in a subordinate position in an organization in which subordinates believe that their superiors are "out to get them" will interpret many incidents in this light, though the incidents themselves may not seem, either to the other party in the interaction or to the observer, to indicate such malevolence. Any such mythology will distort people's view of events to such a degree that they will report as fact things which have not occurred, but which seem to them to have occurred. Students, for example, frequently invent sets of rules to govern their relations with teachers, and, although the teacher may never have heard of such rules, regard the teachers as malicious when they "disobey" them. The point is that things may be reported in an interview through such a distorting lens, and the interviewer may have no way of knowing what is fact and what is distortion of this kind; participant observation makes it possible to check such points. The following is a particularly clear example.

Much of the daily teaching was done, and practical work of medical students supervised, in a particular department of the hospital, by the house residents. A great deal of animosity has grown up between the particular group of students I was with at the time and these residents, the students believing that the residents would, for various malicious reasons, subordinate them and embarrass them at

every opportunity. Before I joined the group, several of the students told me that the residents were "mean," "nasty," "bitchy," and so on, and had backed these characterizations up with evidence of particular actions.

After I began participating daily with the students on this service, a number of incidents made it clear that the situation was not quite like this. Finally, the matter came completely into the open. I was present when one of the residents suggested a technique that might have prevented a minor relapse in a patient assigned to one of the students; he made it clear that he did not think the relapse in any way the student's fault, but rather that he was simply passing on what he felt to be a good tip. Shortly afterward, this student reported to several other students that the resident had "chewed him out" for failing to use this technique: "What the hell business has he got chewing me out about that for? No one ever told me I was supposed to do it that way." I interrupted to say, "He didn't really chew you out. I thought he was pretty decent about it." Another student said, "Any time they say anything at all to us I consider it a chewing out. Any time they say anything about how we did things, they are chewing us out, no matter how God damn nice they are about it."

In short, participant observation makes it possible to check description against fact and, noting discrepancies, become aware of systematic distortions made by the person under study; such distortions are less likely to be discovered by interviewing alone. This point, let us repeat, is only relevant when the interview is used as a source of information about situations and events the researcher himself has not seen. It is not relevant when it is the person's behavior in the interview itself that is under analysis.

INFERENCE, PROCESS AND CONTEXT

We have seen, in the previous sections of this paper, some of the ways in which even very good interviews may go astray, at least from the perspective of the field observer. We turn now to a consideration of the more general areas of difference between the two methods, suggesting basic ways in which the gathering and handling of data in each differ.

Since we tend to talk in our analyses about much the same order of thing whether we work from interviews or from participant-observational materials, and to draw conclusions about social relations and the interaction that goes on within them whether we have actually seen these things or only been told about them, it should be clear that in working with interviews we must necessarily infer a great many things we could have observed had we only been in a position to do so. The kinds of errors we have discussed above are primarily errors of inference, errors which arise from the necessity of making assumptions about the relation of interview statements to actual events which may or may not be true; for what we have solid observable evidence on in the first case we have only secondhand reports and indices of in the second, and the gap must be bridged by inference. We must assume, when faced with an account or transcription of an interview, that we understand the meaning of the everyday words used, that the interviewee is able to talk about the things we are interested in, and that his account will be more or less accurate. The examples detailed above suggest that these assumptions do not always hold and that the process of inference involved in interpreting interviews should always be made explicit and checked, where possible, against what can be discovered through observation. Where, as in often the case, this is not possible, conclusions should be limited to those matters the data directly describe.

Let us be quite specific, and return to the earlier example of resident-student hostility. In describing this relationship from interviews with the students alone we might have assumed their description to be accurate and made the inference that the residents were in fact "mean." Observation proved that this inference would have been incorrect, but this does not destroy the analytic usefulness of the original statements made to the fieldworker in an informal interview. It does shift the area in which we can make deductions from this datum, however, for we can see that such statements, while incorrect factually, are perfectly good statements of the perspective from which these students interpreted the events in which they were involved. We could not know without observation whether their descriptions were true or false; with the aid of observation we know that the facts of the matter are some-

times quite different, and that the students' perspective is strong enough to override such variant facts. But from the interview alone we could know, not what actually happened in such cases, but what the students thought happened and how they felt about it, and this is the kind of inference we should make. We add to the accuracy of our data when we substitute observable fact for inference. More important, we open the way for the discovery of new hypotheses for the fact we observe may not be the fact we expected to observe. When this happens we face a new problem requiring new hypothetical explanations which can then be further tested in the field.

Substitution of an inference about something for an observation of that thing occurs most frequently in discussions of social process and change, an area in which the advantages of observation over an extended period of time are particularly great. Much sociological writing is concerned, openly or otherwise, with problems of process: The analysis of shifts in group structure, individual self-conception and similar matters. But studies of such phenomena in natural social contexts are typically based on data that tell only part of the story. The analysis may be made from a person's retrospective account, in a single interview, of changes that have taken place; or, more rarely, it is based on a series of interviews, the differences between successive interviews providing the bench marks of change. In either case, many crucial steps in the process and important mechanisms of change must be arrived at through inferences which can be no more than educated guesses.

The difficulties in analyzing change and process on the basis of interview·material are particularly important because it is precisely in discussing changes in themselves and their surroundings that interviewees are least likely or able to give an accurate account of events. Changes in the social environment and in the self inevitably produce transformations of perspective, and it is characteristic of such transformations that the person finds it difficult or impossible to remember his former actions, outlook, or feelings. Reinterpreting things from his new perspective, he cannot give an accurate account of the past, for the concepts in which he thinks about it have changed and with them his perceptions and memories.[8] Similarly, a person in the midst of such change may find it difficult to describe what is happening, for he has not developed a perspective or concepts which would allow him to think and talk about these things coherently; the earlier discussion of changes in medical school fraternity life is a case in point.

Participant observation does not have so many difficulties of this sort. One can observe actual changes in behavior over a period of time and note the events which precede and follow them. Similarly, one can carry on a conversation running over weeks and months with the people he is studying and thus become aware of shifts in perspective as they occur. In short, attention can be focused both on what has happened and on what the person says about what has happened. Some inference as to actual steps in the process or mechanisms involved is still required, but the amount of inference necessary is considerably reduced. Again, accuracy is increased and the possibility of new discoveries being made is likewise increased, as the observer becomes aware of more phenomena requiring explanation.

The participant observer is both more aware of these problems of inference and more equipped to deal with them because he operates, when gathering data, in a social context rich in cues and information of all kinds. Because he sees and hears the people he studies in many situations of the kind that normally occur for them, rather than just in an isolated and formal interview, he builds an evergrowing fund of impressions, many of them at the subliminal level, which give him an extensive base for the interpretation and analytic use of any particular datum. This wealth of information and impression sensitizes him to subtleties which might pass unnoticed in an interview and forces him to raise continually new and different questions, which he brings to and tries to answer in succeeding observations.

The biggest difference in the two methods, then, may be not so much that participant observation provides the opportunity for avoiding the errors we have discussed, but that it does this by providing a rich experiential context which causes him to become aware of incongruous or unexplained facts, makes him sensitive to their possible implications and connections with other observed facts, and thus pushes him continually to revise and adapt his theoretical orientation and specific problems in the direction of greater relevance to the phenomena under study. Though this kind of context and its attendant benefits cannot be reproduced in interviewing (and the same degree of sensitivity and sense of problem produced in the interviewer), interviewers can profit from an awareness of those limitations of their method suggested by this comparison and perhaps improve their batting average by taking account of them.[9]

---

[8] Anselm L. Strauss, "The Development and Transformation of Monetary Meanings in the Child," *American Sociological Review*, 17 (June, 1952), 275–86, and *An Essay on Identity* (unpublished manuscript), *passim*.

[9] We are aware that participant observation raises as many technical problems as it solves. (See, for instance, the discussions in Morris S. Schwartz and Charlotte Green Schwartz, "Problems in Participant Observation," *American Journal of Sociology*, 60 (Jan., 1955), 343–53, and Vidich, *op cit.*) We feel, however, that there is considerable value in using the strong points of one method to illuminate the shortcomings of another.

Manford H. Kuhn &
Thomas S. McPartland

An Empirical Investigation of Self-Attitudes

Although the self has long been the central concept in the symbolic interaction approach to social psychology, little if anything has been done to employ it directly in empirical research. There are several reasons for this, one of the most important of which is that there has been no consensus regarding the class of phenomena to which the self ought to be operationally ordered. The self has been called an image, a conception, a concept, a feeling, an internalization, a self looking at oneself, and most commonly simply the self (with perhaps the most ambiguous implications of all). One of these many designations of the self has been as *attitudes*. We do not have space here to discuss the theoretical clarification which results from the conscious conceptualization of the self as a set of attitudes[1] except to point out that this conceptualization is most consistent with Mead's view of the self as an object which is in most respects like all other objects, and with his further view that an object is a plan of action (an attitude).

If, as we suppose, human behavior is *organized* and *directed,* and if, as we further suppose, the organization and direction are supplied by the individual's *attitudes toward himself,* it ought to be of crucial significance to social psychology to be able to identify and measure self-attitudes. This paper is intended to provide an initial demonstration of the advantages to empirical research from thus treating the self as attitudes.

PROBLEMS IN THE DEVELOPMENT OF A SELF-ATTITUDES TEST

The obvious first step in the application of self-theory to empirical research is the construction and standardization of a test which will identify and measure self-attitudes.

The initial consideration in designing such a test is the question of accessibility. Would people give to investigators the statements which are operative in identifying themselves and therefore in organizing and directing their behavior? Or would they be inclined to hide their significant self-attitudes behind innocuous and conventional fronts? Those following symbolic interaction orientation have apparently guessed the latter to be the case for they have seldom if ever asked direct questions regarding self-attitudes, and have tended to assemble self-attitudes of those they were studying from diverse kinds of statements and behavior through the use of long and dubious chains of inference.

One of the present authors, in an earlier attempt to identify and measure self-attitudes

Manford H. Kuhn and Thomas S. McPartland, "An Empirical Investigation of Self-Attitudes," *American Sociological Review,* vol. 19 (February 1954), pp. 68–76. Reprinted by permission.

The investigation on which this paper is based was made possible by a grant from the Graduate College of the State University of Iowa. The paper is a part of an extended examination of self-theory given before the social psychology section of the Midwest Sociological Society at Omaha, April 25, 1953.

[1] A paper dealing with this view is being prepared by the present authors for publication elsewhere.

among groups of Amish, Mennonite and Gentile school children,[2] made the assumption that self-attitudes might be studied in a fairly direct manner by collecting statements of role preference and role avoidance, role expectations, models for the self, and the like. While this investigation yielded results which corresponded to the cultural differences involved, it was clear that the self-statements which the children gave were specific to the role situations asked for and that therefore *general* self-attitudes still had to be (somewhat tenuously) inferred from them.

Subsequent pilot studies were made comparing the contents of extended autobiographies of university students with paragraphs written in answer to the question "Who are you?" These paragraphs contained virtually all the items which were yielded by rough content analyses of the self-attitudes in their corresponding autobiographies. This applied to painful and self-derogatory materials as well as to self-enhancing materials. Thus we concluded that it might be profitable to construct a test which was aimed directly at self-attitudes.[3]

The device which we then used, and upon the use of which this research report is in major part based, consisted of a single sheet of paper headed by these instructions:

"There are twenty numbered blanks on the page below. Please write twenty answers to the simple question 'Who am I?' in the blanks. Just give twenty different answers to this question. Answer as if you were giving the answers to yourself, not to somebody else. Write the answers in the order that they occur to you. Don't worry about logic or 'importance.' Go along fairly fast, for time is limited."

APPLICATION OF THE "TWENTY-STATEMENTS" TEST

This test was given to 288 undergraduate students at the State University of Iowa. It was administered during regular class meetings of introductory courses given in the Department of Sociology and Anthropology at various times during the spring of 1952. In a few classes the instructions were presented orally rather than in writing. In every instance students were given twelve minutes in which to complete the test. The students were naïve in the sense that they had not received instruction in the area to which this research was directed.

The number of responses per respondent evoked by these instructions varied from the twenty requested to one or two (with the median being seventeen responses). The responses took the general form "I am . . ." Frequently "I am" was omitted, the responses consisting of phrases (*e.g.*, "a student," "an athlete," "a blonde") or of single words (*e.g.*, "girl," "married," "religious").

The responses were dealt with by a form of content analysis. They were categorized dichotomously either as *consensual* references or as *subconsensual* references.[4] These content categories distinguish between statements which refer to groups and classes whose limits and conditions of membership are matters of common knowledge, *i.e., consensual;* and those which refer to groups, classes, attributes, traits, or any other matters which would require interpretation by the respondent to be precise or to place him relative to other people, *i.e., subconsensual.* Examples of the consensual variety are "student," "girl," "husband," "Baptist," "from Chicago," "premed," "daughter," "oldest child," "studying engi-

[2] Manford H. Kuhn, "Family Impact upon Personality," Chapter Five of *Problems in Social Psychology: An Interdisciplinary Inquiry*, edited by J. E. Hulett, Jr., and Ross Stagner, Urbana: University of Illinois Press, 1953, esp. pp. 50–52. A more comprehensive report of this study is to be included in a symposium on culture and personality, edited by Francis L. K. Hsu, to be published in the spring of 1954.

[3] The social scientist, unlike the Freudian, assumes that most human behavior is organized and directed by internalized but consciously held role recipes. See, for example, Theodore Newcomb, *Social Psychology*, New York: Dryden, 1950, for his excellent discussion of the relation of attitudes and symbols to the *direction* of behavior (pp. 77–78, 82), and his discussion of the *directive* (versus the expressive) organization of behavior (pp. 343–344). Those absorbed in the present fashion of projective testing would seem to have the cart before the horse, for relatively few of their subjects have been studied in terms of their directive and overt attitudes. It would seem much more reasonable to run out the implications of findings tests of such attitudes before attempting to uncover deeplying, unconscious or guarded attitudes. We have concluded that much time is wasted debating *in advance* to what extent people will hide their "true attitudes," whether they be self-attitudes or attitudes toward other objects or states of affairs.

[4] The precise working definitions of the two categories are given in detail in Thomas S. McPartland, *The Self and Social Structure: An Empirical Approach*, Iowa City: State University of Iowa Library, 1953, p. 147, Ph.D. Dissertation, microfilm.

neering"; that is, statements referring to consensually defined statuses and classes. Examples of the subconsensual category are "happy," "bored," "pretty good student," "too heavy," "good wife," "interesting"; that is, statements without positional reference, or with references to consensual classes obscured by ambiguous modifiers.

The assignment of responses to these dichotomous content categories was highly reliable between different analysts, differences in categorization between two judges occurring less than three times in one hundred responses.

When the content was dichotomized in this way several interesting and useful features emerged:

First, from the ordering of responses on the page it was evident that *respondents tended to exhaust all of the consensual references they would make before they made (if at all) any subconsensual ones;* that is, having once begun to make subconsensual references they tended to make no more consensual references (if indeed they had made any at all). This ordering of responses held whether a respondent made as many as nineteen consensual references or a few as one.

Second, the number of consensual references made by respondents varied from twenty to none. Similarly the number of subconsensual references made by respondents varied from twenty to none. However, the number of consensual and subconsensual references made by any given respondent did not stand in a simple arithmetic relation (such as the number of consensual references plus the number of subconsensual references equals twenty). This resulted from the fact that many respondents made fewer than twenty statements. For example, a respondent might make ten consensual statements and then leave the remaining ten spaces blank, while another might make two consensual references, twelve subconsensual references, and then leave the last six spaces blank.[5]

In the analysis on which this report is based, all consensual references are on one side of the dichotomy, while "no-responses" are combined with subconsensual references on the other. An individual's "locus score" is simply the number of consensual references he makes on the "Twenty-Statements" Test.

These characteristics of the responses to the "Twenty-Statements" Test satisfy the definition of a Guttman scale. "The scalogram hypothesis is that the items have an order such that, ideally, *persons who answer a given question favorably all have higher ranks on the scale than persons who answer the same question unfavorably.*"[6] In applying this criterion it is necessary to keep in mind that "a given question" refers in this case to a specified one (by order) of the twenty statements, and that a "favorable response" would refer to a statement with a consensual reference—one that places the individual in a social system.

"The items used in a scalogram analysis must have a special *cumulative property.*"[7] Again it must be kept in mind that "the items" must in this case be interpreted in terms of the content analysis and not in terms of the raw responses to the open-ended question. Since a person who, let us say, makes a consensual statement as his seventh has also (in more than ninety percent of the instances) made consensual statements in his first six, and since "consensuality" or "locus" refers to anchorage or self-identification in a social system, a variable which is numerically cumulative, we may regard the criterion of cumulativeness as being satisfied in this test. Guttman states, "A third equivalent definition of a scale is the one upon which our practical scalogram analysis procedures are directly based. It requires that each person's responses should be reproducible from the rank alone. A more technical statement of the condition is that each item shall be a simple function of the persons' ranks."[8] This is true for the test under consideration.

---

[5] The variables which result from these characteristics of responses to the "Twenty-Statements" Test are presently being utilized in further research with special reference to clinical use. There are some interesting indications that those with few if any *consensual* statements to make have symptoms of emotional disturbance, while those having few statements *of any kind* to make are of Riesman's "radar" type, taking their cues from each specific situation, and (in the phrase of John Gould) "taking their 'immediate others' to be their 'significant others.'"

[6] S. A. Stouffer, L. Guttman, E. A. Suchman, P. F. Lazarsfeld, S. A. Star, and J. A. Clausen, *Studies in Social Psychology in World War II, Volume IV: Measurement and Prediction,* Princeton: Princeton University Press, 1950, p. 9.

[7] *Ibid.,* p. 10.

[8] *Ibid.,* p. 62.

TABLE 7.1. The scale of locus, showing scale-types, frequency, total responses[1] in each scale type and the coefficient of reproducibility for each scale type

Scale Type	Frequency	Total Response	Errors	C.R.
20	19	380	41	.892
19	5	100	13	.870
18	1	20	1	.950
17	4	80	7	.913
16	1	20	3	.850
15	6	120	24	.800
14	8	160	9	.937
13	8	160	19	.875
12	4	80	10	.875
11	13	260	21	.915
10	7	140	15	.893
9	9	180	19	.895
8	9	180	15	.912
7	7	140	9	.936
6	10	200	15	.925
5	11	220	24	.891
4	8	160	11	.932
3	12	240	24	.900
2	2	40	5	.875
1	4	80	8	.900
0	3	60	0	1.000
	151	3020	293	.903

[1] Includes failure to respond to a blank as a response.

Scores can therefore be assigned which indicate not only *how many* consensual references were made by each respondent, but *which* of his responses fell into the consensual category. The coefficient of reproducibility for this scale, based on 151 respondents, is .903. The test-retest reliability of the scale scores is approximately + .85.

Both for convenience and because consensual references are references to subjective identification by social position we have called the consensual-subconsensual variable the *locus* variable. Table 7.1 is a summary of the "scale of locus," and shows among other things the number of respondents approximating each scale type. For example, the first row in Table 7.1 indicates that 19 respondents most closely approximated Scale Type 20, *i.e.*, making twenty statements of the consensual reference variety. Of their 380 responses there were 41 errors (that is, randomly distributed nonconsensual statements), giving a coef-

ficient of reproducibility of .892 for this scale type. At the other end of the scale there were three respondents who belonged in Scale Type O, which is that of making no consensual statements, thus giving a perfect coefficient of reproducibility, 1.00.

VALIDITY OF THE TEST

The problem of validity of a test in a hitherto uninvestigated area is a difficult one. There are generally recognized to be two related but distinct methods of assessing validity. One is by examining the logical relatedness of the test with the body of theory on which it rests. This subsumes the test of validity by correlating test results with the criterion behavior indicated by the theory. The other method is through correlation of the results of the test with other (already standardized) tests of the problem under investigation. When—as in this case—an area has not been previously investigated by inductive research there are no other tests to use as correlation checks. We need not be held up unduly by this consideration, however, for this is apparently a very much misused method of assessing validity in the field of personality research.[9]

There are two kinds of demonstration required to deal properly with the problem of the

[9] There has been a considerable tendency to validate each new personality test by correlating its results with those obtained by the already existent ones, without inquiring into *their* validity. See Leonard W. Ferguson, *Personality Measurement*, New York: McGraw-Hill, 1952. Ferguson points out (p. 178) that the Bernreuter Personality Inventory was validated by correlating its scales with scores on the Allport Ascendance-Submission scale, the Bernreuter Self-Sufficiency Scale, the Laird Introversion-Extroversion Schedule and the Thurstone Personality Inventory. The correlations were high. But the Laird and Thurstone tests had been through *no validation process whatsoever*, and the other two were unsatisfactorily validated! He points out, later, that the Bell Adjustment Inventory was validated against the Allport, Thurstone and Bernreuter tests (p. 232), thus pyramiding still another validation on the original shaky base. And so it goes until people have completely forgotten all details of the construction of the earliest tests on whose validity the whole series rests as far as this variety of validation is concerned.

We should note parenthetically that we were not interested in validating this test operation of ours against any of the existent personality tests not alone for the reasons involved in the argument above, but more basically because these other tests were designed from orientations quite foreign to ours. One has only to check the items on any current personality test to see how seldom is there any logical relation to self-theory.

consistency of the test with its antecedent body of orientational theory. One is that of making explicit the chains of logic which went into the designing of the test, the test operations and the manipulations of the data obtained through its application. The other is that of showing that the test results correlate in some consistent patterns with the kinds of behavior which the orientation asserts are related.

With respect to the first kind of demonstration we need indicate only that the question "Who am I?" is one which might logically be expected to elicit statements about *one's identity;* that is, his social statuses, and the attributes which are in his view relevant to these. To ask him to give these statements "as if to himself" is an endeavor to obtain from him *general* self-attitudes rather than simply ones which might be idiosyncratic to the test situation or those which might be uniquely held toward himself in his relation to the test administrator. The request in the test for as many as twenty statements of self-identity stems from a recognition by the investigators of the *complex* and *multifarious* nature of an individual's statuses, their curiosity regarding the question of whether the *ordering of responses* correlates with the individual's particular anchoring in society, and their interest in exploring the *range* of self-attitudes.

The manipulation of the responses by assigning them to dichotomous categories, that of consensual reference and that of subconsensual reference, rests on the self-theory view that the self is an interiorization of one's positions in social systems. One may assume from this orientation that variations in such self-identifications are equivalents of variations in the ways in which the individuals in a society such as ours have cast their lot within the range of possible reference groups.

There is an alternative hypothetical mechanism which might be advanced to explain the salience of the consensual reference statement. It is this: Our society requires such a volume of census information from its citizens that the salience of consensual references in the replies to the "Twenty-Statements" Test is according to this hypothesis, simply a superficial carry-over from other questionnaires and forms. On this view those responses which are treated in our investigation as subconsensual are "deeper" self-

attitudes, and hence those which lie closer to the "authentic individual."

We do not agree with this view. It is our belief that the ordering of responses is a reflection of the make-up of the self-conception.[10] The fact that the volume of consensual responses (corresponding to social anchorings) varies greatly from respondent to respondent is taken to give indirect confirmation of our position. Another and more direct empirical confirmation is to be found in the fact that three- and four-year-old children when asked "Who are you?" give, in addition to their names, their sex and occasionally their ages; in their instances one cannot allege a carry-over from the giving of census data. Of course only the pragmatic success or failure of the technique here under consideration will give a dependable answer, and the latter part of this report is devoted to an account of one such pragmatic test. This pragmatic test of the usefulness of the scale scores of the "locus" component of self-attitudes may serve also as the second kind of demonstration of the validity of the instrument.

VARIATIONS IN SELF-ATTITUDES BY "KNOWN GROUPS"

The behavior which we tested for correlation with locus scores derived from our self-attitudes test is that of differential religious affiliation. It is simply one of a multitude of possible investigations which now need to be undertaken to answer

[10] In the ordering of responses we are dealing essentially with the dimension of *salience* of self-attitudes. Theodore Newcomb (in his *Social Psychology,* New York: Dryden, 1950, p. 151) says of salience that it "refers to a person's readiness to respond in a certain way. The more salient a person's attitude the more readily will it be expressed with a minimum of outer stimulation. It seems reasonable to assume that a very salient attitude—one expressed with great spontaneity—has more importance for the person expressing it than does an attitude which he expresses only after a good deal of prodding or questioning. The weakness of direct questions is that they provide no way of measuring the salience of an attitude; we never know whether the attitude would have been expressed at all, or in the same way, apart from the direct question." Thus when a respondent, in reply to the "Who am I?" question on the "Twenty-Statements" Test, writes "I am a man," "I am a student," "I am a football player," it is reasonable to believe that we have far more solid knowledge of the attitudes which organize and direct his behavior than if, on a checklist and among other questions, we had asked "Do you think of yourself as a man?" "Do you think of yourself as a student?" and "Do you think of yourself as an athlete?"

TABLE 7.2. Variations in self-attitudes by religious affiliation: the significance of observed differences between locus scores of affiliates of various religious denominations

Denomination	N[1]	Denominational Mean	Significance of Difference[2]	Significance of Difference[3]
Roman Catholic	38	11.89	. .	P < .001
"Small Sects"[4]	20	11.00	not sig.	P < .01
"Protestant"	21	10.47	not sig.	P < .01
Congregationalist	13	10.30	not sig.	P < .01
Lutheran	33	10.09	not sig.	P < .01
"Christian"	11	9.81	not sig.	P < .02
Jewish	19	9.57	not sig.	P < .05
Methodist	73	8.94	P < .02	not sig.
Presbyterian	32	8.18	P < .01	not sig.
"None"	28	5.75	P < .001*	. .

[1] The total N is 288. These 288 include the 151 on whom the locus scale, reported in Table 7.1, was established, plus 137 cases obtained subsequently.
[2] Computed from the Roman Catholic group mean as the base.
[3] Computed from the group means of "Nones" as the base.
[4] Includes Baptists, Episcopalians, Evangelicals, Mennonites, Nazarenes, Reorganized Latter Day Saints, Unitarians.
* While this and the other measures of statistical significance of difference are such as to give great confidence that the differences are not due to chance, it will only be through repeated correlations of locus scores with other behavior with respect to representative samples that we will be able to discover the theoretical import of the *magnitude* of the difference.

the larger question "What values of this variable (locus) are related to what kinds of behavior and to what trains of social experience?"

Our orientation indicates that the self-conception should vary with differential social anchorage in (a) large, conventional, "respectable," accepted and influential groups; (b) small, weak or different, ambivalently viewed, marginal or dissident groups; or (c) no groups at all (in institutional areas in which a large fraction of the society's membership belongs and is identified by status in one or another of the existent groups). Religious groups and corresponding affiliation by our respondents fitted this model admirably so that we might check differentials in their self-attitudes against differentials in their religious group affiliations. Some religious groups in our society are "majority groups," while others are groups whose subcultures contain norms which set their members at odds with the norms of the larger society. Then, too, a large fraction of the population either has no religious reference group or no religious group membership.

Reports of membership in religious groups in our sample were collected by means of the

direct question: "What is your religious affiliation or preference?" The numbers of each variety of affiliation are given in the column under the heading "N" in Table 7.2. The mean locus scale scores were computed for each of these religious groups and are given in the next column. The mean scale scores ranged from 11.89 (for Catholics) to 5.75 (for "nones"). These scale scores are simply the mean number of consensual reference statements made by respondents in each of the religious groups.

Analysis of variance revealed a relation between religious affiliation and scale scores significant beyond the one percent level. The differences between group means of Roman Catholics on the one hand and Methodists, Presbyterians, and persons reporting no affiliation on the other, were significant beyond the two percent level. Taking the group reporting no affiliation as the base, we found significant differences between this group-mean and the group-means of Roman Catholics, "small sects," "Protestants," Congregationalists, Lutherans, Christians, and Jews. Although the N's were relatively large, Methodists and Presbyterians did not differ signif-

TABLE 7.3. Differential self-anchorage in religious groups: the significance of observed differences between mean salience scores of religious references among affiliates of various religious denominations

Denomination	Denominational Mean	Significance of Difference[1]
Roman Catholic	7.39	. .
Lutheran	7.09	not significant
"Small Sects"	7.04	not significant
Jewish	6.68	not significant
Congregationalist	5.54	not significant
Presbyterian	4.47	$P < .01$
Methodist	3.22	$P < .01$
"Christian"	1.82	$P < .01$

[1] Computed from the Roman Catholic group mean as a base.

TABLE 7.4. Reference group evidence: the dichotomous division of 116 respondents on the basis of religious affiliation and identification with religious groups

	Religious Reference Present	Religious Reference Absent	
Catholics and Jews	13 (5.5)	7 (14.5)	20
All others	19 (26.5)	77 (69.5)	96
Total	32	84	116

Chi Square:	17.03
Q:	.875
P less than	.0001

icantly from "nones" at any usually accepted level of statistical significance. The results of this analysis appear in the last two columns in Table 7.2.

These results indicate clear differences in the relative strength of the more directly socially anchored component of the self-conception among affiliates of certain religious subcultures, but leave open the question of the antecedent correlates of these differences. If one postulates that Roman Catholics have in common with members of small Protestant denominations, Lutherans and Jews the characteristic that religious affiliation is picked out as "important" and differentiating; and that Methodists, Presbyterians, and "indifferentists" have in common the characteristic that religious affiliation is not "important" or that it is taken

for granted, then the two clusters of denominations by scale scores make sense.

If this postulate is sound, then Roman Catholics, Jews, and members of small sects should carry religious references more saliently in the self-conception. The "Twenty-Statements" Test provides data on this point.[11]

The salience of a self-reference may be understood as the relative spontaneity with which a particular reference will be used as an orientation in the organization of behavior.[12] In this

[11] This, obviously, is a use of data from the "Twenty-Statements" Test in an altogether different way than through the use of them to obtain locus scores. There are, in fact, almost unlimited numbers of ways in which these self-statements may be treated, but each would constitute essentially a new test.

[12] The comments and quotation in footnote 10 above apply equally here.

TABLE 7.5.   Reference group evidence on the gradient of differentism: the dichotomous division of respondents by religious identification against a trichotomous division by religious affiliation

	Religious Reference Present	Religious Reference Absent	
Catholics and Jews	13 (6.2)	7 (13.8)	20
"Small Sects"	9 (6.2)	11 (13.8)	20
"Large Denominations"	10 (19.6)	53 (43.4)	63
Total	32	71	103

Chi Square: 19.45
T: .37
P less than   .0001

research, salience of religious reference in the self-conception was measured by the rank of religious reference (if any was made) on the page of twenty statements, mention of religious affiliation in the first place being scored 20, mention in last place scoring 1, and omission of reference to religious affiliation arbitrarily scored zero.

The mean salience of religious references on the "Twenty-Statements" Test ranged from 7.4 from Roman Catholics to 1.82 for "Christians." Analysis of variance of religious references showed salience scores to be related to religious affiliation beyond the one per cent level. The analysis of the significance of the difference between group means appears in Table 7.3.

A completely independent operation was conducted to test this finding of the relation between the social "importance" of group affiliation and "importance" in the self-conception; 116 undergraduates, whose religious affiliations were known, were asked to answer one of two alternative "reference-group" questions: "With what groups do you feel most closely identified?" or "I am proudest of my membership in ——." When respondents were cross-classified (a) by religious affiliation and (b) by their giving or not giving religious affiliation references in response to these direct questions, Table 7.4 resulted. Since we had obtained, from the self-attitudes research done previously, an empirically derived gradient of "differentism," we used this to make a finer subdivision of these responses, which yielded Table 7.5.

These independently derived data support the hypothesized relation between salience in the self-conception and socially defined importance of group membership at high levels of statistical significance.

CONCLUSIONS

The evidence provided by the "Twenty-Statements" Self-Attitudes Test and by its application to "known groups," in this case religious groups, gives support to the following empirically grounded inferences which have, in our view, rather large theoretical implications:

1. The consensual (more directly socially anchored) component of the self-conception is the more salient component. Stated differently, consensually supported self-attitudes are at the top of the hierarchy of self-attitudes.
2. Persons vary over a rather wide range in the relative volume of consensual and subconsensual components in their self-conceptions. It is in this finding that our empirical investigation has given the greatest advance over the purely deductive and more or less literary formulations of George Herbert Mead. Stated in terms of the language of this test, people have locus scores which range from 0 to 20. The variable involved here is one which we can correlate with a wide variety of other attitudes and behavior.
3. The variation indicated in (1) and (2) can be established and measured by the empirical

techniques of attitude research—specifically, the Guttman scaling technique. This gives a dual advantage in that it furthers the presumption that the locus variable is a unitary one and also in that it facilitates the further manipulation of values of the variable with respect to other quantitative problems.

4. Locus scores vary with religious affiliation, as our initial validation test shows, members of the "differentistic" religious groups having significantly higher locus scores than do members of the "conventional" religious groups (using an independent source of information to establish the fact of membership in religious groups).

5. Religious affiliation references are significantly more salient among the self-attitudes of members of "differentistic" religious groups than among members of "majority" or conventional religious groups.

6. Corroboratively, the religious group as a reference group appears far more frequently as an answer to a direct, reference-group type of question among those made by members of "differentistic" religious groups.

This is a first (and only partially completed) effort to build a personality test consistent with the assumptions and findings of social science. The social science view is that people organize and direct their behavior in terms of their subjectively defined identifications. These in turn are seen as internalizations of the objective social statuses they occupy, but for prediction we need to have the *subjective* definitions of identity, in view of the looseness between the social systems and the individual occupants of statuses in them in a society such as ours, characterized by alternatives, change, and collective behavior—in short, a society toward the secular end of the scale. Our test elicits these self-definitions.

To complete a comprehensive personality test on this basis we will need to know, in addition to the subjects' subjective identifications in terms of statuses, their roles, role preferences and avoidances and role expectations, their areas of self-threat and vulnerability, their self-enhancing evaluations, their patterns of reference-group election (their "negative others" as well as their "positive others"), and probably their self-dissociated attitudes. Questions such as "What do you do?" "Who do you wish you were?" "What do

you intend to do?" "What do you take the most pride in?" "As a member of what groups or categories would you like to count yourself?" are a few of the indicated types in the directions suggested of building a soundly grounded approach to a science of personality and culture.

SELECTED REFERENCES
PART ONE

Baldwin, James Mark. *The Individual and Society; or Psychology and Sociology.* Boston: R. G. Badger, 1911. By a somewhat neglected early symbolic interactionist.

Blumer, Herbert. *Symbolic Interactionism: Perspective and Method.* Englewood Cliffs, N.J.: Prentice-Hall, Inc., 1969. A collection of writings by the chief progenitor of the Chicago School of symbolic interactionism.

Cooley, Charles Horton. "The Roots of Social Knowledge." *The American Journal of Sociology,* vol. 32 (July 1926), pp. 59–79. A classic statement of the "sympathetic introspection" method in the study of human behavior.

Denzin, Norman K. *The Research Act.* Chicago: Aldine Publishing Company, 1970. The most comprehensive exposition available on methods appropriate to the perspective of symbolic interactionism. See also the set of readings edited by Denzin, *Sociological Methods: A Sourcebook.* Chicago: Aldine Publishing Company, 1970.

Garfinkel, Harold. *Studies in Ethnomethodology.* Englewood Cliffs, N.J.: Prentice-Hall, Inc., 1967. By a major exponent of a variant form of symbolic interactionism, this is one of several recent books expounding ethnomethodology.

Hewitt, John P. *Self and Society: A Symbolic Interactionist Psychology.* Boston: Allyn and Bacon, Inc., 1976. Basic concepts and their interrelationships in readable, useful form.

Hickman, C. Addison, and Manford H. Kuhn. *Individuals, Groups, and Economic Behavior.* New York: Dryden Press, 1956, pp. 21–45. A comprehensive statement of self-theory, the Iowa School of symbolic interactionism. Contrasts this approach with Freudian, field, and learning theories.

Kuhn, Manford H. "Kinsey's View of Human Nature." *Social Problems,* vol. 1 (April 1954), pp. 119–125. A devastating critique of the neobehavioristic, zoomorphic assumptions underlying Kinsey's approach to human sexual behavior.

Lewis, J. David. "The Classic American Pragmatists as Forerunners to Symbolic Interactionism," *The Sociological Quarterly*, vol. 17 (Summer, 1976), pp. 347–359. Argues that Mead's writings were more closely aligned with the social realism of Charles Peirce's pragmatism than with the social nominalism of William James' pragmatism.

Mead, George Herbert. *Mind, Self and Society.* Chicago: The University of Chicago Press, 1934. The single most influential book, to date, on symbolic interactionism.

Mehan, Hugh, and Houston Wood. *The Reality of Ethnomethodology.* New York: John Wiley and Sons, 1975. A readable exposition.

Meltzer, Bernard N., John W. Petras, and Larry T. Reynolds. *Symbolic Interactionism: Genesis, Varieties and Criticism.* London: Routledge and Kegan Paul, 1975. A concise and comprehensive summation.

Miller, D. L. *George Herbert Mead.* University of Texas Press, 1973. A comprehensive overview of Mead's ideas.

Morrione, Thomas J. "Symbolic Interactionism and Social Action Theory." *Sociology and Social Research* 59 (April 1975), pp. 200–218. Compares views of Blumer with Talcott Parsons' voluntaristic theory.

Morris, Monica B. *An Excursion into Creative Sociology.* New York: Columbia University Press, 1977. Comparison and contrast of phenomenology, symbolic interactionism, ethnomethodology, and dramaturgical sociology.

Petras, John W. (ed.). *George Herbert Mead: Essays on His Social Philosophy.* New York: Teachers College Press, Columbia University, 1968. A group of articles related to Mead's theory of mind, self, and society, emphasizing his concern with applied pragmatism. Also see the articles by Petras in the *Journal of the History of the Behavioral Sciences* on John Dewey (vol. 4, January 1968, pp. 18–27), James Mark Baldwin and William James (vol. 4, April 1968, pp. 132–142), and W. I. Thomas (vol. 6, January 1970, pp. 70–79).

Psathas, George (ed.). *Phenomenological Sociology: Issues and Applications.* New York: John Wiley and Sons, 1973. A useful collection of original essays.

Schwartz, Morris S., and Charlotte G. Schwartz. "Problems in Participant Observation." *American Journal of Sociology,* vol. 60 (January 1955), pp. 343–353. An evaluation of one of the favorite research techniques of symbolic interactionists.

Shott, Susan. "Society, Self, and Mind in Moral Philosophy: The Scottish Moralists as Precursors of Symbolic Interactionism." *Journal of the History of the Behavioral Sciences,* vol. 12 (1976), pp. 39–46. Shows that many important concepts of symbolic interactionism were anticipated by a group of eighteenth-century thinkers.

Singelmann, Peter. "Exchange as Symbolic Interactionism: Convergences Between Two Theoretical Perspectives." *American Sociological Review,* vol. 37 (August 1972), pp. 414–424. The author reviews assumptions and interpretations while aiming at synthesized theory.

Swanson, Guy E. "Mead and Freud: Their Relevance to Social Psychology." *Sociometry,* vol. 24 (December 1961), pp. 319–339. Uses Freud as a benchmark for assessing Mead's work.

PART two ——————————

Society

One of symbolic interactionism's basic propositions (proposition 3) is: Human society is most usefully conceived as consisting of people in interaction. Thus, symbolic interactionists view society as a process of ongoing activity and varied interactions, not as a relatively static system, structure, or organization. The symbolic interactionist conception of society tends to focus attention on interpersonal relationships rather than on whole societies or groups. As a consequence, some critics have questioned the applicability of the microsociological approach of symbolic interactionism to macrosociological phenomena. They argue that symbolic interactionist concepts, propositions, and methods tend to ignore the importance of large-scale organizations and institutions. The paucity of empirical studies by symbolic interactionists of the nature and impact of government bureaucracies, multinational corporations, the military establishment, and other massive collectivities, lends some substance to their claims. Such criticisms seem particularly appropriate for those who do not differentiate between symbolic interactionism as a sociological and as a social-psychological perspective.

In present American sociology, the developing emphases on structural-functional analysis and on historical and comparative studies have brought a focus on social systems and subsystems. Such analyses have stressed the role of larger social units in shaping component, smaller units. For many exponents of symbolic interactionism, this stress has been accompanied by an unacceptable collective determinism of human conduct. That is, the individual presented in such schemes is often merely a passive, pliant, taken-for-granted recipient of relatively inflexible societal influences.

On two counts, this presentation is held to be inadequate. In the first place, it overlooks the mutual, bilateral relationship between society and the individual. Most symbolic interactionists reject collective determinism almost as strongly as they reject biological determinism. Second, the assumption of a fixed or durable societal structure contradicts the symbolic interactionists' conception of a dynamic society ever in the process of "becoming."

In the essay, "Society as Symbolic Interaction," Herbert Blumer presents the basic premises and methodological implications of this position. He focuses on the distinctive character of human relationships—the learned ability of human beings to construct and share their social worlds. He links this focus with a microsociological approach to understanding human society.

The importance of communication in social life is stressed in the selection by John Dewey. Here Dewey suggests a conception of society as existing in the process of communication. Through communication, individuals are linked in a dynamic social process. The Dewey excerpt, and the succeeding one by Cooley, amplify another basic proposition (proposition 2): The individual becomes humanized through interaction with others.

The excerpt from one of Charles Horton Cooley's books constitutes his classic statement of the centrality of the family and other intimate group relationships in forming what he calls "human nature." This selection, written in 1909, remains valuable despite his obsolete, unfortunate reference to race differences. A fairly good synopsis of Cooley's contributions to social psychology can be gained by reading this selection along with his article in Part III.

Reference group theory, first formulated by Herbert Hyman, has been congruent with the ideas of symbolic interactionism. Tamotsu Shibutani analyzes the ways the concept has been used and points out its specific relevance to communication and social relationships.

The selection by Hans Gerth and C. Wright Mills concerns the ways institutions and roles are treated by symbolic interactionists, considered in the contexts of self-conceptions and interpersonal relations. The closing phrase of this brief excerpt from *Character and Social Structure*, referring to "the social structures within which persons live out their lives," along with the elaboration of this point in their book, prefigured Mills' later analyses in *The Power Elite* and *The Sociological Imagination*. These books offer the reader important insights into the relationship between individuals and society.

Although conformity to group rules is socially approved, every society has its rule-violators. According to some observers, the causes of crime, alcoholism, homosexuality, and other forms of deviance are the genetic or mental flaws of abnormal individuals. In contrast, labeling theory, the basis of several selections in this book, views deviant behavior as a social product. Groups define what is deviant, decide who is deviant, and, through the stigma of derogatory labels, unwittingly maintain deviance. However, an organization's strategy of using stigmatizing labels in order to change deviant behavior toward *conformity* is the subject of the article by Barbara Laslett and Carol A. B. Warren.

A central feature of human groups is the power relationship between individuals in different social positions. One facet of this topic, the connection between role-taking and power, is the theme of an empirical research described in the article by Darwin L. Thomas, David D. Franks, and James M. Calonico. In their study of 888 members of 222 families, they tested the hypothesis that role-taking accuracy is inversely related to power within the family. Their findings cast new light upon family decision-making processes.

In a rather abstract but rewarding essay, Eugene A. Weinstein and Judith M. Tanur consider the impact of social structure upon interaction by means of a frame of reference that draws upon symbolic interactionism, structural-functionalism, and exchange theory. This article directs attention to the important newly emerging concept of "situational identity" as a refinement of role. It merits study both because of its eclectic effort to combine relevant elements of three different perspectives and its concern with bridging the gap between microsociological and macrosociological levels of analysis.

The final article in this section deals with societal interpretations of collective strife and violence. Ralph H. Turner attempts to develop criteria for determining why some of these collective actions are viewed as acceptable social protest, rather than crime or revolutionary upheavals. Following an era of racial riots, antiwar demonstrations, and a host of liberation movements, his analysis of public perceptions and reactions merits our attention.

While differing in focus and technique, the articles in Part II have a common perspective: They suggest that human relationships are neither static nor abstract, but reflect the constructed, emergent quality of human behavior. This central feature helps to account for both the stability and the changeability of human society.

Society as Symbolic Interaction

A view of human society as symbolic interaction has been followed more than it has been formulated. Partial, usually fragmentary, statements of it are to be found in the writings of a number of eminent scholars, some inside the field of sociology and some outside. Among the former we may note such scholars as Charles Horton Cooley, W. I. Thomas, Robert E. Park, E. W. Burgess, Florian Znaniecki, Ellsworth Faris, and James Mickel Williams. Among those outside the discipline we may note William James, John Dewey, and George Herbert Mead. None of these scholars, in my judgment, has presented a systematic statement of the nature of human group life from the standpoint of symbolic interaction. Mead stands out among all of them in laying bare the fundamental premises of the approach, yet he did little to develop its methodological implications for sociological study. Students who seek to depict the position of symbolic interaction may easily give different pictures of it. What I have to present should be regarded as my personal version. My aim is to present the basic premises of the point of view and to develop their methodological consequences for the study of human group life.

The term "symbolic interaction" refers, of course, to the peculiar and distinctive character of interaction as it takes place between human beings. The peculiarity consists in the fact that human beings interpret or "define" each other's actions instead of merely reacting to each other's actions. Their "response" is not made directly to the actions of one another but instead is based on the meaning which they attach to some actions. Thus, human interaction is mediated by the use of symbols, by interpretation, or by ascertaining the meaning of one another's actions. This mediation is equivalent to inserting a process of interpretation between stimulus and response in the case of human behavior.

The simple recognition that human beings interpret each other's actions as the means of acting toward one another has permeated the thought and writings of many scholars of human conduct and of human group life. Yet few of them have endeavored to analyze what such interpretation implies about the nature of the human being or about the nature of human association. They are usually content with a mere recognition that "interpretation" should be caught by the student, or with a simple realization that symbols, such as cultural norms or values, must be introduced into their analyses. Only G. H. Mead, in my judgment, has sought to think through what the act of interpretation implies for an understanding of the human being, human action, and human association. The essentials of his analysis are so penetrating and profound and so important for an understanding of human group life that I wish to spell them out, even though briefly.

The key feature in Mead's analysis is that the human being has a self. This idea should not be cast aside as esoteric or glossed over as something that is obvious and hence not worthy of attention. In declaring that the human being has a self, Mead had in mind chiefly that the human being can be the object of his own actions. He can act toward himself as he might act toward others. Each of us is familiar with actions of this sort in which the human being gets angry with himself, rebuffs himself, takes pride in himself, argues with himself, tries to bolster his own courage, tells himself that he should "do this" or not "do that," sets goals for himself, makes compromises with himself, and plans what he is going to do. That the human being acts toward himself in these and countless other ways is a matter of easy empirical observation. To recognize that the human being can act toward himself is no mystical conjuration.

Mead regards this ability of the human being to act toward himself as the central mechanism with which the human being faces and deals with his world. This mechanism enables the human being to make indication to himself of things in his surroundings and thus to guide his actions by what he notes. Anything of which a human being is conscious is something which he is indicating to himself—the ticking of a clock, a knock at the door, the appearance of a friend, the remark made by a companion, a recognition that he has a task to perform, or the realization that he has a cold. Conversely, anything of which he is not conscious is, *ipso facto,* something which he is not indicating to himself. The conscious life of the human being, from the time that he awakens until he falls asleep, is a continual flow of self-indications—notations of the things with which he deals and takes into account. We are given, then, a picture of the human being as an organism which confronts its world with a mechanism for making indications to himself. This is the mechanism that is involved in interpreting the actions of others. To interpret the actions of another is to point out to oneself that the action has this or that meaning or character.

Now, according to Mead, the significance of making indications to oneself is of paramount importance. The importance lies along two lines. First, to indicate something is to extricate it from its setting, to hold it apart, to give it a meaning or, in Mead's language, to make it into an object. An object—that is to say, anything that an individual indicates to himself—is different from a stimulus; instead of having an intrinsic character which acts on the individual and which can be identified apart from the individual, its character or meaning is conferred on it by the individual. The object is a product of the individual's disposition to act instead of being an antecedent stimulus which evokes the act. Instead of the individual being surrounded by an environment of pre-existing objects which play upon him and call forth his behavior, the proper picture is that he constructs his objects on the basis of his on-going activity. In any of his countless acts—whether minor, like dressing himself, or major, like organizing himself for a professional career—the individual is designating different objects to himself, giving them meaning, judging their suitability to his action, and making decisions on the basis of the judgment. This is what is meant by interpretation or acting on the basis of symbols.

The second important implication of the fact that the human being makes indications to himself is that his action is constructed or built up instead of being a mere release. Whatever the action in which he is engaged, the human individual proceeds by pointing out to himself the divergent things which have to be taken into account in the course of his action. He has to note what he wants to do and how he is to do it; he has to point out to himself the various conditions which may be instrumental to his action and those which may obstruct his action; he has to take account of the demands, the expectations, the prohibitions, and the threats as they may arise in the situation in which he is acting. His action is built up step by step through a process of such self-indication. The human individual pieces together and guides his action by taking account of different things and interpreting their significance for his prospective action. There is no instance of conscious action of which this is not true.

The process of constructing action through making indications to oneself cannot be swallowed up in any of the conventional psychological categories. This process is distinct from and different from what is spoken of as the "ego"—just as it is different from any other conception which conceives of the self in terms of composition or organization. Self-indication is a moving communicative process in which the individual notes things, assesses them, gives them a meaning, and decides to act on the basis of the meaning. The human being stands over against the world, or against "alters," with such a process and not with a mere ego. Further, the process of self-indication cannot be subsumed under the forces, whether from the outside or inside, which are presumed to play upon the individual to produce his behavior. Environmental pressures, external stimuli, organic drives, wishes, attitudes, feelings, ideas, and their like do not cover or explain the process of self-indication. The process of self-indication stands over against them in that the individual points out to himself and interprets the appearance or expression of such things, noting a given social demand that is made on him, recognizing a command, observing that he is hungry, realizing that he wishes to buy something, aware that he has a given feeling, conscious that he dislikes eating with someone he despises, or aware that he is thinking of doing some given things. By virtue of indicating such things to himself, he places himself over against them and is able to act back against them, accepting them, rejecting them, or transforming them in accordance with how he defines or interprets them. His behavior, accordingly, is not a result of such things as environmental pressures, stimuli, motives, attitudes, and ideas but arises instead from how he interprets and handles these things in the action which he is constructing. The process of self-indication by means of which human action is formed cannot be accounted for by factors which precede the act. The process of self-indication exists in its own right and must be accepted and studied as such. It is through this process that the human being constructs his conscious action.

Now Mead recognizes that the formation of action by the individual through a process of self-indication always takes place in a social context. Since this matter is so vital to an understanding of symbolic interaction it needs to be explained carefully. Fundamentally, group action takes the form of a fitting together of individual lines of action. Each individual aligns his action to the action of others by ascertaining what they are doing or what they intend to do—that is, by getting the meaning of their acts. For Mead, this is done by the individual "taking the role" of others—either the role of a specific person or the role of a group (Mead's "generalized other"). In taking such roles the individual seeks to ascertain the intention or direction of the acts of others. He forms and aligns his own action on the basis of such interpretation of the acts of others. This is the fundamental way in which group action takes place in human society.

The foregoing are the essential features, as I see them, in Mead's analysis of the bases of symbolic interaction. They presuppose the following: that human society is made up of individuals who have selves (that is, make indications to themselves); that individual action is a construction and not a release, being built up by the individual through noting and interpreting features of the situations in which he acts; that group or collective action consists of the aligning of individual actions, brought about by the individuals' interpreting or taking into account each other's actions. Since my purpose is to present and not to defend the position of symbolic interaction I shall not endeavor in this essay to advance support for the three premises which I have just indicated. I wish merely to say that the three premises can be easily verified empirically. I know of no instance of human group action to which the three premises do not apply. The reader is challenged to find or think of a single instance which they do not fit.

I wish now to point out that sociological views of human society are, in general, markedly at variance with the premises which I have indicated as underlying symbolic interaction. Indeed, the predominant number of such views, especially those in vogue at the present time, do not see or treat human society as symbolic interaction. Wedded, as they tend to be, to some form of sociological determinism, they adopt images of human society, of individuals in it, and of group action which do not square with the premises of symbolic interaction. I wish to say a few words about the major lines of variance.

Sociological thought rarely recognizes or treats human societies as composed of individuals who have selves. Instead, they assume human beings to be merely organisms with some kind of organization, responding to forces which play upon them. Generally, although not exclusively, these forces are lodged in the make-up of the society, as in the case of "social system," "social structure," "culture," "status position," "social role," "custom," "institution," "collective representation," "social situation," "social norm," and "values." The assumption is that the behavior of people as members *of a society* is an expression of the play on them of these kinds of factors or forces. This, of course, is the logical position which is necessarily taken when the scholar explains their behavior or phases of their behavior in terms of one or other of such social factors. The individuals who compose a human society are treated as the media through which such factors operate, and the social action of such individuals is regarded as an expression of such factors. This approach or point of view denies, or at least ignores, that human beings have selves—that they act by making indications to themselves. Incidentally, the "self" is not brought into the picture by introducing such items as organic drives, motives, attitudes, feelings, internalized social factors, or psychological components. Such psychological factors have the same status as the social factors mentioned: they are regarded as factors which play on the individual to produce his action. They do not constitute the process of self-indication. The process of self-indication stands over against them, just as it stands over against the social factors which play on the human being. Practically all sociological conceptions of human society fail to recognize that the individuals who compose it have selves in the sense spoken of.

Correspondingly, such sociological conceptions do not regard the social actions of individuals in human society as being constructed by them through a process of interpretation. Instead, action is treated as a product of factors which play on and through individuals. The social behavior of people is not seen as built up by them through an interpretation of objects, situations, or the actions of others. If a place is given to "interpretation," the interpretation is regarded as merely an expression of other factors (such as motives) which precede the act, and accordingly disappears as a factor in its own right. Hence, the social action of people is treated as an outward flow or expression of forces playing on them rather than as acts which are built up by people through their interpretation of the situations in which they are placed.

These remarks suggest another significant line of difference between general sociological views and the position of symbolic interaction. These two sets of views differ in where they lodge social action. Under the perspective of symbolic interaction, social action is lodged in acting individuals who fit their respective lines of action to one another through a process of interpretation; group action is the collective action of such individuals. As opposed to this view, sociological conceptions generally lodge social action in the action of society or in some unit of society. Examples of this are legion. Let me cite a few. Some conceptions, in treating societies or human groups as "social systems," regard group action as an expression of a system, either in a state of balance or seeking to achieve balance. Or group action is conceived as an expression of the "functions" of a society or of a group. Or group action is regarded as the outward expression of elements lodged in society or the group such as cultural demands, societal purposes, social values, or institutional stresses. These typical conceptions ignore or blot out a view of group life or of group action as consisting of the collective or concerted actions of individuals seeking to meet their life situations. If recognized at all, the efforts of people to develop collective acts to meet their situations are subsumed under the play of underlying or transcending forces which are lodged in society or its parts. The individuals composing the society or the group become "carriers," or media for the expression of such forces; and the interpretative behavior by means of which people form their actions is merely a coerced link in the play of such forces.

The indication of the foregoing lines of variance should help to put the position of symbolic interaction in better perspective. In the remaining discussion I wish to sketch somewhat more fully how human society appears in terms of symbolic interaction and to point out some methodological implications.

Human society is to be seen as consisting of acting people, and the life of the society is to be seen as consisting of their actions. The acting units may be separate individuals, collectivities whose members are acting together on a common quest, or organizations acting on behalf of a constituency. Respective examples are individual purchasers in a market, a play group or missionary band, and a business corporation or a national professional association. There is no empirically observable activity in a human society that does not spring from some acting unit. This banal statement needs to be stressed in light of the common practice of sociologists of reducing human society to social units that do not act—for example, social classes in modern society. Obviously, there are ways of viewing human society other than in terms of the acting units that compose it. I merely wish to point out that in respect to concrete or empirical activity human society must necessarily be seen in terms of the acting units that form it. I would add that any scheme of human society claiming to be a realistic analysis has to respect and be congruent with the empirical recognition that a human society consists of acting units.

Corresponding respect must be shown to the conditions under which such units act. One primary condition is that action takes place in and with regard to a situation. Whatever be the acting unit—an individual, a family, a school, a church, a business firm, a labor union, a legislature, and so on—any particular action is formed in the light of the situation in which it takes place. This leads to the recognition of a second major condition, namely, that the action is formed or constructed by interpreting the situation. The acting unit necessarily has to identify the things which it has to take into account—tasks, opportunities, obstacles, means, demands, discomforts, dangers, and the like; it has to assess them in some fashion and it has to make decisions on the basis of the assessment. Such interpretative behavior may take place in the individual guiding his own action, in a collectivity of individuals acting in concert, or in "agents" acting on behalf of a group or organization. Group life consists of acting units developing acts to meet the situations in which they are placed.

Usually, most of the situations encountered by people in a given society are defined or "structured" by them in the same way. Through previous interaction they develop and acquire common understandings or definitions of how to act in this or that situation. These common definitions enable people to act alike. The common repetitive behavior of people in such situations should not mislead the student into believing that no process of interpretation is in play; on the contrary, even though fixed, the actions of the participating people are constructed by them through a process of interpretation. Since ready-made and commonly accepted definitions are at hand, little strain is placed on people in guiding and organizing their acts. However, many other situations may not be defined in a single way by the participating people. In this event, their lines of action do not fit together readily and collective action is blocked. Interpretations have to be developed and effective accommodation of the participants to one another has to be worked out. In the case of such "undefined" situations, it is necessary to trace and study the emerging process of definition which is brought into play.

Insofar as sociologists or students of human society are concerned with the behavior of acting units, the position of symbolic interaction requires the student to catch the process of interpretation through which they construct their actions. This process is not to be caught merely by turning to conditions which are antecedent to the process. Such antecedent conditions are helpful in understanding the process insofar as they enter into it, but as mentioned previously they do not constitute the process. No can one catch the process merely by inferring its nature from the overt action which is its product. To catch the process, the student must take the role of the acting unit whose behavior he is studying. Since the interpretation is being made by the acting unit in terms of objects designated and appraised, meanings acquired, and decisions made, the process has to be seen from the standpoint of the acting unit. It is the recognition of this fact that makes the research work of such scholars as R. E. Park and W. I. Thomas so notable. To try to catch the interpretative process by remaining aloof as a so-called "objective" observer and refusing to take the role of the acting unit is to risk the worst kind of subjectivism—the objective observer is likely to fill in the process of interpretation with his own surmises in place of catching the process as it occurs in the experience of the acting unit which uses it.

By and large, of course, sociologists do not study human society in terms of its acting units. Instead, they are disposed to view human society in terms of structure or organization and to treat social action as an expression of such structure or organization. Thus, reliance is placed on such structural categories as social system, culture, norms, values, social stratification, status positions, social roles and institutional organization. These are used both to analyze human society and to account for social action within it. Other major interests of sociological scholars center around this focal theme of organization. One line of interest is to view organization in terms of the functions it is supposed to perform. Another line of interest is to study societal organization as a system seeking equilibrium; here the scholar endeavors to detect mechanisms which are indigenous to the system. Another line of interest is to identify forces which play upon organization to bring about changes in it; here the scholar endeavors, especially through comparative study, to isolate a relation between causative factors and structural results. These various lines of sociological perspective and interest, which are so strongly entrenched today, leap over the acting units of a society and bypass the interpretative process by which such acting units build up their actions.

These respective concerns with organization on one hand and with acting units on the other hand set the essential difference between conventional views of human society and the view of it implied in symbolic interaction. The latter view recognizes the presence of organization in human society and respects its importance. However, it sees and treats organization differently. The difference is along two major lines. First, from the standpoint of symbolic interaction the organization of a human society is the framework inside of which social action takes place and is not the determinant of that action. Second, such organization and changes in it are the product of the activity of acting units and not of "forces" which leave such acting units out of account. Each of these two major lines of difference should be explained briefly in order to obtain a better understanding of how human society appears in terms of symbolic interaction.

From the standpoint of symbolic interaction, social organization is a framework inside of which acting units develop their actions. Structural features, such as "culture," "social systems," "social stratification," or "social roles," set conditions for their action but do not determine their action. People—that is, acting units—do not act toward culture, social structure or the like; they act toward situations. Social organization enters into action only to the extent to which it shapes situations in which people act, and to the extent to which it supplies fixed sets of symbols which people use in interpreting their situations. These two forms of influence of social organization are important. In the case of settled and stabilized societies, such as isolated primitive tribes and peasant communities, the influence is certain to be profound. In the case of human societies, particularly modern societies, in which streams of new situations arise and old situations become unstable, the influence of organization decreases. One should bear in mind that the most important element confronting an acting unit in situations is the actions of other acting units. In modern society, with its increasing crisscrossing of lines of action, it is common for situations to arise in which the actions of participants are not previously regularized and standardized. To this extent, existing social organization does not shape the situations. Correspondingly, the symbols or tools of interpretation used by acting units in such situations may vary and shift considerably. For these reasons, social action may go beyond, or depart from, existing organization in any of its structural dimensions. The organization of a human society is not to be identified with the process of interpretation used by its acting units; even though it affects that process, it does not embrace or cover the process.

Perhaps the most outstanding consequence of viewing human society as organization is to overlook the part played by acting units in social change. The conventional procedure of sociologists is (a) to identify human society (or some part of it) in terms of an established or organized form, (b) to identify some factor or condition of change playing upon the human society or the given part of it, and (c) to identify the new form assumed by the society following upon the play of the factor of change. Such observations permit the student to couch propositions to the effect that a given factor of change playing upon a given organized form results in a given new organized form. Examples ranging from crude to refined statements are legion, such as that an economic depression increases solidarity in the families of workingmen or that industrialization replaces extended families by nuclear families. My concern here is not with the validity of such propositions but with the methodological position which they presuppose. Essentially, such propositions either ignore the role of the interpretative behavior of acting units in the given instance of change, or else regard the interpretative behavior as coerced by the factor of change. I wish to point out that any line of social change, since it involves change in human action, is necessarily mediated by interpretation on the part of the people caught up in the change—the change appears in the form of new situations in which people have to construct new forms of action. Also, in line with what has been said previously, interpretations of new situations are not predetermined by conditions antecedent to the situations but depend on what is taken into account and assessed in the actual situations in which behavior is formed. Variations in interpretation may readily occur as different acting units cut out different objects in the situation, or give different weight to the objects which they note, or piece objects together in different patterns. In formulating propositions of social change, it would be wise to recognize that any given line of such change is mediated by acting units interpreting the situations with which they are confronted.

Students of human society will have to face the question of whether their preoccupation with categories of structure and organization can be squared with the interpretative process by means of which human beings, individually and collectively, act in human society. It is the discrepancy between the two which plagues such students in their efforts to attain scientific propositions of the sort achieved in the physical and biological sciences. It is this discrepancy, further, which is chiefly responsible for their difficulty in fitting hypothetical propositions to new arrays of empirical data. Efforts are made, of course, to overcome these shortcomings by devising new structural categories, by formulating new structural hypotheses, by developing more refined techniques of research, and even by formulating new methodological schemes of a structural character. These efforts continue to ignore or to explain away the interpretative process by which people act, individually and collectively, in society. The question remains whether human society or social action can be successfully analyzed by schemes which refuse to recognize human beings as they are, namely, as persons constructing individual and collective action through an interpretation of the situations which confront them.

Communication, Individual and Society

We often fancy that institutions, social custom, collective habit, have been formed by the consolidation of individual habits. In the main this supposition is false to fact. To a considerable extent customs, or widespread uniformities of habit, exist because individuals face the same situation and react in like fashion. But to a larger extent customs persist because individuals form their personal habits under conditions set by prior customs. An individual usually acquires the morality as he inherits the speech of his social group. The activities of the group are already there, and some assimilation of his own acts to their pattern is a prerequisite of a share therein, and hence of having any part in what is going on. Each person is born an infant, and every infant is subject from the first breath he draws and the first cry he utters to the attentions and demands of others. These others are not just persons in general with minds in general. They are beings with habits, and beings who upon the whole esteem the habits they have, if for no other reason than that, having them, their imagination is thereby limited. The nature of habit is to be assertive, insistent, self-perpetuating. There is no miracle in the fact that if a child learns any language he learns the language that those about him speak and teach, especially since his ability to speak that language is a pre-condition of his entering into effective connection with them, making wants known and getting them satisfied. Fond parents and relatives frequently pick up a few of the child's spontaneous modes of speech and for a time at least they are portions of the speech of the group. But the ratio which such words bear to the total vocabulary in use gives a fair measure of the part played by purely individual habit in forming custom in comparison with the part played by custom in forming individual habits. Few persons have either the energy or the wealth to build private roads to travel upon. They find it convenient, "natural," to use the roads that are already there; while unless their private roads connect at some point with the highway they cannot build them even if they would.

These simple facts seems to me to give a simple explanation of matters that are often surrounded with mystery. To talk about the priority of "society" to *the* individual is to indulge in nonsensical metaphysics. But to say that some pre-existent association of human beings is prior to every particular human being who is born into the world is to mention a commonplace. These associations are definite modes of interaction of persons with one another; that is to say they form customs, institutions. There is no problem in all history so artificial as that of how "individuals" manage to form "society." The problem is due to the pleasure taken in manipulating concepts, and discussion goes on because concepts are kept from inconvenient contact with facts. The facts of infancy and sex have only to be called to mind to see how manufactured are the conceptions which enter into this particular problem.

The problem, however, of how those established and more or less deeply grooved systems of interaction which we call social groups, big and small, modify the activities of individuals who perforce are caught up within them, and how the activities of component individuals remake and redirect previously established customs is a deeply significant one. Viewed from the standpoint of custom and its priority to the formation of habits in human beings who are born babies and gradually grow to maturity, the facts which are now usually assembled under the conceptions of collective minds, group-minds, national-minds, crowd-minds, etc., etc., lose the mysterious air they exhale when mind is thought of (as orthodox psychology teaches us to think of it) as something which precedes action. It is difficult to see that collective mind means anything more than a custom brought at some point to explicit, emphatic consciousness, emotional or intellectual.[1]

The family into which one is born is a family in a village or city which interacts with other more or less integrated systems of activity, and which includes a diversity of groupings within itself, say, churches, political parties, clubs, cliques, partnerships, trade-unions, corporations, etc. If we start with the traditional notion of mind as something complete in itself, then we may well be perplexed by the problem of how a common mind, common ways of feeling and believing and purposing, comes into existence and then forms these groups. The case is quite otherwise if we recognize that in any case we must start with grouped action, that is, with some fairly settled system of interaction among individuals. The problem of origin and development of the various groupings, or definite customs, in existence at any particular time in any particular place is not solved by reference to psychic causes, elements, forces. It is to be solved by reference to facts of action, demand for food, for houses, for a mate, for someone to talk to and to listen to one talk, for control of others, demands which are all intensified by the fact already mentioned that each person begins a helpless, dependent creature. I do not mean of course that hunger, fear, sexual love, gregariousness, sympathy, parental love, love of bossing and of being ordered about, imitation, etc., play no part. But I do mean that these words do not express elements or forces which are psychic or mental in their first intention. They denote *ways of behavior*. These ways of behaving involve interaction, that is to say, and prior groupings. And to understand the existence of organized ways or habits we surely need to go to physics, chemistry and physiology rather than to psychology.

There is doubtless a great mystery as to why any such thing as being conscious should exist at all. But *if* consciousness exists at all, there is no mystery in its being connected with what it is connected with. That is to say, if an activity which is an interaction of various factors, or a grouped activity, comes to consciousness it seems natural that it should take the form of an emotion, belief or purpose that reflects the interaction, that it should be an "our" consciousness or a "my" consciousness. And by this is meant both that it will be shared by those who are implicated in the associative custom, or more or less alike in them all, and that it will be felt or thought to concern others as well as one's self. A family-custom or organized habit of action comes into contact and conflict for example with that of some other family. The emotions of ruffled pride, the belief about superi-

[1] Mob psychology comes under the same principles, but in a negative aspect. The crowd and mob express a disintegration of habits which releases impulse and renders persons susceptible to immediate stimuli, rather than such a functioning of habits as is found in the mind of a club or school of thought or a political party. Leaders of an organization, that is of an interaction having settled habits, may, however, in order to put over some schemes, deliberately resort to stimuli which will break through the crust of ordinary custom and release impulses on such a scale as to create a mob psychology. Since fear is a normal reaction to the unfamiliar, dread and suspicion are the forces most played upon to accomplish this result, together with vast vague contrary hopes. This is an ordinary technique in excited political campaigns, in starting war, etc. But an assimilation like that of Le Bon of the psychology of democracy to the psychology of a crowd in overriding individual judgment shows lack of psychological insight. A political democracy exhibits an overriding of thought like that seen in any convention or institution. That is, thought is submerged in habit. In a crowd and mob, it is submerged in undefined emotion. China and Japan exhibit crowd psychology more frequently than do western democratic countries. Not in my judgment because of any essentially Oriental psychology but because of a nearer background of rigid and solid customs conjoined with the phenomena of a period of transition. The introduction of many novel stimuli creates occasions where habits afford no ballast. Hence great waves of emotion easily sweep through masses. Sometimes they are waves of enthusiasm for the new; sometimes of violent reaction against it—both equally undiscriminating. The war has left behind it a somewhat similar situation in western countries.

ority or being "as good as other people," the intention to hold one's own are naturally *our* feeling and idea of *our* treatment and position. Substitute the Republican party or the American nation for the family and the general situation remains the same. The conditions which determine the nature and extent of the particular grouping in question are matters of supreme import. But they are not, as such, subject-matter of psychology, but of the history of politics, law, religion, economics, invention, the technology of communication and intercourse. Psychology comes in as an indispensable tool. But it enters into the matter of understanding these various special topics, not into the question of what psychic forces form a collective mind and therefore a social group. That way of stating the case puts the cart a long way before the horse, and naturally gathers obscurities and mysteries to itself. In short, the primary facts of social psychology center about collective habit, custom. In addition to the general psychology of habit—which *is* general not individual in any intelligible sense of that word—we need to find out just how different customs shape the desires, beliefs, purpose of those who are affected by them. The problem of social psychology is not how either individual or collective mind forms social groups and customs, but how different customs, established interacting arrangements, form and nurture different minds.

Charles Horton Cooley   **10**

Primary Group and Human Nature

Primary groups are primary in the sense that they give the individual his earliest and completest experience of social unity, and also in the sense that they do not change in the same degree as more elaborate relations, but form a comparatively permanent source out of which the latter are ever springing. Of course they are not independent of the larger society, but to some extent reflect its spirit; as the German family and the German school bear somewhat distinctly the print of German militarism. But this, after all, is like the tide setting back into creeks, and does not commonly go very far. Among the German, and still more among the Russian, peasantry are

Reprinted by permission of Charles Scribner's Sons from *Social Organization*, pages 26–31, by Charles Horton Cooley. Copyright 1909 Charles Scribner's Sons; renewal copyright 1937 Elsie Jones Cooley.

found habits of free cooperation and discussion almost uninfluenced by the character of the state; and it is a familiar and well-supported view that the village commune, self-governing as regards local affairs and habituated to discussion, is a very widespread institution in settled communities, and the continuator of a similar autonomy previously existing in the clan. "It is man who makes monarchies and establishes republics, but the commune seems to come directly from the hand of God."[1]

In our own cities the crowded tenements and the general economic and social confusion have sorely wounded the family and the neighborhood, but it is remarkable, in view of these conditions, what vitality they show; and there is nothing

[1] De Tocqueville, *Democracy in America*, vol. i, chap. 5.

upon which the conscience of the time is more determined than upon restoring them to health.

These groups, then, are springs of life, not only for the individual but for social institutions. They are only in part molded by special traditions, and, in larger degree, express a universal nature. The religion or government of other civilizations may seem alien to us, but the children or the family group wear the common life, and with them we can always make ourselves at home.

By human nature, I suppose, we may understand those sentiments and impulses that are human in being superior to those of lower animals, and also in the sense that they belong to mankind at large, and not to any particular race or time. It means, particularly, sympathy and the innumerable sentiments into which sympathy enters, such as love, resentment, ambition, vanity, hero-worship, and the feeling of social right and wrong.[2]

Human nature in this sense is justly regarded as a comparatively permanent element in society. Always and everywhere men seek honor and dread ridicule, defer to public opinion, cherish their goods and their children, and admire courage, generosity, and success. It is always safe to assume that people are and have been human.

It is true, no doubt, that there are differences of race capacity, so great that a large part of mankind are possibly incapable of any high kind of social organization. But these differences, like those among individuals of the same race, are subtle, depending upon some obscure intellectual deficiency, some want of vigor, or slackness of moral fibre, and do not involve unlikeness in the generic impulses of human nature. In all these races are very much alike. The more insight one gets into the life of savages, even those that are reckoned the lowest, the more human, the more like ourselves, they appear. Take for instance the natives of Central Australia, as described by Spencer and Gillen,[3] tribes having no definite government or worship and scarcely able to count to five. They are generous to one another, emulous of virtue

as they understand it, kind to their children and to the aged, and by no means harsh to women. Their faces as shown in the photographs are wholly human and many of them attractive.

And when we come to a comparison between different stages in the development of the same race, between ourselves, for instance, and the Teutonic tribes of the time of Caesar, the difference is neither in human nature nor in capacity, but in organization, in the range and complexity of relations, in the diverse expression of powers and passions essentially much the same.

There is no better proof of this generic likeness of human nature than in the ease and joy with which the modern man makes himself at home in literature depicting the most remote and varied phases of life—in Homer, in the Nibelung tales, in the Hebrew Scriptures, in the legends of the American Indians, in stories of frontier life, of soldiers and sailors, of criminals and tramps, and so on. The more penetratingly any phase of human life is studied the more an essential likeness to ourselves is revealed.

To return to primary groups: the view here maintained is that human nature is not something existing separately in the individual, but a *group-nature or primary phase of society*, a relatively simple and general condition of the social mind. It is something more, on the one hand, than the mere instinct that is born in us—though that enters into it—and something less, on the other, than the more elaborate development of ideas and sentiments that makes up institutions. It is the nature which is developed and expressed in those simple, face-to-face groups that are somewhat alike in all societies; groups of the family, the playground, and the neighborhood. In the essential similarity of these is to be found the basis, in experience, for similar ideas and sentiments in the human mind. In these, everywhere, human nature comes into existence. Man does not have it at birth; he cannot acquire it except through fellowship, and it decays in isolation.

If this view does not recommend itself to common sense I do not know that elaboration will be of much avail. It simply means the application at this point of the idea that society and individuals are inseparable phases of a common whole, so that wherever we find an individual

---

[2] These matters are expounded at some length in the writer's *Human Nature and the Social Order.*
[3] *The Native Tribes of Central Australia.* Compare also Darwin's views and examples given in chap. 7 of his *Descent of Man.*

fact we may look for a social fact to go with it. If there is a universal nature in persons there must be something universal in association to correspond to it.

What else can human nature be than a trait of primary groups? Surely not an attribute of the separate individual—supposing there were any such thing—since its typical characteristics, such as affection, ambition, vanity, and resentment, are inconceivable apart from society. If it belongs, then, to man in association, what kind or degree of association is required to develop it? Evidently nothing elaborate, because elaborate phases of society are transient and diverse, while human nature is comparatively stable and universal. In short the family and neighborhood life is essential to its genesis and nothing more is.

Here as everywhere in the study of society we must learn to see mankind in psychical wholes, rather than in artificial separation. We must see and feel the communal life of family and local groups as immediate facts, not as combinations of something else. And perhaps we shall do this best by recalling our own experience and extending it through sympathetic observation. What, in our life, is the family and the fellowship; what do we know of the we-feeling? Thought of this kind may help us to get a concrete perception of that primary group-nature of which everything social is the outgrowth.

Tamotsu Shibutani **11**

Reference Groups as Perspectives

Although Hyman coined the term scarcely more than a decade ago, the concept of reference group has become one of the central analytic tools in social psychology, being used in the construction of hypotheses concerning a variety of social phenomena. The inconsistency in behavior as a person moves from one social context to another is accounted for in terms of a change in reference groups; the exploits of juvenile delinquents, especially in interstitial areas, are being explained by the expectations of peer-group gangs; modifications in social attitudes are found to be related to changes in associations. The concept has been particularly useful in accounting for the choices made among apparent alternatives, particularly where the selections seem to be contrary to the "best interests" of the actor. Status problems—aspirations of social climbers, conflicts in group loyalty, the dilemmas of marginal men—have also been analyzed in terms of reference groups, as have the differential sensitivity and reaction of various segments of an audience to mass communication. It is recognized that the same generic processes are involved in these phenomenally diverse events, and the increasing popularity of the concept attests to its utility in analysis.

As might be expected during the exploratory phases in any field of inquiry, however, there is some confusion involved in the use of this concept, arising largely from vagueness of signification. The available formal definitions are inconsistent, and sometimes formal definitions are

Tamotsu Shibutani, "Reference Groups as Perspectives," *American Journal of Sociology,* vol. 60 (May 1955), pp. 562–569, by permission of The University of Chicago Press. Copyright 1955 by The University of Chicago.

contradicted in usage. The fact that social psychologists can understand one another in spite of these ambiguities, however, implies an intuitive recognition of some central meaning, and an explicit statement of this will enhance the utility of the concept as an analytic tool. The literature reveals that all discussions of reference groups involve some identifiable grouping to which an actor is related in some manner and the norms and values shared in that group. However, the relationship between these three terms is not always clear. Our initial task, then, is to examine the conceptions of reference group implicit in actual usage, irrespective of formal definitions.

One common usage of the concept is in the designation of that group which serves as the point of reference in making comparisons or contrasts, especially in forming judgments about one's self. In the original use of the concept Hyman spoke of reference groups as points of comparison in evaluating one's own status, and he found that the estimates varied according to the group with which the respondent compared himself. Merton and Kitt, in their reformulation of Stouffer's theory of relative deprivation, also use the concept in this manner; the judgments of rear-echelon soldiers overseas concerning their fate varied, depending upon whether they compared themselves to soldiers who were still at home or men in combat. They also propose concrete research operations in which respondents are to be asked to compare themselves with various groups. The study of aspiration levels by Chapman and Volkmann, frequently cited in discussions of reference-group theory, also involves variations in judgment arising from a comparison of one's own group with others.[1] In this mode of application, then, a reference group is a standard or check point which an actor uses in forming his estimate of the situation, particularly his own position within it. Logically, then, *any* group with which

an actor is familiar may become a reference group.

A second referent of the concept is that group in which the actor aspires to gain or maintain acceptance: hence, a group whose claims are paramount in situations requiring choice. The reference group of the socially ambitious is said to consist of people of higher strata whose status symbols are imitated. Merton and Kitt interpret the expressions of willingness and felt readiness for combat on the part of inexperienced troops, as opposed to the humility of battle-hardened veterans, as the efforts of newcomers to identify themselves with veterans to whom they had mistakenly imputed certain values.[2] Thus, the concept is used to point to an association of human beings among whom one seeks to gain, maintain, or enhance his status; a reference group is that group in which one desires to participate.

In a third usage the concept signifies that group whose perspective constitutes the frame of reference of the actor. Thus, Sherif speaks of reference groups as groups whose norms are used as anchoring points in structuring the perceptual field,[3] and Merton and Kitt speak of a "social frame of reference" for interpretations.[4] Through direct or vicarious participation in a group one comes to perceive the world from its standpoint. Yet this group need not be one in which he aspires for acceptance; a member of some minority group may despise it but still see the world largely through its eyes. When used in this manner, the concept of reference group points more to a psychological phenomenon than to an objectively existing group of men; it refers to an organization of the actor's experience. That is to say, it is a structuring of his perceptual field. In this usage a reference group becomes any collectivity, real or imagined, envied or despised, whose perspective is assumed by the actor.

Thus, an examination of current usage discloses three distinct referents for a single concept: (1) groups which serve as comparison points; (2)

[1] H. H. Hyman, "The Psychology of Status," *Archives of Psychology*, XXXVII (1942), 15; R. K. Merton and A. Kitt, "Contributions to the Theory of Reference Group Behavior," in R. K. Merton and P. F. Lazarsfeld (eds.), *Studies in the Scope and Method of "The American Soldier"* (Glencoe, Ill.: Free Press, 1950), pp. 42–53, 69; D. W. Chapman and J. Volkmann, "A Social Determinant of the Level of Aspiration," *Journal of Abnormal and Social Psychology*, XXXIV (1939), 225–38.

[2] *Op. cit.*, pp. 75–76.

[3] M. Sherif, "The Concept of Reference Groups in Human Relations," in M. Sherif and M. O. Wilson (eds.), *Group Relations at the Crossroads* (New York: Harper & Bros., 1953), pp. 203–31.

[4] *Op. cit.*, pp. 49–50.

groups to which men aspire; and (3) groups whose perspectives are assumed by the actor. Although these terms may be related, treating together what should be clearly delineated as generically different can lead only to further confusion. It is the contention of this paper that the restriction of the concept of reference group to the third alternative—that group whose perspective constitutes the frame of reference of the actor—will increase its usefulness in research. Any group or object may be used for comparisons, and one need not assume the role of those with whom he compares his fate; hence, the first usage serves a quite different purpose and may be eliminated from further consideration. Under some circumstances, however, group loyalties and aspirations are related to perspectives assumed, and the character of this relationship calls for further exploration. Such a discussion necessitates a restatement of the familiar, but, in view of the difficulties in some of the work on reference groups, repetition may not be entirely out of order. In spite of the enthusiasm of some proponents there is actually nothing new in reference-group theory.

CULTURE AND PERSONAL CONTROLS

Thomas pointed out many years ago that what a man does depends largely upon his definition of the situation. One may add that the manner in which one consistently defines a succession of situations depends upon his organized perspective. A perspective is an ordered view of one's world—what is taken for granted about the attributes of various objects, events, and human nature. It is an order of things remembered and expected as well as things actually perceived, an organized conception of what is plausible and what is possible; it constitutes the matrix through which one perceives his environment. The fact that men have such ordered perspectives enables them to conceive of their ever changing world as relatively stable, orderly, and predictable. As Riezler puts it, one's perspective is an outline scheme which, running ahead of experience, defines and guides it.

There is abundant experimental evidence to show that perception is selective; that the organi-

zation of perceptual experience depends in part upon what is anticipated and what is taken for granted. Judgments rest upon perspectives, and people with different outlooks define identical situations differently, responding selectively to the environment. Thus, a prostitute and a social worker walking through a slum area notice different things; a sociologist should perceive relationships that others fail to observe. Any change of perspectives—becoming a parent for the first time, learning that one will die in a few months, or suffering the failure of well-laid plans—leads one to notice things previously overlooked and to see the familiar world in a different light. As Goethe contended, history is continually rewritten, not so much because of the discovery of new documentary evidence, but because the changing perspectives of historians lead to new selections from the data.

Culture, as the concept is used by Redfield, refers to a perspective that is shared by those in a particular group; it consists of those "conventional understandings, manifest in act and artifact, that characterize societies."[5] Since these conventional understandings are the premises of action, those who share a common culture engage in common modes of action. Culture is not a static entity but a continuing process; norms are creatively reaffirmed from day to day in social interaction. Those taking part in collective transactions approach one another with set expectations, and the realization of what is anticipated successively confirms and reinforces their perspectives. In this way, people in each cultural group are continuously supporting one another's perspectives, each by responding to the others in expected ways. In this sense culture is a product of communication.

In his discussion of endopsychic social control Mead spoke of men "taking the role of the generalized other," meaning by that that each person approaches his world from the standpoint of the culture of his group. Each perceives, thinks, forms

[5] R. Redfield, *The Folk Culture of Yucatan* (Chicago: University of Chicago Press, 1941), p. 132. For a more explicit presentation of a behavioristic theory of culture see *The Selected Writings of Edward Sapir in Language, Culture and Personality*, ed. D. G. Mandelbaum (Berkeley: University of California Press, 1949), pp. 104–9, 308–31, 544–59.

judgments, and controls himself according to the frame of reference of the group in which he is participating. Since he defines objects, other people, the world, and himself from the perspective that he shares with others, he can visualize his proposed line of action from this generalized standpoint, anticipate the reactions of others, inhibit undesirable impulses, and thus guide his conduct. The socialized person is a society in miniature; he sets the same standards of conduct for himself as he sets for others, and he judges himself in the same terms. He can define situations properly and meet his obligations, even in the absence of other people, because, as already noted, his perspective always takes into account the expectations of others. Thus, it is the ability to define situations from the same standpoint as others that makes personal controls possible.[6] When Mead spoke of assuming the role of the generalized other, he was not referring to people but to perspectives shared with others in a transaction.

The consistency in the behavior of a man in a wide variety of social contexts is to be accounted for, then, in terms of his organized perspective. Once one has incorporated a particular outlook from his group, it becomes his orientation toward the world, and he brings this frame of reference to bear on all new situations. Thus, immigrants and tourists often misinterpret the strange things they see, and a disciplined Communist would define each situation differently from the non-Communist. Although reference-group behavior is generally studied in situations where choices seem possible, the actor himself is often unaware that there are alternatives.

The proposition that men think, feel, and see things from a standpoint peculiar to the group in which they participate is an old one, repeatedly emphasized by students of anthropology and of the sociology of knowledge. Why, then, the sudden concern with reference-group theory during the past decade? The concept of reference group actually introduces a minor refinement in the long

familiar theory, made necessary by the special characteristics of modern mass societies. First of all, in modern societies special problems arise from the fact that men sometimes use the standards of groups in which they are *not* recognized members, sometimes of groups in which they have never participated directly, and sometimes of groups that do not exist at all. Second, in our mass society, characterized as it is by cultural pluralism, each person internalizes several perspectives, and this occasionally gives rise to embarrassing dilemmas which call for systematic study. Finally, the development of reference-group theory has been facilitated by the increasing interest in social psychology and the subjective aspects of group life, a shift from a predominant concern with objective social structures to an interest in the experiences of the participants whose regularized activities make such structures discernible.

A reference group, then, is that group whose outlook is used by the actor as the frame of reference in the organization of his perceptual field. All kinds of groupings, with great variations in size, composition, and structure, may become reference groups. Of greatest importance for most people are those groups in which they participate directly—what have been called membership groups—especially those containing a number of persons with whom one stands in a primary relationship. But in some transactions one may assume the perspective attributed to some social category—a social class, an ethnic group, those in a given community, or those concerned with some special interest. On the other hand, reference groups may be imaginary, as in the case of artists who are "born ahead of their times," scientists who work for "humanity," or philanthropists who give for "posterity." Such persons estimate their endeavors from a postulated perspective imputed to people who have not yet been born. There are others who live for a distant past, idealizing some period in history and longing for "the good old days," criticizing current events from a standpoint imputed to people long since dead. Reference groups, then, arise through the internalization of norms; they constitute the structure of expectations imputed to some audience for whom one organizes his conduct.

[6] G. H. Mead, "The Genesis of the Self and Social Control," *International Journal of Ethics*, XXXV (1925), 251–77, and *Mind, Self and Society* (Chicago: University of Chicago Press, 1934), pp. 152–64. Cf. T. Parsons, "The Superego and the Theory of Social Systems," *Psychiatry*, XV (1952), 15–25.

THE CONSTRUCTION OF SOCIAL WORLDS

As Dewey emphasized, society exists in and through communication; common perspectives—common cultures—emerge through participation in common communication channels. It is through social participation that the perspectives shared in a group are internalized. Despite the frequent recitation of this proposition, its full implications, especially for the analysis of mass societies, are not often appreciated. Variations in outlook arise through differential contact and association; the maintenance of social distance—through segregation, conflict, or simply the reading of different literature—leads to the formation of distinct cultures. Thus, people in different social classes develop different modes of life and outlook, not because of anything inherent in economic position, but because similarity of occupation and limitations set by income level dispose them to certain restricted communication channels. Those in different ethnic groups form their own distinctive cultures because their identifications incline them to interact intimately with each other and to maintain reserve before outsiders. Different intellectual traditions within social psychology—psychoanalysis, scale analysis, *Gestalt*, pragmatism—will remain separated as long as those in each tradition restrict their sympathetic attention to works of their own school and view others with contempt or hostility. Some social scientists are out of touch with the masses of the American people because they eschew the mass media, especially television, or expose themselves only condescendingly. Even the outlook that the *avant-garde* regards as "cosmopolitan" is culture-bound, for it also is a product of participation in restricted communication channels—books, magazines, meetings, exhibits, and taverns which are out of bounds for most people in the middle classes. Social participation may even be vicarious, as it is in the case of a medievalist who acquires his perspective solely through books.

Even casual observation reveals the amazing variety of standards by which Americans live. The inconsistencies and contradictions which charac-

terize modern mass societies are products of the multitude of communication channels and the ease of participation in them. Studying relatively isolated societies, anthropologists can speak meaningfully of "culture areas" in geographical terms; in such societies common cultures have a territorial base, for only those who live together can interact. In modern industrial societies, however, because of the development of rapid transportation and the media of mass communication, people who are geographically dispersed can communicate effectively. Culture areas are coterminous with communication channels; since communication networks are no longer coterminous with territorial boundaries, culture areas overlap and have lost their territorial bases. Thus, next-door neighbors may be complete strangers; even in common parlance there is an intuitive recognition of the diversity of perspectives, and we speak meaningfully of people living in different social worlds—the academic world, the world of children, the world of fashion.

Modern mass societies, indeed, are made up of a bewildering variety of social worlds. Each is an organized outlook, built up by people in their interaction with one another; hence, each communication channel gives rise to a separate world. Probably the greatest sense of identification and solidarity is to be found in the various communal structures—the underworld, ethnic minorities, the social elite. Such communities are frequently spatially segregated, which isolates them further from the outer world, while the "grapevine" and foreign-language presses provide internal contacts. Another common type of social world consists of the associational structures—the world of medicine, of organized labor, of the theater, of café society. These are held together not only by various voluntary associations within each locality but also by periodicals like *Variety*, specialized journals, and feature sections in newspapers. Finally, there are the loosely connected universes of special interest—the world of sports, of the stamp collector, of the daytime serial—serviced by mass media programs and magazines like *Field and Stream*. Each of these worlds is a unity of order, a universe of regularized mutual response. Each is an area in which there is some structure which permits reasonable anticipation of the behavior of others, hence, an area in which one may act with a sense of security and confidence.[7] Each social world, then, is a culture area, the boundaries of which are set neither by territory nor by formal group membership but by the limits of effective communication.

Since there is a variety of communication channels, differing in stability and extent, social worlds differ in composition, size, and the territorial distribution of the participants. Some, like local cults, are small and concentrated; others, like the intellectual world, are vast and the participants dispersed. Worlds differ in the extent and clarity of their boundaries; each is confined by some kind of horizon, but this may be wide or narrow, clear or vague. The fact that social worlds are not coterminous with the universe of men is recognized; those in the underworld are well aware of the fact that outsiders do not share their values Worlds differ in exclusiveness and in the extent to which they demand the loyalty of their participants. Most important of all, social worlds are not static entities; shared perspectives are continually being reconstituted. Worlds come into existence with the establishment of communication channels; when life conditions change, social relationships may also change, and these worlds may disappear.

Every social world has some kind of communication system—often nothing more than differential association—in which there develops a special universe of discourse, sometimes an argot. Special meanings and symbols further accentuate differences and increase social distance from outsiders. In each world there are special norms of conduct, a set of values, a special prestige ladder, characteristic career lines, and a common outlook toward life—a *Weltanschauung*. In the case of elites there may even arise a code of honor which holds only for those who belong, while others are dismissed as beings somewhat less than human

from whom bad manners may be expected. A social world, then, is an order conceived which serves as the stage on which each participant seeks to carve out his career and to maintain and enhance his status.

One of the characteristics of life in modern mass societies is simultaneous participation in a variety of social worlds. Because of the ease with which the individual may expose himself to a number of communication channels, he may lead a segmentalized life, participating successively in a number of unrelated activities. Furthermore, the particular combination of social worlds differs from person to person; this is what led Simmel to declare that each stands at the point at which a unique combination of social circles intersects. The geometric analogy is a happy one, for it enables us to conceive the numerous possibilities of combinations and the different degrees of participation in each circle. To understand what a man does, we must get at his unique perspective—what he takes for granted and how he defines the situation—but in mass societies we must learn in addition the social world in which he is participating in a given act.

LOYALTY AND SELECTIVE RESPONSIVENESS

In a mass society where each person internalizes numerous perspectives there are bound to be some incongruities and conflicts. The overlapping of group affiliation and participation, however, need not lead to difficulties and is usually unnoticed. The reference groups of most persons are mutually sustaining. Thus, the soldier who volunteers for hazardous duty on the battlefield may provoke anxiety in his family but is not acting contrary to their values; both his family and his comrades admire courage and disdain cowardice. Behavior may be inconsistent, as in the case of the proverbial office tyrant who is meek before his wife, but it is not noticed if the transactions occur in dissociated contexts. Most people live more or less compartmentalized lives, shifting from one social world to another as they participate in a succession of transactions. In each world

[7] Cf. Riezler, *Man: Mutable and Immutable* (Chicago: Henry Regnery Co., 1950), pp. 62–72; L. Landgrebe, "The World as a Phenomenological Problem," *Philosophy and Phenomenological Research,* I (1940), 38–58; and A. Schuetz, "The Stranger: An Essay in Social Psychology," *American Journal of Sociology,* XLIX (1944), 499–507.

their roles are different, their relations to other participants are different, and they reveal a different facet of their personalities. Men have become so accustomed to this mode of life that they manage to conceive of themselves as reasonably consistent human beings in spite of this segmentalization and are generally not aware of the fact that their acts do not fit into a coherent pattern.

People become acutely aware of the existence of different outlooks only when they are successively caught in situations in which conflicting demands are made upon them, all of which cannot possibly be satisfied. While men generally avoid making difficult decisions, these dilemmas and contradictions of status may force a choice between two social worlds. These conflicts are essentially alternative ways of defining the same situation, arising from several possible perspectives. In the words of William James, "As a man I pity you, but as an official I must show you no mercy; as a politician I regard him as an ally, but as a moralist I loathe him." In playing roles in different social worlds, one imputes different expectations to others whose differences cannot always be compromised. The problem is that of selecting the perspective for defining the situation. In Mead's terminology, which generalized other's role is to be taken? It is only in situations where alternative definitions are possible that problems of loyalty arise.

Generally such conflicts are ephemeral; in critical situations contradictions otherwise unnoticed are brought into the open, and painful choices are forced. In poorly integrated societies, however, some people find themselves continually beset with such conflicts. The Negro intellectual, children of mixed marriages or of immigrants, the foreman in a factory, the professional woman, the military chaplain—all live in the interstices of well-organized structures and are marginal men.[8] In most instances they manage to make their way through their compartmentalized lives, although personal mal-

adjustments are apparently frequent. In extreme cases amnesia and dissociation of personality can occur.

Much of the interest in reference groups arises out of concern with situations in which a person is confronted with the necessity of choosing between two or more organized perspectives. The hypothesis has been advanced that the choice of reference groups—conformity to the norms of the group whose perspective is assumed—is a function of one's interpersonal relations; to what extent the culture of a group serves as the matrix for the organization of perceptual experience depends upon one's relationship and personal loyalty to others who share that outlook. Thus, when personal relations to others in the group deteriorate, as sometimes happens in a military unit after continued defeat, the norms become less binding, and the unit may disintegrate in panic. Similarly, with the transformation of personal relationships between parent and child in late adolescence, the desires and standards of the parents often become less obligatory.

It has been suggested further that choice of reference groups rests upon personal loyalty to significant others of that social world. "Significant others," for Sullivan, are those persons directly responsible for the internalization of norms. Socialization is a product of a gradual accumulation of experiences with certain people, particularly those with whom we stand in primary relations, and significant others are those who are actually involved in the cultivation of abilities, values, and outlook.[9] Crucial, apparently, is the character of one's emotional ties with them. Those who think the significant others have treated them with affection and consideration have a sense of personal obligation that is binding under all circumstances, and they will be loyal even at great personal sacrifice. Since primary relations are not necessarily satisfactory, however, the reactions may be negative. A person who is well aware of the expectations of significant others may go out of his way to reject them. This may account for the bifurcation of orientation in minority groups, where

[8] Cf. E. C. Hughes, "Dilemmas and Contradictions of Status," *American Journal of Sociology,* L (1945), 353–59, and E. V. Stonequist, *The Marginal Man* (New York: Charles Scribner's Sons, 1937).

[9] H. S. Sullivan, *Conceptions of Modern Psychiatry* (Washington, D.C.: W. H. White Psychiatric Foundation, 1947), pp. 18–22.

some remain loyal to the parental culture while others seek desperately to become assimilated in the larger world. Some who withdraw from the uncertainties of real life may establish loyalties to perspectives acquired through vicarious relationships with characters encountered in books.[10]

Perspectives are continually subjected to the test of reality. All perception is hypothetical. Because of what is taken for granted from each standpoint, each situation is approached with a set of expectations; if transactions actually take place as anticipated, the perspective itself is reinforced. It is thus the confirming responses of other people that provide support for perspectives.[11] But in mass societies the responses of others vary, and in the study of reference groups the problem is that of ascertaining *whose* confirming responses will sustain a given point of view.

THE STUDY OF MASS SOCIETIES

Because of the differentiated character of modern mass societies, the concept of reference group, or some suitable substitute, will always have a central place in any realistic conceptual scheme for its analysis. As is pointed out above, it will be most useful if it is used to designate that group whose perspective is assumed by the actor as the frame of reference for the organization of his perceptual experience. Organized perspectives arise in and become shared through participation in common communication channels, and the diversity of mass societies arises from the multiplicity of channels and the ease with which one may participate in them.

Mass societies are not only diversified and pluralistic but also continually changing. The successive modification of life-conditions compels changes in social relationships, and any adequate

[10] Cf. R. R. Grinker and J. P. Spiegel, *Men under Stress* (Philadelphia: Blakiston Co., 1945), pp. 122–26; and E. A. Shils and M. Janowitz, "Cohesion and Disintegration in the Wehrmacht in World War II," *Public Opinion Quarterly*, XII (1948), 280–315.

[11] Cf. G. H. Mead, *The Philosophy of the Act* (Chicago: University of Chicago Press, 1938), pp. 107–73; and L. Postman, "Toward a General Theory of Cognition," in J. H. Rohrer and M. Sherif (eds.), *Social Psychology at the Crossroads* (New York: Harper & Bros., 1951), pp. 242–72.

analysis requires a study of these transformational processes themselves. Here the concept of reference group can be of crucial importance. For example, all forms of social mobility, from sudden conversions to gradual assimilation, may be regarded essentially as displacements of reference groups, for they involve a loss of responsiveness to the demands of one social world and the adoption of the perspective of another. It may be hypothesized that the disaffection occurs first on the level of personal relations, followed by a weakening sense of obligation, a rejection of old claims, and the establishment of new loyalties and incorporation of a new perspective. The conflicts that characterize all persons in marginal roles are of special interest in that they provide opportunities for cross-sectional analyses of the processes of social change.

In the analysis of the behavior of men in mass societies the crucial problem is that of ascertaining how a person defines the situation, which perspective he uses in arriving at such a definition, and who constitutes the audience whose responses provide the necessary confirmation and support for his position. This calls for focusing attention upon the expectations the actor imputes to others, the communication channels in which he participates, and his relations with those with whom he identifies himself. In the study of conflict, imagery provides a fertile source of data. At moments of indecision, when in doubt and confusion, who appears in imagery? In this manner the significant other can be identified.

An adequate analysis of modern mass societies requires the development of concepts and operations for the description of the manner in which each actor's orientation toward his world is successively reconstituted. Since perception is selective and perspectives differ, different items are noticed and progressively diverse set of images arises, even among those exposed to the same media of mass communication. The concept of reference group summarizes differential associations and loyalties and thus facilitates the study of selective perception. It becomes, therefore, an indispensable tool for comprehending the diversity and dynamic character of the kind of society in which we live.

Institutions and Persons

If we shift our view from the external behavior of individual organisms and from explanations of such behavior in terms of physiological elements and mechanisms, and view man as a person who acts with and against other persons, we may then (1) examine the patterns of conduct which men enact together, and (2) avail ourselves of the direct experiences which persons have of one another and of themselves. At its minimum, social conduct consists of the actions of one person oriented to another, and most of the actions of men are of this sort. Man's action is interpersonal. It is often informed by awareness of other actors and directly oriented to their expectations and to anticipations of their behavior.

Out of the metaphors of poets and philosophers, who have likened man's conduct to that of the stage actor, sociologists have fashioned analytical tools. Long-used phrases readily come to mind: "playing a role" in the "great theater of public life," to move "in the limelight," the "theater of War," the "stage is all set." More technically, the concept "role" refers to (1) units of conduct which by their recurrence stand out as regularities and (2) which are oriented to the conduct of other actors. These recurrent interactions form patterns of mutually oriented conduct.

By definition, roles are interpersonal, that is, oriented to the conduct and expectations of others. These others, who expect things of us, are also playing roles: we expect them to do things

From *Character and Social Structure: The Psychology of Social Institutions* by Hans Gerth and C. Wright Mills, copyright 1953 by Harcourt Brace Jovanovich, Inc. Reprinted by permission of the publishers.

in certain ways and to refrain from doing and feeling things in other ways. Interpersonal situations are thus built up and sets of roles held in line by mutual expectation, approbation, and disfavor.

Much of our social conduct, as we know from direct experience, is enacted in order to meet the expectations of others. In this sense, our enemies often control us as much as our friends. The father of a patriarchal family is expected by his wife and children to act in certain ways when confronted with given situations, and he in turn expects them to act in certain regular ways. Being acquainted with these simple facts about patriarchal families we expect regularities of conduct from each of their members, and having experienced family situations, we expect, with some degree of probability, that each of these members will experience his place and his self in a certain way.

Man as a person is an historical creation, and can most readily be understood in terms of the roles which he enacts and incorporates. These roles are limited by the kind of social institutions in which he happens to be born and in which he matures into an adult. His memory, his sense of time and space, his perception, his motives, his conception of his self . . . his psychological functions are shaped and steered by the specific configuration of roles which he incorporates from his society.

Perhaps the most important of these features of man is his image of his self, his idea of what kind of person he is. This experience of self is a crucially interpersonal one. Its basic organization is reflected from surrounding persons to whose approbation and criticism one pays attention.

What we think of ourselves is decisively influenced by what others think of us. Their attitudes of approval and of disapproval guide us in learning to play the roles we are assigned or which we assume. By internalizing these attitudes of others toward us and our conduct we not only gain new roles, but in time an image of our selves. Of course, man's "looking-glass self" may be a true or a distorted reflection of his actual self. Yet those from whom a man continually seeks approval are important determinants of what kind of man he is becoming. If a young lawyer begins to feel satisfaction from the approval of the boss of the local political machine, if the labels which this boss uses to describe his behavior matter a lot to the lawyer, he is being steered into new roles and into a new image of his self by the party machine and its boss. Their values may in time become his own and he will apply them not only to other men but to his own actions as well.[1] The self, Harry Stack Sullivan once said, is made up of the reflected appraisals of others.[2]

The concept of role does not of course imply a one person–one role equation. One person may play many different roles, and each of these roles may be a segment of the different institutions and interpersonal situations in which the person moves. A corporation executive acts differently in his office than in his child's nursery. An adolescent girl enacts a different role when she is at a party composed of members of her own clique than when she is at her family's breakfast table. Moreover, the luxury of a certain image of self

implied in the party role is not often possible in her family circle. In the family circle the party role might be amusing, as a charming attempt at sophistication "beyond her age and experience," but at the party it might bring prestige and even the adulation of young males. She cannot, usually, act out the self-conception of a long-suffering lover before her grandfather, but she can when she is alone with her young man.

The chance to display emotional gestures, and even to feel them, varies with one's status and class position. For emotional gestures, expected by others and by one's self, form important features of many social roles. The Victorian lady could dramatize certain emotions in a way that today would be considered silly, if not hysterical. Yet the working girl who was her contemporary was not as likely to faint as was the lady; there would probably not have been anyone to catch the working girl. During the nineties in America it was expected that women who were also ladies, that is, members of an upper status group, would faint upon very exciting occasions. The role of the delicate and fainting lady was involved in the very being of a lady.[3] But the "same" occasions would not elicit fainting on the part of the ladies' maid, who did not conceive of her "place," and of her self, as a fainting lady; fainting requires a certain amount of leisure and gentlemanly attention, and accordingly offers opportunities to the gentleman to demonstrate that chivalry is not dead.

The roles allowed and expected, the self-images which they entail, and the consequences of these roles and images on the persons we are with are firmly embedded in a social context. Inner psychological changes and the institutional controls of a society are thus interlinked.

An institution is an organization of roles, which means that the roles carry different degrees of authority, so that one of the roles—we may call it the "head" role—is understood and accepted by the members of the other roles as guaranteeing the relative permanence of the total conduct pattern. An *institution* is thus (1) an organization of roles, (2) one or more of which is

---

[1] The mechanism by which persons thus internalize roles and the attitudes of others is language. Language is composed of gestures, normally verbal, which call forth similar responses in two individuals. Without such gestures man could not incorporate the attitudes of others, and could not so easily make these attitudes a condition of his own learning and enactment of roles of his own image of self.

These conceptions will be discussed in greater detail in Chapters III: Organism and Psychic Structure and IV: The Person. Here we are only concerned with setting forth in the most general way the sociological model of explanation. [Ed. Note: reference is to chapters in *Character and Social Structure*.]

[2] "Conceptions of Modern Psychiatry," *Psychiatry*, Vol. III, No. 1 (February 1949), pp. 10–11. Compare also C. H. Cooley's *Human Nature and the Social Order* (rev. ed.; New York: Scribner's, 1922). The tradition is well documented by Fay B. Karpf, *American Social Psychology* (New York: McGraw-Hill, 1932).

[3] Cf. Ralph Linton, *The Study of Man* (New York: Appleton-Century, 1936).

understood to serve the maintenance of the total set of roles.

The "head role" of an institution is very important in the psychic life of the other members of the institution. What "the head" thinks of them in their respective roles, or what they conceive him to think, is internalized, that is, taken over, by them. In a strictly patriarchal family, the head, the father, is looked up to; his is the most important attitude toward the child that may determine the child's attitude toward his, the child's, own conduct and perhaps toward his self: in taking over this attitude the child builds up an "other" within his self, and the attitude he conceives this other to have toward him is a condition for his attitude toward his own self. Other persons in other roles also have attitudes toward him and each of these may be internalized, and eventually form segments of his self-conception. But the attitude of the head of the major institution in which we play a role is a decisive one in our own maturation. If "he says it is all right," we feel secure in what we are doing and how we are conceiving our self. When his attitudes are taken over into the self, this head constitutes in a concrete form, a "particular other." But he is not seen merely as a particular person; he is the symbol and the "mouth piece" of the entire institution. In him is focused the "final" attitudes toward our major roles and our self within this institution; he sums them up, and when we take over these attitudes and expectations we control our institutional conduct in terms of them. It is by means of such internalized others that our conduct, our playing of roles within institutions, is "self-controlled."

By choosing the social role as a major concept we are able to reconstruct the inner experience of the person as well as the institutions which make up an historical social structure. For man as a *person* (from the Latin *persona*, meaning "mask") is composed of the specific roles which he enacts and of the effects of enacting these roles upon his self. And society as a *social structure* is composed of roles as segments variously combined in its total circle of institutions. The organization of roles is important in building up a particular social structure; it also has psychological implications for the persons who act out the social structure.

Most of the various interpersonal situations in which we are involved exist within institutions, which make up a social structure; and changes of social structure make up the main course of human history. In order to understand men's conduct and experience we must reconstruct the historical social structures in which they play roles and acquire selves. For such regularity of conduct, and of the motives for this conduct, as we may find will rest upon the historical regularities of these social structures, rather than upon any suprahistorical, biological elements assumed to be innate and constant within the organism. From the sociological point of view, man as a person is a social-historical creation. If his view of his self and of his motives is intimately connected with the roles which are available to him and which he incorporates, then we may not expect to learn much that is very concrete about individual men unless we investigate a number of his specific roles in a number of varied social-historical settings.

Rather than constant elements within a physiological organism, the sociologist rests his primary model of explanation upon the interpersonal situations, and in the last analysis, the social structures within which persons live out their lives.

Barbara Laslett &
Carol A. B. Warren

13

Losing Weight: The Organizational Promotion of Behavior Change

Fatness, or as it is more politely called in our society "obesity,"[1] is both a medical and a social problem, since in our society the fat are stigmatized. However, unlike other forms of deviant behavior such as check forgery and shoplifting, obesity is not against the law. Reaction to this deviant status and behavior cannot, therefore, be channeled through the criminal justice system as a means of control.

One purpose of this analysis is to explore the sociological dimensions of obesity as a type of deviance by applying the concept of stigma, as developed by Goffman (1963), to the strategies used by one voluntary weight loss organization[2] to combat obesity. In this organization, efforts to change the behavior of fat people so that they would become thin included, as a central feature,

the application of stigmatizing labels. The insights which this analysis provides will then be used to specify variation in the meanings, uses and consequences of applying stigmatizing labels.

The use of stigma as a strategy for changing behavior from deviant to normal presents a challenge to labeling theory in general, and in particular to Lemert's (1967) theory of secondary deviation which assumes that further deviance follows from the application of stigmatizing labels. We will argue that the social labeling involved in stigmatization may also be used to change behavior in the opposite direction, i.e., toward normalcy. If this is true, then whether a stigmatizing label has a positive or negative effect on behavior will depend on other features of the situation than the labeling process alone. The empirical example upon which this analysis is based presents some suggestions of what these features may be, and they will be discussed in the concluding section of the paper.

Barbara Laslett and Carol A. B. Warren, "Losing Weight: The Organizational Promotion of Behavior Change," *Social Problems* 23:1 (October 1975) pp. 69–80. Reprinted by permission.

An earlier version of this paper was read at the 1973 meetings of the Pacific Sociological Association, Scottsdale, Arizona. This research was supported by the Social Science Research Institute, University of Southern California.

[1] Under the more technical rubric "obesity," two types of problem are included: overfat and overweight. A person can be slender and overfat, and overweight but not overfat. For example, a football player may weigh more than ideal for his height, as specified by life insurance company tables, but his body may not have any excess fat over muscle. A slender, sedentary person may, in contrast, have an excess of fat cells in his or her body and be "overfat" but not overweight. We use the terms "fat" and "obese" interchangeably to refer to persons who are perceived as too large by significant others and who perceive themselves that way as well.

[2] Permission to use the name of the organization studies was denied. Therefore, we refer only to the "weight loss organization" in the discussion.

STIGMA AND OBESITY

Stigma, as Goffman (1963 : 3) puts it, is "an attribute that is deeply discrediting." In Lemert's terms, it is a negative label. Goffman distinguishes three types of stigma: (1) perceived "blemishes of individual character," such as criminality, (2) the "tribal stigma of race, nation and religion" and (3) "abominations of the body—various physical deformities." Obesity is one type of "abomination of the body" which is particularly affected by cultural definitions. Not only do physiologically based definitions of obesity vary, but definitions of beauty—where obesity may or may not be discrediting—are particularly liable to cultural and historical variation.[3] In our society, although slimness is a general societal ideal, definitions of fat and slim vary according to social class, ethnicity, age and geographical area. Adolescents are more inclined to view themselves as fat than are adults, females more than males, and people of higher socio-economic status more than lower status (Dwyer et al. 1970). Fatness can also affect socio-economic opportunities: in New York, the extremely obese may go on welfare permanently since they are regarded as essentially unemployable, and in one California city, teachers may not be more than 25% overweight.[4]

Goffman (1963:3–4) emphasizes that while stigma might be seen in terms of individual characteristics, "a language of relationships, not attributes is really needed." The social meaning of obesity is derived in interaction with others, not from the attribute alone. It is for this reason that Goffman's further distinction of discrediting features that are or are not visible to others is relevant to the study of obesity.

For stigmatization to occur, the discrediting attribute must be known by the others with whom interaction takes place. Some stigmatizing attributes, like criminality and homosexuality, are not immediately apparent. Goffman (1963:4) refers to those persons whose stigma is invisible as *discreditable*. Other attributes, such as obesity, provide visible cues to stigma: their bearers are *discredited*. The obese cannot "pass" as thin; they must either lose weight or remain stigmatized.

Obesity as a source of stigma in contemporary American society has been documented in both the popular and professional literature (Stuart and Davis, 1972; Allon, 1973). Dwyer et al. (1970) point out that "normal" persons (using the term as Goffman does, to contrast with the stigmatized) stereotype fat persons as weak willed, ugly, awkward and immoral and the fat themselves have negative self-images to match the stereotypes. Fat people in contemporary American society, therefore, are the subject of the stigmatizing labels used by others and themselves.[5]

THE LABELING PERSPECTIVE

The labeling perspective defines deviance and normalcy in terms of the reactions of social audiences.[6] Lemert (1967:41) extends this perspective to the theory of secondary deviation.

The essence of the theory of secondary deviation is contained in two propositions, one explicit and one implicit: (1) Further deviance is promoted by audience labeling of persons as deviant, and (2) the "further deviance" promoted by labeling is made up of a deviant identity, deviant behavior, and a deviant way of life *which vary together*. This study questions these propositions by showing that *the use of negative or stigmatizing labels, in this case the label "fat," can be used to promote the normalization of deviant behavior, i.e., to make fat people thin*. Additionally, we question the logically assumed connection between identity, behavior and way of life.

METHODOLOGY

The data were collected in six months of systematic participant observation by the two authors in two different groups of the organization's weekly meetings. We observed three lecturers

---

[3] In classical Hawaiian culture, for example, a man's wealth, and a woman's beauty, were both measured by the amount of fat accumulated.

[4] Occupational health standards of such large-scale employers as the Los Angeles City School system, and the Los Angeles City and County governments include as one criteria for employment in *all* jobs, that the individual be within a range of weight specified as normal for a given age, height, and sex group, usually according to Metropolitan Life Insurance Company tables. (See Metropolitan Life Insurance Co., New York: 1969.)

[5] The only counter-trend to the negative labeling of obesity is the development of a "fat power" movement to destigmatize the *category* "fat persons" rather than to destigmatize fat persons by making them thin. (See Allon, 1973).

[6] "Stigma" encompasses the same phenomena as "deviant," except that (1) stigma focuses more clearly on the audience reaction than deviance (and more than the labeling theory of deviance, which includes the definitionally illegitimate concept "secret deviance"), and (2) stigma encompasses "bodily abominations" and "tribal stigma" whereas deviance is generally restricted to "defects of character."

and several hundred members in interaction. One of the authors had been a long-term member of the organization (for over three years), and could provide additional informal data on more than 6 other lecturers. The other author joined the organization for the purpose of the research.

Each observer participated as a member, and it was only as a member that access to the organization was permitted. Leaders of the weight loss organization itself suggested the tactic of becoming a member when a representative denied our request for permission to do overt research. The authors were therefore in the unusual situation of doing secret research with the implicit permission of the institution involved.

The lack of overt permission did present certain problems for data collection. Each observer attempted to take notes in the field on the content of the weekly meetings. During one meeting, however, another member (who, to our knowledge, was not a researcher) was asked not to take down what the lecturer was saying, despite her claim that she was just practicing her shorthand. Note-taking therefore was covert. The themes, however, were frequently reiterated in the lectures, facilitating accurate field notes.

The focus of analysis was the organization's strategies for promoting behavior change, particularly the use of a stigmatized identity label as a way of promoting normalized behavior and a normal way of life. Using Glaser and Strauss' (1967) model for the generation of grounded theory, the analytic categories were generated during data collection and preliminary analysis.

STIGMATIZING IDENTITY AS A STRATEGY FOR BEHAVIOR CHANGE

The major strategy used by the organization to promote the desired behavior (adoption of a rigidly defined program of eating) is *intensive stigmatization of the members as fat persons and the continued application of the label "fat" as an essential identity.* Members are told that the world is dichotomized into two types of people with reference to food and weight: the fat, and the "civilians" (the slender). The stigmatized identity of the fat person is permanent. It cannot

be erased by weight loss, although it can be shifted from a visible stigma to an invisible one—from discrediting to discreditable. For the fat person who has become thin, weight loss is always potentially reversible and is an ever-dangerous invisible stigma which threatens the individual:

Lecturer: *I am a fat person who got thin.*
Member *(250 lb. loser): I still think of myself as really heavy.*

At most, then, the fat person can expect a partial destigmatization: the destigmatization of behavior reflected in appearance, but not the destigmatization of identity.[7] According to the weight loss organization, a change of identity from fat to thin would remove one of the best safeguards the fat person has against future weight gains. The continual awareness of an essential fat identity, whether visible (in pounds and fat) or invisible, acts as a warning device against the type of eating behavior promoting the discredited fat state.

Lecturer: *One doctor at UCLA says that he wishes that the word "obese" would appear on fat people's foreheads when they become 5% overweight, since that much body weight changes chemistry so you can't use the same drugs. Furthermore, fat can be concealed by clothes. It is those women with lovely faces and good dress sense who are worse off than anyone, because they can put it on and not even notice.*

Although identity cannot and should not be changed, eating behavior is amenable to change. The behavior change promoted by the organization is a permanent change in the quality and quantity of the food consumed so that external slenderness can be maintained for life. The threat of compulsive eating, however, is always present. Therefore compulsive eating behavior must be changed, either toward more moderation in eating habits or toward less fattening objects:

Lecturer: *You will learn moderation here, too— to have ½ cup of ice cream and feel satisfied*

[7] For a general discussion of the phenomenon of destigmatization, see Warren, 1975.

with it. You will learn that 4 teaspoons of sour cream will be plenty on a baked potato and 1 teaspoon of cream cheese is enough on your bagel.

Lecturer:　*I am still a compulsive eater, but now I eat lettuce compulsively.*

The fact that food must be consumed to live gives the weight loss organization a tactical problem in promoting the desired behavior change unlike the self-help organizations for smokers, drug addicts and alcoholics which forbid the undesirable behavior. Instead, an exactly opposite mechanism is substituted—continuously focusing on food and stressing to the members that they *must* eat. Members who do not eat breakfast or who have a skimpy lunch are lectured to about the dangers of not eating enough. For fat people, being hungry is a violation of their essential self. They must be sure both to eat regularly so that they do not become hungry, and to exercise constant vigilance over food.

Lecturer:　*(to a member who complained about having to eat the weekly liver portion which is required): You must eat it. Everything you put in your mouth does not have to be a thrill of a lifetime.*

Lecturer:　*Set up a barrier between you and food. A barrier that thin people have automatically, but for you it must be a conscious matter.*

Being hungry is a violation of the essential self, and carries with it the danger to which fat people are always exposed: the "bad," uncontrolled eating which may occur if the member gets too hungry. The organization promotes the conception of food as a vital force in a person's life. Meetings are characterized by this focus on food, which also contributes to reinforcing the individual's identity as fat, since fat people are seen as preoccupied with eating.

The organization encourages a change in behavior where one set of foodstuffs (thinning, good, "treats") are substituted for another (fattening, bad, "monsters"). There is an emphasis on traditional recipes using "legal" ingredients, like lobster newburg made with blended cauliflower for sauce, rather than completely different foods.

Members are forbidden to use dietetic foods except for sugar-free soda and substitute sweeteners. So while stressing the significance of a total change in eating habits, the organization attempts to charm the members by focusing on their favorite vice, food, as a central symbol and by promising slenderness through this "totally new way" of using old recipes. The sin of gluttony can be satisfied through the back door. One of the organization's slogans is "you will never be hungry on our program."

The preoccupation with food and eating, which comprises a large part of the program's rhetoric, of lecturers' materials, and informal interaction at the weekly meetings, relates to this common feature of fat people's essential identity. The weight loss organization's goal is to change the eating behavior of the obese. One of their strategies to achieve their end is to emphasize the identity of "being a fatty" and fat people's obsession with food and eating. Negative labels, then, which *reinforce the essential identity of the fat as fat*, are used as a means of *changing behavior from deviant to normal*, thereby presenting a challenge to the theory of secondary deviation, which would predict an escalation of deviant behavior to follow from the act of stigmatization.

LIFESTYLE CHANGE

"Lifestyle" or "way of life" are ill-defined terms, used by both Lemert (1967) and the weight loss organization to describe the types of behavior change persons undergo that are related to but are not composed of the behavior under consideration. Persons losing weight are presented by the organization as undergoing not only behavior change related to eating but also to change in other personal attributes and the social life that accompanies both eating and a size that is stigmatized in our society.

Lecturer:　*When I was fat, I could never balance my check book. My husband had to do it for me. But now I am more independent and more able to take care of myself. You have to be more independent and you can do it.*

The organization reinforces the image that the lifestyle of fat people is full of embarrassing and self-demeaning experiences. Lecturers tell of getting stuck in theatre seats and behind the wheel of a car, or requiring other people to push as one tries to pull oneself out of a pool. They tell stories of not going places they really wanted to go because of having to sit in the back seat of a small car and fearing they would not be able to get out of it, or not having clothes that fit. They also emphasize that fat people are self-deluding and make irrational excuses for themselves and their stigma:

Member: *I have to have cookies in the house in case my grandchildren come to visit.*

Lecturer: *Where do your grandchildren live?*

Member: *In New York! (This study was done in California.)*

While such stories are often told to amuse the membership, their serious meaning is clear: until fat people reduce their weight they will live with painfully reduced self-esteem in a restricted range of activities, and a correspondingly unsatisfactory lifestyle. Lecturers promote an imagery and provide examples of the "better" way of life automatically accruing to fat persons as they become slender. For instance, lecturers state that a variety of positive changes accompanied their weight loss—sparkling wit at parties, more energy, a greater ability to cope with life's vicissitudes. They suggest greater business and professional, as well as social, success are a consequence of eliminating the visible stigma of fat. Thus, there is no need to force members to exercise, quit smoking, or have better human relationships: these good things will automatically follow from the transformation in lifestyle accompanying weight loss.

The organization is concerned with life style in the context of attributes and activities unconnected with eating behavior; it also claims that a lifelong commitment to its weight loss and loss-maintenance program must become part of the individual's way of life. Because the person's essential fat identity is always present, the threat of returning to "bad" eating behavior is always possible. This lifelong commitment is expressed linguistically in the organization's distinction between a "diet" and a "program."

A "diet" is what fat people go on and off; it involves a temporary behavior change followed by relapse. A "program" is a changed lifestyle and pattern of eating lasting a lifetime. A "diet" implies the illusory promise of the destigmatizing of the individual, the shedding of the fat self for a reborn thin one. A "program" establishes the alternative ideal of a lifelong struggle to divorce eating behavior and way of life from an inevitably fat identity.

Linked with the concept of "program" is a view of time encompassing a whole past, present and future of eating habits. The lifetime program is divided into three stages the initiate must pass through before the attainment of a stigma which is discreditable only: the basic weight loss program, the "leveling" program (beginning when the person is within 10 lbs of goal weight) and the "maintenance" program theoretically continued for the remainder of the person's future. Free lifetime membership in the organization accrues to people who have achieved their goal weight, complete the "maintenance" program, weigh in monthly and do not gain more than 2 pounds above their goal weight. Initiates to the organization are given a master plan for their entire life, divided into four distinct time tracks: three as a member of the organization and one (always in the past) as a discredited fat person.

A tactical problem for the organization is posed, however, by the fact that members do not follow the master plan: they do not always lose weight (or worse still, sometimes gain) during the time they attend meetings. They return to the organization after losing forty pounds and regaining fifty. For such contingencies the organization has another perspective on time: it is the present only, just the immediate day or even meal at hand, which counts—not the past, and not the future. The members are told, on the one hand, that the program is a master plan for their entire lives, and on the other hand that no past action constitutes failure. This paradox is illustrated by two quotes from an organizational pamphlet: "If you do the best and the most you can today, don't worry about tomorrow"; "Perfection is attained by slow degrees; she requires the hand of time." Since all acts will eventually become past, success is always possible and organizational membership is always available. No matter how often one joins or rejoins, lecturers tell new members "Today is the first day of the rest of your life."

The mixed perspective on time and an emphasis on the permanence of their fat identity enables the weight loss organization to place the responsibility for failure on the individual and not the organization. The membership, at any one time, includes many former members who failed to lose weight, or who lost weight and later regained it. They are welcomed back and reassured that behavior change is always possible. Through the use of stigma as a strategy for individual behavior change, the organization constructs a foolproof ideology: success comes from following the organization's program, while failure is the responsibility of the individual member reflecting his or her essential identity.

Lemert's theory of secondary deviation implies that a deviant identity, deviant behavior and a deviant way of life vary together. The weight loss organization's separation of identity, behavior and lifestyle—through its use of stigma both as a means of changing behavior and as a basis on which to attribute responsibility for failure to individual members—presents a further challenge to the theory as it has been formulated. Not only can a stigmatized identity lead to non-deviant behavior, but "normal" behavior can lead to a "normal" way of life despite the retention of an identity which bears a negative label. A lifestyle change is only possible, though, when the stigma becomes discreditable (i.e., when it is no longer visible).

ORGANIZATIONAL STRATEGIES FOR THE PROMOTION OF BEHAVIOR CHANGE

The two major strategies of change employed by the organization to promote and reinforce a stigmatized fat identity, normalized eating behavior and a better lifestyle are (1) the fostering of an ingroup–outgroup sentiment and (2) the use of change agents who are themselves successful graduates of the program.

The ingroup–outgroup differentiation is dual: between fat members and fat nonmembers of the organization, and, more important, between fat "foodaholics" and thin "civilians." Civilians are regarded, much as Goffman defines them: as "normals." Fat non-members are unenlightened potential members; if they are not attempting to become thin they are slothful and immoral. At best they are to be pitied, and members may serve as models to help them to a future in which they may be discreditable rather than discredited persons. If they are following some other weight program, such as diet pills, they are doomed to failure. Whatever the case, they are potential converts through efforts of both members and organizational advertising.

Unlike some behavior changing institutions such as Synanon, the weight loss organization is not a total institution (Goffman, 1961), and cannot set up walls between the membership and the civilian world. Worse, housewives form a large proportion of the membership; they have the traditional female role tasks of making meals for their families—meals which include desserts, cookies, potatoes and creamy salad dressings. So the members are encouraged to *quarantine* themselves, either physically or mentally from the surrounding temptations of their everyday lives.

Quarantine involves both removal from the non-quarantined and association with other quarantined persons (the ingroup impulse). Unlike Alcoholics Anonymous, though, the organization can rarely suggest that the members socialize only with those who do not use the substance, both because everyone uses food, and because so much of the member's lives are involved with food preparation for and consumption with "civilians." But the members are exhorted mentally to disassociate themselves from civilians, who are pictured as dedicated to the members' failure.

Lecturer: *Friends want us to fail because that is the only way they can succeed . . . you have to be prepared for them . . . or they may be a civilian, and then they do not understand.*

Weekly organization meetings are presented as a kind of inoculation against external pressures which weaken will-power and resolve: waitresses in restaurants, children begging for homemade cookies, husbands asserting that they like cuddly women, are all threats:

Lecturer: *We must have free will not to eat and resist others . . . fat people are afraid of asserting themselves in the face of pressures to eat by restaurants, hostesses, fat people and others. Besides, they don't want to resist pressure. When you say "no" and mean it there is a tone in your voice that says you mean it. But a fat person's "no" to a second helping may be accompanied by salivating and panting.*

While the outgroup is the non-fat world, the ingroup is the world of foodaholics, and most particularly the membership of the organization. In the early days of the organization, there was more stress on ingroup participation (for example, members tempted to eat would telephone another member for moral support), but at the present time the organization has become so large that the notion of "interdependence of members' goals" is not used as a social control mechanism. Unlike other self-help groups such as Synanon and AA, group therapy and other group dynamics take at most a secondary place to the lecture as a primary focus of organizational meetings (see Crosbie et al., 1972). The difference may lie in the profit-making nature of the weight loss organization. Having more and smaller groups would reduce the money which the organization makes by increasing staff (lecturers, weighers and clerks) and hall rental costs.

In addition to quarantining and inoculation, which promote ingroup–outgroup differentiation, ingroup sentiment is fostered by organizational rituals. Among the most important of these are group rituals instituted by the organization to reward persons who lose weight; these include graduation ceremonies from the three phases of the program, special pins, and certificates of merit. Other rituals, which socialize and cement the group as an institution, are the semi-public weekly weighing of each member, shows of hands of persons who had gained, lost or remained at the same

weight during the week, and rounds of hand clapping both for persons who had lost weight and others who were "trying."

Since goal interdependence and ingroup sentiment is hard to manage in a nontotal institution of a large size which cannot forbid the addictive substance to members, the organization stresses the theme of self-discipline considerably more than that of discipline by peers: "it's up to you" is a phrase constantly used by the lecturers. Along with the theme of self-discipline, however, there is the continuing suggestion that pressures from the outgroup—the non-fat civilian society—is the source of external pressure on the individual:

Lecturer: *We are victims of patterns taught us in childhood of obeying our mothers and eating it all up because of the starving people in so-and-so country, but we must no longer be victims.*

As with many other self-help behavior modification groups, however, the pursuit of "causes" such as this hypothetical one remains completely secondary to the "major" goal of changing behavior in the here and now.

Lecturer: *I am not concerned with why you are fat because of past factors. You are rolling in mud because of your own choice. But if there are deep reasons for that, you should go to a doctor who can take care of you up here (points to his head).*

As an enterprise, this weight loss organization has an additional reason to refrain from seeking the hidden psychological and medical causes of obesity: legal responsibility. Lecturers constantly stress that they are not psychiatrists and will not dispense psychiatric advice, nor will they dispense authoritative nutritional, medical or scientific knowledge about obesity. Members with special problems are always told to consult their doctors. A denial of scientific expertise is yet another way of establishing the organization's lack of responsibility for any member's failure, and of placing the blame on the individual. Thus they cannot be held accountable for a failure of the program (the product) which they sell.

THE CHANGE AGENT

We found the change agent to be one of the most important facilitators for the "escalation" of behavior from deviant to normal (as defined by the organization). All the lecturers and other organizational personnel are fat persons turned thin-on-the-outside: they provide a vital symbol of identification for persons who believe that "no one ever loses weight and keeps it off." The major ways in which the lecturers accomplish such identification for the members are *stigma display* (linking the past of the lecturer with the soon-to-be-past of the member) and *deviance display* (linking the lecturer's present with the members').

Stigma display is the constant reiteration by the lecturers of their own identity as essentially fat persons, once discredited but now discreditable. This is accomplished in various ways: display of "before" and "after" pictures of the lecturer, anecdotes of the past sins of eating, and sad tales of the lifelong misery of the discredited fat and the counterpoint happiness of the discreditable (leavened quite often with humor):

Lecturer: *F told a story about how her husband had given her (now that she is thin) a black lace night gown and black satin sheets for Xmas. "Before, when I was a fat lady, we had a king size bed. He stayed on his side and I stayed on mine and we didn't meet in the middle very often. Satin sheets are very slippery. You slide off them."*

As Hurvitz (1968:4) notes, such identification of the change agents' past with the members' trials and tribulations is a fundamental aspect of most self-help type organizations.

But a sorry past does not always qualify one to win present peer identification, as studies of drug addicts who become "fat cat" bureaucrats have shown. Lecturers in this organization use a second tactic to promote members' identification with the change agent's *present* experience: *deviance display,* a tactic forbidden organizations as AA which ban the use of the deviant substance. Change agents underline the fact of lifelong temptation by food by indicating that they, too, are sometimes tempted and fail (but that the or-

ganization gives them the ability to recoup failures quickly and effectively):

Lecturer: *I ate three barrels of sauerkraut over the weekend and gained seven pounds, but now I know what to do and have taken almost all of it back off.*

Deviance display serves to promote identification, underlines the *continued* necessity of organizational membership, and highlights the necessity for changed behavior and an ultimate commitment to "a new way of life," at the same time as it reinforces the stigmatized essential identity.

SUMMARY AND CONCLUSIONS

Our data lead us to the conclusion that an empirically grounded elaboration of Lemert's theory of secondary deviation is both possible and needs to be tested in various behavior change settings. Our elaboration of Lemert's theory of secondary deviation or, as would be more accurate in the situation described here, a *theory of secondary normalization,* adds the following propositions which delineate those features of the labeling situation which make secondary normalization more probable than secondary deviation.

1. The central change strategy in organizations which use "ex's" as change agents is the permanent acceptance of a stigmatized identity. This strategy is in opposition to the strategy of the promotion of a "cured" or "normal" identity, attempted by organizations which are staffed by professional agents, such as mental hospitals and jails. Successful behavior change under the conditions described above, however, may require lifetime organizational membership to enable the stigmatized identity to be reinforced as a "positive" feature of normal behavior and a normal way of life.

2. Individuals may change their behavior and way of life from deviant to normal on some relevant dimension, but may retain a stigmatized identity connected with that same dimension.

The ideal test of the theory of secondary normalization, would, like a test of the theory of secondary deviation, involve a long-term evaluative follow-up study of organizational graduates, something which has never been fully accomplished with any organization.[8] Since the weight loss organization does not give permission for social or medical research, it was not possible to obtain information permitting us to evaluate the success which they claim for their program.

This stance is typical of behavior-changing organizations, which generally resist independent evaluation of their success and failure rates. Some behavior changing organizations keep their own statistics of success and failure; this weight loss organization claims not to keep systematic records of any kind, and only occasionally gives any indication of the success or failure of the members. For example, the lecturers sometimes quoted gross total weight losses for the class (or for the city), but these were often misleading since gross weight gain was not subtracted. In one class where this *was* done, the gross class weight loss for the month was over a hundred pounds, but the gross weight gain was nearly a hundred—leaving a total weight loss of a few pounds to be distributed among sixty or so members!

Failing the ideal test of Lemert's theory of secondary deviation (independently measured rates of success and failure when negative labels are used as a strategy for changing deviant behavior) this analysis suggests that the self-help organization studied here does not accept the view that escalation to deviant behavior always follows negative social labels. Furthermore, under certain conditions, such labeling can be used as a means to normalize deviant behavior. It is also clear that, in conflict with the traditional formulation of the theory of secondary deviation, stigmatization or normalization of identity can be viewed as

independent of and not coterminous with deviant or normal behavior and way of life.

In summary, negative social labeling, or stigmatization, may have fateful consequences for the individual, but these are not always in the expected direction. In an expanded study of many behavior change groups dealing with drug use and child abuse as well as obesity, we found that *groups who used ex's as change agents all used strategies of identity stigmatization in order to facilitate normalization of members' behavior* (Warren, 1974). Such data give further empirical thrust to the conclusion that normal or deviant identity, way of life and behavior are empirically separable phenomena, erroneously analyzed under the umbrella "secondary deviation."

REFERENCES

Allon, Natalie. "Group Dieting Rituals." *Society* 10 (January–February 1973): 36–42.

Becker, Howard S. *Outsiders*. Glencoe, Illinois: Free Press, 1963.

Berger, Peter I., and Thomas Luckmann. *The Social Construction of Reality*. New York: Doubleday, 1967.

Dwyer, Johanna T., Jacob J. Feldman, and Jean Mayer. "The Social Psychology of Dieting." *Journal of Health and Social Behavior* 11 (December 1970): 269–287.

Fisher, Sethard. "Stigma and Deviant Careers in Schools." *Social Problems* 20 (Summer 1972): 78–83.

Foster, Jack D., Simon Dinitz, and Walter C. Reckless. "Perceptions of Stigma Following Public Intervention for Deviant Behavior." *Social Problems* 20 (Fall 1972): 202–209.

Goffman, Erving. *Asylums*. New York: Doubleday, 1961.

———. *Stigma*. Englewood Cliffs, N.J.: Prentice-Hall, 1963.

Hurvitz, Nathan. "The Characteristics of Peer Self-help Psychotherapy Groups and Their Implications for the Theory and Practice of Psychiatry." Paper presented at the San Francisco convention of The American Psychological Association, 1968.

Lemert, Edwin. *Human Deviance, Social Problems and Social Control*. Englewood Cliffs, N.J.: Prentice-Hall, 1967.

---

[8] A few empirical (but not organizational-evaluative) studies of the effects of stigma do, however, exist. These studies illustrate that the process of stigmatization involves the exchange of meanings between participants and is not simply a matter of label-sticking and passive receiving. Furthermore, "mental labeling" or stereotyping is not the same thing as the behavior that is directed toward the person so labeled. (See for example, Fisher, 1972; Foster et al., 1972; Schwartz and Stryker, 1970.)

Metropolitan Life Insurance Co. "New Weight Standards for Men and Women." *Statistical Bulletin* 20 (November–December 1969).

Schur, Edwin. *Labeling Deviant Behavior: Its Sociological Implications.* New York: Harper and Row, 1971.

Schwartz, Michael, and Sheldon Stryker. *Deviance, Selves and Others.* Washington, D.C.: American Sociological Association, 1970.

Stuart, Richard B., and Barbara Davis. *Slim Chance in a Fat World.* Champaign, Illinois: Research Press Co., 1972.

Warren, Carol A. B. "The Use of Stigmatizing Labels in Conventionalizing Deviant Behavior." *Sociology and Social Research* 58 (April 1974): 303–311.

———. "Destigmatization: Acts, Identities, and Categories." Unpublished paper, 1975.

Darwin L. Thomas,
David D. Franks, &
James M. Calonico

14

Role-taking and Power in Social Psychology

THEORETICAL RATIONALE

Role-Taking. From a sociological orientation in social psychology, few concepts rival role-taking in theoretical importance. It is a truly interactive concept (Turner, 1962), and at the same time it plays a critical role in a sociological view of the development of self as well as in a theory of social control (Shibutani, 1961:194–201). The "biological" individual becomes a member of a social community when he becomes self-conscious about his own actions from society's stand-

Darwin L. Thomas, David D. Franks, and James M. Calonico, "Role-Taking and Power in Social Psychology," *American Sociological Review*, vol. 37, October 1972, pp. 605–614. Reprinted by permission.

An earlier version of this paper was presented at the Rocky Mountain Social Science Association Meetings, Salt Lake City, Utah, 1972. This research was supported in part by NSF Grant GS 2650. We wish to thank Viktor Gecas and Andrew J. Weigert for helpful suggestions on earlier versions of this paper and to Bernard Babbitt, Marlene Huntsinger and Lorrie Rippee for computer programming assistance.

point. This makes him distinctively human and roots his social nature in the interactive process. "The biologic individual must be able to call out in himself the response his gesture calls out in the other, and then utilize this imagined response of the other for the control of his own further conduct. The ability to call out the same response in both self and other gives the content necessary for community of meaning." (Mead, 1934, p. xxi)

Self is not a biological given but emerges in social interaction. The child develops a self (becomes self-conscious) only to the extent that he can see himself as others do (role-taking) and use this to monitor his behavior with others. One becomes an object to himself through being able to take others' perspectives. This depends on significant symbols or shared meanings (language) which actors use in a given reference group. Paradoxically, only through an inherently social process of role-taking can one develop a viable sense of individuality.

In view of the central nature of the theoretical construct of role-taking, (see Cotrell, 1950; Stryker, 1971) one would expect sociologists interested in individual conduct to continue to contribute at both the theoretical and hypothesis testing levels. Such is not the case. The theoretical potential of the concept has not been matched by attention at the operational and research level (Stone and Farberman, 1970; Kuhn, 1964). Stryker (1971) laments the absence of sociologically oriented theory and research in his recent review of the latest *Handbook of Social Psychology.* Both theoretically and empirically, the relationship between role-taking and power is a potentially fruitful area of investigation in social psychology.

Role-Taking and Power. Often in theoretical discussions of interpersonal behavior along the dimension of power, an important distinction in levels of analysis is overlooked. Sociologists are appropriately interested in clarifying the interactional nature of power relations (see Wrong, 1968:673; Emerson, 1962:31–32). They emphasize that subordinates can have "power" since they can and do constrain superiors. Thus Emerson describes one of four types of "balancing operations"[1] which:

> . . . increases the weaker member's power to control the formerly more powerful member through increasing the latter's motivational investment in the relation. This is normally accomplished through giving him status recognition in one . . . of its many forms, from ego-gratifications to monetary differential. The ego rewards . . . are highly valued . . . while given at a low cost to the giver. (p. 39)

This theoretical formulation is important, but the broad use of "power" tends to obscure the distinction between resources stemming from one's social *position* and those stemming from an individual's self-system. Resources accruing from the

self-system are potentially available to all persons depending on their individual competencies in interpersonal relations.[2]

Granted that both subordinates and superordinates have at their disposal potentials for controlling each other, *power* will refer to potentials given by one's structural position vis à vis the other; and the term *influence* will be used to refer to potential for control based on one's interpersonal skill, independent of his social position. Power and influence are fundamentally distinct modes of gaining control, the former utilizing a relatively enduring[3] structure and the latter the reservoir of interpersonal abilities.

For the social psychologist how are power and role-taking related? Following Goffman (1959), role-taking not only socializes the individual, but it is used to control others' responses by pleasing them on their own terms. A premium is placed on *accuracy* in role-taking when the subordinate utilizes controls based on interpersonal abilities. Such control is more particularized than the use of power. The subordinate must role-take accurately if he is not to destroy his potential control say, by misjudging the superordinate's response and becoming identified as an "ingratiator."

The general proposition is that persons in higher power positions do not need to and therefore do not use role-taking to the same degree as persons of lower power positions. This is not to say that controlling others through power does not involve role-taking. However, once a person

---

[1] See Secord and Backman (1964) for a summary of the main concepts concerning power relations used here. ". . . an unbalanced (power) relation is unstable since it encourages the use of power, which in turn sets into motion processes that Emerson, (1962) has called cost reduction and balancing operations." (Parentheses are ours.) The balancing operation of interest here is Emerson's *third* one.

[2] Secord and Backman (1964:293) emphasize this feature. "Various interpersonal strategies are employed to shift the balance of power either in fact or perceptually. People may disguise their dependency, pretend to have many desirable alternatives, increase the investment of the other by raising his status, or invoke norms that restrict the other person's alternatives." They go on to discuss interpersonal attraction as a source of "power," while we would prefer the term influence.

[3] The emphasis on enduring sources of control is often isolated as an important feature of potential power in a structural framework. Since behavior on the interactional level is situated and episodic, power, to be enduring, must be seen as having the quality of potential. Structural power in our terminology has this enduring quality because it is transsituational. For a discussion of this see Dennis Wrong, 1968. Our use of the term power is similar to Emerson (1962) and Wolfe's (1959) "authority" concept, which has connotations similar to "legitimate power" as used by Smith (1970) and others.

in power has correctly identified a resource desired by the other, it is more important for the subordinate to act according to the desires and orientations of the power holder than vice versa. Rose (1969) has enunciated a similar idea using the term empathy instead of role-taking:

It may be that persons who are members of minority groups are forced, because of their underprivileged positions, to develop an empathetic ability as a condition of their adjustment to the subtle expression of dominance by members of superordinate groups. Thus, Negroes in minority situations have been characterized as having a more accurate perception of white mentality than whites have of Negro mentality. . . . One of the privileges of power, perhaps an often overlooked one, is the privilege of insensitivity to the negative attitudes of others. (p. 476)

Rose also generalizes the basic idea by proposing that women should be more accurate role-takers than men. Subordinate status in a situated role-set should be characterized by role-taking accuracy among members of different social categories.

Hypotheses. One could deduce from this that children would tend to be more accurate in intrafamilial role-taking than their parents. Furthermore, in families in male dominant societies, the females should be more accurate in their role-taking ability than the males. By combining the two propositions, one can deduce the following hypothesis: *Accuracy in role-taking will exhibit the following pattern among family members: father < mother < male child < female child.*

Note that the hypothesis that children will be better role-takers than their parents is not a common-sense notion. One could maintain that their greater fund of knowledge and experience about theirs and their children's lives would make parents better role-takers. Indeed, parents are often forced to anticipate their child's behavior to protect against possible danger or produce a desired outcome.

A second hypothesis can be generated from this basic link between role-taking and power which will allow for an investigation of the effect of personal power style on role-taking. Individuals in a particular social position will vary on the degree of power they exercise and hence on the degree to which others in that social group perceive them as powerful. If personal power style is related to role-taking as structural power is in the above theoretical rationale, then *children who perceive their fathers and mothers as highly powerful individuals should be better role-takers than children who perceive their fathers and mothers as low power individuals.* By the same reasoning *husbands and wives who exercise a high degree of power in the conjugal relationship should be less accurate role-takers than those with low conjugal power.*

METHODOLOGY

Sample. In order to test the hypothesized relationships, data were gathered from both parents and children in intact nuclear families. A "face-sheet" requesting necessary information about the respondent and his family was administered to around a thousand undergraduate students at a large western state university. From these responses a sample of the student population was drawn which represented the student body on the following characteristics: sex, year in school, major field of study and grade point average. Further requirements for inclusion in the study were intact families composed of mother, father, high school aged child and college aged child. A random sample of three hundred qualifying families was drawn from the families meeting the necessary criteria.

During the summer a packet of materials was sent to each family chosen. Each packet contained four questionnaires, one for each family member, along with a cover letter and instructions to assist respondents in completing and returning questionnaires. Separate return envelopes were included for each respondent to allow as much privacy as possible. Four mailed follow-ups were sent to families at approximately ten-day intervals, the first being sent ten days after the family received the original packet. At the beginning of data analysis, questionnaires had been returned by 82.8% (994) of the sample's 1,200 family members (four members in each of three hundred families).

Comparisons were made with the non-respondents using information gathered on the initial "face-sheet," and those families not returning their questionnaires were found not to differ significantly on SES level, family size, religious affiliation, and parents' education level.

Since the current analysis required the use of both parents and children's responses, we decided to use only the scores of "completed" families, i.e., scores from all four family members. For the present analysis, 222 completed families were available necessitating the use of only the role-taking scale. This represents 74% of the three hundred families in the original sample. Where analysis required using both the role-taking and power (as measured by the semantic differential) scales, 70.7% (212) of the completed families were available. This difference occurs because some persons completed only one of the two scales, invalidating the use of that family for the particular analysis.

Finally, a measure of conjugal power was obtained in the second phase of data collection, a telephone follow-up six months after the beginning of the first phase. A number of families could not be contacted during this follow-up; thus, for the analysis requiring both role-taking and conjugal power scores, 56.3% (169) of the completed families could be included.

Role-Taking Measure. This scale was developed specifically for the current work. Judgment tests usually employ either a "trait-rating" procedure (Bronfenbrenner, Harding and Gallwey, 1958; Fiedler, 1954; Fiedler, Blaisdell and Warrington, 1952) or a direct prediction of another's response to attitude items (Byrne and Blaylock, 1963). The present effort differs from these and most other types of "judging instruments" (see Cline, 1964:224) in its attempt to approximate role-taking more closely. It is a modification of the dilemma resolution technique previously used in parent-child research (see Thomas and Weigert, 1971). The role-taking measure is most easily understood by considering the following item from the scale.

A young man about to graduate from college is opposed to military service but is sure he will be drafted shortly after he graduates. He is trying to decide whether to allow himself to be drafted and serve in the armed forces or to unlawfully resist the draft, thereby risking the chance of arrest and imprisonment.

a. I would advise this young man to allow himself to be drafted and serve in the armed forces.
   1. no
   2. probably no
   3. probably yes
   4. yes
b. In my opinion, my father (older child) would advise this young man to allow himself to be drafted and serve in the armed forces.
   4. yes
   3. probably yes
   2. probably no
   1. no
c. In my opinion my mother (younger child) would advise this young man to allow himself to be drafted and serve in the armed forces.
   1. no
   2. probably no
   3. probably yes
   4. yes

Each of the ten items presents a hypothetical situation in which an abstract other, i.e., neither actor nor the specific person whose role he is taking, is placed in a behavioral dilemma. The abstract other is shown as perceiving two possible responses to his dilemma. The actor must indicate how he would advise the abstract other to respond. He must then indicate how each of two significant others, persons whose roles he is taking, would advise the abstract other to respond. Parents were asked to take the role of each of the two participating children and each child was asked to take the role of each parent. The names of specific family members were written into the questions so that the person would know whose role he was taking.

A role-taking accuracy or difference score is computed for each respondent by comparing the other's actual response with the actor's prediction of that response. Thus the range of absolute difference between any two subjects on any item is

TABLE 14.1. Principal axis factor analysis of role-taking scale

Item	Factor Loading
1. Military Draft[1]	.59*
2. Homosexual as Security Risk	.55*
3. Communist Teacher	.52*
4. Search Warrant	.34*
5. Marriage at College-Age	.32*
6. Spanking of Children	.28
7. Employee Theft	.18
8. Atheism of College Student	.11
9. Prisoner as Parole Risk	.08
10. Police Shooting of Burglar	.06

* Those items used in the role-taking score (see Footnote 5).
[1] For exact wording of the items used in this scale, write the authors.

from zero to three. *Higher scores* denote greater role-taking *inaccuracy.*

These absolute scores were factor analyzed Table 14.1 presents the factor loadings obtained by means of principal axis factor analysis.[4] From these results, role-taking scores[5] were created by including those items with a factor loading $\geq$ .30.

[4] Since our primary concern was to identify a major underlying role-taking factor from the difference scores on each of the ten items, we used the principal axis factor analysis. Three factors were produced in this analysis with the values in Table 14–1 coming from the first. The second and third accounted for less total variance in the role-taking scale than did factor one, and some items (marriage, parole, search warrant) loaded on more than one factor. In an attempt to analyze for other possible factor structures, the verimax factor rotation solution was used to identify orthogonal factors. The first orthogonal factor consisted of three items: draft, homosexual, communist. These three items had the strongest loadings on the first factor from the principal axis factor analysis. The second and third orthogonal factors were a mixture of the remaining seven items. Thus the results of the orthogonal factor analysis seemed to support the decision to use the principal axis factor analysis in constructing the role-taking scores.

[5] Scale scores are created by first standardizing each variable (item) to have a mean of zero. Then, for any subject, the value of each variable in his original score which is to be included in his scale score is multiplied by its corresponding factor loading. The products are then summed to constitute his scale score. This weights each item in the score by the size of its factor loading. In addition, the mean of the factor analysis scale scores is set to zero; thus, for the present work, the more *positive* an individual's scale score the more inaccurate is his role-taking; and the more *negative* his scale score the more accurate is his role-taking.

Power Measures. In the test of the first hypothesis, the individual's position in the family was taken as an index of his power in the family. The position rank on the power dimension is father $>$ mother $>$ male child $>$ female child.

In the test of the second hypothesis, two power measures were used. In the first, each family member rated himself and each other member on ten adjective pairs. Through factor analysis of the semantic differential, two adjective pairs, stern-mild and powerful-powerless, emerged for constructing a power measure.[6] Fathers and mothers were divided at the median into high and low power groups according to the children's perception. For the present work, role-taking scores of children who perceived their mothers and fathers as high on power were compared with children who perceived their parents as low on power.

A second power measure (conjugal power) was constructed by using the responses to four questions asked of the wife in four areas of decision making: when you and your husband disagree over (money, religion, furnishing the house, and disciplining the children) who has the final say? 1. mother always, 2. mother more than father, 3. mother and father about equal, 4. father more than mother, 5. father always. A second scoring scheme (DS scale or degree of Shared Authority Index) was developed where the 1 and 5 response categories received a one, the 2 and 4 response categories received a two; and the 3 response category received a three; these two indices of power were combined (RS-Relative Power Index) to produce the four conjugal power types developed by Wolfe (1959): namely, mother dominant, father dominant, syncratic and autonomic.[7] These four types are pictured graphi-

[6] Factor analysis of the ten adjective pairs produced a potency factor (using three factor verimax solution) consisting of these two items having the highest loadings, .81 for stern-mild and .51 for powerful-powerless.

[7] Since four items were used in the present study, different cut off points from either the Detroit Study (Blood and Wolfe, 1960) or the Los Angeles Study (Centers *et al.*, 1971) were used. In this research (see Figure 14.1) Mother Dominance was defined as the bottom 25% on the relative authority scale (RA) and Father Dominance was the top 25% on the RA Scale. Syncratic was defined as anyone scoring in the middle 50% on the RA Scale and the top 50% on the DS Scale. Autonomic was anyone falling in the middle 50% on the RA Scale and the bottom 50% on the DS Scale.

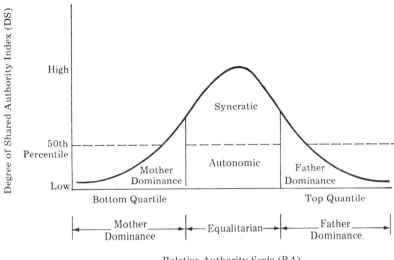

FIGURE 14.1. *Construction of Conjugal Power Types*

cally in Figure 14.1. The father is hypothesized as being most powerful in the father dominant type and least powerful in the mother dominant. The mother is seen as most powerful in the mother dominant and least powerful in the father dominant families. The autonomic and syncratic types are conceptualized as middle power types for both the father and mother, since they both tend to make decisions in different areas (autonomic) or share in joint decision making (syncratic). As indicated previously, 169 families were available for this phase of the analysis.

FINDINGS

The first hypothesis (on the basis of power differences) predicts the following order on role-taking across family positions: father < mother < male child < female child. Table 14.2 presents the mean role-taking scores and significance levels for t-tests between adjacent positions on the power continuum. The pattern of the data supports the hypothesized relationship. Fathers are significantly less accurate role-takers than mothers (p < .001) and mothers significantly less accurate than male children (p < .001; section A, Ta-

ble 14.2). The difference between the mean role-taking scores of male and female children is in the predicted direction, but it is not statistically significant.

The literature on the sociology of the family contains the idea that order of birth is important in ascribing positions of power to children (see Thomas and Calonico, 1972; Reiss, 1967:154). Older children in families are seen as occupying positions of both power and responsibility compared to younger children. If this reasoning is correct, younger children should be better role-takers than older children. To further test the proposition relating role-taking to power, the effect of birth order on sibling role-taking was investigated. Table 14.2, section B, presents these results. The pattern between the means indicates that younger children are better role-takers than older children, but again the difference is not statistically significant. At this juncture we reasoned that if both order of birth (older and younger) and sex were combined, the oldest male child might be significantly less accurate in role-taking than the youngest female child. Section C in Table 14.2 presents the mean scores. It can be seen that the absolute difference in means is increased when the effects of order of birth and sex are

TABLE 14.2. Mean role-taking scores and significance levels for t-test by position in the family

			Position in the Family			
				A		
		Fathers		*Mothers*	*Male Children*	*Female Children*
Mean Role-Taking Scores[1]		.682	***	.168 ***	−.408	−.442
N		222		222	221	223
				B		
		Fathers		*Mothers*	*Older[2] Children*	*Younger[3] Children*
Mean Role-Taking Scores		.682	***	.168 ***	−.371	−.478
N		222		222	222	222

				C			
				Older Male Children	*Older Female Children*	*Younger Male Children*	*Younger Female Children*
	Fathers		*Mothers*				
Mean Role-Taking Scores	.682 ***		.168 ***	−.325	−.407	−.473	−.486
N	222		222	97	125	124	98

*** = $p < .001$ for one tailed t-test computed between adjacent means.
[1] When factor analysis scale scores are created, the distribution of the scores is reconstituted to set the mean of the distribution at zero. For the analysis here, the more negative a score is, the more accurate the role-taking and the more positive a score is, the less accurate the role-taking.
[2] These children are college age: mostly Freshmen and Sophomore with a mean age of 19.5.
[3] These children are high school age: with a mean age of 15.9.

combined, but none of the differences between adjacent means is statistically significant. When a separate t-test was calculated between the mean score of older male children with that of younger female children, the difference was not statistically significant.

The second hypothesis predicts that children in families with high power fathers and mothers will be significantly better role-takers than children in families of low power fathers and mothers. Table 14.3 presents the mean role-taking scores for high and low power fathers and mothers as perceived by their children. The relationships among the mean role-taking scores for the female children are as predicted. None of the differences in means is statistically significant, but the difference in mean role-taking scores for female children in low and high power mother homes approaches the .05 level of significance. The difference in means for male children is small, and

TABLE 14.3. Children's mean role-taking scores by parental power and sex

	Level of Perceived Parental Power			
	Father's Power		*Mother's Power*	
	Low	*High*	*Low*	*High*
Female Children	−.278	−.344	−.008	−.246
N =	113	95	117	91
Male Children	−.163	−.115	−.314	−.238
N =	109	107	111	105

The difference in means of female children in high and low power mother groups is the only comparison which approaches significance at the .05 level ($t = 1.52$).

TABLE 14.4. Parents' mean role-taking scores by conjugal power type

	Husband Dominant	Conjugal Power Syncratic	Autonomic		Wife Dominant
N	(40)	(76)	(18)		(35)
Fathers' Mean Score[1]	.660	.469	1.132		.704
Mothers' Mean Score	.295	−.013	−.507	**	.414

[1] None of the differences between any of the adjacent means are statistically significant.

** = p < .025 for one tailed t-test computed between adjacent means.

their role-taking scores of father and mother are in the opposite predicted direction.

The test of the second hypothesis using conjugal power scores as a measure of the husband's and wife's relative power in the conjugal relationship is presented in Table 14.4. The hypothesized relationship that fathers (husbands) with low power (wife dominant conjugal relations) will be more accurate than fathers with high power (father dominant conjugal relations) is not supported. Fathers with low relative power in the conjugal relationship are not the most accurate role-takers. Neither are fathers with high power in the conjugal relationship the least accurate. None of the differences between the means is statistically significant.

It will be noted from Table 14.4 that the hypothesized relationship that mothers (wives) high on power would be the least accurate role-takers is supported. However, the most accurate role-takers are mothers (wives) who come from autonomic conjugal power structures. The difference in means between wife dominant and autonomic groups is statistically significant at the .025 level.

DISCUSSION AND CONCLUSIONS

The major findings of this research, that fathers are significantly less accurate role-takers than mothers and mothers significantly less accurate role-takers than their children, support the theory guiding this research.[8] The data trends for

children, that positions having the least power in the family (younger female children) are more accurate role-takers than positions having more power (older male children) also support the theoretical proposition that role-taking ability varies inversely with the degree of power ascribed to social positions. This basic theoretical proposition should now be tested on other social groups to determine the generalizability of the findings.

The family as a social group differs on important dimensions from other social groups, and it is possible that findings reported here apply only to variations in role-taking ability among different family members. The family is a social group having a history important in the functioning of its members. It is also characterized by strong emotional bonds between and within generations. Therefore, attempts to generalize these findings to other social groups are risky. Despite these differences between the family and other social groups we believe the findings are not group specific.

This judgment derives from previous analyses of the data along with possible interpretations of it presented in this report. The emotional dimension characteristic of the family was not found to be an important predictor of role-taking ability (see Calonico and Thomas, 1972).

[8] However, one should not claim too much for power as indexed by position in the family in this research. Given the relatively large N's used here, one should not overestimate the importance

of the statistical significance. Computing Omega Squared [Ω^2] (see Hayes, 1965:327) as a measure of association based on the t value between mean role-taking scores of fathers and younger female children, yields a value of .085. Thus knowing that a person is a father or a female child will allow one to account for about nine percent of the variance in role-taking scores. Clearly much work remains for the researcher interested in accounting for variance in role-taking ability.

Variation in the amount of emotional support children received from parents was only related to role-taking when parents and children did not share similar value orientations. Such children from families with high parent-child affect were not accurate role-takers. The explanation offered for this finding was that with high emotional support from parents, children could not accurately take the role of parents because they assumed parents were like themselves, when in fact parents and children did not share similar values. That finding combined with the data in this research suggests that persons in low power positions who share similar values with persons of high power, and who have a high positive emotional bond with people in power will be accurate role-takers. However, if persons in low power positions do not share similar value positions with persons in high power positions, but have high positive emotional bonds with them, they will be inaccurate role-takers. This relationship is posited to hold for any group which has interacted long enough for bonds of emotional support to have developed.

The major findings in this research cannot be explained by differences between the generations. True, the data show that children are better role-takers than parents but mothers are significantly better than fathers a fact which argues against differences in generations being the cause of the findings. Also, mothers in wife dominant families are less accurate in role-taking abilities than mothers in autonomic families. Differences between generations would not help explain this finding; thus, the power explanation becomes more credible.

The finding for wives that the autonomic conjugal power structure rather than the husband dominant produces the most accurate role-taker requires some comment. The theoretical underpinnings may require modification. Further research is needed to untangle methodological problems associated with different power measures from theoretical inadequacies. The conjugal power measure asks about decision making in the husband-wife dyad, while the role-taking measure is between the parent's and children's generations. It is not clear why this power measure is related to the wife's but not the husband's ability

to accurately take the role of their children. Research concentrating on exercise of power and role-taking across and within family generations could contribute important knowledge about the functioning of families as well as other groups.

Our theoretical orientation leads us to assume that rather than individual characteristics the superordinate-subordinate characteristic of social structure should predict differences in role-taking ability. This interpretation receives some support in the data. The nuclear family positions arrayed on a power continuum produce significant differences in role-taking, while the group members' perceptions along the powerful-powerless dimension are not consistently related to role-taking. The trend in the data seems to suggest that perception of others' power characteristics may be important for women's role-taking ability but not for men's (note that it is the wife's perception in the conjugal power dimension and the female child's perception of parents' power that seem related to role-taking.) This fact suggests that in American society women may become more adept at perceiving their own as well as others' power characteristics in order to role-take more accurately. Thus the autonomic wife must role-take accurately to make and carry out decisions in her areas of power. Her position as wife does not automatically carry this power with it. The power must be won. Accurate role-taking is one way of winning it. Further research could clarify these and other relationships.

An important aspect of this research is the type of investigations that it points toward. It calls for research to isolate the personal dimension from the structural. If our theorizing is accurate, any individual should be a more accurate role-taker of people in superordinate rather than subordinate positions in the group. Academic institutions, hospitals or any other hierarchically organized structure would provide ample tests for a number of propositions. Would department chairmen be better role-takers of deans than vice versa? Would deans better take the role of vice presidents than of their department chairmen? If an individual tends to develop these different abilities to take the other's role on the basis of power differences emerging in specific role sets, then one should probably not emphasize personality traits or characteristics but rather systemic qualities of the social structure. Such research could begin to identify the contributions of the individual and social structure in the basic social psychological role-taking process.

REFERENCES

Blood, R. O. and D. M. Wolfe. *Husbands and Wives: The Dynamics of Married Living.* Glencoe, Illinois: The Free Press, 1960.

Bronfenbrenner, U., J. Harding and M. Gallwey. "The Measurement of Skill in Social Perception." *Talent and Society.* Edited by D. C. McClelland *et al.* New York: Van Nostrand, 1958, pp. 20–111.

Byrne, D. and B. Blaylock. "Similarity and Assumed Similarity of Attitudes Between Husbands and Wives." *Journal of Abnormal and Social Psychology* 67 (1963):636–40.

Calonico, James M. and Darwin L. Thomas. "Role Taking as a Function of Value Similarity and Affect in the Nuclear Family." Unpublished. Washington State University, 1972.

Centers, Richard, Bertram H. Raven and Aroldo Rodrigues. "Conjugal Power Structure: A Re-examination." *American Sociological Review* 36 (April 1971):264–78.

Cline, V. B. "Interpersonal Perception." *Progress in Experimental Research.* Edited by Brendan A. Maker. New York: Academic Press, 1964, pp. 221–284.

Cottrell, Leonard S. "Some Neglected Problems in Social Psychology." *American Sociological Review* 6 (December 1950):705–12.

Emerson, Richard M. "Power-dependence Relations." *American Sociological Review* 27 (February 1962):31–41.

Fiedler, F. E. "Assumed Similarity Measures as Predictors of Team Effectiveness." *Journal of Abnormal and Social Psychology* 49 (1954):381–88.

Fiedler, F. E., E. L. Blaisdell and W. G. Warrington. "Unconscious Attitudes as Correlates of Sociometric Choice in a Social Group." *Journal of Abnormal and Social Psychology* 47 (1952):790–96.

Goffman, Erving. *The Presentation of Self in Everyday Life.* Garden City, New York: Doubleday Anchor, 1959.

Hays, William L. *Statistics for Psychologists.* New York: Holt, Rinehart and Winston, 1963.

Kuhn, Manford H. "Major Trends in Symbolic Interaction Theory in the Past Twenty-five Years." *Sociological Quarterly* 5 (Winter 1964):61–84.

Mead, George H. *Mind, Self and Society.* Edited with introduction by Charles W. Morris. Chicago: University of Chicago Press, 1934.

Reiss, Ira. *The Social Context of Premarital Sexual Permissiveness.* New York: Holt, Rinehart and Winston, 1967.

Rose, Jerry D. "The Role of the Other in Self-evaluation." *The Sociological Quarterly* 10 (Fall 1969): 470–79.

Secord, Paul F. and Carl W. Backman. *Social Psychology.* New York: McGraw-Hill, 1964.

Shibutani, Tamotsu. *Society and Personality.* Englewood Cliffs, New Jersey, Prentice-Hall, 1961.

Smith, Thomas Ewin. "Foundations of Parental Influence Upon Adolescents: An Application of Social Power Theory." *American Sociological Review* 35 (October 1970):860–73.

Stone, Gregory P. and Harvey A. Farberman. *Social Psychology Through Symbolic Interaction.* Waltham, Massachusetts: Ginn Blaisdell, 1970.

Stryker, Sheldon. "Review of the Handbook of Social Psychology." *The American Sociological Review* 36 (October 1971):894–98.

Thomas, Darwin L. and James M. Calonico. "Birth Order and Family Sociology: A Reassessment." *Social Science* 47 (Winter 1972):48–50.

Thomas, Darwin L. and Andrew J. Weigert. "Socialization and Adolescent Conformity to Significant Others: A Cross-national Analysis." *American Sociological Review* 36 (October 1971):835–47.

Turner, Ralph H. "Role-taking: Process Versus Conformity." *Human Behavior and Social Processes.* Edited by A. M. Rose. Boston: Houghton Mifflin, 1962, pp. 20–40.

Wolfe, D. M. "Power and Authority in the Family." *Studies in Social Power.* Edited by Dorwin Cartwright. Ann Arbor, Michigan: Institute for Social Research, 1959, pp. 99–117.

Wrong, Dennis H. "Some Problems in Defining Social Power." *American Journal of Sociology* 73 (May 1968):673–81.

Eugene A. Weinstein &
Judith M. Tanur

15

Meanings, Purposes, and Structural Resources in Social Interaction

Three orientations compete for dominance among sociologists concerned with accounting for social interaction. The first, symbolic interactionism, argues for the primacy of such subjective determinants as the perceptions of the situation and of one another that interactants form. The second, exchange theory, focuses on the interests of those engaged in interaction, and assigns primacy to the interplay of those interests. The third, structural-functionalism, emphasizes maintenance requirements for aggregate social entities. It sees the ways individuals are implicated in networks meeting those requirements as the primary determinant of interactive behavior. Various spokesmen for each position ignore criticisms made by others or respond with much rancor, usually writing past one another. By lining up concepts side by side and applying some tinkering, it seems possible to generate a scheme for the analysis of interaction that does violence to none of the essential tenets of these approaches and yet preserves their special strengths. This pa-

Eugene A. Weinstein and Judith M. Tanur, "Meanings, Purposes, and Structural Resources in Social Interaction." Reprinted from *The Cornell Journal of Social Relations*, volume 11, no. 1 (Spring 1976), pp. 105–110.

Note to the reader: We wish to thank the National Institute of Mental Health for their generous support of this work (Grant MH16952). We also wish to thank Philip Blumstein, Aaron Cicourel, Steven Cole, O. Andrew Collver, Rose Coser, Forest Dill, Kenneth Feldman, Norman Goodman, Hanan Selvin, Jerome Singer, Sheldon Stryker, Gerald Suttles, John Weiler and Sasha Weitman, as well as other colleagues and students for their helpful comments on an earlier version of this paper. Its flaws remain our responsibility, of course.

per is devoted to that task. It points to a direction that we believe social psychology must take if it is to inform sociology and itself.

Historically, some of the debates between orientations developed from a change in focus in sociology from process to structure. In turn-of-the-century sociology it was fashionable to argue that society *is* social process—that social interaction is the locus of social order. This concern with social process developed in two directions. One movement emphasized the forms of social interaction, independent of their content (association, dissociation, accommodation, etc.). In so doing, this school marched bravely into a taxonomic blind alley. (Simmel is a clear exception to the sterility of Formalism in sociology. However, his most fruitful insights came from his sensitive observations of the substance of social interaction rather than a classification of its forms.) Little is heard from them save for lists of definitions to be memorized by students in introductory sociology courses. The second movement was more directly concerned with the substance or content of interaction. Stemming from an amalgam of German phenomenology and American pragmatism, this movement was concerned with substance as it was experienced by those involved in the interaction process. The principal inheritors of this orientation in contemporary sociology are the symbolic interactionists, who remain persistent evangelists for the point of view that societies are unending streams of interaction process (see Blumer, 1962:179–192).

We have no quarrel with the symbolic interactionist's emphasis on process. Indeed, we share it. The real strength of symbolic interaction is in its sensitivity to the *emergent* properties of interaction. The episode of interaction (Goffman's "encounter") becomes a temporary word in itself for the participants. And, of course, it is in such worlds that social structure finds its concrete expression.

However, in an overemphasis on these strengths, at least one wing of symbolic interactionism (The Neo-Blumerians) commit two excesses that are not inherent in all versions (or practice) of the perspective. Symbolic interaction sees social processes as the interplay of minded individuals, both conscious and self-conscious. Its concepts are fully rooted in the interaction itself, and linked to the contents of the participants' consciousness, as in, for example, such constructs as the definition of the situation, role-taking, and awareness contexts. This emphasis on consciousness by the symbolic interactionists is the source of the first excess they commit. Just because the contents of consciousness are qualitative, does not mean that their exterior expression cannot be coded, classified, even counted, much as the individual himself codes, classifies, and counts in dealing with the qualitative richness of his own experience. No one, not even the most micro-oriented ethnomethodologist, can attend to all of the potential information that is simultaneously available to him; categoric systems for collapsing and coding information is what makes minds possible in the first place, and informal counting of occurrences accumulate to what we call experience. In any research endeavor there is a possible trade-off between a qualitative but vague richness, dependent upon the perceptive skills of the individual analyst, and a more precise and more replicable, but more narrow, identification of patterns.

Thus orthodox symbolic interactionists beg the question of this trade-off by making the injunction against quantitative analysis an article of faith rather than a matter of style. (There are notable exceptions to this methodological stance. The research careers of S. Stryker and C. N. Alexander provide exemplary instances.) In practice, this has led to a proliferation of sensitizing concepts for describing the contents of people's consciousness. Of particular concern are people's images of and orientation toward the social scenes in which they are involved. At its best, this work results in sensitive and compelling understanding of the perspectives of the participants; at its worst, it wanders precariously close to the taxonomic trap of Formalism, obscuring the essential distinction between definition and explanation.

The sensitizing orientation of symbolic interaction can lead to work that is prospective, quantitative, and oriented to explanation rather than only retrospective, qualitative, and oriented toward understanding. This can be accomplished by using the insights gained by taking a phenomonological stance and casting them, self-consciously and explicitly, into a framework of measurement rather than description. This recasting, while retaining the phenomonologists' sensitivity to the dependence of meaning on context, allows for two potential gains. First, it makes it possible to assess the degree of consensus in intersubjectivity (that is, estimate reliability). Thus, reliance on the perceptions of a single analyst is reduced. Second, the results of phenomonologically premised investigation can be incorporated into quantitative modes of analysis.

Symbolic interaction has used informal content analysis for the generation of qualitatively differentiated types. Formal coding procedures are not used to establish the types. Rather a documentary method uses instances-in-context as indexical particulars signifying the essential connotative meaning. The same documentary approach can be used to make comparative *ratings* of how much of a particular quality is represented by an observation of content-in-context rather than the more basic decision as to whether the content falls within the type. However, ethnomethodologists, among others, point out serious problems in any content analytic procedure, whether qualitative or quantitative (cf. Aaron Cicourel, 1964, *Method and Measurement in Sociology*, New York: The Free Press). Ethnomethodologists are rightfully upset about the assumed isomorphism between the communicative intent of the actor and the perception of it by the coder. This assumption rests in turn upon the further assumption of a common communicative culture between actor and analyst. Sensitivity to context-dependence of meaning does not obviate the problem. In some respects, the problem is insoluble. As we note later, there are always unlocatable limits to the extent of intersubjectivity. Perhaps it is most reasonable to view a communicative act as a resource available for sense-making in the elaboration of meaning by a "normal member." Thus the analyst does not take the role of the source of communication but of the category of persons to whom the communication is directed. Or the analyst can participate directly in the process under investigation in which case he "takes his own role" as the source of information about communication directed toward himself. This orientation is more interactive in nature and shifts the focus from intent to potential effect. It does not, however, eliminate two difficulties which can plague any research operation in which meanings are the object of study. First, there is the danger that the analyst's theoretical scheme will interfere with his capacity to take the role of the "normal member." Second, the assumption that communication is being addressed to a "normal member" is not always tenable in established relationships which may have generated their own communicative culture.

Not that quantification is to be regarded as an end in itself. It is merely a means of making available techniques which add power and sensitivity to individual judgment when one attempts to detect and describe *patterning* in a set of observations. Through using the most powerful tools available, some purchase can be obtained on the complex interplay among the conditions characterizing a social scene, the participants' attribution of meanings to the scene, and their actions toward one another. Why throw away anything helpful? And, equally to the point, why insist that only understanding is possible without exploring the potentials for explanation available in one's own framework?

By concentrating its analysis almost exclusively on events interior to an episode of interaction and to the people within it, symbolic interaction almost completely neglects the connectedness of episodes to each other. But episodes *are* connected. The very fact that a particular episode occurs, the identities of the particular participants who populate it, the context within which it occurs including the resources, both material and cultural, available to the participants are not matters of happenstance. These matters are the results of the aggregated outcomes of many prior episodes of interaction.

It is the aggregated outcomes that form the linkages among episodes of interaction that are the concern of sociology qua sociology. Social order is dependent not only on the prevention of universal aggression, but on the existence of some measure of coordination. And the maintenance of effective coordination in even the simplest of social institutions requires a base of informal understandings, codified rules, shared meanings, and material resources that is enormous both in magnitude and complexity. As an example, consider the specialized sort of interaction that takes place within the institution called collective bargaining. Any bargaining session clearly must begin with and make use of the outcomes of previous sessions between the particular participants. There is an emergent culture generated out of these prior episodes that is specific to this set of relationships and that evolves during this particular session. But the participants must also work within a shared framework that takes into account prior interactions between others, which have left such residues or resources as labor laws, previous contracts, the possibility of arbitration, a common language (both general and specialized), the ethic of good faith, the solvency of management (or its lack) that sets broad limits on the terms of settlement, the reality of strike threats, expectation for currently accepted contract terms, and the very notion of a contract. The list stretches on to include the total content of both the culture of the relationship between these parties and the larger culture within which that mini-culture is situated.

Of course, any collective bargaining session—or to return to our main argument, any episode of interaction—can be described on the basis of its unique parameters. It is undeniably true that there is only one time in the history of the universe when these particular participants met in this precise setting, in these very special frames of mind, to discuss these very aspects of these specific issues. But it is probably an impossible task, and certainly an unproductive one, to perform all the tracebacks necessary to explain a current episode of interaction in terms of its unique links with other concrete episodes.

Economy of description and the possibility of generalization exist only when abstraction of the properties of a particular episode and their aggregation with properties of other such episodes has taken place. To thus examine the aggregate properties of episodes of interaction and to see them as analytically representable as a social system is a legitimate enterprise. It is possible, without Durkheimian reification, to see these aggregate properties as contributing to the resources available to participants in any concrete episode. Further, it is possible to do so without denying that it is indeed within the episode that resources become manifest, mediated through the consciousness of the participants. Neither is it necessary to insist on the reduction of social structure to individual consciousness. The concept of social structure is necessary to deal with the incredible density and complexity of relations through which episodes of interaction are interconnected. So we are perfectly comfortable with Merton's statement that "Determinants of social life . . . are not necessarily evident to those engaged in it" (1972:41).

Structural-functional orientations towards interaction, on the other hand, start from this aggregate level. They assume a set of coordinating functions linking together elements of a structure into an integrated, coordinated network. People located at given positions in the structure then carry the structural imperatives as at least partial recipes for their activities in ongoing interaction. The strength of structural-functional theories is in their emphasis on the mode of coordination, that is on the consequences of aggregation, and on using system maintenance requirements as simplifying assumptions for accounting for the nature of interaction process itself.

Within this framework, the concepts linking structure and process are status and role. People are attached to structure in everyday interaction through normatively scripted roles. These normative scripts (role expectations) are part of the necessary equipment individuals possess for partici-

pation in the social process, equipment acquired by individuals during socialization, a process which is itself normatively scripted. These role expectations are internalized by individuals, they operate as self-regulatory mechanisms, and they become manifest in interaction with other individuals possessing complementary equipment.

The burden that must be carried by the concept of role in structural-functional accounts of interaction is clearly too heavy. It is possible, however, to modify the position-role treatment of the individual to include both contextual and processual components. The concept of *situational identity* serves this purpose. A person's situational identity is the locus of all attributes and characteristics imputed to him by those present in a particular encounter. Any social position one occupies is a candidate for inclusion in a situational identity. But so are dispositional tendencies, elements of biography including prior actions in the present encounter, and any characteristics we possess. Situational identities serve as bases both for expectations and actions. Some social position may be predominant in organizing the elements of a situational identity as in typical status activation. Even so, status elements may only set broad boundaries for behavior; these boundaries may be sufficiently broad that they are of limited importance in determining which behavior will take place toward what end.

Cicourel (1972) goes further along these lines by asserting that the structural-functional treatment of interaction is analytically incomplete; it fails to specify the details of *how*, in process, roles become manifest. How do people signal to one another the roles they will carry out and the complementary roles that others ought to carry out? How do they achieve consensus as to which roles are relevant and what matters are outside the domain of relevance in any particular episode of interaction? How, if indeed it is the case, is the sharedness of role definitions recognized and built upon? Cicourel notes that by asserting that roles structure social situations, one automatically imposes, rather than investigates, the fit between structural imagery and manifest social process.

In empirical investigations, this imagery is translated into a set of coding operations that tend to exclude the problematic aspects of interaction, or even worse, to treat them as merely unilluminating examples of a limited range of permitted variation in role activity. Thus the fit between data and theory becomes tautological. Instead, the "roledness" of a social encounter should be, itself, taken as problematic and worthy of investigation. Norms and roles then become part but not the totality, of the pool of meanings accessible to "normal members," to be used as resources in the mundane process of getting through the day. The extent, the conditions and the means by which such structural resources are brought into play, are thus investigated within a context of discovery rather than serving as the analyst's arbitrarily imposed metaphor.

Social locations bear still another burden in structural-functional analysis. At the aggregate level, interests pattern according to structural location. But how interests operate at the level of ongoing process is less clearly developed. Numerous conceptual treatments of role omit any direct inclusion of purposes as part of the core meaning of the concept. At best one might be able to squeeze purposive connotations out of such terms as "rights" and "obligations." But one would have to squeeze very hard and, in practice, the enterprise is rarely undertaken. Instead, roles are defined almost exclusively in terms of the three "P's,"—prescribed, proscribed, and permitted—behavior associated with social positions. Perhaps if one could assume that personal goals and structured roles were always in harmony, the problem would not be so serious. By behaving in socially appropriate ways one would automatically be pursuing one's own interests. But to assume so again resolves by fiat what is essentially an empirical issue. Indeed, there is clear recognition in functionalism that goals and roles may not be articulated.

Exchange theory provides an alternative orientation to the analyzing of the interplay of interests. In exchange theory, rather than as bearers of normative scripts, people are seen as packages of hierarchically arranged interests. Positional location, which in structural-functional analysis would be seen as the major warrant for claims on resources, is, in exchange theory, only one of several possible sources of legitimating claims. Others, such as distributive justice, no less norma-

tive, then can supercede or subsume social location.

The discussion of preference orderings or outcome values by exchange theorists has an atomistic flavor; there is little in the way of pointing out how values for outcomes are interrelated *within* the individual. They probably are. A useful way of dealing with the interrelationships is to view them as integrated with the self-system. Singleman (1972) emphasizes the importance of "selves" to exchange theory. The overt manifestation of this system in interaction is the individual's situational identity. Situational identities *per se* can be loci of rewards and costs. As we have noted elsewhere (Weinstein, 1969), the actor may have highly specific objectives in the encounter such as touching another for a five dollar loan. Who he can be or has to be in order to get the five dollars will constitute an important set of costs for him. It would be only in the most secondary and impersonal encounters that the situational identities of the parties would not be the principal nexus of rewards and costs. Often, they are precisely and completely that. A person's principal motivation may be to get affirmation from the other(s) for an identity he desires or requires for himself, e.g., worthy of esteem. Or establishing a particular situational identify can be a prerequisite means for pursuing other types of purposes as in getting oneself defined as essential to the group for future leverage in it. In either case, whatever the more specific goals of exchange in interaction, underlying them are negotiations, and subsequent renegotiations as well, about who is "really" whom in the current situation.

Further, to see exchange as the *modus operandi* of social relations does not require glossing over the linkage intervening between individual interests and society-at-large as some exchange theorists are wont to do. Interests do not get exchanged in the abstract, but in the marketplaces of everyday social encounters. There is a level of analysis between social structures and individual interests, the level of concrete social process. And just as there are concepts and propositions at the sociological and at the psychological levels, so too must there be propositions and concepts dealing with the level of everyday interaction itself. Goffman has made a major contribution to the development of such a conceptual framework with such notions as "working consensus" (1959), "realized resources" and rules of relevance and irrelevance (1961). Symbolic interactionism, ethnomethodology, and the tradition of field-work have made contributions as well, contributions that not only sensitize us to the processes by which social structures are actualized in interaction, but alert us to ways in which the outcomes of exchange are conditioned to reduce society immediately to the interplay of individual interests, as does much of exchange theory, is to neglect a critical level of analysis.

We have now pointed to many questions raised about the completeness or adequacy of some existing paradigms of social interaction. In the process, we have noted the possibility of generating a framework for analyzing interaction incorporating the capacity of symbolic interactionism to deal with meanings and with the emergent aspects of interaction, the ability of structural-functionalism to deal with linkages among episodes of interaction, and the strength of exchange theory in dealing with coordination of contingencies in the pursuit of individual interests. Let us now draw together the essential aspects of such a framework.

First, interaction is an analytically separable level, not the epiphenomenon of individual interests or consciousness, or of structural residues (Swanson, 1965). On this level the focal unit of analysis is the episode of interaction—Goffman's "encounter," a contained social world within a stream of such worlds. Encounters occur when people make themselves available to one another for communicative contact, and terminate when that availability is withdrawn. (Purposive ignoring during co-presence is a special instance which fits ordinary definitions of interaction but would be excluded under this definition.)

Second, the pursuit of personal purposes is what these episodes of social interaction are all about. This assumption of purposiveness is a universal feature of all theoretical schemes for accounting for social action. From Aristotle to Schutz, from Homans to Parsons, from needs to values, some form of hedonic assumption is necessary to render social activity as sensible. There

need not be any assumption that purposes are transitive, either within individuals or across them, or any assumption of conscious, let alone self-conscious, rationality. One need not be an orthodox Freudian to be convinced that people can have purposes of which they are unaware and pursue them vigorously. What *is* important to emphasize is that, by definition, *interaction* entails not only the activity of one person pursuing his own interests, but the responsive behavior of others to that activity. Goal seeking in interaction, then, is a process involving both these defining features; *personal purposes* must get pursued through controlling or directing the *responses that others make* to one's own activity. As such, these responsive actions themselves become goals of interpersonal activity.

The responses of another intended by one person may be quite overt, as when one hands another money or covert, as when one thinks another to be a good person. But whether overt or covert, intended consciously or wished subconsciously, they are the objects around which people's everyday social activities are organized. *Interpersonal task* is a generic term to denote the response from another that a person's activities are directed to elicit. The purposive activities themselves are *lines of action.*

Third, expanding Goffman's analysis to general social theory suggests that the fundamental process in encounters is the transformation of resource potentials into realized resources. (The implications of "Fun in Games," (Goffman, 1961) extend beyond the construction of reality in the encounter to a general theory of the interchange between social structure and social process. Much of this paper is merely tracing out and attempting to generalize those implications. Perhaps fools rush in where angels fear to tread.)

The potential resources of an encounter are functions of the physical context of the encounter, and the participants themselves, with their characteristics, purposes, interests and schemes for constructing sense. Taken together, these potential resources determine what is available for realization. For example, each of the participants occupies a number of different social locations vis-à-vis the other. While all these locations are part of the potential resources, only some will be relevant to the joint definition of the situation that emerges and thus become realized resources.

In the above example, the realization of resources are used as equivalent to Merton's "status activation." But Goffman's idea of resources is broader and not limited only to social locations. Any value, preference, expectation presumed by one participant to be held by another can be made an object of joint attention, explicitly agreed upon as irrelevant, or go ignored because the focus of joint attention is placed on other values, preferences or expectations. Other potential resources include any individual characteristic of the co-participants, any action or event in the history of their co-participation, and the cultural implications of such events for attributing traits or dispositions. And each of these additional resources carries the possibility for focus or disregard.

The problem for theory at the interactional level is to account for the specific transformations (or realizations) that take place. What are the processes involved in selecting from among the various constructions that could be placed upon an encounter the one to which its participants tacitly subscribe? What are the determinants of how these processes turn out? Which resources will become realized through incorporation into the joint definition of the situation—"working consensus"—that serves as the prerequisite base for maintenance of interaction? And which of the lines of action available within this larger frame will be expressed, thus becoming both a realized resource and a new potential one for predicating further lines of action?

Fourth, the location of an individual in an encounter cannot be adequately described only in terms of the structural locations he occupies; that list is both too long and too short. It must be shortened to exclude those social positions that are only potential and not realized resources, and it must be lengthened to include all the other realized resources, and it must be lengthened to include all the other realized resources attaching to the person. This total set of realized resources is an individual's *situational identity*. Status activation is thus subsumed under the construction of situational identities and situational identities are, in turn, central but not exhaustive elements of a working consensus.

Fifth, the working consensus itself is usefully analyzed as the outcome of exchange processes.[1] Each participant may have somewhat different interests in which of the particular "events" that *could* be created out of the "stuff" (potential resources) of the present occasion becomes manifest. To establish a working consensus, therefore, involves negotiating agreement on meanings, particularly the implications for action to be ascribed to elements in the pool of resources. (This is roughly equivalent to involvement with the indexical status of any specific element.) The form that the pursuit of interests takes is this negotiating over meanings. (It is important to note that the "negotiation" may involve nothing more than tacit assent to the common-cultural implications of some element of context or action-in-context. Negotiations can thus take place over which potential elements of situational identities (including which of the various structural positions each of the participants occupies vis-à-vis the others) is to be appropriate for the current occasion. What, for example, should be the implications of prior episodes involving these participants for who they are now? Or for what should "rightfully" engage their attention? Or which of the possible norms (also part of potential resources) for supporting claims and counterclaims that participants can make on one another are appropriately invocable on the basis of situational identities?

Presumably, people will negotiate aspects of the working consensus on the basis of how it will

---

[1] Goffman implicitly rests his discussion of the working consensus on exchange. "Each participant is allowed to establish the tentative official ruling regarding matters which are vital to him . . . In exchange for this courtesy he remains silent or noncommittal on matters important to others . . ." (1959:9). Our treatment is a bit less passive. Interestingly Goffman (1969:38) subsequently raised objections to the idea of the exchangeability of intangibles such as esteem. We disagree. While the tactics used to elicit expressions of esteem may not be direct, it seems unparsimonious to require that the cognitive processes involved in evaluating the satisfactions likely to occur as a consequence of our actions are different for intangible than for tangible outcomes. Nor does it seem necessary to provide a separate account for the process of *choice* of actions designed to overtly produce outcomes that may not even be overtly expressed. People can and do act in ways which they can only assume are leading others to value them. Admittedly, it is often gauche (and foolish) to bargain for their overt expression since that expression is easily faked and may be mandatory as a matter of tact.

affect their interpersonal tasks. Indeed, the establishment of some particular working consensus is always an interpersonal task in itself. Power has its impact in this process. Power has its roots in the capacity of one person to affect the interests of another (both inside of the current encounter and in possible other encounters. This is ultimately reducible to terms of affecting the probability of success in interpersonal tasks.) That capacity may not be equally distributed among participants, so that some may be at an advantage in negotiating meetings. (This is the interpersonal analog of the functioning of power in the aggregate social construction of reality, Berger and Luckman, 1966.) However, power may be limited in its exercise by the reluctance of its holder to use it because of its implications for the situational identities of both its user and its target. (Blau (1964) makes a similar point in discussing the limits of power in which one with greater power may exchange fairness for esteem.) Thus, one who exercises power may be limited by his desire to avoid being seen as one who would "take advantage" of his position. And its target may be reluctant to accept the identity of one who would be exploited by superior power. (Using somewhat different terms, Thibaut and Kelley [1959] talk about the tendency to transform what they call fate control into mutual behavior control.)

These niceties may not always obtain; coercive power exists and is unhesitantly used by some. But, as long as constraints of legitimacy and altruism exist, differential power alone is insufficient to predict the results of negotiation over meaning. So, ultimately, the pursuit of personal purposes always involves negotiation over meanings, whether tacit or explicit. Here symbolic interaction, with its emphasis on the continuous construction of meaning, merges with exchange theory when that construction becomes a joint process. For negotiation over meanings does not stop with the establishment of the working consensus. Each act, each event occurring in the encounter, not only adds to, but in part may transform, the pool of resources for constructing and retrospectively reconstructing meaning. An exchange already made can no longer be held up as a contingency. Or an event can cause a person

to discover that his interests are not where he thought they lay.

Sixth, all interaction is inherently problematic; the definition of the situation may never be assumed to be necessarily "given." The idea of the inherently problematic nature of situational definitions runs counter to some versions of structural-functionalism and to much of our unexamined everyday experience. In those versions of structural-functionalism, problematic definitions are usually treated as either the result of malarticulation in the social structure (some forms of role conflict) or as a residual category stemming from the wide range of latitude permitted in status-linked behavior. In our everyday experience, we often go into contexts for which there exist prior coordinating arrangements (e.g., schedules, agendas, appointments) for our being there, which include agreements as to the nature of the future working consensus. We come, we act as if such were indeed the arrangements, so do our co-participants, so where is the problem? Indeed, the omnipresence of the possibility of problems has generated a variety of interactive techniques (e.g., tact) for protection of encounters against the failure of expectations. The existence of such elaborate routines (like the existence of incest taboos) is testimony to the *importance* of untoward events, not necessarily their commonness.

Any situation, however, may become problematic at any time. Exogenous occurrences may upset the balance of interests that originally produced a working consensus. Or, the interests of some participants may be perceived as not being sufficiently satisfied by an upcoming arrangement. Renegotiation, incremental or radical, of the terms of the previous working consensus then becomes the object of bargaining (Goode, 1960). In order for us to experience a situation as non-problematic, it is necessary for initial action to convey the meta-message that all is to proceed along expected lines. And it is necessary that no information be introduced countering such presuppositions (including assumptions about the status elements in situational identities). When our subjective expectancies are exceedingly high, we are likely to falsely assign zero probability to such exceptions and hence see the situation as non-problematic.

Another place under which problems are buried is the heap of unexamined assumptions whose very unexamined status makes social life possible (Garfinkel, 1967). These include the assumption of a single, ultimately knowable "reality" and the tendency to overattribute intersubjectivity from the evidence of similar linguistic practices. Common words may have elements of uncommon meaning. We do not have sufficient attention to focus both on consensus and on examining the possibilities of having "talked past one another." As long as there is sufficient appearance of commonality to manage the practical aspects of coordination, we do not tend to question our assumption that accurate role-taking is common to the co-participants. But inconsistencies crop up, and what we had been taking for granted all along may require reinterpretation.

We are not denying the possibility of partial identity of meanings. To do so would be to deny culture itself. What we are implying is that the myriad elements of the situation vary in the level of consensus that exists about their categoric placement and the ease of such placement. One important consequence of the partial lack of intersubjectivity is, as Goffman emphasizes, that we must ultimately rely on impressions and thus are constantly vulnerable to being duped. But it has another consequence as well. It means that definitions of the situation are not totally and immediately fixed for all by the "givens" of immediate experience. And this leaves open the possibility of mutual negotiation over meanings and their implications for appropriate behavior as avenues for pursuing personal interests.

This is not to imply that the social process *is only* meaning negotiation, or that exchange of objects as well as of implications for identity does not take place. Nor do the everpresent possibilities of surprise, discovery, or renegotiation deny the occurrence of the regular, the expected, or, in short, the degree of stability *necessary* for the *continued existence and functioning of social structure*. Interaction, it occurrence, its forms, and its outcomes are not random but patterned. This patterning comes from the aggregate outcomes of inummerable encounters. Their traces (in concrete objects, in records, and in the recall of those who participated) and the cultural meanings and normative implications of those objects and recalled events are a large share of the potential resources of any encounter. The remaining share consists of the co-presence of this particular set of participants with their particular interests and frameworks for organizing experience. But even the agendas that brought these co-participants together are influenced by the ways these people are implicated in social structure. In particular, the social positions people can claim to occupy and the interests that they have as a result of these positions strongly affect the agendas for their rounds of everyday encounters.

The impact of social structure upon interaction is thus not *direct*. Its juncture with social process is in the potential resources available in any encounter for constructive definitions of the situation. And the work of social process is transforming structurally provided potentials into realized resources. Taken collectively, the outcomes of that realization process aggregate into social structure.

REFERENCES

Barnsley, John H. 1972. "On the Hobbesian Problem of Order: A Comment." *American Sociological Review*, 37 3(June):369–373.

Berger, P. L., and T. Luckman. 1966. *The Social Construction of Reality*. New York: Doubleday.

Blau, Peter. 1964. "Justice in Social Exchange." *Sociological Inquiry*, 26:183–193.

Blumer, Herbert. 1962. "Society as Symbolic Interaction." Pp. 179–192 in Arnold M. Rose (ed.), *Human Behavior and Social Process*. Boston: Houghton Mifflin Co.

Cicourel, Aaron. 1972. "Basic and Normative Rules in the Negotiation of Status and Role." Pp. 229–258 in David Sudnow (ed.), *Studies in Social Interaction*. New York: The Free Press.

Ellis, Desmond P. 1971. "On the Hobbesian Problem of Order: A Critical Reappraisal of the Normative Solution." *American Sociological Review*, 36:692–703.

Garfinkel, H. 1967. *Studies in Ethnomethodology*. New York: Prentice-Hall.

Goffman, Erving. 1959. *The Presentation of Self in Everyday Life*. Garden City, New York: Doubleday.

————. 1961. "Fun in Games." Pp. 17–84 in *Encounters.* Indianapolis: Bobbs-Merrill.

————. 1969. *Strategic Interaction.* Philadelphia: University of Pennsylvania Press.

Goode, William J. 1960. "Norm Commitment and Conformity to Role Status Obligations." *American Journal of Sociology,* 66:246–258.

Merton, Robert. 1957. "Social Structure and Anomie." Pp. 131–194 in *Social Theory and Social Structure.* Glencoe, Illinois: The Free Press.

————. 1972. "Insiders and Outsiders." *American Journal of Sociology,* 78 1:41.

Singleman, Fred. 1972. "Exchange as Symbolic Interaction." *American Sociological Review,* 37:414–424.

Swanson, Guy E. 1956. "On Explanations of Social Interaction." *Sociometry,* 28:101–123.

Thibaut, John W., and Harold H. Kelley. 1959. *The Social Psychology of Groups.* New York: John Wiley & Sons.

Weinstein, Eugene. 1969. "The Development of Interpersonal Competence." In David Goslin (ed.), *Handbook of Socialization Theory and Research.* Chicago: Rand McNally.

Ralph H. Turner   **16**

The Public Perception of Protest

The year 1965 marked a dramatic turning point in American reactions to racial disorder. Starting with Watts, dominant community sentiment and the verdicts of politically sensitive commissions have identified mass violence by blacks primarily as acts of social protest. In spite of its well advertised failings, the McCone Commission (Governor's Commission on the Los Angeles Riots, 1965) devoted most of its attention to reporting the justified complaints of Negroes and proposing their amelioration. The Kerner Report

Ralph H. Turner, "The Public Perception of Protest," *American Sociological Review,* vol. 34, December 1969, pp. 815–831. Reprinted by permission.

Prepared as Presidential Address, 64th Annual Meetings of the American Sociological Association, September 3, 1969. The author is grateful for the searching critiques of an earlier version of the paper by Herbert Blumer, John Horton, Lewis Killian, Leo Kuper, Kurt Lang, Melvin Seeman, Neil Smelser, and Samuel Surace.

(National Advisory Commission on Civil Disorders, 1968) went further in predicating recommendations for action on the assumption that disorders must be understood as acts of social protest, and not merely as crime, anti-social violence, or revolutionary threats to law and order. A few earlier bodies had seen minority protest as a component in racial disorders (Silver, 1968), but in most cases these commissions were far removed from the political process. Even when whites had perpetrated most of the violence, public officials before 1965 typically vented their most intense anger against Negroes, Negro leaders, and their white allies (Lee and Humphreys, 1943; Rudwick, 1964). If comparable data were available from earlier racial disturbances, it is unlikely they would match Morris and Jeffries' (1967:5) finding that 54% in a sample of white Los Angeles residents viewed the disturbance as Negro protest.

The aim of this paper is to suggest several theoretical vantage points from which to predict when a public will and will not view a major disturbance as an act of social protest. Historically, labor strife has sometimes been understood as protest and sometimes not. Apparently the protest meaning in the activities of Cesar Chavez and his farm laborers is discounted by most Americans today. A gang *rumble* is seldom viewed as protest, even when Puerto Ricans and other minorities are prominently involved. Three-fourths of an unspecified sample of Los Angeles residents in May, 1969, are reported to have seen disorders in secondary schools as the work of agitators and not as social protest, (Los Angeles Times, May 19, 1969), even though Mexican-Americans and blacks have played the leading roles. Events of early 1969 hint at a rising movement to redefine all racial and youthful disturbances in other terms than social protest. Hence, it is of both current and continuing sociological interest to advance our understanding of these variable public definitions, in broad terms that might apply to all kinds of disturbances, and eventually to other cultures and eras.

The Meaning of Protest. Protest has been defined as "an expression or declaration of objection, disapproval, or dissent, often in opposition to something a person is powerless to prevent or avoid." (Random House Dictionary, 1967). An act of protest includes the following elements: the action expresses a grievance, a conviction of wrong or injustice; the protestors are unable to correct the condition directly by their own efforts; the action is intended to draw attention to the grievances; the action is further meant to provoke ameliorative steps by some target group; and the protestors depend upon some combination of sympathy and fear to move the target group in their behalf. Protest ranges from relatively persuasive to relatively coercive combinations (Bayley, 1962), but always includes both. Many forms of protest involve no violence or disruption, but these will not concern us further in this paper.

The term protest is sometimes applied to trivial and chronic challenges that are more indicative of a reaction style than of deep grievance. For instance, we speak of a child who protests

every command from parent or teacher in the hope of gaining occasional small concessions. It is in this sense that the protestations by some groups in society are popularly discounted because "they just protest everything." But the subject of this analysis is *social protest*, by which we mean protest that is serious in the feeling of grievance that moves it and in the intent to provoke ameliorative action.

When violence and disorder are identified as social protest, they constitute a mode of communication more than a form of direct action. Looting is not primarily a means of acquiring property, as it is normally viewed in disaster situations (Dynes and Quarantelli, 1968); breaking store windows and burning buildings is not merely a perverted form of amusement or immoral vengeance like the usual vandalism and arson; threats of violence and injury to persons are not simply criminal actions. All are expressions of outrage against injustice of sufficient magnitude and duration to render the resort to such exceptional means of communication understandable to the observer.

In identifying the principal alternatives to protest we must first differentiate crime and deviance on the one hand and rebellion and revolution on the other. The latter may or may not express a generally understandable grievance, but they constitute direct action rather than communication and their aim is to destroy the authority of the existing system either totally or so far as the rebellious group is concerned. Thus protest and rebellion are distinguished according to their ultimate goal and according to whether the disruptions are meant as communication or direct action. Deviance and crime are actions identified chiefly according to their nonconforming, illegal, or harmful character. Deviance and crime are seen principally in individual terms, and while there may be "social" causes that require attention, the harmful or nonconforming features of the behavior are the primary concern. The distinctions are not absolute. Extortion, "power plays," and similar ideas fall between crime and protest. Nor can the line between protest and rebellion be drawn precisely. Attributing disorders to agitators is another common variation, in which either criminal or rebellious meaning is ascribed to the agitators, but any criminal, protest, or rebellious meaning is blunted for the mass of participants.

In deciding that individuals view a disturbance as social protest, it is helpful but not conclusive to note whether they apply the term protest. Defining a disturbance as protest does not preclude disapproving the violence or disorder by which the protest is expressed, nor does it preclude advocating immediate measures to control and suppress the disturbance. Thus Marvin Olsen's (1968) study of the legitimacy that individuals assign to various types of protest activities is related to the present question, but makes a somewhat different distinction. The principal indicators of a protest definition are concerned with identifying the grievances as the most adequate way of accounting for the disturbance and the belief that the main treatment indicated is to ameliorate the unjust conditions. Fogelson (1968:37–38) offers an exceptionally explicit statement of this mode of interpreting racial disorder: ". . . the riots of the 1960's are articulate protests against genuine grievances in the Negro ghettos. The riots are protests because they are attempts to call the attention of white society to the Negroes' widespread dissatisfaction with racial subordination and segregation in urban America. The riots are also articulate because they are restrained, selective, and perhaps even more important, directed at the sources of the Negroes' most immediate and profound grievances."

Definitions by Publics.   We assume that individuals and groups of individuals assign simplifying meanings to events, and then adjust their perceptions of detail to these comprehensive interpretations. Lemert's (1951) pioneering examination of deviance as a label applied by society's agents serves as a valuable prototype for the analysis of responses to public disturbances. We scrupulously avoid assuming that there are objectifiable phenomena that must be classified as deviance, as protest, or as rebellion. We further assume that participant motivations are complex and diverse, so that a given disturbance is not simply protest, or not protest, according to participant motives. Just as Negroes and whites used different labels for the Watts disturbance (Tomlin-

son and Sears, 1967), we also assume that publics will often interpret the events quite differently from the participants.

This concern with public definitions contrasts—but is not incompatible—with studies in which protest is defined and examined as an objective phenomenon. For example, Lipsky's (1968) careful statement of the prospects and limitations in the use of protest as a political tool deals with an objectively identified set of tactics rather than a subjective category. Irving Horowitz and Martin Liebowitz (1968:285) argue that "The line between the social deviant and the political marginal is fading." The political marginal engages in social protest, in our sense, and the authors are pointing out that much of what sociologists heretofore understood as deviance is now taking on the character of social protest, either as objectively defined or according to the motives of the subject individuals.

The question of labeling disturbances has been examined by other investigators from somewhat different points of view. Lang and Lang (1968) have observed that the label "riot" is used to identify quite different kinds of events that are similar only in the kind of official response they evoke. Grimshaw (1968) pointed out the different labels attached to recent disturbances according to whether they are seen as racial clashes, class conflict, or civil disturbances in which the theme of intergroup conflict is de-emphasized.

The nature of the public definition undoubtedly has consequences for the course and recurrence of the disturbance, and for short- and long-term suppression or facilitation of reform. One of the most important consequences is probably that a protest definition spurs efforts to make legitimate and nonviolent methods for promoting reform more available than they had been previously, while other definitions are followed by even more restricted access to legitimate means for promoting change (Turner and Killian, 1957:327–329). Persons to whom the Joseph McCarthy movement was a massive protest against threats to our national integrity were unwilling to oppose the Senator actively even when they acknowledged that his methods were improper. Following the recent student disruption of a Regents meeting at UCLA, a faculty member who perceived the activity as protest against academic injustice advised the Academic Senate to listen more to what the students were saying and less to the tone of voice in which they said it. But the important tasks of specifying and verifying the consequences of protest definition fall beyond the limits of this paper. Any judgment that protest definition is "good" or "bad" must depend upon the findings of such investigation and on such other considerations as one's evaluation of the cause and one's preferred strategy for change.

The rest of this paper will be devoted to suggesting five theoretical vantage points from which it is possible to formulate hypotheses regarding the conditions under which one group of people will define as disturbances and some other group as social protest. First, publics test events for *credibility* in relation to folk-conceptions of social protest and justice. Second, disturbances communicate some combination of *appeal and threat,* and the balance is important in determining whether the disturbances are regarded as social protest. Third, disturbances instigate conflict with a target group, who may define them as social protest in the course of attempted *conciliation* to avoid full scale conflict. Fourth, defining disturbances as protest is an invitation from a third party for the troublemaking group to form a *coalition.* And fifth, acting as if the disturbances were social protest can be a step by public officials in establishing a *bargaining* relationship.

The paper offers theoretical proposals and not tested findings. The proposals are not a complete catalogue of causes for protest interpretation; notably omitted are such variables as understanding, empathy, and kindness. The proposals generally assume that there is no well-established tradition of disruptive or violent protest (Silver, 1968), that the society is not sharply polarized, and that the disturbances emanate from a clearly subordinated segment of the society.

CREDIBILITY AND COMMUNICATIONS

If a disturbance is to be viewed as social protest, it must somehow look and sound like social protest to the people witnessing it. If they see that the events are widely at variance from their conception of social protest, they are unlikely to identify the disturbance as social protest in spite of any intergroup process in which they are involved. On the other hand, if events are clearly seen to correspond precisely with people's idea of social protest, intergroup processes will have to operate with exceptional force to bring about a different definition. It is within the limits imposed by these two extreme conditions that the intergroup process variables may assume paramount importance. Hence it is appropriate to begin our analysis by examining these limiting considerations.

Our first two theoretical perspectives concern this preliminary question, whether the events will be recognizable as social protest or not. First, there are the viewer's preconceptions about protest that render believable the claim that what he sees is protest. We look to the predispositions of individuals and groups to ascertain what characteristics a disturbance must exhibit if it is to be *credible* as protest. Second, the ability of the observer to attend to one or another of the melange of potential messages communicated to him will be affected by the specific nature of the disturbance. For example, the balance between *appeal and threat* messages seems especially crucial for whether observers see the disturbance as social protest.

Credibility: The Folk Concept. The main outlines of a *folk concept* (Turner, 1957) of social protest appear to be identifiable in contemporary American culture. The folk concept is only partially explicit, and is best identified by examining the arguments people make for viewing events and treating troublemakers in one way or another. Letters to newspapers and editorial and feature columns supply abundant material in which to conduct such a search. More explicit statements are to be found in essays that present reasoned arguments for viewing disturbances as protest (Boskin, 1968). The folk concept supplies the criteria against which people judge whether what they see looks like social protest or not. Often the process works in reverse: people who are predisposed to interpret a disturbance as protest, or as criminal rioting, perceive events selectively so as to correspond with the respective folk concept. But in so far as there is any testing of the events to see whether they look like protest, crime, or rebellion, the folk concepts are the key. The folk concept will not necessarily correspond with what sociologists would find in a study of objectively defined protest behavior.

Several components of the folk concept of social protest emerge from examination of relevant materials. To be credible as protestors, troublemakers must seem to constitute a major part of a group whose grievances are already well documented, who are believed to be individually or collectively powerless to correct their grievances, and who show some signs of moral virtue that render them "deserving." Any indication that only few participated or felt sympathy with the disturbances predisposes observers to see the activities as deviance or as revolutionary activity by a small cadre of agitators. The claim that a group's conditions explain their resort to unusual means for gaining public attention to their plight is undermined when it appears that many persons in identical situations will not join or support the protest.

Common arguments against protest interpretation take the following form: "Unemployed? Let him go out, walk the streets, and find a job the way I did!" "They have one vote each the same as we do!" Powerlessness and grievance probably cannot be effectively communicated for the first time in a large-scale disturbance. To be credible as protest, a disturbance must follow an extended period in which both the powerlessness and the grievances have already been repeatedly and emphatically advertised.

Any weak individual or group who comes with a plea to more powerful personages is normally required to be more circumspect and more virtuous than those to whom he appeals. The normative principle would not be endorsed in this explicit form by majority groups. But the *de facto* principle operates because the sincerity and justifiability of the pleader's claim is subject to investigation and test while there is no investigation of the other's legitimacy. Since violence and disruption immediately call virtue into question, there must be offsetting indications of goodness in the group's past or current behavior. The group in question must be customarily law-abiding and must have used acceptable means and exercised

restraint on other occasions. Nonviolent movements that precede violent disruptions help to establish the credibility of protest. Widespread support and sympathy for the objectives of protest coupled with the group's principled rejection of the violent means employed by a few of their members help to establish the deserving nature of the group without undermining the pervasive character of their grievances.

To be credible as protest, the disturbance itself must be seen either as a spontaneous, unplanned, and naive outburst, or as an openly organized protest of more limited nature that got tragically out of hand. Any evidence of covert planning, conspiracy, or seriously intended threats of violence before the event would weaken the credibility of the protest interpretation. On the other hand, naive expressions of rage, released under the stimulus of rumor and crowd excitement, are consistent with a folk-image of protest. In this connection the protest interpretation is supported by demonstrating that what triggered the disturbances was some incident or act of provocation, and that a succession of recent provocations had prepared the ground for an eruption.

To be credible as protest, indications of the use of riots for self-aggrandizement, the settlement of private feuds, or enjoyment of violence and destruction must be subordinated to naive anger and desperation. Looting for personal gain and the attitude that rioting is "having a ball" are two features of the racial disturbances since 1965 that have repeatedly detracted from the image of social protest. In a widely read article typical of many such statements, Eric Sevareid (1967) challenged the protest definition by describing the carnival atmosphere at certain stages in many of the disturbances.

Finally, some indications of restraint are important cues to interpretation as protest. A belief that only property and not personal injury was the object of attack, that deaths and severe injuries to persons resulted only under special circumstances of confusion and provocation, and that rioters went to exceptional lengths in a few dramatic instances to protect a white person or guarantee a college administrator safe passage is often salient in the imagery of persons defining the activity as protest.

Credibility: The Admission of Injustice.
Interpretations of disruptive activity as protest
invoke conceptions of justice and injustice. Homans (1961) and Blau (1964a and 1964b) are
among those who interpret the sense of injustice
as a feeling of inadequate reciprocation in social
exchange. Runciman (1966), applying Merton and
Kitt's (1950) conception of relative deprivation,
proposes that the selection of reference groups
determines whether there is a sense of injustice
with respect to the rewards of position. But these
theories do not answer the question: when is it
possible and probable that one group will see another group's position as unjust to the point of
accepting violence and disruption as the natural
expression of that injustice?

If we assume that each group tends to employ
its own situation as the point of reference in assessing another group's claims of injustice, we are
led to the conclusion that groups who are clearly
advantaged by comparison with the "protestors"
can find the claim of injustice more credible than
groups less advantaged. Crucial here is the assumption that objective and detached comparison
between the situations of the troublemakers and
the target groups is less powerful in shaping the
assessment of injustice than the observing group's
position vis-à-vis the troublemakers. Consequently, the great middle segment of American
population finds it easier to identify black ghetto
disturbances as social protest than to interpret
college student demonstrations in the same sense.
Similarly, black student demonstrations are less
amenable to interpretation as protest than ghetto
demonstrations.

According to this view, groups who see themselves as even more disadvantaged than the protestors are least likely to grant their claim. Viewed
from below, disturbances are most easily compre-
hended as power plays or as deviance. Groups
who see their situation as about the same as that
of the protestors likewise do not find it easy to
accord the protest interpretation. Leaders in such
groups commonly attempt to weld alliances based
on mutual appreciation, and these sometimes
work as political devices. But they are hindered
rather than helped by the spontaneous reaction
to disruptive activity by a group whose position
is apparently no worse than that of the group

passing judgment. Olsen's (1968) finding that persons who score high on measures of political inca-
pability and political disability are least willing
to adjudge direct action to correct grievances as
legitimate may also be consistent with this
reasoning.

*Credibility: Crediting Crime, Protest, Re-
bellion.* The credibility of a disturbance as protest also reflects the variable strength of resist-
ances against believing that massive crime,
protest, or rebellion is taking place. Each person's
security system is anchored in some fashion in
the assumption that he is part of an integral society. This anchorage poses obstacles to believing
that any of these conditions is widespread. But
each interpretation of disorder has different implications for societal integrity. Rebellion is difficult to credit by all but those whose disaffection
with the social order is such that they delight in
the threat of its disintegration. When crime and
deviance become extensive and blatant, the assumption of a society integrated on the basis of
consensus over major values is shaken. Hence,
people whose personal security is rooted in the
conviction of a fundamental consensus are resistant to admitting widespread crime and deviance.
People who understand society as a sort of jungle
accommodation will find it easier to interpret disturbances as criminal outbursts. In contrast,
protestors—even when they resort occasionally
to desperate means—need not reject the values
of those to whom they protest. They may share
the same values and seek only their share of what
others already have. Therefore, the belief in widespread protest calls into question the mechanics
of society's operation, but not necessarily the
value consensus.

When judgments by different socioeconomic
strata are compared, the middle strata find it
more difficult to credit massive deviance and
crime and less difficult to acknowledge protest
because of their commitment to society as a system of values. The lower strata have more day-
to-day experience of crime and the rejection of
societal values, and are forced to anchor their security to a less consensual image of society. Hence
they do not find massive crime so difficult to believe. If these assumptions about credibility are

correct, and if we have characterized the strata accurately, investigators should find middle class populations readier to make protest interpretations than working class groups.

APPEAL AND THREAT MESSAGES

It is a reasonable assumption that most observers could, under appropriate circumstances, see both an *appeal* and a *threat* in a violent disturbance. If this combination of messages is present, reading the disturbance as protest means that the appeal component is more salient to the observer than the threat component. For we can safely assume that when the preoccupation with threat to self and to those objects identified with self is foremost, appeals are no longer heard. Threat so often monopolizes attention to the exclusion of appeals, and acknowledging justice in the appeals weakens the foundation for defensive efforts required to meet the threat. Thus we are led to the proposition that disruptions are interpreted as protest only when the experience of threat is not excessive.

The foregoing observation however is incomplete. Somehow the appeal message must command attention, and resistance to acknowledging the protest message must be overcome. The *credibility* requirements we have just outlined are so restrictive that a positive incentive is required to overlook some of the criteria. An appeal by itself is normally a weak attention-getter; threat is much stronger in this respect. A combination of threat and appeal serves to gain attention and to create the sense of urgency necessary to overcome the resistance to acknowledging protest. When threat is insufficient, the events can be disregarded or written off as deviance, to be contained by the established systems of social control. An optimal combination of threat and appeal is necessary for the probability of seeing disturbance as protest. When the threat component falls below the optimal range, the most likely interpretation is deviance; above the optimal range, preoccupation with threat makes rebellion the probable interpretation.

This approach suggests several hypotheses relating interpretation as protest to the nature

and bounds of the disorder and to the position of various population segments reacting to the disorders. Certainly the threat posed by disorders during the last half decade has been sufficient to gain attention and force examination of the message. At the same time, threat has been limited by the localization of disorders in the ghettos and by the minimization of direct personal confrontation between whites and blacks. Without replicable measurements of the magnitude of threat and appeal components, predictions regarding specific situations can only be formed intuitively. Intuition suggests that either pitched battles leading to death and injury of any substantial number of whites, or spread of the disorders outside of the boundaries of black neighborhoods and especially into white residence areas, would substantially reduce the likelihood of disorders being interpreted as a form of protest and would seriously divert attention away from black grievances.

Differential perception of threat by population segments is affected by a combination of personal involvement and proximity to the events and of ability to perceive the limits and patterns of disorder realistically. On this basis it is easiest for groups who live a safe distance from black neighborhoods and who have no stake in ghetto businesses to turn their attention toward the appeal component of the disturbance message. But we must also take note of the principle suggested by Diggory's (1956) findings regarding a rabid fox scare in Pennsylvania. While fear was greater among persons near to the rumored center of rabid fox sightings, the tendency to exaggerate the extent of the menace was less. Persons closest to the events were able to form a more realistic picture. Similarly, whites closest to the disturbances may be better able to discount inflated reports of violence against the persons of whites, and to see a pattern in the properties attacked and protected. Thus persons close enough to fear any spread of disorders but not close enough to correct exaggerated reports from personal experience may find it most difficult to see the activities as protest.

After the 1964 riots, Harper's (1968) Rochester *suburban* subjects were most likely to acknowledge that Negroes had a right to complain; city residents living more than one block from a Negro family were least likely to grant Negroes this right; and subjects living within one block of a Negro family were intermediate in their responses. After the 1965 Watts disorder, Morris and Jeffries (1967) found upper-middle-class Pacific Palisades residents most likely to identify the events as Negro protest and all-white low socioeconomic status Bell residents least likely, among the six white areas of Los Angeles County sampled.

The experience of threat is not entirely an individual matter. The self-conception is made up of group memberships, and the individual is threatened whenever an important membership group seems to be the object of threat. Consequently, we should expect members of such groups as small merchants, police, and firemen, even though they were personally unaffected by the disturbances, to experience much threat because of their identification with these same groups immediately involved in the confrontation. Police and merchants within the ghettos were not generally disposed to view racial disorder as social protest (Rossi, et al., 1968). It would be surprising to discover many people among these groups in the larger community who see the events primarily as protest.

It is possible to overlook what others see as threat because one rejects identification with the group under attack. The phenomenon of a few Jews who supported Hitler and were able to discount his antisemitic policies as threats to themselves suggests such a mechanism. The radical repudiation of Jewish identity, labeled self-hatred by Kurt Lewin (1941), may have been strong enough in these individuals that they were unable to conceive of the attacks as being directed toward themselves. There are many whites who radically reject any identification with American society. For those to whom disidentification with conventional society and conventional people is a strong component of the self-conception, threats directed toward white society, toward *honkies*, or toward *whitey* are unlikely to be perceived as referring to themselves. Hence the personal threat is minimized, and it is easiest for such persons to identify the disturbances as protest.

Finally, according to the assumption of an optimal mixture of threat and appeal, it may be difficult to keep the awareness of protest dominant for an extended period of time. We have noted that escalation of violence is likely to preclude protest definition because of preoccupation with the threat. But repeated threat that is not followed by tangible injury to the threatened loses its impact. The diminishing force of repeated destructive activity confined to ghettos lessens the concern that originally directed attention toward the appeal component. Hence, repeated unescalated disturbances are likely to be accompanied by decreasing degrees of interpretation as protest, replaced by increasing tendencies to see the events as deviance.

Except for understanding protest interpretation as a means to protect the observer from seeing a serious lack of consensus in society, we have thus far treated protest interpretation as a passive matter. But the observation that some of the most unsympathetic interpretations abound among groups far removed from the disorders is difficult to understand with the principles outlined. It is true that small town and rural dwellers often feel somewhat deprived relative to large city dwellers, and therefore may have difficulty seeing justice in the complaints even of ghetto dwellers. They also lack the incentive of the large city dwellers to avoid acknowledging widespread crime by interpreting disturbances as protest. But perhaps the protest interpretation is part of a more active stance, brought about by involvement in a relationship with the troublemaking group. Crime and rebellion are in an important sense easier interpretations to make since they can be inferred from the most conspicuous and superficial aspects of behavior, without a search for the motives and grievances behind the violence and disruption. Our remaining three approaches rest on this assumption.

CONCILIATION OF CONFLICT

A more complex basis for predicting the assignment of meaning to disorders is supplied by viewing the protestors and the interpreters as engaged in a real or potential process of conflict. The aggressive initiative of the moment lies with the protestors. Interpreting the disturbances as protest can then usefully be seen as a *gesture of conciliation,* an action to forestall the incipient conflict or to reduce or conclude the conflict without victory or surrender. We can justify this assertion and use it to suggest conditions leading to protest interpretation only after briefly reviewing the nature of the conflict process.

We shall use the term "conflict," not in the broad sense that includes all disagreements and all efforts by people or groups to pursue incompatible goals, but in the tradition of Simmel (1955), von Wiese (1932:246) and Park and Burgess (1921). In Coser's (1968:232) definition of conflict as "a struggle over values or claims to status, power, and scarce resources, in which the claims of the conflicting parties are not only to gain the desired values but also to neutralize, injure, or eliminate their rivals," we underline the latter portion. Conflict has properties that distinguish it from other processes revolving about disagreement because there is an autonomous goal of injuring the antagonist—autonomous in the sense that efforts to injure the antagonist are not fully subjected to the test of effectiveness in promoting the other ostensible goals of the conflicting party. Conflict exists when the relationship between groups is based on the premise that whatever enhances the well-being of one group lessens the well-being of the other, and that impairing the well-being of the antagonist is a favored means for enhancing the well-being of one's own group.

The strategy of conflict centers about injuring the other without simultaneously injuring the self, while inhibiting and defending against retaliatory injury from the opponent. Consequently, conflict tends, particularly as it persists and intensifies, to be volatile and comprehensive with respect to the issues that divide the combatants. Combatants must be able to shift grounds and issues as necessary to fight on terrains that are strategically favorable for them. There has probably never been a war or violent revolution in which the question of what either side was fighting for did not become unclear, nor in which the issue at the close of fighting was defined in the same way as at the start of combat.

When conflict occurs between groups regarded as members of some common social order, the process is circumscribed by a somewhat distinctive set of conflict norms. In certain respects the conflict normative system grants license not available to other relationships. In other respects it imposes stricter obligations, such as those requiring demonstrations of ingroup loyalty. Two consequences of assimilation of conflict to a normative order have bearing on our subsequent discussion of conciliation.

First, because conflict involves inflicting injury on persons who are part of a common social order, a course of action that is not normatively sanctioned except within a recognized conflict relationship, the preoccupation with normative considerations is heightened. There is special attention to painting the antagonist as villainous and to establishing the virtuousness of the protagonist group. An important aspect of conflict strategy is to manipulate the normative aspects of the exchange so as to justify the claim to a reserve of moral credit upon which the combatant can draw when he engages in what might otherwise be considered shocking or reprehensible behavior.

Second, a great deal of conflict is fought symbolically with symbolic injuries in the form of insults and threats and symbolic defenses against such injuries. Much of the symbolic conflict consists of testing the other and jockeying for position. But because the combatants are members of a social order, the effective use of symbols so as to place the other in an unfavorable light is a way of inflicting injury upon him. Thus, what Waller and Hill (1951) called "manipulation of morality" in family conflict is an important part of the repertoire of symbolic tactics available for use in any conflict.

There is frequently confusion between the steps from disagreement toward agreement and the process of conflict resolution. Conflict resolution is more complicated because the combatants must cope with both disagreement and the pattern of reciprocal injury. The past and projected mutual injury is the more fundamental problem since it is possible to resolve conflict without agreement on substantive issues, but agreement on these issues does not erase the injury that each has done to the other in the course of the conflict.

The latter supplies independent momentum for the continuation of conflict. Hence the key to all conflict resolution is the repair of previous injury and protection against future injury. When conflict resolution is by surrender, the victor disarms the vanquished and extracts reparations. The vanquished party cannot usually exact compensation in repairing the injury to himself, but he normally surrenders under the assumption that once he no longer offers any threat of injury to the victor, he will be immune from further injury by the victor. When conflict resolution occurs without surrender, both parties must give assurances against doing harm in the future and both must take steps to ameliorate the injury that each has already done to the other. Since surrender is an unlikely response to current disorders, our interest is in conflict resolutions characterized by some degree of mutuality.

We shall refer to any act whose aim is to avert or discontinue conflict without either asking or offering surrender as conciliation. To be effective, a conciliatory act must incorporate both an offer to discontinue attacks and a tender of help to correct the harm already done. To the extent to which the conflict is being fought at the symbolic level, the remedies are partially symbolic. With respect to the exchange of threats and insults (i.e., symbolic conflict), conciliation is an offer to discontinue such attacks and to discount the meaning of prior threats and insults. In order to participate in conciliatory exchange, the combatant must be prepared to believe that the other did not fully mean what he said, that his threats were not really meant to be carried out, and that his insults did not express his more enduring feelings and views. Hence an act of conciliation must provide the other with a basis on which such beliefs are credible.

We are now prepared to see reaction to public disturbances as response in a situation of potential conflict. The disturbance involves physical injury and threats of further damage to the property and persons of the dominant white group, the college faculty or administration, management and ownership of industry, or colonial powers. In addition, it conveys insulting characterizations and promises of escalating disrespect. Faced with potential conflict, the dominant group has several alternatives, though not all are viable in any given situation. An effort can be made to ignore or depreciate the conflict significance of the disturbances by interpreting them as deviance. The challenge of conflict can be accepted, in which case the disturbance is defined as rebellion and the appropriate response is retaliatory suppression. This was plainly the dominating white reaction in earlier race riots such as St. Louis in 1919 and Detroit in 1943, when whites not only turned the encounters into massive attacks on Negroes but continued to take punitive action for weeks after the riots were finished and after the evidence of disproportionate injury to Negroes was plain to all (Lee and Humphreys, 1943; Rudwick, 1964). It is also common for some individuals to respond by repudiating their own group identification and joining with the dissidents, at least symbolically. Here too the definition is rebellion, but from the opposite side of the conflict. This position normally includes recognition of the protest orientation, though the identity problems involved in this position often cause the protest theme to become secondary in importance to the aim of discrediting one's group and disidentifying from it. Some of the difficulties in this response are represented when white students have attempted to participate in black protests, and when the Hell's Angels have offered support to conservative protesters against militant youth.

If we omit the possibility of surrender, the remaining alternative is to extend an offer of conciliation. The prospect of conflict is accepted as real, but the aim is to interrupt the reciprocation of attack that locks the combatants into full-scale conflict. The conciliator offers public acknowledgement that he has done injury to the protestor, promising repentence and corrective actions. By making this acknowledgement he grants that there is some justification for the other's hostility toward him, and he also supplies the basis for believing that the other's antagonism is not unalterable and is not personal to himself or his group. The white man can say that the black's antagonism is not really directed against the white man, but merely against those people who happen to be doing the black an injustice at a particular time. Conciliation is thereby rendered a viable posture, because there is no reason to expect the other to continue his attacks once he is assured of compensation and security from further injury.

Interpreting violent and disruptive action as protest is following exactly this pattern. It means assuming that the intent to do injury is secondary in importance to the effort to secure redress, and it means acknowledging that there is some basis in the behavior of one's own group for the antagonism displayed by the protestor.

If we have correctly identified the process, we must predict the protest interpretation by specifying the conditions that lead to acts of conciliation. Individuals and groups seek to avert conflict for four reasons: to avoid the risk of injury (or further injury) to themselves; to avoid the risk of injury or further injury to the potential opponent; to protect the relationship between the potential combatants from damage or increased damage; and to avoid the diversion of resources and energy into the conduct of conflict at the expense of other activities. The view of protest interpretation as conciliation and the reasons for conciliation suggest several correlates of protest interpretation.

First, protest interpretation is more likely to occur when there is some apparent danger to the group than when there is none. Second, the stronger the norms, values, or sentiments against doing injury to others, the greater the likelihood of interpreting disorder as protest. Third, the greater the interdependency between groups, the greater the likelihood of protest interpretation. The interdependency may be ecological or social; the solidarity, organic or mechanical in nature. If breaking or weakening the bonds between the groups is threatening, the likelihood of offering the conciliatory protest interpretation will be increased.

Fourth, the greater the commitment to activities and resources that may have to be sacrificed in order to carry on the conflict, the greater the readiness to make a protest interpretation. If there is a greater tolerance for conflict in lower socioeconomic strata and less exploration of conciliatory approaches, it may be because there is less at stake in the disruption of the standard round of life than there is in the higher social strata. Some groups are flexibly organized so that conflict can be sustained alongside of continuing normal activities. Private industry was long able to avoid treating labor unrest as social protest because private police could be hired to isolate the conflict while production continued. Universities are not equipped in this fashion, and must therefore face disruption of their normal functions under even mild conflict. Hence, universities are relatively quick to interpret internal disturbances as social protest.

Fifth, the less the anticipated costs of conciliation, the greater the tendency to see disturbance as protest. College officials who believe that discontinuing an R.O.T.C. program is sufficient to bring an end to campus conflict find it easy to see student activism as social protest, rather than as rebellious confrontation.

Because of the tendency for moralistic perspectives to be an inseparable part of conflict, an offer of conciliation is typically viewed by the conciliator as an act of generosity, going beyond what could be expected or required of him. Under the reciprocity principle (Gouldner, 1960) the act of placing a more generous than necessary interpretation on the other's actions obligates the latter to make generous response. Because the normative system of conflict permits a combatant to place a less favorable interpretation on the other's actions, the sense of self-righteous virtue attached to protest interpretation can be great. Furthermore, the protest interpretation with its clearly implied admission of fault places the conciliator in a precarious position, for his admission of prejudice, militarism, or insensitivity to student needs, for instance, can be used against him later if the other does not respond in kind. The risk he knows he is taking enhances the conciliator's self-righteousness. Hence, there is a strong tendency for conciliatory gestures to be withdrawn and replaced by active promotion of conflict when there is no discontinuance of insults and threats and no retraction of earlier attacks.

Hence we are led again (as under the appeal-threat perspective) to the generalization that interpretation of disorder as protest is a conditional and unstable response. According to the conflict model, it readily gives way to the interpretation of disorder as rebellion when it is not soon followed by subsidence of disorder and threat. On the other hand, without the prospect of involve-

ment in conflict, there is no occasion for conciliation, and crime or deviance is the most natural
interpretation.

THIRD PARTY POINT OF VIEW

From both the appeal-threat and conflict-
conciliation approaches comes the hint that a
third party may under some circumstances find
it easier to interpret disturbance as protest than
does the group against whom the disturbance is
directed. For the target group, the merit of conciliation rather than accepting the challenge of conflict declines as the prospective costs of conciliation increase. Furthermore, whenever group
membership is a salient aspect of personal identity, it is difficult to accept group fault without
offsetting the admission by assessing equal or
greater fault to the protestors. But a third party
is not so directly threatened and does not pay
most of the costs of conciliation and, consequently, is able to sustain a protest view of the
disturbances after such an interpretation ceases
to be tenable for the target group.

To account for third party protest interpretation, we must first ask why the third party should
be sufficiently concerned about a conflict, in
which they are bystanders, to acknowledge grievances and take a sympathetic stand. The question
implies the answer: that protest interpretations
by third parties are only likely to occur when
there is some threat of third party involvement
in the conflict or a strong basis for identification
with one of the two parties. American people seldom concerned themselves sufficiently to make
any interpretation of student riots abroad until
student disorders became an immediate concern
at home. Labor-management strife in the United
States today attracts sufficient attention only
when it threatens the supply of goods and services
to the community

Third party protest interpretations indicate
either the defense of neutrality against the threat
of partisan involvement in conflict or the active
acceptance of partisanship on the side of the
protestors. The bystander who is endangered by
conflict is not inclined toward a sympathetic interpretation of either side, but rather toward wishing

"a plague on both your houses!" Only when identities or interests pull him in one direction or the
other can the threat of involvement press him
to see the disturbance as protest.

Defining disturbance as protest can be a
defense of neutrality for the third party for some
of the same reasons that it can be a means of
conciliation for the target group. Acknowledging
valid grievances while condemning improper
means is a way of giving something to each side.
Protest definition as a defense of neutrality occurs
when (1) strong pressures toward partisan involvement play on the third party but (2) partisanship on either side is a costly prospect.

Protest definition as *partisanship* differs from
a similar definition as a form of neutrality in ignoring or de-emphasizing concern with the legitimacy of means employed to register protest. Partisan protest interpretation is likely under two
conditions: shared membership group identities
and circumstances that facilitate coalition formation. We have already observed that objectively
similar plights are not usually enough to lead to
partisan support. The poor white man is often
the last to view black activism as social protest,
and the large Mexican-American vote in Los Angeles was a liability rather than an asset for the
black candidate for mayor in 1969. Identification
through a common membership group that is a
salient component of the self-conception is required for partisanship.

The protest interpretation is understandable
as an invitation to form a coalition, or preparation
to enter into a coalition. When the possibility of
a mutually acceptable coalition for mutual gain
seems to be present, the third party is inclined
toward understanding the disruption as social protest. Lipsky (1968) proposes that activating third
parties is the principal way in which protest by
weak groups can hope for some success. The complexities of coalition theory are elaborations of a
principle of self-interest. In the broadest of terms,
coalitions are formed when the allies can do better together than they can separately vis-à-vis
some other group and when they can arrange
between them an acceptable division of the advantages that accrue from the coalition (Caplow,
1968). On this basis other disadvantaged minority
groups might support the efforts of militant

blacks, if they could be reasonably sure of gaining a substantial share of whatever concessions militancy wins from the target group. But since the concessions are likely to fall short of meeting black wants, they are unlikely to be divided. On the other hand, forming an alliance with the powerful target group may offer the prospect of greater rewards than an alliance with blacks. It is clear that contradictory tendencies are at work in this situation but that the problem of distributing limited benefits works against strong coalitions and against interpreting the other minority group's activism as social protest.

Coalitions with disruptive groups are more likely to be favorable for groups of higher standing whose own position is strengthened by adding the threat of disorder from the protesting group to their own established power. Groups and agencies who are in a position to serve as the intermediate link in distributing benefits to protestors may invite the protestors into a coalition by announcing acknowledgement of the latter's grievances. In return for support of the protestors, they offer the power of their own position in helping to legitimate the grievance claims and in applying pressure on the target group.

It is interesting that several principles converge to predict the overwhelming tendency for college and university faculties to view campus disruptions as social protest. First, the credibility-injustice principle is invoked by the faculty position of superordination to the students. Through constant contact and intimate familiarity with the circumstances of student life, faculty members readily understand the grievances of students by comparison with their own more favorable position. Second, the earlier student disorders were directed almost wholly against college administrations rather than faculty, making the latter a third party. Structurally, the faculty position makes them subject to strong pressures toward partisan involvement but makes partisanship on either side costly. Organizationally, the faculty belong to the same side as the administration but their contacts with students are more frequent and more crucial to the success of their teaching and research activities on the day to day basis. As third parties, faculty members sought neutrality by interpreting student disturbances as protest. Third,

by virtue of the residue of resentments from their own relationships with administrators, some faculty members were inclined to proffer a coalition to the students. On the basis that the higher status partner in a coalition ultimately gains more if the coalition lasts, this could be an effective tactic in strengthening the faculty position vis-à-vis administration. However, all of these principles operate differently when students take faculty as the target for their disruptions. Threat soon becomes more salient than appeal; neutrality is no longer attainable; and the only available coalition for faculty is with the administration. If it is true that the faculty have been the principal carriers for the protest interpretation of student disorders, the current move toward including faculty as targets of student disorder may have profound effects on the way these activities are seen in American society.

We have spoken as if the target group were precisely designated and the line between the target group and third parties were precise. But the protest message is usually vague and with varying targets, leaving considerable latitude for identifying the boundaries. Existing cleavages within the more broadly defined target group then mark off as third parties those segments to whom coalitions with the protestors would enhance their position in internecine strife. Thus "anti-establishment" whites may ally themselves symbolically with blacks in identifying "whitey" as referring only to "establishment" whites. Interpreting ghetto disorder as protest can then serve as an invitation to blacks to join them in a coalition.

OFFICIAL ACTIONS

We have spoken of the predisposition by various groups to identify disturbances under varying circumstances as social protest. But we have neglected thus far to assign enough importance to the actions of officials and formal leaders who must react conspicuously. On the basis of well established principles in the study of public opinion, opinion leadership and keynoting by officials should be a substantial determinant of public definitions (Katz and Lazarsfeld, 1955).

The problem of officials in the face of disturbance differs from the problem of others as action differs from attitude. The adoption of an attitude by itself has no consequences, and for most people its public enunciation has very little effect. But official action has consequences with respect to effectiveness, reactions provoked, and public commitments made. Hence, the public definition exhibited by officials is only a simple application of their private views when two conditions are met: the community definitions are overwhelmingly homogeneous; and officials have the resources to be certain their efforts are effective. When Federal Bureau of Investigation officials set out in the 1930's to eradicate gangster leaders, these conditions prevailed, and there was no need to explore the possibility that gangsterism was a protest against ethnic discrimination, cultural assimilation, and poverty. But when these conditions do not prevail, treating disturbances as protest can serve as a hedging tactic. It permits a restrained handling that does not create the expectation of immediate suppression of disturbances, without forestalling a shift toward a harder line after community sentiment and official capability have been tested. Official protest interpretation can serve as an effective hedge only in societies and communities where humanitarian values are strong relative to toughness values, so that failure of official action in the service of humanitarianism is excusable. But since this is true in many parts of American society, and because of the volatility of protest groups and the undependability of community support, official acknowledgment that disturbances are a form of protest has become progressively more common during the span of the last five years. This observation applies to almost all kinds of disturbances, and goes considerably beyond Etzioni's (1969) parallel observation that demonstrations have come increasingly to be accepted as a legitimate tactic of political persuasion.

The effect of these official responses is initially to keynote and legitimate the protest interpretation by various community segments. When these responses coincide with substantial prestigious community definitions of the events, the effect is further to establish a situational norm identifying the proper or publicly acceptable interpreta-

tion. Views that the disturbances are simply crime on a larger scale demanding strengthened law enforcement, or that they are sinister rebellions to be handled as internal wars, tend to be suppressed, even though many individuals and groups incline toward such views. The result is an unstable situation in which temporarily the socially sanctioned view sees disturbance as protest, while dissident views subsist as an audible rumbling in the background.

A strong government with assured community support is unlikely to tolerate massive disruption to the extent of viewing it as social protest. But when the grievance is not so limited and specific that it can be easily and quickly righted, when complete confidence in official capability to suppress massive crime or rebellion is lacking, or when community support is uncertain, the standard official approach is to explore the possibilities of resolving the confrontation through bargaining. Accounts of the 1967 racial disorders indicate repeated efforts to identify black representatives who could bargain for the protestors, and numerous instances of tentative bargains that failed because agents on one side or the other could not command the support of the group they were supposed to represent. Official entry into a bargaining relationship serves initially to validate a public definition of the disturbances as social protest, acknowledging the merit of some grievances.

When the potential for disturbances persists, the tendency is to move toward an accommodation through a system of routinized bargaining, such as we practice between management and labor unions or through the sensitive ward organization of machine politics. But the effect of a *routinized* bargaining relationship is to erode the protest meanings. Routinized bargaining and the protest interpretation are incompatible for several reasons. Protest tends to define open-ended commitments: no one can tell how much effort and money will ultimately be required to correct racial inequities in the United States. But bargaining can only occur with respect to specific and delimited demands, permitting concessions to be weighed against costs. The bargainer must view the exchange impersonally, seeing the other's demands as tactics. He cannot afford the sentimentality of viewing them as legitimate grievances. The attributes of spontaneity and naiveté that inhere in the folk concept of social protest are no longer met by organized, routinized disorders. Quite a different concept of protest, for instance, is involved in the routinized disorders of the London mobs described by Hobsbaum (1959).

As it becomes evident that the official approach is now the impersonal approach of bargaining, public sanction for the protest interpretation weakens. The result is either to free the suppressed unsympathetic interpretations in the pattern known as "backlash," or to accept the relationship as one of impersonal bargaining. If the former happens, there is pressure on public officials to discontinue bargaining. At the time of this writing this is clearly happening in connection with the pattern of bargaining by university officials with militant student groups. If the latter happens, minor disturbances come to be accepted as recurring minor annoyances. As in most contemporary labor disputes, public attitude is "what are they asking for this time?" assuming that the aim is competitive betterment rather than grievance correction.

Once again, if our theorizing is correct, the protest interpretation is inherently unstable, tending to transform into another definition as disturbances continue and recur.

CONCLUSION

A speculative analysis of this sort should be completed by bringing together all of the predictions and indicating where the sets of assumptions are redundant, where they are contradictory, and where they are complementary. But neither the theories nor the variables can be designated precisely enough at the present time to support this type of summation. Three observations will underline the main thrust of the approach we have employed.

First, the analysis exemplifies the assumption that meanings are attached to events as an aspect of intergroup process. The meaning attributed to a public disturbance expresses in large part the current and anticipated interaction between the various relevant groups. Meanings change both currently and retrospectively as the process unfolds and as intergroup relationships change.

Second, there are important shades of differences in protest interpretations that correspond with the specific types of intergroup process in which the interpreters are involved. Three kinds of relationships have been reviewed. One group may become *partisans* in conflict with the troublemakers, either because they belong to a group that can usefully make common cause against the target group while maintaining an advantageous position in a coalition with the troublemakers, or because of disaffection from their own group so that they ally with its enemies. Concern of the former with the protestors' grievances is constantly tinged with a comparison of benefits that each group gains from the coalition. For the latter, orientation toward conflict is the salient bond, and discomfiture of the target group easily becomes a more important aim than ameliorating the condition of the troublemakers.

A second group may see themselves as prime target for attack or as neutrals in danger of being drawn into conflict with the troublemakers, and thus respond with an offer of conciliation. Conciliation involves a generous interpretation of the troublemakers' activities, acknowledging their grievances, admitting fault, and identifying their activity as social protest. Grievances must be identified if conciliation is to proceed. But the salient condition easily becomes protection of the target group, and the protest interpretation is highly vulnerable in the event that conciliation is not reciprocated.

A third group, consisting of public officials and spokesmen, engages in bargaining by offering some amelioration in return for guarantees against further violence and disorder. But the impersonal and calculating nature of bargaining, especially as it recurs and is routinized, works against seeing the trouble as social protest. The disturbance soon becomes a move in a competitive game, to be met by minimal and calculated concessions. And as the masters of urban political machines have long understood, "buying off" protest leaders, directly, tends to be a less costly and more immediately effective tactic of bargaining than offering programs for amelioration of underlying grievances.

Our third and final observation is that interpreting public disorders as social protest is an unstable and precarious condition. It requires an optimally balanced set of conditions, and is difficult to maintain over an extended period of time. Insofar as such interpretations are favorable to social reform, it appears that they must be capitalized quickly, while conditions are favorable, through programs that can be implemented on a continuing basis by a more routinized and impersonal bargaining. Perhaps a residue of understanding that can be favorable to future reforms may remain in spite of community redefinition. Perhaps, also, reformers should not overestimate what can be gained by disorderly protest in relation to the many other means for effecting change.

REFERENCES

Bayley, David H. "The Pedagogy of Democracy: Coercive Public Protest in India." *American Political Science Review* 56 (September 1962): 663–672.

Blau, Peter. "Justice in Social Exchange." *Sociological Inquiry* 34 (Spring 1964a):193–206.

———. *Exchange and Power in Social Life.* New York: John Wiley and Sons, 1964b.

Blumer, Herbert. "Collective Behavior." *An Outline of the Principles of Sociology.* Edited by Robert E. Park. New York: Barnes and Noble, 1939, pp. 221–280.

Boskin, Joseph. "Violence in the Ghettoes: A Consensus of Attitudes." *New Mexico Quarterly* 37 (Winter 1968):317–334.

Caplow, Theodore. *Two Against One: Coalitions in Triads.* Englewood Cliffs, N.J.: Prentice-Hall, Inc., 1968.

Coser, Lewis. "Conflict: Social Aspects." *International Encyclopedia of the Social Sciences,* Vol. 3, 1968, pp. 232–236.

Diggory, James C. "Some Consequences of Proximity to a Disease Threat." *Sociometry* 19 (March 1956):47–53.

Dynes, Russell and Enrico L. Quarantelli. "What Looting in Civil Disturbances Really Means." *Trans-action* 5 (May 1968):9–14.

Etzioni, Amitai. "Demonstrations Becoming a Legitimate Mode of Expression." *Los Angeles Times* (May 18, 1968):Section F, p. 2.

Fogelson, Robert M. "Violence as Protest." *Urban Riots: Violence and Social Change.* Edited by Robert H. Connery. New York: Academy of Political Science, 1968, pp. 25–41.

Gouldner, Alvin W. "The Norm of Reciprocity: A Preliminary Statement." *American Sociological Review* 25 (April 1960):161–178.

Governor's Commission on the Los Angeles Riots. *Violence in the City—An End or a Beginning?* Los Angeles, 1965.

Grimshaw, Allen D. "Three Views of Urban Violence: Civil Disturbance, Racial Revolt, Class Assault." *Riots and Rebellion.* Edited by Louis H. Masotti and Don R. Bowen. Beverly Hills, California: Sage Publications, 1968, pp. 103–119.

Harper, Dean. "White Reactions to a Riot." *Riots and Rebellion.* Edited by Louis H. Masotti and Don R. Bowen. Beverly Hills, California: Sage Publications, 1968, pp. 307–314.

Hobsbaum, Eric J. *Social Bandits and Primitive Rebels.* Glencoe, Ill.: Free Press, 1959.

Homans, George. *Social Behavior: Its Elementary Norms.* New York: Harcourt, Brace, and World, 1961.

Horowitz, Irving L. and Martin Liebowitz. "Social Deviance and Political Marginality: Toward a Redefinition of the Relation Between Sociology and Politics." *Social Problems* 15 (Winter 1968):280–296.

Katz, Elihu and Paul Lazarsfeld. *Personal Influence.* Glencoe, Ill.: Free Press, 1955.

Kelley, Harold H. "Attribution Theory in Social Psychology." Pp. 192–238 in Nebraska Symposium on Motivation, 1967.

Lang, Kurt and Gladys E. Lang. "Racial Disturbances as Collective Protest." *Riots and Rebellion.* Edited by Louis H. Masoti and Don R. Bowen. Beverly Hills, Calif.: Sage Publications, 1968, pp. 121–130.

Lee, Alfred McClung and Norman D. Humphrey. *Race Riot.* New York: Dryden Press, 1943.

Lemert, Edwin. *Social Pathology.* New York: McGraw-Hill, 1951.

Lewin, Kurt. "Self-hatred Among Jews." *Contemporary Jewish Record* 4 (1941):219–232.

Lipsky, Michael. "Protest as a Political Resource." *American Political Science Review* 62 (December, 1968): 1144–1158.

Merton, Robert K. "The Self-fulfilling Prophecy." *Antioch Review* 8 (Summer 1948):193–210.

Merton, Robert K. and Alice S. Kitt. "Contributions to the Theory of Reference Group Behavior." *Studies* in the Scope and Method of "The American Soldier." Edited by Merton and Paul F. Lazarsfeld. Glencoe, Ill.: Free Press, 1950, pp. 40–105.

Morris, Richard T. and Vincent Jeffries. Los Angeles Riot Study: The White Reaction Study. Los Angeles: U.C.L.A. Institute of Government and Public Affairs, 1967.

National Advisory Commission on Civil Disorders. Report of the National Advisory Commission on Civil Disorders (The Kerner Report). Washington: U.S. Government Printing Office, 1968.

Olsen, Marvin E. "Perceived Legitimacy of Social Protest Actions." Social Problems 15 (Winter 1968):297–310.

Park, Robert E. and Ernest W. Burgess. Introduction to the Science of Sociology. Chicago: University of Chicago Press, 1921.

Random House. Random House Dictionary of the English Language. New York: Random House, 1967.

Rossi, Peter H., Richard A. Berk, David P. Boesel, Bettye K. Eidson, and W. Eugene Groves. "Between White and Black: The Faces of American Institutions in the Ghetto." Pp. 69–215 in Supplemental Studies for the National Advisory Commission on Civil Disorders. Washington: U.S. Government Printing Office, 1968.

Rudwick, Elliott M. Race Riot in East St. Louis, July 2, 1917. Carbondale: Southern Illinois University Press, 1964.

Runciman, W. G. Relative Deprivation and Social Justice. Berkeley: University of California Press, 1966.

Sevareid, Eric. "Dissent or Destruction?" Look 31 (September 5, 1967):21 ff.

Silver, Allan A. "Official Interpretations of Racial Riots." Urban Riots: Violence and Social Change. Edited by Robert H. Connery. New York: Academy of Political Science, 1968.

Simmel, Georg. Conflict and the Web of Group-Affiliations. Translated by Kurt Wolff and Reinhard Bendix. New York: Free Press, 1955.

Smelser, Neil J. Theory of Collective Behavior. New York: Free Press, 1963.

Tomlinson, T. M. and David O. Sears. Los Angeles Riot Study: Negro Attitudes Toward the Riot. Los Angeles: U.C.L.A. Institute of Government and Public Affairs, 1967.

Turner, Ralph H. "The Normative Coherence of Folk Concepts." Research Studies of the State College of Washington 25 (1957):127–136.

———. "Collective Behavior and Conflict: New Theoretical Frameworks." Sociological Quarterly 5 (Spring 1964):122–132.

Turner, Ralph H. and Lewis M. Killian. Collective Behavior. Englewood Cliffs, N.J.: Prentice-Hall, 1957.

von Wiese, Leopold. Systematic Sociology. Adapted and amplified by Howard Becker. New York: John Wiley and Sons, 1932.

Waller, Willard and Reuben Hill. The Family: A Dynamic Interpretation. New York: Dryden Press, 1951.

SELECTED REFERENCES
PART TWO

Blumer, Herbert. "Social Problems as Collective Behavior." Social Problems 18 (Winter 1971), pp. 298–306. Social problems viewed as subjective interpretations and group responses.

Briedis, Catherine. "Marginal Deviants: Teenage Girls Experience Community Response to Premarital Sex and Pregnancy." Social Problems 22 (April 1975), pp. 480–493. Parental and community reaction to deviant behavior.

Couch, Carl J. "Dimensions of Association in Collective Behavior Episodes." Sociometry, vol. 33 (December 1970), pp. 457–471. Challenges the need for a special set of concepts in the examination of collective, as opposed to societal, behavior.

Davis, Fred. "The Cab Driver and His Fare: Facets of a Fleeting Relationship." American Journal of Sociology, vol. 65 (September 1959), pp. 158–165. Participant-observation study of a special kind of human encounter.

Denzin, Norman K. "The Significant Others of a College Population." Sociological Quarterly, vol. 7 (Summer 1966), pp. 298–310. Based on a distinction made by Kuhn, the article identifies role-specific "significant others" and "orientation others."

Farberman, Harvey H. "A Criminogenic Market Structure: The Automobile Industry." The Sociological Quarterly, vol. 16 (Autumn 1975), pp. 438–457. A symbolic interactionist perspective on illegal actions by an established organization.

Garfinkel, Harold. "Conditions of Successful Degradation Ceremonies." American Journal of Sociology, vol. 61 (March 1956), pp. 420–424. An early precursor of ethnomethodology and labeling.

————. "Studies of the Routine Grounds of Everyday Activities." *Social Problems*, vol. 11 (Winter 1964), pp. 225–250. Inspired by Alfred Schuetz's phenomenology. An insightful delineation of taken-for-granted elements in everyday human relationships.

Goffman, Erving. *Asylums.* Garden City, New York: Doubleday & Company, Inc., 1961. Description of "total institutions" (prisons, mental hospitals, convents, orphanages, and other societies-in-miniature) and the kinds of interaction typifying them.

————. "On Face-Work: An Analysis of Ritual Elements in Social Interaction." *Psychiatry*, vol. 18 (August 1955), pp. 213–231. Discusses the elaborate social rituals that function primarily to reduce the likelihood of invalidation of self-image, particularly in casual contacts.

Gross, Edward, and Gregory P. Stone. "Embarrassment and the Analysis of Role Requirements." *American Journal of Sociology*, vol. 60 (July 1964), pp. 1–15. Study of 1,000 instances of recalled embarrassment, revealing some major sociological functions of deliberate embarrassment.

Hall, Peter M. "A Symbolic Interactionist Analysis of Politics." *Sociological Inquiry* 42, (3–4, 1972), pp. 35–70. A detailed application of concepts to the political process.

Kuhn, Manford H. "The Reference Group Reconsidered." *The Sociological Quarterly*, vol. 5 (Winter 1964), pp. 6–21. Distinguishing between "group" and "category," Kuhn proposes new ways of defining the idea of "the other."

Lauer, Robert H. "Social Movements: An Interactionist Analysis." *Sociological Quarterly*, vol. 13 (Summer 1972), pp. 315–328. A study of the LSD movement led by Timothy Leary.

Manis, Jerome G. "The Concept of Social Problems: Vox Populi and Sociological Analysis." *Social Problems*, vol. 21 (1974), pp. 305–315. A contrasting position to the article by Blumer cited above.

Martin, William B. "The Negotiated Order of Teachers in Team Teaching Situations." *Sociology of Education*, 40 (Spring 1975), pp. 202–222. Analysis of classroom behavior.

McPhail, Clark. "Student Walkout: A Fortuitous Examination of Elementary Collective Behavior." *Social Problems*, vol. 16 (Spring 1969), pp. 441–455. An empirical challenge to the customary separations of explanations of collective "unstructured" behavior and routine social behavior.

Mead, George Herbert. *Mind, Self and Society.* Chicago: The University of Chicago Press, 1934, pp. 260–328. Mead here explores the complex relationship between society and the individual.

Scheff, Thomas. "Negotiating Reality: Notes on Power in the Assessment of Responsibility." *Social Problems,* vol. 16 (Summer 1968), pp. 3–17. A symbolic-interactionist view of power.

Schmitt, Raymond L. *The Reference Other Orientation: An Extension of the Reference Group Concept.* Carbondale and Edwardsville: Southern Illinois University Press, 1972. A careful examination of the concept of "reference group."

Stryker, Sheldon. "Relationships of Married Offspring and Parent: A Test of Mead's Theory." *American Journal of Sociology*, vol. 62 (November 1956), pp. 308–319. Empirical tests of hypotheses on role-taking drawn from propositions of Mead.

Turner, Ralph H. "Role-Taking: Process versus Conformity." In Arnold M. Rose (ed.) *Human Behavior and Social Processes.* Boston: Houghton Mifflin Company, 1962, pp. 20–40. Makes an important distinction between role-taking and role-making.

————. "Role-Taking, Role Standpoint, and Reference-Group Behavior." *American Journal of Sociology*, vol. 61 (January 1956), pp. 316–328. Clarification of certain important social-psychological concepts.

Urry, John. *Reference Groups and Theory of Revolution.* London: Routledge and Kegan Paul, 1973. Uses the postulates of symbolic interactionism in studying the genesis of revolutionary consciousness in Indonesia in the twentieth century.

Warriner, Charles K. *The Emergence of Society.* Homewood, Illinois: Dorsey Press, 1970. Examines the social-psychological phenomena involved in the formation and persistence of social forms and processes.

PART three

Self

Among the concepts of symbolic interactionism, none has received more discussion and investigation than that of the "self." During the past few decades a host of books and articles by social psychologists, both symbolic interactionists and others, have explored this concept. The formation of the self is a crucially important aspect of the process of socialization (see proposition 2). Moreover, the concept of the self is fundamental to the major symbolic interactionist principle expressed in proposition 4: Human beings are active in shaping their own behavior.

As we pointed out in the Introduction to this book, the idea of self received considerable attention by some of the late nineteenth- and early twentieth-century philosophers and psychologists. To William James, Josiah Royce, James Mark Baldwin, and others, the development and functioning of the self were central to the study of social life. With the rise of Watsonian behaviorism, however, the concept was rejected as subjective and unscientific. In turn, behaviorism has been criticized for neglecting important, though covert, aspects of human behavior.

Mead's social behaviorism stressed the process by which individuals become aware of and learn to guide their behavior. The article by Meltzer summarizing Mead's approach (in Part One) discussed the major contributions and problems of his concept of self. The ambiguity of Mead's work has been paralleled by recent divergences among social psychologists in defining and empirically studying the idea of the self. Among current symbolic interactionists, those who see the self as a dynamic process—of viewing and responding to one's own behavior—emphasize participant-observation, interviews, and Cooley's "sympathetic introspection." Those who see the self as a structure of internalized roles stress such devices as the "Who Am I" Test (also known as the Twenty-Statements Test). Finally, some investigators, conceiving the self as a set of attitudes or evaluations, use self-rating scales in their research.

The first two selections in Part III deal with two distinct facets of the self: object and actor. The selection from Cooley's work describes how individuals come to experience themselves as objects. Through the attitudes of others, persons learn to "see" and to evaluate their appearance, attitudes, and behavior. It is in this sense that the self is sometimes defined as "the individual as known to the individual." Cooley terms this self-reflective process, which closely resembles his recommended method for the acquisition of social knowledge, the "looking-glass self."

The Erving Goffman article concerns the individual as subject rather than object. Here the self is considered in its active aspect. Individuals are capable not only of viewing their own behavior, but also of directing and guiding this behavior and of shaping the images of themselves available to others. In explaining his view of the self, Goffman draws on drama, literature, and observation. His perspective is dramaturgical—interpreting the individual as an actor in a theatrical performance.

Gregg S. Wilkinson uses the dramaturgical perspective as a way of interpreting behavior that psychiatrists diagnose as mental illness. Though Wilkinson uses the term "identity," rather than self or self-identity, his analysis of the individual as actor reveals the importance of one's skills in the presentation of self to others. His data suggest that dramaturgic incompetence—mismanaged performances—appears to be used as evidence of psychiatric disorder. Moreover, degree of dramaturgic incompetence, and its components, is found to be associated with diagnosed degree of psychiatric disorder. On these grounds, Wilkinson suggests alternative conceptualizations to the medical model of mental "illness."

William L. Kolb's article evaluates two of Mead's central concepts that have received scant study. Although the "I" and the "Me" have been analytically useful, Kolb points out their basic lack of clarity. He suggests that their ambiguity stems from the complexity of the relationship between social and biological phenomena.

A series of experiments by John Kinch was designed to test a proposition he derived from the Mead-Cooley theory of self-conception. He developed four hypotheses to test the basic proposition that individuals' self-conceptions are based on their conception of others' behavior toward them.

Early contributors to symbolic interactionism were much concerned with the development of the self. While stressing the dynamic and diverse nature of self-conceptions, their emphasis was placed upon the socialization process in childhood. More recently, attention has been given to the critical changes in self-conceptions which take place during the adult years. An example is the article by Helena Znaniecki Lopata. She examines the impact of marriage and widowhood upon women's self-identities. One of her noteworthy, and perhaps surprising, findings concerns the stronger consequences these life-stages have upon the self-identities of the more highly educated women in her sample.

E. L. Quarantelli and Joseph Cooper describe a study of professional self-conception and its relation to the generalized other. Using a structured questionnaire, a technique not often employed by symbolic interactionists, they apply a ten-point scale to measure development of the professional self-image.

No theory of human behavior can be restricted to a single human grouping. Edwin D. Driver's comparison of self-conceptions in India and the United States, however, is among the few cross-cultural studies. His data are used to assess the validity of the Twenty-Statements Test.

Some of the selections composing this Part employ concepts and techniques devised by Manford H. Kuhn. Charles W. Tucker's article raises crucial questions about Kuhn's self-theory and its most common research tool. Dealing with such problems as the "situationality" of responses to the Twenty-Statements Test, and the questionable content-analysis procedures used in analyzing the responses, he points out a lack of fit between the theory and the technique. Tucker's analysis thereby makes a valuable contribution to what he has called the "age of inquiry" in symbolic interactionism.

While these articles represent substantial divergences in interpretation and research orientation, they agree in their central thesis that self-conceptions are largely derived from experiences with others and are crucial sources of individual and interpersonal behavior. These articles are only a small segment of the rapidly growing theoretical and empirical literature on what might be considered the core of the human personality.

Looking-Glass Self

In a very large and interesting class of cases the social reference takes the form of a somewhat definite imagination of how one's self—that is any idea he appropriates—appears in a particular mind, and the kind of self-feeling one has is determined by the attitude toward this attributed to that other mind. A social self of this sort might be called the reflected or looking-glass self:

"Each to each a looking-glass
Reflects the other that doth pass."

As we see our face, figure, and dress in the glass, and are interested in them because they are ours, and pleased or otherwise with them according as they do or do not answer to what we should like them to be; so in imagination we perceive in another's mind some thought of our appearance, manners, aims, deeds, character, friends, and so on, and are variously affected by it.

A self-idea of this sort seems to have three principal elements: the imagination of our appearance to the other person; the imagination of his judgment of that appearance, and some sort of self-feeling, such as pride or mortification. The comparison with a looking-glass hardly suggests the second element, the imagined judgment, which is quite essential. The thing that moves us to pride or shame is not the mere mechanical reflection of ourselves, but an imputed sentiment, the imagined effect of this reflection upon another's mind. This is evident from the fact that the character and weight of that other, in whose mind we see ourselves, makes all the difference with

Reprinted by permission of Charles Scribner's Sons from *Human Nature and the Social Order* by Charles Horton Cooley.

our feeling. We are ashamed to seem evasive in the presence of a straightforward man, cowardly in the presence of a brave one, gross in the eyes of a refined one, and so on. We always imagine, and in imagining share, the judgments of the other mind. A man will boast to one person of an action—say some sharp transaction in trade—which he would be ashamed to own to another.

. . .

The process by which self-feeling of the looking-glass sort develops in children may be followed without much difficulty. Studying the movements of others as closely as they do they soon see a connection between their own acts and changes in those movements; that is, they perceive their own influence or power over persons. The child appropriates the visible actions of his parent or nurse, over which he finds he has some control, in quite the same way as he appropriates one of his own members or a plaything, and he will try to do things with this new possession, just as he will with his hand or his rattle. A girl six months old will attempt in the most evident and deliberate manner to attract attention to herself, to set going by her actions some of those movements of other persons that she has appropriated. She has tasted the joy of being a cause, of exerting social power, and wishes more of it. She will tug at her mother's skirts, wriggle, gurgle, stretch out her arms, etc., all the time watching for the hoped-for effect. These performances often give the child, even at this age, an appearance of what is called affectation, that is, she seems to be unduly preoccupied with what other people think of her.

Affectation, at any age, exists when the passion to influence others seems to overbalance the established character and give it an obvious twist or pose. It is instructive to find that even Darwin was, in his childhood, capable of departing from truth for the sake of making an impression. "For instance," he says in his autobiography, "I once gathered much valuable fruit from my father's trees and hid it in the shrubbery, and then ran in breathless haste to spread the news that I had discovered a hoard of stolen fruit."[1]

The young performer soon learns to be different things to different people, showing that he begins to apprehend personality and to foresee its operation. If the mother or nurse is more tender than just, she will almost certainly be "worked" by systematic weeping. It is a matter of common observation that children often behave worse with their mother than with other and less sympathetic people. Of the new persons that a child sees, it is evident that some make a strong impression and awaken a desire to interest and please them, while others are indifferent or repugnant. Sometimes the reason can be perceived or guessed, sometimes not; but the fact of selective interest, admiration, prestige, is obvious before the end of the second year. By that time a child already cares much for the reflection of himself upon one personality and little for that upon another. Moreover, he soon claims intimate and tractable persons as *mine,* classes them among his other possessions, and maintains his ownership against all comers. M., at three years of age, vigorously resented R.'s claim upon their mother. The latter was *"my* mamma," whenever the point was raised.

Strong joy and grief depend upon the treatment this rudimentary social self receives. In the case of M. I noticed as early as the fourth month a "hurt" way of crying which seemed to indicate a sense of personal slight. It was quite different from the cry of pain or that of anger, but seemed about the same as the cry of fright. The slightest tone of reproof would produce it. On the other hand, if people took notice and laughed and encouraged, she was hilarious. At about fifteen months old she had become "a perfect little actress," seeming to live largely in imaginations of

her effect upon other people. She constantly and obviously laid traps for attention, and looked abashed or wept at any signs of disapproval or indifference. At times it would seem as if she could not get over these repulses, but would cry long in a grieved way, refusing to be comforted. If she hit upon any little trick that made people laugh she would be sure to repeat it, laughing loudly and affectedly in imitation. She had quite a repertory of these small performances, which she would display to a sympathetic audience, or even try upon strangers. I have seen her at sixteen months, when R. refused to give her the scissors, sit down and make-believe cry, putting up her under lip and snuffling, meanwhile looking up now and then to see what effect she was producing.[2]

In such phenomena we have plainly enough, it seems to me, the germ of personal ambition of every sort. Imagination co-operating with instinctive self-feeling has already created a social "I," and this has become a principal object of interest and endeavor.

Progress from this point is chiefly in the way of a greater definiteness, fulness, and inwardness in the imagination of the other's state of mind. A little child thinks of and tries to elicit certain visible or audible phenomena, and does not go back of them; but what a grown-up person desires to produce in others is an internal, invisible condition which his own richer experience enables him to imagine, and of which expression is only the sign. Even adults, however, make no separation between what other people think and the visible expression of that thought. They imagine the whole thing at once, and their idea differs from that of a child chiefly in the comparative richness and complexity of the elements that accompany and interpret the visible or audible sign. There is also a progress from the naive to the subtle in socially self-assertive action. A child obviously and simply, at first, does things for effect. Later there is an endeavor to suppress the appearance of doing so; affection, indifference, contempt, etc., are simulated to hide the real wish to affect the self-image. It is perceived that an obvious seeking after good opinion is weak and disagreeable.

---

[1] *Life and Letters of Charles Darwin,* by F. Darwin, p. 27.

[2] This sort of thing is very familiar to observers of children. See, for instance, Miss Shinn's Notes on the Development of a Child, p. 153.

The Presentation of Self to Others

When an individual enters the presence of others, they commonly seek to acquire information about him or to bring into play information about him already possessed. They will be interested in his general socio-economic status, his conception of self, his attitude toward them, his competence, his trustworthiness, etc. Although some of this information seems to be sought almost as an end in itself, there are usually quite practical reasons for acquiring it. Information about the individual helps to define the situation, enabling others to know in advance what he will expect of them and what they may expect of him. Informed in these ways, the others will know how best to act in order to call forth a desired response from him.

For those present, many sources of information become accessible and many carriers (or "sign-vehicles") become available for conveying this information. If unacquainted with the individual, observers can glean clues from his conduct and appearance which allow them to apply their previous experience with individuals roughly similar to the one before them or, more important, to apply untested stereotypes to him. They can also assume from past experience that only individuals of a particular kind are likely to be found in a given social setting. They can rely on what the individual says about himself or on documentary evidence he provides as to who and what he is. If they know, or know of, the individual by virtue of experience prior to the interaction, they can rely on assumptions as to the persistence and generality of psychological traits as a means of predicting his present and future behavior.

However, during the period in which the individual is in the immediate presence of the others, few events may occur which directly provide the others with the conclusive information they will need if they are to direct wisely their own activity. Many crucial facts lie beyond the time and place of interaction or lie concealed within it. For example, the "true" or "real" attitudes, beliefs, and emotions of the individual can be ascertained only indirectly, through his avowals or through what appears to be involuntary expressive behavior. Similarly, if the individual offers the others a product or service, they will often find that during the interaction there will be no time and place immediately available for eating the pudding that the proof can be found in. They will be forced to accept some events as conventional or natural signs of something not directly available to the senses. In Ichheiser's terms,[1] the individual will have to act so that he intentionally or unintentionally *expresses* himself, and the others will in turn have to be *impressed* in some way by him.

The expressiveness of the individual (and therefore his capacity to give impressions) appears to involve two radically different kinds of sign activity: the expression that he *gives*, and the expression that he *gives off*. The first involves verbal symbols or their substitutes which he uses admittedly and solely to convey the information that he and the others are known to attach to

[1] Gustav Ichheiser, "Misunderstandings in Human Relations," Supplement to *The American Journal of Sociology.* LV (September 1949), pp. 6–7.

these symbols. This is communication in the traditional and narrow sense. The second involves a wide range of action that others can treat as symptomatic of the actor, the expectation being that the action was performed for reasons other than the information conveyed in this way. As we shall have to see, this distinction has an only initial validity. The individual does of course intentionally convey misinformation by means of both of these types of communication, the first involving deceit, the second feigning.

Taking communication in both its narrow and broad sense, one finds that when the individual is in the immediate presence of others, his activity will have a promissory character. The others are likely to find that they must accept the individual on faith, offering him a just return while he is present before them in exchange for something whose true value will not be established until after he has left their presence. (Of course, the others also live by inference in their dealings with the physical world, but it is only in the world of social interaction that the objects about which they make inferences will purposely facilitate and hinder this inferential process.) The security that they justifiably feel in making inferences about the individual will vary, of course, depending on such factors as the amount of information they already possess about him, but no amount of such past evidence can entirely obviate the necessity of acting on the basis of inferences. As William I. Thomas suggested:

> It is also highly important for us to realize that we do not as a matter of fact lead our lives, make our decisions, and reach our goals in everyday life either statistically or scientifically. We live by inference. I am, let us say, your guest. You do not know, you cannot determine scientifically, that I will not steal your money or your spoons. But inferentially I will not, and inferentially you have me as a guest.[2]

Let us now turn from the others to the point of view of the individual who presents himself before them. He may wish them to think highly of him, or to think that he thinks highly of them, or to perceive how in fact he feels toward them, or to obtain no clear-cut impression; he may wish to ensure sufficient harmony so that the interaction can be sustained, or to defraud, get rid of, confuse, mislead, antagonize, or insult them. Regardless of the particular objective which the individual has in mind and of his motive for having this objective, it will be in his interests to control the conduct of the others, especially their responsive treatment of him.[3] This control is achieved largely by influencing the definition of the situation which the others come to formulate, and he can influence this definition by expressing himself in such a way as to give them the kind of impression that will lead them to act voluntarily in accordance with his own plan. Thus, when an individual appears in the presence of others, there will usually be some reason for him to mobilize his activity so that it will convey an impression to others which it is in his interests to convey. Since a girl's dormitory mates will glean evidence of her popularity from the calls she receives on the phone, we can suspect that some girls will arrange for calls to be made, and Willard Waller's finding can be anticipated:

> It has been reported by many observers that a girl who is called to the telephone in the dormitories will often allow herself to be called several times, in order to give all the other girls ample opportunity to hear her paged.[4]

Of the two kinds of communication—expressions given and expressions given off—this report will be primarily concerned with the latter, with the more theatrical and contextual kind, the nonverbal, presumably unintentional kind, whether this communication be purposely engineered or not. As an example of what we must try to examine, I would like to cite at length a novelistic incident in which Preedy, a vacationing Englishman,

---

[2] Quoted in E. H. Volkart, editor, *Social Behavior and Personality.* Contributions of W. I. Thomas to Theory and Social Research (New York: Social Science Research Council, 1951), p. 5.

[3] Here I owe much to an unpublished paper by Tom Burns of the University of Edinburgh. He presents the argument that in all interaction a basic underlying theme is the desire of each participant to guide and control the responses made by the others present. A similar argument has been advanced by Jay Haley in a recent unpublished paper, but in regard to a special kind of control, that having to do with defining the nature of the relationship of those involved in the interaction.

[4] Willard Waller, "The Rating and Dating Complex," *American Sociological Review,* II, p. 730.

makes his first appearance on the beach of his summer hotel in Spain:

> But in any case he took care to avoid catching anyone's eye. First of all, he had to make it clear to those potential companions of his holiday that they were of no concern to him whatsoever. He stared through them, round them, over them—eyes lost in space. The beach might have been empty. If by chance a ball was thrown his way, he looked surprised; then let a smile of amusement lighten his face (Kindly Preedy), looked round dazed to see that there *were* people on the beach, tossed it back with a smile to himself and not a smile *at* the people, and then resumed carelessly his nonchalant survey of space.
>
> But it was time to institute a little parade, the parade of the Ideal Preedy. By devious handlings he gave any who wanted to look a chance to see the title of his book—a Spanish translation of Homer, classic thus, but not daring, cosmopolitan too—and then gathered together his beach-wrap and bag into a neat sand-resistant pile (Methodical and Sensible Preedy), rose slowly to stretch at ease his huge frame (Big-Cat Preedy), and tossed aside his sandals (Carefree Preedy, after all).
>
> The marriage of Preedy and the sea! There were alternative rituals. The first involved the stroll that turns into a run and a dive straight into the water, thereafter smoothing into a strong splashless crawl towards the horizon. But of course not really to the horizon. Quite suddenly he would turn on to his back and thrash great white splashes with his legs, somehow thus showing that he could have swum further had he wanted to, and then would stand up a quarter out of water for all to see who it was.
>
> The alternative course was simpler, it avoided the cold-water shock and it avoided the risk of appearing too high-spirited. The point was to appear to be so used to the sea, the Mediterranean, and this particular beach, that one might as well be in the sea as out of it. It involved a slow stroll down and into the edge of the water—not even noticing his toes were wet, land and water all the same to *him!*—with his eyes up at the sky gravely surveying portents, invisible to others, of the weather (Local Fisherman Preedy).[5]

The novelist means us to see that Preedy is improperly concerned with the extensive impressions he feels his sheer bodily action is giving off to those around him. We can malign Preedy further by assuming that he has acted merely in order to give a particular impression, that this is a

[5] William Sansom, *A Contest of Ladies* (London: Hogarth, 1956), pp. 230–32.

false impression, and that the others present receive either no impression at all, or worse still, the impression that Preedy is affectedly trying to cause them to receive this particular impression. But the important point for us here is that the kind of impression Preedy thinks he is making is in fact the kind of impression that others correctly and incorrectly glean from someone in their midst.

I have said that when an individual appears before others his actions will influence the definition of the situation which they come to have. Sometimes the individual will act in a thoroughly calculating manner, expressing himself in a given way solely in order to give the kind of impression to others that is likely to evoke from them a specific response he is concerned to obtain. Sometimes the individual will be calculating in his activity but be relatively unaware that this is the case. Sometimes he will intentionally and consciously express himself in a particular way, but chiefly because the tradition of his group or social status require this kind of expression and not because of any particular response (other than vague acceptance or approval) that is likely to be evoked from those impressed by the expression. Sometimes the traditions of an individual's role will lead him to give a well-designed impression of a particular kind and yet he may be neither consciously nor unconsciously disposed to create such an impression. The others, in their turn, may be suitably impressed by the individual's efforts to convey something, or may misunderstand the situation and come to conclusions that are warranted neither by the individual's intent nor by the facts. In any case, in so far as the others act *as if* the individual had conveyed a particular impression, we may take a functional or pragmatic view and say that the individual has "effectively" projected a given definition of the situation and "effectively" fostered the understanding that a given state of affairs obtains.

There is one aspect of the others' response that bears special comment here. Knowing that the individual is likely to present himself in a light that is favorable to him, the others may divide what they witness into two parts; a part that is relatively easy for the individual to manipulate at will, being chiefly his verbal assertions, and a part in regard to which he seems to have little concern or control, being chiefly derived from the expressions he gives off. The others may then use what are considered to be the ungovernable aspects of his expressive behavior as a check upon the validity of what is conveyed by the governable aspects. In this a fundamental asymmetry is demonstrated in the communication process, the individual presumably being aware of only one stream of his communication, the witnesses of this stream and one other. For example, in Shetland Isle one crofter's wife, in serving native dishes to a visitor from the mainland of Britain, would listen with a polite smile to his polite claims of liking what he was eating; at the same time she would take note of the rapidity with which the visitor lifted his fork or spoon to his mouth, the eagerness with which he passed food into his mouth, and the gusto expressed in chewing the food, using these signs as a check on the stated feelings of the eater. The same woman, in order to discover what one acquaintance (A) "actually" thought of another acquaintance (B), would wait until B was in the presence of A but engaged in conversation with still another person (C). She would then covertly examine the facial expressions of A as he regarded B in conversation with C. Not being in conversation with B, and not being directly observed by him, A would sometimes relax usual constraints and tactful deceptions, and freely express what he was "actually" feeling about B. This Shetlander, in short, would observe the unobserved observer.

Now given the fact that others are likely to check up on the more controllable aspects of behavior by means of the less controllable, one can expect that sometimes the individual will try to exploit this very possibility, guiding the impression he makes through behavior felt to be reliably informing.[6] For example, in gaining admission to a tight social circle, the participant observer may not only wear an accepting look while listening to an informant, but may also be careful to wear the same look when observing the informant talking to others, observers of the observer will then not as easily discover where he actually stands. A specific illustration may be cited from Shetland Isle. When a neighbor dropped in to have a cup of tea, he would ordinarily wear at least a hint of an expectant warm smile as he passed through the door into the cottage. Since lack of physical obstructions outside the cottage and lack of light within it usually made it possible to observe the visitor unobserved as he approached the house, islanders sometimes took pleasure in watching the visitor drop whatever expression he was manifesting and replace it with a sociable one just before reaching the door. However, some visitors, in appreciating that this examination was occurring, would blindly adopt a social face a long distance from the house, thus ensuring the projection of a constant image.

This kind of control upon the part of the individual reinstates the symmetry of the communication process, and sets the stage for a kind of information game—a potentially infinite cycle of concealment, discovery, false revelation, and rediscovery. It should be added that since the others are likely to be relatively unsuspicious of the presumably unguided aspect of the individual's conduct, he can gain much by controlling it. The others of course may sense that the individual is manipulating the presumably spontaneous aspects of his behavior, and seek in this very act of manipulation some shading of conduct that the individual has not managed to control. This again provides a check upon the individual's behavior, this time his presumably uncalculated behavior, thus re-establishing the asymmetry of the communication process. Here I would like only to add the suggestion that the arts of piercing an individual's effort at calculated unintentionality seem better developed than our capacity to manipulate our own behavior, so that regardless of how many steps have occurred in the information game, the witness is likely to have the advantage over the actor, and the initial asymmetry of the communication process is likely to be retained.

When we allow that the individual projects a definition of the situation when he appears before others, we must also see that the others, however passive their role may seem to be, will themselves effectively project a definition of the

[6] The widely read and rather sound writings of Stephen Potter are concerned in part with signs that can be engineered to give a shrewd observer the apparently incidental cues he needs to discover concealed virtues the gamesman does not in fact possess.

situation by virtue of their response to the individual and by virtue of any lines of action they initiate to him. Ordinarily the definitions of the situation projected by the several different participants are sufficiently attuned to one another so that open contradiction will not occur. I do not mean that there will be the kind of consensus that arises when each individual present candidly expresses what he really feels and honestly agrees with the expressed feelings of the others present. This kind of harmony is an optimistic ideal and in any case not necessary for the smooth working of society. Rather, each participant is expected to suppress his immediate heartfelt feelings, conveying a view of the situation which he feels the others will be able to find at least temporarily acceptable. The maintenance of this surface of agreement, this veneer of consensus, is facilitated by each participant concealing his own wants behind statements which assert values to which everyone present feels obliged to give lip service. Further, there is usually a kind of division of definitional labor. Each participant is allowed to establish the tentative official ruling regarding matters which are vital to him but not immediately important to others, e.g., the rationalizations and justifications by which he accounts for his past activity. In exchange for this courtesy he remains silent or non-committal on matters important to others but not immediately important to him. We have then a kind of interactional *modus vivendi*. Together the participants contribute to a single overall definition of the situation which involves not so much a real agreement as to what exists but rather a real agreement as to whose claims concerning what issues will be temporarily honored. Real agreement will also exist concerning the desirability of avoiding an open conflict of definitions of the situation.[7] I will refer to this level of agreement as a "working consensus." It is to be understood that the working consensus established in one interaction setting will be quite different in content from the working consensus established in a different type of setting. Thus, between two friends at lunch, a reciprocal show of affection, respect, and concern for the other is maintained. In service occupations, on the other hand, the specialist often maintains an image of disinterested involvement in the problem of the client, while the client responds with a show of respect for the competence and integrity of the specialist. Regardless of such differences in content, however, the general form of these working arrangements is the same.

In noting the tendency for a participant to accept the definitional claims made by the others present, we can appreciate the crucial importance of the information that the individual *initially* possesses or acquires concerning his fellow participants, for it is on the basis of this initial information that the individual starts to define the situation and starts to build up lines of responsive action. The individual's initial projection commits him to what he is proposing to be and requires him to drop all pretenses of being other things. As the interaction among the participants progresses, additions and modifications in this initial informational state will of course occur, but it is essential that these later developments be related without contradiction to, and even built up from, the initial positions taken by the several participants. It would seem that an individual can more easily make a choice as to what line of treatment to demand from and extend to the others present at the beginning of an encounter than he can alter the line of treatment that is being pursued once the interaction is underway.

In everyday life, of course, there is a clear understanding that first impressions are important. Thus, the work adjustment of those in service occupations will often hinge upon a capacity to seize and hold the initiative in the service relation, a capacity that will require subtle aggressiveness on the part of the server when he is of lower socio-economic status than his client. W. F. Whyte suggests the waitress as an example:

[7] An interaction can be purposely set up as a time and place for voicing differences in opinion, but in such cases participants must be careful to agree not to disagree on the proper tone of voice, vocabulary, and degree of seriousness in which all arguments are to be phrased, and upon the mutual respect which disagreeing participants must carefully continue to express toward one another. This debaters' or academic definition of the situation may also be invoked suddenly and judiciously as a way of translating a serious conflict of views into one that can be handled within a framework acceptable to all present.

The first point that stands out is that the waitress who bears up under pressure does not simply respond to her customers. She acts with some skill to control their behavior. The first question to ask when we look at the customer relationship is, "Does the waitress get the jump on the customer, or does the customer get the jump on the waitress?" The skilled waitress realizes the crucial nature of this question . . .

The skilled waitress tackles the customer with confidence and without hesitation. For example, she may find that a new customer has seated himself before she could clear off the dirty dishes and change the cloth. He is now leaning on the table studying the menu. She greets him, says, "May I change the cover, please?" and, without waiting for an answer, takes his menu away from him so that he moves back from the table, and she goes about her work. The relationship is handled politely but firmly, and there is never any question as to who is in charge.[8]

When the interaction that is initiated by "first impressions" is itself merely the initial interaction in an extended series of interactions involving the same participants, we speak of "getting off on the right foot" and feel that it is crucial that we do so. Thus, one learns that some teachers take the following view:

You can't ever let them get the upper hand on you or you're through. So I start out tough. The first day I get a new class in, I let them know who's boss . . . You've got to start off tough, then you can ease up as you go along. If you start out easy-going, when you try to get tough, they'll just look at you and laugh.[9]

Similarly, attendants in mental institutions may feel that if the new patient is sharply put in his place the first day on the ward and made to see who is boss, much future difficulty will be prevented.[10]

Given the fact that the individual effectively projects a definition of the situation when he enters the presence of others, we can assume that events may occur within the interaction which contradict, discredit, or otherwise throw doubt upon this projection. When these disruptive events occur, the interaction itself may come to a confused and embarrassed halt. Some of the assumptions upon which the responses of the participants had been predicated become untenable, and the participants find themselves lodged in an interaction for which the situation has been wrongly defined and is now no longer defined. At such moments the individual whose presentation has been discredited may feel ashamed while the others present may feel hostile, and all the participants may come to feel ill at ease, nonplussed, out of countenance, embarrassed, experiencing the kind of anomy that is generated when the minute social system of face-to-face interaction breaks down.

In stressing the fact that the initial definition of the situation projected by an individual tends to provide a plan for the co-operative activity that follows—in stressing this action point of view—we must not overlook the crucial fact that any projected definition of the situation also has a distinctive moral character. It is this moral character of projections that will chiefly concern us in this report. Society is organized on the principle that any individual who possesses certain social characteristics has a moral right to expect that others will value and treat him in an appropriate way. Connected with this principle is a second, namely that an individual who implicitly or explicitly signifies that he has certain social characteristics ought in fact to be what he claims he is. In consequence, when an individual projects a definition of the situation and thereby makes an implicit or explicit claim to be a person of a particular kind, he automatically exerts a moral demand upon the others, obliging them to value and treat him in the manner that persons of his kind have a right to expect. He also implicitly forgoes all claims to be things he does not appear to be[11] and hence forgoes the treatment that would be appropriate for such individuals. The others find,

[8] W. F. Whyte, "When Workers and Customers Meet," Chap. VII, *Industry and Society*, ed. W. F. Whyte (New York: McGraw-Hill, 1946), pp. 132–33.

[9] Teacher interview quoted by Howard S. Becker, "Social Class Variations in the Teacher-Pupil Relationship," *Journal of Educational Sociology*, XXV, p. 459.

[10] Harold Taxel, "Authority Structure in a Mental Hospital Ward" (unpublished Master's thesis, Department of Sociology, University of Chicago, 1953).

[11] This role of the witness in limiting what it is the individual can be has been stressed by Existentialists, who see it as a basic threat to individual freedom. See Jean-Paul Sartre, *Being and Nothingness*, trans. by Hazel E. Barnes (New York: Philosophical Library, 1956), p. 365 ff.

then, that the individual has informed them as to what is and as to what they *ought* to see as the "is."

One cannot judge the importance of definitional disruptions by the frequency with which they occur, for apparently they would occur more frequently were not constant precautions taken. We find that preventive practices are constantly employed to avoid these embarrassments and that corrective practices are constantly employed to compensate for discrediting occurrences that have not been successfully avoided. When the individual employs these strategies and tactics to protect his own projections, we may refer to them as "defensive practices"; when a participant employs them to save the definition of the situation projected by another, we speak of "protective practices" or "tact." Together, defensive and protective practices comprise the techniques employed to safeguard the impression fostered by an individual during his presence before others. It should be added that while we may be ready to see that no fostered impression would survive if defensive practices were not employed, we are less ready perhaps to see that few impressions could survive if those who received the impression did not exert tact in their reception of it.

In addition to the fact that precautions are taken to prevent disruption of projected definitions, we may also note that an intense interest in these disruptions comes to play a significant role in the social life of the group. Practical jokes and social games are played in which embarrassments which are to be taken unseriously are purposely engineered.[12] Fantasies are created in which devastating exposures occur. Anecdotes from the past—real, embroidered, or fictitious— are told and retold, detailing disruptions which occurred, almost occurred, or occurred and were admirably resolved. There seems to be no grouping which does not have a ready supply of these games, reveries, and cautionary tales, to be used as a source of humor, a catharsis for anxieties, and a sanction for inducing individuals to be modest in their claims and reasonable in their projected expectations. The individual may tell himself through dreams of getting into impossible positions. Families tell of the time a guest got his dates mixed and arrived when neither the house nor anyone in it was ready for him. Journalists tell of times when an all-too-meaningful misprint occurred, and the paper's assumption of objectivity or decorum was humorously discredited. Public servants tell of times a client ridiculously misunderstood form instructions, giving answers which implied an unanticipated and bizarre definition of the situation.[13] Seamen, whose home away from home is rigorously he-man, tell stories of coming back home and inadvertently asking mother to "pass the fucking butter."[14] Diplomats tell of the time a near-sighted queen asked a republican ambassador about the health of his king.[15]

To summarize, then, I assume that when an individual appears before others he will have many motives for trying to control the impression they receive of the situation. This report is concerned with some of the common techniques that persons employ to sustain such impressions and with some of the common contingencies associated with the employment of these techniques. The specific content of any activity presented by the individual participant, or the role it plays in the interdependent activities of an on-going social system, will not be at issue; I shall be concerned only with the participant's dramaturgical problems of presenting the activity before others. The issues dealt with by stagecraft and stage management are sometimes trivial but they are quite general; they seem to occur everywhere in social life, providing a clear-cut dimension for formal sociological analysis.

It will be convenient to end this introduction with some definitions that are implied in what has gone before and required for what is to follow. For the purpose of this report, interaction (that is, face-to-face interaction) may be roughly defined as the reciprocal influence of individuals

---

[12] Goffman, *op. cit.*, pp. 319–27.

[13] Peter Blau, "Dynamics of Bureaucracy" (Ph.D. dissertation, Department of Sociology, Columbia University, forthcoming, University of Chicago Press), pp. 127–29.

[14] Walter M. Beattie, Jr., "The Merchant Seaman" (unpublished M. A. Report, Department of Sociology, University of Chicago, 1950), p. 35.

[15] Sir Frederick Ponsonby, *Recollections of Three Reigns* (New York: Dutton 1952), p. 46.

upon one another's actions when in one another's immediate physical presence. An interaction may be defined as all the interaction which occurs throughout any one occasion when a given set of individuals are in one another's continuous presence; the term "an encounter" would do as well. A "performance" may be defined as all the activity of a given participant on a given occasion which serves to influence in any way any of the other participants. Taking a particular participant and his performance as a basic point of reference, we may refer to those who contribute the other performances as the audience, observers, or co-participants. The pre-established pattern of action which is unfolded during a performance and which may be presented or played through on other occasions may be called a "part" or "rou-

tine."[16] These situational terms can easily be related to conventional structural ones. When an individual or performer plays the same part to the same audience on different occasions, a social relationship is likely to arise. Defining social role as the enactment of rights and duties attached to a given status, we can say that a social role will involve one or more parts and that each of these different parts may be presented by the performer on a series of occasions to the same kinds of audience or to an audience of the same persons.

[16] For comments on the importance of distinguishing between a routine of interaction and any particular instance when this routine is played through, see John von Neumann and Oskar Morgenstern, *The Theory of Games and Economic Behavior* (2nd ed.; Princeton: Princeton University Press, 1947), p. 49.

Gregg S. Wilkinson **19**

Psychiatric Disorder Dramaturgically Considered

In the past, a number of scholars have noted the importance of social interaction for considerations of psychiatric disorder. For instance, Sullivan

Gregg S. Wilkinson, "Psychiatric Disorder Dramaturgically Considered," *The Sociological Quarterly*, vol. 15 (Winter 1974), pp. 143–158. Reprinted by permission.

This paper was made possible by support received from PHS Training Grant No. HS00019, National Center for Health Services Research and Development, Saxon Graham, Director; and by a NIMH Postdoctoral Fellowship in Sociology and Psychiatry, No. IToIMH13112, George Maddox, Director. During various stages of its inception, this work has received the benefit of advice and criticisms from Daniel Yutzy, Dennis Brissett, Gregory P. Stone, Richard Zeller, Saxon Graham, Tai S. Kang as well as the continuing support of Jacqueline N. Wilkinson. Secretarial assistance was provided by Valerie Hawkins.

(1953) advocated viewing mental disorders as primarily a disruption of communication which always occurred within an "interpersonal field." Gough (1968) has argued that psychopathy results largely from empathic deficiency on the part of psychopathic individuals. E. Becker (1968) views schizophrenia as inadequate social performance in the rituals which characterize any given culture, resulting from faulty socialization. Rose (1968) has offered an explanation of involutional neurosis based upon loss of roles which departs from the often cited hormonal theories. Lemert (1968) has shown that paranoid individuals do not contrive the conspiracies they often argue exist against them, but rather actually experience a series of interactional episodes, including a withdrawal by others of interpersonal contact, which could be interpreted as conspiratorial in nature. Goffman (1967:141) argues that psychosis might be viewed as situationally improper behavior which disrupts social gatherings (Goffman, 1963a:242–248). Scheff (1966, 1968) has developed a sociological theory of mental illness emphasizing the reactions of others to acts of "residual deviance" which help to stabilize deviant roles. Although of diverse nature, social interaction constitutes an important theme in all of the above conceptualizations.

It also has been argued that mental illness may be fruitfully conceptualized as dramaturgic incompetence (Wilkinson, 1973a) insofar as it comprises an interactional phenomenon. This paper is concerned with reporting the results of an investigation into the empirical applicability of such a model.

Dramaturgical thought has been depicted as a branch of the symbolic interactionist school (Kuhn, 1970). Similar to symbolic interaction, much of its foundation is based upon the thought of Mead (1934), Cooley (1902), James (1892), and Dewey (1922). The dramaturgical emphasis is probably most evident in the formulations of Burke (1965; 1969a, b), Duncan (1968), Goffman (1959; 1961a, b; 1963a, b; 1967; 1971), Stone (1970), Foote (1967), Brissett (1968), and perhaps E. Becker (1962).[1] Building upon the work of the above as well as numerous others, I have attempted to achieve some degree of operationalization and have endeavored to apply such a mode of thought to the description and analysis of mental disorders.

Human behavior dramaturgically considered entails explicit cognizance of performers, those before whom they perform, and the influence exerted by each upon the other. More specifically, dramaturgical analysis requires explication of: activities and elements which affect or contribute to the actions of individual performers; characteristics, modes of action, and influences experienced and exerted by audiences; dimensions emanating

from the symbiotic relationship of performer and audiences; and finally, aspects of the all pervading influence exerted by the nutrient social matrix in which these elements are immersed.[2] In attempting to apply such a mode of thought to a consideration of psychiatric disorder, the concept dramaturgic incompetence was developed.[3] Before exploring this notion in detail, however, it may be appropriate to consider its opposite—dramaturgic competence.

Dramaturgic Competence

Numerous investigators have noted the importance of identity (e.g., Goffman, 1963; Stone, 1970) and identification (e.g., Foote, 1967; Thomas, 1967; Strauss, 1959) for human interaction. Identity refers to one's existence as a social entity, i.e., what and where an individual is (Stone, 1970:399), whereas identification consists of recognition of an object's existence and imputation of a symbolic label thereby enabling one to act toward and in terms of a given entity.

Identities are presented during interactional encounters and are subject to confirmation by the audience before whom they are performed. If interaction process between performer and audience is to continue, validation of the presented identity must be forthcoming. Those situations in which identities are announced, confirmed, and in which interaction proceeds smoothly may be interpreted as dramaturgically competent encounters. Those in which audience confirmation is not forthcoming, resulting in disruption of interaction flow, may be viewed as dramaturgically incompetent.

Dramaturgic competence consists of five core elements or stages. The first, performative competence, refers to activities associated with the presentation and staging of social performances

---

[1] For critical appraisals of this approach see Messinger et al. (1962) and Dewey (1969). The writings of Strauss (1959) especially as it relates to identity could also be interpreted as of a dramaturgic nature.

[2] The most definitive statements of dramaturgical thought and its core elements are to be found in Burke (1965; 1969a, b) and Duncan (1968). Goffman (1959; 1963b) and Stone (1970) deal with specific concepts such as self and identity from this orientation.

[3] The term dramaturgic incompetence was first brought to the author's attention by Dennis Brissett.

(see Goffman, 1959). The second, empathic competence, is concerned with processes of empathy including reflexive activities manifested in the interactional experiences of actor and audience. The phenomenon of "taking the role of the other" is probably the most important aspect of empathic process (see Mead, 1934; Foote and Cottrell, 1955; Sarbin, 1954; Scheff, 1968). The third stage, motive competence, refers to the facility with which vocabularies of motive (Mills, 1967) are employed to account for staged performances. Contextual motive manipulation is either anticipatory or explanatory in nature (see also, Burke, 1969a, b; Scott and Lyman, 1970; Blum and McHugh, 1971). In the fourth stage, substantive meaning is invested in the performance which enables the audience to respond to those events previously occurring.[4] If the above stages have taken place, the fifth and final stage consisting of confirmation of the actor's identity probably will occur. As a consequence, the performer becomes socially situated, a social identity has been achieved, and social process continues without interruption.

Dramaturgic Incompetence

Interactional encounters, however, being continuously subject to various kinds of disruptions are fraught with difficulty. If, for instance, a performance is incorrectly or improperly staged, the encounter might be characterized as performatively incompetent. Examples of such performances would include inappropriate use of cosmetic equipment, stage props (Goffman, 1959), or flooding out (Goffman, 1961b). An incompetent performance having occurred, the audience is likely to experience empathetic difficulties—i.e., an inability to take the role of actor (see e.g., Mead, 1934; Sarbin, 1954). If such should be the case, we may speak of the encounter as exhibiting empathic incompetence. Upon ascertaining an incompetent performance and having experienced difficulty in assuming the role of the actor, the audience may challenge the motives or motivation which presumably underlie the performer's

actions. At this time the actor is expected to justify his behavior by offering a suitable explanation (Mills, 1967; Scott and Lyman, 1970; Blum and McHugh, 1971). In the event an actor is unable or unwilling to account for his behavior in a satisfactory manner, the encounter may be described as displaying motive incompetence.[5] Lacking receipt of a suitable explanation, the performance loses all meaning for the audience who as a consequence is unable to respond. Meaning loss prevails over the interactional encounter. The end result is a withholding of confirmation by the audience and a questioning of the performer's identity. The actor, in a very real sense, experiences identity loss.[6]

A dramaturgically incompetent encounter then, is characterized by a mismanaged performance, an inability of the audience to anticipate future actions and to act toward or in terms of the performer, and a disruption or cessation of interaction process (Wilkinson, 1973a). Performers who are unfortunate enough to experience such a train of events are provided with an identity maintained by society specifically for such situations—that of mentally ill persons. Having been identified as such, a set of socially prescribed responses is called forth allowing interaction to proceed once again.

Some would argue (e.g., Foote, 1967; Thomas, 1967; Strauss, 1959) that before one may act toward or with respect to a given object, that object must first be identified. This implies that identification of the acting other constitutes a necessary requirement for interaction between humans. It is achieved by attributing an identity from performances and proffered vocabularies of motive. If an actor's identity is questioned or not validated he must be given another before audiences find it possible to incorporate him into the ongoing social process. In our society, a psychiat-

[4] One might argue that performances also must be meaningful for the performer. For discussions of meaning and interaction see Mead (1934), Becker (1962), and Blumer (1969).

[5] Motive incompetence is based upon the notion, motive loss, originated by Charles Edgley (1970) in his dissertation: Vocabularies of Motive and the Social Definition of Schizophrenia. Buffalo: SUNY.

[6] All is not necessarily lost. A performer upon having his identity challenged will usually immediately adopt and announce another. One engages in identity manipulation. It is only when one runs out of identities to adopt or announces an identity so contextually inappropriate that no amount of switching will save the encounter that one undergoes identity loss. (This concept was first suggested to the author by Dennis Brissett.)

ric identity constitutes a substitute identity which may be appropriated in such situations thereby allowing the audience to define the situation and act accordingly.[7]

DRAMATURGIC INCOMPETENCE AND PSYCHIATRIC DIAGNOSIS

It was hypothesized that each component of dramaturgic incompetence as well as dramaturgic incompetence in general would be positively associated with degree of diagnosed psychiatric disturbance and general diagnosis. Performances of a bizarre, severely incompetent, or totally out of context nature are more likely to be taken as evidence of severe psychiatric impairment than are those which seem merely eccentric, strange, or slightly out of frame. Likewise, the degree to which one is able to empathize with a performance similarly would be related to psychiatric diagnosis. Performers who display a total lack of motive competence or who offer no motives will appear more handicapped than will those who occasionally submit wrong or slightly implausible motives. Also, performances completely void of meaning are likely to seem more disturbed than those in which meaning is confused or ambiguous. Finally, total identity loss will correspond with diagnoses of a severe nature.

It also was hypothesized that each event would occur in the following order: performative incompetence first, empathic incompetence second, motive incompetence third, meaning loss fourth, and identity loss fifth.

Method

Patients and a significant audience were interviewed by means of an open-ended structured interview schedule as they were processed through the psychiatric screening facility of Northeastern County Hospital.[8] This agency served as a screening and referral service for all public psychiatric facilities in the county. Interviews were conducted during the intake phase as part of the regular screening procedure. All types of patients, both first and readmissions, were selected with only drug abuse and alcoholism cases being eliminated. The audience proved to be an amorphous category including at times: friends, relatives, acquaintances, close family members, spouses, parents, social workers, police, and hospital personnel. The significance of the audience was determined on the basis of who initiated hospital screening. Hospital records were examined later for information pertaining to diagnosis. Interest was focused upon elaboration of the series of interactional events leading to hospitalization and culminating in an initial psychiatric diagnosis.

A total of 87 interviews were completed. Although the original intention was to obtain a universe, this was not achieved for the following reasons: 1) a large number of patients did not enter with significant audiences and as such were inappropriate· 2) some patients were so obstreperous they immediately were sent to an inpatient ward; 3) at times the influx of patients was so great that not all of them could be interviewed; and 4) 24-hour coverage was not possible. As a result, it was necessary to characterize the sample as a pseudo-universe (i.e., a universe that was not, in a strict sense, achieved). For this reason, only nonparametric forms of measurement were considered appropriate.

Criteria for each component were devised; data were coded in terms of presence or nonpresence, with a value of 1 indicating presence and 0 nonpresence; scores were summed; the mean was computed; and scores were categorized as either above or below the mean for each variable examined.[9] Classification in this manner provided

---

[7] The present conceptualization is complementary to Scheff's (1966; 1968) theory of mental illness in that both deal with role, audience response, and labelling (identification). However, several points of divergence are present. The current formulation is focused upon identity. Furthermore, whereas Scheff admittedly skips over the individual while emphasizing the social, the present model attempts to capture both the performer and his audience engaged in the interactive process. As such, the current argument is similar in many respects to Sarbin's (1954) treatment of role, self, and identification, and may be interpreted as an extension of Scheff's (1966) argument.

[8] A pseudonym. This was a large county hospital affiliated with a university medical school, located in a metropolitan urban area of a densely populated state in the northeastern United States. The psychiatric facility was primarily an acute care facility with the average length of stay for patients being approximately 2 to 3 weeks.

[9] The coding protocol is included in an appendix. The interview schedule may be obtained from the author.

a crude form of ordinal measurement. Degree of psychiatric disturbance also may be interpreted as constituting a crude form of ordinal measurement in that patients were ranked by psychiatric staff on a scale ranging from severely disturbed to no disturbance. It could be argued, however, that such a form of classification does not really meet ordinal criteria since it is based upon the subjective evaluations of staff, and since it seems highly questionable whether one can determine (in a reliable manner) whether a patient is slightly, moderately, or highly disturbed. It does seem possible for one to distinguish in a fairly consistent manner between the severely disturbed and the slightly disturbed. Therefore, for the purposes of the present study, evaluations were collapsed into two categories: high and low disturbance. General diagnosis may be interpreted in similar fashion if psychosis is viewed as being more severe than neurosis.

Statistical analysis entailed the use of P-R-E related measures: gamma, dyx, and Tau beta. Such statistics are superior to chi-square based measures in that chi-square indicates only presence or nonpresence of an association. P-R-E measures, however, not only demonstrate presence, but also direction, relative strength, and form (see e.g., Kang, 1972, 1973; Kim, 1971). Therefore, rather than being limited to monotonic biconditional associations, as we are by chi-square, conditional and weak biconditional relationships become suitable material for analysis.

Results

A strong relationship was found between each of the elements comprising dramaturgic incompetence and psychiatric diagnosis. In all cases very high gammas were observed with values for dyx and τ_b being on the average 2 to 3 points lower. This information when combined with examination of the cross-tabular distributions indicates the following: 1) in terms of degree of psychiatric disturbance most distributions could be interpreted as variants of weak, monotonic, biconditional forms with the exception of meaning loss which is more appropriately interpreted as a strong conditional association. Thus, with the ex-clusion of meaning loss, there is a pronounced tendency for high incompetence or loss to be related to high disturbance. In the case of meaning loss, no responses occurred in the high loss-low disturbance cell, with most observations falling along the major diagonal and a lesser number occurring in the low meaning loss-high disturbance cell. This indicates that high loss rarely contributes to diagnoses of low disturbance whereas low loss may be present when high disturbance is diagnosed. 2) General diagnosis in terms of psychosis versus neurosis follows a similar pattern although the values are slightly lower than was the case with degree of disturbance.

When considered in its entirety, dramaturgic incompetence was found to be strongly associated with psychiatric diagnosis as might be expected from the previous findings.[10] A weak, monotonic, biconditional relationship in the predicted direction appears when degree of disturbance is examined, while general diagnosis approaches a strong conditional association in the predicted direction. The number of observations falling in each of the cells comprising the minor diagonal is less than 10 percent for degree of psychiatric disturbance, which may be attributed to error, measurement crudity, variations in diagnosis, or a combination of all three. However, in the case of general diagnosis, which approaches a conditional association, it is interesting to note that approximately 13 percent of the observations fall in the low incompetence-psychosis cell. This may indicate a tendency for psychiatric staff to render a diagnosis of a more severe nature (psychosis) in ambiguous circumstances, an interpretation that is equally plausible for degree of disturbance. In any event, the evidence in this case appears to support the contention that dramaturgic incompetence is positively associated with psychiatric diagnosis.

With respect to order of placement, a definite trend was found in the hypothesized direction. It is interesting to note in Table 19.3 that deviations from the primary diagonal tend to occur before, rather than after, the hypothesized stage. With the exception of identity loss, which does not offer such a possibility, only performative in-

---

[10] Dramaturgic incompetence was computed by summing the raw scores for each of its components, computing a grand mean, and categorizing in terms of this mean as either high or low.

TABLE 19.1. Association between elements comprising dramaturgic incompetence and psychiatric diagnosis*

Degree of Psychiatric Disturbance	Performative Incompetence		Empathic Incompetence		Motive Incompetence		Meaning Loss		Identity Loss	
	High	Low	High	Low	High	Low	High	Low	High	Low
High	51.2	11.6	54.8	9.5	54.1	9.4	50.0	15.9	57.3	7.3
Low	3.5	33.7	2.4	33.3	5.9	30.6	.0	34.1	7.3	28.0
γ	.95		.97		.94		1.0		.94	
d_{yx}	.68		.74		.67		.68		.68	
τ_b	.70 p < .001		.76 p < .001		.68 p < .001		.72 p < .001		.68 p < .001	
General Diagnosis										
Psychosis	50.0	15.5	54.9	12.2	54.2	12.0	50.0	18.8	58.7	8.7
Neurosis	6.0	28.8	3.7	29.3	7.2	26.5	1.2	30.0	7.5	25.0
γ	.88		.95		.89		.97		.91	
d_{yx}	.54		.64		.57		.59		.63	
τ_b	.57 p < .001		.67 p < .001		.59 p < .001		.64 p < .001		.63 p < .001	

* High and low cells are in percents.

TABLE 19.2. Association between dramaturgic incompetence and psychiatric diagnosis*

Dramaturgic Incompetence

		High	Low	
Degree of Psychiatric Disturbance	High	53.5	9.3	γ .98 d_{yx} .75
	Low	2.3	34.9	τ_b .77 p < .001
General Diagnosis	Psychosis	51.2	12.8	$\gamma = .93$
	Neurosis	4.7	27.9	d_{yx} .63
	No disturbance	0	3.5	$\tau_b = .64$ p < .001
			N = 86	

* High and low cells are in percents.

TABLE 19.3. Association between elements comprising dramaturgic incompetence and order of occurrence

Elements	Stage of Occurrence					
	1st	2nd	3rd	4th	5th	Uncodable
Performative Incompetence	83	1	0	0	0	3
Empathic Incompetence	5	66	0	0	0	17
Motive Incompetence	2	16	64	0	0	5
Meaning Loss	0	4	8	61	0	14
Identity Loss	0	4	8	7	58	10

$\chi^2 = 1265.84$ for 16 df, p < .001
$\gamma = .95$
$d_{yx} = .79$
$\tau_b = .78$, p < .001

competence presents an error after the predicted stage, and in this case no possibility exists for an error of precedence.

Those cases which could not be assigned a specific placement with respect to other stages were categorized as uncodable. Such observations constitute another form of error. It is interesting to note that empathic incompetence and meaning loss demonstrate the highest frequency of un-

codable observations. This may indicate the necessity for further refinement since it is precisely these two variables which are most difficult to operationalize.

When presence and nonpresence of a perfect sequence was examined in terms of degree of disturbance and general diagnosis, it was found that presence was strongly associated with high disturbance and a diagnosis of psychosis. This indicates that the sequence as hypothesized is more descriptive of psychosis than neurosis.

PSYCHIATRIC DISORDER DRAMATURGICALLY CONSIDERED

It has been possible to demonstrate that dramaturgic incompetence and each of its components are positively associated with severity of psychiatric diagnosis. It also has been demonstrated that each component tends to occur in the predicted sequence which gives us some insight into the nature of the dynamics involved. The importance of interpersonal processes in the development of psychiatric identities is strongly implied. Furthermore, the development of mental illness has been viewed as a social phenomenon involving both a performer and an audience. Each are necesary for the end result, a psychiatric identity, to occur. It is distorting to concentrate upon one without taking into account the other.

The mutual engagement of performer and audience in a social encounter may be designated as an interactional frame. Theoretically speaking, the means by which interactional frames are sustained and social performances carried to completion entails the processes of identification and identity negotiation. If an identity, upon being presented, fails to receive audience validation, the interactional frame is broken resulting in interaction breakdown and disruption of social drama.

Social life is comprised of many dramas from the basic dyad to complex collectivities. It might be argued that macro processes ultimately rest upon minute everyday dramas. If these are in some way disrupted, the breakdown in social process might eventually achieve macro dimensions with concomitant implications for the public order. Maintenance of social order implies more than traffic laws, regulation of economic transactions, criminal penalties, etc. Also included are acceptable definitions of reality, rules governing social performance, and standards for behavior in general. Existence of such normative requirements serves as an effective mode of control contributing to maintenance of the public order. One of the most important facets of this control aspect

is the requirement that presented identities conform to the situation in which they occur. It is impossible to cite all situations and correspondingly acceptable identities since they are too numerous, many are unknown, they are often contextually related, and they are often situationally constructed. It is quite evident, however, that one may present himself as Atilla the Hun on the formal stage but not on the stage of everyday social life.

A measure of social control is implied merely through the restrictions placed upon the use of identities. Once an individual has been provided with an identity, audiences pertinent to that particular situation are able to direct their behavior toward him in a manner corresponding to the individual's validated identity.

An individual's perception of his identity, however, may differ from that of the audience, or he may prove unable to present an identity which achieves audience satisfaction. Such circumstances have been defined as dramaturgically incompetent. Those individuals characterized by high dramaturgic incompetence are more likely to be diagnosed as psychotic whereas those displaying lower degrees of dramaturgic incompetence are more likely to be considered neurotic. This may indicate: 1) the presence of pathology or indwelling behavioral limitations on the part of the performer before entering the encounter (see Gough, 1968; Sarbin, 1954); 2) the importance of interactional processes in human behavior; and/or 3) a manner in which societal restraints upon human behavior are exercised. The evidence in this paper is limited to interpretations 2 and 3 above.

Dramaturgic incompetence as conceived in this investigation appears to occupy a prominent position in the development of psychiatric identities although it is necessary to recognize that it may not be the only factor. As an interactional phenomenon, dramaturgic incompetence constitutes a dimension that cannot be accounted for by physiological, psychic, or sociostructural factors alone. It is an entirely different phenomenon comprised of but superceding these factors. This does not mean that it is possible to rule out entirely the plausible contributions of such elements to human behavior. It is conceivable that a chemical imbalance or neurogenic trauma could lead to manifestation of dramaturgically incompetent behavior. In the case of syphilitic psychosis, a delimiting factor influencing performance is indeed present. Furthermore, psychic states and culturally learned patterns of behavior do indeed influence social performance. However, whereas it is possible to demonstrate dramaturgical parameters in all instances of mental illness—especially psychosis—not all psychoses result from chemical imbalance or neurogenic trauma. On this basis, it could be argued that biologically induced forms of psychiatric disorder constitute a subset of the larger set dramaturgic incompetence. Therefore, a reconceptualization of mental illness as dramaturgic incompetence would not be epistemologically or empirically unsound especially since it allows consideration of the influence exerted by the audience without disregarding the individual himself. In other words, the potential exists for a true interactional model of mental illness and human behavior.

Numerous investigators have documented that certain psychoses (especially schizophrenia) occur more frequently among the lower social classes (e.g., Hollingshead and Redlich, 1958; Rushing, 1971). The problem has been how to explain such findings, and explanations have included mobility, isolation, stress, culture conflict, deprivation, and frames of reference. Applying the findings of the present study, one could speculate that dramaturgic incompetence may provide a clue to the link between social class and psychiatric disorder, at least in some cases. Given that high incompetence occurs more frequently among lower status individuals (Wilkinson, 1973a), one might argue that lower educational achievement, with concomitant limitations of a symbolic nature, combines with relative lack of social power as manifested by low occupational prestige to produce the inverse connections between social class and mental illness. Those who possess a preponderance of social power (higher status groups) are able to set behavioral standards of both an overt and symbolic nature to which others must conform. On the other hand, lower status individuals, hampered by lack of education and limited symbolic skills are not only more likely to appear severely disturbed to psychiatric

diagnosticians (who are likely to possess highly developed symbolic skills), but also are likely to be at a disadvantage in terms of performance, motive manipulation, and identity negotiation. The disadvantage stems from limited interactional skills, divergent cultural experiences, and lack of social power. It is possible that dramaturgic incompetence, as it has been defined, taps these dimensions in a crude way.[11]

Identities and Identification: A Crucial Process

The concept dramaturgic incompetence is especially appropriate when identity serves as the focus of attention. Evidence obtained in this investigation has demonstrated not only the existence of the elements mentioned in behavior adjudged psychiatrically impaired and the order in which they occur during the process of attaining a psychiatric identity, but also the crucial nature of identification processes and concomitant identities.[12] In order for interactants to take part in social drama, the interactional situation must first be defined by the interactants. Performative, empathic, motive incompetence, meaning, and identity loss tend to impede defining the situation and in this manner hamper social process.

Defining the situation entails identifying objects and ascribing some type of identity to them. This allows an individual to incorporate an object which has been identified and attributed an identity into his program of action. It is precisely this process which has been documented in the development of psychiatric identities. Audiences, upon encountering strange or bizarrely performing individuals, are unable to identify them with respect to the social context at hand. As a conse-

[11] Of course, since we have not been concerned with distinguishing between those groups demonstrating high and low incompetence, such notions must be regarded as highly speculative. Nevertheless, such an explanation seems plausible although it disregards performative limitations that may be of somatic origin. Such limitations would not seem to be sensitive to status designations, however, unless they were of an endogenous nature in which case race or ethnic origin would be more valid indicators than would status per se.

[12] It must be emphasized that this investigation and discussion is limited to the topic of identity attainment. Interpretations, conclusions, claims, and projections based upon the data presented are subject to this limitation.

quence, they are unable to provide them with identities which would allow the audience to act toward, upon, and with the individuals in question. In order to do so, some type of identity must be ascribed. Under such circumstances, the performer may be identified as mentally ill which permits audience incorporation of the performer into the interactional world.[13]

During a social encounter a performer announces his identity in either a manifest or latent fashion and conducts a performance appropriate for the identity presented. If one's identity and performance do not jibe or are not contextually proper, one is likely to encounter interactional problems. For instance, a hobo who attempts to pass himself off as a millionaire, or an illiterate field worker who claims he is a physician, or a maid who claims she is the Virgin Mary are likely to be held suspect. Audiences often find that such identities do not fit their frames of reference, expectations, or repertoires of social experience. Mental illness serves as a handy catchall mode of identification that can be applied whenever identities are questioned and the encounter threatened. It is a substitute identity of extreme flexibility—especially in western industrialized societies[14]—that is used to fill the void created by identity loss.

Implications are forthcoming from such findings bearing upon the more general topic of identity construction and negotiation in social life at large. If psychiatric identities result from dramaturgic incompetence—it seems reasonable to suspect that in the absence of incompetence or presence of competence—so-called normal identities will be presented, validated, sustained, and interaction process will continue unimpeded. One must exercise caution, however, in generalizing from the data presented in this report since it was obtained only from individuals who came in contact with psychiatric facilities.

Attribution of psychiatric identities fulfills a required societal function. It provides for maintenance of our social gatherings (Goffman, 1967) and facilitates continuation of interactional processes. A taken-for-granted norm seems to exist that social process should flow unimpeded and interaction between performers should be smooth and without interruption (Goffman, 1968; Szasz, 1970). We cannot at this time say why this exists—only that it does.

Limitations

A number of qualifications should be cited concerning the findings of this investigation and the methods used. First, the concepts and measuring devices are crude and require further refinement. Second, operationalization has been inadequate in a number of instances—especially in tapping the dimensions of empathic process and meaning loss. Third, although an attempt was made to sample a universe, because of limitations encountered at the research site, it proved impossible. Therefore, in a strict sense the sample comprises neither a random sample nor a universe. However, when one considers the refusal rate encountered in most surveys and the return rate of most questionnaire studies, the present study has achieved as strong a sample, if not stronger, as is usually achieved. Fourth, the interviews were directed toward ascertaining the interactional events which preceded psychiatric screening and in this sense are retrospective. However, the problem of conducting an investigation into the phenomena considered in other than a retrospective fashion constitutes a serious dilemma. Finally, although concerned with process, a certain amount of reification is present as a result of linguistic limitations. It should be explicitly understood that the model presented is processual and not structural.

Several theoretical limitations also should be mentioned. In the first place, the present conceptualization of audience is too simplistic. It has become obvious that any given individual performs before many audiences even under further specific circumstances such as achieving a psychiatric identity. Therefore further specification of the au-

---

[13] We are faced with the task of explaining why one identity comes to be accepted over another. This may be in part, a function of social power; i.e., those who are able to marshal a preponderance of social support receive confirmation of their definitions of others as well as validation of their own identity presentations.

[14] A psychiatrist once mentioned to the author that psychiatric impairment could be found in anyone if one wanted to look far enough—a statement which is sobering indeed!

dience(s) involved would greatly strengthen subsequent research efforts. A possible strategy could
entail refinement in the manner of Duncan
(1968). Another limitation concerns the manner
in which empathic incompetence was approached. In contrast to prior conceptions of this
concept, it was viewed as an attribute of the audience rather than a characteristic of the performer. It could also be argued that empathic incompetence characterizes the performer thereby
affecting his performance (see Gough, 1968; Sarbin, 1954). Finally, we have not adequately accounted for why some individuals are able to receive validation for their identities—given similar
types of performances—whereas others are not.
A structural approach to this type of problem
might prove illuminating not only in terms of
whose definition comes to prevail, but also in
terms of role expectations and corresponding social situations.

SUMMARY

Dramaturgical thought has been criticized by
Kuhn (1970) for its phenomenological characteristics and unoperationalized nature. This investigation was in part an attempt to operationalize
dramaturgical thought and in part an attempt to
conceptualize mental illness in dramaturgical
terms. A measure of initial success has been
achieved. Evidence was presented in support of
the proposition that individuals identified as psychiatrically impaired display dramaturgic incom-
petentence. It has also been shown that the separate components of dramaturgic incompetence
tend to occur in the specified order, especially
in those circumstances whereby individuals come
to be identified as psychotic or severely disturbed.
Further refinement and elaboration of the concepts employed in this investigation are required.
Nevertheless, it has been demonstrated that conceptualization of mental illness in dramaturgic
terms is plausible and may prove to be a worthwhile direction for subsequent research. In this
manner, interactional dimensions of psychiatric
disorder in particular will be illuminated as well
as explication of social drama in general.

APPENDIX

Method Employed in Coding & Computing Dramaturgic Incompetence[15]

I. Performative Incompetence   Score 1 for
presence, 0 for nonpresence
   A. Value Dimension
      1. Violations of rules of relevance and
         irrelevance   _____
      2. Violations of residual rules   _____
      3. Improper management of expressive
         equipment   _____
      4. Improper management of structural
         props   _____
      5. Involvement in situational improprie-
         ties   _____

                                        _____
                          Σ of items present

   B. Mood Dimension
      1. Improper engrossment-involvement

                                        _____
      2. Violations of personal ease-tension
         continuum   _____
      3. Contributes to interactional tension

                                        _____
      4. Flooding out   _____

                                        _____
                          Σ of items present
Total Performative Incompetence = A + B

II. Empathic Incompetence
      1. Patient unable to understand how he
         should have acted   _____
      2. Patient unable to understand what consti-
         tutes proper behavior   _____
      3. Patient seems unable to take role of the
         other   _____

---

[15] Performative incompetence is based upon the following
sources: rules of relevance and irrelevance (Goffman, 1961b);
residual rules (Scheff, 1966); expressive equipment and structural props (Goffman, 1967); situational improprieties (Goffman,
1967); engrossment-involvement (Goffman, 1963a); personal
ease-tension, interactional tension, and flooding out (Goffman,
1961b); value-mood dimension (Stone, 1970). Empathic incompetence was developed from Mead (1934) and Sullivan
(1953). Motive incompetence was derived from Burke (1965,
1969a, b), Mills (1967), Scott and Lyman (1970), and Edgley
(1970). Meaning loss is based on Becker (1962), Blumer (1969),
as well as Mead (1934). Identity loss is an extension of Stone
(1970) and Goffman (1963b). For a more detailed discussion
of identity loss and its components as well as all of the above,
see Wilkinson (1973a).

4. Patient unable to successfully manage role obligations _____
5. Audience unable to understand patients behavior _____
6. Audience unable to take role of patient _____

_____
Σ of items present

III. Motive Incompetence
1. Patient unable to offer any motives justifying his behavior _____
2. Patient offers wrong motives _____
3. Audience rejects proffered motives _____
4. Audience unable to understand proffered motives _____
5. Patient engages in motive confusion. (Offers several or many motives which confuse rather than explain) _____

_____
Σ of items present

IV. Audience Meaning Loss
1. Audience unable to respond to performer's announced identity (apparent) _____
2. Audience unable to respond to performer's announced identity (discursive) _____
3. Audience able to respond to performer's announced identity only in psychiatric terms _____
4. Audience able to respond to performer's announced identity only in terms of illness _____
5. Audience experiences meaning confusion/ ambivalence _____

_____
Σ of items present

V. Identity Loss
1. Involuntary rather than voluntary commitment _____
2. Presentation as somatically ill rather than mentally ill _____
3. Confused as to time, location, whom one is _____
4. Presentation as sane rather than disturbed _____
5. Presentation as requiring less help than audience defines as needing _____
6. Presentation as well rather than ill _____
7. General confusion as to what is occurring _____
8. Audience ascription of an identity different from that announced _____

_____
Σ of items present

Dramaturgic Incompetence $= \Sigma$ of Performative Incompetence $+ \Sigma$ of Empathic Incompetence $+ \Sigma$ of Motive Incompetence $+ \Sigma$ of Meaning Loss $+ \Sigma$ of Identity Loss

REFERENCES

Blum, A. F., and P. McHugh. "The Social Ascription of Motives." *American Sociological Review* 35 (February 1971):98–108.

Blumer, Herbert. *Symbolic Interactionism.* Englewood Cliffs: Prentice Hall, 1969.

Becker, Ernest. "Socialization, Command of Performance, and Mental Illness." *The Mental Patient: Studies in The Sociology of Deviance.* Edited by Stephan P. Spitzer and Norman K. Denzin. New York: McGraw-Hill, 1968, pp. 31–40.

————. *The Birth and Death of Meaning.* New York: The Free Press, 1962.

Brissett, D. "Collective Behavior: The Sense of a Rubric." *American Journal of Sociology* 74 (July 1968):70–78.

Burke, Kenneth. *A Grammar of Motives.* Berkeley & Los Angeles: University of California Press, 1969a.

————. *A Rhetoric of Motives.* Berkeley & Los Angeles: University of California Press, 1969b.

————. *Permanence and Change.* New York: Bobbs Merrill, 1965.

Cooley, Charles H. *Human Nature and the Social Order.* New York: Charles Scribner' Sons, 1902.

Dewey, John. *Human Nature and Conduct.* New York: Holt, Rinehart and Winston, 1922.

Dewey, R. "The Theatrical Analogy Reconsidered." *The American Sociologist* (November 1969):307–311.

Duncan, Hugh D. *Symbols in Society.* New York: Oxford University Press, 1968.

Dunham, H. Warren and Robert E. L. Faris. *Mental Disorders in Urban Areas.* Chicago; University of Chicago Press, 1939.

Foote, Nelson and Leonard S. Cottrell, Jr. *Identity and Interpersonal Competence.* Chicago: University of Chicago Press, 1955.

Foote, Nelson. "Identification as the Basis for a Theory of Motivation." *Symbolic Interaction.* Edited by Jerome G. Manis and Bernard N. Meltzer. Boston: Allyn and Bacon, 1967, pp. 343–354.

Goffman, Erving. *Relations in Public.* New York: Harper and Row, 1971.

———. *Interaction Ritual*, Garden City, New York: Doubleday and Company, 1967.

———. *Behavior in Public Places*. New York: The Free Press, 1963a.

———. *Stigma*. Englewood Cliffs, New Jersey: Prentice Hall, 1963b.

———. *Asylums*. Garden City, New York: Doubleday and Company, 1961a.

———. *Encounters*. New York: Bobbs Merrill, 1961b.

———. *The Presentation of Self in Everyday Life*. Garden City, New York: Doubleday, 1959.

Gough, Harrison G. "A Sociological Theory of Psychopathy." *The Mental Patient: Studies in the Sociology of Deviance*. Edited by Stephan P. Spitzer and Norman K. Denzin. New York: McGraw Hill, 1968, pp. 60–68.

Hollingshead, August B. and Fredrick C. Redlich. *Social Class and Mental Illness*. New York: John Wiley, 1958.

Hunt, R. G. "Socio-cultural Factors in Mental Disorders." *Behavioral Science* 4 (April 1959):96–106.

James, William. *Psychology*. New York: Henry Holt and Company, 1892.

Kang, T. S. "Ordinal Measures of Association and Form of Hypotheses." *Sociological Quarterly* 14 (Spring 1973):235–248.

———. "Linking Forms of Hypothesis to Type of Statistics: An Application of Goodman's z." *American Sociological Review* 37 (June 1972):357–365.

Kim, J. O. "Predictive Measures of Ordinal Association." *American Journal of Sociology* 76 (March 1971):891–907.

Kuhn, Manford H. "Major Trends in Symbolic Interaction Theory in the Past Twenty-five Years." *Social Psychology Through Symbolic Interaction*. Edited by Gregory P. Stone and Harvey A. Farberman. Waltham, Mass.: Ginn-Blaisdell, 1970, pp. 70–87.

Lemert, Edwin M. "Paranoia and the Dynamics of Exclusion." *The Mental Patient: Studies in the Sociology of Deviance*. Edited by Stephan P. Spitzer and Norman K. Denzin. New York: McGraw Hill, 1968, pp. 68–84.

Manis, Jerome G., and Bernard N. Meltzer. *Symbolic Interaction*. Boston: Allyn and Bacon, 1967.

Mead, George H. *Mind, Self, and Society*. Chicago: University of Chicago Press, 1934.

Messinger, S. L., with H. Sampson and R. D. Tonne. "Life as Theater: Some Notes on the Dramaturgical Approach to Social Reality." *Sociometry* 25 (March 1962):98–110.

Mills, C. Wright. "Situated Actions and Vocabularies of Motive." *Symbolic Interaction*. Edited by Jerome G. Manis and Bernard N. Meltzer. Boston: Allyn and Bacon, 1967, pp. 355–366.

Rose, Arnold M. "A Social-psychological Theory of Neurosis." *The Mental Patient: Studies in the Sociology of Deviance*. Edited by Stephan P. Spitzer and Norman K. Denzin. New York: McGraw Hill, 1968, pp. 52–59.

Sabin, Theodore R. "Role Theory." *Handbook of Social Psychology*. Edited by Gardner Lindzey. Cambridge, Mass.: Addison-Wesley, 1954, pp. 223–258.

Scheff, Thomas J. "The Role of the Mentally Ill and the Dynamics of Mental Disorder: A Research Framework." *The Mental Patient: Studies in the Sociology of Deviance*. Edited by Stephen P. Spitzer and Norman K. Denzin. New York: McGraw Hill, 1968, pp. 8–22.

———. *Being Mentally Ill: A Sociological Theory*. Chicago: Aldine, 1966.

Scott, Marvin B., and Stanford M. Lyman. "Accounts." *Social Psychology Through Symbolic Interaction*. Edited by Gregory P. Stone and Harvey A. Farberman. Waltham, Mass.: Ginn-Blaisdell, 1970, pp. 489–509.

Stone, Gregory P. "Appearance and the Self." *Social Psychology Through Symbolic Interaction*. Edited by Gregory P. Stone and Harvey A. Farberman. Waltham, Mass.: Ginn-Blaisdell, 1970, pp. 394–414.

Strauss, Anselm. *Mirrors and Masks*. New York: Free Press of Glencoe, 1959.

Sullivan, Harry S. *The Interpersonal Theory of Psychiatry*. New York: W. W. Norton, 1953.

Thomas, William I. "The Definition of the Situation." Pp. 315–321 in *Symbolic Interaction*. Edited by Jerome G. Manis and Bernard N. Meltzer. Boston: Allyn and Bacon, 1967, pp. 315–321.

Wilkinson, Gregg S. "The Social Construction of Psychiatric Disorders: Mental Illness as Dramaturgic Incompetence." Unpublished Ph.D. dissertation State University of New York at Buffalo, 1973a.

———. "Patient-audience Social Class and the Social Construction of Psychiatric Disorders." Paper presented to American Sociological Association Annual Meeting. New York, 1973b.

A Critical Evaluation of Mead's "I" and "Me" Concepts

Social scientists have finally come to the realization that the task of a specific systematic science is not the exhaustive explanation of the empirical reality from which it draws its data, but rather the verifying of a series of abstract hypotheses which can then be used in conjunction with the concepts of other sciences to explain a specific situation in reality.[1] The infinite divisibility of reality makes any other approach impossible; any empirical situation is made up of a multiplicity of systems, physical, biological and social. These variables combine in determining the structure of the situation, and any attempt to explain this tangled web of phenomena within the frame of reference offered by any one science can only end in disaster. Conversely, any attempt to construct a systematic science on the basis of all these variables can only result in the crudest form of eclecticism and inconsistent systematization. The social psychologist has been one of the most persistent offenders of this unalterable canon of science. This inability or disinclination to deal only with that which falls properly within the sphere of social psychology is reflected in the unsystematic character of textbooks that are purported

to be systematic analyses of personality or of other social psychological phenomena.[2]

Of all social psychologists the one that would seem least guilty of this desire to explain everything about personality is G. H. Mead.[3] Yet, even here, it is possible to discover the results of an attempt to explain aspects of personality and self that more properly belong to other sciences. In his logical development of a systematic theory of the social nature of the growth of the self and of the personality through social interaction and role-taking, Mead gives no explicit explanation of the facts of social change or of the fact that the actions of individuals never exactly correspond to the roles which they are expected to play, prior to the introduction of the "I" and "me" concepts. If he had closed his system without taking these phenomena into consideration, the personality and social structures formed by processes delineated in his analysis would have been con-

Reprinted from *Social Forces*, vol. 22 (March 1944), pp. 291–296. "A Critical Evaluation of Mead's 'I' and 'Me' Concepts" by William L. Kolb. Copyright © The University of North Carolina Press.

[1] Cf. Talcott Parsons, *The Structure of Social Action* (New York, 1937), pp. 3–42. Here the emphasis is on the relation between a given body of theory and empirical fact. See also Florian Znaniecki, *The Method of Sociology* (New York, 1934), *passim*. Both of these works are concerned with the necessity of abstraction in what might be called sociology proper, but their strictures are applicable to any systematic body of knowledge.

[2] Since the writer is unfamiliar with any social psychology text which has not been conceived in too grandiose a fashion, it is unfair to single out any particular offender, but for a somewhat similar criticism pointed at a specific text see H. H. Gerth's review of Steuart Henderson Britt, *Social Psychology of Modern Life* (New York, 1941), in *American Sociological Review*, 6 (December 1941), 915–916.

[3] G. H. Mead, *Mind, Self, and Society* (Chicago 1934). See also his "The Social Self," *Journal of Philosophy, Psychology and Scientific Method*, X (1913), 374–380; "The Mechanism of Social Consciousness," *Journal of Philosophy, Psychology and Scientific Method*, IX (1912), 401–406; "What Social Objects Must Psychology Presuppose," *Journal of Philosophy, Psychology and Scientific Method*, VII (1910), 174–180; "A Behavioristic Account of the Significant Symbol," *Journal of Philosophy*, XIX (1922), 157–163; and, "Genesis of the Self and Social Control," *International Journal of Ethics*, XXXV (1924–1925), 251–277.

stant, i.e., personality would not vary from the various roles defined by the culture of the society. This is not an a priori impossibility, since as we have seen, a systematic science may not explain everything concerning a particular phenomenon, and thus all differences in personality not accounted for by differentiated roles might conceivably be due to differences generated by other than social factors. Nevertheless, Mead was perfectly justified in attempting to discover whether or not some of these differences could be explained within his frame of reference. In so doing, however, he erred in attempting to explain these residual phenomena under one concept, the "I," and in attempting to close his system by enclosing within it heterogeneous phenomena. The "I" becomes accountable for everything that cannot be explained by the organized set of roles which the individual takes over in the processes of social interaction.[4] This conceptualizing of a residual category of phenomena as being homogeneous has been a source of confusion for both Mead and his interpreters; the nature of this confusion can be demonstrated by an analysis of the characteristics which have been attributed to the "I" as opposed to the "me."

The first characteristic of the "I," that we do not experience it until it passes into memory, fails to distinguish it from the "me," if we define the latter behavioristically. Since this point of view involves defining attitude as an early stage of an act, the "me," which consists of organized internalized attitudes of others, can and must be regarded, unless one is willing to disregard the behavioristic aspects of Mead's work, as realizing itself only in responses. In other words, unless one regards the aspects of the active "me" as existing in various responses called out by various stimuli, including earlier actions of the individual, the "me" becomes merely a fictional concept, useful,

perhaps, but unrelated to a behavioristic psychology.[5] If then we are unconscious of what we are doing until we respond to our doing it, as Mead assumed when he speaks of our consciousness of the "I," we are unconscious of any specific active aspect of the "me" until we have responded to it. This being true, the first criterion by means of which we can distinguish the "I" from the "me" becomes meaningless: the assumption that we become conscious of the "I" only when it has passed into experience and become part of the "me." If we use a behavioristic definition of the "me" as outlined above, the "me" and the "I" become hopelessly confused because we are conscious of neither of them until they have passed into experience, i.e., until we respond to them.

Another criterion used to identify the "I" can, if properly developed, be used to differentiate between sectors of the self, but can hardly be used to account for the uniqueness of response which it is supposed to explain. We are told that one of the distinguishing characteristics of the "I" is that around it persists ". . . the sense of individuality of our own movements in relation to outer objects or persons, and of our activity in regard to these internalized "me's.""[6] If we use this conception of the "I" it becomes differentiated from the "me" only in that it is that segment of attitudes which will issue in overt action unless modified by the responses of other segments of attitudes. What is one time the "I" may next time be the "me." If, for example, a man sees someone beating a woman, his definition of the situation may be of such a nature that his immediate impulse is to strike the woman-beater; but this impulse calls out in him an attitude of discretion,[7]

---

[4] For Mead's basic discussion of the "I" see *Mind, Self, and Society*, pp. 173–178 and 192–199. It should be noted that the chronological development of Mead's thinking is not involved here. It may well be that Mead first made the distinction between the "I" and "me" long before other elements of his system had been chronologically developed; but the fact remains, the reader of *Mind, Self, and Society* is more interested in the logic of Mead's discussion as it is developed in this book; and in the logical argument social change and personal uniquenesses are only accounted for after the "I" and "me" have been introduced on p. 173. After the "I" is introduced it is then used as an explanation of the emergence of the novel, pp. 196–200.

[5] *Ibid.*, pp. 1–41. In a social psychology devoted purely to the content of personality structures, i.e., those devoted to such phenomena as value hierarchies and their effect on action, little attention need be paid to this technical psychological point, for this relation between psychology and social action can be assumed; but it forms the center of a systematic analysis which is directed toward an explanation of the dynamics of personality and self-development.

[6] Kimball Young, *Personality and Problems of Adjustment* (New York, 1940), p. 175. *Cf.* Mead, *op. cit.*, pp. 177–178.

[7] No social action is as simple as this example might lead one to believe, but there still remains a convenient distinction to be drawn between the initial impulse to act and the various "me's" which are drawn out by it; it is the function of this example to illustrate this distinction in its simplest form.

which may lead to inaction. In that case the "I" would be the anti-woman beating attitude, and the "me" would be the attitude of caution which nullified the active impulse. If, however, his wife does something of which he disapproves there may be called out in him a wife-beating response, which in turn may call out an anti-woman beating response of the nature described above. In that event, the "I" would consist of the wife-beating impulse, and the "me" of the anti-woman beating response. Thus this differentiation is merely a convenient method of distinguishing the original impulse from the modifying attitudes which prevent its fruition in overt action. Both attitudes are part of the generalized pattern of attitudes or generalized other which make up the personality of the individual, and offer no explanation of uniqueness of overt action.[8]

The third distinguishing feature of the "I" is that it is unpredictable. Thus we are given the illustration of the baseball player whose "me" calls for a throw to first base when a ground ball is hit in his direction, but who actually may either succeed in throwing the ball directly to his man or ten feet over his head.[9] It is in this example that we must take care not to fall into an erroneous conception of the relations of the various segments of the action: it is not the action of throwing the ball and throwing it ten feet over the first baseman's head which are related socially, but rather the attitude of throwing the ball to first base and the actual throwing of the ball that are bound together. If the "I" concept is meaningful at all in this case it must consist of the attitude which is called forth by the internalized attitudes of others, and its relation to the subsequent action. If we accept this as sound, there may or may not

be a relation between the attitudes involved and the fact that the ball was thrown wild. If there is such a relation it can be explained only in terms of the uniqueness of the organized set of attitudes in terms of which the player was acting.[10] Any other explanation involves the appeal to another system of causation. Thus if the player in throwing had slipped on a banana peel, there would have been no relationship between the wild throw and the attitude which we have designated as the "I." To force the banana peel or an organic rheumatic twinge in the thrower's arm into a social frame of reference would of course be sheer nonsense.[11] There is then no significance to the concept of the "I" as the unpredictable unless we regard the "I" as that attitude, located in the generalized system of attitudes, which was called out by the situation and by the attitudes of the other players internalized in the same system. If this is so, then the problem becomes one of the analysis of the determinants of the uniqueness of the attitude configuration or of a specific attitude which renders unnecessary any division of the self into the "I" and the "me" unless it is used in the manner exemplified above, i.e., as a means of distinguishing between that attitude which is called out in any specific situation and all those others which respond to it and perhaps modify it.

This still leaves us, however, with the problem of the definite residual category that Mead introduced when he had practically finished his analysis. It is necessary to carve out of the category those sectors which contain factors related to the unpredictability of human behavior which can be analyzed within Mead's scheme and to separate them from those sectors which can only be handled within a different frame of reference. This is not an easy task to perform and the following schematization must be regarded as preliminary and provisional in nature.

Physical factors, of course, can be most easily eliminated, since the social psychologist has never insisted on including phenomena in his research

---

[8] In this analysis the sense of individuality would grow out of the set of attitudes which one took toward one's self as distinct from other objects in the environment, and not out of some mystical concept of "being." Thus this approach is a line with Mead's analysis of how the individual becomes self-conscious, but refutes any attempt to account for later self-consciousness in terms of the "I." Another somewhat related, although not identical, conception of the "I" is that it is that attitude which is issuing into response at any instant of time. In this case the conception "I" would be compatible with the "I" as not directly experienced, but would be undistinguishable from the "me" except as the latter concept is used to refer to attitudes in their *latent* state. This conception may be useful for some purposes, but cannot be used to explain the residual category of phenomena which it is intended to explain.

[9] Mead, *op. cit.*, pp. 175–76.

[10] Again we see that the concept of the "I" becomes functionally useless, since it is either part of the generalized other, or is part of another system of relations that has no place within a social frame of reference.

[11] If the banana peel and the rheumatic twinge become defined within the system of attitudes which constitutes the generalized other of the player, then they may be interpreted within sociological theory of personality, but not until that time.

that can only be explained on the basis of physical laws. Thus human behavior which is rendered deviant from expectations by changes in the physical environment must merely be regarded as something that complicates the task of prediction within the empirical sphere and about which nothing can be done within the framework of a systematic social psychology. Our ball player who slipped on a banana peel must be regarded as a phenomenon unexplainable in terms of our frame of reference, and we must recognize that the "I" has nothing to do with the outcome of a situation in which a man is kept from reaching his goal by reason of the fact that he is bound by iron chains.

When we come to the realm of biological phenomena, however, the problem becomes somewhat more complicated, since the relationship prevailing between biological and social phenomena is much more complex and subtle, and the effect of the biological is discernible even on that fundamentally social phenomenon, the pattern of integrated attitudes which Mead calls the "generalized other." While Mead himself attached no explicit biological significance to the "I," others have attempted to explain the "I" as being composed of basically biological elements. Young, for example, finds the roots of the "I" partly located in the biological or constitutional foundations of action.[12] While there is some validity in this conception of the "I," the issue is still basically confused. We cannot think of the "I" as being a biological response to the "generalized other" which is social in nature, since we know that the actual response is made up of an attitude called out from this generalized system of attitudes, and hence if they are social it too must be regarded as social. The solution to this dilemma is to be found in analyzing the "generalized other" as the product of social interaction in which an individual with certain biological characteristics has engaged. Thus the "me" or the "generalized other" of a given individual is unique in that as a biological specimen he is unique.

The question then arises as to the possibility of explaining this uniqueness within a social frame of reference. It is the writer's position that this

is an impossibility if we intend to develop a systematic social psychology of personality. Since the set of attitudes is the product of both biological and social factors which present almost infinite possibilities of combining with one another, attempts to explain the importance of shifting biological conditions while at the same time analyzing the effect of socialization can only result in the conclusion that each personality is incapable of being compared with any other. This does not mean, however, that we should ignore the biological, but rather that we should assess it as a constant.[13] We must take the typical biological characteristics of man as man and consider them as dynamic factors in the development of personality, not merely as the preconditions of social development. In doing this we forego the urge to explain differences of behavior rising within the same social group as a product of biological differences between the members, but we are enabled to open up a new realm of research to Mead's frame of reference: the phenomenon which Kardiner calls basic personality structure.[14]

Thus we find a connective link between the work of a cultural psychoanalyst and Mead, which will make Mead's work more dynamic and the research of Kardiner more relevant for the sociologist and the social psychologist. If Mead's theory is used as an explanation of the process of social-

[12] Young, op. cit., p. 178

[13] Mead treats the biologic individual as a constant, but tends to emphasize the nondynamic aspects of the constant. See Mind, Self and Society, p. 139, 347–353, and passim.

[14] Abram Kardiner, The Individual and His Society (New York, 1939). Basic personality structure is defined by Linton in the foreword of Kardiner's study as "the constellation of personality characteristics which would appear to be congenial with the total range of institutions comprised within a given culture." p. vi. The importance of this concept is that with it Kardiner emphasizes the dynamic relationships existing between the demands of the society and the basic biological characteristics of man. This is not a reversion to instinct theory, since it is recognized that the drives are generalized and that all that is necessary is that they be satisfied some way, not in any specific. Thus: "If, in a particular culture, the biological need for sexual gratification is systematically interfered with, from infancy on, from our knowledge of human nature we can expect that this will give rise to a series of reactions, and that these reactions may eventually become petrified in institutions which offer some expression for the effects created by the frustrations concerned." p. 11. Since any institution is the result of human action we have here a situation in which the internalization of attitudes interfering with a basic drive result in something new: a culture complex which was not present before, and which is due to just this dynamic interaction between internalized attitude and biological drives.

ization Kardiner's work used as a means of de-lineating the dynamic relationship between the socially incorporated attitudes and the constant biological drives of men, there is some possibility of the two theories merging into one.[15] Even if this is not accomplished, there is still some benefit to be derived from the addition of a dynamic bio-logic element to Mead's theory; and the work of tracing the relation between socially derived atti-tudes, the basic personality structure, and the sec-ondary institutions, which are the product of the dynamic interaction of basic drives and social atti-tudes, will not suffer because of an increased knowledge of how the incorporation of social atti-tudes into the personality actually takes place. Attempts to reconcile different bodies of theory that stem from such divergent origins as do these two is obviously dangerous, but since the psy-choanalysts are gradually approaching a social point of view the gap between the two bodies of theory is much more apparent than real.[16]

The application of this point of view which considers biological factors as dynamic elements in the formation of the personality also makes it possible to explain widely divergent overt behav-ior where the difference between the social atti-tudes involved seems very slight. If one family adds just a slightly higher degree of emphasis on anti-masturbation attitudes than does another, with the result that the sexual behavior of the offspring of the two families varies widely, it might be possible to explain this difference on the basis of the relation between the sex drive and the two sets of attitudes.

In all the above analysis of the relation of biological factors to social factors in the formation of unique attitudes and behavior, we have ap-proached the central problem which faces us, but have not quite come to grips with it. That problem is, of course, whether there is any source of uniqueness of attitudes and behavior that is de-finitively social in nature, and that does not in-volve extra-social considerations. The generic an-swer to this question is probably in the negative. Given absolutely the same biological makeup, the identical geographic environment, a constancy in the time element, and identical physical condi-tions, there seems no reason to believe that there is anything in the process of socialization that would lead to divergent attitudes and hence to divergent behavior. This, however, is scarcely a relevant answer. Once a process of attitude differ-entiation sets in, for whatever reason, it should be obvious that the operation of purely social fac-tors will increase that differentiation. This is most apparent in the social interaction that takes place between people who have divergent back-grounds. The personality structures of both are modified, usually in an unpredictable direction, and in a direction which perhaps has never been manifested before in either of the social groups from which the individuals originated. If either of these individuals returns to his group the result is the differentiation of attitudes within the group, provided the individual is not removed in order to remove the danger of change. The literature which we have accumulated concerning culture contact, acculturation, and social change within a society bears witness to this analysis. Thus a unique set of attitudes is the product of the social interaction in which one engages with an individ-ual who has a different set of attitudes, and at least part of this change can be viewed as brought about by purely social factors.

The result of continued differentiation of this sort is a growing discrepancy between the various basic attitudes which are the common property of the group, and a child born into this type of society is likely to inherit a set of attitudes which are not consistently related to one another. The analysis of this situation is best carried out in terms of Mead's theory of internal conversation.[17] When a situation arises which is governed by conflicting attitudes, unless the self of the individual is com-

---

[15] It must be remembered that this convergence becomes pos-sible only after we have reopened Mead's system by throwing out the concept of the "I" and re-examining the residual cate-gory of phenomena which Mead cloaked with this concept.

[16] The dangers inherent in the reconciling of divergent bodies of theory grow primarily from two sources: premature reconcil-iation and crude eclecticism. This attempt to bring together the work of Kardiner and Mead may be somewhat premature since the cultural psychoanalysts are still hazy in their ideas concerning the influence and nature of social factors, and since such convergence also depends on the validity of the writer's arguments concerning the "I"; but it certainly does not suffer from eclecticism since there is no picking and choosing in-volved, but rather a conjunction of the theories in their totality has been suggested.

[17] Mead, *op cit.*, pp. 61–75.

partmentalized, a conversation between various aspects of the self ensues and the resultant attitude is likely to diverge significantly from both of the previously existing ones, so that the overt action may be greatly different from what anyone expected.

Finally, there are shifts in attitudes which occur as a result of success or failure in reaching the goals or values defined by the attitudes so that the behavior becomes unpredictable. Success is almost certain to result in the reinforcement of the attitude, but prolonged and persistent failure may result in shifts in attitudes in at least two basic fashions. The first is simply that if the defined value is important enough, the ethically enjoined attitudes toward the means will gradually lose their strength so that the goal may be sought by a new pattern of activity.[18] The second involves an evaluation of failure. If, for example, the culture places a high premium on success, prolonged failure is likely to result in self-condemnation which in turn violates basic security attitudes. In turn the interaction of these attitudes may result in what Horney has called neurotic trends, set up to protect the individual.[19] The nature of this trend is likely to depend on other techniques for gaining security which are approved by the society.

It is manifestly impossible to present all the various forms of attitude differentiation which arise out of the dynamic interplay between differing social attitudes and the situation in which they are expressed, but we have succeeded, perhaps, in pointing out the scientific benefits to be derived from the breaking down of the residual category which Mead called the "I" into some of its various components. We have discovered that some uniquenesses in behavior are unexplainable in terms of a social frame of reference; that others can be explained only in terms of the dynamic interaction of a constant biological factor and various social factors; and finally, that there does exist a realm of attitude differentiation which analytically belongs wholly within the field of social interaction. We must remember that these various forms are intermixed in the world, but nevertheless, they are analytically separable.

One more result of this breakdown of the residual category should now be apparent: Within the framework of Mead's theory certain aspects of behavior which were unexplainable except by the use of the ambiguous concepts of the "I" and the "me" are now not only explainable but have been processed so that they may to some extent even become predictable. If we recognize the basic social factors at work in attitude differentiation, it should be possible to discover predictable features in their recurrence. The way has already been opened by the cultural psychoanalysts, and with the reopening of Mead's system to include the basic findings of these researchers, it seems plausible to expect that future research will discover that variation from the dominant sets of attitudes of any society are not random but follow a pattern that can be discovered, provided one stays within the limits of the social frame of reference. That there always will be unexplainable differences in attitude and action is obvious, but that the area not only of theoretical unpredictability but of empirical unpredictability will be cut down can certainly be anticipated. In that case the extremely high probabilities that of necessity accompany all theoretical prediction will be of more significance, in that they will serve to increase the somewhat low probabilities which attend our present efforts at empirical prediction. We shall never know all about reality, but if we recognize the nature of systematic science and its limitations, we can approach closer and closer to the goal.

[18] An analysis of this type of attitude shift is to be found in Robert K. Merton's article, "Social Structure and Anomie," *American Sociological Review*, III (1938), 672–682.

[19] While the cultural psychoanalysis of Kardiner is oriented about the interplay of biological and social factors, Karen Horney's studies are concerned with the nature of conflict between social attitudes within the individual. If we disregard her undue emphasis on security, her research delineates quite clearly certain types of personality conflict based on the presence of conflicting attitudes, or of attitudes conflicting with actual performance, and traces the conflicts back to their origin in the culture pattern of our society. The same things may be said of the possible convergence of Horney's theory with that of Mead as were said in the case of Kardiner and Mead, except that in this case Horney offers a technique for unraveling the relations existing between conflicting attitudes within Mead's frame of reference. See Karen Horney, *New Ways in Psychoanalysis* (New York, 1939); *The Neurotic Personality of Our Time* (New York, 1937); and "Culture and Neurosis," *American Sociological Review*, I (1936), pp. 221–230.

Experiments on Factors Related to Self-Concept Change

A. THEORETICAL FRAMEWORK

The Cooley-Mead formulations concerning the self-concept are primarily focused on the relationships between other persons' responses to an individual and his conception of himself. More specifically, they argue that a person's conception of himself comes about as a result of the way he perceives the responses of others toward him [Cooley's "looking-glass self" (5) and Mead's "taking-the-role-of-the-other" (14)]. This, they aver, is particularly important, since the way the individual sees himself (his self-concept) has the function of directing, or influencing, the way he will behave.

This approach has had wide acceptance among social psychologists, but not without some reservations. The vague concepts and general propositions make its application very difficult. However, when the basic ideas are used as a general framework from which more specific statements are developed, the theory is most fruitful. These extensions or elaborations are not necessarily derived from the theory in a logical sense, but are intervening claims that reduce the generality or abstractness of the framework and bring it conceptually closer to the specific phenomena it purports to explain.

In the study reported here, previous work

John W. Kinch, "Experiments on Factors Related to Self-Concept Change," *Journal of Social Psychology,* vol. 74 (1968), pp. 251–258. Reprinted by permission.

on one of the propositions is used as a framework from which specific hypotheses are developed to be tested. The proposition may be stated as follows: *The individual's conception of himself is based on his perception of the way others are responding to him.* There is ample research evidence supporting this general relationship between individuals' perceptions of others and their self-concepts. However, few writers in this tradition have paid specific attention to how this process works. It is obvious that the theorists are not arguing that every time a new response is directed toward an individual there will be a corresponding change in his self-concept. What is needed is an expansion of this general proposition so that the relationships are made explicit. The basic question seems to be: *Under what conditions do the perceptions of the others' responses have an effect on the individual's self-conception?*

The theoretical framework and what evidence there is available in the literature suggest that the effect of perceived responses on the self-concept is a function of a series of factors involved in interpersonal contacts. They are *(a)* the *frequency* of responses in the course of these interpersonal contacts, *(b)* the perceived *importance* of the contacts, *(c)* the *temporal proximity* of the contacts, and *(d)* the *consistency* of the responses resulting from the contacts. It should be understood that each of the hypotheses that follows is preceded by an implied "other-factors-being-equal."

1. Hypothesis 1 (Frequency)

The more frequently the individual perceives others as responding toward him in a particular way, the more likely he is to align his self-concept with the perceived responses.

Although very little attention is given to the direct test of this notion, there are many studies that implicitly do so. For example, experimental studies have for the most part given the subjects specific ratings or evaluations which, in effect, increase the frequency of these responses, thus indirectly testing this hypothesis (4, 9, 13, 17).

2. Hypothesis 2 (Importance)

The more important the individual perceives the contact between himself and the others to be, the more likely it is that the individual's perceptions of the responses of the others will be used in defining his self-image. It is widely accepted that contacts with "significant others" are required before the individual's self-concept will be affected. These "significant others" may take the form of prestigeful persons (experts) or of personal acquaintances (friends). However, the research evidence available is not completely consistent on this subject (4, 10, 11).

3. Hypothesis 3 (Temporal Proximity)

The individual's concept of himself is a function of (a) the earliest evaluations he receives on a particular attribute and (b) the most immediate evaluations. This hypothesis has two parts. First, it is contended that the *first contacts* which the individual perceives as favoring a particular self-concept are of extreme importance. Self-conceptions that develop in early childhood are likely to persist throughout life. No direct evidence is available on this hypothesis, but there is considerable indirect evidence when one considers the *selective* aspect of early evaluations. If the author's basic contention is true that the responses of others are used in the original formation of the self-concept, there is ample evidence in the literature to suggest that persons choose friends and join groups which they perceive as evaluating them congruently with their perception of themselves

(2, 3, 8, 15). Therefore, once an individual develops a conception of himself, he will interact as much as possible with others who will reinforce this conception for him. The second part of Hypothesis 3 suggests that those *most immediate contacts* are important in understanding the individual's self-concept at any given time. Almost without exception those studies which have compared perceived responses of others to self-concepts have dealt with responses of others in the immediate situation (7, 16). In one study that directly confronted this issue, it was found that the most exaggerated changes were observed immediately following the experiment. However, some significant change still remained six weeks following the experiment, which suggests some lasting effects (9).

4. Hypothesis 4 (Consistency)

The more the individual perceives a consistent pattern in the responses of others, the more likely he is to let this affect his self-concept.

B. RESEARCH DESIGN

The research presented here empirically evaluates certain aspects of the hypotheses suggested above. It employs a series of experiments—each following the classical design with before and after tests on both experimental and control groups. The dependent variable concerns changes in one aspect of an individual's self-concept and the independent, or experimental, variables consist of the "factors" (frequency, importance, temporal proximity, and consistency) which are varied, one at time, in the experimental situations.

In the present study the notion of the self-concept is defined as the *organization of qualities which the individual attributes to himself.* Although this self-concept is "organized," it cannot be measured on a single continuum of self-regard (as many social psychologists have used the concept), but must be analyzed in terms of individual attributes or clusters of attributes. There seems to be substantial evidence for this contention (1, 6, 13, 17). In the present study, subjects were required to evaluate themselves on several descriptive objectives by use of a seven-point scale. Rather than attempt to accumulate these self-evaluations, the investigation concentrated on one adjective, "leadership."

As in other experimental studies of the self, the subjects were asked to evaluate themselves before and after they were involved in an experimental situation. In the set of experiments, conditions were varied in order to demonstrate the effect of those factors which the hypotheses suggest should influence self-concept change. In order to specify the procedure more clearly, a detailed description follows: Each experiment followed a design whereby all participants, with one exception, were confederates of the investigator. During the activity in the experimental setting, the one naive student was assigned a position of leadership and was required to direct the others. On completion of this activity the confederates were presented to the naive subject as students who were experts in organizational dynamics, all having taken advanced courses on the subject. They were then asked by the investigator to rate the naive subject's performance as a leader. This was done according to a prearranged system, *independent of the subject's actual performance.* The ratings were communicated by the verbal response of each confederate and were marked on a scale on the blackboard in front of all the participants. The confederates were pre-instructed to perform the task reasonably well regardless of the naive subject's orders, so that the prearranged ratings did not appear out of line.

Four variations in the confederates' ratings made up what were called "experimental conditions" and were designed to test several of the hypotheses. In Experimental Condition 1, each subject was rated favorably by all experts with very little variation in ratings. In the second condition (E.C. 2) each subject was involved in two sessions, thus doubling the number of evaluations which they received. Experimental Conditions 3 and 4 followed the same pattern as E.C. 1, except that in E.C. 3 only five confederates were used and a sixth rating was given by the investigator conducting the experiment, and in E.C. 4 the six

ratings were more dispersed and less consistent than in E.C. 1, although the average ratings were the same for both. These categories were compared with a control group: a matched category of students who did not participate in the experiment.

All the prearranged ratings were *higher* than the individual had rated himself before the experiment. The question of the consequence of lower ratings was not examined. In a limited experiment in which negative ratings were given a number of subjects, the results seemed to suggest that these ratings were even more influential in changing self-concepts than were the positive ratings. However, for ethical reasons this study was limited to only a few students and was not continued after the first responses were considered (12). About half of the naive students were interviewed and questioned about their impressions of the experiment. Although there were several reasons for these interviews, one major concern was with establishing some idea of the subjects' perception of the ratings they were given. Since the theory suggests that it is the way the individual *perceives* the responses of others that changes his self-concept, it was felt that the investigators must make certain that the favorable ratings which were given the subjects were perceived as such.

The difficulty of setting up an experiment that would test the hypotheses of this theory is apparent. The experimental situation had to be somewhat artificial. The ratings were rather formal compared with the ratings that one gets in everyday life. The student participation in the experiment took a relatively short time (10 minutes). Four to five weeks elapsed between the before and after tests. During that time these freshmen in college were experiencing many other situations relevant to their self-concept. For these reasons the sensitivity of the experiment and its significance for the respondents was seen as one of the major problems to be dealt with in the research presented here. Several devices were employed to increase the significance of the situation for the subjects. The subjects were required to work with the other members of the experiment "as a team," and it was this "team" that rated them. In other experiments of this type, the subjects were rated by some *one* (expert, stranger, or friend) who was not engaged with them in the experiment. In the interviews, the subjects indicated considerable concern over what ratings they received and considered the ratings as favorable. This suggests that the others in the experiment were significant to them.

The problem of sample size is particularly difficult in this type of design, since, for each subject, there must be a separate experiment, plus complete before and after test information. When the total number of cases is divided into four experimental conditions and a control group, the number of cases in any one condition is likely to be cut seriously low. This was the case in the present study, which started with 105 subjects, 21 assigned to each of the four experimental conditions and 21 to the control group. Some of the disadvantages of the small numbers were reduced by precision matching and randomization of assignments.

C. RESULTS

By comparing before-after changes in self-concept ratings on leadership for the subjects in each of the conditions, evidence is brought to bear on at least part of three of the four hypotheses mentioned above. The complete results are reported in Table 21.1.

There are several ways in which these data may be applied to Hypothesis 1. In this hypothesis it is suggested that the more frequently a person perceives a particular type of response directed toward him, the more likely he is to use that response in changing his self-concept. Since all those taking part in the experiments had a particular type of response (favorable ratings on leadership) directed toward them, we can assume that "on the average" this group has had more of this type of response than the control group. Therefore, one test of the hypothesis is a simple comparison of those in the experimental groups with those in the control group. The results are in the expected direction with mean changes of $+.65$ of a unit on the rating scale for those in the experimental groups ($N=71$). and only $+.23$ of a unit for the control group ($N=21$). The differences between the two changes are statistically significant at the .05 level of significance ($t=1.76$, difference between independent mean test).

A more refined test on this hypothesis involves comparing those in E.C. 2 with those in E.C. 1 and the control group, since the subjects in E.C. 2 had more of a particular type of response directed toward them than did the subjects in E.C. 1. The results support the hypothesis. Those who performed under E.C. 2 showed a mean change in their self-conceptions of one complete unit on the rating scale, while those in E.C. 1

TABLE 21.1. Mean self-ratings on leadership before and after experimental evaluations by experimental conditions

Experimental Condition	N	Before		After		Before-After Differences		t
		M	SD	M	SD	M	SD	
E.C. 1 (Standard)	19	4.26	1.02	4.63	.93	.37	.98	1.59
E.C. 2 (Repeat)	18	4.28	1.04	5.28	.73	1.00	1.15	3.57**
E.C. 3 (Importance)	19	4.26	1.12	4.89	.73	.63	.74	3.62**
E.C. 4 (Dispersed)	15	4.20	1.11	4.80	.83	.60	.92	2.36*
All experimental conditions	71	4.25	1.07	4.90	.83	.65	.99	5.45**
Control group	21	4.29	1.16	4.52	.96	.23	.75	1.42

Note: All tests are one-tailed. The t's above refer to the difference between the before and after means of dependent samples.
* $p<.05$.
** $p<.01$.

changed only .37 of a unit. This difference is statistically significant ($t = 2.29$, difference between independent mean test).

From Hypothesis 2 (Importance) it was felt that the added prestige of the investigator's rating in E.C. 3 would lead to greater changes than in the comparable E.C. 1. Here the results are in the expected direction; however, the difference between the two experimental groups was small and not statistically significant (means of .37 and .63 for E.C. 1 and 3, respectively—$t = .93$).

Hypothesis 4 suggests that the consistency of responses is important and would lead to the expectation of a greater before-after difference in E.C. 1 than in E.C.4. Here the results show just the opposite. Those students who were given about the same ratings by all the raters changed less than those subjects who were given more dispersed ratings (mean changes of .37 in E.C. 1 as compared with a change of .60 in E.C. 4).

D. SUMMARY

The study described here is one in a series of studies proposed by the author designed to vary systematically factors relevant to changes in self-conceptions. Although experimental studies of this type are hampered by the several difficulties apparent in this report, the valuable manipulative power that the investigator has over his variables allows crucial tests which could not be accomplished by other methods. The need for systematic empirical support or investigation of social psychological theory is recognized by all. This study has attempted to provide that type of support for the Mead-Cooley notions about the self-concept.

REFERENCES

1. Akeret, R. U. Interrelationships among various dimensions of the self concept. *J. Counsel, Psychol.*, 1959, 6, 199–201.

2. Backman, C. W., & Secord, P. F. The effect of perceived liking on interpersonal attraction. *Hum. Relat.*, 1959, 12, 379–384.

3. ———. Liking, selective interaction, and misperception in congruent interpersonal relations. *Sociometry*, 1962, 25, 321–335.

4. Bergin, A. The effect of dissonant persuasive communications upon changes in a self-referring attitude. *J. Personal.*, 1962, 30, 423–438.

5. Cooley, C. H. *Human Nature and the Social Order.* New York: Scribner, 1902.

6. Couch, C. Family role specialization and self-attitudes in children. *Sociolog. Quart.*, 1962, 3, 115–122.

7. Davidson, H. H., & Lang, G. Children's perceptions of their teachers' feelings toward them related to self-perception, school achievement and behavior. *J. Exper. Educ.*, 1960, 29, 107–118.

8. Dittes, J. E. Attractiveness of group as a function of self-esteem and acceptance by group. *J. Abn. & Soc. Psychol.*, 1959, 59, 77–82.

9. Haas, H. L., & Moehr, M. L. Two experiments on the concept of self and reactions of others. *J. Personal. & Soc. Psychol.*, 1965, 1, 100–105.

10. Harvey, O. J., Kelley, H. H., & Shapiro, M. M. Reactions to unfavorable evaluations of the self made by other persons. *J. Personal.*, 1957, 25, 393–411.

11. Kennedy, J. L., & Lasswell, H. D. A cross-cultural test of self-image. *Hum. Organization*, 1958, 17, 41–43.

12. Kinch, J. W. The manipulation of subjects in experiments. Unpublished paper presented at the Pacific Sociological Association Meetings, Vancouver, British Columbia, Canada, 1966.

13. Maehr, M., Mensing, J., & Nafager, S. Concept of self and the reaction of others. *Sociometry*, 1962, 25, 353–357.

14. Mead, G. H. *Mind, Self and Society.* Chicago, Ill.: Univ. Chicago Press, 1934.

15. Reese, H. W. Relationships between self-acceptance and sociometric choices. *J. Abn. & Soc. Psychol.*, 1961, 62, 472–474.

16. Rosengren, W. R. The self in the emotionally disturbed. *Amer. J. Sociol.*, 1961, 66, 454–462.

17. Videbeck, R. Self-conception and the reaction of others. *Sociometry*, 1960, 23, 351–359

Self-Identity in Marriage and Widowhood

This paper examines some of the processes by which women re-define their identities in marriage and in widowhood, and the influence that their educational achievement has upon the processes and the results. Theories of symbolic interaction and ethnomethodology provide certain basic assumptions about the construction of social reality, including self-identity, as it emerges in social interaction (Berger and Luckman, 1966; Blumer, 1969; Goffman, 1963, 1967; McCall and Simmons, 1966). These assumptions are: 1) that identities are formulated in a complicated process of social interaction which involves symbolic definitions of the self, the other, and the situation; 2) that repeated interaction with the same other in similar situations, as in long-term significant relations, results in rather definite and stabilized self and

Helena Znaniecki Lopata, "Self-Identity in Marriage and Widowhood," *The Sociological Quarterly*, vol. 14 (Summer 1973), pp. 407–418. Reprinted by permission.

This article was first presented as a paper at the American Sociological Association meetings in Denver, August, 1971. The first set of studies, that of role definitions of several samples of married women living in metropolitan Chicago, was facilitated by fellowships and grants from *The Chicago Tribune*, The Midwest Council for Social Research on Aging, and Roosevelt University, and is summarized elsewhere (1971a). The second, consisting of interviews with a modified area probability sample of 301 metropolitan Chicago widows aged 50 and over, drawn by the National Opinion Research Center, was supported in part by an Administration on Aging grant, a division of the Department of Health, Education and Welfare (Grant No. AA–4–67–030–01–A1) and in part by Roosevelt University. I am grateful to Herbert Blalock, Richard Hill, Eileen Markley Znaniecki, David Maines, and Frank Steinhart for helping me with this paper.

other identities; 3) that these identities are modified as the self, the other, or the definition of the situation change; and 4) that the removal of the significant other from interaction with the self will necessitate a reformulation of the identities in which he or she was involved. The more important and pervasive the relation with the other, the more the actor's entrance into it, and exit from it, will involve reformulation of prior identities.

Two sets of studies are used here to question some of the assumptions about the pervasiveness and the depth of identity reformulations with entrance into and exit from a major social relation, the nuclear family marriage. One set of studies has examined the role and self-definitions of 571 urban and suburban housewives and working women, and the descriptions of life and self changes which were produced by major events in the past of another 205 respondents. The second involved interviews with a modified area probability sample of 301 widows residing in metropolitan Chicago.

Most observers of the American urban scene consider marriage to be one of the major social relations for both partners, but particularly for women.[1] Only the parent-child relation is ex-

[1] Edmund Volkhart (1965:272–293) explains in detail the factors contributing to shifts in the structure and functions of the nuclear family in his discussion of why its members are so vulnerable to bereavement. Most of his comments are directed to parent-child relations, but they certainly fit those between husband and wife

pected to approximate it in importance. There is no agreement as to whether these two sets of relations are equal or, if they are not, which is the more important one in the lives of women.[2] According to Berger and Kellner (1970), entrance into such an intense relation as modern marriage requires cooperative objectification of a common world, including reformulation of the identities of the husband and the wife. The identity changes result not only from their interaction in the dyad, as described by Berger and Kellner, but also from the common front they present toward the world and the influence of their marriage upon other relations. The process can be expected to have a profound influence upon a wife for several reasons, all embedded in the family institution. In the first place, although girls are socialized into individualistic personality identities, married women and mothers are expected to be oriented primarily toward family welfare. Secondly, the roles of wife and mother are considered the basic and the only really important ones for adult women.[3] The addition of the roles of husband and father are not expected to produce an equivalently significant shift in the role cluster of men. Finally, the reality constructed by a couple symbolically and in actual life-style tends to be built around the husband's occupational role outside of the home.[4] This is particularly true if

his occupation has, or is expected to achieve, high status in the community, such as foreman or craftsman in the blue-collar community or practically any type of professional or managerial worker in middle- or upper-class neighborhoods. Although there may be a trend decreasing this heavy stress on male employment in American society, most people agree that residence and style of life, including the daily rhythm, possessions, vocations, friendships, etc., should be built around the man's job. After all, goes the argument, without it the family could not be maintained.

The importance of marriage in the life of a woman is symbolized by her name change. In effect, becoming Mrs. Harry Jones wipes out the whole past of Mary Smith, her family, her ethnic and personal achievement identities. In the historical past this was accompanied by a complete shift into the husband's family-life-style, and even now continuity of identity without change is almost impossible as new relations, residence, economic base, and fresh responsibilities are thrust upon the wife.

The influence of marriage upon the self-identity of women emerged as a fact in the studies of the housewives and the working women living in metropolitan Chicago, leading to the prediction that the abrupt ending of marriage through the death of the husband would also result in a dramatic identity reformulation. However, an additional fact emerged from these studies, leading to a re-examination of the assumptions about the influence of marriage upon the construction of social reality. The women whose self and role definitions were examined varied considerably in the extent to which they felt their identities were influenced by marriage and by the identities of their husbands. The basic factor affecting their

---

[2] The role hierarchy of American metropolitan women was tapped in two different ways within several research projects. First, the suburban full-time housewives were asked to list, in order of importance, the most important roles of women. The next study isolated 13 roles mentioned by the respondents to the first study and asked for a ranking of all in relation to the others. The several different patterns of ranking were found to be dependent upon education of the woman and several socioeconomic factors (Lopata, 1965).

[3] There is considerable evidence that American women do not take seriously their obligations to society. They justify work as merely a means of getting more money for the home and are very unreliable as voluntary workers. *Occupation: Housewife* respondents ranked the roles of worker, self expressive (i.e., writer) member of community, and member of a religious organization at the bottom of the rank order of importance of women's roles, ranking mother, wife, woman, housewife, daughter, grandmother, sister, neighbor and friend above these (Lopata, 1971a and 1971b).

[4] Ogburn (1922) built a theory of social change around the thesis that the economic technological institution is the focal one within a society and is the first to change, forcing adjustments on other institutions, with cultural lag on the part of the family. He was generalizing only from American social life, since there

have been, and still are, societies focusing around other institutions. It is quite probable that the low status of women in societies with complex industrialized and urbanized cultures and a strong focus on the economic institution is due to the fact that they are not expected to take an important part in that segment of life. Their *Second Sex* location can be seen as peripheral to the masculine sex whose primary contribution is within the focal institution. (See also Friedan, 1963, de Beauvoir, 1953, Greer, 1971, Janeway, 1971, Klein, 1949, Komarovsky, 1953, and 1950).

awareness and expression of identity reformulation in marriage and their involvement in a common world with their husbands proved to be the level of formal education which they had achieved.[5] There were several pieces of evidence leading to this conclusion. The less educated women often forgot to list marriage as a major event of the past, focusing rather on the birth of the first and of subsequent children. The less education women have, the less apt they are to list the role of wife as being of primary importance in the lives of women; they concentrate instead on the role of mother. They now see life in much the same way they had visualized it in adolescence, commenting chiefly on its economic features. These women do not feel that they share in the work-life of the husband. They believe that they have no influence on it or else that their only contribution is to feed their husband well at home and to nag him—or not nag, as the case may be—to get a better job and bring home more money. The lower the education of the respondent, the more the difference between the man's and the woman's lives appeared in the selection of friends, in child-rearing, and in participation in the neighborhood and the community. Rather than building a common world with their husbands, they exist in segregated, though often parallel hemispheres, with little knowledge or understanding of the other half (see also, Rainwater et al., 1959).

On the other hand, the more educated a woman is, the more influence she assigns in her identity formulation to being married, to being married to this particular husband, and to being part of this couple. She is very apt to list marriage as a major event and to explain carefully the changes she experienced in herself as a result of it. She assigns the role of wife first place in a rank order of importance or explains her emphasis on the role of mother as temporarily necessitated by the age of her children. She does not think

she is now leading the kind of life she visualized in adolescence, re-defining her prior interest in an occupation as unrealistic.[6] The more educated woman feels that she influences her husband's performance at work either directly, through specific tasks or entertainment, or indirectly by understanding his problems and being able to discuss them. She shares with him a definition of the world, or of a large part of it, and builds a set of social relations which involve him, including couple-companionate friendships, neighboring, membership in voluntary associations, etc.

Thus, these studies of urban and suburban housewives and working women indicated that there are differences in the degrees to which wives weave being married and the identities of their husbands into their world constructs, resulting in a reformulation of their own identities. Awareness of these variations led, in a study of widows aged 50 and over, to a hypothesis concerned directly with identity reformulation. The hypothesis is that the higher the education of a woman as measured by formal schooling, the more she will be affected by widowhood, because with this event she will undertake a more complete reconstruction of reality and identity than her less educated counterpart will. This hypothesis actually contains two components of identity formulation: the abstracted and constructed reality, and the extent to which this reality is woven around the presence of a husband, the presence of this particular husband, and participation as a member of this couple.

Theoretically, the death of the husband is bound to produce direct and secondary changes in the identities of American metropolitan women, particularly if prior to that event he was residing with the wife and sharing a life-style and

---

[5] Komarovsky (1967) also found that the higher the educational level, even within *Blue-Collar Marriage*, the greater the communication between marital partners. Some of our less educated respondents did not even know how many years of schooling their husbands had completed, or where his relatives are living now, or the names of his married sisters.

[6] As late as 1965 Rossi (1965:180) reported that most women college students were not seriously preparing for a variety of occupational roles. Most either planned on becoming housewives or entering traditional fields. Only 7 percent declared an interest in fields of knowledge in which they were "pioneers" because of their sexual identities. It is possible that the new trends in the women's movement will have a direct effect on the young couples who will construct their world to include more complex identities for women and convert the abstractions into concrete plans for implementing occupational aspirations (see also Rose, 1961).

social relations with her.[7] The stronger the bond with the husband and the more varied the sets of relations she had with him—e.g., couple-companionate friendships, neighboring, serving as a daughter-in-law to his parents, as a salesman's wife to his sales manager, etc.—the more complex and significant the changes which could be expected to follow in her life and identities with his death.

The study of widowhood in the Chicago area brought forth several reasons why a woman experiences changes with the death of her husband. In the first place, she loses the partner with whom she has shared the on-going process of defining the world.[8] Living alone, as most older widows do (and women are apt to become widowed when they grow older), she gradually loses the memory of her husband's definitions. She will often report that, as new situations arise, she tries to imagine what her husband would have said were he alive, but the dialogue becomes difficult over time. She may hang on to her husband's image of her, as she had perceived it, but that, too, fades or becomes harder to revive, as her mirror and others note the changes.

Identity reformulation is also a consequence of the changes in daily life. The absence of the husband dramatically or gradually changes the routine, what is thought about, and what is felt in response to events, including those on television. Furthermore, his absence cuts off the help upon which the woman depended in their division of labor. She has no object for her work, and since marriage created a system of specialization in knowledge and skills, she has definite gaps in her abilities. Many widows report strong feelings of inadequacy and frustration because of their inability to handle money transactions or to maintain an automobile. In addition, no one is available to act as a man around the house, and widows feel very unfeminine doing things previously undertaken by the husband. For many women the division of tasks into "his" or "hers" creates a real void, which has repercussions upon her feeling as an incomplete person.

It is in interaction with others that widows are most apt to report identity problems. Two aspects of interaction are of special significance: without her husband, the woman cannot reproduce certain interactional sequences, and other people do not treat her the same way as before. Their image of her is that of a widow and not that of a wife, while she frequently wants to retain her prior identity. If they knew her husband well, they see her as the widow of that particular man, a constant reminder of the mortality of men. Some respondents report being literally shunned, because the late husband's friends are made so uncomfortable by their presence. Others report that their mutual friends now regard them as dangerous objects around their still living husbands, assuming the widow to be out to get another mate, in marriage or sexually only. Respondents sense that friends are also afraid of the demands they might be making for sympathy or services, which the associates define as unreasonable in the framework of the past relation. Widows often feel that their married friends no longer trust them or seem unwilling to meet their needs. What also seems to happen is that a new widow is undergoing a "status passage" with no clearly defined end product. What is a widow in American society? There is no single, predictable pattern of behavior associated with that status. It is not a role in the sense that it was in traditional India. The associates of a woman whose husband has recently died know that she is undergoing changes, but they often cannot predict the results of the process of modification. Many alternative identities are available to modern women who are widows, but

[7] There have been several studies of the problems of the widowed, including Marris (1958) in London, England and Berardo (1967, 1968a, 1968b) of both men and women in the state of Washington, U.S.A. Townsend (1968) and Turnstall (1966) also talk of these problems. Some of the psychiatrists and related social scientists of the Harvard Medical School studied grief intensively (Maddison, 1968; Maddison and Walker, 1967; Parkes, 1964, 1965; Parkes and Benjamin, 1967). See also Jackson's (1959, 1969) discussion of death and grief. See also Lopata (1972).

[8] Many of the "Forms of Loneliness" (Lopata, 1969) reported by the Chicago area widows really focus upon identity problems which are ignored because grief is culturally defined as a pining for the deceased, without analysis of what this means. McCall and Simmons (1966) point out, however, that marriage or another diadic relation constructs a person's agenda so that "The two persons are not merely disjointed individuals but constitute a unit, a collective unit of which they are members . . . (175). Married people are invited to events not as persons but as couples (176)."

the future they choose is often a surprise to friends. In most cases, any real change takes or pushes her away from them. Thus, since the recently bereaved woman is not a stable identity, she threatens the identities of others.

A major variation in the perceived changes in her identities lies in the manner in which a widow's late husband served as a link between her and society, the extent to which their world was built around him, and his outside identities. Chicago area respondents report a decrease in social life, if it was dependent on his business contact, or because they are afraid to go out at night alone, hesitant about entering public places without a male escort, unable to reach distant events, and in general helpless in many social situations. The undercurrent of many complaints about the problems of widowhood thus consists of three segments: a feeling of incompetence and incompleteness as persons, being shunned by others, and experiences of strain in social interaction. There are strong stigmatic aspects to these feelings, often camouflaged by descriptions of what grief means, but resembling attitudes toward the self felt by people who are adjusting to a major physical or social disfigurement (Goffman, 1963).[9]

Although these sentiments are reported as a direct consequence of the death of the husband, there are women in the sample who still experience negative self-feelings after years of widowhood. However, most of the women who are aware of changes in themselves report positive identity reformulations after the initial "grief work" is completed (see Lindemann, 1944;

Parkes, 1964, and 1965; Maddison, 1968; Maddison and Walker, 1967). When questioned: "Many women tell us that they change after becoming widows. How do you think you have changed?", 54 percent of the respondents listed at least one change. Sixty-three percent of those who list a first or only change believe themselves to be more independent and competent now than while their husbands were living. Another 10 percent report that they are freer and more active individuals. Only 18 percent view the major change in negative terms. They find themselves prone to worry or to be less sociable, and 2 percent are more suspicious of other people. One hundred widows list a second change in themselves and of these, 18 percent explain it as being a freer person, 47 percent as being more active, and 23 percent as being more worried and suspicious. Finally, 62 respondents list a third change in answer to this open-end question: 31 percent of them are more socially engaged individuals, but 68 percent report being more worried and concerned about themselves and their lives, with only one woman reporting an increase of suspicion. Thus, the overwhelming proportion of widows who recognize or admit change in their personalities or identities consider themselves fuller and freer people than before the death of their husbands. They have rounded out their personalities, previously restricted or limited as a result of marriage. This does not mean necessarily that they had bad marriages, as these are the very same individuals who list loneliness, rather than money or other troubles as the worst problem of widowhood, and miss their husband most as a person or a partner, rather than as a breadwinner, worker, or a presence in the house. This is the form of loneliness most often experienced (Lopata, 1969). Also, the fact that they now feel fuller and more competent identities does not mean that the interim period was easy, since worry, strain in relations, and grief were a part of it.

Of special concern to this discussion are the women who reject the idea of change in themselves in widowhood. Those who claim not to have been changed by the death of their husband contravene all the theoretical propositions of symbolic interaction and ethnomethodology, as well as the logic of life in American urban centers.

---

[9] The needs and the problems of identity reformulation in widowhood are neglected by sociologists and other social scientists, who really should know better than to make the assumptions such neglect implies. Cumming and Henry (1961) claimed that widowhood is easier for women than retirement is for men, because there is no loss of status in the former case. Riley and associates (1969:968) even state that "Bereavement is not a threat to the self-image (in the same sense as retirement), because it results neither from the individual's failure nor from his loss of capacity to perform the functions of the role." This statement neglects the loss of capacity and identity following the death, let alone the guilt feelings connected with it. Even psychologists studying "grief work," as Lindemann (1944) called it, under-value the extent to which it involves identity reformulation. They may mention it (Flesch, 1969) in passing, but they never return to it nor have they investigated the process or the end result.

TABLE 22.1. Association between education and reported change in the self since the death of the husband

Education	Change in Self in Widowhood	
	No Change N = 138 %	Change N = 162 %
Less than 8th grade (N = 76)	33	18
Eighth grade (N = 69)	25	22
Some high school (N = 61)	18	22
High school graduate (N = 62)	17	24
More than high school (N = 32)	7	14
	100	100

$\chi^2 = 12.15$; d.f. = 4; level of significance $< .01$
Kendall's Tau B = 0.179; level of significance $< .001$

There could be several reasons why women refuse to admit change in themselves in spite of the fact that, throughout the interview, they make frequent references to relation problems and the need to develop skills, change friends, move, go to work, etc. In the first place, American culture, particularly that shared at the lower socioeconomic levels, contains fixed personality imagery. Adults are regarded as possessing stable traits. Secondly, permanence of identity into widowhood performs the important traditional function of sanctifying the dead. The wife remains the same as before—"in his memory." A third reason may be non-involvement in identity reformulation in marriage and absence of a strong dependence of life-style on the husband, in that he was not an integral part of the wife's life. A fourth reason may be the absence of social interaction with people able and willing to record change in the widow. An isolated woman may not have anyone aware of whether she is changing or not; an uneducated one may have companions who also lack the conceptualization skills required to note patterns of behavior in her. Those hypotheses would lead to the expectation that the women reporting no change in their identity as a result of the death of their husband would be uneducated, lacking a strong interpersonal social life, not highly dependent upon the husband when he was living, and currently socially isolated.

The distributions of the widows reporting change in themselves or rejecting the idea are significant and support the conclusions reached by the study of married women and the hypotheses drawn from the theoretical bases. The variables which have the strongest significant associations with each other in connection with reported change in the self following the death of the husband turned out to be: education of the woman, occupation of her husband, social isolation, and reported change in the level and quality of social life.[10]

The respondents who report no change in themselves as a result of widowhood are less educated, more socially isolated and less dependent in their social life on the presence of their husband than are the women who have consciously experienced identity reformulation. The educational differences are very strong (see Table 22.1). Also, women reporting "no change" scored high

[10] Several factors which I expected to be of significance in differentiating between women who report change in themselves as a result of widowhood and those who reject the idea proved insignificant. For example, the number of children a woman has, or their total absence, and the number of people with whom she is currently living do not influence her perception of identity modifications. Neither does the length of widowhood, most ˙ because so few respondents were recently bereaved. A˙ widowhood is influential only in the oldest age categor 65 and over, but this trend is also related to educˑ husband's education, which have a much stronger with reported change.

TABLE 22.2. Association between perceived change since the death of the husband and score on the social isolation scale

| | Change in Self | |
| | No Change
N = 138
% | Change
N = 162
% |
Level of Social Isolation		
Low (N = 52)	10	24
Medium (N = 210)	71	69
High (N = 38)	19	7
	100	100

$\chi^2 = 15.35$; d.f. = 2; level of significance $< .005$
Kendall's Tau B = $-.22$; level of significance $< .001$

TABLE 22.3. Association between perceived change in the self since death of husband and changes in social life

| | Change in Self | |
| | No Change
N = 130
% | Change
N = 157
% |
Change in Social Life		
Less Now (N = 113)	32	45
Same (N = 126)	58	32
More (N = 34)	8	15
Different People or Activity (N = 14)	2	8
	100	100

$\chi^2 = 23.38$; d.f. = 3; level of significance $< .001$

on the social isolation scale, based on the absence of a variety of potential social relations at the time of the interview (see Table 22.2).

In addition, the social isolation of these women is not a consequence of the absence of the husband, but seems to be a chronic state, since these women report themselves as having the same type, in quality and quantity, of social life as they had when he was living (see Table 22.3). In fact, 97 percent of the highly isolated women, compared to 43 percent of the medium isolated and 41 percent of those scoring "low" on the social isolation scale report their social life to be the same as before the death of the husband. These are strong contrasts. Those who report an increase in social life, interestingly enough, tend

to score "medium" on the social isolation scale rather than "low." The low scorers are the more educated women, who nevertheless report a change or decrease in social life with widowhood. It is likely that they re-engaged in society in different types of activities than before, since they are the same women who report independence and feeling freer than in the past. That social life and other engagement relations affect self-identity is indicated by the fact that women who report change in themselves as a result of losing the husband are the most apt to report either a lessening of social life or an increase. They are very unlikely to claim it to be the same.

Table 22.4 summarizes in greater detail the general trends. The importance of education

TABLE 22.4. Association between social isolation and education for women reporting change in themselves as a result of widowhood and those reporting no change

	Change			Total		No-Change			Total	
	Social Isolation			Reporting Change		Social Isolation			Reporting No Change	
Education	Low %	Medium %	High %	%*	N	Low %	Medium %	High %	%**	N
Less than 8	0	90	10	40	30	2	67	30	60	46
8	26	60	14	51	35	9	71	21	49	34
9–11	14	81	6	59	36	12	80	8	41	25
12	38	59	3	63	39	9	78	13	37	23
More than 12	41	54	4	69	22	50	50	0	31	10
N	26	98	14							

$\chi^2 = 23.52$; d.f. = 8; l.s. = .003 $\chi^2 = 27.08$; d.f. = 8; l.s. = .007
Kendall's Tau B = −.27; l.s. = .0001   Kendall's Tau B = −.29; l.s. = .001
The percentages in column * are of the total number of people in that educational category who report change. 100% is obtained by adding * and **.

comes out in the rotation of all five of the significant variables—education, occupation of husband, social isolation, reported changes in social life, and reported changes in the self. The occupation of the husband is associated with social isolation most strongly for women with less than an eighth grade education, but for highly trained women the husband's job has less influence on isolation and felt reformulation of life and self. The relation between the variables which emerges from such a rotation is as follows: A minimal educational achievement restricts a woman's ability to obtain a husband with whom she will become fully involved in the reconstruction of reality and self-identity and also her ability to become socially active with or without him. The less educated woman does not consciously reformulate self-identities in conjunction with her husband and is thus less affected by his presence or absence than is the more educated woman. The higher the education of the wife, the greater her involvement in identity reconstruction in marriage and widowhood. This kind of woman reports change in social life, in quality or quantity, without becoming socially isolated, and feels that she has changed in consequence of widowhood. The change was painful in the process, but now she feels like a fuller human being, more independent and competent than in the past.

SUMMARY

The education, social isolation, and reported changes in the social life package indicate that women differ in their degree of involvement with their husband and that these differences are reflected in their self-identities. Women at the lower end of the socioeconomic scale, particularly those who do not have much formal education in abstractly organizing their worlds, do not engage in the process described by ethnomethodologists (Berger and Kellner, 1970) as strongly as the more educated wives of white collar husbands. It is probable that they lack both complexity and structure in their construction of reality, which includes their self identities, and that they do not go through a self-conscious process of re-structuring and objectifying their reality upon marriage, so that they do not need or are not inclined to re-structure it in widowhood. They are less affected in their conscious identities by the presence and world constructs of their husband than are the more educated women. They communicate with the mate less; his entrance into, and exit from their lives does not require conscious reformulation of their own identities and location in the constructed world.

One conclusion of this paper is that the construction process and the end product of self identity and world formulation vary by the formal education achieved by a woman and by the social class of her life style. The second is that marriage and widowhood are less disorganizing to the identities of lower-class women than for those with higher training and life style, because the better educated women devote more time and resources to constructing a world view around the presence and with the help of the man they marry than do their less educated counterparts.

REFERENCES

Berardo, Felix. "Widowhood Status in the United States: Perspective on a Neglected Aspect of the Family Life-cycle." The Family Coordinator 17 (July 1968a):191–203.

———. "Survivorship and Social Isolation. The Case of the Aged Widower." (Manuscript), 1968b.

———. "Social Adaptation to Widowhood among a Rural-Urban Population." Washington State University, College of Agriculture: Agricultural Experiment Station Bulletin 689 (December 1967).

Berger, Peter, and Hansfried Kellner. "Marriage and the Construction of Reality." Recent Sociology #2. Edited by Hans Dreitzel. London: Collier-Macmillan, 1970, pp. 50–73.

Berger, Peter and Thomas Luckman. The Social Construction of Reality. Garden City, N.Y.: Doubleday Anchor Books, 1966.

Blumer, Herbert. Symbolic Interactionism: Perspective and Method. Englewood Cliffs, N.J.: Prentice-Hall, 1969.

Cumming, Elaine, and William E. Henry. Growing Old: The Process of Disengagement. New York: Basic Books, 1961.

de Beauvoir, Simone. The Second Sex. New York: Alfred Knopf, 1953.

Flesch, Regina. "The Condolence Call." Death and Bereavement. Edited by Austin H. Kutscher. Springfield, Ill.: Charles C. Thomas, 1969, pp. 236–248.

Friedan, Betty. The Feminine Mystique. New York: W. W. Norton, 1963.

Goffman, Erving. Interaction Ritual. Garden City, N.Y.: Anchor Books, 1967.

———. Stigma: Notes on the Management of Spoiled Identity. Englewood Cliffs, N.J.: Prentice-Hall, Inc., 1963.

———. Encounters. Indianapolis: Bobbs-Merrill, 1961.

Greer, Germain. The Female Eunuch. New York: McGraw-Hill, 1971.

Jackson, Edgar N. "Attitudes toward Death in our Culture." Death and Bereavement. Edited by Austin H. Kutscher. Springfield, Ill.: Charles C Thomas, 1969, pp. 204–206.

———. "Grief and Religion." The Meaning of Death. Edited by Herman Feifel. New York: McGraw-Hill, 1959, pp. 218–233.

Janeway, Elizabeth. Man's World Woman's Place: A Study in Social Mythology. New York: William Morrow, 1971.

Klein, Viola. The Feminine Character: History of an Ideology. New York: International Universities Press, 1949.

Komarovsky, Mirra. Blue-Collar Marriage. New York: Random House, 1967.

———. Women in the Modern World: Their Education and Their Dilemmas. Boston: Little, Brown, and Co., 1953.

———. "Functional Analysis of Sex Roles." American Sociological Review (August 1950):508–516.

Lindemann, E. "Symptomology and Management of Acute Grief." American Journal of Psychiatry 101 (July 1944):141–148.

Lopata, Helena Znaniecki. Widowhood in an American City. Cambridge, Mass.: Schenkman Publishing Company, 1972.

———. Occupation: Housewife. New York: Oxford University Press, 1971.

———. "Loneliness: Forms and Components." Social Problems 17 (Fall 1969):248–262.

———. "The Secondary Features of a Primary Relationship." Human Organization 24 (Summer 1965):116–123.

Lopata, H. Z. and F. Steinhart. "Work Histories of American Urban Women." The Gerontologist (Winter 1971):27–36.

Maddison, D. "The Relevance of Conjugal Bereavement for Preventative Psychiatry." British Journal of Psychiatry 41 (September 1968):223–233.

Maddison, D., and W. L. Walker. "Factors Affecting the Outcome of Conjugal Bereavement." British Journal of Psychiatry 113 (October 1967):1057–1067.

Marris, Peter. Widows and Their Families. London: Routledge and Kegan Paul, Ltd., 1958.

McCall, George, and J. L. Simmons. Identities and Interactions. New York: The Free Press, 1966.

Ogburn, William. Social Change. New York: The Viking Press, 1922.

Parkes, M. "Bereavement and Mental Illness: A Clinical Study." *British Journal of Medical Psychology, Part I*, 38 (1965):1–12 and Part II, 38 (1965):13–26.

——. "Effects of Bereavement on Physical and Mental Health: A Study of the Medical Records of Widows." *British Medical Journal* 2 (August 1964):272–279.

Parkes, M. and B. Benjamin. "Bereavement." *British Medical Journal* 3 (July–September 1967):232–233.

Rainwater, Lee, Richard Coleman and Gerald Handel. *Workingman's Wife*. New York: Oceana Publications, 1959.

Riley, Matilda White and Associates. "Socialization for the Middle and Later Years." *Handbook of Socialization Theory and Research*. Edited by David A. Goslin. Chicago: Rand McNally Co., 1968, pp. 951–982.

Rose, A. "The Inadequacy of Women's Expectations for Adult Roles." *Social Forces* 30 (October 1961):69–77.

Rossi, Alice. "Barriers to the Career Choice of Engineering, Medicine or Science among American Women." *Women and the Scientific Professions*. Edited by Jacquelyn A. Mattfelt and Carol G. Van Aken. Cambridge, Mass.: M.I.T. Press, 1965, pp. 55–127.

Townsend, Peter. "Isolation, Desolation and Loneliness." *Old People in Three Industrial Societies*. Edited by Ethel Shanas, Dorothy Wedderburn, Henning Friis, Poul Mithoj, Jan Stehoumer. New York: Atherton Press, 1968, pp. 258–285.

Tunstall, Jeremy. *Old and Alone*. London: Routledge and Kegan Paul, Ltd., 1966.

Volkhart, Edmund H. and Stanley T. Michael. "Bereavement and Mental Health." *Death and Identity*. Edited by Robert Fulton. New York: John Wiley and Sons, 1965, pp. 272–293.

E. L. Quarantelli
& Joseph Cooper   **23**

Self-Conceptions and Others: A Further Test of Meadian Hypotheses

In this paper we attempt to do the following with respect to the symbolic interactionist approach to social psychological phenomena: (1) to add to its relatively meager empirical base; (2) to develop a neglected aspect of the position, namely, the time dimension; and (3) to contribute to both the replication and the extension of the limited systematic research which has used this

E. L. Quarantelli and Joseph Cooper, "Self-Conceptions and Others: A Further Test of Meadian Hypotheses," *The Sociological Quarterly*, vol. 7, no. 3 (Summer 1966), pp. 281–297. Reprinted by permission.

This investigation was supported in part by Public Health Service Research Grant DH-00014–04, The Division of Dental Public Health and Resources. Margaret Helfrich played an important role in gathering a major part of the data used in the analysis. The authors are also indebted to Albert Schwartz for his suggestions and advice on earlier drafts. James Ross helped with some of the data processing.

particular framework to focus on the key concept of self.

That the symbolic interactionist approach does not rest on a substantial body of empirical research has been noted by even such a sympathetic critic as Merton.[1] Proponents of the approach have tended to substitute discursive illustrations for hypothesis testing especially when setting forth the ideas of George H. Mead, the major progenitor of the scheme. In fact, some of the major commentators on Mead have at times suggested that his prime contribution is an abstract frame of reference with which an observer can look at behavior rather than a set of specific hypotheses to be tested.[2] We try to show it is possible to test a key Meadian notion on the relationship between self-conception and social others, through an examination of concrete data.

Stryker has noted the general paucity of symbolic interactionist studies which systematically deal with the time dimension in the stream of human conducts.[3] This is a telling criticism, since the processual aspects of behavior are central to the interactionist frame of reference. Recent efforts to formulate and test hypotheses based on Mead's view of the self as product of social interaction are cases in point.[4] Although these studies

unambiguously view self-conceptions as dynamic consequences of interaction, self-attitudes are typically analyzed either with reference to some static instant or against a time period of short duration.[5] In contrast, our study utilizes data covering time periods of up to two years.

Finally, the symbolic interactionist approach suffers, as does most sociology, from a lack of replication and cumulation. To be sure, findings from innumerable studies can be interpreted in Meadian terms. However, such analyses do not represent any kind of systematic testing of the framework. Even a number of the studies recently brought together by Rose, as being within the symbolic interactionist framework, are neither clearly drawn from the basic propositions in the formulation nor built upon earlier research.[6] This paper instead reports a partial replication of two prior studies specifically testing hypotheses based on Mead's notion of the social origins of the self. It also extends the range of these earlier studies by offering data in support of derived hypotheses which focus on future oriented self-conceptions.

THEORETICAL BACKGROUND

As many observers have noted, the dynamic nature of the symbolic interactionist framework has made its empirical test exceedingly difficult. This has been particularly true with respect to a central thesis of the scheme, the view that the self is social in that it is derived from responses of other persons. Nevertheless, some aspects of this particular idea have been investigated, first

[1] Robert K. Merton, *Social Theory and Social Structure*, rev. and enlarged (Glencoe, Ill.: Free Press, 1957), p. 239. See also Manford Kuhn, "Major Trends in Symbolic Interaction Theory in the Past Twenty-Five Years," *Sociological Quarterly*, 5:61–84 (Winter, 1964).

[2] For example, Strauss once wrote in a preface to a compilation of Mead's work: "The truth of the matter seems to be that Mead offers us not so much specific hypotheses, or even a theory, as a rather abstract frame of reference." See Anselm Strauss (ed.), *The Social Psychology of George Herbert Mead* (Chicago: Univ. of Chicago Press, 1956), p. xvi. These remarks are not in the preface to the 1964 second edition of the same book entitled *George Herbert Mead on Social Psychology*. See also, Guy E. Swanson, "Mead and Freud: Their Relevance for Social Psychology," *Sociometry*, 24: 319–39 (Dec., 1961). A somewhat contrasting viewpoint is presented by John Kinch, "A Formalized Theory of the Self Concept," *American Journal of Sociology*, 68:481–86 (Jan., 1963).

[3] Sheldon Stryker, "The Interactional and Situational Approaches" in Harold Christensen (ed.), *Handbook of Marriage and the Family* (Chicago: Rand McNally, 1964), p. 162. Neglect of the time dimension in sociological studies has been stressed by Wilbert Moore in his *Man, Time and Society* (New York: Wiley, 1963).

[4] For example, S. Frank Miyamoto and Sanford Dornbusch, "A Test of the Symbolic Interactionist Hypothesis of Self-Conception," *American Journal of Sociology*, 617:399–403 (Mar., 1956);

Lee Reeder, George Donohue, and Arturo Biblarz, "Conceptions of Self and Others," *American Journal of Sociology*, 66:153–59 (Sept., 1960); Carl Couch, "Self-Attitude and Degree of Agreement with Immediate Others," *American Journal of Sociology*, 63:491–96 (Mar., 1958); Martin Maehn, Josef Mensing and Samuel Nafager, "Concept of Self and the Reactions of Others," *Sociometry*, 25:353–57 (Dec., 1962); and John J. Sherwood, "Self Identity and Referent Others," *Sociometry*, 28:66–81 (Mar., 1965).

[5] At most the time period is a matter of weeks. For example, a six week period was used by Melvin Manis in "Social Interaction and the Self Concept," *Journal of Abnormal and Social Psychology*, 51:362–70 (Nov., 1955).

[6] Arnold Rose (ed.), *Human Behavior and Social Processes* (Boston: Houghton Mifflin, 1962).

by Miyamoto and Dornbusch and later by Reeder, Donohue, and Biblarz.[7]

Miyamoto and Dornbusch, using ten somewhat miscellaneous semigroupings from fraternities, sororities, and college sociology classes, ask their respondents to give self-ratings and also to rate every other group member on four specified personal characteristics. They conclude that their findings from 195 individuals not only show the possibility of empirically studying self-conception within the symbolic interactionist framework, but also support three general propositions. First, the response of others is related to self-conceptions; second, the subject's perception of that response is more closely related to self-conceptions than the actual response of others; and third, an individual's self-conception is more closely related to his estimate of the generalized attitude toward him than to the perceived responses of members of a particular group.

Reeder, Donohue, and Biblarz are particularly interested in the relation between self-conception and both the actual and the perceived ratings by members of given groups. They report on nine work crews (totaling 54 enlisted men), at a small military base. Each respondent was asked to rank every member of his crew (including himself) in terms of two criteria: best worker and best leader. Further, each respondent was asked to indicate how he thought most of the men in his group would rank him on these dimensions. Reeder and his co-workers find, in general, that the responses of others have "an influence in shaping one's self-definition" and that his self-definition is "derived chiefly from the perception of the generalized other."[8] In essence, the findings parallel those reported by Miyamoto and Dornbusch.

Both sets of authors judge their research as supporting key notions implicit in the Meadian conception of the social nature of the self. Yet both acknowledge the limited conclusions of their studies, while also indicating that future research should go beyond duplicating their own work. Hence our work is not merely a replication of

their research on a different and much larger population. More important, we try to develop three lines of new research suggested to us by these previous studies.

First, a better indicator of self-conception is desirable. Miyamoto and Dornbusch use self-ratings of intelligence, self-confidence, physical attractiveness and likableness as an index of self-conception. But no evidence is presented that any or all of these features were salient in the self-conception of their respondents. While there is no reason to question that some of these characteristics were central to parts of the self-definition of some of their subjects,[9] their centrality to the selves of all the participants in the study is neither subjectively nor objectively argued or documented. Similarly, Reeder and his co-workers do not particularly justify their use of ranking along the dimensions of best leader and best worker as a valid measure of the individual's self-conception. They simply say that "it is assumed that the self-rank is an expression of the individual's self-conception."[10] An index of self-conception for which a case for saliency in the life of the individual can be made would be more in keeping with Mead's view.

Second, neither of the previous studies takes into account the time dimension in the emergence and maintenance of the self. The questions put to respondents are confined to the instant of questioning. If the Meadian formulation—that the individual learns to define and to identify himself as he begins to perceive (and later to share) the responses of others toward him—is correct, this neglect of time is a serious omission in the research design. There are two ways to remedy this oversight. One way is through a longitudinal study which catches the individual's self-conceptions at two or more points in time. Another way is by having the respondent project his self-conceptions at future times. The latter procedure has the advantage of being less likely to be confused by the attempts of individuals to reconcile what

[7] Miyamoto and Dornbusch, *op. cit.;* Reeder, Donohue, and Biblarz, *op. cit.*

[8] *Ibid.,* p. 158.

[9] Studies that have used the "Who Am I?" instrument would cast some doubt about the saliency of all four characteristics in the self-conceptions of many persons. See Manford Kuhn, "Self-Attitudes by Age, Sex, and Professional Training," *Sociological Quarterly,* 1:40–55 (Jan., 1960).

[10] Reeder, Donohue, and Biblarz, *op. cit.,* p. 154.

they wish they were with what they perceive themselves to be.

Third, both previous studies struggle to operationalize the somewhat abstract concept of the "generalized other" and seem, in part, to deviate from what its originator had in mind. Miyamoto and Dornbusch take the position that Mead treats the "generalized other" as the individual's conception of the organized social process of which he is a part, and that he sees it "composed of numerous specialized roles."[11] They note, however, that persons often enter into social relationships wherein there is a response to a "generalized other," but where the organization of roles is obscure or minimal. In fact, the Miyamoto and Dornbusch study relies upon social groupings "whose members were, at best, loosely joined by friendships and had no definite organized group activity within which to identify their respective roles."[12] Accordingly, their index of the generalized other is based on the respondent's perception of the *typical* attitudes of others toward him. Operationally, they ask: "How intelligent . . . do most people think you are?"[13]

In other words, Miyamoto and Dornbusch use the term "generalized other" to refer to the nonparticular other taken into account by the individual in situations which are lacking organization for him.[14] This seems a partial, albeit conscious, departure from the Meadian formulation. Mead, in a frequently cited passage, speaks of the generalized other as the process whereby the person "takes the attitudes of the organized social group to which he belongs."[15] As suggested in his account on the game stage in the development of the self, the internalization of the generalized other requires the individual to define and regulate his conduct with regard for the expectations of a complexly organized multiplicity of other actors.

Reeder and his co-workers capture part of this formulation. As an index of the generalized

other, they use the participant's "estimated objective group rating." In turn, this rating is based on the respondent's indication of the rank which he thinks most of his work group assign him with respect to two criteria—leadership and workmanship. Unlike the procedure used by Miyamoto and Dornbusch, this technique has the merit of conceiving the generalized other in terms of the attitudes of an organized and on-going group.

Reeder and his co-authors, however, assume "that the individual, in making an estimate of how the group ranks him, is taking the role of the generalized other."[16] In this research the group is treated as the equivalent of the small number of immediately present individuals in any given work crew. This is not inconsistent with one of Mead's two somewhat different uses of the term "organization." In the research of Reeder and his colleagues, the work crews seem analogous to Mead's famous example of the ball team, where the team is seen as the generalized other "insofar as it enters—as an organized process or social activity—into the experience of any one of the individual members."[17] Mead's other use of the term "organization," however, appears to place greater stress on the actor's organizing of attitudes towards himself than on the possibility that these attitudes may be derived from an organized activity. Even while discussing games, it is noted: "We get then an organization of attitudes of those involved in the same process."[18] Clearly the process can extend beyond any group. In fact, most of Mead's discussion of the generalized other is in terms of the socialization of the child. In this context, the child's organization of the attitudes of others is of greater importance than the organized nature of the activity wherein he draws his self-conception.

At still another point, Mead observes that the individual enters into two kinds of social relations: "Some of them are concrete social classes or subgroups. . . . The others are abstract social classes or subgroups . . . in terms of which their individual members are related to one another only more or less indirectly and which only more or less indi-

---

[11] Miyamoto and Dornbusch, *op. cit.*, p. 400.

[12] *Ibid.*

[13] *Ibid.*, p. 410. There is an interesting assumption here that the "typical" is equivalent to the "most."

[14] *Ibid.*, p. 400.

[15] Charles W. Morris (ed.), *Mind, Self and Society* (Chicago: University of Chicago Press, 1934), p. 155.

[16] Reeder, Donohue, and Biblarz, *op. cit.*, p. 154.

[17] Morris, *op. cit.*, p. 154.

[18] *Ibid.*, p. 154.

rectly function as social units. . . ."[19] A research effort centered on the latter formulation seems called for. The generalized other would be viewed as the individual's perception of the responses of others as he sees them with regard to some salient aspect of himself. The perceiving individual and the others whose responses he organizes need not be members of any particular group. They do, however, stand in some role relationship to him (e.g., as friend or teacher). Analysis along these lines emphasizes process rather than structure. Such an analysis proceeds from the actor's point of view and not from the standpoint of an outside observer.

Given these considerations, this study seeks to develop a more salient index of self-conception, to incorporate the temporal aspect of the process of self-identification and to operationalize the generalized other so as to reflect Mead's concern with the self-as-process.

METHODS AND TECHNIQUES

We draw data for this study from a much broader investigation of factors influencing the professionalization of dental students. In the larger effort on career lines, we are following two successive waves of students panel-like from the time of entrance into dental school until graduation. (Two other waves are under study for shorter periods.) This report is based on a small segment of the extensive questionnaire data obtained from all students at the very beginning of each academic year. The larger study is still in progress; but data are available from 600 freshmen (waves 1, 2, 3, 4) and from 450 sophomores (waves 1, 2, 3).[20] No doubt our findings would be strengthened if all the longitudinal data (ultimately to cover the entire four years' experience of 300 dental students) were available. However, the particular hypotheses to be examined are testable just as readily with the information already in hand; that is, with data covering one year's actual experience, as well as a two-year projection of self-ratings.

[19] *Ibid.*, p. 157.
[20] Because of dropouts and failures to answer relevant questions we have data for only 594 freshmen and 432 sophomores.

Among many other questions, we asked each student at the start of every academic year to complete the following professional labeling scale. The line in the diagram represents an arbitrary distance between a dental student and a dentist.

```
DENTAL     1 2 3 4 5 6 7 8 9 10
STUDENT  |_|_|_|_|_|_|_|_|_|_|  DENTIST
```

Using *ONE* of the *WHOLE* numbers on this line write in *below:*

A. Where would you place yourself at this time?———
B. Which point on the line is closest to where you think you will be one year from now?———
C. In general, where do you think you will be about two years from now, i.e., when you start to work in the clinic?———
D. Where do you think that the dental faculty now sees you?———
E. Where do you think that the faculty will expect you to be one year from now?———
F. Where do you think your parents now see you?———
G. (IF MARRIED) Where do you think your wife now sees you?———
H. Where do you think that your non-dental school friends and acquaintances now see you?———
I. Where do you think that your classmates now see you?———
J. Where do you think that the advanced dental students now see you?———

We use the respondent's self-placement on the scale (Item A) as a salient index of self-conception. The student's very presence in a professional school is taken as a firm indication that a dental career is of considerable importance to him. Entering dental school is not only a voluntary act on the part of the student but it also follows upon a series of necessarily rather self-conscious decisions. Even without assuming total or identical commitment to the profession, the embarkation upon a long and expensive educational career argues for the importance of the undertaking to the participant. In this respect the dental student differs from the typical social club member, the

TABLE 23.1. Means of actual and projected ratings by self and others

	Freshmen					
	High		Low		Total	
	$\bar{x}$	N	$\bar{x}$	N	$\bar{x}$	N
Self-ratings						
Current	3.18	91	1.00	503	1.33	594
Projection						
One-Year	4.90	91	2.87	502	3.18	593
Two-Year	6.86	91	5.46	499	5.67	590
Perceived Ratings by Others						
Current						
Faculty	2.12	89	1.04	494	1.21	583
Upperclassmen	2.07	91	1.05	501	1.20	592
Classmates	2.80	91	1.12	492	1.39	583
Nondental Friends	3.95	91	2.46	501	2.69	592
Parents	4.15	88	2.31	495	2.58	583
Wives	4.60	20	1.88	130	2.25	150
Aggregate 1*	3.08	—	1.61	—	1.84	—
Aggregate 2†	3.15	—	1.73	—	1.94	—
Projection						
One-Year Faculty	4.36	91	2.91	502	3.13	593
Actual Ratings by Faculty						
Current	1.71	80	1.71	80	1.71	80
Projection						
One-Year	2.94	80	2.94	80	2.94	80
Two-Year	4.96	80	4.96	80	4.96	80

* Includes classmates.
† Excludes classmates.

student in a sociology class, or the worker on a military crew.

In addition to recording his current location (or actual self-conception) on the professional labeling scale, each respondent projected the locations he expected to occupy in one or two years' time (Items B-C). We discuss these as projected self-ratings or self-conceptions. Further, each respondent noted his perception of current and projected placements by a variety of others: (Items D-J) these we treat as *perceived*—actual or projected—ratings by others. A parallel questionnaire completed by 86 percent of the dental school's faculty (N-93), provides data on the actual faculty ratings of the students at three points in their academic careers: these data we refer to

as the *actual* ratings—current or projected—by others. Table 23.1 summarizes the data considered in this study. The means of both current and projected ratings at the onset of two academic years are recorded for three analytical categories: self-ratings, perceived ratings by others, and actual ratings by faculty.[21]

We distinguish between particular others and the generalized other. Particular others are specific social alters we assume to be saliently related to our respondents in their role as dental students. Six categories of particular others are used: faculty, classmates, upperclassmen, nondental school friends, parents, and in appropriate cases, wives.

[21] We do not have comparable faculty ratings of sophomores.

TABLE 23.1. (cont.)

	Sophomores					
	High		Low		Total	
	$\bar{x}$	N	$\bar{x}$	N	$\bar{x}$	N
Self-ratings						
Current	3.56	214	1.84	218	2.69	432
Projection						
One-Year	6.14	214	4.26	218	5.19	432
Two-Year	—	—	—	—	—	—
Perceived Ratings by Others						
Current						
Faculty	2.94	213	1.78	216	2.36	431
Upperclassmen	3.22	212	1.85	216	2.54	428
Classmates	3.62	2.0	2.14	2.4	2.89	424
Nondental Friends	5.07	208	4.27	217	4.66	425
Parents	5.03	203	4.02	214	4.51	417
Wives	4.73	73	3.00	80	3.81	153
Aggregate 1*	4.01	—	2.83	—	3.41	—
Aggregate 2†	4.10	—	2.98	—	3.53	—
Projection						
One-Year Faculty	5.80	213	4.47	216	5.13	429
Actual Ratings by Faculty						
Current	—	—	—	—	—	—
Projection						
One-Year	—	—	—	—	—	—
Two-Year	—	—	—	—	—	—

* Includes classmates.
† Excludes classmates.

Potentially at least, these categories appear to exhaust the likely sources of major interaction within which the process of self-identification could be developed. Furthermore, and important to our case, we take the perceived responses of these others toward a salient aspect of the student self-conception—his position on the professional labeling scale.

We operationally define the generalized other as the aggregate of the student's perceptions of the ratings awarded to him by particular others. This definition of the generalized other differs from the concept as it appears in the work of Miyamoto and Dornbusch and in the paper by Reeder, Donohue, and Biblarz. As noted above, the earlier studies exhibit a partial adher-

ence to the Meadian formulation. The present operationalization, however, has a somewhat different focus. We assume the aggregated data to relate to the respondent's organization of ratings by others of a salient part of himself. We think this is consistent with one reading of the Meadian formulation, and in combination with the time element discussed before, may better capture the processual aspect supposedly involved in the emergence of salient self-conceptions. We claim no more.

Following the analytical lead provided in the two previous studies, we classify (where appropriate) the average ratings of our respondents into "high" and "low." In the case of the freshmen we treat statistical means of one as "low," all others as "high." For sophomores, we classify means of three and over as "high," all below that figure as "low."[22]

HYPOTHESES AND FINDINGS

Hypothesis 1. Self-conception is closer to the mean perceived response of others to the actor than to the mean actual response of others. Drawn directly from Miyamoto and Dornbusch, this hypothesis rests on the assumption that the perceived behavior of others towards the actor has a more direct influence than their actual behavior. For purposes of testing this notion, we match the mean self-rating of freshmen against their perception of faculty rankings, as well as against actual faculty rating of students.

Our data fully support the hypothesis. Freshmen perceive themselves at a mean of 1.33 on the scale; they think the faculty sees them at 1.21; the faculty actually ranks them at 1.71. Thus, there is only a mean difference of .12 (in the direction of a lower estimate) between perceived rating by faculty and self-rating in contrast to a mean difference of .38 between self-rating and actual rating by faculty members.

Although partly dictated by its easier accessibility, the choice of data from faculty members to test this hypothesis is also guided by a substantive consideration. In one respect, it seems reasonable to expect that freshmen might be more sensitive to faculty judgments of their relative position on the path to becoming a dentist, than they are to the judgment of most others. The institutional structure is such that, by virtue of the assignment of grades, only faculty members decide whether a freshman can move through the professional school. This is a point sometimes explicitly made by students in personal interviews. Other persons may influence what a student thinks of himself, but only faculty members, particularly in the crucial first year, decide if a freshman can even remain on the path to becoming

a dentist. (The poor underestimation by freshmen of how far along faculty members actually see them is of course the kind of finding that would be anticipated by this kind of reasoning.)

Hypothesis 2. The mean of the perceived responses by others is higher for those persons with high self-rating than for those with low self-rating. This hypothesis is also directly drawn from Miyamoto and Dornbusch.[23] The reasoning here is that if self-conceptions are primarily determined by the perceived responses of others toward the person, those seeing themselves accorded higher ranking should reflect a higher self-evaluation than those visualizing themselves as less highly regarded.

In our examination of this hypothesis, we not only choose to focus on the perceived rather than the actual responses of others, but attempt to strengthen the testing of the hypothesis by taking into account the range of others that could likely be salient to our students. Thus, we examine how both freshmen and sophomores perceive the rating accorded them by faculty members, upperclassmen, classmates, nondental-school friends, parents, wives. Without pretending that all possible others who might be important for every single respondent is included, it seems reasonable to argue that we encompass in our categories most all who would be salient—in the sense of being an "other"—to the mass of our students.

As indicated in Table 23.1 this hypothesis is supported for each category of others (i.e., faculty, etc.). High self-raters perceive all others as according them a higher rank than do low self-raters. This is equally true for freshmen and sophomores with no mean difference in the twelve comparisons made lower than .80. If is of interest that low self-raters as sophomores perceive themselves ranked higher by only one other category (nondental-school friends), than do high self-raters see others ranking them as freshmen.

Whereas the previous hypotheses were confined to a particular point in time, the following set of hypotheses deals with projections through time.

[22] The rationale for treating sophomores in this fashion is that it gives us an approximate median distribution of the respondents. Unfortunately our data, as was also true in the case of the data obtained by Miyamoto and Dornbusch, and by Reeder and his co-workers, preclude the application of tests of significance. Consequently, as they did, we primarily search for gross differences in examining the validity of the hypotheses.

[23] Most of the hypotheses said to be set forth by Miyamoto and Dornbusch are more directly stated also by Reeder and his co-workers.

Hypothesis 3. Anticipated self-rating is closer to the mean perceived future response of others to the actor than to the mean actual future response of others. Of course this is an extension of Hypothesis 1 through time. It assumes that even in future projections, the perceived rather than the actual behavior of others is the more important influence as far as self-conception is concerned.

We again use faculty members as the example of the other in the test of the hypothesis. We contrast the self-ratings which the freshmen project into their sophomore year, first, with their perceptions of the faculty's projected ratings, and second, with the faculty's actual anticipation.

The mean anticipated self-rating is 3.18. The perception of the projected rating by the faculty is 3.13; the actual projected rating is 2.94. Thus, the mean differences between self and perceived projected faculty rating is .05, but it is .24 between self and actual projected faculty rating. Thus, Hypothesis 3 is supported, though perhaps not as strongly as Hypothesis 1.

Hypothesis 4. The mean of the perceived future responses by others is higher for those persons with high present self-rating than for those with present low self-rating. This hypothesis makes the same basic assumption as is made in Hypothesis 2. It differs only in that it involves a projection into the future. The hypothesis assumes that those presently according themselves a high self-rating compared with those who visualize themselves as lower on the scale, will project a higher future self-ranking by others.

We test this hypothesis for both freshmen and sophomores. That is, we examine the freshmen's perceptions of the faculty's projected placement of them as sophomores and the sophomore's perceptions of the faculty's expectations of them as juniors. For this hypothesis, unfortunately, we do not have perceived projections by the students of all possible salient others as we do have for Hypothesis 2.

We find that the high self-raters project a sophomore mean score by others of 4.36 whereas the low self-raters see others as only rating them 2.91. This is a mean difference of 1.45 in the direction of supporting the hypothesis. The same relationship holds for sophomore perceived projec-

tions by the faculty into the junior year. The high self-raters project a junior mean score by the faculty of 5.80; the low self-raters see the professional staff as rating them but 4.47. The mean difference here is 1.33. Thus, both sets of data support Hypothesis 4.

Hypothesis 5. The mean anticipated self-rating is higher for those whose present self-rating is high than for those whose present self-rating is low. This hypothesis derives from some of our previous findings. We observe that the anticipated self-conception of our respondents appears to be related to their perception of the future response of others towards them. Likewise, we note that the perceived future responses of others seems to be linked to whether or not the respondent presently rates himself high or low. It follows then that there ought to be some relationship between anticipated self-rating and present high or low self-rating. In the light of Hypothesis 4, the proposition is stated as above.

In testing this hypothesis, we examine the freshman respondents' projected self-ratings as sophomores and as juniors. Present high self-raters project a mean rank of 4.90 as sophomores, whereas low self-raters foresee a mean rank of 2.87: the mean difference of 2.03 is substantial. The mean difference for projected junior ranking is also high, being 1.40. The present high self-raters give themselves an anticipated mean rank of 6.86, but the low self-raters only 5.46. The general hypothesis is thus supported. Similarly, the sophomores who are low self-raters project a self-rating of 4.26 as juniors, while their high self-rating peers anticipate a rating of 6.14. Thus, all comparisons allowed by our data point to a relationship between present self-conception and future oriented self-expectations.

Hypothesis 6. Those persons who have high self-rating have a higher mean perception of the generalized other than those with low self-rating. Although our formulation of the generalized other is somewhat different from theirs, this hypothesis is also directly drawn from Miyamoto and Dornbusch. Basically, however, the hypothesis tests the notion that self-conception is derived from multiple perspectives, and that persons seeing themselves accorded generally higher ranking should reflect a higher self-evaluation than those visualizing themselves as in general less highly regarded.

We test this hypothesis by comparing summations of the respondents' perceptions of ratings assigned to them by others. In this instance, all other categories are utilized in the analysis of the effects of the generalized other. Both freshman and sophomore data are examined.

The results are clear-cut. The high freshman self-raters have an aggregate mean score of 3.08 while the low self-raters have a score of 1.61. This mean difference of 1.47 compares with a mean difference of 1.18 among the sophomores. In that group, the high self-raters have an aggregate mean score of 4.01 whereas the low self-raters have a mean score of 2.83. Thus both freshman and sophomore high self-raters perceive themselves as being ranked higher from multiple perspectives than do low self-raters. We thus find support for Hypothesis 6.

Hypothesis 7. Self-conception corresponds more closely to the mean perception of the generalized other than to the mean of the perceived response of particular others. Again this is a hypothesis derived from Miyamoto and Dornbusch. Its rests on the assumption that self-conception as a whole emerges from interaction in divergent relationships. Thus, self-conception should more closely reflect the way most potentially meaningful others are perceived as viewing the subject than the perception of the responses of any particular collection of individuals to the actor.

In testing this hypothesis, we treat the student's classmates as particular others. The rationale for this is that classmates represent those persons with whom the freshman in the dental school has the most social contact, at least in the quantitative sense. (Also, in using this group we have the nearest equivalent in our study to the fraternity, sorority, and school class groupings Miyamoto and Dornbusch used, and the work teams Reeder and his co-workers employed in their study.) For purposes of this analysis, the category of classmates is left out of the aggregated data for the generalized other.

The data do *not* support the hypothesis. Both for freshmen and sophomores the mean per-

ceived response of particular others (i.e., classmates) are closer to the actual self-conception of students than the mean perception of the generalized other. Among freshmen the mean difference between self and particular others is only .06, but it is .61 between self and generalized other. Among sophomores the mean difference between the self and generalized other is .84, whereas it is only .20 between self and particular other. Thus, Hypothesis 7 is not supported.

It is significant that both prior studies of which ours is a partial replication also encountered some unexpected findings in testing variants of this hypothesis. Miyamoto and Dornbusch find that only for the characteristic of self-confidence was there "marked deviations from the expected direction."[24] That is, the findings were not much better than chance when ratings on self-confidence were used to test the hypothesis that self-conceptions should correspond more closely with the generalized other than with the mean of the perceived response of others (i.e., how each individual predicted every other member of his grouping ranked him as to self-confidence). As distinguished from intelligence, physical attractiveness, and likeableness, self-confidence is the one characteristic which most closely approximates the index of self we use in our study—where our subjects rank themselves on a dental student to dentist scale. Hence, the absence of a positive finding along these lines in both studies may be more than a coincidence.

As part of their demonstration of the weight to be given to the perceived response of the generalized other in accounting for self-conception, Reeder and his co-researchers compare subject self-rating with the rankings actually awarded them by work-related others. They find a difference between high and low self-raters. They attribute this difference to the possibility that high self-raters have more reference groups than low self-raters, and thus are less responsive to the actual attitudes of particular others towards the self. (In their study this would be the actual attitudes of the other members of the work crews.)

Following the lead of Reeder and his co-workers, we also examine our data to see if there

---

[24] Miyamoto and Dornbusch, *op. cit.*, p. 403.

is a similar high-low self-rating difference. We proceed as in testing Hypothesis 7, except that we divide our subjects into high and low self-raters.

The results are not consistent. For the freshmen we find the same difference found by Reeder and co-workers. That is, the mean self-conception of the low self-raters corresponds more closely to the perceived mean attributed to particular others than to the generalized other. The high self-raters show a reverse pattern. However, the pattern does not hold for the sophomores, where the mean self-conception of the high self-raters corresponds more closely to the perceived mean attributed to particular others than to their perceptions of ratings by the generalized other. The low self-raters among the sophomore students exhibit the same pattern. These findings are not a direct test of the observation by Reeder and his co-workers (i.e., that there is considerable correspondence between self-conception and the actual response of others only for persons who rate themselves low and not for those whose self-rating is high). They, however, do raise questions about its generality.

It is of interest that both prior studies and ours have encountered unhypothesized results when examining roughly the same general proposition.[25] At least it is suggestive of the possibility that the findings are not idiosyncratic to particular pieces of research or specific analytical procedures. It could indicate that something more fundamental may be involved. However, it would probably be most fruitful in future research to attempt to get at the relationship between the generalized other and particular others in still some different way. For instance, it may be that the findings in all three studies are confounded by a research failure to separate the category of significant other from particular others. If this is what accounts for the findings, the basic hypothesis may only require modification and may not need a major alteration.

[25] Vaughan, in a test of three hypotheses which are similar in some respects to the hypothesis in question above, also failed to find anticipated results. See Ted R. Vaughan, "Group Determinants of Self-Conception: An Empirical Assessment of Symbolic Interaction Theory," (Unpublished Ph. D. dissertation, University of Texas, 1964), pp. 102–6.

CONCLUSION

The results of our study reinforce the suggestion of the earlier researchers that it is possible to test and also to find some empirical support for those aspects of the symbolic interactionist framework examined. The posited relationships are clearly supported for six of the seven major hypotheses, even when in our opinion a more rigorous index of self-conception is introduced, when the neglected time dimension is incorporated into some of the data, and when a somewhat different operational measure of the generalized other is utilized.

As did Miyamoto and Dornbusch, we find that it is the perceived rather than the actual response of others that is the more important in the formation of self-conception. Furthermore, this holds true not only for self-conception at a given point in time, but also for anticipated self-rating. It is the same whether a general comparison is made or whether subjects are divided into high and low self-raters. Furthermore, the data indicate that not only is self-definition chiefly derived from the perceived rather than the actual response of others, but that it is also a reflection of the perceived response of the generalized other. The latter statement, however, has to be qualified insofar as the key hypothesis concerning it is not fully supported. Since there have been difficulties with variants of this hypothesis in prior studies, the need for future research to take this as a prime point of attack is obvious.

The possibility of attaining empirical results should be of some comfort to many who, while advocating the symbolic interactionist position, have been bothered with the suspicion that there was no way of either confirming or disproving the basic notions involved. We hope our research, crude and gross as it is, will encourage others towards far more systematic and more rigorous empirical testing not only of the ideas of Mead examined in this paper, but of many others. After all, whether in the course of the development of sociology, Mead is to be eventually ranked with the alchemists or as a Lavoisier is yet to be decided.

Self-Conceptions in India and the United States: A Cross-Cultural Validation of the Twenty Statement Test

The Twenty Statement Test (TST) was first reported by Kuhn and McPartland (1954) as a valid instrument for identifying and measuring self-attitudes as they are defined in the self theory of C. H. Cooley, G. H. Mead, H. S. Sullivan, T. Newcomb, and others. Since 1954 the TST has been used in studies of the general adult population, businessmen, students, the professions, and other populations in order to learn how self-conceptions vary and how they are related to changes in age, the reference set, and other social variables. Although this instrument and its associated theory have been assessed in several ways (see Wylie, 1961; Kuhn, 1964; Kemper, 1966), it has not been assessed in terms of its cross-cultural adequacy in eliciting self-conceptions. Yet, this evaluation is quite important both because self theory is not viewed as having subcultural or cultural boundaries and because the users of the TST implicitly suggest its rather general applicability.

PURPOSE AND METHOD

We are therefore interested in determining the validity of the TST when used in India, a

Edwin D. Driver, "Self-Conceptions in India and the United States: A Cross-Cultural Validation of the Twenty Statements Test," *The Sociological Quarterly*, vol. 10, no. 3 (Summer 1969), pp. 341–354. Reprinted by permission.

society whose cultural system differs appreciably from that of the United States. The data for this study were collected in 1966 as a part of a larger project, involving interviews with a stratified sample of 440 adults residing in a large city, small town, and three small and contiguous villages in South India. Except for the use of interviews rather than questionnaires, we have replicated as closely as possible the procedures of Kuhn and McPartland. In order to prevent the influence of answers to direct questions in the interview on TST responses, the TST material was sought at the beginning of the interview. The TST responses were "content analyzed" by the Beta system devised by Kuhn (n.d.), which requires placement of each statement of a respondent in one of the five categories: "(1) social groups and classifications (the statuses and roles of the subject); (2) ideological beliefs (his explanation of the cosmos, life, society—and his part in them); (3) interests (approach and avoidance with respect to social objects—the familiar adience-abience of the psychologist); (4) ambitions (status and role intentions; anticipations and expectations respecting positions in the social system); (5) self-evaluations ('a kind of pride or mortification over the way the subject imagines he appears to others who matter to him')." The second part of the "content analysis" involved assigning the statements to either the consensual group or the sub-consensual group. The difference between them is that the former type is a reference which unquestionably and pointedly places the individual in a social system, whereas the latter type requires interpretation by the speaker before its relevance to a social system, if any, can be ascertained. In establishing the two groups, we have simply merged together statements of self-evaluation, ideological beliefs, ambitions, and interests to form the subconsensual reference. Both the five-fold and the two-fold systems of classifying the responses were necessary in order to show the unique features of the India protocols and to examine the cross-cultural validity of the claims made for the TST.

What then are the claims made for the TST and how do they relate to the theoretical position of the symbolic-interactionist school, as represented primarily by Kuhn and McPartland? The claims (propositions) for the TST, or what it in effect elicits, are explicitly stated in the conclusions drawn by Kuhn and McPartland (1954:75–76) from their study of university students:

1) The consensual (more directly socially anchored) component of the self-conception is the more salient component. Stated differently, consensually supported self-attitudes are at the top of the hierarchy of self-attitudes.
2) Persons vary over a rather wide range in the relative volume of consensual and subconsensual components in their self-conceptions . . .
3) The variation indicated in 1) and 2) can be established and measured by the empirical techniques of attitude research—specifically, the Guttman scaling technique. This . . . furthers the presumption that the locus variable is a unitary one . . .[1]
4) Locus scores vary with differential social anchorage in (a) large, conventional . . . and influential groups; (b) small, weak, or . . . ambivalently viewed . . . groups; or (c) no groups at all . . .[2]

[1] Kuhn and McPartland point out that a respondent tends to exhaust his consensual references before giving any subconsensual ones and it is therefore possible to assign a score (the locus variable) which indicates both the number of consensual references made by the respondent and their positions among the twenty statements. If, for example, the last consensual statement is his seventh statement, then it is very probable (9/10 cases) that the preceding six statements are also consensual ones (Kuhn and McPartland, 1954:70–71).

[2] This is the one conclusion which we have drastically reconstructed. It originally read: "Locus scores vary with religious

5) Religious affiliation references are significantly more salient among the self-attitudes of members of "differentistic" religious groups than among members of "majority" or conventional religious groups.
6) Corroboratively, the religious group as a reference group appears far more frequently . . . among members of "differentistic" religious groups.

These conclusions seem then to correspond with some key ideas of self theory: "man is an object to himself—an object whose meaning to himself and others can only be derived from the system of social objects in which he is enmeshed" (Kuhn, 1960:53), the most important objects being his roles and statuses in the social system (Conclusions 1, 2, and 3); individuals in a society vary in the ways in which "they have cast their lot within the range of possible reference groups" (Kuhn and McPartland, 1954:72), and in what they interiorize from them (Conclusions 2, 4, 5, and 6); and the "self," defined as a set of attitudes (plans for action)[3] which the individual holds toward himself, is organized (Conclusions 1 and 3) (Kuhn and McPartland, 1954:69).

FINDINGS

In order to confirm the cross-cultural validity of the TST our India data must, then, support the above mentioned propositions.

affiliation, as our initial validation test shows, members of the 'differentistic' religious groups having significantly higher locus scores than do members of the 'conventional' religious groups" (Kuhn and McPartland, 1954:75). What we have given as the fourth conclusion is the merging of parts of two quotes from Kuhn and McPartland (1954:73, 75) which we feel communicate the larger propositions which the writers seemingly viewed as central to the validation of the TST, namely: the type of religious affiliation may be regarded as an index of majority group affiliation; persons having majority group affiliation are believed to have greater social anchorage in general than persons having minority group affiliation; and it follows, therefore, that persons who are known to have majority religious affiliation will have high locus scores if the TST is a valid measure of social anchorage.

[3] Kuhn and McPartland (1954:68) note that the "self" has been called an image, a conception, a concept, a feeling, a self looking at oneself, and so on. They believe that their conceptualization of the 'self' as a set of attitudes is most consistent with Mead's view and further that it has certain theoretical advantages. For other conceptualizations of the self, see Lowe (1961).

General Pattern of Responses. The total responses per respondent range from one for two persons to twenty—the maximum—for 121 persons, with the median number being 12.3. (The median is 17.0 in the Kuhn-McPartland study.) Responses are mainly subconsensual ones, especially of the self-evaluative kind (see Table 24.1), and these patterns are vivid contrasts to those observed for United States respondents. Among the Indian respondents, there are, however, wide variations in the ratios of consensual to subconsensual responses, and this finding confirms proposition two.

Detailed analysis of the consensual responses suggests that the TST has successfully elicited information on each of the five general kinds of statuses which, according to Ralph Linton (1954), are found in every society. The percentage of respondents mentioning each of these statuses is as follows: 1) 18.7 and 12.5 for age and sex categories, respectively; 2) 54.7 for family groups (kinship); 3) 12.5 and 8.4 for primary group and secondary group identities, respectively (voluntary association); 4) 27.9 for specialized occupational groups; 5) 27.8 and 7.5 for social class and caste identities, respectively (the ordering of individuals or prestige systems).

The Pattern of Consensual Responses. Consensual statements constitute 16.9 percent

TABLE 24.1. Percentage distribution of 440 respondents in India to the Twenty Statement Test, according to number of responses and Kuhn's five inclusive categories

Number of Responses	Consensual Statements	Subconsensual Statements				
	Social Groups and Categories	Self-Evaluative Statements	Ideological Beliefs	Ambitions	Interests	Total
0	25.23	1.59	56.36	83.86	39.55	...
1	25.23	2.50	33.64	12.50	18.41	0.45
2	14.55	5.91	8.18	2.73	10.91	0.91
3	12.05	6.36	1.36	0.45	7.95	1.14
4	8.18	12.27	0.23	...	4.55	5.23
5	6.14	9.77	...	...	5.68	6.36
6	2.95	10.23	...	...	4.55	5.91
7	2.50	8.41	...	0.23	2.95	7.73
8	1.14	6.36	0.23	...	2.05	5.91
9	1.14	6.14	...	0.23	1.82	4.55
10	0.45	5.00	...	...	1.14	7.05
11	...	4.32	...	...	0.23	3.64
12	0.23	4.09	...	...	0.23	3.64
13	0.23	3.64	...	...	...	1.59
14	...	3.41	...	...	...	3.18
15	...	2.95	...	...	...	2.50
16	...	1.82	...	...	...	2.95
17	...	1.82	...	...	...	4.55
18	...	2.05	...	...	...	2.73
19	...	0.45	...	...	...	2.50
20	...	0.91	...	...	...	27.50
Total	100.0	100.0	100.0	100.0	100.0	100.0
Mean	2.19	7.65	0.57	0.23	2.08	12.72
S.D.	2.26	4.53	0.81	0.72	2.61	5.60
S.E.	0.11	0.22	0.04	0.03	0.12	0.29

of the total responses but 29.9 percent of the first responses, 22.3 percent of the second responses, and 20.9 percent of the third responses. Consensual references are, then, more salient than are the subconsensual ones. But, the strength of this pattern for our India respondents is much less than it is for Kuhn and McPartland's respondents and as a result the India data do not show the same scalability (see Table 24.2). These findings confirm the first proposition (the salience of consensual references), but are too weak statistically to support the third proposition (the scalability of consensual-subconsensual statements).

The data also confirm the fourth proposition: persons having majority, i.e., dominant, group affiliation have relatively high locus scores. Using education as an index to majority group affiliation,[4] we find that the highly educated—the dominant group—have appreciably higher scores than those having less education and those without any education (see Table 24.3). *Religious Affiliation and Identification.* "Other Religions"—Christians (85.0 percent of total), Muslims, Sikhs, Jains, and Parsis—are viewed by us as the minority or "differentistic" religious groups in India. Compared with Hinduism, they stress congregate worship and other forms of grouping and they do not provide comprehensive philosophies and codes of living.[5] As might be expected, and in support of propositions five and six, members of the "Other Religions" make many more references to their religion (see Table 24.4) and these references are more salient[6]—the difference between their

[4] There are high intercorrelations among education, occupation, and caste in India (See Driver, 1962; Gist, 1954).

[5] Hinduism does not provide the individual with a standard form of worship or what to worship. One has a choice among 1) the Absolute (which is the highest form), 2) a personal god, 3) incarnations like Rama, Krishna, Buddha, 4) deities and sages, 5) petty forces and spirits. Further, "while fixed intellectual beliefs mark off one religion from another, Hinduism sets itself no such limits. Intellect is subordinated to intuition, dogma to experience, outer expression to inner realization. . . . Religion is a specific attitude of the self, itself, and no other, though it is mixed up generally with intellectual views, aesthetic forms, and moral valuations" (Radhakrishnan, 1927:15, 32). (See also Wach, 1944.)

[6] Following Kuhn and McPartland (1954:74), the score on the 'salience of religious reference' is simply the mean of the *ranks* of "religious reference (if any was made) on the page of twenty statements, mention of religious affiliation in first place being scored 20, mention in last place scoring 1, and omission of reference to religious affiliation arbitrarily scored zero."

mean score of 1.500 and that of Hindus, 0.618, having a probability of less than .01.

DISCUSSION AND INTERPRETATION

The India data, then, confirm all the propositions stated by Kuhn and McPartland in validating the TST except the one relating to the scalability of responses. One way of explaining the non-scalability of the India responses is to point to the small number of consensual references (an average of 2.2 in contrast to the average of 10.0 in Kuhn and McPartland's study) and to argue that scalability is, to a degree, a function of the number of consensual references. We will not go into the merits of this argument because the non-scalability of the India responses seems more strongly to suggest reformulation of one part of Kuhn and McPartland's statement of self theory than an adequate reason for rejecting the cross-cultural applicability of the TST. What we do wish to consider is whether the small number and lesser salience of consensual statements in the India data can be explained either by 1) our difference with Kuhn and McPartland in methodology; or 2) the fact that consensual references are not, really, primary aspects of self-conceptions in India to the same degree that they are in the United States.

Methodological Issues. In the area of methodology we differ from Kuhn and McPartland in using interviews rather than questionnaires and in having to "content analyze" materials obtained in a bilingual context. If our findings are associated with simply the interviewing process, then this would mean that the TST merely elicits the attitudes which the person holds toward himself in relation to the test administrator. We are inclined to reject this kind of "situationality" as an explanation of TST findings on the following grounds: the self-conceptions of persons in the United States are quite similar when presented in autobiographical material and in interview or questionnaire responses to the TST; and the oral and written responses of persons in India to the TST are quite similar.

The second methodological issue, bilingualism, is a very complex matter and its possible im-

TABLE 24.2. The scale of locus, showing scale-types, frequency, total responses* in each scale type and the coefficient of reproducibility for each scale type, United States and India

		*United States***		
Scale Type	Frequency	Total Responses	Errors	C. R.
20	19	380	41	.892
19	5	100	13	.870
18	1	20	1	.950
17	4	80	7	.913
16	1	20	3	.850
15	6	120	24	.800
14	8	160	9	.937
13	8	160	19	.875
12	4	80	10	.875
11	13	260	21	.915
10	7	140	15	.893
9	9	180	19	.895
8	9	180	15	.912
7	7	140	9	.936
6	10	200	15	.925
5	11	220	24	.891
4	8	160	11	.932
3	12	240	24	.900
2	2	40	5	.875
1	4	80	8	.900
0	3	60	0	1.000
	151	3020	293	.903

pact on the TST content can be considered here in only the most general manner. As we mentioned earlier, our interviews were recorded in English but the interviewer employed English, Tamil, Telegu, or another language common to him and the interviewee in giving the TST instruction and clarifying statements. Thus, the oral communications might be in the *mother-tongue* of both the interviewer and the interviewee, or neither, or of one but not the other. Bias, which in this instance means the use of terms which unintentionally connote other than the desired meaning may, therefore arise with the interviewee or interviewer: the former as he translates instructions or self-conceptions from the common language into his mother-tongue, and vice versa; and the latter as he translates the interviewee's statements into his own mother-tongue and then into English. Bias would most often arise where there is not equivalence between English and the other language(s) in vocabulary, idiom, or grammar.[7] This could give rise to two kinds of distortion in meaning. On the one hand, conceptions of a consensual kind may appear as subconsensual statements, or vice versa;[8] on the other

[7] Examples of the lack of equivalence between the English language and the languages of India are the English words: uncle, aunt, and cousin. As one writer puts it, they "are the most confusing to a Hindu. One can never know what relation is meant" (Karve, 1965:114).

[8] Kuhn certainly gave attention to the Sapir-Whorf-Cassirer 'language and culture orientation' but, in our opinion, did not stress strongly the subtleties of language within a culture and across cultures.

In analyzing our data we have become acutely aware that many terms connote a mixture of sentiment, and obligation or expectation. It is our belief that this is one of the more fruitful areas for investigation by persons involved in recording and analyzing TST material. It may very well be that terms which are now classified as consensual are really intended by the speaker to convey primarily his sentiment rather than obligation

TABLE 24.2. (cont.)

India

Scale Type	Frequency	Total Responses	Errors	C. R.
20	16	320	246	.23
19	16	320	217	.48
18	10	200	129	.36
17	14	280	184	.34
16	14	280	167	.40
15	8	160	80	.50
14	14	280	130	.54
13	11	220	103	.53
12	14	280	112	.60
11	10	200	77	.62
10	18	360	118	.68
9	20	400	129	.68
8	16	320	81	.75
7	17	340	73	.79
6	14	280	61	.79
5	15	300	44	.85
4	21	420	42	.90
3	21	420	25	.94
2	27	540	17	.97
1	30	600	0	1.00
0	114	2280	0	1.00
	440	8800	2035	.77

* We followed the procedure of Kuhn and McPartland in counting the failure to respond to a blank as a response to the subconsensual type.
** From Table 1 of Kuhn and McPartland (1954: 71).

hand, a given type of consensual or subconsensual conceptualization may appear as a different type when stated verbally or in writing. The manner in which the latter problem could arise may be seen by reference to the terms in Tamil for father. The sets of terms include: 1) *tantai, tantay, entai, muntai;* 2) *ai, aiyan;* 3) *appā, appaṇ, appu, takappan;* 4) *annan, annā;* 5) *attaṇ, accan;* 6) *ammān.* "Except *tantai* all the words . . . seem to be used for any elderly or powerful or respected person and only gradually seem to have acquired their fairly [clear] definition. Even now the connotation is not as definite as, e.g., the word *pitā* in Sanskrit" (Karve, 1965:228, 230). Further, the term *annā* is also used to denote elder brother (Karve, 1965:245). Confronted with the complex meaning of *annā,* for example, and the lack of an equivalent term in the other languages of India, including English, the translator must decide what aspect of its meaning he wishes to convey. A correct decision in South India seems to depend, as it does in North India, on knowledge of usage by localities and social strata (Gumperz, 1958).

toward another person. The manner in which the sentiment component is expressed in choosing a term of reference from a group of terms which are usually considered to be synonymous is well-documented by Schneider and Homans (1955). Another writer (Ghurye, 1955:93) observes that the sentiments-system is closely integrated with even affinal relatives in some kinship terminologies. But, Karve (1965:242) states that the dichotomy of status and sentiments found in certain North India terms is absent in the South. Lastly, Kuhn (1960:55), after noting that fifteen to thirty percent of the responses of his groups were explicitly of a self-evaluation nature, states that "many of the other responses explicitly referring to status have an implicit self-evaluation dimension."

TABLE 24.3.   Mean scores on "locus variable" by educational groups*

| | No.** | Mean Score on "Locus Variable"*** | Significance of Difference in Means, Computed from | |
			Matriculation or Above	Uneducated
Matriculation or Above	192	2.7	...	P < .0001
Below Matriculation	166	2.0	P < .0046	P < .05
Uneducated	81	1.5	P < .001	...

* The level of education is viewed by us as an index of one's affiliation with the majority, i.e. dominant, group in India.
** Excludes one person whose education is unknown.
*** Our procedure for establishing these mean scores is identical with that used by Kuhn and McPartland. The score is "simply the mean number of consensual reference statements made by respondents."

TABLE 24.4.   Religious affiliation and identification with religious groups

| | Identification | | |
	Yes	No	Total
Hinduism	14 (20.1)*	326 (319.9)	340
Other Religions	12 (5.9)	88 (94.1)	100
Total	26	414	440

Chi Square: 8.69. .01 > p > .001; Q = .523.
* Figures in parentheses are expected frequencies.

The extent to which our findings are biased because of bilingualism cannot be precisely measured. But, two procedures convince us that the bias does not nearly approach the high level which is possible in such material. First, we sometimes had a second interviewer, who differed in mother-tongue from the first one, re-interview various persons; and secondly, we have compared the TST content with some "known characteristics" (such as caste and membership in voluntary associations) of the interviewee. Neither procedure, and we do not contend that they alone are adequate for the purpose at hand, yielded any great discrepancy between the two measurements being compared.

Substantive Issues.   We may now turn to the second question which we asked at the beginning of this section: is the low frequency and salience of consensual statements in our data related to the fact that groups are not, really, primary aspects of self-conceptions in India to the same degree that they are in the United States? The writings of Morris, Hsu, McClelland, and Coehlo suggest an affirmative answer to this question.

There are sharp differences among students in the United States, China, and India in their responses to the "Ways of Living" document devised by Charles Morris. Factor analysis of the thirteen "ways" yields the same five factors for all three societies, and this suggests that there may be a common "value space" for them. But, the societies differ in their rankings on the factors, with the United States having first place on factor e, self-indulgence, and with India having first place on factor a, social restraint and self-control. When asked to give their comments on the adequacy of the document, the few United States students who complied showed a dissatisfaction with all the "ways," a rejection of all definite codes for living, and said that the "ways" needed to stress more "orientation to self" and personal possessions. The most general criticism of the document was that it did not stress *social co-operation* enough. The comments of the India students were twice as numerous, did not reject any of the "ways" and formulated some new "ways." They, in particular, emphasized "service to one's fellow men" and the need of combining the "cultivation of the inner life with outward and socially responsible action" (Morris, 1956:36, 44, 46, 47, 53–54).

Somewhat similar contrasts between persons in the two countries are provided by Hsu (1963) and McClelland (1967). Hsu compares them in terms of responses to Cards 1 and 12 BG of the Thematic Apperception Test and finds that the images of United States students more often show *involvement with other persons (especially peers),* insensitivity to the physical environment, and an absence of mutability. The India students more often pictured themselves as *being alone* in general and even when the specific response (to Card 12BG) is Enjoyment. "In addition . . . there is a kind of Enjoyment response which is highly impersonal that the Indians give but the Chinese and Americans do not give" (Hsu, 1963:263–311, especially Tables A-2, A-3, A-6).

Using different measuring procedures, McClelland (1967:198) likewise finds more United States boys than India boys emphasizing group activity and egocentric virtue—Morris' self-indulgence factor. It is important to note, finally, that the intercultural differences found by Morris, Hsu, and McClelland are based on their studies of populations which are very similar in age, sex, education, and social class.

Possible reasons for the consensual-subconsensual variation between the United States and India may be adduced from the writings of Hsu and McClelland. Hsu provides evidence of the universality of sociability, security, and status as primary social needs and says that the type of cultural system affects the degree to which the family (the basic organization everywhere) or other organizations fulfill these needs. Further, cultural systems may be differentiated by the degree to which they stress one of the social needs

over the others. An unusual emphasis on sociability and its corollary, membership in many voluntary associations, or "clubs," exists in the United States. In India and China, the respective combinations are caste and status, and kinship and security.[9]

McClelland attributes the tendency of persons to affiliate themselves with many organizations, and quite often with each one on a short-term basis, with the strong other-directed orientation which is now present in the United States. Voluntary associations, "particularly those in school, may serve the important social function of training people to pay attention to the wishes and opinions of others." In turn, the development of other-directedness, or the tendency of ego to be motivated to interact on the basis of pressures primarily from peers, probably heightens the need for sociability and the stress on self-development values (McClelland, 1967:201). In traditional, or less other-directed, societies such as India, there is "less dependence on the opinion of others, therefore less need for group activities to make people sensitive to such opinions, and correspondingly greater stress on such sociocentric virtues as kindness, loyalty, and obligations to others as defined and prescribed in traditional social institutions" (McClelland, 1967:201). The strength of tradition in India is evident from the way in which many people even today turn to the *Ramayana, Mahabharata,* and other classics for cultural models, norms, and values.[10]

The preceding evidence lends considerable support to our belief that the low frequency and salience of consensual references in the TST protocols of respondents in India may actually reflect a cultural system which does not stress sociability

---

[9] See Hsu (1963), especially Chapter 10, "Culture pattern and human grouping." The contrasts have led Hsu to characterize the societies in Durkheim's terms of 'kinship solidarity' (premodern China), 'hierarchic solidarity' (India), and 'contractual solidarity' (United States).

Other researchers confirm the U.S. emphasis on peer group, or nonhierarchical, relations (See, Dahlberg and Stone, 1966:589–602; Kluckhohn and Strodtbeck, *et al.,* 1961:144, 147).

[10] Sanskritization, or the process whereby groups low in status or groups just being assimilated into Hinduism from a tribal background adopt the ideology, rituals and customs of high castes, strengthens the traditional orientation. Sanskritization is strong today and raises questions about the actual impact of Westernization (see Srinivas, 1966).

as strongly as the United States system. If culture is such a key variable, then one might reasonably expect that long exposure of a person to a new cultural system would modify his self-conceptions.

The studies of the Useems (1955: esp. Chapter 2, "Change in the character and outlook of the individual"), Hsu, and Coehlo (see also Lambert and Bressler, 1956:80–89) suggest that such changes, or acculturation, do, in fact, occur after long and intensive exposure to a different culture. Hsu observes how the TST responses of persons in India who have experienced United States culture through the educational system or the Indo-American Society resemble those of persons in the United States. The study by Coehlo (1958) of students from India presents some dramatic shifts in the dominance of certain themes and reference groups as the exposure to United States culture increases. From initial contact—one week or less—with the host culture to last contact—four years or more—there is a decline in themes which are diplomatic-political, educational-cultural, and economic-industrial, and an increase in the themes which are social-personal and religious-philosophical-theoretical. Persons who mentioned reference groups in the United States initially spoke of either the "average middle-class American" (67 percent) or the University Group (27 percent), but at the end of their stay they spoke of friends (13 percent), localized groups (27 percent), and the international group (27 percent). At the end, the University Group is as strong a reference as it was in the beginning but the undifferentiated "middle-class American" disappears altogether (Coehlo, 1958:8, 21, 31, 35, 68–70). The shifts in the organization of content do not occur smoothly and the student customarily experiences what Erik Erikson calls an "identity crisis" toward the end of phase two, i.e., from three to nine months in the United States. For the Indian students who continue their sojourn here the crisis is resolved through a greater assimilation of United States culture, with the result that in phase four they show the same "privatistic outlook" (Coehlo, 1958:103) as do other United States students (Dahlberg and Stone, 1966:601). As Coehlo (1958:88) remarks, "the major characteristic of Phase 4 is that the Indian student devotes an intense, if not exclusive, attention to his social and personal relations with those around him."

CONCLUSIONS

Our data for respondents in India indicate, therefore, that the TST is a valid instrument for eliciting self-conceptions in different cultural settings. We were able to confirm five of the six propositions which Kuhn and McPartland offered as evidence of the validity of the test for United States respondents. The one proposition which is not supported is not a crucial one insofar as validation is concerned, but its non-verification suggests that self theory, as presented by Kuhn, needs to be modified so as to view consensual (social system) references as central in only some cultural systems rather than universally. This modification in theory formulation is suggested not only by our data but also by an early study of Kuhn's in which an unexpected and glaringly high percentage of Amish, in contrast to Mennonites and "Gentiles," mentioned abstract moral and religious attributes rather than primary group or secondary group models when asked to define ideal persons as well as persons whom they would least like to be (Kuhn, 1954:57–59, 63).

In addition to assessing the cross-cultural validity of the TST, our data have also permitted us to make comparisons of self-conceptions in India and the United States. These comparisons bring out many similarities with respect to anchorage in both consensual and subconsensual types of objects and also the vivid contrast between the two societies with respect to emphasis on self-evaluation and involvement with groups.

REFERENCES

Coehlo, George V. 1958. Changing Images of America. Glencoe: The Free Press.

Dahlberg, Francis M. and Philip J. Stone. 1966. "Cross-cultural contrasts in interpersonal structure." Pp. 589–602 in Philip J. Stone et al., The General Inquirer: A Computer Approach to Content Analysis. Cambridge: Massachusetts Institute of Technology Press.

Driver, E. D. 1962. "Caste and occupational structure in central India." Social Forces 41:26–31.

Ghurye, Govind S. 1955. Family and Kin in Indo-Aryan Culture. University of Bombay Publications in Sociology Series No. 4. Bombay: Oxford University Press.

Gist, N. P. 1954. "Caste differentials in south India." American Sociological Review 19:126–137.

Gumperz, J. J. 1958. "Dialect differences and social stratification in a north Indian village." American Anthropologist 60:668–682.

Hsu, Francis L. K. 1963. Clan, Caste and Club. Princeton: D. Van Nostrand Company.

Karve, Irawate. 1965. Kinship Organization in India. Second Revised Edition. Bombay: Asia Publishing House.

Kemper, T. D. 1966. "Self-conceptions and the expectation of significant others." The Sociological Quarterly 7:323–343.

Kluckhohn, Florence Rockwood; Fred L. Strodtbeck, et al. 1961. Variations in Value Orientations. Evanston: Row, Peterson and Company.

Kuhn, Manford H. 1964. "Major trends in symbolic interaction theory in the past twenty-five years." The Sociological Quarterly 5:61–84.

———. 1960. "Self attitudes by age, sex, and professional training." The Sociological Quarterly 1:53.

———. 1954. "Factors in personality: socio-cultural determinants as seen through the Amish." Pp. 43–65 in Francis L. K. Hsu (ed.), Aspects of Culture and Personality. New York: Abelard-Schuman.

———. (n.d.) "Procedure for Content Analysis of the TST in Five Inclusive Categories." Mimeographed paper. Ames: Iowa State University.

Kuhn, M. H. and T. S. McPartland. 1954. "An empirical investigation on self-attitudes." American Sociological Review 19:68–77.

Lambert, Richard D. and Marvin Bressler. 1956. Indian Students on an American Campus. Minneapolis: University of Minnesota Press.

Linton, Ralph. 1954. "What we know and what we don't know about society, culture and the individual." Pp. 187–210 in Francis L. K. Hsu (ed.), Aspects of Culture and Personality. New York: Abelard-Schuman.

Lowe, C. M. 1961. "The self-concept: fact or artifact?" Psychological Bulletin 58:325–336.

McClelland, David C. 1967. The Achieving Society. New York: The Free Press.

Morris, Charles W. 1956. Varieties of Human Value. Chicago: University of Chicago Press.

Radhakrishnan, Sarvepalli. 1927. The Hindu View of Life. London: George Allen and Unwin.

Schneider, D. M. and G. C. Homans. 1955. "Kinship terminology and the American kinship system." American Anthropologist 57:1194–1208.

Srinivas, Mysore N. 1966. Social Change in Modern India. Berkeley and Los Angeles: University of California Press.

Useem, John and Ruth Hill Useem. 1955. The Western-Educated Man in India. New York: Dryden Press.

Wach, Joachim. 1944. The Sociology of Religion. Chicago: University of Chicago Press.

Wylie, Ruth C. 1961. The Self Concept: A Critical Survey of Pertinent Research Literature. Lincoln: University of Nebraska Press.

Some Methodological Problems of Kuhn's Self Theory

Manford Kuhn in his review of twenty-five years of symbolic interaction theory noted that the "oral tradition" had sustained the theory during the years preceding the "age of inquiry."[1] And, as Kuhn has accurately noted, this "age of inquiry" has utilized different subtheories and there was little consensus or "formalization" which preceded the empirical studies.[2] This is true for Kuhn's own theory as well as for the other subtheories of the orientation.

It is the purpose of this paper to correct this condition for Kuhn's theory. In doing this I have brought together, in a systematic manner, the ideas, definitions, assumptions, and propositions of the work of Kuhn and his students.[3] With this foundation, I discuss several methodological problems of the theory which have not been previously investigated. It is hoped that this effort will contribute to the "age of inquiry" in Symbolic Interaction Theory.

Charles W. Tucker, Some Methodological Problems of Kuhn's Self Theory," *The Sociological Quarterly*, vol. 7, no. 3 (Summer 1966), pp. 345–358. Reprinted by permission.

[1] Manford H. Kuhn, "Major Trends in Symbolic Interaction Theory in the Past Twenty-five Years," *Sociological Quarterly*, 5:61–84 (Winter, 1964).

[2] *Ibid.*, p. 63.

[3] For a list of studies by Kuhn's students see Harold A. Mulford and Winfield W. Salisbury II, "Self-Conceptions in a General Population," *Sociological Quarterly*, 5:35–46 (Winter, 1964). In addition, for titles of dissertations by Kuhn's students see footnotes 20–25, and 33–36 in Kuhn *op. cit., ibid.*

I

This part includes the assumptions, propositions and terms of the theory.[4] Initially, it is important to recognize that Kuhn distinguished between the cultural-institutional view and the social-psychological view of human activity. He considered the latter view, which he held, to be a complement to the former, rather than a substitute for it. The social-psychological view attempts to account for human behavior in situations not completely structured, while the other view assumes structured or rigidly normative situations. In order to predict a person's behavior in a variety of situations it is necessary, according to Kuhn, that we measure "an individual's own hierarchy of identities at a time of rapid social change."[5] So, assuming this distinction regarding views of human behavior and the purpose of the social-psychological view, Kuhn set out his theoretical formulation.

According to this theory, society as ongoing human behavior, precedes any individual. The child is born into some specific family "context" where the procedures of living are being estab-

[4] As the reader will notice, I am using C. A. Hickman and M. H. Kuhn, *Individuals, Groups, and Economic Behavior* (New York: Holt, Rinehart and Winston, 1956) extensively in the formulation of this theory. Although this book is seldom mentioned in the discussions of self theory, it seems to be the most complete treatment of this theory yet published.

[5] Hickman and Kuhn, *op. cit.*, p. 46.

lished. Then by means of simple act symbols the child learns the appropriate behaviors from others. As part of this process, a child is shown what to do with the objects in his environment. In fact, it is assumed that any introduction to an object is by use of the appropriate behaviors for employing that object. Hence, all objects are social *before* they are physical.

From these basic notions, the self theorist makes the following assumptions regarding human behavior:[6]

> Man lives in a universe of events and objects which do not have intrinsic meaning for human experience and behavior. Rather, the universe is endowed with meaning, by man himself, through social definitions in language.
>
> The meaning of any object is in terms of the behavior that is taken with regard to that object. "Those concatenations of events which we think of as objects have become objects as a result of structuring by language." So, the name for an object is simply a way of collapsing the meaning for the object.
>
> "The individual is not a passive agent who *automatically* responds to the group-assigned meaning of objects. Rather, he is constantly engaged in telling himself what he must pay attention to, what he must look for, what the significance of some object is, and how he must act on the basis of the objects about him."
>
> The process indicated above is commonly called "thinking." Thinking, it is assumed, is made possible through man's ability to internally manipulate language symbols. These language symbols are acquired by the person through his interaction with others. Therefore, his thinking is limited by his language and further, by the "others" who have interacted with him.

From these assumptions we go to the basic concepts and propositions of this theory.

First, the definition of "self" or "self-conception" as used in the theory is "the individual's attitudes (plans of action) toward his own mind and body, viewed as an object";[7] or similarly, "the individual as viewed (defined) by the individual, a social object among social objects."[8] The classes

of "attitudes" may include identities, in terms of roles and statuses, interests and aversions, conceptions of goals, an ideological view, and evaluative statements.[9] The phrase "among social objects" implies a "context of behavior" or "situation" in which the self-attitudes are observed. Hence, unless the "situation" is specified the self-attitudes given by a person are meaningless.

With this definition of self we turn to a general statement of the theory:

> A person obtains attitudes toward himself from his "orientational others." These attitudes are similar to those he has obtained regarding other social objects. But, the self as a social object, unlike other objects, is present in all situations. This being the case, self-attitudes are anchoring attitudes or the "common frame of reference" upon which other attitudes are founded. Therefore, the self serves as the basis from which a person makes judgements and subsequent "plans of action" toward the many other objects that appear in each specific situation.[10]

Two propositions can be derived from this general statement. They are (1) a person's self is based on the behaviors that his "orientational others" direct toward him; (2) the self serves as the basis from which a person's behaviors are directed toward other objects. From these propositions, we derive a third proposition: The behavior of "orientational others" that are directed toward a person determines his behavior regarding all objects, including himself.[11] Now, the terms which seem to need defining in this theory are object, atti-

---

[6] *Ibid.*, pp. 25 f, 43.

[7] *Ibid.*, p. 43.

[8] Manford H. Kuhn, "Self," in *A Dictionary of the Social Sciences,* ed. by J. Gould and W. L. Kolb (New York: The Free Press, 1964), p. 629. Most of the definitions by Kuhn in this volume had previously appeared in his "Definitions in Symbolic Interaction Theory," Department of Sociology, State University of Iowa, 1955 (mimeograph), which he utilized in his teaching.

[9] Manford H. Kuhn, "Self-Conception," *op. cit.,* p. 631.

[10] Hickman and Kuhn, *op. cit.,* pp. 21–45 *passim.*

[11] The difference between the above "formalization" and that of John Kinch in "A Formalized Theory of the Self-Concept," *American Journal of Sociology,* 68:481–86 (Jan., 1963), is seen clearly in his third proposition, which states: "The individual's perception of the responses of others toward him reflects the actual responses of others toward him" (p. 482). This proposition would, it seems to me, be questionable in Kuhn's theory, for he contends that *"per*ception is *inextricably* bound up with *con*ception, the conceptions have been learned with the language," therefore, "the individual acts not in terms of an intrinsically coercive and resistant outer reality, but in terms of the meanings he ascribes to units of that reality, as they are selected and defined for him by the symbols which constitute his language" (Hickman and Kuhn, *op. cit.,* p. 23). So, with this assertion there is no separation between "perceived" and "actual" which implies a dualistic notion of reality, but rather, what man *conceives* is reality.

tudes, and "orientational others." I will begin with the most important of these:

Object. As stated earlier, self theory asserts that man's experience in the world is in terms of objects. And, according to the theory, an object which is experienced must have been socially defined, and hence is called a "social object." It refers to

> any distinguishable aspect of social reality. It may be a thing, a quality, an event, or a state of affairs. All that is necessary is that it have been given unity and disjunctiveness from other matters by having been given a name which distinguishes it and assigns it a meaning. The sum total of one's social objects constitute his social reality.[12]

Hence, it is asserted that the world man experiences is the world he symbolically or linguistically designates; there is no other world. And accordingly, the world varies according to the symbolic systems of designation which are utilized by men.

Related to the conception of social objects is the notion of "meaning" in self theory. The meaning of an object is "primarily a property of behavior and only secondarily a property of objects."[13] More specifically:

> The meaning of any object is only in part a set of assumptions or ascriptions regarding its nature—how it works, what it is made of, etc. It is also in part a prescription for behavior toward that object—how much it is valued, for what kinds of activity it has meaning, what one is supposed to do with it, etc. The language which we use to define an object or an event, regardless of how abstract, general, formal or objective it is, always indicates something about the object or event.[14]

Meaning is always relative to the "norms" of the group in which the activities are taking place. "The norms of the group constitute the relational 'plans of action' which gives meaning to (or creates) the object."[15] So, the meaning of any object

[12] Manford H. Kuhn, "Social Object," in Gould and Kolb, *op. cit.,* p. 659.

[13] See T. Shibutani, *Society and Personality* (Englewood Cliffs, N.J.: Prentice-Hall, 1961), pp. 98 f. for a discussion of these ideas.

[14] Hickman and Kuhn, *op. cit.,* p. 24.

[15] Kuhn, "Social Object," *loc. cit.*

is dependent upon the behavioral relationships and they are the limiting "factors" of meaning.

Attitudes. The behaviors which are observed as directed toward objects are called "plans of action." As Kuhn states:

> By "plan of action" we mean considerably more than seeking out or avoiding of an object. We mean also the ways in which the object is thought to behave, for these naturally have a bearing on the individual's own behavior toward or away from the object or state of affairs in question. And, too, we mean the affects (feelings and emotions) which the individual manifests in relation to others.[16]

All behaviors that are taken with regard to objects are considered as "plans of action." But not all "plans of action" are attitudes. Attitudes are

> verbal statements that constitute blueprints for behavior in that they indicate the ends toward which action is directed, the justification for holding these ends, the proper feelings and evaluations regarding the degree of success and failure in achieving them.[17]

The main point is that attitudes, as used in this theory, are overt, observable behavior which are directly amenable to scientific investigation. They are considered to be verbal statements which can organize and direct other behavior.[18]

Orientational Others. In a recent article, Kuhn "reconsidered" the concept of "reference group."[19] He indicated that Merton, Hyman, and others have used this concept to refer to *cate-*

[16] Hickman and Kuhn, *op. cit.,* p. 223.

[17] *Ibid.,* p. 87.

[18] Hickman and Kuhn expand on this notion in the following: "Such distinctions (between opinion and attitude) seem not only useless but misleading, first, because words constitute a great deal—probably most—of man's activity, and hence, cannot be distinguished from deeds; and secondly, because we believe, like Merton, that nonverbal overt acts can be and frequently are deceptive, as in the sense of 'posturing' or 'keeping up a front.' Finally, if men's verbally communicated plans of action were not in fact fairly accurate blueprints of their action, human societies could not exist. Societies rest on reciprocal role-playing and consensual definitions of each situation" (p. 224).

[19] Manford H. Kuhn, "The Reference Group Reconsidered," *Sociological Quarterly,* 5:5–21 (Winter, 1964).

gories of others rather than *groups* of others. To make a clear distinction between groups and categories, he proposed a "new" concept which takes into account the ideas of those who originally put forth the notion of "others" (e.g., Cooley, Dewey, and Mead.) These "others" he called "orientational others," which is defined by the following attributes:[20] (1) The term refers to the others to whom the individual is most fully, broadly and basically committed, emotionally and psychologically. (2) It refers to the others who have provided him with his general vocabulary, including his most basic and crucial concepts and categories. (3) It refers to the others who have provided and continue to provide him with his categories of self and other, and with meaningful roles to which such assignment refer. (4) It refers to the others in communication with whom his self-conception is basically sustained and/or changes. From this class of others, Kuhn specified several types or subclasses of others which could be employed in research. For example there are "contemporary others" and "past others"; "proximal others" and "distal others"; and "present others" and "absent others," and the like. Kuhn believed that if we approach the investigation of "others" with this notion of orientational others the empirical findings will be much more relevant to ongoing human behavior than the approach which is now being used in social psychology. Only empirical study can assess the correctness of this "belief."

In the above I have attempted to summarize Kuhn's self theory by using the Hickman and Kuhn book and incorporating some of Kuhn's last notions regarding the theory. In order to discuss the methodological problems of the theory it is necessary to look at some of the studies that have employed the Twenty Statements Test as an operational specification for the conception of self.[21] I will not consider each study separately, but I consider the problems mentioned as common to all the studies which employed this theory and technique. Therefore, the many "technical" problems which have plagued the self theorist will not be considered, but only those problems which

clearly relate to the connection between the operational specifications and the theoretical framework. These connections will be specified in the section following the discussion of the Twenty Statements Test.

II

First, the question and the administration procedures of the Twenty Statements Test. Each prospective respondent is given a sheet of paper with twenty blank lines on it and a single question at the top of the page. The question usually reads as follows:

> In the spaces below, please give twenty different answers to the question, "Who Am I?" Give these as if you were giving them to yourself, not to somebody else. Write fairly rapidly, for the time is limited.

The respondents usually have a limited amount of time to answer the question. After the time limit has elapsed, the respondents are asked to complete other questions (e.g., face-data type questions), but told not to return to the self question. The instruments are collected after their completion.

By inspecting the question carefully we can note several assumptions which are implied by it. Then we can note whether these assumptions are consistent with the theoretical formulation. First, the respondent is asked to answer the question "Who Am I?" but he is to answer this question under a special circumstance. He is asked to answer the question "as if you were giving them (the answers) to yourself, *not to anyone else.*" If the directions are followed the person should refer to himself as an object. This specification seems to be consistent with the conception of self in this theory.

With further consideration, there is an assumption that the self theorist makes which is not always clearly stated. This assumption is stated by McPartland in a manual designed for using the Twenty Statements Test.[22] In order to answer

---

[20] *Ibid.,* p. 18.

[21] See note 3, above.

[22] T. S. McPartland, "Manual for the Twenty-Statements Problem" (Department of Research: The Greater Kansas City Mental Health Foundation, Jan. 3, 1959, mimeograph).

the question it must be assumed that the person "knows" who he is and puts this "knowledge" into words. As McPartland states: ". . . respondents are confronted with the problem of identifying themselves and left to decide for themselves how this identification will be made."[23] This assumption is necessary for the self theorist and is not essentially inconsistent with the theory.

In addition to having a rather epistemological "tone" to it, the above assumption is related to several others which seem to be theoretically necessary. It is assumed that the person's "knowledge" of himself will be dependent upon the situation in which he finds himself. As stated, this "knowledge" comes from the behavior of the "orientational others" in various situations. Therefore, it is necessary to discard the notions of many personality theorists and "self-concept" theorists who employ "trait" notions with regard to their concepts. The self theorist finds this notion contrary to his assumptions.[24]

Secondly, the assumption that a person "knows" who he is precludes the use of a set of fixed responses to obtain theoretically meaningful information regarding the self. Giving the person a set of responses regarding himself assumes either (1) that the person does not "know" who he is or (2) that the researcher has the "knowledge" regarding the respondent's self-attitudes in this situation. The first alternative clearly contradicts the assumption of the self theorist, and the second alternative would question the necessity of any research on the problem. As Kuhn states, "responses resulting from suggestion have no predictive utility (regarding the self as defined in this theoretical framework) for they do not indicate the plans by which the individual organizes and directs his behavior."[25] So it is assumed that the "Who Am I?" question does not suggest specific answers to the respondent. Therefore, all the answers that are given are the respondent's own "plans of action" which can direct his subsequent behavior.

Finally, another assumption, related to the above is made by the self theorist. It is assumed

that the question "Who Am I?" is general enough as not to elicit responses which are unique or particular to a limited situation, especially the testing situation. If this assumption was not made the responses to the question would have limited "predictive utility." That is, one could say very little about the person's behavior in a variety of circumstances with the information gathered from this question. This would, of course, make the theory so specific as to cast doubts on its scientific utility (i.e., the ability to make general statements regarding human behavior). So, as in the instance mentioned above, this final assumption seems to be required within the framework of self theory.

In summary, the following assumptions and assertions are made by the self theorist when he uses the Twenty Statements Test to operationalize the concept of self:

1. The person will refer the question "Who Am I?" to himself and not to anyone else.
2. The person is aware ("knows") of himself and he puts this "knowledge" into words.
3. The person's awareness of himself is dependent upon the behaviors of others in a situation and not a matter of "traits" or "instincts."
4. The person's awareness of himself precludes the use of any fixed responses; the responses must be the person's own plans of action.
5. The responses to the question are not limited to the testing situation, but have applicability in a variety of situations.

It seems that each of these assumptions or assertions, taken separately, is necessary within the theoretical framework and not essentially inconsistent with it.

The other area of importance regarding the Twenty Statements Test is the procedures that have been used for analyzing the data. I will discuss the procedures which have provided a *foundation* for the variety of analysis systems that have been employed. In this discussion, I will point out several assumptions which have not been mentioned previously. As before, I will assess the adequacy of these assumptions in terms of the theory.

Each answer of the respondent is content analyzed. Every statement is assigned to one of two

[23] *Ibid.*, p. 2.
[24] Hickman and Kuhn, *op. cit.*, p. 243.
[25] *Ibid.*

categories: consensual or subconsensual (this latter category is sometimes called "nonconsensual"). Consensual statements are those which "require no further explanation in order to be understood by the analyst, or, for that matter, by anyone."[26] Examples are: "I am a man," "I am a student," or "I am a teacher." It is assumed that there is consensus by everyone regarding an object which is identified by this type of statement. The consensus is in terms of the behavior that one would take with regard to the object so identified. Another way of saying this is that the object, so identified, would have a common meaning for all concerned.

All statements which are not identified by the analyst as consensual are considered to be subconsensual. These statements refer to "groups, classes, attributes, traits, or any other matters which require interpretation by the respondent to be precise or to place him relative to other people."[27] They refer to "norms which may vary and into which the analyst must inquire if he is to grasp the denotation of the statements."[28] Examples of this type of statement are: "I am a good student," "I am an angry person," and so on. It is asserted, in these instances, that there is little consensus of meaning with regard to objects identified in a subconsensual manner. That is, others will not know how to behave consistently toward objects which are identified in these terms. This, of course, is the direct opposite of the interpretation for consensual statements.

One can see, I think, how the above analysis procedures relate to self theory. The main focus in these procedures is on the meaning of social objects. As mentioned earlier, meaning is defined in terms of behavior taken with regard to objects. Those objects which are identified in a consensual fashion will elicit the same responses from all who come in contact with them. So the person who has identified himself consensually can expect all others to behave toward him in a similar manner in a variety of situations. If that is so, it is further reasoned that those with the largest number of

consensual statements have behaved in a greater number of different situations. They are, in other words, "socially anchored" in a variety of situations. And, the number of consensual statements "is a reflection of the degree to which a person is effectively anchored in the main (consensually agreed to) culture" and has "achieved a stable identification by, and in terms of, the larger culture."[29] All of these assumptions and assertions seem to be in accord with the theory and particularly the concepts of "social object" and "meaning." Now, with this discussion in mind, the next section will point out some methodological problems that appear between the theory and the procedures employed to investigate its notions.

III

The first problem to be discussed is what can be called "situationality." This problem is not only evident in self theory but it has plagued many a social scientist, especially social psychologist, for years. Essentially, the problem of "situationality" is concerned with the question: How do the social factors (i.e., behavior of others), *within the testing situation,* affect the observable behaviors one obtains from the respondent(s)?[30] I think the investigation of this question can be shown to be crucial to the development of social self theory.

From the statements of the self theorists it can be seen that this problem is clearly relevant to their theory. Kuhn criticizes those who assume that the testing situation is "neutral," especially in an experimental study. He states that the researcher "must determine the subject's attitudes toward objects to be manipulated in the experiment . . . in order to have full knowledge of the variables."[31] Further, in the definitions of self and orientational others it is noted that these concepts

---

[26] *Ibid.,* p. 244.

[27] Manford H. Kuhn and Thomas S. McPartland, "An Empirical Investigation of Self-Attitudes," *American Sociological Review,* 19:64 (Feb., 1954).

[28] Hickman and Kuhn, *op. cit.,* p. 244.

[29] Robert L. Stewart and Glenn M. Vernon, "Four Correlates of Empathy in the Dating Situation," *Sociology and Social Research,* 43:284 (Mar., 1959).

[30] For an extended discussion of the issues involved in this question see Aaron V. Cicourel, *Method and Measurement in Sociology* (New York: The Free Press, 1964), pp. 157–171. This discussion should be useful to anyone concerned with the problems of social research, especially the type of research that obtains observations by asking people questions.

[31] Hickman and Kuhn, *op. cit.,* p. 26.

are relative to the "definition of the situation." Finally, in one of Kuhn's latest articles, he points to this problem as one which has been "neglected" in symbolic interaction theory.[32] Yet, even with this recognition, the problem seems to have been ignored in most of the research. The question comes to mind: How could this "state of affairs" possibly have developed?

I think the problem developed from the "style" in which the theory was originally presented. The self theorist seldom attempted to order his theory as it has been done above. When he took each assumption and assertion *separately,* he could not discover the contrary assumptions which appear in the theory and research relationship. But when they are considered together the contradictions are quite noticeable.

To cite a case, one can see a direct contradiction between several ideas in self theory. First, is the idea that knowledge of the person's self-attitudes will enable an observer to predict that person's behavior in a variety of situations. This notion implies that there is a "core" self or a particular set of "basic self-attitudes" that a person utilizes in all, or at least a variety of, situations. This same notion is held by some "self-concept" theorists and is consistent *within their framework.*[33] But, *within this theoretical framework,* it is contradictory to the explicit and firm rejection of the "trait" notions of personality.

In fact, it was one of Kuhn's expressed purposes to devise a theory which would show that the ideas of "traits" or "instincts" in human behavior are clearly metaphysical and beyond scientific investigation. But, it seems that the very ideas which he intended to challenge are to be found in his theory, particularly in the notion of "social anchoring" self-attitudes.

This same contradiction can be noted in the research operations. This appears when two ideas are contrasted. First is the idea that self-attitudes are derived within a particular "context of behav-

ior" and are "meaningless" without the explication of that "context." But, in a contrary manner, it is assumed that the responses from the question "Who Am I?" are applicable to a *variety of situations.* This assumes that the others who are "present" and "contemporary" are irrelevant to the person's behavior. Now, it may be the case that *some* of the responses are applicable to the testing situation, while other responses are relevant to a variety of situations beyond the testing situation. But, it seems to me, before we can establish this assertion, an empirical investigation of the testing situation must be conducted.[34]

The second problem concerns the content analysis procedures that have been consistently used in the studies. Although this may appear to be a mere "technical" problem, I think that it can be demonstrated that these procedures are derived from the theory. This being the case, whatever problems that appear with these procedures have definite consequences for the development and utility of the theory.[35]

The content analysis categories and their assumptions were described briefly in the preceding part of this paper. As stated there, the ideas for these procedures were derived from the concepts of "meaning" and "social object." The statements obtained on the Twenty Statements Test are expected to refer to the respondent as an object. If the "meaning" of the statement has a high degree of agreement it is consensual; if not, then it is subconsensual. Now, because these procedures are related to several important ideas of the theory, we should take a closer look at them.

We noted that the self theorist assumes or asserts the following: (1) that fixed responses have little predictive utility; (2) that the person's

---

[32] Manford H. Kuhn, "Major Trends in Symbolic Interaction Theory," p. 78.

[33] The theorists who use this type of framework are reviewed in Ruth Wylie, *The Self-Concept* (Lincoln: The University of Nebraska Press, 1961), and in C. Marshall Lowe, "The Self-Concept: Fact or Artifact?" *Psychological Bulletin,* 58:325–336 (1961).

[34] At the present time, procedures are being devised to obtain observations which will be relevant to this problem. The main deviation from the previous operations include the use of post-test interview with respondents who have answered the "Who Am I?" question.

[35] The more "technical" problems which will not be discussed in the text of the paper include (1) the lack of any consistent set of coding instructions across all of the studies using the Twenty Statements Test, and (2) the lack of inter-coder reliability procedures which are clearly specified and reported in the studies under consideration here. Regarding this last issue, some studies have reported figures for inter-coder reliability, but the procedures used to obtain these figures were never clearly reported.

"knowledge" of himself is contained in the responses on the Twenty Statement Test; (3) that the person's own perspective and "plans of action" is the focus of study. It was mentioned that the Twenty Statements Test does not violate any of these assumptions or assertions. But when it comes to the analysis of these statements from the Twenty Statements Test, the analyst *imposes the meaning on each of them from his own perspective*. In many theories this procedure would be appropriate. That is, they do not assume that the perspective or viewpoint of the respondent (actor) is the focus of study. In these theories the experience of the analyst is the focus of study. But, as the statements above point out, in self theory the experiences of the respondents are the focus of study. Therefore, the procedures employed in content analysis seem to contradict the assumptions and assertions of the theory.

Let us take a closer look at this contradiction. It seems that the self-theorist–researcher is using his notions of meaning on two different levels. On one level, the researcher assumes that the person knows the meaning of himself and obtains that information on the Twenty Statements Test. But, at another point, the researcher determines the meaning for each of these responses without taking the person's perspective into account. He decides which responses have consensus in terms of another context (e.g., his own, the "culture," the "society," etc.) which *may* be irrelevant for the person who made the responses. The analyst's standard for consensus seems to be "common-sense," but as Cicourel points out,

> The social scientist cannot afford to rely upon his own common-sense understanding for his content analysis of communications. To do so would make it impossible for him to differentiate between what he can understand because of his theoretical framework and what he can understand as a member of the same society (or even the same audience) in which the communication was presented.[36]

Again, I think this problem stems from a lack of "systematic" formulation in the theory. In order to employ a content analysis type of procedure the theory should be precise. I agree with Cicourel when he states:

The problem for the content analyst is to employ a theory which is sufficiently precise to enable the researcher to specify in advance what he should look for in some set of materials, how he is to identify and extract the material, how he must code it, and, finally, how its significance is to be decided.[37]

Even though the theory, as presented here, seems to be more "systematic" than others, in its original form it was not. If it had been, the self theorist might have noticed these problems. So, if these criticisms are valid, it seems that the self theorist should either investigate the notion of consensus or completely discard it.[38]

IV

Undoubtedly, those who have worked with this theory have thought of these and many other problems. Some other problems that could be explored are implied in the following questions:

1. Is there systematic empirical support for the assumptions and assertions that the self theorist states regarding the "self indication process"?
2. Is there systematic empirical support for the "interpretative process" that the self theorist and others posit as the basic process of social action?
3. What are the consequences for the theory of employing different types of questions, under a variety of conditions, which ask the respondent to refer to himself as an object?

These questions are rather "obvious" for those who have employed this theory in their research. But, as far as I know, the rationale for these questions, and the other problems mentioned in this paper, have not been specified by them. I think it is time for the self theorist to become openly "self-conscious" about his own work and limit the amount of effort expended on criticizing the other

[36] Cicourel, *op. cit.*, p. 155.

[37] *Ibid.*, p. 144.

[38] Several unpublished exploratory studies have been done regarding this problem. They include S. Clark McPhail, "Perceived Consensus Regarding Statements about the Self in Response to the Question, 'Who Am I?' " read at the Ohio Valley Sociological Society Meetings, Columbus, Ohio, 1964; and Charles W. Tucker, "The Dimensions of Self-Attitudes: A Working Paper" (mimeograph, 1965, Department of Sociology, Michigan State University).

theories of social behavior. It is hoped that this paper is one minor step in that direction.

In summary, this paper has attempted to accomplish several tasks. First, it organizes the various ideas, assumptions, definitions, and propositions of Kuhn's self theory. Then, using this as a base, it points out two major methodological problems which have not been previously mentioned or investigated by the self theorists. These problems deal with the effects of the testing situation on the responses to the self question and the content analysis procedures which have been employed by the self-theorist–researchers. By indicating these problems in this way it is expected that further empirical work can be done with this theory on a more sturdy foundation than was heretofore available.

SELECTED REFERENCES
PART THREE

Bain, Read. "The Self-and-Other Words of a Child." *American Journal of Sociology*, vol. 41 (May 1936), pp. 767–775. Explores the relationship of society and self through the medium of language.

Baumann, Bedrich. "George H. Mead and Luigi Pirandello, Some Parallels Between the Theoretical and Artistic Presentation of the Social Role Concept." *Social Research*, vol. 34 (Autumn 1967), pp. 563–607. A lengthy and, at times, difficult illustration of the convergence between artistic and scientific expositions of human behavior.

Braroe, Niels Winther. *Indian and White: Self-Image and Interaction in a Canadian Plains Community.* Stanford, California: Stanford University Press, 1975. Application of Goffman's perspective in an anthropological field study.

Clifton, Rodney A. "Self-Concept and Attitudes: A Comparison of Canadian Indian and Non-Indian Students." *Canadian Review of Sociology and Anthropology*, vol. 12 (November 1975), pp. 577–584. Discrimination does not appear to have harmed self-images.

Cooley, Charles Horton. "A Study of the Early Use of Self-Words by a Child." *Psychological Review*, vol. 15 (November 1908), pp. 339–357. Forerunner of the study described by Bain, above.

Couch, Carl J. "Family Role Specialization and Self-Attitudes in Children," *The Sociological Quarterly*, vol. 3 (April 1962), pp. 115–121. Uses the Twenty Statements Test to explore the relationship between family roles and individual self-image.

Denzin, Norman K. "Play, Games and Interaction: The Contents of Childhood Socialization." *Sociological Quarterly*, vol. 16 (Autumn 1975), pp. 458–478. Observational study of socialization and interaction in early childhood.

Denzin, Norman K. "The Genesis of Self in Early Childhood." *Sociological Quarterly*, 13 (Winter 1972), pp. 291–314. Empirical data on development of the self.

Kinch, John W. "A Formalized Theory of the Self-Concept." *American Sociological Review*, vol. 68 (January 1963), pp. 481–486. From the basic postulates of self-theory, the author deduces their logical consequences.

Mahoney, E. R. "The Processual Characteristics of Self-Conception." *Sociological Quarterly*, vol. 14 (Autumn 1973), pp. 517–533. Uses the Twenty Statements Test to compare the validity of three views of the self.

McPhail, Clark, and Charles W. Tucker. "Classification and Ordering of Responses to 'WAI'." *Sociological Quarterly*, vol. 13 (Summer 1972), pp. 329–347. Assessment of the "Who Am I" test in terms of certain basic principles of self theory.

Mead, George Herbert. *Mind, Self and Society.* Chicago: The University of Chicago Press, 1934, pp. 144–178. Mead's exposition of the genesis of the self.

Merrill, Francis E. "Stendhal and the Self: A Study in the Sociology of Literature." *American Journal of Sociology*, vol. 66 (March 1961), pp. 446–453. Presents an interpretive humanistic inquiry into the interactionist conception of the self in Stendhal's novel, *The Red and the Black.*

Miyamoto, S. Frank, and Sanford M. Dornbusch. "A Test of Interactionist Hypothesis of Self-Conception." *American Journal of Sociology*, vol. 61 (March 1956), pp. 399–403. Study of the relation of self-conceptions to the behavior of others, perception of others, and perception of the generalized other.

Pfuetze, Paul E. *The Social Self.* New York: Bookman Associates, 1954. A comparison and synthesis of Mead's ideas on the self with those of the eminent theologian Martin Buber.

Reeder, Leo G., George A. Donohue, and Arturo Biblarz. "Conceptions of Self and Others." *American*

Journal of Sociology, vol. 66 (September 1960), pp. 153–159. Research among military personnel, comparing self-concepts with ratings by others in the group.

Rosenberg, Morris. "Which Significant Others?" *American Behavioral Scientist,* vol. 16 (July/August 1973), pp. 57–65. The impact of valuation and credibility upon interpersonal relationships.

Schaefer, Robert, Rito Braito and Joe M. Bahley. "Self-Concept and the Reactions of 'Significant Others'." *Sociological Inquiry,* vol. 46 (1976), pp. 57–65. Survey sample data raises questions about the reflective self-conception.

Schmitt, Raymond L. "Major Role Change and Self Change." *Sociological Quarterly,* vol. 7 (Summer 1966), pp. 311–322. Study of 48 girls in the process of becoming Catholic nuns.

Sherwood, J. J. "Self-Identity and Referent Others." *Sociometry,* vol. 28 (March 1965), pp. 66–81. Tests the proposition that "the individual's self-identity (and his self-evaluation) is dependent upon his subjectively held version of the peer group's actual ratings of him."

Simmons, Roberta G., Florence Rosenberg, Morris Rosenberg. "Disturbance in the Self-Image at Adolescence." *American Sociological Review,* 38 (October 1973), pp. 553–568. Quantitative analysis of survey data reveals turmoil of adolescent development.

Spitzer, Stephan P. "Test Equivalence of Unstructured Self-Evaluation Instruments." *Sociological Quarterly,* vol. 10 (Spring 1969), pp. 204–215. Compares findings for six open-ended self-conception measures.

PART four

Mind

The basic symbolic interactionist proposition most relevant to this Part is our fifth one, which states: Consciousness, or thinking, involves interaction with oneself. For symbolic interactionists, then, "mind" refers to the processes through which persons carry on transactions with their environment. These processes, consisting of designations to oneself by means of symbols, enable individuals to direct and manage their acts while performing them and to carve out the objects constituting their environment. As we stated earlier, in more terse propositional form (proposition 6): Human beings construct their behavior in the course of its execution.

The concept of mind refers to a mental process or activity, not a physical entity like the brain. Although the activity is covert, it is behavior which closely resembles the overt communication between individuals. The inner processes of thought rely on the same symbols used in observable behavior. As we have previously indicated, thinking can be viewed as a process of internal conversation—of symbolic interaction between the individual and himself/herself.

William Lewis Troyer's brief article presents Mead's major ideas on mind, stressing its social genesis and its adaptive, processual character. In a straightforward and compact way, he examines the internal organization of the act, the meaning of meaning, and the selective quality of our perceptions of objective conditions. The crucial role of significant symbols in "minded behavior" emerges clearly in this summary.

The selection by John Dewey further underscores the functional view of mind. This pragmatic, instrumental conception stands in sharp contrast to the conception of mind in substantive terms. While this article focuses on the relation of mind to behavior, Dewey also stresses the importance of society and communication in developing the human mind (see his article in Part II).

The excerpt from William I. Thomas' book discusses the indications to oneself entailed in thought processes. That human beings act on the basis of their "definitions of the situation" is, of course, axiomatic for the symbolic-interactionist perspective. Using illustrations derived from his classic study (with Florian Znaniecki) of *The Polish Peasant in Europe and America,* Thomas relates the individual's definition of the situation to family and community sources.

Both Robert A. Stebbins and Harold Garfinkel present empirical studies of Thomas' concept, while Joan P. Emerson uses illustrative incidents in analyzing the same phenomena. The selection by Stebbins shows how useful the concept can be in the explanation of motivated behavior. It also distinguishes cultural, or consensual, definitions of the situation from unique personal, or nonconsensual, ones. Stebbins points out that his own definition of the situation affected his research strategy and its outcome. Emerson's article deals with the problem of maintaining shared definitions of situations. She shows that these shared definitions may play an important part in the labeling of behavior as deviant.

The article by Garfinkel applies what he calls the documentary method of interpretation to the study of commonsense knowledge of social structures. By documentary method, he means an interpretive analysis, rather than a literal description, of people's statements or actions. His provocative experiment, so characteristic of ethnomethodology, shows how individuals define their situations by instilling their own meanings into the instructions of the experimenter.

The crucial place of language in human thought and behavior is evidenced in the excerpt from Kurt Goldstein's classic book on aphasia. Studying the speech patterns of patients with brain lesions, Goldstein uncovered some of the critical consequences of diminished symbolic capability by human beings. Language is more than a simple tool. It is the basis of our ability to name, explain, and understand. Without language skills, memory, communication, and action are confined to the narrow boundaries of concrete sensations.

The selections by C. Wright Mills and by John P. Hewitt and Randall Stokes grapple with "motive," a concept that has proved troublesome to students of human behavior and relationships. It should be recalled, incidentally, that Stebbins' article addresses this concept. Mills and Hewitt and Stokes indicate the usefulness of treating motives as labels, or definitions, that humans apply to their own conduct and to the conduct of others. For Mills, language provides the individual with the vocabularies of motive appropriate for explaining behavior in specific situations. Thus, one's purpose in going to college is said to be to add to one's knowledge or to acquire a vocation. Hewitt and Stokes follow up Mills' point with their concept of "disclaimers," the ways that individuals interpret and justify their projected actions. They are verbal techniques, built out of socially acceptable words, phrases, and typifications, for avoiding potential criticism or blame.

These articles in Part IV should dispel the notion that mind is inevitably a mystical, unanalyzable phenomenon. To the symbolic interactionist, the term refers to an important process without which human behavior and society cannot be adequately understood. Indeed, understanding by social psychologists involves the same process as understanding by their subjects. The process of mind refers to the capacity of **each** socialized individual to communicate with himself/herself just as he/she is able to communicate with others. While inner communication is not readily observable, the following articles reveal its importance and suggest techniques for its observation and analysis.

Mead's Social and Functional Theory of Mind

The development of an adequate theory of mind in relation to nature was a central interest of the late George Herbert Mead's philosophical career. His general position is best designated with the term "social behaviorism." The basic datum from this point of view is the social act. But this datum is by no means an obvious and simple element for observation. Before it can be used to explore and understand the nature and function of mind, supporting theories of society and of self require elaboration. Hence, the natural order of Mead's own thinking seems to have been that of society-self-mind, instead of the reverse as suggested by the title of the edited volume of his famous lectures in social psychology.[1] A well-proportioned and discerning outline of Mead's position should culminate rather than begin with his understanding of mind

THE INTERNAL ORGANIZATION OF THE ACT

Mead, like John Dewey, was very critical of that form of behaviorism set forth by John Watson and his followers. These latter, he believed, had played a positive role in the development of a science of psychology but had, nevertheless, greatly oversimplified the concept and, consequently, the analysis of the act. They failed to take full account of the social character of the act, and what was worse yet, they limited analysis to fragmentary portions of the act. A thoroughgoing behaviorism would include within its purview the *complete* act, and particularly that portion of it which goes on "in the central nervous system as the beginning of the individual's act and as the organization of the act."[2] This larger inclusiveness would necessarily take the investigator beyond the field of direct observation, Watson's stopping point. An earlier retort that such procedure goes beyond science loses force in the light of a modern subatomic physics and a biochemistry of colloids and viruses.

Mead's criticism and his constructive development both begin with the concept of the reflex, or so-called stimulus-response arc. His position is essentially the same as that advanced by Dewey in his well-known article of 1896.[3] Both Mead and Dewey insisted that action is present in the living organism from the very outset. What has to be accounted for is not action but the direction which action takes. The process of responding is present in the entire act determining the very entertainment of stimuli. The living organism, in other words,

. . . is not a sensitive protoplasm that is simply receiving these stimuli from without and then responding to them. It is primarily *seeking* for certain stimuli.

William Lewis Troyer, "Mead's Social and Functional Theory of Mind," *American Sociological Review*, vol. 11 (April 1946), pp. 198–202. Reprinted by permission.
[1] G. H. Mead, *Mind, Self, and Society* (Chicago: University of Chicago Press, 1934).

[2] *Ibid.*, p. 11.
[3] John Dewey, "The Reflex Arc Concept in Psychology," *Psychological Review*, III (July 1896), 357–370.

. . . Whatever we are doing determines the sort of a stimulus which will set free certain responses which are merely ready for expression, and it is the *attitude* of action which determines for us what the stimulus will be.[4]

The use of the term "attitude" in this connection is highly important. Mead recognized that the functioning of the nervous system is as yet only partially explored, but he regarded the results already obtained as substantial enough to indicate an organization of the act in terms of social attitudes. Thus, he declared:

There is an organization of the various parts of the nervous system that are going to be responsible for acts, an organization which represents not only that which is immediately taking place, but also the later stages that are to take place. If one approaches a distant object, he approaches it with reference to what he is going to do when he arrives there. If one is approaching a hammer, he is muscularly all ready to seize the handle of the hammer. *The later stages of the act are present in the early stages—* not simply in the sense that they are ready to go off, but in the sense that *they serve to control the process itself.* They determine how we are going to approach the object, and the steps in our early manipulation of it.[5]

Whatever may be found by biological research to be the actual physiological pattern of functioning in the nervous system, the important point emphasized by Mead probably will not be gainsaid; that is, that the complete act is present as a determining factor in the beginning of the overt phase of the act. The attitude, as Mead uses the term, stands simply for this internal organization of the act.

A closely associated fact, brought to emphasis in Mead's outlook, is that the central nervous system, among human beings at least, provides a mechanism of *implicit* response. Not only does the human organism select its stimuli on the basis of attitudes, but it may also test out implicitly the various possible completions of an already initiated act in advance of the actual completion of that act. This it does through the employment of significant symbols. There is thus interposed between stimulus and response a process of selection. Mead referred to this phenomenon as "delayed reaction." To him this seemed to be the basis upon which it is legitimate to speak of choice and conscious control of behavior. It is this process, when considered in conjunction with the development of social attitudes, which constitutes intelligence or mind.[6] Obviously, this is far removed from the behaviorism of Watson; yet it is thoroughly behavioristic. It imports nothing from outside the act itself. It simply refuses to conceive the act narrowly as a mechanistic and individualistic reaction to external pressures.

BIOLOGICAL AND SOCIAL BASES OF MIND

Now, it should be clear from the foregoing that Mead emphasized the indispensability of the physiological organism in his account of mind. Individual experience and behavior was, in his thought, "physiologically basic" to social experience and behavior, and the processes and mechanisms essential to the origin and continued existence of society, self, and mind were dependent upon the social functioning of that which is physiologically individual.[7]

The individual members of even the most advanced invertebrate societies do not possess sufficient physiological capacities for developing minds or selves, consciousness or intelligence, out of their social relations and interactions with one another; and hence these societies cannot attain either the degree of complexity which would be presupposed by the emergence of minds and selves within them, or the further degree of complexity which would be possible only if minds and selves had emerged or arisen within them. Only the individual members of human societies possess the required physiological capacities for such development of minds and selves, and hence only human societies are able to reach the level of complexity, in their structure and organization, which becomes possible as the result of the emergence of minds and selves in their individual members.[8]

[4] G. H. Mead, *Movements of Thought in the Nineteenth Century* (Chicago: University of Chicago Press, 1936), pp. 389–390 (italics not in the original).

[5] Mead, *Mind, Self, and Society*, p. 11 (italics not in the original).

[6] *Ibid.*, pp. 99–100; 117–118.

[7] *Ibid.*, pp. 1–2.

[8] *Ibid.*, p. 236 (footnote).

For Mead the central nervous system, and particularly the cortex, furnished the physiological mechanism by means of which the "genesis of minds and selves out of the human social processes of experience and behavior—out of the human matrix of social relations and interactions—is made biologically possible in human individuals." Minds do not occur without brains. Looked at from the physiological angle, therefore, mind is an extraordinarily complex adjustment mechanism; an extension of distance receptors and motor effectors, a refined type of antennae, so to speak, by more efficient adaptation of organism and environment as achieved.

Important as this grounding of mind and selfhood in physiology is, however, the repeated reference in the above quotations to *social relations and interactions* must be fully appreciated if Mead's notion of mind is not to be gravely misunderstood. Brains are necessary to the emergence of mind, but brains, *per se,* do not make mind. It is society—social interaction—using brains, which makes mind. Intelligent human behavior is "essentially and fundamentally social";

> . . . it involves and presupposes an ever on-going social life-process; and . . . the unity of that on-going social process—or any one of its component acts—is irreducible, and in particular cannot be adequately analyzed simply into a number of discrete nerve elements.[9]

If this be true, it follows that the psychologist should study social relations and social behavior primarily, rather than physiology, if he would know what mind is and how it functions.

In pursuing this line of approach, Mead took his students over ground dealing with the emergence of human society and the self. He focused attention on the gesture, particularly the *vocal gesture,* and especially upon the vocal gesture at the point where it becomes a *significant symbol.* He declared that mentality "resides in the ability of the organism to indicate that in the environment which answers to his responses, so that he can control these responses in various ways."[10]

In his discussion of society and the self this indicating process is designated as "taking the role of the other" or participation in the "conversation of attitudes." As a self can arise only in a society where there is communication, so mind can arise only in a self or personality within which this conversation of attitudes or social participation is taking place. It is this conversation, this symbolic interaction, interposed as an integral part of the act, which constitutes mind.[11] Looked at from one standpoint, it is mind; from another, it is communication. Functioning within the organismic processes and social activities of the specific individual, communication is mind. It is symbolic social interaction, the process which makes human life distinctive.

The concrete import of such a theory of mind cannot be better summarized than in Mead's own words.

> In defending a social theory of mind we are defending a functional, as opposed to any form of substantive or entitative view as to its nature. And in particular, we are opposing all intracranial or intraepidermal views as to its character and locus. For it follows from our social theory of mind that the field of mind must be co-extensive with, and include all the components of, the field of the social process or experience and behavior: i.e., the matrix of social relations and interactions among individuals, which is presupposed by it, and out of which it arises or comes into being. If mind is socially constituted, then the field or locus of any given individual mind must extend as far as the social activity or apparatus of social relations which constitutes it extends; and hence that field cannot be bounded by the skin of the individual organism to which it belongs.[12]

The advantage of this view of mind resides in its plausibility as an account and explanation of the genesis and development of mind without postulation of supernatural endowment or special Being.[13] It thoroughly naturalizes mind in such a way as to give the concept of mind heuristic value in any full-fledged science of human nature. In so far as originality can be assigned to Mead, this achievement in understanding, if sustained by later criticism, may well rank with those of

---

[9] *Ibid.,* p. 118 (footnote).

[10] *Ibid.,* p. 132.

[11] Mead, *Movements of Thought,* pp. 384–385.

[12] Mead, *Mind, Self, and Society,* p. 223 (footnote).

[13] *Ibid.,* pp. 223–225.

Newton and Darwin in its importance to mankind.

THE OBJECT AS A COLLAPSED ACT

Mead's discussion of the self as an object to itself and also of the possibility of social responses toward inanimate objects raises a question as to the nature of objects and how they are known. While the ramifications of this phase of his thought are too varied for appropriate summary here, the matter does involve the concept of meaning and, therefore, warrants some consideration in the presentation of any rounded understanding of Mead's theory of mind.

In Mead's way of thinking, meaning arises only through communication. The significance of a gesture (symbol), for instance, is found in the response of others to it as a part of a social act. The various acts of individuals presuppose the social process, and

> . . . the gesture arises as a separable element in the social act, by virtue of the fact that it is selected out by the sensitivities of other organisms to it; it does not exist as a gesture merely in the experience of the single individual. The meaning of a gesture by one organism . . . is found in the response of another organism to what would be the completion of the act of the first organism which that gesture initiates and indicates.[14]

The relationship, in other words, between a stimulus as a gesture and the later phases of the social act constitutes the field within which meaning originates and exists.

What is particularly of significance in such a statement is that meaning, as thus considered, is a development *objectively there* as a relation between certain phases of the social act. It is not to be thought of as a psychical addition" to the act. It is no mere "idea" in the traditional sense.[15] Meaning is implicit wherever there is present a certain "triadic relation of a gesture of one individual, a response to that gesture by a second individual, and completion of the given social act

initiated by the gesture of the first individual."[16] Meaning is, therefore, thoroughly social in origin and nature.

According to Mead gestures may be either significant or non-significant. Below the human level of life the conversation of gestures is largely, if not completely, non-significant, non-meaningful, because it is not *self*-conscious. A lower organism acts, but its activity, from its own standpoint, or from that of any other non-human organism, is meaningless. There is gesture and response, as in the dog-fight, and things happen, but there is no self and no other; that is, no designation of objects. Any such designation would imply symbolic interaction. Meaning, as the object-matter of such symbolic interaction, or thought,

> . . . arises in experience through the individual stimulating himself to take the attitude of the other in his reaction toward the object. *Meaning is that which can be indicated to others while it is by the same process indicated to the indicating individual.*[17]

This point of view may be put in other terms. Mead laid emphasis, for example, upon the selective quality of organic activity. The living organism, within limits, but nevertheless definitely, selects or carves out its own environment. Among human beings this environment is distinctive in that it is composed of objects. At first the environment, or the world, is one of social objects, but as self and social other are acquired, physical objects and relationships may also be constructed by a process of abstraction. In this latter process the human hand, in conjunction with the eye, plays a major role.

Mead did not question that nature—or the extra-human world—is objectively there regardless of our experience of it. He was a pragmatist, not an idealist, in philosophy. He consequently held, however, that all objects are defined as such in and through human experience. Objective nature thereby comes to possess certain characteristics by virtue of its relationship to human experiencing or mind which it would not possess otherwise, or apart from this relationship. These

---

[14] *Ibid.,* pp. 145–146.
[15] *Ibid.,* pp. 75–76.

[16] *Ibid.,* p. 81.
[17] *Ibid.,* p. 89 (italics not in the original).

characteristics, Mead held, constitute the meanings of objects to us, and to all intents and purposes, give definition and functional reality to the objects themselves.[18] An object is always in this sense a "construct," a resultant, the kind of response which will ensue after a certain type of activity. A blackboard, for example, is what it is for us, has certain properties associated with writing in black and white, because that is the way it responds to our activity. As a symbol, an object, it stands for certain consequences in activity. Certain qualities are there, but as parts of an act, and not of some independently existing "essence" or "extension." From this standpoint, an object may be defined as a "collapsed act"; the sign of what would happen if the act were carried to completion.[19]

Following this point to its conclusion, Mead declared:

. . . The earliest objects are social objects, and all objects are social objects. Later experience differentiates the social from the physical objects, but the mechanism of the experience of things over against self as an object is the social mechanism. The identification of the individual with physical objects which appear in the effective occupation of space is a derivative of this.[20]

An object, thus, becomes a meaningful reality to a human being because of his ability to make indications, either imaginatively to himself, or directly to others. All objects, all symbols with semantic reference, represent telescoped acts. By means of the conversation of attitudes and the use of significant symbols—essentially a social process—the world (both social and physical) of each individual comes into being. Viewed, indeed, as consisting of objects and their relationships, the world is an out-and-out social world, as self and mind are also social, that is emergent within the human social process of activity itself. As Charles W. Morris, to whose labors we owe much for the possession of Mead's thought in print, declares in the introduction to the latest of the posthumous volumes,

. . . Mind, as involving the symbolic internalization of the complete or social act, and the self, as an object that has itself for an object, are on this view seen as social emergents made possible through the process of linguistic communication within the social act. . . . In man, animal impulse becomes enormously elaborated and intelligently guided, sensitivity to stimuli becomes the perception of enduring objects, manipulation is elaborated into the physical world of science, and communication shares in the elaboration of impulse and its illumination through reason. Animals live in a world of events; man lives in a world of common meanings—and meaning for Mead is socially generated and sustained.[21]

---

[18] *Ibid.*, p. 131.
[19] G. H. Mead, *The Philosophy of the Act* (Chicago: University of Chicago Press, 1938), pp. 368–370.
[20] *Ibid.*, pp. 428–430.

[21] *Ibid.*, pp. ix–x.

Mind, Experience, and Behavior

Let us begin with the technical side—the change in psychology. We are only just now commencing to appreciate how completely exploded is the psychology that dominated philosophy throughout the eighteenth and nineteenth centuries. According to this theory, mental life originated in sensations which are separately and passively received, and which are formed, through laws of retention and association, into a mosaic of images, perceptions and conceptions. The senses were regarded as gateways or avenues of knowledge. Except in combining atomic sensations, the mind was wholly passive and acquiescent in knowing. Volition, action, emotion, and desire follow in the wake of sensations and images. The intellectual or cognitive factor comes first and emotional and volitional life is only a consequent conjunction of ideas with sensations of pleasure and pain.

The effect of the development of biology has been to reverse the picture. Wherever there is life, there is behavior, activity. In order that life may persist, this activity has to be both continuous and adapted to the environment. This adaptive adjustment, moreover, is not wholly passive; is not a mere matter of the moulding of the organism by the environment. Even a clam acts upon the environment and modifies it to some extent. It selects materials for food and for the shell that protects it. It does something to the environment as well as has something done to itself. There is no such thing in a living creature as mere con-

formity to conditions, though parasitic forms may approach this limit. In the interests of the maintenance of life there is transformation of some elements in the surrounding medium. The higher the form of life, the more important is the active reconstruction of the medium. This increased control may be illustrated by the contrast of savage with civilized man. Suppose the two are living in a wilderness. With the savage there is the maximum of accommodation to given conditions; the minimum of what we may call hitting back. The savage takes things "as they are," and by using caves and roots and occasional pools leads a meagre and precarious existence. The civilized man goes to distant mountains and dams streams. He builds reservoirs, digs channels, and conducts the water to what had been a desert. He searches the world to find plants and animals that will thrive. He takes native plants and by selection and cross-fertilization improves them. He introduces machinery to till the soil and care for the harvest. By such means he may succeed in making the wilderness blossom like the rose.

Such transformation scenes are so familiar that we overlook their meaning. We forget that the inherent power of life is illustrated in them. Note what a change this point of view entails in the traditional notions of experience. Experience becomes an affair primarily of doing. The organism does not stand about, Micawberlike, waiting for something to turn up. It does not wait passive and inert for something to impress itself upon it from without. The organism acts in accordance with its own structure, simple or complex, upon its surroundings. As a consequence the changes

From *Reconstruction in Philosophy*, pp. 84–87, 90–92, by John Dewey, copyright 1948 by Beacon Press.

produced in the environment react upon the organism and its activities. The living creature undergoes, suffers, the consequences of its own behavior. This close connection between doing and suffering or undergoing forms what we call experience. Disconnected doing and disconnected suffering are neither of them experiences. Suppose fire encroaches upon a man when he is asleep. Part of his body is burned away. The burn does not perceptibly result from what he has done. There is nothing which in any instructive way can be named experience. Or again there is a series of mere activities, like twitchings of muscles in a spasm. The movements amount to nothing; they have no consequences for life. Or, if they have, these consequences are not connected with prior doing. There is no experience, no learning, no cumulative process. But suppose a busy infant puts his finger in the fire; the doing is random, aimless, without intention or reflection. But something happens in consequence. The child undergoes heat, he suffers pain. The doing and undergoing, the reaching and the burn, are connected. One comes to suggest and mean the other. Then there is experience in a vital and significant sense.

Certain important implications for philosophy follow. In the first place, the interaction of organism and environment, resulting in some adaptation which secures utilization of the latter, is the primary fact, the basic category. Knowledge is relegated to a derived position, secondary in origin, even if its importance, when once it is established, is overshadowing. Knowledge is not something separate and self-sufficing, but is involved in the process by which life is sustained and evolved. The senses lose their place as gateways of knowing to take their rightful place as stimuli to action. To an animal an affection of the eye or ear is not an idle piece of information about something indifferently going on in the world. It is an invitation and inducement to act in a needed way. It is a clue in behavior, a directive factor in adaptation of life in its surroundings. It is urgent not cognitive in quality. The whole controversy between empiricism and rationalism as to the intellectual worth of sensations is rendered strangely obsolete. The discussion of sensations belongs under the head of immediate stimulus and reponse, not under the head of knowledge.

. . .

When experience is aligned with the life-process and sensations are seen to be points of readjustment, the alleged atomism of sensations totally disappears. With this disappearance is abolished the need for a synthetic faculty of super-empirical reason to connect them. Philosophy is not any longer confronted with the hopeless problem of finding a way in which separate grains of sand may be woven into a strong and coherent rope—or into the illusion and pretence of one. When the isolated and simple existences of Locke and Hume are seen not to be truly empirical at all but to answer to certain demands of their theory of mind, the necessity ceases for the elaborate Kantian and post-Kantian machinery of *a priori* concepts and categories to synthesize the alleged stuff of experience. The true "stuff" of experience is recognized to be adaptive courses of action, habits, active functions, connections of doing and undergoing; sensori-motor co-ordinations. Experience carries principles of connection and organization within itself. These principles are none the worse because they are vital and practical rather than epistemological. Some degree of organization is indispensible to even the lowest grade of life. Even an amoeba must have some continuity in time in its activity and some adaptation to its environment in space. Its life and experience cannot possibly consist in momentary, atomic, and self-enclosed sensations. Its activity has reference to its surroundings and to what goes before and what comes after. This organization intrinsic to life renders unnecessary a super-natural and super-empirical synthesis. It affords the basis and material for a positive evolution of intelligence as an organizing factor within experience.

Nor is it entirely aside from the subject to point out the extent in which social as well as biological organization enters into the formation of human experience. Probably one thing that strengthened the idea that the mind is passive and receptive in knowing was the observation of the helplessness of the human infant. But the observation points in quite another direction. Because of his physical dependence and impotency, the contacts of the little child with nature are mediated by other persons. Mother and nurse, father and older children, determine what experiences the child shall have; they constantly instruct him as to the meaning of what he does and undergoes. The conceptions that are socially current and important become the child's principles of interpretation and estimation long before he attains to personal and deliberate control of con-

duct. Things come to him clothed in language, not in physical nakedness, and this garb of communication makes him a sharer in the beliefs of those about him. These beliefs coming to him as so many facts form his mind; they furnish the centres about which his own personal expeditions and perceptions are ordered. Here we have "categories" of connection and unification as important as those of Kant, but empirical not mythological.

William I. Thomas **28**

The Definition of the Situation

One of the most important powers gained during the evolution of animal life is the ability to make decisions from within instead of having them imposed from without. Very low forms of life do not make decisions, as we understand this term, but are pushed and pulled by chemical substances, heat, light, etc., much as iron filings are attracted or repelled by a magnet. They do tend to behave properly in given conditions—a group of small crustaceans will flee as in a panic if a bit of strychnia is placed in the basin containing them and will rush toward a drop of beef juice like hogs crowding around swill—but they do this as an expression of organic affinity for the one substance and repugnance for the other, and not as an expression of choice or "free will." There are, so to speak, rules of behavior but these represent a sort of fortunate mechanistic adjustment

From *The Unadjusted Girl*, pp. 41–50, by William I. Thomas (Boston: Little, Brown and Company, 1931), reprinted by permission of Social Science Research Council.

of the organism to typically recurring situations, and the organism cannot change the rule.

On the other hand, the higher animals, and above all man, have the power of refusing to obey a stimulation which they followed at an earlier time. Response to the earlier stimulation may have had painful consequences and so the rule or habit in this situation is changed. We call this ability the power of inhibition, and it is dependent on the fact that the nervous system carries memories or records of past experiences. At this point the determination of action no longer comes exclusively from outside sources but is located within the organism itself.

Preliminary to any self-determined act of behavior there is always a stage of examination and deliberation which we may call *the definition of the situation*. And actually not only concrete acts are dependent on the definition of the situation, but gradually a whole life-policy and the personality of the individual himself follow from a series of such definitions.

But the child is always born into a group of people among whom all the general types of situation which may arise have already been defined and corresponding rules of conduct developed, and where he has not the slightest chance of making his definitions and following his wishes without interference. Men have always lived together in groups. Whether mankind has a true herd instinct or whether groups are held together because this has worked out to advantage is of no importance. Certainly the wishes in general are such that they can be satisfied only in a society. But we have only to refer to the criminal code to appreciate the variety of ways in which the wishes of the individual may conflict with the wishes of society. And the criminal code takes no account of the many unsanctioned expressions of the wishes which society attempts to regulate by persuasion and gossip.

There is therefore always a rivalry between the spontaneous definitions of the situation made by the member of an organized society and the definitions which his society has provided for him. The individual tends to a hedonistic selection of activity, pleasure first; and society to a utilitarian selection, safety first. Society wishes its member to be laborious, dependable, regular, sober, orderly, self-sacrificing; while the individual wishes less of this and more of new experience. And organized society seeks also to regulate the conflict and competition inevitable between its members in the pursuit of their wishes. The desire to have wealth, for example, or any other socially sanctioned wish, may not be accomplished at the expense of another member of the society—by murder, theft, lying, swindling, blackmail, etc.

It is in this connection that a moral code arises, which is a set of rules or behavior norms, regulating the expression of the wishes, and which is built up by successive definitions of the situation. In practice the abuse arises first and the rule is made to prevent its recurrence. Morality is thus the generally accepted definition of the situation, whether expressed in public opinion and the unwritten law, in a formal legal code, or in religious commandments and prohibitions.

The family is the smallest social unit and the primary defining agency. As soon as the child has free motion and begins to pull, tear, pry, meddle, and prowl, the parents begin to define the situation through speech and other signs and pressures: "Be quiet," "Sit up straight," "Blow your nose," "Wash your face," "Mind your mother," "Be kind to sister," etc. This is the real significance of Wordsworth's phrase, "Shades of the prison house begin to close upon the growing child." His wishes and activities begin to be inhibited, and gradually, by definitions within the family, by playmates, in the school, in the Sunday school, in the community, through reading, by formal instruction, by informal signs of approval and disapproval, the growing member learns the code of his society.

In addition to the family we have the community as a defining agency. At present the community is so weak and vague that it gives us no idea of the former power of the local group in regulating behavior. Originally the community was practically the whole world of its members. It was composed of families related by blood and marriage and was not so large that all the members could not come together; it was a face-to-face group. I asked a Polish peasant what was the extent of an "okolica" or neighborhood—how far it reached. "It reaches," he said, "as far as the report of a man reaches—as far as a man is talked about." And it was in communities of this kind that the moral code which we now recognize as valid originated. The customs of the community are "folkways," and both state and church have in their more formal codes mainly recognized and incorporated these folkways.

The typical community is vanishing and it would be neither possible nor desirable to restore it in its old form. It does not correspond with the present direction of social evolution and it would now be a distressing condition in which to live. But in the immediacy of relationships and the participation of everybody in everything, it represents an element which we have lost and which we shall probably have to restore in some form of cooperation in order to secure a balanced and normal society—some arrangement corresponding with human nature.

Very elemental examples of the definition of the situation by the community as a whole, corresponding to mob action as we know it and to our trial by jury, are found among European peasants.

The three documents following, all relating to the Russian community or *mir,* give some idea of the conditions under which a whole community, a public, formerly defined a situation.

25. We who are unacquainted with peasant speech, manners and method of expressing thought—mimicry—if we should be present at a division of land or some settlement among the peasants, would never understand anything. Hearing fragmentary, disconnected exclamations, endless quarreling, with repetition of some single word; hearing this racket of a seemingly senseless, noisy crowd that counts up or measures off something, we should conclude that they would not get together, or arrive at any result in an age. . . . Yet wait until the end and you will see that the division has been made with mathematical accuracy—that the measure, the quality of the soil, the slope of the field, the distance from the village—everything in short has been taken into account, that the reckoning has been correctly done and, what is most important, that every one of those present who were interested in the division is certain of the correctness of the division or settlement. The cry, the noise, the racket do not subside until every one is satisfied and no doubter is left.

The same thing is true concerning the discussion of some question by the *mir.* There are no speeches, no debates, no votes. They shout, they abuse each other, they seem on the point of coming to blows. Apparently they riot in the most senseless manner. Some one preserves silence, silence, and then suddenly puts in a word, one word, or an ejaculation, and by this word, this ejaculation, he turns the whole thing upside down. In the end, you look into it and find that an admirable decision has been formed and, what is most important, a unanimous decision.[1]

26. As I approached the village, there hung over it such a mixed, varied violent shouting, that no well brought-up parliament would agree to recognize itself, even in the abstract, as analogous to this gathering of peasant deputies. It was clearly a full meeting today. . . . At other more quiet village meetings I had been able to make out very little, but this was a real lesson to me. I felt only a continuous, indistinguishable roaring in my ears, sometimes pierced by a particularly violent phrase that broke out from the general roar. I saw in front of me the "immediate" man, in all his beauty. What struck me first of all was his remarkable frankness; the more "immediate" he is, the less able is he to mask his thoughts and feelings; once he is stirred up the emotion seizes him quickly and he flares up then and there, and does not quiet down till he has poured out before

you all the substance of his soul. He does not feel embarrassment before anybody; there are no indications here of diplomacy. Further, he opens up his whole soul, and he will tell everything that he may ever have known about you, and not only about you, but about your father, grandfather, and great-grandfather. Here everything is clear water, as the peasants say, and everything stands out plainly. If any one, out of smallness of soul, or for some ulterior motive, thinks to get out of something by keeping silent, they force him out into clear water without pity. And there are very few such small-souled persons at important village meetings. I have seen the most peaceable, irresponsible peasants, who at other times would not have thought of saying a word against any one, absolutely changed at these meetings, at these moments of general excitement. They believed in the saying, "On people even death is beautiful," and they got up so much courage that they were able to answer back the peasants commonly recognized as audacious. At the moment of its height the meeting becomes simply an open mutual confessional and mutual disclosure, the display of the widest publicity. At these moments when, it would seem, the private interests of each reach the highest tension, public interests and justice in turn reach the highest degree of control.[2]

27. In front of the volost administration building there stands a crowd of some one hundred and fifty men. This means that a volost meeting has been called to consider the verdict of the Kusmin rural commune "regarding the handing over to the [state] authorities of the peasant Gregori Siedov, caught red-handed and convicted of horse-stealing." Siedov had already been held for judical inquiry; the evidence against him was irrefutable and he would undoubtedly be sentenced to the penitentiary. In view of this I endeavor to explain that the verdict in regard to his exile is wholly superfluous and will only cause a deal of trouble; and that at the termination of the sentence of imprisonment of Siedov the commune will unfailingly be asked whether it wants him back or prefers that he be exiled. Then, I said, in any event it would be necessary to formulate a verdict in regard to the "non-reception" of Siedov, while at this stage all the trouble was premature and could lead to nothing. But the meeting did not believe my words, did not trust the court and wanted to settle the matter right then and there; the general hatred of horse-thieves was too keen. . . .

The decisive moment has arrived; the head-man "drives" all the judges-elect to one side; the crowd stands with a gloomy air, trying not to look at Siedov and his wife, who are crawling before the *mir* on their knees. "Old men, whoever pities Gregori, will

[1] A. N. Engelgardt: "Iz Derevni: 12 Pisem" ("From the Country; 12 Letters"), p. 315.

[2] N. N. Zlatovratsky: "Ocherki Krestyanskoy Obshchiny" ("Sketches of the Peasant Commune"), p. 127.

remain in his place, and whoever does not forgive him will step to the right," cries the head man. The crowd wavered and rocked, but remained dead still on the spot; no one dared to be first to take the fatal step. Gregori feverishly ran over the faces of his judges with his eyes, trying to read in these faces pity for him. His wife wept bitterly, her face close to the ground; beside her, finger in mouth and on the point of screaming, stood a three-year-old youngster (at home Gregori had four more children). . . . But straightway one peasant steps out of the crowd; two years before some one had stolen a horse from him. "Why should we pity him? Did he pity us?" says the old man, and stooping goes over to the right side. "That is true; bad grass must be torn from the field," says another one from the crowd, and follows the old man. The beginning had been made; at first individually and then in whole groups the judges-elect proceeded to go over to the right. The man condemned by public opinion ran his head into the ground, beat his breast with his fists, seized those passed him by their coat-tails, crying: "Ivan Timofeich! Uncle Leksander! Vasinka, dear kinsman! Wait, kinsmen, let me say a word. . . . Petrushenka." But, without stopping and with stern faces, the members of the *mir* dodged the unfortunates, who were crawling at their feet. . . . At last the wailing of Gregori stopped; around him for the space of three *sazen* the place was empty; there was no one to implore. All the judges-elect, with the exception of one, an uncle of the man to be exiled, had gone over to the right. The woman cried sorrowfully, while Gregori stood motionless on his knees, his head lowered, stupidly looking at the ground.[3]

The essential point in reaching a communal decision, just as in the case of our jury system, is unanimity. In some cases the whole community mobilizes around a stubborn individual to conform him to the general wish.

> 28. It sometimes happens that all except one may agree but the motion is never carried if that one refuses to agree to it. In such cases all endeavor to talk over and persuade the stiff-necked one. Often they even call to their aid his wife, his children, his relatives, his father-in-law, and his mother, that they may prevail upon him to say yes. Then all assail him, and say to him from time to time; "Come now, God help you, agree with us too, that this may take place as we wish it, that the house may not be cast into disorder, that we may not be talked about by the people, that the neighbors may not hear of it, that the world may not make sport of us!" It seldom occurs in such cases that unanimity is not attained.[4]

[3] "V. Volostnikh Pisaryakh" ("A Village Secretary"), p. 283.
[4] F. S. Krauss: "Sitte und Brauch der Südslaven," p. 103.

A less formal but not less powerful means of defining the situation employed by the community is gossip. The Polish peasant's statement that a community reaches as far as a man is talked about was significant, for the community regulates the behavior of its members largely by talking about them. Gossip has a bad name because it is sometimes malicious and false and designed to improve the status of the gossiper and degrade its object, but gossip is in the main true and is an organizing force. It is a mode of defining the situation in a given case and of attaching praise or blame. It is one of the means by which the status of the individual and of his family is fixed.

The community also, particularly in connection with gossip, knows how to attach opprobrium to persons and actions by using epithets which are at the same time brief and emotional definitions of the situation. "Bastard," "whore," "traitor," "coward," "skunk" "scab," "snob," "kike," etc., are such epithets. In "Faust" the community said of Margaret, "She stinks." The people are here employing a device known in psychology as the "conditioned reflex." If, for example, you place before a child (say six months old) an agreeable object, a kitten, and at the same time pinch the child, and if this is repeated several times, the child will immediately cry at the sight of the kitten without being pinched; or if a dead rat were always served beside a man's plate of soup he would eventually have a disgust for soup when served separately. If the word "stinks" is associated on people's tongues with Margaret, Margaret will never again smell sweet. Many evil consequences, as the psychoanalysts claim, have resulted from making the whole of sex life a "dirty" subject, but the device has worked in a powerful, sometimes a paralyzing way on the sexual behavior of women.

Winks, shrugs, nudges, laughter, sneers, haughtiness, coldness, "giving the once over" are also language defining the situation and painfully felt as unfavorable recognition. The sneer, for example, is incipient vomiting, meaning, "you make me sick."

And eventually the violation of the code even in an act of no intrinsic importance, as in carrying food to the mouth with the knife, provokes condemnation and disgust. The fork is not a better instrument for conveying food than the knife, at least it has no moral superiority, but the situation has been defined in favor of the fork. To smack with the lips in eating is bad manners with us, but the Indian has more logically defined the situation in the opposite way; with him smacking is a compliment to the host.

In this whole connection fear is used by the group to produce the desired attitudes in its member. Praise is used also but more sparingly. And the whole body of habits and emotions is so much a community and family product that disapproval or separation is almost unbearable.

Robert A. Stebbins **29**

Studying the Definition of the Situation: Theory and Field Research Strategies

For over forty years, since Thomas and Znaniecki published *The Polish Peasant,* the phrase "the definition of the situation" has been in the American sociologist's lexicon. What is remarkable, given this longevity, is the paucity of research that focuses on the definitions of specific situations by groups of actors as explanations for the behaviour of these actors in the immediate environment. Those few studies that have been carried out under the name of definition of the situation (for example, Gorden, 1952; Lerner and Becker, 1962; Deutscher, 1964) have either inadequately operationalized this notion or have considered as the situation to be defined something far larger and less specific than a typical instance

of ongoing social interaction.[1] However, it should be noted that there is one very recent exception to this indictment, and we shall consider it briefly later on. It is Peter McHugh's ingenious laboratory study of the definition of the situation (1968).

It seems that tradition as well as genuine conceptual and measurement difficulties have combined to produce a reluctance to investigate, in a systematic fashion, people's definitions of situations. The myth, outside and to some extent within the field of symbolic interactionism, that the ideas of George Herbert Mead (and therefore those of his followers) cannot be empirically examined still lingers. There is the very real problem of concretizing or establishing working definitions for a concept so subjective and abstract as the definition of the situation. Finally, there has been the tendency to consider the definition of the situ-

Robert A. Stebbins, "Studying the Definition of the Situation: Theory and Field Research Strategies." Reprinted from *The Canadian Review of Sociology and Anthropology,* 6:4 (1969), by permission of the author and the publisher.

The author wishes to express his gratitude to Professors Jean L. Briggs, Frank E. Jones, and Robert W. Habenstein for their helpful comments on various drafts of the manuscript.

[1] It is this latter kind of situation in which we are interested. It has been defined more formally by Stebbins (1967:150) as the "subjective situation" or "the immediate social and physical surroundings and the current physiological and psychological state of the actor . . . *as seen by him.*"

ation in terms of the single individual who holds it, a practice not conducive to the development of nomothetic science. With respect to this last point, we must strive instead to make general statements about *classes* of definitions used by identifiable *groups* of men in particular but recurrent situations.

Although it will be a long time before anything like "grounded" theories of the definitions of specific kinds of situations by specific categories of actors appear, it is evident that a set of research strategies must be devised to assist us in our efforts to reach this goal. The aim of this paper is to offer, along with certain strategies for research, some refinements in the theory of the definition of the situation that was presented in an earlier essay by the author (Stebbins, 1967). An exploratory type of field experimental demonstration follows this discussion, and we conclude with a review of the implications of the refined theory for sociological motivation.

THEORY AND RESEARCH STRATEGIES

The goal of making general statements about classes of definitions used by identifiable groups of men in particular but recurrent situations, is best attained by employing the following concepts. The groups of men to be studied are those in different *social identities*, the conventionally recognized categories in community life into which human actors place themselves and others.[2] Most of our definitions of the countless situations that we enter, whatever identity we are in, may be classified as belonging to one of the following modes: *cultural definitions* (Wolff, 1965:182), *habitual personal definitions*, or *unique personal definitions*.[3] The chief difference between the first two lies in the distinction between consensual and non-consensual sharing of meanings. Cultural definitions are collective rep

[2] "Identity" is preferred over closely related ideas such as "status," "position," and "rank" because of its apparently broader scope. For example, one can have the identity of neighbour, but we would not ordinarily call this a position or a status.

[3] These three modes of the definition of the situation represent an expansion of the "cultural" and "personal definitions" discussed by the author in his earlier paper (Stebbins, 1967:158)

resentations; the standard meanings of events embedded in the community culture as a whole or some sub-part of it (sub-culture) that we learn either through primary socialization or secondary socialization or both. A given cultural definition is consensually shared to the extent that those who are members of a particular group are aware that others in it recognize and utilize that definition in the same way that they do. Thus, in North America bar rooms are generally defined as places where people drink alcoholic beverages and talk sociably with others, and offices at places of work are typically conceived as locations for occupationally related activity—two widely held cultural definitions.

But sharing of the definition need not be consensual. The non-consensual sharing characteristic of the habitual personal definition refers to the circumstances in which the same category of situation holds roughly the same meaning for a particular class of actor participating in it, but in which each individual participant is more or less *unaware* that people like him who are having the same kind of experiences elsewhere define them in the same way. Present research by the author into the ways teachers define certain classroom situations has disclosed that they are largely unaware of how their colleagues deal with routine instances of disorderly behaviour. That Johnny was discovered whispering the other day or that Susan was daydreaming this morning are apparently not of sufficient importance to the teachers investigated so far in the project to warrant comment to other teachers in the same kind of setting. Still, each teacher defined situations such as these, usually as calling for a specific action designed to curb the undesirable behaviour of the student or students involved.

Habitual definitions are the regular meanings employed by categories of actors in specific kinds of periodic situations that for one reason or another (such as, the insignificance of the event or the unavailability of like actors to each other while behaving in the situation) are not communicated. These meanings can be distinguished from unique personal definitions, which refer to the person's interpretation of events rarely or never encountered in the community. To wit, events that occur for which, so far as he is concerned, no cultural or habitual meaning exists. Thus, he must improvise his own interpretation, usually basing his synthesis on the nearest personal or collective equivalent. Presumably, the recent earth tremors in the midwestern portion of North America led to many unique definitions of that situation.

Although they are infrequent, unique personal definitions are apparently shared on a nonconsensual basis under some circumstances. Hill and Hansen (1962:186), after examining several studies concerning the family in disasters, concluded that there is a general tendency for family members to seek each other under these circumstances, if geographical location does not prevent this. It seems that people's definitions of disaster situations regularly include family considerations, if their families are believed to be in any danger.

The relationship between these three modes of definitions of the situation is complicated and must await empirical specification. Because they are multidimensional they cannot be placed on a single continuum. At this stage of the development of the theory, they are best viewed as ideal types, functioning heuristically to inform us how closely a given empirical case approximates the pure conceptualization of the phenomenon.

The aim of research in this field should be the development of "grounded theories" of definitions of recurrent situations encountered by the incumbents of a particular identity.[4] Since cultural and habitual definitions are seen as forming the foundation on which actors build unique definitions, and since they refer to recurrent settings, it should be clear that we must begin any research program with the aim just suggested by concentrating initially on the first two modes of definitions. And by studying the definitions of situations of those in a given identity, a theoretical link to the social structure of the community is also gained, thereby permitting us as well to view our findings in terms of their relevance at the macrosociological level of analysis.

A cultural definition, since it is categorical and impersonal, must be given additional specification by the actor using it with reference to any

particular setting. Once a cultural definition is determined to be relevant for the events at hand, it is idiosyncratically tailored so as to better serve the user. As we shall indicate shortly, this is done, in part, through activated predispositions. The usage of the term "predisposition" in this paper is similar to the modern conceptualization of Newcomb, Turner, and Converse (1965:40–46, 67–73) and Campbell (1963:97–112). Campbell, who limits his statement strictly to acquired states, stresses the importance of the fact that predispositions (he calls them "acquired behavioural dispositions") are enduring and that they remain dormant until activated by situational stimuli. When activated, these products of past experience impinge upon our awareness, equip us with a specific view of the world, and guide behaviour in the immediate present.

The following sequential model indicates the location of the definition of the situation in relation to the initial reaction of the individual to the setting.[5] 1. Typical actors in a given identity enter a typical setting with a specific intention or action orientation in mind. 2. Certain aspects of these surroundings, some of which are related to the intention, activate or awaken some of the predispositions the actors characteristically carry with them. 3. The aspects of the surroundings, the intention, and the activated predispositions, when considered together, lead to the selection of a cultural or habitual definition. 4. This definition directs subsequent action in the situation, at least until a reinterpretation occurs.

From what has been said so far, it is possible to formulate two research problems to guide actual study. 1. What cultural or habitual definitions are available to those in a given social identity for use in one or more specified kinds of recurring situations? 2. For classes of actors within an identity, what common predispositions are activated by elements in the ongoing setting that influence the selection of one of these definitions instead of another?[6]

---

[4] Grounded theory is theory discovered "from data systematically obtained from social research" (Glaser and Strauss, 1967:2).

[5] This is, of course, a highly simplified version of a more complicated process. For a more detailed discussion of this model, see Stebbins (1967).

[6] McHugh's treatment of the process of "emergence" seems to come closest in meaning to the cultural and habitual definitions, when compared with the rest of the concepts in our framework. Following Mead, emergence refers to the past and future

Operationalization

Once one discovers some of the more important recurring situations for the actors in an identity (by means of some form of observation), one can, if not already aware of them, begin to search for the cultural or habitual definitions available for each setting. This can be done most efficaciously by a combination of further direct observation and questionnaire interviewing. Here observation performs a single important function: it gives the investigator a crude idea of the definition that the subject has chosen in response to the situation at hand. Having acquired this knowledge it is possible for the former to question the latter about that event, the intention being to establish a more detailed and consequently more valid picture of the meaning that the incident held for the respondent. In order to avert problems of recall, interviewing should take place as soon as possible after the situation under observation has ended.

The interviewing, if it is to fulfil its function, must be conducted along the lines of programmatically developed statements operationalizing the concept of the definition of the situation, thirteen of which are listed below. Each of these has been theorized and often empirically demonstrated by social psychologists to play an important role in situationally based and situationally focused explanations of behaviour.[7] The merit of the theory of the definition of the situation is that it pulls together these theoretical strands, which are in themselves incomplete as explanations, within a more coherent and comprehensive framework (some of which we have yet to discuss). There is a degree of overlap between some of the statements, but for our purposes this may be advantageous. 1. Identification by the identity incumbents of the relevant others present (Ball, forthcoming; Foote, 1951: 17–21; McHugh, 1968:43; Stone, 1962:89–90; Strauss, 1959:47; Turner, 1956; Weinstein and Deutschberger, 1963; 1964).[8] 2. The incumbents' perception of the evaluation that those others have made of the situation, including the moral and emotional or sentimental connotations of the immediate setting as they are established with reference to the others' identification of themselves (Ball, forthcoming; Jones and Davis, 1965;226–227; McHugh, 1968:44; Newcomb, 1958:180; Shand, 1920; Shibutani, 1961:332–334; Stone, 1962:97–101; Strauss, 1959:59; Thomas, 1951:69; Turner, 1956:321; Weber, 1947:90–95). 3. The incumbents' perception of the goals or intentions of the others while in the setting (Ball, forthcoming; Jones and Davis, 1965:222–223; Schutz, 1964:32; Strauss, 1959:59; Turner, 1956; Weber, 1947:90–95). 4. The incumbents' perception of the plans of action (strategies for reaching the goals) of the relevant others (Turner, 1956:321). 5. The incumbents' perception of the justifications or vocabularies of motives associated with the others' plans of action (Mills, 1940; Schutz, 1964:32). 6. The incumbents' evaluation of the situation (Ball, forthcoming; Cooley, 1922:183–184; Foote, 1951:20–21; McCall and Simmons, 1966:136; Shand, 1920; Shibutani, 1961:332–334; Stone, 1962:93, 97–101; Strauss, 1959:59; Turner, 1956:322). 7. The incumbents' plans of action (Jones and Thibaut, 1958:158–174). 8. The incumbents' justifications of the plans (Burke, 1945; 1950; MacIver, 1964:293; Mills, 1940; Schutz, 1964:11).

---

influence on contemporary behaviour (McHugh, 1968;24–25). The process of emergence partly manifests itself in everyday life by leading the actor to expect a familiar "theme" in all or most of his dealings with others (McHugh, 1968:37). The other major parameter of the definition of the situation found in McHugh's study is that of the "relativity" of standpoints from which we judge the setting (1968:28, 42–45). However, his evidence suggests that relativity, as he uses this term, operates mostly where the assumption of a theme breaks down. This approaches our notion of unique personal definition, which is peripheral to our interests here. While there are several places where aspects of the process of emergence and those of the cultural or habitual definition seem to correspond, we shall retain the operational terminology developed earlier. It better relates to the previously developed theory and, because of its greater comprehensiveness, better serves field research.

[7] The phrase "situationally based and situationally focused explanations" refers to those propositions in social psychology that fix on behaviour in the immediate setting and that are consistent with the assumption that human action is, at least in part, a product of what is happening there. They are clearly of a different genre than constitutionally based or social structurally based explanations.

---

[8] The citations at the end of each of these statements refer to some of the relevant theoretical and empirical literature. They do not, in any way, represent an exhaustive inventory of pertinent entries. Also the operational statements presented in this paper are occasionally couched in language rather different from that found in the works cited.

And as through the looking glass: 9. The identity incumbents' perception of the identification of them by the relevant others (McCall and Simmons, 1966:140–142; Stone, 1962:93; Turner, 1956:321–323; 1962:34). 10. The incumbents' perception of the evaluation of the situation imputed to them by the others (Cooley, 1922:183–184; Jones, 1964; Stone, 1962:97–101; Turner, 1956:321–323; 1962:34). 11. The incumbents' perception of the intentions imputed to them while in the situation (Jones, 1964; Turner, 1956:321–323; 1962:34). 12. The incumbents' perception of the plans of action imputed to them (Foote, 1951; Strauss, 1959:51; Turner, 1956:321–323). 13. The incumbents' perception of the justifications of the plans imputed to them (Mills, 1940; Schutz, 1964:32–33; Strauss, 1959:52).

All of these perceptions by a given set of identity holders can, theoretically, be said to be part of their definitions of a particular kind of situation. However, not all of them will necessarily be obtained in any given investigation, for the actors may not be able to get such information for their own use in the interaction. They might, for example, be able to identify the relevant others, their meanings, and their intentions, but they might not have time to reflect about their plans of action or their justifications for them.

Moreover, we may not need or desire the type of knowledge contained in each of these perceptions. We, as social persons, require only *adequate* knowledge about the others present and their perceptions of us so that we can act; additional information, while perhaps desirable, is less essential.[9] Jones and Thibaut (1958:151–152) cite research demonstrating that not all information is equally useful in assessing other actors in the environment. They believe that much of the perceiver's energy will be directed toward his own future response (his plan of action) and not toward the stable characteristics of the others present (Jones and Thibaut, 1958:74). Ichheiser (1949:46–48) points out that there is a tendency to overestimate the role of personal factors in the environment, while underestimating the role of situa-

tional factors. We are often blind to situational factors as others see them. Finally, it has been suggested by Gerth and Mills (1954:115) that unless one's anticipated behaviour is contrary to the expectations of those present, there is no felt need to justify it.

The investigator can isolate the cultural or habitual definitions used by those in an identity in certain circumstances by combining their responses to the operational statements as they appear in the questionnaire. This is exemplified in the field experiment reported later. Such a procedure permits one to obtain something of the actors' organic views of the immediate circumstances, which is in keeping with the belief that a definition or meaning of the situation is a synthesis, interpretation, and interrelation of predispositions, intentions, and elements of the setting (Stebbins, 1967:158).

Phases of the Definition of the Situation

In our sequential model presented earlier we stated that on the basis of the situational factors, the actors' predispositions, and their goals, a cultural or habitual personal mode of definition was selected. Although generally correct this statement is oversimplified. In actuality, the choice of standard definitions seems to take place in two phases occurring in rapid succession. Phase I is that of identifying the ongoing events as an instance of some category of situation. Here the incumbents have a choice; (i) a set of events is for them an instance of "X" category of situation, or (ii) a set is not such an instance and therefore is an instance of another category of situation (say, situation "A," "B," or "C"). However, recurrent situations are not free from associated meanings in the individual mind; they do not occur as neutral, uninterpreted happenings. In the very process of identifying the category of setting we are in, we have also selected a portion of our cultural or habitual definition because it is associated by means of socialization with the events at hand. More specifically, some or all of operational statements 1 through 5 and 9 through 13 appear simultaneously merely from identifying a set of events as "X" or "B" or whatever.

[9] Or, lacking direct information one may assume a certain amount about the others, relying on what Simmel (1950:318) called "confidence" in their meanings, intentions, etc. These assumptions are still part of the definition of the situation.

Phase II of the selection of a cultural or habitual definition amounts to choosing a standard personal evaluation, plan of action, and justification (operational statements 6 through 8). This can only be done after some answers, no matter how tentative, have been provided to the questions posed by the operational statements that comprise Phase I. There must be a modicum of information about the situation to evaluate, and to respond to with a plan of action. In Phase II, choice is guided by the immediate intentions of the actors, the actors' identification of the setting in Phase I, and the activated predispositions resulting from this identification.[10] When the intentions and activated predispositions play a role in the selection of a certain cultural definition (as compared with a habitual definition), they also direct the tailoring of that definition to the individual user. In this subjective sense the intentions and the predispositions are very much a part of the definition of the situation (both as a process and a product).

There are a couple of formulations in the literature that speak for the tenability of conceptualizing the defining of a situation in terms of two rapidly occurring successive phases. For instance, Fritz Heider (1958:76) has enunciated the general principle that perception influences action by arousing motivational states in the actor. Shand's theory of emotional expression (1920) also fits our model: as manifestations of underlying sentiments, behaviour-directing emotions are responses to certain kinds of settings. If I hate the man next door, I will be revolted when I see him in his garden and pleased when I notice that he has a flat tire.

Once we have identified one or more common purposes for a set of identity incumbents

in any typical situation, then, having observed the events there, our problem is just as we stated earlier: to isolate the activated predispositions for classes of actors. These predispositions, which are many and varied (e.g., attitudes, values, general life goals, ideal self-conceptions, internalized role expectations, interests, and so forth),[11] can be measured in almost as many diverse ways. The most critical procedural problem facing the researcher in this area is how to record this activation of predispositions. Its solution demands much more than simply finding out which people hold a particular attitude or self-conception. Rather it involves determining if that disposition has played a role in the selection of a particular cultural or habitual definition. Fortunately, we are aided by common sense here, since it will be obvious to the long-time occupants of an identity (and to the observer who taps their knowledge) that some predispositions are not usually associated with certain social situations, while others are. Thus, teacher attitudes toward other races are not likely to be activated in an all-white classroom situation where mathematics is being taught.

Appropriate knowledge about an identity, then, enables us to be reasonably confident that a relevant predisposition has been activated and has been a factor in the selection of a particular definition when those who have chosen it are found to hold both the disposition and the definition in a significantly greater proportion than we would expect from their observed frequency in the study sample.

Parenthetically, it should be noted that any cultural or habitual definition may be replaced by another if, for some reason, the events in the setting change in some significant way. If this happens, then the same processes of selection recur (also see Ball's discussion of this point, forthcoming). Major changes in the affairs of the moment have been said, in fact, to signal the emergence of a new situation. The problems of establishing temporal, social, and physical boundaries of situa-

---

[10] In the interest of clarity it should be pointed out that the immediate intentions with which an actor enters the setting and his general life goals or long-range goals are two distinct, albeit, related ideas. A general life goal is a predisposition that is too complex and abstract from the individual's point of view to be realized in one or a few situations. The immediate intention, on the other hand, although it may be in service of a long-range goal is envisaged by the actor as being realized in the ongoing setting or in a short sequence of such settings. This latter type of goal is not a predisposition because it is not an enduring state that may be activated from time to time or that equips us with a special view of the world.

[11] A longer though still incomplete list is available in Campbell (1963:100–101). In fact, some phenomena that traditionally have been considered in objective terms, can also be treated as predispositions. See, for example, the author's papers on interpersonal relationships and social networks and subjective career (Stebbins, 1969; 1970).

tions, both old and new, are considered by Stebbins (1967:151–154).

A FIELD EXPERIMENT

The experiment was conducted during a series of controversial lectures on the theory of evolution in an introductory sociology and anthropology course in a community where religious matters are taken seriously. Although there were no outright contests between instructor and students, it was clear that the latter were taking an unusual interest in the lecture material of the former, thereby indicating its concern (both positive and negative) to them.

With the co-operation of the instructor, two well-dressed male sociology students, ages 22 and 38, entered the lecture hall just before class was to begin and sat in the front row. After the instructor had begun summarizing some of his previous lectures on evolution, one of the men abruptly interrupted him with a contentious question about the validity of his information. For approximately five minutes a heated debate raged between instructor and the experimenter's confederates over the merits of the biblical versus the scientific versions of creation and the development of man. The instructor, not from the community in which the university is located, was branded, among other things, an outsider, an atheist, and a Communist. He was accused of defiling the minds of students and inciting pernicious social change. In the end the interlopers were expelled without ceremony.

The experimenter (who was listening outside the door) appeared immediately, and disclosed the true nature of the preceding events. Thereupon each student was asked to fill in a questionnaire containing a small number of open-ended items which were constructed along the lines of some of the thirteen operational statements of the definition of the situation.[12] Although individ-

ual interviewing would have been preferable, this procedure was successful enough to provide some definitive information about their interpretation of the experimental situation. Most students were able to complete the form in approximately twenty minutes.

An hour later (at the second meeting of that class) each student was requested to take, in the order of their appearance here, the Kuhn-McPartland Twenty-Statements Test, an interest ranking test, and a goal ranking test.[13] These measures provided the experimenter with a modicum of data about the predispositions of the students. The Twenty-Statements Test, though successfully administered, was unusable because the numbers of respondents, even in the largest cells, were not sufficient for meaningful cross tabulation. With respect to the other tests the students were asked to rank order six major interests: theoretical, economic, aesthetic, social, political, and religious. There were also ten general life goals to be ranked (see Newcomb, 1961:39–40).

Results

The following six operational statements were used: (i) identification of the two men; (ii) their perceived evaluation of the class and its activities; (iii) their perceived intentions; (iv) the students' evaluation of the behaviour of the men; (v) the students' plans of action; and (vi) their justifications for them. Tables 29.1 through 29.4 summarize the distribution of responses to the questionnaire items constructed with reference to the first four of these. These were not enough responses to the items on plans of action and their justifications to be useful for our purposes.

By cross tabulating the data in Table 29.1 with those in Tables 29.2 through 29.4, two cultural definitions were isolated.

Definition I. These two men are religious figures of some sort. Their beliefs are being seriously threatened by the lectures, and as a result

---

[12] The instructions that appeared at the top of the first page, which were also read aloud to the students, requested that they record only those reactions to the two men that they had *up to the time the experimenter entered the room.* By means of this procedure it was hoped that retrospective definitions would be minimized.

[13] Both the interest ranking and goal ranking tests were taken from Newcomb (1961:39–40).

TABLE 29.1. Student identifications of the two men

Identifications	Number	Percent
Religious figures (clergymen, zealous laymen, theology students, etc.)	25	20.8
Non-student intruders or outsiders	16	13.3
Troublemakers, fanatics, cranks, etc.	10	8.3
Narrow-minded, conservative men	7	5.8
Know them by name	3	2.5
Suspect or know they are students	8	6.7
Newcomers to the course	6	5.0
Have been invited by the instructor (teaching assistants, graduate students, professors, etc.)	7	5.8
More than one identification	2	1.7
Other	2	1.7
Unable to make any identification	34	28.4
Totals	120	100.0

TABLE 29.2. Student perceptions of the evaluation of the class by the men

Perceived Evaluations	Number	Percent
The lectures threaten their beliefs	63	52.5
The lectures have a bad influence on the students	14	11.7
The lectures will promote social and cultural change in the community	13	10.8
The lectures have made them curious about the class	5	4.2
An opportunity to make a disturbance or to show off	3	2.5
Other	3	2.5
Unable to establish any meaning	19	15.8
Totals	120	100.0

they want them either corrected or stopped. Their activities are outrageous and highly resented.

Definition II. These two men are only non-student intruders. They somehow feel that the lectures are having a bad influence upon us students, and as a result want them either corrected or stopped. Their activities are mildly disgusting.

For Definition I, 44.2 percent of those who identified the two men as religious figures also felt that the lectures posed a threat to their beliefs, whereas the expected proportion was only 29.2 percent as based on the marginal totals of the over-all cross tabulation between Tables 29.1 and 29.2. Using the chi-square one-sample test, this association can be expected by chance in

less than 3 percent of the cases ($\chi^2 = 4.60$; $0.025 > p > 0.01$).[14] Similarly, 52.7 percent of those who identified the men as religious figures also identified them as wanting to correct the instructor's views, while the expected proportion was only 30.5 percent ($\chi^2 = 4.36$; $0.025 > p > 0.01$). Finally, 50.0 percent of those

[14] All of the chi-squares reported here are one-tailed. This practice is justified by the observation that, for a cross tabulation to yield a meaningful association, it has to be of a *higher* frequency than expected from the margin totals. Also, in three of the chi-square tests presented in this paper, one of the expected frequencies was slightly below 5, the minimum allowed for their optimal application. The decision was made to use them in spite of this weakness since the research is only demonstrative, and the only alternative appeared to be the binomial test, which with our data is prohibitively laborious. See Siegel (1956:36–47).

TABLE 29.3. Student perceptions of the men's intentions

Perceived Intentions	Number	Percent
They have come to correct the instructor's views	21	17.5
They have come to encourage the students to reject the lectures	5	4.2
They have come to test the student's reaction to the lectures	7	5.8
They have come to make a disturbance, harass, or to show off	25	20.8
They have come at the instructor's invitation to stimulate discussion	5	4.2
Other	3	2.5
Unable to establish any intentions	54	45.0
Totals	120	100.0

TABLE 29.4. Student feelings about the activities of the two men

Feelings	Number	Percent
Ambivalence, confusion	4	3.3
Disgust, dislike	56	46.7
Disappointment, shame, embarrassment that this happens in our community	6	5.0
Outrage, anger, resentment	17	14.2
Surprise, shock	3	2.5
Amusement	5	4.2
More than one sentiment (sequentially)	7	5.8
Other	4	3.3
No answer	18	15.0
Totals	120	100.0

identifying the men as religious figures felt that their activities and intentions were highly outrageous, although this was expected in only 29.1 percent of those cases ($\chi^2 = 2.53$; $0.10 > p > 0.05$). If these proportions seem low, it must be remembered that sizeable percentages of respondents were either unable to establish meaning or intention or else did not answer the questions. Hence, the proportions presented above would have been considerably higher if we had chosen to state them in relation to the total number of respondents who answered each item.

The association between the operational statements in Definition II is weaker because there were smaller numbers of respondents to work with and the ratios between observed and expected proportions were low in two of the three instances. Thirty-three percent of those who identified the two men as non-student intruders also saw them as holding the view that the lectures

were a bad influence on the students. This was expected in only 19.1 percent of the cases ($\chi^2 = 1.22$; $0.15 > p > 0.10$). Those making this same identification of the men perceived them as intending to correct the instructor's ideas in 21.1 percent of the cases, whereas this was expected in only 15.3 percent of them ($\chi^2 = 0.39$; $0.35 > p > 0.25$). Thirty-one percent of those who looked on the men as intruders harboured feelings of mild disgust toward their activities, though this was expected in only 20.3 percent of their responses ($\chi^2 = 3.87$; $0.025 > p > 0.01$).

Only in the case of Definition I were we able to link it with a generally held predisposition, and this was only partially successful. By cross-tabulating the responses of those who placed religious interests either first, second, or third (out of six possible ranks) with the data presented in Tables 29.1 through 29.4, we were able to discover two associations. Thus, those who ranked religious interest in one of these positions were found to identify the two men as religious figures more often than expected; 64.0 percent were observed in contrast to the 55.0 percent expected ($\chi^2 = 0.78$; $0.25 > p > 0.15$). They also imputed the intention of wanting to correct the instructor's views beyond the frequency expected; 89.9 percent were observed as compared with an expected 55.0 percent ($\chi^2 = 5.63$; $0.01 > p > 0.005$). A similar response pattern was found in the ordering of the general life goal "living in accordance with religious principles." For the ranking of both goals and interests, no association was discernible with the perceived evaluation of the class by the two men or with the feelings that the students had toward their activities. In conclusion, common sense leads us to anticipate that religious predispositions will be found to be linked to our four operational statements, but the data only partly bear this out. Hopefully, the use of more precise data gathering techniques would eradicate this discrepancy in the findings in favour of our expectations.

Discussion

The field experiment presented in this section was expressly designed to demonstrate some of the research strategies discussed in the preceding pages. However, as usually happens in exploratory undertakings such as this, one learns a great deal in the process of carrying them out, the significance of which sometimes embarrasses his earlier ideas. This has happened here. The research strategies presented earlier are, in part, remodelled products of hindsight made possible by the experiment.

For example, the demonstration was planned with the notion in mind that it should be a startlingly different experience so that one could observe the creative defining of a situation. This strategy was adopted when the author was still labouring under the belief that study of the innovative and therefore relatively idiosyncratic aspects of interpreting events, that is, the study of unique personal definitions, was the best way to make an initial thrust into the complexities of this area. In spite of these intentions a good case can be made for cultural definitions of situations such

as the one contrived here for experimental purposes, since outbursts by the religiously conservative are not uncommon in this community. However, there was no program of observation over time that could help us determine if such cultural definitions do exist among students. For the sake of demonstration we have referred to the standard definitions of the situation that appeared in the experiment as cultural definitions, despite this shortcoming. Also, only six of the thirteen operational statements were employed because the remaining ones were conceived too late to incorporate them into the questionnaire.

Our demonstration of the research strategies has probably raised many more questions than it has solved. Space limitations allow us to deal with only two of these.

First of all, those engaged in studying definitions of situations empirically will find themselves in something of a dilemma with respect to the form of interviewing they choose to do. If the investigator has observed a large number of people define a situation, he is committed to using some type of self-administered questionnaire in order to obviate problems of recall, since it would be impossible to interrogate each person individually. This form of data collection enables one to survey all who are willing to participate in the project in a short period of time, perhaps much closer to the actual occurrence of the event under consideration, than if a special appointment had to be made for a face-to-face interview. However, it does restrict one to certain operational statements. Statements 9 through 13 are more subtle than the rest, and require additional explanation for most subjects; they would only spawn confusion in a self-administered form of questionnaire. Moreover, since the investigator depends entirely upon the benevolence of his respondents for cooperation and accurate reporting of their views, he must take care not to antagonize them. This means that he must eliminate not only subtle (and hence confusing) items from his instruments, but also ones that appear to be repetitious because the differences are not large enough for laymen to discriminate. Several of the operational statements, when transformed into questionnaire items, could easily seem repetitious to the average respondent.

When only one or a few persons are observed

as they define situations, the author's more recent experiences in this field indicate that the personal interview is the more desirable method of gathering information relating to the operational statements. However, this approach is more time consuming, although it is also more thorough since the ambiguities and ambivalences typical of human definitions of situations can be examined by careful probing.

This dilemma concerning the more appropriate kind of data collection can only be solved through extensive research, where we have the advantage of viewing the strengths and weaknesses of both techniques. It is true, no doubt, that the relative novelty of our experimental situation contributed to the presence of a large variety of answers to the questions. More familiar events probably would not invite such a range of responses.

The second question also pertains to the amount of novelty in our experiment. Presumably it was this feature of it that led to the large number of "no answer" and "don't know" responses. Some of the students simply needed more time to reflect on the events that had just unfolded before their eyes. Had they been given this time they would have, by answering our questions, expanded the size of some of the substantive categories, while the size of the "no answer" and "don't know" cells would have shrunk.

Actually, we can expect a certain proportion of these responses in research involving definitions of the situation, even when we are dealing with recurrent settings. For not all of the recurring situations encountered by those in an identity will be equally familiar. Some reflection will be needed to sort out and interpret the novel elements present (which occur in every situation in some degree), and the more that is required the greater the number of incomplete questionnaires that will be turned in. Waiting for this reflection to take place before beginning the interviewing or distributing the questionnaire forms is not a solution either, since there will be the tendency for those who have already selected a definition to think further about the event, thereby changing its initial meaning through retrospective interpretation. This in itself is an interesting aspect of human behaviour which is worthy of study.

But it is the ongoing definition of the situation that interests us and that guides behaviour in the immediate setting. In investigating it, it is wise to keep it as separate as possible from subsequent redefinitions beyond that setting.

IMPLICATIONS FOR A SOCIOLOGICAL THEORY OF MOTIVATION

When we speak of definition of the situation, we speak of motivation according to Nelson Foote (1951:15):

> In a sentence, we take motivation to refer to the degree to which a human being, as a participant in the ongoing social process in which he necessarily finds himself, defines a problematic situation as calling for performance of a particular act, with more or less anticipated consummations and consequences, and *thereby* his organism releases the energy appropriate to performing it.

Foote's paper and an earlier one by C. Wright Mills (1940) have been the two most significant advances in sociology's attempt to develop a situational theory of motivation. Yet, two curious facts exist: the last major theoretical progress was nearly twenty years ago, and there has been very little, if any, empirical work on this approach to motivation either before or since.[15] There are, no doubt many reasons for this situation including, perhaps, the vicissitudes of the fads of social science. The explanations given at the beginning of this paper for the lack of research on the definition of the situation could also be cited. Finally, there is still another reason, and it is this one that we shall consider now.

It seems that, in their haste to denounce the place of predispositions in a sociological theory of motivation, Mills and Foote worked themselves, and consequently the possibilities for further development of such a theory, into a logical *cul-de-sac*. Foote launched the strongest attack. As we have just seen he looked on motivation as a definition of a situation, though it should be

---

[15] This statement refers only to progress toward a theory of motivation in the name of such a theory. There have been many advances in closely related areas such as identification, situational studies, and, as I intend to show here, the social psychology of predispositions.

added that he placed special emphasis on the process of identification of self and others within that setting. Predispositions were allowed into this scheme only as "memory . . . by virtue of which we call up in the present images of past consummations of acts" (1951:20). Memory plus organic mobilization (after the definition of the situation) were said to equal motivation.

This reaction against the inclusion of predispositions was reasonable fifteen years ago, but recent thought on their nature and on their location in a theory of the definition of the situation makes such a position untenable today. Foote (and Mills) appeared to be reacting to the organismically based, situation-free models of predispositions and motivation. But in this paper, following Campbell (1963), their prior activation by stimuli within the situation is taken as essential for their influence on behaviour. Here predispositions are viewed as developing from past experience, and once activated they are seen to impinge upon our awareness as specialized views of the world. There is little in this conceptualization with which a sociologist can disagree.

Nevertheless, the sociologist might assert that there is still no place in the theory of the definition of the situation for predispositions. Foote, for example, believed that "definitions of the situation account for attitudes, not the reverse" (1951:15). Our earlier discussion, however, indicates that defining a situation is a complicated process that takes place in two phases; and that predispositions do enter into the second phase, both in directing the selection of the cultural definition and in tailoring that definition to the peculiar requirements of the individual.

Predispositions as they have been incorporated into the model used in this paper are considerably more than just general "memory" of past acts. They are those peculiar (activated) perspectives in any immediate present so characteristic of the interchanges among men, although, of course, memory serves to make them available to us in the ongoing setting. Because they are enduring states, their recurrent activation also helps explain why human beings are motivated in the same way in the same class of situation at various points in time. Predisposing orientations such as attitudes of racial prejudice or ideals

such as fair play or self-conceptions such as "I am a competent golfer," are impossible to ignore in any theory of motivation.[16] It is doubtful that Mills or Foote intended to do this either, but the state of knowledge about predispositions at that time led them toward a blind alley.

The problem of motivation is "to account for the *patterning, timing, and direction of behavior*, especially for persistent movement toward a goal" (Shibutani, 1961:181). There is good reason to believe that the theory of the definition of the situation is the best solution available; that is, as long as we include an adequate up-to-date statement about the nature and location of predispositions within it.

SUMMARY AND CONCLUSIONS

Contrary to some long-established beliefs, the definition of the situation can be studied empirically. That is, it can be studied with the aid of a certain number of research strategies, which it has been the objective of this paper to provide. Two problems should guide the investigator in this field. 1. What cultural or habitual personal definitions are available to those in a given social identity for use in one or more specified kinds of recurring situations? 2. For classes of actors within an identity, what predispositions are activated by elements in the ongoing setting that lead to the selection of one of these definitions instead of another? Observation is an indispensable part of any research program focusing on definitions of situations. When carried out over time it gives the social scientist a rough idea of the standard definitions identity incumbents have to choose from in typical situations. Later it facilitates precision in the interviewing when one begins to sharpen his picture of these definitions by questioning the actors along the lines of the various operationalizations with respect to specific ongoing settings. Cultural and habitual definitions are

[16] The use of "predisposition" here is compatible with the general scheme presented by Shibutani. He includes under the section heading of "motivation" discussion of self-concept, reference groups as perspectives, and the internalization of social control (1961:179–319). All of these have predispositional qualities about them.

constructed by combining the responses to these questions. Theoretically, it is believed that selecting such definitions occurs in two relatively distinct temporal phases occurring in rapid succession.

At its present stage of technical development and theoretical accumulation, research on the definition of the situation can amount to little more than a program of description. Without knowledge of the cultural and habitual definitions available to sets of actors within an identity and without knowledge of their patterns of choice of these definitions in given kinds of situations, we have little on which to base prediction or higher-order explanation. Until such substantive propositions are established, we can only provide descriptive data. Through time and in conjunction with the general theory of the definition of the situation, bodies of descriptive data will form the bases for grounded theories of definitions of situations for particular identities.

Description of standard definitions and recurrent situations is probably best carried out by means of some type of field research. However, once a substantive theory begins to take shape, experimentation as a mode of testing hypotheses becomes a feasible alternative. But until we know a particular kind of situation in sufficient detail, it will be impossible to simulate it adequately in the laboratory. We also need an elementary knowledge of the possible cultural and habitual definitions available to the incumbents in such a situation so that we know which variables we wish to control.

This discussion of the definition of the situation has certain implications for a sociological theory of motivation. There is good reason to believe that the theory of the definition of the situation is the best explanation for motivated behaviour that is available; that is, as long as we include an adequate and contemporary statement about the nature and location of predispositions within it.

REFERENCES

Ball, D. W. Forthcoming. "The definition of the situation: some theoretical and methodological conse-

quences of taking W. I. Thomas seriously," in J. D. Douglas (ed.), Existential Sociology. New York: Appleton-Century-Crofts.

Burke, K. 1945. A Grammar of Motives. New York: Prentice-Hall.

———. 1950. A Rhetoric of Motives. New York: Prentice-Hall.

Campbell, D. T. 1963. "Social attitudes and other acquired behavioral dispositions." Pp. 94–172 in S. Koch (ed.), Psychology: A Study of a Science, vol. 6. New York: McGraw-Hill.

Cooley, C. H. 1922. Human Nature and the Social Order. New York: Charles Scribner's Sons.

Deutscher, I. 1964. "The quality of postparental life: definitions of the situation." Journal of Marriage and the Family 26:52–59.

Foote, N. N. 1951. "Identification as the basis for a theory of motivation." American Sociological Review 16:14–21.

Gerth, H. and C. W. Mills. 1954. Character and Social Structure. London: Routledge & Kegan Paul.

Glaser, B. G. and A. L. Strauss. 1967. The Discovery of Grounded Theory. Chicago: Aldine.

Gorden, R. L. 1952. "Interaction between attitude and the definition of the situation in the expression of opinion." American Sociological Review 17:50–58.

Heider, F. 1958. The Psychology of Interpersonal Relations. New York: John Wiley.

Hill, R. and D. A. Hansen. 1962. "Families in Disaster," pp. 185–221 in G. W. Baker and D. W. Chapman (eds.), Man and Society in Disaster. New York: Basic Books.

Ichheiser, G. 1949. "Misunderstandings in human relations." American Journal of Sociology 55 (September, Part II): 1–70.

Jones, E. E. 1964. Ingratiation. New York: Appleton-Century-Crofts.

Jones, E. E. and K. E. Davis. 1965. "From acts to dispositions." Pp. 220–266 in L. Berkowitz (ed.), Advances in Experimental Social Psychology, Vol. 2. New York: Academic Press.

Jones, E. E. and J. W. Thibaut. 1958. "Interaction goals as bases of inference in interpersonal perception." Pp. 151–178 in R. Tagiuri and L. Petrullo (eds.), Person Perception and Interpersonal Behavior. Stanford, Calif.: Stanford University Press.

Lerner, M. J. and S. Becker. 1962. "Interpersonal choice as a function of ascribed similarity and definition of the situation." Human Relations 15:27–34.

McCall, G. J. and J. L. Simmons. 1966. Identities and Interactions. New York: The Free Press.

McHugh, P. 1968. Defining the Situation. Indianapolis: Bobbs-Merrill.

MacIver, R. M. 1964. Social Causation (rev. ed.). New York: Harper & Row.

Mills, C. W. 1940. "Situated actions and vocabularies of motives." American Sociological Review 5:904–913.

Newcomb, T. M. 1958. "The cognition of persons as cognizers." Pp. 179–190 in R. Tagiuri and L. Petrullo (eds.), Person Perception and Interpersonal Behavior. Stanford, Calif.: Stanford University Press.

———. 1961. The Acquaintance Process. New York: Holt, Rinehart & Winston, Inc.

Newcomb, T. M., R. H. Turner, and P. E. Converse. 1965. Social Psychology: The Study of Human Relations. New York: Holt, Rinehart & Winston.

Schutz, A. 1964. Collected Papers II: Studies in Social Theory. The Hague: Martinus Nijhoff.

Shand, A. F. 1920. The Foundations of Character. London: Macmillan, Ltd.

Shibutani, T. 1961. Society and Personality. Englewood Cliffs, N.J.: Prentice-Hall.

Siegel, S. 1956. Nonparametric Statistics for the Behavioral Sciences. New York: McGraw-Hill.

Simmel, G. 1950. The Sociology of Georg Simmel. New York: The Free Press.

Stebbins. R. A. 1967. "A theory of the definition of the situation." The Canadian Review of Sociology and Anthropology 4:148–164.

———. 1969. "Social network as a subjective construct: a new application for an old idea." The Canadian Review of Sociology and Anthropology 6:1–14.

———. 1970. "Career: the subjective approach." The Sociological Quarterly, forthcoming.

Stone, G. P. 1962. "Appearance and the self." Pp. 86–118 in A. M. Rose (ed.), Human Behavior and Social Processes. Boston: Houghton Mifflin.

Strauss, A. L. 1959. Mirrors and Masks. New York: The Free Press.

Thomas, W. I. 1951. Social Behavior and Personality, ed., E. H. Volkart. New York: Social Science Research Council.

Turner, R. H. 1956. "Role-taking, role standpoint, and reference-group behavior." American Journal of Sociology 61:316–328.

———. 1962. "Role-taking: process versus conformity." Pp. 20–40 in A. M. Rose (ed.), Human Behavior and Social Processes. Boston: Houghton Mifflin.

Weber, M. 1947. The Theory of Social and Economic Organization. New York: Oxford University Press.

Weinstein, E. A. and P. Deutschberger. 1963. "Some dimensions of altercasting." Sociometry 26:454–466.

———. 1964. "Tasks, bargains, and identities in social interaction." Social Forces 42:451–456.

Wolff, K. H. 1964. "Definition of the situation." P. 182 in J. Gould and W. L. Kolb (eds.), A Dictionary of the Social Sciences. New York: The Free Press.

"Nothing Unusual Is Happening"

The societal reaction theory of deviance, disputing earlier approaches which assumed deviance to be an intrinsic quality of behavior, stresses the interaction between actor and audience. A deviant label is the product of an exchange between an actor and someone who charges the actor with rule violations, perhaps with ratification by third parties. How is social reality constructed by the participants so that an event comes to constitute a rule violation?[1]

Participants in any encounter take stances on the expectedness of the events; these stances are referred to in this paper as "nothing unusual is happening" and "something unusual is happening." These orientations are expressed through a person's demeanor and do not necessarily reflect his private assessment of the situation. A member of the audience who undertakes labeling first must establish that "something unusual is happening" in order to define an event as a rule violation.[2] This stance sets the appropriate tone, just as the participants might effuse gaiety or being emotionally touched to carry off other events. In the framework of "something unusual," the labeler must establish the following propositions: (1) "You have committed an act of such-and-such a nature"; (2) "We recognize a prohibition on acts of this kind"; (3) "Therefore, you have committed a prohibited act." The validity of the labeler's premises may be challenged in terms of the kind of act that took place, the actor's responsibility for it, the existence of the rule, or the applicability of the rule. However, it may be more effective to prevent the establishment of the prerequisite "something unusual" framework.

This paper will consider the "nothing unusual is happening" stance as it affects the labeling of deviance. The central hypothesis is that social interaction has intrinsic properties that routinely bias negotiations toward the "nothing unusual" stance; this bias inhibits the application of deviant labels. The paper will suggest circumstances under which the "nothing unusual" stance is assumed and examine in detail two examples of negotiation. Finally, it will explore the structure of interaction affecting the outcome of such negotiations.

THE "NOTHING UNUSUAL" STANCE

In many situations persons assume a stance routinely. But at times it is not clear which stance to assume, or persons may not agree on how to proceed. There are two sets of circumstances relevant to labeling in which the stance is negotiated. First, persons may confront events which are particularly suitable for labeling within an acknowledged framework of rules. Second, persons may negotiate to transform an encounter from one normative framework to another.

Joan P. Emerson, "Nothing Unusual Is Happening." From *Human Nature and Collective Behavior: Papers in Honor of Herbert Blumer,* edited by Tamotsu Shibutani (Englewood Cliffs, N.J.: Prentice-Hall, Inc., 1970), pp. 208–222.

[1] Cf. Howard S. Becker, *Outsiders: Studies in the Sociology of Deviance* (New York: The Free Press of Glencoe, Inc., 1963); and Peter Berger and Thomas Luckmann, *The Social Construction of Reality* (New York: Doubleday & Company, Inc., 1966).

[2] Harold Garfinkel, "Conditions of Successful Degradation Ceremonies," *American Journal of Sociology,* LXI (1956), 420–24.

Persons acknowledging a framework of rules must decide whether or not each particular event constitutes a violation. Although any event may be interpreted as a violation, for some events the interpretive work and winning of acceptance for the definition are easier. For such labeling-prone events the "nothing unusual" stance is particularly important. For example, a man feigning accident but deliberately caressing the body of a strange woman in a crowd trades on the woman's embarrassment, should she publicly invoke a "something unusual" stance. Rather than call attention to the situation at such a high price, the woman may cooperate by pretending she thinks the touching is merely an accident unavoidable in such a tightly packed crowd. The more a person can influence the evolving definition of what is happening, the more he can work the system by undertaking action he thinks would be appropriately defined as deviant and deliberately creating an alternate definition.

When others believe that the actor did not intend to break a rule, they may be especially ready to ignore potential violations. In any situation where a person reveals information about himself which challenges the image he is projecting, loses his self-control, or violates body decorum, others may tactfully act as if nothing unusual were happening.[3] In another example, dying patients typically are treated as though they had as assured a future as anyone else; Barney Glaser and Anselm Strauss speak of "situation as normal" interaction tactics in this connection.[4]

Surprisingly, persons also may react to bizarre behavior, such as delusional statements, with similar tact. The writer repeatedly observed staff members respond blandly to temporarily disoriented, senile, and brain-damaged patients on a medical-surgical ward of a general hospital and later gossip about the patients' "weird" behavior. The staff sustained an ordinary demeanor when a patient in a leg cast and traction claimed to have walked around the ward; when a 90 year old patient refused x-rays because her children

were too young to have the money to pay; when a senile woman asked a young nurse, "Was the meat done when you looked at it?"; and when an elderly man after a stroke said he was a boyscout and made a tent of his bed sheet. On an obstetrics ward of another hospital, nurses advised the writer not to contradict a patient who claimed John the Baptist as the father of her baby. In everyday life as well people are inclined to acquiesce to statements which sound incredible or paranoid. Cautious because of uncertainty about what the behavior means, persons avoid a fuss by continuing their "nothing unusual" stance even in response to bizarre gestures.

So far negotiations about interpretations of particular events have been discussed. Negotiations about the system of interpretation itself, however, have more radical import. When persons are invited to change their normative framework, interpretations of numerous events may be affected over a long period of time.

The most common circumstance in which a person is invited to change his normative framework occurs during socialization into an unfamiliar subculture. As persons move into new settings, they meet unanticipated experiences which initially they may regard as undesirable. Novices learn that the experiences are both customary and desirable in the new situation. Members of the subculture exhort, perhaps implicitly: "Now you see what we actually do here; I urge you to go along even though you weren't prepared to go along with such matters when you entered the situation." The "nothing unusual" stance is often a claim of expertise: "We know more about what usually happens in this situation than you do because we have been here time and time again when you have not."

A good illustration is Howard Becker's article on how experienced drug users present a "nothing unusual" definition to comrades undergoing drug-induced experiences which the latter are tempted to interpret as insanity.[5] In settings where homosexuals are dancing, flirting, and caressing, participants and heterosexual observers

[3] Erving Goffman, *The Presentation of Self in Everyday Life* (New York Doubleday & Company, Inc., 1957).

[4] Barney Glaser and Anselm Strauss, "Awareness Contexts and Social Interaction." *American Sociological Review*, XXIX (1964), 672.

[5] Howard S. Becker, "History, Culture and Subjective Experience: An Exploration of the Social Bases of Drug-Induced Experiences," *Journal of Health and Social Behavior*, VIII (1967), 163–76.

act as if nothing remarkable were occurring. Visitors at nudist camps remark that it seems just like an ordinary resort and that everyone seems to feel natural about not wearing clothes in public.[6] Members of occult groups, when expounding beliefs about magic, reincarnation, communication with other planets, and other matters outrageous to current scientific opinion, speak with the same casualness they use for generally accepted topics.[7]

Consider the prevailing demeanor in night clubs and topless bars. Risqué entertainment derives its impact from trifling with customary taboos, particularly about exposure of the body. Yet, while surrounded by nudity, participants strive to suggest a situation that is no different than it would be were all fully clothed. In bars where pickups occur, the participants' "situation as normal" style implies that they would be amazed to learn that the modes of introduction they were practicing would not be acceptable to Emily Post.

But it is not only in words generally regarded as offbeat that newcomers meet a "nothing unusual" stance. Observers in any setting, such as the medical world, find the same thing. A patient may look upon his medical condition and the technical procedures it elicits as highly unusual events, while the staff is reassuringly nonchalant. In a gynecological examination, for example, the staff members do not acknowledge as applicable the taboo exhibited in most other situations about private parts of the body; they act as though the procedure were as matter-of-course as an examination of the ear.[8]

Because people so frequently meet a "nothing unusual" stance from others they accept as legitimate socializing agents, they are prepared by analogy to accede to the stance under less legitimate circumstances. The "nothing unusual" stance is a claim about the standpoint of a subculture. Persons may insinuate that the suggestions

they make to others are normal in a subculture when in fact this is not the case. This may happen when persons are recruited for situations they are hesitant to enter; it also may happen when two or more persons evolve private understandings. For example, the visibly handicapped, learning to manage the uneasiness of others' responses to them, attempt to negotiate a stance of "nothing unusual is happening."[9] Persons may approach each other in ways which may not fit the elaborate set of conventions surrounding introductions and the initiation of encounters. Prostitutes and clients, disattending the commercial aspect of their transaction, may attribute their encounter to friendship.

> Moreover, much of the interaction of "john" (client) with girl (prostitute) is specifically oriented toward the reduction of the stigma attached to both roles, each pretending that the other is fulfilling a role more obscure than that which is apparent.[10]

Yet participants in these settings remain aware of the outsider's perspective. Thus: "Nudists envision themselves as being labeled deviant by members of the clothed society."[11] "Fringe (occult) group members as usually keenly aware of the fact that the larger culture disagrees with their view of the world. . . ."[12] It is difficult to forget the outsider's perspective when one must continually engage in practices which implicitly acknowledge it. For example, nudist camps discourage the presence of single men, require civil inattention to nude bodies, prohibit bodily contact, and regulate photography.[13]

Underlying the overt "nothing unusual" stance may be simultaneous cues acknowledging "something unusual." Participants may devote elaborate attention to enforcing a "nothing unusual" definition, thus intensifying their interac-

---

[6] Martin Weinberg, "Becoming a Nudist," in *Deviance: The Interactionist Perspective*. eds. Earl Rubington and Martin Weinberg (New York: The Macmillan Company, Publishers, 1968), pp. 240–51.

[7] Leon Festinger, Henry Riechen, and Stanley Schachter. *When Prophesy Fails* (New York: Harper and Row, Publishers, 1964).

[8] Joan Emerson, "Social Functions of Humor in a Hospital Setting" (Doctoral dissertation, University of California at Berkeley, 1963), chap. 4.

[9] Fred Davis, "Deviance Disavowal: The Management of Strained Interaction by the Visibly Handicapped," *Social Problems*, IX (1961), 120–32.

[10] James Bryan, "Occupational Ideologies and Individual Attitudes of Call Girls," in Rubington and Weinberg, *op. cit.*, p. 294.

[11] Weinberg, *op. cit.*, p. 249.

[12] J. L. Simmons, "Maintaining Deviant Beliefs," in Rubington and Weinberg. *op. cit.*, p. 284.

[13] Martin Weinberg, "Sexual Modesty and the Nudist Camp," in Rubington and Weinberg, *op. cit.*, pp. 275–77.

tive alertness, guardedness, and calculation. The behavior being defined as "nothing unusual" may become the intensive focus of attention, as when a person breaks down in tears in a setting (such as a psychotherapeutic one) which claims to tolerate such behavior. Even a verbal acknowledgment of "something unusual" may occur, often accompanied by a negation. For example, a man picking up a woman in a coffee house may remark, "I wouldn't be doing this except that I've been drinking all afternoon." Or before and after the event the participants may take a "something unusual" stance, as in the strained kidding which may accompany the decision to visit a topless bar and the even more forced jollity or the awkward silence on exit.

All parties may find it convenient to adopt a "nothing unusual" stance, and yet the alternate definition presses for some kind of recognition. At other times it may be possible to convince someone to accept a "nothing unusual" stance only if it is qualified by "something unusual" cues. Such cues may serve as a bargaining concession by those adamant about constructing a "nothing unusual" stance.

THE PROCESS OF NEGOTIATION

Examining the process of negotiation a "nothing unusual" stance may provide insight into how definitions of reality are constructed and sustained in social interaction. In most settings novices quietly cooperate with seasoned participants in sustaining a "nothing unusual" stance. In the instance described below, however, the novice declined to cooperate. As a result, the process of negotiation about the framework for the interaction is more explicit than in most encounters.

Incident I. Gynecological Examination

The writer observed a highly atypical examination on the gynecological ward of a general hospital.[14] A twenty-six year old unmarried

[14] For the complete field account of this incident see Emerson, *loc. cit.*

woman balks at one of her first pelvic examinations; rarely do patients complain about unpleasant features of the hospital to this degree. This particular encounter may be viewed as a continual negotiation about whether to take a "nothing unusual" or "something unusual" stance. The parties come to no resolution during the procedure, although shortly afterward the patient indicates to the nurse a partial capitulation.

The patient's demeanor disconcerts the staff, especially the doctor (actually a fourth year medical student), so that the staff members proceed through the episode in a guarded fashion, especially alerted to social as opposed to technical aspects, handling the patient with kid gloves, and cooperating more closely with each other. Thus, while the staff members overtly assert "a nothing unusual" stance, their guardedness conveys an underlying countertheme of "something unusual." Actually, the nurse partially acknowledges a "something unusual" stance at one point when the patient demonstrates pain. This acknowledgment serves as a bargaining offer to the patient: "Okay, we'll go along with you at this point, if you'll go along with us the rest of the time." The patient refuses this offer, for otherwise she implicitly would be agreeing that the unusual element was the pain rather than the invasion of privacy in a gynecological examination.

Six excerpts from the writer's field notes on this examination will now be analyzed.

At 8:50 p.m. the doctor enters, says "hi" in a friendly, nonprofessional way.

PATIENT TO DOCTOR: *"The blood is just gushing out of me."*

DOCTOR, WITH SURPRISE: *"Gushing out?"*

Shortly after this the doctor remarks to the nurse that the patient has her period.

The doctor opens with a casual greeting which asserts a "nothing unusual" stance. The patient counters with a remark implying that her body is in a state nonroutine to the staff. At several other points the patient makes remarks ("Shouldn't I wash before he examines me? The doctor won't be able to examine me with such a heavy flow of blood"), which hint that, because the staff members are mistakenly defining her body state as routine, they are neglecting to take action which is essential if they are to cope with her medical condition. In response the doctor expresses surprise at a move contrary to his proposed definition, attempting to discount the patient's stance. Later the doctor discounts the patient's stance more forcefully by defining her body state as routine, as he also does elsewhere in the episode.

PATIENT TO DOCTOR: *"Do you go through this every day?"*
DOCTOR: *"What?"*
PATIENT: *"This examining."*
DOCTOR: *"Oh yes."*

The patient suggests the possibility that gynecological examinations are nonroutine to the staff. The doctor, by failing to comprehend a move so contrary to his proposed definition, refuses to validate the patient's "something unusual" stance. When the patient supplies clarification, the doctor explicitly denies the patient's suggestion.

DOCTOR: *"I'll tell you what I'm going to do. I'm going to take a Pap smear. This is a routine test we do in this clinic."*
PATIENT: *"Do you take anything out?"*
The nurse explains.

The doctor identifies the steps of the technical procedure beforehand, as he does at numerous other points, and directly states that the procedure is routine. The patient asks a worried question about the technical procedure, a question which implies, "Am I safe in your hands?" This move counters the "nothing unusual" stance. The nurse attempts to reinstate "nothing unusual" by a reassuring explanation.

DOCTOR: *"You have some pain already, huh?"*
PATIENT: *"It's just that I hate this."*
DOCTOR: *"Okay, try to spread your legs apart. Okay, I'm going to try to touch this and see where it is."*

The doctor establishes a framework for the patient to report neutrally about discomfort. The patient ignores the suggested framework and offers a negative comment on the event in strong, emotional language. (At several other points the patient does the same thing; earlier she has said to the nurse: "I hate this. I wish I could go home.") The doctor ignores the patient's move and attempts to reassert his definition by neutral technical instructions and explanations.

DOCTOR: *"Okay, this is the speculum and it's going to feel a little cold."*
PATIENT: *"Oh."*
DOCTOR: *"'Oh' what?"*
NURSE TO PATIENT: *"Okay, take a few deep breaths and try to concentrate on something else. I know it's hard; that's sort of a focal point."*
DOCTOR: *"Does that hurt very much?"*
PATIENT: *"Yes, very much."*
SOON THE PATIENT REMARKS: *"I won't be able to sit down for a week."*
NURSE WITH AN AMUSED AIR: *"You underestimate yourself."*
DOCTOR, WITH AN AMUSED AIR: *"How will you go home?"*

The doctor offers a brief explanation of the technical procedure in a casual style. The patient then demonstrates discomfort in a "something unusual" style. To negate this, the doctor claims that he fails to comprehend the patient's move. The nurse reinforces the doctor's stance by giving technical instructions, but her style and sympathetic remark constitute a compromise in the direction of "something unusual," a move that the patient has already rejected earlier. The doctor again establishes a framework for the patient to report neutrally about discomfort, and again the patient repudiates it, this time by an overt statement of pain in a "something unusual" style. Taking the offensive, the patient hints that the staff is mutilating her body. The staff attempts to discount the hint by couching the message, "You exaggerate," in a joking framework.

DOCTOR: *"I'm going to do a rectal exam."*

PATIENT: *"No, no, no."*

DOCTOR: *"We have to do it; it's part of the examination."*

PATIENT: *"Why can't you give me a sedative first?"*

The doctor announces the next step of the technical procedure. The patient protests this step in a highly emotional style. The doctor claims that both he and the patient are compelled by the standards of good medical practice: "I am merely an agent following the prescribed rules of the system," he suggests. He further emphasizes the routine nature of the procedure. The patient attempts to undermine the doctor's stance by suggesting directly how the technical procedure should be conducted. By asking that she be made insensitive to the experience via a drug, the patient implies that the staff is imposing unnecessary discomfort on her.

In each excerpt one sees a struggle over the stance to be taken. The patient insists that "something unusual is happening," and the staff tells her how routine it is. At one point the patient implies the event is unusual by asking, "Do a lot of women go through this?" Several times she challenges the staff definition by explicit references to topics taboo within the framework the staff is asserting. For example, she wonders if her body odor will repel others. The staff members attempt to establish the medical framework by discussing nonchalantly technical equipment among themselves, asking the patient technical questions in a casual style, and directly assuring the patient it will not be as bad as she anticipates.

Incident II. Attempted Holdup

Sometimes persons need to establish a "something unusual" stance in order to bring off a performance. The audience's "nothing unusual" stance in the following newspaper account undermines the robbers' performance so much that it collapses.

THEIR STORY JUST DIDN'T HOLD UP
Stockton—The worst possible fate befell two young masked robbers here last night. They tried to hold up a party of thirty-six prominent, middle-aged women, but couldn't get anybody to believe they were for real.

One of the women actually grabbed the gun held by one of the youths.

"Why," she said, "that's not wood or plastic. It must be metal."

"Lady," pleaded the man. "I've been trying to tell you, it IS real. This is a holdup."

"Ah, you're putting me on," she replied cheerfully.

The robbers' moment of frustration came about 9 P.M. at the home of Mrs. Florence Tout, wife of a prominent Stockton tax attorney, as she was entertaining at what is called a "hi-jinks" party.

Jokes and pranks filled the evening. Thus not one of the ladies turned a hair when the two men, clad in black, walked in.

"All right now, ladies, put your rings on the table," ordered the gunman.

"What for?" one of the guests demanded.

"This is a stickup. I'm SERIOUS!" he cried.

All the ladies laughed.

One of them playfully shoved one of the men. He shoved her back.

As the ringing laughter continued, the men looked at each other, shrugged, and left empty-handed.[15]

In order to proceed, the robbers must crack the joking framework already established in the setting; if they had been willing to escalate, as by shooting someone, the outcome would have been different. Two sequences in this story will be analyzed.

In the first sequence, the lady who grabs the gun expresses surprise that the gun is metal. Defining the holdup as make-believe, the lady checks out a piece of evidence. In a make-believe holdup the guns are also make-believe, perhaps made of wood or plastic; in a real holdup the guns are real, made of metal. By expressing surprise at evidence contrary to her definition, the lady attempts to negate the challenge to her proposal. The robber immediately issues another challenge by directly stating the contrary definition: "Lady, I've been trying to tell you, it IS real. This is a holdup." The lady tries to negate this attempt by claiming the other is not really committed to the definition he is asserting: "Ah, you're putting me on."

In the second sequence, the robber opens with, "All right now, ladies, put your rings on

[15] *San Francisco Examiner,* April 4, 1968.

the table." Thus, he performs an act which would logically flow from the definition he is asserting. The response, "What for?" asks for a clarification of this act, suggesting that the act is meaningless because the proposed definition from which it is supposed to follow is not accepted. The robber provides clarification by a direct statement of his definition: "This is a stickup. I'm SERIOUS!" By laughing, the ladies propose a humorous framework for the robber's assertion and succeed in discounting the definition of the situation as a holdup.

The process of negotiating the stances of "something unusual" and "nothing unusual" consists of direct assertions and counterassertions, implications and counterimplications. It also involves the establishment of frameworks for the other's subsequent moves and techniques for discounting the other's moves. Such techniques include incomprehension, surprise, humor, and accusing the other of a lack of investment in his own move. In the remainder of this discussion, conditions biasing the negotiations toward a "nothing unusual" stance will be explored.

NEGOTIATING ACCEPTANCE OF A "NOTHING UNUSUAL" STANCE

Whoever performs a "something unusual" stance has some advantage, because his dramatic intensity is difficult to ignore. But maintaining the stance of "nothing unusual" quickly becomes untenable unless all participants corroborate it. Despite this advantage for "something unusual," however, observation suggests that a "nothing unusual" stance more often prevails in a problematic situation. Why is this so?

The "nothing unusual" advocate capitalizes on the ambiguity of events. In the movies the music swells up to signal "something unusual," the weather may change dramatically, and the crowd starts moving toward the focus of attention. Should the audience miss these cues, they can hardly miss the camera zooming in upon the actors' reactions to the unexpected event. In real life people almost expect the concomitants found in the movies, and their absence creates uncertainty about the meaning of the situation.

In the face of uncertainty, the actor may take the easiest way out. "Nothing unusual" provides a definite prescription for behavior: just continue to act in a routine manner. Actors can avoid the effort of creating a unique response. A "something unusual" definition may call for unpleasant emotions which people prefer to avoid—embarrassment and indignation, for example. People are often nonplused by events which could be defined as unusual, and they are inexperienced in managing such events. So they may be willing to take cues from others.

If one person firmly commits himself to a stand, others are likely to acquiesce. An effective strategy is to make a firm commitment to a "nothing unusual" stance immediately, without entering negotiations. An alternate strategy is to wait but decline the other's implicit "something unusual" offers, so the other concedes to "nothing unusual" to avoid a deadlock.

The ambiguity of events provides one condition favoring a "nothing unusual" stance. Conventions about maintaining social order provide another. Most social interaction is predicated on the desirability of avoiding a fuss. Many social practices rest on the assumption that it is wise to acquiesce to a person in his presence, regardless of one's private opinion. If a person has invested himself heavily in a certain definition of reality, others avoid challenging it. In particular, persons are reluctant to challenge another's claim about himself.

Since persons generally aim to maintain order in a particular situation, they invoke particular rules as relevant to the process of maintaining this situationally located order. Defining an event as a rule violation may shatter the view of reality that the participants have taken for granted. So, if invoking a particular rule would create disorder instead of maintaining order, it makes no sense to invoke the rule in that instance.

A third condition favoring a "nothing unusual" stance is the vulnerability of the would-be labeler to adverse consequences from his move. If the labeler's word must be weighed against the actor's, it may be difficult to convince third parties that a violation has occurred. In this as well as other cases, the would-be labeler's move opens him to counterdenunciation. Suppose, as in a Candid Camera sequence, a girl asks a man to help her carry a suitcase. The girl acts as if it were an ordinary suitcase, but actually it is filled with metal.[16] If the man remarks, "This suitcase is too heavy for anyone to carry," the girl might respond, "No, you must be a weak man because I have carried it myself for three blocks." Thus, a "something unusual" claim can be countered by, "No, it is you who cannot cope with this ordinary situation." Not only is a charge of inadequacy possible but, should someone persist in taking a "something unusual" stance, he could be labeled "emotionally disturbed" for displaying a demeanor too involved and for making the occasion into one more momentous than it really is.

Even if the labeler escapes counterdenunciation and succeeds in defining an event as a rule violation, this definition may reflect negatively on himself. Acknowledging the rule violation may involve a loss of face or self-derogation for the labeler. Any deviant act raises the question for observers: "Who am I that this should happen around me?" Many deviant acts are taken as an insult to others. To avoid the insult, what could be defined as a deviant act may be interpreted otherwise.

But under certain conditions others are less likely to assent to a "nothing unusual" stance. If a man comes home and discovers his wife in bed with another man, he is not inclined to accept their nonchalant invitation to join them in the living room for coffee. The following factors press for noncompliance: (1) the more persons are overwhelmed with emotion and cannot maintain the casual demeanor required; (2) the more complex the performance expected if they cooperate with the "nothing unusual" stance (civil inattention is more feasible than active participation); (3) the more certain they are of the definition of the situation that "something unusual is happening"; (4) the more committed they are to upholding rules which they think are being violated; (5) the more experienced they are at imposing the definition "something unusual is happening" in similar situations; (6) the less favorably disposed they are to the "nothing unusual" advocate; (7) the higher their status is compared with the "nothing unusual" advocate, the less they are accustomed to

following his lead, and the less respect they have for his judgment; and (8) the less drastic the action required by the "something unusual" stance.

THE DEVIANT AS A MONSTER

In the preceding section some factors inhibiting movement of the interaction in the direction of a "something unusual" stance and labeling were described. Labeling results from the application of a set of procedures for assessing situations and deciding how to proceed. From a closer examination of this set of procedures, an additional explanation for the structural inhibition against labeling emerges. The explanation is based on the inadequacy of certain commonsense conceptualizations to handle actual experience with potentially deviant behavior.

The set of procedures for assessing situations includes steps for recognizing divergent behavior. As a practical necessity any workable set of instructions singles out a few relevant features of a situation and ignores the rest. Forgetting that this selection has occurred, persons then come to think of the entire event as composed of the few features in focus. So the commonsense model has black and white categories for deviance. Both events and persons are viewed as either entirely deviant or entirely conforming.

A problematic act which persons might negotiate to define as deviant occurs in the context of numerous acts taken for granted as conforming.[17] In a bar pickup, for instance, the only questionable element may be the mode of introduction, while conduct within the exchange may be seen as entirely conforming to proper behavior for striking up an acquaintance with a stranger at a party. When one thinks about the situation in a commonsense perspective, one focuses on the offense and virtually ignores the norm-conforming context.

Because in the light of the commonsense perspective a person has been led to expect an of-

---

[16] Cited in Eugene Webb, Donald Campbell, Richard Schwartz, and Lee Sechrest, *Unobtrusive Measures: Nonreactive Research in the Social Sciences* (Chicago: Rand McNally and Company, 1966), p. 156.

[17] In discussing factors which impede the labeling process, Yarrow, *et al.*, make a similar point by calling the behavior of the candidate for the mental illness label a "fluctuating stimulus," at times symptomatic and at times ordinary. Marian Yarrow, Charlotte Schwartz, Harriet Murphy, and Leila Deasy, "The Psychological Meaning of Mental Illness in the Family," in Rubington and Weinberg, *op. cit.*, p. 38.

fense to stand out markedly and overshadow any norm-conforming elements present, he is surprised at how comparatively dwarfed the possible violation is. Those pressing for a "nothing unusual" definition take advantage of this initial surprise and the moment of uncertainty it entails. Inasmuch as a person revises his expectation to take into account the norm-conforming context, he still might expect all facets of the exchange to be modified to correspond with the norm-violating note. Thus, in a bar pickup he might expect an exaggerated behavior between the couple, in which allusions to sex are blatant, the exchange has a wild, uncontrolled quality, and gestures of respect for the other person are suspended. When these expectations are contradicted by actual experience in a bar, a person's assessment procedures are thrown into confusion. Using ordinary procedures for assessing whether behavior is divergent he is led to the conclusion the behavior is not divergent because it is obscured by norm-conforming elements.[18]

The commonsense perspective leads a person to expect that a deviant, at least in the setting where he engages in norm-violations, behaves in a way an ordinary person would not behave. Thus, victims do not suspect con men. "A deviant could not possibly be a person like you and me" is an underlying assumption. On the contrary, the deviant is a monster with whom we have nothing in common and who is so grotesque as to be incomprehensible to us.[19]

[18] Jackson makes this point about labeling the alcoholic over a period of time. "The inaccuracies of the cultural stereotype of the alcoholic—particularly that he is in a constant state of inebriation—also contribute to the family's rejection of the idea of alcoholism as the husband seems to demonstrate from time to time that he can control his drinking." Joan Jackson, "The Adjustment of the Family to the Crisis of Alcoholism," in Rubington and Weinberg, op. cit., p. 56.

[19] Garfinkel suggests this view is a necessary condition for a successful degradation ceremony: "Finally, the denounced person must be ritually separated from a place in the legitimate order, i.e., he must be defined as standing at a place opposed to it. He must be placed 'outside,' he must be made 'strange.'" Garfinkel, op. cit., p. 423.

Suppose an actor has earned a reputation as an acceptable human being before he commits a labeling-prone act. Even without such a reputation, suppose he presents his act in a conforming context with "nothing unusual" cues. Such an event is experienced as not fitting the deviant-as-monster assumption. To reconcile the discrepancy, people can hold one of the following:

1. the actor is a monster;
2. the "deviant is a monster" assumption is not correct;
3. the actor is not deviant; or
4. the actor is deviant, but the case is an exception to the "deviant is a monster" assumption.

Alternatives 3 and 4 cause the least social disruption and therefore have the lowest cost. Thus, the person responding is inclined to choose 3 or 4. If he decides the actor is not deviant, then the actor escapes labeling entirely. If he decides the actor is deviant but not a monster, then the actor's total identity is not discredited.

To summarize, definitions of reality, such as "nothing unusual is happening" and "something unusual is happening," are negotiated. Ambiguity allows more scope for negotiations. Ambiguity is produced by over-simplified conceptual schemes contradicted by experience. The more difficult it is to use the prevailing conceptual scheme to make sense of experience, the more the social situation will be thrown into confusion and left to *ad hoc* negotiations. Negotiations provide the opportunity for persons to elude labeling when otherwise these persons might be sanctioned.

Black and white categories about deviance may at times serve to discourage behavior which risks labeling by exaggerating the horrors of crossing the line from good to bad. But when the categories are undermined, risky behavior may flourish. And the more simple any system of categories, the more likely it is to be undermined by the complexity of events.

Common Sense Knowledge
of Social Structures: The
Documentary
Method of Interpretation

Sociologically speaking, "common culture" refers to the socially sanctioned grounds of inference and action that people use in their everyday affairs[1] and which they assume that other members of the group use in the same way. Socially-sanctioned - facts - of - life - in - society - that - any-bona-fide-member-of-the-society-knows depict such matters as conduct of family life; market organization; distributions of honor, competence, responsibility, goodwill, income, motives among members; frequency, causes of, and remedies for trouble; and the presence of good and evil purposes behind the apparent workings of things. Such socially sanctioned facts of social life consist of descriptions from the point of view of the collectivity member's[2] interests in the management of his practical affairs. Basing our usage upon the work of Alfred Schutz,[3] we shall call such knowledge of socially organized environments of concerted actions "common sense knowledge of social structures."

The discovery of common culture consists of the discovery *from within* the society by social scientists of the existence of common-sense knowledge of social structures, and the treatment by social scientists of knowledge, and of the procedures that societal members use for its assembly,

Reprinted with permission of Macmillan Publishing Co., Inc. from *Theories of the Mind* edited by Jordan Scher. Copyright © 1962 by The Free Press of Glencoe, a Division of The Macmillan Company.

This investigation was supported by a Senior Research Fellowship SF-81 from the U.S. Public Health Service. The materials for this paper are taken from a book in preparation by the author, *Common-Sense Actions as Topic and Features of Sociological Inquiry*. I wish to thank my colleagues Egon Bittner, Aaron V. Cicourel, and Eleanor Bernert Sheldon for many conversations about these materials. Thanks are due to Peter McHugh for his help with the experiment and for many useful ideas in his report.

[1] The concept "everyday affairs" is intended in strict accord with Alfred Schutz' usage in his articles, "On multiple realities," *Philosophy and Phenomenological Research*, 1945, 4:533–575; "Common sense and scientific interpretation of human action," *Philosophy and Phenomenological Research*, 1953, 14:1–37.

[2] The concept of "collectivity membership" is intended in strict accord with Talcott Parsons' usage in *The Social System*, The Free Press of Glencoe, New York, 1951, and in *Theories of Society*, Vol. I, Part Two, The Free Press of Glencoe, New York, 1961, pp. 239–240.

[3] Alfred Schutz, *Der sinnhafte Aufbau der sozialen Welt*, Verlag von Julius Springer, Wien, 1932; "The problem of rationality in the social world," *Economica*, 1943, 10:130–149; "Some leading concepts in phenomenology," *Social Research*, 1945, 12:77–97; "On multiple realities," *Philosophy and Phenomenological Research*, 1945, 4:533–575; "Choosing among projects of action," *Philosophy and Phenomenological Research*, 1951, 12:161–184; "Common sense and scientific interpretation of human action," *Philosophy and Phenomenological Research*, 1953, 14:1–37; "Concept and theory formation in the social sciences," *American Journal of Philosophy*, 1954, 51:257–274; "Symbol, reality, and society," *Symbols and Society*, Fourteenth Symposium of the Conference of Science, Philosophy, and Religion, edited by Lyman Bryson and others, Harper and Brothers, New York, 1955, pp. 135–202.

test, management, and transmission as objects of mere theoretical sociological interest.

This paper is concerned with common-sense knowledge of social structures as an object of theoretical sociological interest. It is concerned with descriptions of a society that its members, *sociologists included,* as a condition of their enforceable rights to manage and communicate decisions of meaning, fact, method, and causal texture without interference, use and treat as known in common with other members, and with other members take for granted.

As an object of theoretical sociological interest, such knowledge is both a topic as well as a feature of sociological inquiry. One facet of this assertion will be treated in this paper. Its interests are directed to a description of the work whereby decisions of meaning and fact are managed, and a body of factual knowledge of social structures is assembled in common-sense situations of choice.

THE DOCUMENTARY METHOD OF INTERPRETATION

There are innumerable situations of sociological inquiry in which the investigator—whether he be a professional sociologist or a person undertaking an inquiry about social structures in the interests of managing his practical everyday affairs—can assign witnessed actual appearances to the status of an event of conduct only by imputing biography and prospects to the appearances, which he does by embedding the appearances in presupposed knowledge of social structures. Thus it frequently happens that in order for the investigator to decide what he is now looking at he must wait for future developments, only to find that these futures in turn are informed by *their* history and future. By waiting to see what will have happened he learns what it was that he previously saw. Either that, or he takes imputed history and prospects for granted. Motivated actions, for example, have exactly these troublesome properties.

It, therefore, occurs that the investigator frequently must elect among alternative courses of interpretation and inquiry to the end of deciding

matters of fact, hypothesis, conjecture, fancy, and the rest despite the fact that in the calculable sense of the term "know," he does not and even cannot "know" what he is doing *prior to or while he is doing it.* Field workers, most particularly those doing ethnographic and linguistic studies in settings where they cannot presuppose a knowledge of social structures, are perhaps best acquainted with such situations, but other types of professional sociological inquiry are not exempt.

Nevertheless, a body of knowledge of social structures is somehow assembled. Somehow decisions of meaning, facts, method, and causal texture are made. How, in the course of the inquiry during which such decisions must be made, does this occur?

In his concern for the sociologist's problem of achieving an adequate description of cultural events, an important case of which would be Weber's familiar "behaviors with a subjective meaning attached and governed thereby in their course," Karl Mannheim[4] furnished an approximate description of one process. Mannheim called it "the documentary method of interpretation." It contrasts with the methods of literal observation, yet it has a recognizable fit with what many sociological researchers, lay and professional, actually do.

According to Mannheim, the documentary method involves the search for ". . . an identical, homologous pattern underlying a vast variety of totally different realizations of meaning."[5]

The method consists of treating an actual appearance as "the document of," as "pointing to," as "standing on behalf of" a presupposed underlying pattern. Not only is the underlying pattern derived from its individual documentary evidences, the individual documentary evidences, in their turn, are interpreted on the basis of "what is known" about the underlying pattern. Each is used to elaborate the other.

The method is recognizable for the everyday necessities of recognizing what a person is "talk-

---

[4] Karl Mannheim, "On the interpretation of weltanschauung," *Essays on the Sociology of Knowledge,* translated and edited by Paul Kecskemeti, Oxford University Press, New York, 1952, pp. 53–63.

[5] *Ibid.,* p. 57.

ing about" given that he doesn't say exactly what he means, or in recognizing such common occurrences as mailmen, friendly gestures, and promises. It is recognizable as well in deciding the sociologically analyzed occurrence of events like Goffman's strategies for the management of impressions, Erikson's identity crises, Riesman's types of conformity, Florence Kluckhohn's value premises, Malinowski's magical practices, Bales' interaction counts, Merton's types of deviance, Lazarsfeld's latent structure of attitudes, and the U.S. Census' occupational categories.

How is it done by the investigator that from replies to a questionnaire he finds the respondent's "attitude"; that via interviews with office personnel he reports their "bureaucratically organized activities"; that by consulting crimes known to the police, estimates are made of the parameters of "real crime"? More literally, what is the work whereby the investigator sets the observed occurrence and the intended occurrence into a correspondence of meaning such that the investigator finds it reasonable to treat witnessed actual appearances as evidences of the event he means to be studying?

To answer these questions it is necessary to detail the work of the documentary method. To this end a demonstration of the documentary method was designed to exaggerate the features of this method in use and to catch the work of "fact production" in flight.

AN EXPERIMENT

Ten undergraduates were solicited by telling them that research was being done in the Department of Psychiatry to explore alternative means to psychotherapy "as a way of giving persons advice about their personal problems" [sic]. Each subject was seen individually by an experimenter who was falsely represented as a student counselor in training. The subject was asked to first discuss the background to some serious problem on which he would like advice, and then to address to the "counselor" a series of questions each of which would permit a "yes" or "no" answer. The subject was promised that the "counselor" would attempt to answer to the best of his ability. The

experimenter-counselor heard the questions and gave his answers from an adjoining room, via an intercommunication system. After describing his problem and furnishing some background to it, the subject asked his first question. After a standard pause, the experimenter announced his answer, "yes" or "no." According to instructions, the subject then removed a wall plug connecting him with the counselor so that the "counselor will not hear your remarks" and tape-recorded his comments on the exchange. After these were completed, the subject plugged the microphone in and asked his next question. After he received the answer, he again recorded his comments, and thus proceeded through at least ten questions and answers. The subject had been told, "Most people want to ask at least ten questions."

The sequence of answers, evenly divided between yes's and no's, was predecided with a table of random numbers. All subjects asking the same number of questions were administered the same series of yes and no answers. Following the exchange of questions and answers the subject was asked to summarize his impressions of the entire exchange. An interview followed.

The following are illustrative unedited protocols.

Case 1

SUBJECT: *Ok, this is the situation that I am presented with. I happen to be of the Jewish faith and I have been dating a Gentile girl now for about two months. My dad is not directly opposed to this situation, but I feel at the same time that he is not exactly pleased with it. Mother feels that as long as dad is not directly opposed to this situation that I should go ahead and continue dating until he makes some direct statement to the contrary. My reason for feeling why he is not too pleased with this is that he has never said don't date her, but at the same time he will come up with digs and sayings that make me feel very ill at ease about dating the girl. My question is, do you feel under the present circumstances that I should continue or stop dating this girl? Let me put that in a positive way. Do you feel that I should continue dating this girl?*

EXPERIMENTER: *My answer is no.*

SUBJECT: *No. Well, that is kind of interesting. I kinda feel that there is really no great animosity between Dad and I but well perhaps he feels that greater dislike will grow out of this. I suppose or may be it is easier for an outsider to see certain things that I am blind to at this moment.*

I would like to ask my second question now.

EXPERIMENTER: *Okay.*

SUBJECT: *Do you feel that I should have a further discussion with Dad about this situation or not? Should I have further discussion with Dad over this subject about dating the Gentile girl?*

EXPERIMENTER: *My answer is yes.*

SUBJECT: *Well I feel that it is reasonable but I really don't know what to say to him. I mean he seems to be not really too understanding. In other words he seems to be afraid really to discuss the situation. I mean at least it appears that way to me so far. But I guess if it is worthwhile to me, if I really want to continue to date her that I will go on and have this discussion with Dad. I really don't know what to say because I mean I am dating her. I am not in love with her or anything but I really never know what is going to come out. I guess we should have a discussion based on what the future possibilities might be and how he would feel about that. He may not be too strongly opposed now because we are only dating but perhaps he sees future complications that he would really like to get off his chest at the moment. I am ready for my third question now.*

If after having my conversation with Dad and he says to continue dating her but at the same time he gives me an impression that he is really not, he really does not want me to date her, but he is only doing it because he wants to be a good dad, should under these conditions, should I still date the girl?

EXPERIMENTER: *My answer is yes.*

SUBJECT: *Well I am actually surprised at the answer. I expected a no answer on that. Perhaps this is because you are not quite aware of my dad and his reactions and he seems to be the type of person that is sensitive and therefore he is very careful in the way that he will handle things.*

Even though he might have said go ahead and date her I perhaps would feel guilty in knowing that he really did not want me to continue to date her. Though I don't know that it would actually help the situation any. So, well, perhaps we will look into this further and that is another question. I am ready for the fourth question now.

If after having this discussion with Dad and getting a positive answer from him but at the same time felt that this was not his honest opinion do you think that it would be proper for me to have my mother have a serious talk with him and therefore try and get a truer reaction to Dad's opinion on the situation?

EXPERIMENTER: *My answer is yes.*

SUBJECT: *Well this seems fair to me. I feel perhaps that he would be honester with Mother about the situation. Of course that might present a problem. Would Mother come back and be completely honest with me? She seems to be more liberal than Dad, not to say that Mother would lie about it, but she would be a little more liberal about things like this and perhaps in her course of conversation with Dad she would try and present my side to him and therefore once again I get two answers. If I look at it that way I don't think that I am going to get to first base anyway, but at least I feel that we are moving along some way. I am ready for my fifth question now.*

Do you think I should tell this Gentile girl who I am dating the problem that I am having with my folks at home or should I wait until, well that is another question. Do you feel that I should tell the girl that I am dating the problems that I am having at home over her religion?

EXPERIMENTER: *My answer is no.*

SUBJECT: *Well once again I am surprised. Of course, that might depend on how much you care for the girl and how much longer I feel that I am going to be dating her. But I personally feel that it is only right to tell her for if she is perhaps thinking more serious than I am, she might, it might be best for us to understand the full situation and if she feels that this will be a block then I feel perhaps that would end the situation right there without telling her. I feel that perhaps I am going to show this in different ways and she will be unaware of what the real situation* is and perhaps react back to me in a certain way spoiling our dating and everything else like that. I am ready for my sixth question.

If I was to fall in love with this girl and want to make plans for marriage do you feel that it is fair that I should ask her to change her religion over to my belief?

EXPERIMENTER: *My answer is no.*

SUBJECT: *Well, no. Well, this has me stymied. No. Well, I honestly feel that I have been brought up in a certain way and I believe that she has too, and I feel pretty strong about the way that I believe. Not that I am completely orthodox or anything, but of course there is always family pressure and things like that. And I am quite sure that she feels, unfortunately I have never seen a family with a split in religion that really has been able to make a success out of it. So I don't know. I think that perhaps I would be tempted to ask her to change. I don't think that I would be able to really. I am ready for number seven.*

Do you feel that it would be a better situation if we were to get married and neither one of us were willing to talk about the religious difference or to give in on either one side, that we bring our children up in a neutral religion other than the two that we believe in?

EXPERIMENTER: *My answer is yes.*

SUBJECT: *Well perhaps this would be a solution. If we could find a religion that would incorporate our two beliefs to a certain extent. I realize that perhaps this might be literally impossible to do. Perhaps in a sense this neutral religion might be something almost made up by ourselves because I honestly feel that religious training no matter which belief it is if not carried to extremes is good, for everyone should have a certain amount of religious training along these lines. Perhaps this might be a solution to the problem. I guess I should follow this along a little bit further and see exactly what happens. I am ready for number eight.*

If we were to get married would it be best for us to live in a new community where we will not be in contact with our parents if we were getting a lot of family pressure over religious differences?

EXPERIMENTER: *My answer is no.*

SUBJECT: *Well, I kinda tend to agree with this answer. I feel that you wouldn't be accomplishing too much by running away from the issue and that perhaps it would be one of those things in life that eventually you would just be willing to accept it and that the families and we would get along harmoniously together. At least I hope it would work out if that situation comes about. I think it would be best for both families together that we are not going to work it out if we run away from our problem. So we best remain there and try and work it out. I am ready for number nine.*

If we did get married and were to raise our children do you think that we should explain and tell our children that we once had this religious difference or would we just bring them up in this new religion, that is their religion, that we talked about, and let them believe that that is what we originally believe in?

EXPERIMENTER: *My answer is no.*

SUBJECT: *Once again I kinda agree with this. I think they should be told because undoubtedly they will find out. And if they did find out that there was this difference that we once had they would feel that we were sneaking or trying to hide something from them and this would not be the best situation either. So I believe this would be the best situation. I am ready for number ten.*

Do you feel that our children, if there were any, would have any religious problems themselves because of us the parents and our difficulties?

EXPERIMENTER: *My answer is no.*

SUBJECT: *Well I really don't know if I agree with that or not. Perhaps they would have trouble if confusion set in and they were to feel that they did not know which is right and which is wrong or what side to pick if they did not want to stick with their religion. But I kinda feel that if their religion was a wholesome one which supplied the needs of a religion and that which a religion does supply that there would not be any problems with them. But I suppose that only time will tell if such problems would come about. I am finished with my comments now.*

EXPERIMENTER: *Okay, I will be right in.*

The experimenter appeared in the room with the subject, handed him a list of points that he might comment on, and left the room. The subject commented as follows.

SUBJECT: *Well the conversation seemed to be one-sided because I was doing it all. But, I feel that it was extremely difficult for Mr. McHugh to answer these questions fully without having a complete understanding of the personalities of the different people involved and exactly how involved the situation was itself. The answers I received I must say that the majority of them were answered perhaps in the same way that I would answer them to myself knowing the differences in types of people. One or two of them did come as a surprise to me and I felt that the reason perhaps he answered these questions the way he did is for the reason that he is not aware of the personalities involved and how they are reacting or would react to a certain situation. The answers that I received were most of them I felt that he was for the most part aware of the situation as we moved along in that I was interpreting his answers even though they were yes or no answers as fully meditating over these situations that I presented to him and they had a lot of meaning to me. I felt that his answers as a whole were helpful and that he was looking out for the benefit to the situation for the most part and not to curtail it or cut it short in any means. I heard what I wanted to hear in most of the situations presented at time. Perhaps I did not hear what I really wanted to hear but perhaps from an objective standpoint they were the best answers because someone involved in a situation is blinded to a certain degree and cannot take this objective viewpoint. And therefore these answers may differ from the person who is involved in the situation and the person who is outside and can take an objective viewpoint. I honestly believe that the answer that he gave me, that he was completely aware of the situation at hand. Perhaps I guess that should be qualified. Perhaps when I said should I talk to Dad for instance he was not positive. When I said should I talk to Dad for instance he was not positive what I was going to talk to Dad about. In a full capacity. He knew the general topic but he is not aware how close I am to*
Dad or how involved the conversation might get. And if his saying "do talk" in knowing that Dad will not listen, well this perhaps isn't best, or if Dad is very willing to listen he says it may not help. Or don't talk. Well this once again is bringing in personalities which he is not aware of. The conversation and the answers given I believe had a lot of meaning to me. I mean it was perhaps what I would have expected for someone who fully understood the situation. And I feel that it had a lot of sense to me and made a lot of sense. Well I felt that the questions that I asked were very pertinent and did help in understanding the situation on both sides, that is myself and the answerer and my reaction to the answers like I have stated before were mostly in agreement. At times I was surprised but understood that because he is not fully aware of the situation and the personalities involved.*

Here is another protocol.

Case 2

SUBJECT: *I would like to know whether or not I should change my major at the present time. I have a physics major with quite a deficit in grade points to bring up to get my C average in physics. I would like to switch over to mathematics. I have a litle difficulty in it but I think maybe I could handle it. I have failed several math courses here at U.C.L.A. but I have always repeated them and had C's. I have come close to getting a B in math in one specific course because I studied a little more than in others but my question is still should I change my major?*

EXPERIMENTER: *My answer is no.*

SUBJECT: *Well he says no. And if I don't then I will have to make up my deficit in grade points which will be awfully difficult because I am not doing too well this semester. If I pull through this semester with seven units of A then I can count on possibly going on to get my degree in physics in February but then I have this stigma of nuclear physics facing me. I thoroughly dislike the study of nuclear physics. Nuclear Physics 124 will be one of my required courses to get a degree in physics.*

Do you think I could get a degree in physics on the basis of this knowledge that I must take Physics 124?

EXPERIMENTER: *My answer is yes.*

SUBJECT: *He says yes. I don't see how I can. I am not that good of a therorist. My study habits are horrible. My reading speed is bad, and I don't spend enough time studying.*

Do you think that I could successfully improve my study habits?

EXPERIMENTER: *My answer is yes.*

SUBJECT: *He says that I can successfully improve my study habits. I have been preached to all along on how to study properly but I don't study properly. I don't have sufficient incentive to go through physics or do I?*

Do you think I have sufficient incentive to get a degree in physics?

EXPERIMENTER: *My answer is yes.*

SUBJECT: *He says my answer is yes. I think possibly so if I didn't have a bad scholastic record behind me to follow me up. It would be awfully difficult to get that degree.*

Do you think I could successfully do my studying while trying to keep happy relations at home with my wife and still get my work done? I don't do my studying well at school and I don't have much incentive to study when I am at home. But when my wife comes home, I like to study. Yet this keeps us from doing things, and whenever she doesn't do things, it gets on my nerves because there is all this work piling up. Do you think I could successfully do my studying at home?

EXPERIMENTER: *My answer is no.*

SUBJECT: *He says no. I don't think so either.*

Should I come to school every night after supper and do my studying?

EXPERIMENTER: *My answer is no.*

SUBJECT: *He says I shouldn't come to school and study. Where should I go? Should I go to the library on campus to do my studying?*

EXPERIMENTER: *My answer is yes.*

SUBJECT: *He says I should go to the library to do my studying. Which library? They may not have all the references there that I may need but that is not always necessary. I need at least three more questions. Do you think I can develop suffi-*

ciently good study habits and incentive to actually achieve developing those habits such that I wouldn't have to stay up late at night and not get the work done in the first place?

EXPERIMENTER: *My answer is no.*

SUBJECT: *He says no. I can't develop the study habits properly to be able to pull myself through. If you don't think that I can develop the proper study habits and carry them through to reach my goal do you on the basis of this still believe that I can get a degree in physics?*

EXPERIMENTER: *My answer is no.*

SUBJECT: *According to that I won't get a degree. What should I do? Are you still there?*

EXPERIMENTER: *Yes, I am.*

SUBJECT: *If you don't think I will make the— achieve the necessary goal of improving my study habits and getting a degree in physics do you recommend that I quit school?*

EXPERIMENTER: *My answer is yes.*

SUBJECT: *He says I should quit school. Are you still there?*

EXPERIMENTER: *Yes.*

SUBJECT: *I have one more question. I would like to get a commission in the Air Force. I have completed the Air Force R.O.T.C. training program but to get a commission I need a degree. If I don't get the degree the chances are very strong that I may not get the commission although there are in's and out's that there is still some possibility that I may still get a commission without a degree, although this is not desirable. The question is, will I get a commission in the Air Force?*

EXPERIMENTER: *My answer is yes.*

SUBJECT: *He says I will get a commission in the Air Force and that is what I am looking forward to, but will I ever get a degree? If I get a commission without a degree will I ever get a degree in anything?*

EXPERIMENTER: *My answer is no.*

SUBJECT: *This leaves me somewhat unhappy although I don't really need a degree in the type of work that I desire to do. Are you there? Come back in.*

The subject commented as follows. Well, as far as what I got from the conversation, it is rather foolish for me to pursue my work any further as far as getting a degree in anything. Actually I have felt all along that the type of work I am interested in which is inventing is not something that requires a degree necessarily. It requires a certain knowledge of math and physics but it doesn't require a degree to do inventing. From the conversation I gather that I should just quit school and go ahead and get my commission but how I don't know. But it would be awfully nice to have a degree. That degree would be able to get me into other schools. Otherwise I will have the statement that I went through college but I never got out. I also get the impression that my study habits will never improve as much as I would like them to anyway. I will not get a degree. I will get a commission and it is fruitless for me to study either at home or at school. Especially in the evening. I wonder if I should do any studying at all, or if I should learn to do all my studying at school. What to do? I have the feeling that my parents would be very unhappy and also my wife's parents would be very unhappy if I never did get a degree or at least especially right now. I have the feeling that this past conversation is based on what one should have learned to do years ago, that is, as a growing child. To ask themselves questions and give himself an answer of some type, yes or no, and to think out reason why either yes or no holds or might hold and upon the validity or the anticipation of the validity of that answer what one should do accomplish his goal or just exist. I personally think I can do better in math than I can in physics. But I won't know until the end of the summer.

Findings

An examination of the protocols revealed the following:

A. *Getting through the exchange.*
   None of the subjects had difficulty in accomplishing the series of ten questions, and in summarizing and evaluating the advice.

B. *Answers were perceived as "answers-to-questions."*
   1. Typically the subjects heard the experimenter's answers as answers-to-the-question. Perceptually, the experimenter's answers were motivated by the question.
   2. Subjects saw directly "what the adviser had in mind." They heard "in a glance" what he was talking about, i.e., what he meant, and not what he had uttered.
   3. The typical subject assumed over the course of the exchange, and during the post-experimental interview, that the answers were advice to the problem, and that this advice as a solution to the problem was to be found via the answers.
   4. All reported the "advice that they had been given" and addressed their appreciation and criticism to that "advice."

C. *There were no pre-programed questions; the next question was motivated by the retrospective-prospective possibilities of the present situation that were altered by each actual exchange.*
   1. No subject administered a pre-programed set of questions.
   2. Present answers altered the sense of previous exchanges.
   3. Over the course of the exchange the assumption seemed to operate that there was an answer to be obtained, and that if the answer was not obvious, that its meaning could be determined by active search, one part of which involved asking another question so as to find out what the adviser "had in mind."
   4. Much effort was devoted to looking for meanings that were intended but were not evident from the immediate answer to the question.
   5. The present answer-to-the-questions motivated the succeeding set of possibilities from among which the next question was selected. The next question emerged as a product of reflections upon the previous course of the conversation and the presupposed underlying problem as the topic whose features each actual exchange documented and extended. The underlying "problem" was elaborated in its features as a function of the exchange. The sense of the problem was progressively accommo-

dated to each present answer, while the answer motivated fresh aspects of the underlying problem.

6. The underlying pattern was elaborated and compounded over the series of exchanges and was accommodated to each present "answer" so as to maintain the "course of advice," to elaborate what has "really been advised" previously, and to motivate the new possibilities as emerging features of the problem.

D. *Answers in search of questions.*

1. Over the course of the exchange, subjects sometimes started with the reply as an answer and altered the previous sense of their question to accommodate this to the reply as the answer to the retrospectively revised question.
2. The identical utterance was capable of answering several different questions simultaneously, and of constituting an answer to a compound question that in terms of the strict logic of propositions did not permit either a yes or no or a single yes or no.
3. The same utterance was used to answer several different questions separated in time. Subjects referred to this as "shedding new light" on the past.
4. Present answers provided answers to further questions that were never asked.

E. *Handling incomplete, inappropriate, and contradictory answers.*

1. Where answers were unsatisfying or incomplete, the questioners were willing to wait for later answers in order to decide the sense of the previous ones.
2. Incomplete answers were treated by subjects as incomplete because of the "deficiencies" of this method of giving advice.
3. Answers that were inappropriate were inappropriate for "a reason." If the reason was found, the sense of the answer was thereupon decided. If an answer made "good sense" this was likely to be what the answerer had "advised."
4. When answers were incongruous or contradictory, subjects were able to continue by finding that the "adviser" had learned more in the meantime, or that he had decided to change his mind, or that perhaps

he was not sufficiently acquainted with the intricacies of the problem, or the fault was in the question so that another phrasing was required.

5. Incongruous answers were resolved by imputing knowledge and intent to the adviser.
6. Contradictories faced the subject with electing the real question that the answer answered which they did by furnishing the question with additional meanings that fit with the meanings "behind" what the adviser was advising.
7. In the case of contradictory answers much effort was devoted to reviewing the possible intent of the answer so as to rid the answer of contradiction or meaninglessness, and to rid the answerer of untrustworthiness.
8. More subjects entertained the possibility of a trick than tested this possibility. All suspicious subjects were reluctant to act under the belief that there was a trick involved. Suspicions were quieted if the adviser's answers made "good sense." Suspicions were most unlikely to continue if the answers accorded with the subject's previous thought about the matter and with his preferred decisions.
9. Suspicions transformed the answer into an event of "mere speech" having the appearance of coincidental occurrence with the occasion of the questioner's question. Subjects found this structure difficult to maintain and manage. Many subjects saw the sense of the answer "anyway."
10. Those who became suspicious simultaneously, though temporarily, withdrew their willingness to continue.

F. *"Search" for and perception of pattern.*

1. Throughout, there was a concern and search for pattern. Pattern, however, was perceived from the very beginning. Pattern was likely to be seen in the first evidence of the "advice."
2. Subjects found it very difficult to grasp the implications of randomness in the utterances. A predetermined utterance was treated as deceit in the answers instead of as an utterance that was decided beforehand and that occurred independently of the subject's questions and interests.
3. When the possibility of deception occurred

to the subjects, the adviser's utterance documented the pattern of the deceit instead of the pattern of advice. Thus the relationship of the utterance to the underlying pattern as its document remained unchanged.

G. *Answers were assigned a scenic source.*

1. Subjects assigned to the adviser as his advice the thought formulated in the subject's questions. For example, when a subject asked, "Should I come to school every night after supper to do my studying," and the experimenter said, "My answer is no," the subject in his comments said, "He said I shouldn't come to school and study." This was very common.

2. All subjects were surprised to find that they contributed so actively and so heavily to the "advice that they had received from the adviser."

3. Upon being told about the deception the subjects were intensely chagrined. In most cases they revised their opinions about the procedure to emphasize its inadequacies for the experimenter's purposes (which they understood still to be an exploration of means of giving advice).

H. *The vagueness of every present situation of further possibilities remained invariant to the clarification furnished by the exchanges of questions and answers.*

1. There was vagueness (a) in the status of the utterance as an answer, (b) in its status as an answer-to-the-question, (c) in its status as a document of advice with respect to the underlying pattern, and (d) in the underlying problem. While, after the course of an exchange, the utterances furnished "advice about the problem," their function of advice also elaborated the entire scheme of problematic possibilities so that the overall effect was that of a transformation of the subject's situation in which the vagueness of its horizons remained unchanged and "problems still remained unanswered."

I. *In their capacity as members, subjects consulted institutionalized features of the collectivity as a scheme of interpretation.*

1. Subjects made specific reference to the social structures in deciding the sensible and

warranted character of the adviser's advice. Such references, however, were not made to any social structures whatever. In the eyes of the subject, if the adviser was to know and demonstrate to the subject that he knew what he was talking about, and if the subject was to consider seriously the adviser's descriptions of his circumstances as grounds of the subject's further thoughts and management of these circumstances, the subject did not permit the adviser, nor was the subject willing to entertain, *any* model of the social structures. References that the subject supplied were to social structures which he treated as actually or potentially known in common with the adviser. And then, not to *any* social structures known in common, but to normatively valued social structures which the subject as a collectivity member accepted as *conditions* that his decisions, with respect to his own sensible and realistic grasp of his circumstances and the "good" character of the adviser's advice, had to satisfy. These social structures consisted of normative features of the social system *seen from within* which, for the subject, were definitive of his memberships in the various collectivities that were referred to.

2. Subjects gave little indication, prior to the occasions of use of the rules for deciding fact and nonfact, what the definitive normative structures were to which their interpretations would make reference. The rules for documenting these definitive normative orders seemed to come into play only after a set of normative features had been motivated in their relevance to his interpretive tasks, and then as a function of the fact that the activities of interpretation were underway.

3. Subjects presupposed known-in-common features of the collectivity as a body of common-sense knowledge subscribed to by both. They drew upon these presupposed patterns in assigning to what they heard the adviser talking about, its status of documentary evidence of the definitive normative features of the collectivity settings of the experiment, family, school, home, occupation, to which the subject's interests were directed. These evidences and the collectivity features were referred

back and forth to each other, with each elaborating and being thereby elaborated in its possibilities.

J. *Deciding warrant was identical with assigning the advice its perceivedly normal sense.*

Through a retrospective-prospective review, subjects justified the "reasonable" sense and sanctionable status of the advice as grounds for managing their affairs. Its "reasonable" character consisted of its compatability with normative orders of social structures presumed to be subscribed to and known between subject and adviser. The subject's task of deciding the warranted character of what was being advised was identical with the task of assigning to what the adviser proposed (1) its status as an instance of a class of events; (2) its likelihood of occurrence; (3) its comparability with past and future events; (4) the conditions of its occurrence; (5) its place in a set of means-ends relationships; and (6) its necessity according to a natural (i.e., moral) order. The subjects assigned these values of typicality, likelihood, comparability, causal texture, technical efficacy, and moral requiredness while using the institutionalized features of the collectivity as a scheme of interpretation. Thus, the subject's task of deciding whether or not what the adviser advised was "true" was identical with the task of assigning to what the adviser proposed its perceivedly normal values.

K. *Perceivedly normal values were not so much "assigned" as managed.*

Through the work of documenting—i.e., by searching for and determining pattern, by treating the adviser's answers as motivated by the intended sense of the question, by waiting for later answers to clarify the sense of previous ones, by finding answers to unasked questions—the perceivedly normal values of what was being advised were established, tested, reviewed, retained, restored; in a word, managed. It is misleading, therefore, to think of the documentary method as a procedure whereby the advice was admitted to membership in a common-sense corpus in the same way that the rule of observation is a procedure whereby propositions are accorded membership in an ideal scientific corpus. Rather the documentary method developed the advice so as to be continually "membershipping" it.

EXAMPLES IN SOCIOLOGICAL INQUIRY

Examples of the use of the documentary method can be cited from every area of sociological investigation.[6] Its obvious application occurs in community studies where warrant is assigned to statements by the criteria of "comprehensive description" and "ring of truth." Its use is found also on the many occasions of survey research when the researcher, in reviewing his interview notes or in editing the answers to a questionnaire, has to decide "what the respondent had in mind." When a researcher is addressed to the "motivated character" of an action, or a theory, or a person's compliance to a legitimate order and the like, he will use what he has actually observed to "document" an "underlying pattern." The documentary method is used whenever selected features of an object are used to epitomize the object. For example, just as the lay person may say of something that "Harry" says, "Isn't that just like Harry?" the investigator may use some observed feature of the thing he is referring to as a characterizing indicator of the intended matter. Complex scenes like industrial establishments, communities, or social movements are frequently described with the aid of "excerpts" from protocols and numerical tables which are used to epitomize the intended events. The documentary method is used whenever the investigator constructs a life history or a "natural history." The task of historicizing the person's biography consists of using the documentary method to select and order past occurrences so as to furnish the present state of affairs its relevant past and prospects.

The use of the documentary method is not confined to cases of "soft" procedures and "partial descriptions." It occurs as well in cases of rigorous

---

[6] In his article, "On the interpretation of weltanschauung," Mannheim argued that the documentary method is peculiar to the social sciences. There exist in the social sciences many terminological ways of referring to it, viz., "the method of understanding," "sympathetic introspection," "method of insight," "method of intuition," "interpretive method," "clinical method," "emphatic understanding," and so on. Attempts by sociologists to identify something called "interpretive sociology" involve the reference to the documentary method as the basis for encountering and warranting its findings.

procedures where descriptions are intended to exhaust a definite field of possible observables. In reading a journal account for the purpose of literal replication, researchers who attempt to reconstruct the relationship between the reported procedures and the results frequently encounter a gap of insufficient information. The gap occurs when the reader asks how the investigator decided the correspondence between what was actually observed and the intended event for which the actual observation is treated as its evidence. The reader's problem consists of having to decide that the reported observation is a literal instance of the intended occurrence, i.e., that the actual observation and the intended occurrence are identical *in sense*. Since the relationship between the two is a sign relationship, the reader must consult some set of grammatical rules to decide this correspondence. This grammar consists of some theory of the intended events on the basis of which the decisions to code the actual observations as findings are recommended. It is at this point that the reader must furnish the account an investment of interpretive work and an assumption of "underlying" matters "just known in common" about the society in terms of which, what the respondent said, is treated as synonymous with what the observer meant. Correct correspondence is apt to be meant and read on reasonable grounds. Correct correspondence is the product of the work of investigator and reader as members of a community of cobelievers. Thus, even in the case of rigorous methods, if a researcher is to recommend, and the reader is to appreciate, published findings as members of the corpus of sociological fact, the work of the documentary method is employed.

SOCIOLOGICAL SITUATIONS OF INQUIRY AS COMMON-SENSE SITUATIONS OF CHOICE

It is not unusual for professional sociologists to speak of their "fact production" procedures as processes of "seeing through" appearances to an underlying reality; of brushing past actual appearances to "grasp the invariant." Where our subjects are concerned, their processes are not appropriately imagined as "seeing through," but consist

instead of coming to terms with a situation in which factual knowledge of social structures—factual in the sense of warranted grounds of further inferences and actions—must be assembled and made available for potential use despite the fact that the situations it purports to describe are, in any calculable sense, unknown; in their actual and intended logical structures are essentially vague; and are modified, elaborated, extended, if not indeed created, by the fact and manner of being addressed.

If many of the features of our subject's documentary work are recognizable in the work of professional sociological fact production, similarly many situations of professional sociological inquiry have precisely the features that our subjects' situations had. Such features of situations of professional sociological inquiry may be more exactly specified as follows.

1. In the course of an interview an investigator is likely to find himself addressing a series of present situations whose *future states that a contemplated course of treatment will produce* are characteristically vague or even unknown. With overwhelming frequency these as of here-and-now possible future states are only sketchily specifiable prior to undertaking the action that is intended to realize them. There is a necessary distinction between a "possible future state of affairs" and a "how-to-bring-it-about-future-from-a-present-state-of-affairs-as-an-actual-point-of-departure." The "possible future state of affairs" may be very clear indeed. But such a future is not the matter of interest. Instead we are concerned with the "how to bring it about from a here-and-now future." It is this state—for convenience, call it an "operational future"—that is characteristically vague or unknown.

An illustration. A trained survey researcher can describe with remarkable clarity and definiteness what questions he wishes answers to in a questionnaire. How actual replies of actual subjects are to be evaluated as "replies to the questions" are incorporated in a set of procedural decisions known as "coding rules." Any distribution of replies to the questions that is possible under the coding rules is a "possible future state of affairs." After suitable exploratory work such distributions are clearly and definitely imaginable to trained field workers. But with overwhelming frequency it occurs that even late in the *actual* course of the inquiry the questions and answers that will *in effect* have been asked and answered under the various ways of evaluating actual subjects' responses as "replies to the question," given the practical exigencies that must be accommodated in accomplishing the actual work of the inquiry, remain sketchy and open to "reasonable decision" even up to the point of composing the results of the inquiry for publication.

2. Given *a* future, any future, that is known in a definite way, the alternative paths to actualize the future state as a set of stepwise operations upon some beginning present state are characteristically sketchy, incoherent, and unelaborated. Again it is necessary to stress the difference between an inventory of available procedures—investigators can talk about these quite definitely and clearly—and the deliberately pre-programmed stepwise procedures, a set of predecided "what-to-do-in-case-of" strategies for the manipulation of a succession of actual present states of affairs *in their course.* In actual practices such a program is characteristically an unelaborated one.

For example, one of the tasks involved in "managing rapport" consists of managing the stepwise course of the conversation in such a way as to permit the investigator to commit his questions in profitable sequence while retaining some control over the unknown and undesirable directions in which affairs, as a function of the course of the actual exchange, may actually move.[7] Characteristically the researcher substitutes for a pre-programed stepwise solution, a set of *ad hoc* tactics for adjusting to present opportunity, with these tactics only generally governed by what the investigator would hope to have finally found out by the end of the conversation. Under these circumstances, it is more accurate to talk of investigators acting in fulfillment of their hopes, or in avoidance of their fears, than of acting in the deliberate and calculated realization of a plan.

3. It frequently occurs that the investigator takes an action, and only upon the actual occurrence of some product of that action do we find him reviewing the accomplished sequences in a retrospective search therein for their decided character. Insofar as the *decision that was taken* is assigned by the work of the retrospective search, the outcome of such situations can be said to occur *before* the decision. Such situations occur with dramatic frequency at the time the journal article is being written.

4. Prior to his actually having to choose among alternative courses of action on the basis of anticipated consequences, the investigator, for various reasons, is frequently unable to anticipate the consequences of his alternative courses of action and may have to rely upon his actual involvement in order to learn what they might be.

5. Frequently, after encountering some actual state of affairs, the investigator may count it as desirable, and thereupon treat it as the goal toward which his previously taken actions, as he reads them retrospectively, were directed "all along" or "after all."

6. It frequently occurs that only in the course of actually manipulating a present situation, and as a function of his actual manipulation, does the nature of an investigator's future state of affairs become clarified. Thus, the goal of the investigation may be progressively defined as the consequence of the investigator's actually taking action toward a goal whose features as of any present state of his investigative action he does not see clearly.

7. Characteristically such situations are ones of imperfect information. The result is that the investigator is unable to assess, let alone calculate, the difference that his ignorance in the situation makes upon the accomplishment of his activities. Nor, prior to having to take action, is he able either to evaluate their consequences or to assess the value of alternative courses of action.

8. The information that he possesses, that serves him as the basis for the election of strategies, is rarely codified. Hence, his estimates of the likelihood of success or failure characteristically have little in common with the rational mathematical concept of probability.

In their investigative activities, investigators characteristically must manage situations with the above features, given the following additional conditions: that some action must be taken; that the action must be taken by a time and in pace, duration, and phasing that is coordinate with the

---

[7] Cf. Robert K. Merton and Patricia L. Kendall, "The focused interview," *American Journal of Sociology,* 1946, 51:541–557.

actions of others; that the risks of unfavorable out-comes must somehow be managed; that the ac-tions taken and their products will be subject to review by others and must be justified to them; that the elections of courses of action and the resultant outcome must be justified within the procedures of "reasonable" review; and that the entire process must occur within the conditions of, and with his motivated compliance to, corpo-rately organized social activity. In their "shop talk" investigators refer to these features of their actual situations of inquiry and to the necessity for managing them as their "practical circum-stances."

Because their features are so easily recog-nized in the activities of daily life, situations with such features may appropriately be called "com-mon-sense situations of choice." The suggestion is recommended that when researchers call upon "reasonableness" in assigning the status of "find-ings" to their research results, they are inviting the use of such features as these as a context of interpretation for deciding sensibility and war-rant. Findings as outcomes of documentary work, decided under circumstances of common-sense situations of choice, define the term "reasonable findings."

THE PROBLEM

Much of "core sociology" consists of "reasonable findings." Many, if not most, situations of sociolog-ical inquiry are common-sense situations of choice. Nevertheless, textbook and journal discus-sions of sociological methods rarely give recogni-tion to the fact that sociological inquiries are car-ried out under common-sense auspices *at the points where decisions about the correspondence between observed appearances and intended events are being made*. Instead, available de-scriptions and conceptions of investigative de-cision-making and problem-solving assign to the decision-maker's situation contrasting features[8] as follows.

1. From the decision-maker's point of view there exists as a feature of each of his here-and-now states of affairs a recognizable goal with specifiable features. Where sociological inquiry is concerned, this goal consists of the investigator's present problem for the solution to which the investigation will have been undertaken. The goal's specifiable features consist of the criteria whereby, as of any present state of affairs, he de-cides the adequacy with which his problem has been formulated. In their terms, too, the event, "adequate solution," is defined as one of a set of possible occurrences.

2. The decision-maker is conceived to have set for himself the task of devising a program of manipulations upon each successive present state of affairs that will alter each present state so that over their succession they are brought into con-formity with an anticipated state, i.e., the goal, the solved problem.[9]

These features may be restated in terms of the rules of evidence. As a calculable state of af-fairs, an investigator's problem may be regarded as a proposition whose "application" for member-ship, i.e., whose warranted status, is under review. The rules of procedure whereby its warranted status is decided thereby operationally define what is meant by "adequate solution." In ideal scientific activities an investigator is required to decide the steps that define an adequate solution prior to his taking the decided steps. He is re-quired to make this decision before he carries out the operations whereby the possibilities that the proposition proposes will be decided as to their having actually occurred or not. The task of deciding an adequate solution thereby has logi-cal precedence over the actual observation. The observation is said thereby to be "programed," or, alternatively, the intended event is given an "operational definition," or, alternatively, the conditions for the occurrence of an intended event are furnished, or, alternatively, a "predic-tion" is made.

---

[8] I wish to thank Drs. Robert Boguslaw and Myron A. Robinson of the System Development Corporation, Santa Monica, Califor-nia, for the many hours of discussion that we had about calcu-lable and noncalculable situations of choice when we were try-ing together to work through the problem of how consistently successful play in chess is possible.

[9] In some cases, students of decision-making have been inter-ested in those programs that represent fully calculated solutions to the decision-maker's problems. In other cases studies have addressed the fact that the decision-maker may invoke proba-bilistic rules to decide the differential likelihood that alternative courses of action would alter a present state of affairs in the desired direction.

A prominent argument on behalf of this emphasis is that the documentary method is a scientifically erroneous procedure; that its use distorts the objective world in a mirror of subjective prejudice; and that where common-sense situations of choice exist they do so as historical nuisances. Protagonists for methods such as those used in survey research and laboratory experimentation, for example, assert their increasing exemption from situations with common-sense characteristics and documentary dealings with them. After World War II a flood of textbooks on methods was written to provide remedies for such situations. These methods are intended to depict the ways of transforming common-sense situations into calculable ones. Most particularly, the use of mathematical models and statistical schemes of inference are invoked as calculable solutions to the problems of deciding sensibility, objectivity, and warrant in a rigorous way. Immense sums of foundation money, criteria defining adequate research designs, and many careers rest on the conviction that this is so.

Yet it is common knowledge that in the overwhelming number of researches that are methodologically acceptable, and, paradoxically, precisely to the extent that rigorous methods are used, dramatic discrepancies are visible between the theoretical properties of the intended *sociological* findings of inquirers and the mathematical assumptions that must be satisfied if the statistical measures are to be used for the literal description of the intended events. The result is that statistical measurements are most frequently used as indicators, as signs of, as representing or standing on behalf of the intended findings rather than as literal descriptions of them. Thus, at the point where sociological findings must be decided from statistical results,[10] rigorous methods are being asserted as solutions to the tasks of literal description on the grounds of "reasonable" considerations.

Even if it is demonstrable that these features are present, let alone prominent, in sociological inquiries, is it not nevertheless true that a situation of inquiry might receive documentary treatment and still the factual status of its products would be decided differently? For example, is it not the case that there are strictures against ex post facto analysis? And is it not so that a field worker who learned after he consulted his notes what problems he had "in the final analysis" obtained answers to, might reapply for a grant to perform a "confirmatory study" of the "hypotheses" that his reflections had yielded? Is there, therefore, any *necessary* connection between the features of common-sense situations of choice, the use of documentary method, and the *corpus of sociological fact?* Must the documentary method necessarily be used by the professional sociologist to decide sensibility, objectivity, and warrant? Is there a necessary connection between the theoretical subject matter of sociology, as this is constituted by the attitude and procedures for "seeing sociologically" on the one hand, and the canons of adequate description, i.e., evidence, on the other?

Between the methods of literal observation and the work of documentary interpretation the investigator can choose the former and achieve rigorous literal description of physical and biological properties of sociological events. This has been demonstrated on many occasions. Thus far the choice has been made at the cost of either neglecting the properties that make events sociological ones, or by using documentary work to deal with the "soft" parts.

The choice has to do with the question of the conditions under which literal observation and documentary work necessarily occur. This involves the formulation of, and solution to, the problem of sociological evidence in terms that permit a descriptive solution. Undoubtedly, scientific sociology is a "fact," but in Felix Kaufmann's sense of fact, i.e., in terms of a set of procedural rules that *actually* govern the use of sociologists' recommended methods and asserted findings as grounds of further inference and inquiries. The problem of evidence consists of the tasks of making this fact intelligible.

[10] The term "results" is used to refer to the set of *mathematical* events that are possible when the procedures of a statistical test, like chi square, for example, are treated as grammatical rules for conceiving, comparing, producing, etc., events in the mathematical domain. The term "findings" is used to refer to the set of *sociological* events that are possible when, under the assumption that the sociological and mathematical domains correspond in their logical structures, sociological events are interpreted in terms of the rules of statistical inference.

Speech and Thinking

The impairment of the abstract attitude is clearly revealed in characteristic changes in the speech of patients with brain lesions. We know various forms of speech defects in such patients and usually class them together as aphasia.[1] No other pathological material can teach us so much about the organization of the human being. Since we cannot deal with all the various types of aphasia, I shall confine the discussion to a special form, known as amnesic aphasia,[2] which in my opinion is particularly well suited to give us an insight into the nature of man.

If one examines a patient with this type of aphasia one observes as a striking symptom that he is totally or partially unable to find names for concrete things. This is especially noticeable in cases where he has the task of naming presented objects, but it is also apparent in his spontaneous language, which is conspicuously lacking in nouns and verbs. Usually this symptom is considered as the characteristic change, but closer examination shows that other changes also occur. Many circumlocutions are used where we would use single words. A patient shown a cup, for example, may respond with, "This is for drinking," or say, on seeing a penholder, "That is for writing," etc. In another case, a patient of mine said, "That is something for the rain," in a situation in which we should merely say, "That is an umbrella." Or she said: "I must have it for the rain," or, "I have three umbrellas at home." In the last sentence she used the right word in her periphrasis, yet she was unable to repeat it in reply to a repeated question, "What is that?" soon afterward. Evidently such a patient has not lost the word itself but for some reason is unable to use it in naming an object. Further, his entire behavior shows peculiarities. All his acting and thinking seems to center, to an unusual degree, around his own personality and its relation to the world. He is acting in the world rather than thinking or speaking about it. His speech is accompanied to a marked degree by expressive movements. Very often we observe that he seems unable to express his meaning by words but can do so quite well by movements.

The change involving the whole behavior appears still more strikingly in special examinations. I shall begin by presenting the results of one examination with a sorting test because the results seem particularly well suited to carry us into the core of our problem, namely, the basic change in patients with amnesic aphasia.

We place before the patient a heap of colored woolen skeins—Holmgren's well-known samples used for testing color efficiency. We ask him to pick out all the red skeins and put them together. (There are, of course, many different shades of

Reprinted by permission of the publishers from *Human Nature in the Light of Psychopathology*, by Kurt Goldstein, Cambridge, Mass: Harvard University Press, Copyright © 1940, 1968 by the President and Fellows of Harvard College.

[1] See Henry Head, *Aphasia and Kindred Disorders of Speech* (New York, 1926); Theodore Weisenburg and Katherine McBride, *Aphasia* (New York, 1935); Kurt Goldstein, *Uber Aphasie* (Zurich, 1927).

[2] See Kurt Goldstein and Adhemar Gelb, *Psychologische Analysen hirnpathologischer Falle* (Leipsig, 1920); Kurt Goldstein, "The Problem of the Meaning of Words Based upon Observation of Aphasic Patients," *Journal of Psychology*, vol. II, 1936; Ernst Cassirer, *Philosophie der symbolischen Formen*, vol. II (Berlin, 1928).

red.) Or we pick out one particular skein—for example, a dark red one—and ask him to choose strands of the same and similar colors.

In the first task a normal person with good color efficiency usually selects a great number of different shades of the same ground color—that is, for example, different reds, without regard to intensity, purity, lightness, etc. In the same task patients with amnesic aphasia behave quite differently, and exhibit varying types of behavior. For example, when he is told to choose all the skeins that are similar to a given skein, one patient chooses only skeins of the very same or of a closely similar shade. Though urged to go on he chooses a small number because there are only a few very similar ones in the heap. Another patient matches a given bright shade of red with a blue skein of similar brightness. At first such a patient may seem to be color-blind, but it can be demonstrated beyond doubt that his color efficiency is normal and that he is able to differentiate very distinctly between colors that are much alike. More precise observations disclose that in this case the choice is determined by a particular color attribute of the given skein, its brightness. We observe, further, that the choice may be decided by a number of different attributes—at one time by brightness, at another by softness, or coldness, warmth, etc. However—and this is a very amazing thing—a patient who seems to be choosing according to a certain attribute is not able to follow this procedure voluntarily if it is demanded of him—that is, if he is asked to choose only bright skeins, etc. Further, we observe that he does not seem to be able to hold to a certain procedure. He has chosen, for instance, some bright skeins. Suddenly he begins selecting on the basis of another attribute—the coldness of the color or some other factor. In another case, the patient arranges the skeins as if guided by a scale of brightness. He begins with a very bright red, then adds one less bright, and so on to a dull one. But if we ask him to place the skeins in a succession according to their brightness he shows himself incapable of the performance, even if it is demonstrated to him.

To understand the behavior of our patients, it is necessary to examine the procedure of normal persons in such tasks. If we normal persons want to choose a color, we select various nuances, even though we see that they have various attributes not equal to one another, because we recognize that they belong together in respect to their *basic* quality. The several shades are merely examples of this quality, and we treat the skeins not as different individual things but as representatives of that one basic color. For the moment we ignore all differences in shade and disregard all singular attributes. We are able to do this because we can abstract and because we can hold fast to a procedure once initiated.

There is another approach, however, which is open to the normal person. We can start with one particular skein and move it about over the heap, *passively* surrendering ourselves to the impressions that emerge. Then either of two things will take place. If we find skeins resembling our sample in *all* attributes, all these immediately cohere in a unitary sensory experience with the sample. If we find skeins which match our sample in some respects, we experience a characteristic unrest concerning the heap, and an alternating sense of relationship between skeins in the heap and the sample, according to different attributes. No matter whether we experience rivalry or matching, the coherence we feel results directly from sense data and takes place passively; we do not experience a definite attitude toward any attribute.

There is an essential difference between the more passive kind of approach and the former, in which we definitely choose a particular color. In the one, a definite ordering principle determines our actions; in the other, there is no such principle, and our actions are passively determined by outer impressions. These two kinds of behavior correspond to what we have called abstract and concrete behavior and what we may now call categorical and concrete behavior.

A particular kind of language belongs to each of these types of behavior. Our behavior is abstract when we give a name to an object. When we speak of "table" we do not mean a special given table with all its accidental properties; we mean table in general. The word is used as a representative of the category "table" even when naming a particular table. Thus, if we are asked to group together all reds, upon hearing the word "red" we are immediately prepared to select colors in a categorical fashion. In this approach language plays a great role, and the particular form it takes here may be designated by Karl Buehler's term, *darstellende Sprache*, which may be translated as "representative speech."

In the second form of behavior language does not play much of a role at all. Our words merely accompany our acts and express a property of the object itself, like other properties, such as color, size, etc. This fact is shown in the particular kind of words we use in such situations. The words are especially adapted to the individuality of the given object. We use words like "rose-red," "violet"; we do not say "red," but "pink," "dark red," "strawberry-red," "sky-blue"; not green but "grass-green," etc. Often we have no word for naming a given object, and then we do it in a roundabout way. Words are used here less as representative of categories than as individual properties which, like other properties, belong to the object in question. We call such words "individual" words.

Now then we consider the behavior of the patient in the light of these elucidations we may say that it is similar to the second approach of normal persons. He is able to assume only the more concrete, the more realistic, attitude. Therefore he chooses identical skeins or skeins which are similar in an outstanding property, such as brightness. This interpretation finds confirmation in the greater concreteness of the patient's general behavior, in the predominance of acting over thinking, in the accompaniment of speech by expressive movements.

Our assumption is finally substantiated by the results of another type of sorting test. If a normal person tries to arrange a number of objects lying before him—say, on the writing table of a very busy man—he may do it in various ways, according to various attitudes. He may arrange them by size, by color, by function, by the importance of their situation, in terms of activity, of thought, etc. Further, he is able both to shift from one attitude and one kind of order to another as the situation demands it, and to effect a particular arrangement on demand. A patient with amnesic aphasia, confronted with miscellaneous objects with the instruction to group them, will exhibit the same behavior as in the color test. He is capable of proceeding only in a manner that indicates that he is guided by *concrete* promptings.

A particularly instructive example is the following. Among a number of different objects there were placed on a table before a patient a corkscrew and a bottle with a cork loosely set in its neck. The patient, asked to arrange these, did not put the bottle and the corkscrew together. Asked if these two objects did not belong together, he said, "No," very positively, backing his answer up with the explanation, "The bottle is already opened." Under these circumstances most normal people would pay no attention to the fact that the cork was not fast. For the immediate task—the grouping together of objects that belong together—it is quite incidental and unimportant whether the cork is loose or fast. With the abstract attitude, in a form of sorting which involves grouping objects according to categories, we assume that bottle and corkscrew belong together, independently of their occurrence in any particular situation. But for the patient who is able to take the objects only as they are given in sense experience, the corkscrew does not belong to the bottle and the cork if the cork is already loose. From this and similar cases it is plain that he takes the concrete attitude toward objects as well—we may say toward all objects, toward the world in its entirety.

Our conclusion is that the patient's inability to name objects is a consequence of his inability to assume the abstract attitude, for this is a prerequisite for the naming of objects. As we have shown in the example of the umbrella, he has not lost the words themselves, but he is unable to use them in situations which demand their use as categories. Often a patient, asked to name a color presented to him, calls out over and over various color names: red, blue, yellow, etc. He may even utter the appropriate name, but in spite of this he is still unable to connect it with the color itself. Furthermore, it does not help him when we say the different color names for him to repeat after us.

But what makes these words unsuitable for use in connection with objects in the normal way—that is, as names? Why can they not be used as symbols for objects? This may be disclosed in observations of patients who utter appropriate words in connection with some objects but, as closer analysis shows, do not use them in a normal categorical fashion. Here we learn that the patients have the same *concrete* attitude toward the words that they have toward objects they are asked to sort.

Asked to mention the names of several different kinds of animals, the patient may be at first unable to do so. In one case it was not until we had given a patient such examples as dog, cat, mouse, that she replied to the question at all. Then suddenly she said: "A polar bear; a brown bear; a lion; a tiger." Asked why she named these particular animals, she said, "If we enter the zoological gardens, we come at first to the polar bear and then to the other animals."[3] Obviously she had recalled the animals as they were situated in the zoological gardens, and had used the words only as belonging to the concrete situation, not as names for objects. It was very characteristic that she did not simply say "bear," a word which represents the category of all bears, and which we would use when asked to name animals, but that instead she selected the words "polar bear," "brown bear." The same fact appeared when the patient was asked to recite different female first names. She said: "Grete, Paula, Clara, Martha," and, asked why she had mentioned these particular names, answered, "These are all G_____s" (G_____ was her family name), and went on, "one sister died of a heart neurosis." The last sentence demonstrates very clearly that the patient did not recite names but only uttered words which belonged to a particular concrete situation, namely, to her family situation.

How very concretely such words are apprehended may be demonstrated by the following example. When, to such a patient of ours, a knife was offered with a pencil, she called the knife a "pencil sharpener"; when the knife was offered with an apple, it was to her an "apple parer"; when offered with a potato, it was a "potato peeler"; in company with a piece of bread, it became a "bread knife"; and with a fork it was "knife and fork." The word "knife" alone she never uttered spontaneously, and when she was asked, "Could we not always call it simply 'knife?'" she replied promptly, "No."

With different mental sets the same word may mean for the normal person different things. For example, in German the word *Anhänger* is used for a lavalier which hangs on a chain around a girl's neck, or for a follower of a personage, or for the second car which is customarily attached to a street-car in Germany. Our patient was unable to use the word in more than one sense or in connection with more than one object. If she understood the word in a particular sense she could not understand that it could be used in another sense. This observation shows clearly that the words themselves are qualitatively different from such patients as compared with normal people, by whom the same word can be used for various totally different objects. By patients with amnesic aphasia they can be used only in a concrete way, for they seem to have lost the characteristic that is necessary if they are to be used in a categorical sense—that is, as symbols. They may be useful as properties belonging to a definite object, but they have become unfit to serve as symbols for ideas. *They have lost their meaning.*

It has usually been assumed, even by those authors who recognize that these patients have lost the categorical attitude toward objects, that the cause of this lack is the loss of words, or a difficulty in evoking works. This cannot be the case. There is no doubt that words provide a very important means of helping us to assume the categorical attitude and of stabilizing concepts, but, as we have explained, our patients have not really lost the words. Instead, the words have lost their character of being usable in the abstract, and this change in language is only one expression of the basic change in our patients, *the lack of the capacity to create any sort of abstraction.*

These observations are important for understanding the character of the capacity for naming objects. This apparently simple performance does not represent a superficial connection between a thing and a word; naming objects presupposes the abstract attitude and is an expression of a very high mental function. But these observations reveal another point still more important for our

[3] Eva Rothmann, "Untersuchung eines Falles von umschriebener Hirnschadigung mit Storungen auf verschiedenen Leistungsgebieten," *Schweizer Archiv fur Neurologie und Psychiatrie*, vol. XXXIII, 1933.

discussion. They show that speech is one of the essential characteristics of human nature, inasmuch as it is tied to man's highest capacity, the capacity for abstract behavior.

Another significant point appears. The patients we have been discussing have not lost the capacity to use words in a concrete way, and from the advantage this type of speech gives them we can infer what role it may play in normal life.

A patient of mine could name pure colors with their respective color names—red, blue, and so on—but she declined to extend the same word to the several shades of a given color. The words were at her disposal only as individual, concrete things belonging to definite objects. In the course of time, after repeated examinations, she came to call various shades by the same name; for instance, she would use the word "red" for all shades of red. Superficially she seemed to behave like a normal person. One might have thought that she had improved, that she had regained the *meaning* of the words. But it was not so. Asked why she now called all these different shades by the same word, she answered, "The doctors have told me that all these colors are named red. Therefore I called them all red." Asked if this was not correct, she laughed and said, "Not one of these colors is red, but I am told to call them by this word." It is clear that she had not used the words as symbols but had learned to build a quite external connection between one word and a diversity of things, a quite meaningless connection, which, however, because she had a good memory, helped her to carry out a task, if only in a very external way.

Thus we must distinguish very definitely between two ways of using words in connection with objects: real naming, which is an expression of the categorical attitude toward the world in general, and pseudo-naming of objects, which is simply a use of words held in memory. The incidence of this pseudo-naming depends on the extent of the individual's verbal possessions. In it words are used as properties of objects just as other properties—color, size, hue—are used; they belong to concrete behavior. To this type of words belong the speech automatisms of ordinary people—the alphabet, numbers in series, the days of the week, and many other longer or shorter speech expres-sions of everyday life. This use of words plays a great role in ordinary speech. In learning a foreign language, for example, as long as we have no real conception of it as a language, we possess its words only by such superficial connections with the words of our own language. If we understand their meaning within the realm of the foreign language itself, then the words achieve an absolutely different character; then they become representative of a category.

Important as these speech possessions are for our everyday language, they obtain their significance only from their position against a background of representational, meaningful speech. This may be gathered from the fact that to a certain extent speech automatisms are developed only if a human being possesses the function of meaning. Certainly a child acquires many automatisms by repeated imitation of his own speech and that of others. If he is not able to use them later in connection with meaningful speech, however, his learning of these words is limited, and he forgets many that he has learned. We know that children with an inborn deficiency in the attitude toward the abstract are not able to develop speech automatisms to any extent, and that they forget them, in spite of a good memory, if the words are not practiced constantly. In the same way, patients with a loss of categorical behavior may lose their speech automatisms if they are not continuously kept in use by the demands of concrete situations. Thus, for example, if the meaning of numbers is lost, these patients lose the ability to count and the knowledge of the simple multiplication table, which are usually regarded as well-established possessions of memory.

Speech automatisms may be designated as "tools," but it is false to consider language in general as a mere tool. Even speech automatisms are dependent upon the categorical attitude both in their building and in their use. This point is most important. The use of speech automatisms alone is not real language. Our patients, despite their lack of the categorical attitude, may be able to use speech automatisms which they acquired at a time when they were capable of the categorical attitude, but the fact that their speech lacks the spontaneity and fluidity which characterizes normal language, and that they are not able to use the words as symbols, demonstrates very clearly that language without a categorical background is not real language. Whenever human beings use language to establish natural connections between themselves and the world, particularly with their fellow men, language is not merely a tool. It is not merely a superficial means of communication, not a simple naming of objects through words; it represents a particular way of building up the world—namely, by means of abstractions. "Language," said Wilhelm von Humboldt, "never represents objects themselves but the concepts which the mind has formed of them in the autonomous activity by which it creates language." It is this that makes language so important, so essential to the development of a culture. It becomes a manifestation both of all that is human, the human being at his deepest, and of man's psychic bond with his fellows; in none of his cultural creations does man reveal himself so fully as in the creation of language itself. It would be impossible for animals to create a language, because they do not have this conceptual approach toward the world. If they had, they would be not animals but human beings. Nothing brings this home to us more strikingly than observing in patients with amnesic aphasia the parallelism between the changes which occur in personality and the loss of the meaning of words.

C. Wright Mills   33

Situated Actions and Vocabularies of Motive

The major reorientation of recent theory and observation in sociology of language emerged with the overthrow of the Wundtian notion that language has as its function the "expression" of prior elements within the individual. The postulate underlying modern study of language is the simple one that we must approach linguistic behavior, not by referring it to private states in individuals, but by observing its social function of coordinating diverse actions. Rather than expressing something which is prior and in the person, language is taken by other persons as an indicator of future actions.[1]

Within this perspective there are suggestions concerning problems of motivation. It is the purpose of this paper to outline an analytic model for the explanation of motives which is based on a sociological theory of language and a sociological psychology.[2]

C. Wright Mills, "Situated Actions and Vocabularies of Motive," *American Sociological Review*, vol. 5 (December 1940), pp. 904–913. Reprinted by permission.
    Revision of a paper read to The Society for Social Research, University of Chicago, August 16–17, 1940.

[1] See C. Wright Mills, "Bibliographical Appendices," Section I, 4: "Sociology of Language" in *Contemporary Social Theory*, Ed. by Barnes, Becker & Becker, New York, 1940.

[2] See G. H. Mead, "Social Psychology as Counterpart of Physiological Psychology," *Psychol. Bul.*, VI: 401–408, 1909; Karl Mannheim, *Man and Society in an Age of Reconstruction*, New York, 1940; L. V. Wiese-Howard Becker, *Systematic Sociology*, part I, New York, 1932; J. Dewey, "All psychology is either biological or social psychology," *Psychol. Rev.*, vol. 24: 276.

As over against the inferential conception of motives as subjective "springs" of action, motives may be considered as typical vocabularies having ascertainable functions in delimited societal situations. Human actors do vocalize and impute motives to themselves and to others. To explain behavior by referring it to an inferrred and abstract "motive" is one thing. To analyze the observable lingual mechanisms of motive imputation and avowal as they function in conduct is quite another. Rather than fixed elements "in" an individual, motives are the terms with which interpretation of conduct *by social actors* proceeds. This imputation and avowal of motives by actors are social phenomena to be explained. The differing reasons men give for their actions are not themselves without reasons.

First, we must demarcate the general conditions under which such motive imputation and avowal seem to occur.[3] Next, we must give a characterization of motive in denotable terms and an explanatory paradigm of why certain motives are verbalized rather than others. Then, we must indicate mechanisms of the linkage of vocabularies of motive to systems of action. What we want is an analysis of the integrating, controlling, and specifying function a certain type of speech fulfils in socially situated actions.

The generic situation in which imputation and avowal of motives arise, involves, first, the *social* conduct or the (stated) programs of languaged creatures, i.e., programs and actions oriented with reference to the actions and talk of others; second, the avowal and imputation of motives is concomitant with the speech form known as the "question." Situations back of questions typically involve *alternative* or *unexpected* programs or actions which phases analytically denote "crises."[4] The question is distinguished in that it usually elicits another *verbal* action, not a motor response. The question is an element in *conversation*. Conversation may be concerned with the factual features of a situation as they are seen or believed to be or it may seek to integrate and promote a set of diverse social actions with reference to the situation and its normative pattern of expectations. It is in this latter assent and dissent phase of conversation that persuasive and dissuasive speech and vocabulary arise. For men live in immediate acts of experience and their attentions are directed outside themselves until acts are in some way frustrated. It is then that awareness of self and of motive occur. The "question" is a lingual index of such conditions. The avowal and imputation of motives are features of such conversations as arise in "question" situations.

Motives are imputed or avowed as answers to questions interrupting acts or programs. Motives are words. Generically, to what do they refer? They do not denote any elements "in" individuals. They stand for anticipated situational consequences of questioned conduct. Intention or purpose (stated as a "program") *is* awareness of anticipated consequence; motives are names for consequential situations, and surrogates for actions leading to them. Behind questions are possible alternative actions with their terminal consequences. "Our introspective words for motives are rough, shorthand descriptions for certain typical patterns of discrepant and conflicting stimuli."[5]

The model of purposive conduct associated with Dewey's name may briefly be stated. Individuals confronted with "alternative acts" perform one or the other of them on the basis of the differential consequences which they anticipate. This nakedly utilitarian schema is inadequate because: (a) the "alternative acts" of *social* conduct "appear" most often in lingual form, as a question, stated by one's self or by another; (b) it is more adequate to say that individuals act in terms of anticipation of named consequences.

---

[3] The importance of this initial task for research is clear. Most researches on the verbal level merely ask abstract questions of individuals, but if we can tentatively delimit the situations in which certain motives *may* be verbalized, we can use that delimitation in the construction of *situational* questions, and we shall be *testing* deductions from our theory.

[4] On the "question" and "conversation," see G. A. DeLaguna, *Speech: Its Function and Development*, 37 (and index), New Haven, 1927. For motives in crises, see J. M. Williams, *The Foundations of Social Science*, 435 ff, New York, 1920.

[5] K. Burke, *Permanence and Change*, 45, New York, 1936. I am indebted to this book for several leads which are systematized into the present statement.

Among such names and in some technologically oriented lines of action there may appear such terms as "useful," "practical," "serviceable," etc., terms so "ultimate" to the pragmatists, and also to certain sectors of the American population in these delimited situations. However, there are other areas of population with different vocabularies of motives. The choice of lines of action is accompanied by representations, and selection among them, of their situational termini. Men discern situations with particular vocabularies, and it is in terms of some delimited vocabulary that they anticipate consequences of conduct.[6] Stable vocabularies of motives link anticipated consequences and specific actions. There is no need to invoke "psychological" terms like "desire" or "wish" as explanatory, since they themselves must be explained socially.[7] Anticipation is a subvocal or overt naming of terminal phases and/or social consequences of conduct. When an individual names consequences, he elicits the behaviors for which the name is a redintegrative cue. In a *societal* situation, implicit in the names for consequences is the social dimension of motives. Through such vocabularies, types of societal controls operate. Also, the terms in which the question is asked often will contain both alternatives: "Love or Duty?" "Business or Pleasure?" Institutionally different situations have different *vocabularies of motive* appropriate to their respective behaviors.

This sociological conception of motives as relatively stable lingual phases of delimited situations is quite consistent with Mead's program to approach conduct socially and from the outside. It keeps clearly in mind that "both motives and actions very often originate not from within but from the situation in which individuals find themselves. . . ."[8] It translates the question of "why"[9] into a "how" that is answerable in terms of a situation and its typical vocabulary of motives, i.e., those which conventionally accompany that type situation and function as cues and justifications for normative actions in it.

It has been indicated that the question is usually an index to the avowal and imputation of motives. Max Weber defines motive as a complex of meaning, which appears to the actor himself or to the observer to be an adequate ground for his conduct.[10] The aspect of motive which this conception grasps is its intrinsically social character. A satisfactory or adequate motive is one that satisfies the questioners of an act or program, whether it be the other's or the actor's. As a word, *a motive tends to be one which is to the actor and to the other members of a situation an unquestioned answer to questions concerning social and lingual conduct.* A stable motive is an ultimate in justificatory conversation. The words which in a type situation will fulfil this function are circumscribed by the vocabulary of motives acceptable for such situations. Motives are accepted justifications for present, future, or past programs or acts.

To term them justification is *not* to deny their efficacy. Often anticipations of acceptable justification will control conduct. ("If I did this, what could I say? What would they say?") Decisions may be, wholly or in part, delimited by answers to such queries.

A man may begin an act for one motive. In the course of it, he may adopt an ancillary motive. This does not mean that the second apologetic motive is inefficacious. The vocalized expectation of an act, its "reason," is not only a mediating condition of the act but it is a proximate and controlling condition for which the term "cause" is not inappropriate. It may strengthen the act of the actor. It may win new allies for his act.

When they appeal to others involved in one's act, motives are strategies of action. In many

[6] See such experiments as C. N. Rexroad's "Verbalization in Multiple Choice Reactions," *Psychol. Rev.*, Vol. 33: 458, 1926.

[7] Cf. J. Dewey, "Theory of Valuation," *Int. Ency. of Unified Science*, New York, 1939.

[8] K. Mannheim, *Man and Society*, 249, London, 1940.

[9] Conventionally answerable by reference to "subjective factors" within individuals. R. M. MacIver, "The Modes of the Question Why," *J. of Soc. Phil.*, April, 1940. Cf. also his "The Imputation of Motives," *Amer. J. Sociol.*, July, 1940.

[10] *Wirtschaft und Gesellschaft*, 5, Tubingen, 1922, "'Motiv' heisst ein Sinnzusammenhang, Welcher dem Handelnden selbst oder dem Beobachtenden als sinnhafter 'Grund' eines Verhaltens in dem Grade heissen, als die Beziehung seiner Bestandteile von uns nach den durchschnittlichen Denk-und Gefühlsgewohnheiten als typischer (wir pflegen in sagen: 'richtiger') Sinzusammenhang bejaht Wird."

social actions, others must agree, tacitly or explicitly. Thus, acts often will be abandoned if no reason can be found that others will accept. Diplomacy in choice of motive often controls the diplomat. Diplomatic choice of motive is part of the attempt to motivate acts for other members in a situation. Such pronounced motives undo snarls and integrate social actions. Such diplomacy does not necessarily imply intentional lies. It merely indicates that an appropriate vocabulary of motives will be utilized—that they are conditions for certain lines of conduct.[11]

When an agent vocalizes or imputes motives, he is not trying to *describe* his experienced social action. He is not merely stating "reasons." He is influencing others—and himself. Often he is finding new "reasons" which will mediate action. Thus, we need not treat an action as discrepant from "its" verbalization, for in many cases, the verbalization is a new act. In such cases, there is not a discrepancy between an act and "its" verbalization, but a difference between two disparate actions, motor-social and verbal.[12] This additional (or *"ex post facto"*) lingualization may involve appeal to a vocabulary of motives associated with a norm with which both members of the situation are in agreement. As such, it is an integrative factor in *future* phases of the original social action or in other acts. By resolving conflicts, motives are efficacious. Often, if "reasons" were not given, an act would not occur, nor would diverse actions be integrated. Motives are common grounds for mediated behaviors.

Perry summarily states the Freudian view of motives "as the view that the real motives of conduct are those which we are ashamed to admit either to ourselves or to others."[13] One can cover the facts by merely saying that scruples (i.e., *moral* vocabularies of motive) are often efficacious and that men will alter and deter their acts in terms of such motives. One of the components of a "generalized other," as a mechanism of societal control, is vocabularies of acceptable motives. For example, a business man joins the Rotary Club and proclaims its public-spirited vocabulary.[14] If this man cannot act out business conduct without so doing, it follows that this vocabulary of motives is an important factor in his behavior.[15] The long acting out of a role, with its appropriate motives, will often induce a man to become what at first he merely sought to appear. Shifts in the vocabularies of motive that are utilized later by an individual disclose an important aspect of various integrations of his actions with concomitantly various groups.

The motives actually used in justifying or criticizing an act definitely link it to situations, integrate one man's action with another's, and line up conduct with norms. The societally sustained motive-surrogates of situations are both constraints and inducements. It is a hypothesis worthy and capable of test that typical vocabularies of motives for different situations are significant determinants of conduct. As lingual segments of social action, motives orient actions by enabling discrimination between their objects. Adjectives such as "good," "pleasant," and "bad" promote action or deter it. When they constitute components of a vocabulary of motives, i.e., are typical and relatively unquestioned accompaniments of typal situations, such words often function as directives and incentives by virtue of their being the judgments of others as anticipated by the actor. In this sense motives are "social instruments, i.e., data by modifying which the agent will be able to influence [himself or others]."[16] The "control" of others is not usually direct but rather through manipulation of a field of objects. We influence a man by naming his acts or imputing motives to them—or to "him." The motives accompanying institutions of war, e.g., are not "the causes" of war, but they do promote continued

---

[11] Of course, since motives are communicated, they may be lies; but this must be proved. Verbalizations are not lies merely because they are socially efficacious. I am here concerned more with the social function of pronounced motives, than with the sincerity of those pronouncing them.

[12] See F. Znaniecki, *Social Actions*, 30, New York, 1936.

[13] *General Theory of Value*, 292–293, New York, 1936.

[14] *Ibid.*, 392.

[15] The "profits motive" of classical economics may be treated as an ideal-typical vocabulary of motives for delimited economic situations and behaviors. For late phases of monopolistic and regulated capitalism, this type requires modification; the profit and commercial vocabularies have acquired other ingredients. See N. R. Danielian's *AT&T*, New York, 1940, for a suggestive account of the *noneconomic* behavior and motives of business bureaucrats.

[16] *Social Actions*, 73.

integrated participation, and they vary from one war to the next. Working vocabularies of motive have careers that are woven through changing institutional fabrics.

Genetically, motives are imputed by others before they are avowed by self. The mother controls the child: "Do not do that, it is greedy." Not only does the child learn what to do, what not to do, but he is given standardized motives which promote prescribed actions and dissuade those proscribed. Along with rules and norms of action for various situations, we learn vocabularies of motives appropriate to them. These are the motives we shall use, since they are a part of our language and components of our behavior.

The quest for "real motives" suppositiously set over against "mere rationalization" is often informed by a metaphysical view that the "real" motives are in some way biological. Accompanying such quests for something more real and back of rationalization is the view held by many sociologists that language is an external manifestation or concomitant of something prior, more genuine, and "deep" in the individual. "Real attitudes" versus "mere verbalization" or "opinion" implies that at best we only infer from his language what "really" is the individual's attitude or motive.

Now what *could we possibly* so infer? Of precisely *what* is verbalization symptomatic? We cannot *infer* physiological processes from lingual phenomena. All we can infer and empirically check[17] is another verbalization of the agent's which we believe was orienting and controlling behavior at the time the act was performed. The only social items that can "lie deeper" are other lingual forms.[18] The "Real Attitude or Motive" is not something different in kind from the verbalization or the "opinion." They turn out to be only relatively and temporally different.

The phrase "unconscious motive" is also unfortunate. All it can mean is that a motive is not explicitly vocalized, but there is no need to infer unconscious motives from such situations and

then posit them in individuals as elements. The phrase is informed by persistence of the unnecessary and unsubstantiated notion that "all action has a motive," and it is promoted by the observation of gaps in the relatively frequent verbalization in everyday situations. The facts to which this phrase is supposedly addressed are covered by the statements that men do not always explicitly articulate motives, and that *all* actions do not pivot around language. I have already indicated the conditions under which motives are typically avowed and imputed.

Within the perspective under consideration, the verbalized motive is not used as an index of something in the individual but *as a basis of inference for a typal vocabulary of motives of a situated action*. When we ask for the "real attitude" rather than the "opinion," for the "real motive" rather than the "rationalization," all we can meaningfully be asking for is the controlling speech form which was incipiently or overtly presented in the performed act or series of acts. There is no way to plumb behind verbalization into an individual and directly check our motive-mongering, but there is an empirical way in which we can guide and limit, in given historical situations, investigations of motives. That is by the construction of typal vocabularies of motives that are extant in types of situations and actions. Imputation of motives may be controlled by reference to the typical constellation of motives which are observed to be societally linked with classes of situated actions. Some of the "real" motives that have been imputed to actors were not even known to them. As I see it, motives are circumscribed by the vocabulary of the actor. The only source for a terminology of motives is the vocabularies of motives actually and usually verbalized by actors in specific situations.

Individualistic, sexual, hedonistic, and pecuniary vocabularies of motives are apparently now dominant in many sectors of twentieth-century urban America. Under such an ethos, verbalization of alternative conduct in these terms is least likely to be challenged among dominant groups. In this milieu, individuals are skeptical of Rockfeller's avowed religious motives for his business conduct because such motives are not *now* terms of the vocabulary conventionally and prominently

---

[17] Of course, we could infer or interpret constructs posited in the individual, but these are not easily checked and they are not explanatory.

[18] Which is not to say that, physiologically, there may not be cramps in the stomach wall or adrenalin in the blood, etc., but the character of the "relation" of such items to social action is quite moot.

accompanying situations of business enterprise. A medieval monk writes that he gave food to a poor but pretty woman because it was "for the glory of God and the eternal salvation of his soul." Why do we tend to question him and impute sexual motives? Because sex is an influential and widespread motive in our society and time. Religious vocabularies of explanation and of motives are now on the wane. In a society in which religious motives have been debunked on rather wide scale, certain thinkers are skeptical of those who ubiquitously proclaim them. Religious motives have lapsed from selected portions of modern populations and other motives have become "ultimate" and operative. But from the monasteries of medieval Europe we have no evidence that religious vocabularies were not operative in many situations.

A labor leader says he performs a certain act because he wants to get higher standards of living for the workers. A business man says that this is rationalization, or a lie; that it is really because he wants more money for himself from the workers. A radical says a college professor will not engage in radical movements because he is afraid for his job, and besides, is a "reactionary." The college professor says it is because he just likes to find out how things work. What is reason for one man is rationalization for another. The variable is the accepted vocabulary of motives, the ultimates of discourse, of each man's dominant group about whose opinion he cares. *Determination of such groups, their location and character, would enable delimitation and methodological control of assignment of motives for specific acts.*

Stress on this idea will lead us to investigations of the compartmentalization of operative motives in personalities according to situation and the general types and conditions of vocabularies of motives in various types of societies. The motivational structures of individuals and the patterns of their purposes are relative to societal frames. We might, e.g., study motives along stratified or occupational lines. Max Weber has observed:

. . . that in a free society the motives which induce people to work vary with . . . different social classes.

. . . There is normally a graduated scale of motives by which men from different social classes are driven to work. When a man changes ranks, he switches from one set of motives to another.[19]

The lingual ties which hold them together react on persons to constitute frameworks of disposition and motive. Recently, Talcott Parsons has indicated, by reference to differences in actions in the professions and in business, that one cannot leap from "economic analysis to ultimate motivations; the institutional patterns *always* constitute one crucial element of the problem."[20] It is my suggestion that we may analyze, index, and gauge this element by focusing upon those specific verbal appendages of variant institutionalized actions which have been referred to as vocabularies of motive.

In folk societies, the constellations of motives connected with various sectors of behavior would tend to be typically stable and remain associated only with their sector. In typically primary, sacred, and rural societies, the motives of persons would be regularly compartmentalized. Vocabularies of motives ordered to different situations stabilize and guide behavior and expectation of the reactions of others. In their appropriate situations, verbalized motives are not typically questioned.[21] In secondary, secular, and urban structures, varying and competing vocabularies of motives operate coterminously and the situations to which they are appropriate are not clearly demarcated. Motives once unquestioned for de-

[19] Paraphrased by K. Mannheim, *op. cit.,* 316–317.

[20] "The Motivation of Economic Activities," 67, in C. W. M. Hart, *Essays in Sociology,* Toronto, 1940.

[21] Among the ethnologists, Ruth Benedict has come up to the edge of a genuinely sociological view of motivation. Her view remains vague because she has not seen clearly the identity of differing "motivations" in differing cultures with the varied extant and approved vocabularies of motive. "The intelligent understanding of the relation of the individual to his society . . . involves always the understanding of the types of human motivations and capacities capitalized in his society . . ." "Configurations of Culture in North America," *Amer. Anthrop.,* 25, Jan.–Mar. 1932; see also: *Patterns of Culture,* 242–243, Boston, 1935. She turns this observation into a quest for the unique "genius" of each culture and stops her research by words like "Apollonian." If she would attempt constructively to observe the vocabularies of motives which precipitate acts to perform, implement programs, and furnish approved motives for them in circumscribed situations, she would be better able to state precise problems and to answer them by further observation.

fined situations are now questioned. Various motives can release similar acts in a given situation. Hence, variously situated persons are confused and guess which motive "activated" the person. Such questioning has resulted intellectually in such movements as psychoanalysis with its dogma of rationalization and its systematic motive-mongering. Such intellectual phenomena are underlaid by split and conflicting sections of an individuated society which is characterized by the existence of competing vocabularies of motive. Intricate constellations of motives, for example, are components of business enterprise in America. Such patterns have encroached on the old style vocabulary of the virtuous relation of men and women: duty, love, kindness. Among certain classes, the romantic, virtuous, and pecuniary motives are confused. The asking of the question: "Marriage for love or money?" is significant, for the pecuniary is now a constant and almost ubiquitous motive, a common denominator of many others.[22]

Back of "mixed motives" and "motivational conflicts" are competing or discrepant situational patterns and their respective vocabularies of motive. With shifting and interstitial situations, each of several alternatives may belong to disparate systems of action which have differing vocabularies of motives appropriate to them. Such conflicts manifest vocabulary patterns that have overlapped in a marginal individual and are not easily compartmentalized in clear-cut situations.

Besides giving promise of explaining an area of lingual and societal fact, a further advantage of this view of motives is that with it we should be able to give sociological accounts of other theories (terminologies) of motivation. This is a task for sociology of knowledge. Here I can refer only to a few theories. I have already referred to the Freudian terminology of motives. It is apparent that these motives are those of an upper bourgeois patriarchal group with strong sexual and individualistic orientation. When introspecting on the couches of Freud, patients used the only vocabulary of motives they knew; Freud got his hunch and guided further talk. Mittenzwey has dealt with similar points at length.[23] Widely diffused in a postwar epoch, psychoanalysis was never popular in France where control of sexual behavior is not puritanical.[24] To converted individuals who have become accustomed to the psychoanalytic terminology of motives, all others seem self-deceptive.[25]

In like manner, to many believers in Marxism's terminology of power, struggle, and economic motives, all others, including Freud's, are due to hypocrisy or ignorance. An individual who has assimilated thoroughly only business congeries of motives will attempt to apply these motives to all situations, home and wife included. It should be noted that the business terminology of motives has its intellectual articulation, even as psychoanalysis and Marxism have.

It is significant that since the Socratic period many "theories of motivation" have been linked with ethical and religious terminologies. Motive is that in man which leads him to do good or evil. Under the aegis of religious institutions, men use vocabularies of moral motives: they call acts and programs "good" and "bad," and impute these qualities to the soul. Such lingual behavior is part of the process of social control. Institutional practices and their vocabularies of motives exercise control over delimited ranges of possible situations. One could make a typal catalog of religious motives from widely read religious texts, and test its explanatory power in various denominations and sects.[26]

In many situations of contemporary America, conduct is controlled and integrated by *hedonistic* language. For large population sectors in certain situations, pleasure and pain are now unquestioned motives. For given periods and socie-

---

[22] Also motives acceptably imputed and avowed for one system of action may be diffused into other domains and gradually come to be accepted by some as a comprehensive portrait of *the* motive of men. This happened in the case of the economic man and his motives.

[23] Kuno Mittenzwey, "Zur Sociologie der psychoanalystischer Erkenntnis," in Max Scheler, ed., *Versuche zu einer Sociologie des Wissens*, 365–375, Munich, 1924.

[24] This fact is interpreted by some as supporting Freudian theories. Nevertheless, it can be just as adequately grasped in the scheme here outlined.

[25] See K. Burke's acute discussion of Freud, *op. cit.*, Part I.

[26] Moral vocabularies deserve a special statement. Within the viewpoint herein outlined many snarls concerning "value-judgments," etc., can be cleared up.

ties, the situations should be empirically determined. Pleasures and pain should not be reified and imputed to human nature as underlying principles of all action. Note that hedonism as a psychological and an ethical doctrine gained impetus in the modern world at about the time when older moral-religious motives were being debunked and simply discarded by "middle class" thinkers. Back of the hedonistic terminology lay an emergent social pattern and a new vocabulary of motives. The shift of unchallenged motives which gripped the communities of Europe was climaxed when, in reconciliation, the older religious and the hedonistic terminologies were identified: the "good" is the "pleasant." The conditioning situation was similar in the Hellenistic world with the hedonism of the Cyrenaics and Epicureans.

What is needed is to take all these *terminologies* of motive and locate them as *vocabularies* of motive in historic epochs and specified situations. Motives are of no value apart from the delimited societal situations for which

they are the appropriate vocabularies. They must be situated. At best, socially unlocated *terminologies* of motives represent unfinished attempts to block out social areas of motive imputation and avowal. Motives vary in content and character with historical epochs and societal structures.

Rather than interpreting actions and languages as external manifestations of subjective and deeper lying elements in individuals, the research task is the locating of particular types of action within typal frames of normative actions and socially situated clusters of motive. There is no explanatory value in subsuming various vocabularies of motives under some terminology or list. Such procedure merely confuses the task of explaining specific cases. The languages of situations as given must be considered a valuable portion of the data to be interpreted and related to their conditions. To simplify these vocabularies of motive into a socially abstracted terminology is to destroy the legitimate use of motive in the explanation of social actions.

John P. Hewitt &
Randall Stokes   34

Disclaimers

INTRODUCTION

Problematic events of varying seriousness occur in the concrete situations of everyday life: people are embarrassed by their own and others'

John P. Hewitt and Randall Stokes, "Disclaimers," *American Sociological Review*, vol. 40, February 1975, pp. 1–11. Reprinted by permission.

We are indebted to Rob Faulkner for his helpful comments on an earlier draft of this paper.

faux pas; serious and trivial departures from role obligations are noticed; rules are broken (or, more properly, certain actions are treated as rule violations); extraordinary, disturbing, or seemingly inexplicable behavior is observed in self or others.

Such problematic events are important for two reasons. First, they affect the course and outcome of social interaction. People gear their words and deeds to the restoration and maintenance of situated and cherished identities. When the violation of rules fractures the context of inter-action, or when the emergent meaning of a situation is disrupted, people endeavor to repair the breaks and restore meaning. Thus, if the direction of social interaction in a given situation is to be well understood, adequate concepts for handling such events are necessary.

Second, a conceptual grasp of the problematic features of identity, social interaction and emergent meaning is crucial to an understanding of the classic problem of social order and cultural continuity. While the sociological treatment of the problem is conventionally anchored in socialization and the internalization of culture, there are several difficulties with such a formulation, most notably that little routine action appears guided by deeply internalized norms. A discussion of problematic events aids in the reformulation of the link between culture and behavior, for it is in relation to such problematic occasions that culture most clearly enters the consciousness of actors, shapes the meaning of their conduct, becomes fundamental to their identities, and is thus made visible and re-affirmed.

Several concepts have been developed to deal with the problem of how actors restore disrupted meaning, repair fractured social interaction, and re-negotiate damaged identities. C. Wright Mills' (1940) conception of "vocabularies of motive"; Marvin Scott and Stanford Lyman's (1968) "accounts"; and John Hewitt and Peter Hall's (1970, 1973) "quasi-theories" each comes to grips with an important aspect of the dual problem of social interaction and culture in problematic situations.

For Mills, the most important feature of motives is that they arise in talk, whether as states of mind the person imputes to others or avows for himself. "As a word, a motive tends to be one which is to the actor and to the other members of a situation an unquestioned answer to questions concerning social and lingual conduct" (Mills, 1940:906). Motive talk is thus important to the ongoing construction of meaning in social interaction, since the continuity of both is sustained (in part) by people's ability to attribute their own and others' acts to "reasons" or "motives." While Mills addresses himself to the issue of how disrupted meaning is restored, his discussion lacks generality, since motive talk, while central to so-cial interaction, is not the only means of dealing with disrupted meaning.

The concepts of accounts and quasi-theories are also addressed, each in a particular way, to problematic meaning. Accounts are the justifications and excuses people offer when the course of interaction has been disrupted by an act or word. Quasi-theories are explanations people construct in social interaction to account for various kinds of problematic situations. Both concepts point to observable features of social interaction in which meaning is restored by efforts undertaken for that purpose. But these concepts are limited because their view of meaning and its reconstruction is largely *retrospective*—they deal with the definition of the past in the present. Neither deals adequately, nor is it intended to do so, with the anticipation of events, with the *prospective* construction of meaning for words and deeds that may be problematic.

This paper introduces, defines and discusses a new concept, the "disclaimer." Its level is that of the account and the quasi-theory: a process that occurs in social interaction in which problematic events that may disrupt emergent meaning are defined and dealt with. Unlike accounts and quasi-theories, which are retrospective in their effect, disclaimers are prospective, defining the future in the present, creating interpretations of potentially problematic events intended to make them unproblematic when they occur.

The Disclaimer

In order to define the disclaimer and describe its forms we must first attend to some major features of problematic meaning. As individuals in social interaction form their conduct in response to one another, meaning in their situation is created and maintained. The individual organizes meaning thematically: as behavior in the situation emerges he seeks to "fit" events to "theme" (McHugh, 1968). The relationship between the theme that organizes meaning and the specific acts or events that fit the theme is a reflexive one: events take on meaning when pattern is imputed to them; pattern is visible

only in the concrete events it is used to interpret. When events or acts no longer seem understandable in terms of the patterns imputed
to them, individuals examine discrepant events
with some care, seeking to determine what has
gone wrong with their understanding of the
situation.

Central to the themes used to organize meaning are identities. Whether defined on the basis
of conventional, named social roles (father, policeman, teacher) or interpersonal roles established
by specific individuals over time in relation to
one another (friend, follower, enemy), situated
identities are established and known to interactants. Indeed, the thematic organization of meaning by interactants usually depends upon their
ability to interpret each others' actions as manifestations of particular identities. It follows that
when events fail to fit themes in interaction, identities may come into focus as problematic: if the
acts of another fail to appear sensible in light of
his identity in the situation, perhaps he is not who
he appears to be.

The crucial place of identities in the organization of meaning points more generally to the importance of the process of typifying and the fact
of typification in social interaction (Schutz, 1964).
In their relations with one another, people search
for and make use of specific cues from others as
a means of typifying them, i.e., of treating them
as kinds of persons. Socialized individuals carry
with them a vast store of information as to how
various types of persons will behave, what they
are like, their typical motives and values, how
to deal with them, etc. In concrete situations they
search for cues from others, invoke a typification
that appears relevant to those cues and rely upon
the store of information organized by the typification in their subsequent interaction with the
other, filling in the "gaps" in the other's self-pres-
entation with the typification. Some typifications
are essentially identical in content to conventional and interpersonal roles (thus we carry typifications of fathers, enemies, policemen), while
others cut across the grain of roles, pointing to
other "types" that may, in given cases, be important, even controlling in social interaction (so, for
example, we carry typifications of the prejudiced,
stupid, incompetent, mentally ill, etc.).

Crucial to the concept of the disclaimer is
the fact that individuals *know* their own acts serve
as the basis for typifying them; they know that
specific acts they undertake will be treated by
others as cues for typification. They know this,
in the simplest sense, because they do it themselves, seeking in others' acts the "keys" that will
unlock the secrets of their behavior. Moreover,
with varying degrees of awareness, individuals
seek to present others with cues that will lead
to desired typifications of them—to present themselves in ways that will lead others to grant their
situated identity claims.

This awareness of typification (in general, if
not in specific cases) plays an important role in
the imaginative preconstructions of conduct that
go on continuously in the mental life of the individual. As individuals construct their acts in imagination, they anticipate the responses of others,
including the typificatory uses to which their acts
will be put. For the individual, any given act is
potentially a basis on which others can typify him.
Put another way, as the individual anticipates the
response to his conduct, he may see it either as
in line with an established identity or as somehow
discrepant, in which case it may be taken as a
cue for some new typification, possibly a negative
one, possibly a more favorable one.

Individuals' anticipation of others' typifications of them are not governed, however, by any
simple principle of seeking positive and avoiding
negative typifications. Life is filled with occasions
on which individuals find it necessary to engage
in acts that undermine the emergent meaning
of situations and make probable the destruction
of their identities in them. Even if they do not
feel constrained to act in such ways, individuals
may perceive opportunities—even legitimate
ones—in lines of action they know others will take
exception to. And on some occasions, individuals
may sense the possibility of being typified in ways
they would like to avoid, but find themselves without any certain way of anticipating the response.
Under such circumstances as these and others,
disclaimers are invoked.

A disclaimer is a verbal device employed to
ward off and defeat in advance doubts and negative typifications which may result from intended
conduct. Disclaimers seek to define forthcoming

conduct as not relevant to the kind of identity-challenge or re-typification for which it might ordinarily serve as the basis. Examples abound and serve to make the abstract concrete: "I know this sounds stupid, but . . ."; "I'm not prejudiced, because some of my best friends are Jews, but . . ."; "This is just off the top of my head, so . . ."; "What I'm going to do may seem strange, so bear with me." "This may make you unhappy, but . . ."; "I realize I'm being anthropomorphic. . . ."

In each of the foregoing examples, individuals display in their speech the expectation of possible responses of others to their impending conduct. In each example, a specific utterance calls the other's attention to a *possible* undesired typification and asks forbearance. Each phrase, in effect, disclaims that the word or deed to follow should be used as a basis for identity challenge and re-typification. The user's clear hope is that his intended act will not disrupt the current relationship, nor undesirably shift the emergent definition of the situation. Each disclaimer is thus a device used to sustain interaction, to manage the flow of meaning in situations, to negotiate a social order in which people can treat one another's acts with discretion, with good judgment, and with deserved good will.

Types of Disclaimers

The examples cited above, as well as others, can best be analyzed by sorting disclaimers into several types, each of which reflects a different set of conditions of use.

Hedging. There are countless situations in which individuals preface statements of fact or opinion, positions in arguments or expressions of belief with disclaimers of the following kind: "I'm no expert, of course, but . . ."; "I could be wrong on my facts, but I think . . ."; "I really haven't thought this through very well, but . . ."; "I'm not sure this is going to work, but let's give it a try"; "Let's play devil's advocate here. . . ."

What does the use of disclaimers of this type indicate about the individual's conduct and his expectations about others' responses? First, each

expression is an intentional signal of minimal commitment to the impending line of conduct, an indication of willingness to receive discrepant information, change opinions, be persuaded otherwise or be better informed. Put otherwise, such an expression indicates the tentative nature of forthcoming action. Second, the tentative or negotiable coloration given subsequent conduct indicates a measure of uncertainty about the likely response to the act. From the standpoint of the individual constructing his act, what he is about to say may be taken seriously and importantly by others, thus confirming his identity; or it may be taken by others as damaging to his identity, even as the basis for some new, controlling typification of him. He does not know. Third, the re-typification that may occur is at least potentially serious. While the individual may suspect that the worst that can happen is that he will be thought ill-informed or wrong-headed, he faces the possibility that his act may fundamentally transform him in the eyes of the other.

Minimal commitment and uncertain response are the defining conditions under which hedging takes place. Where an individual does not know how his act will be received and simultaneously does not think a positive response to his act is essential to his identity or his ends, he will hedge by disclaiming in advance the importance of the act to his identity. "I'm no expert" is a phrase that conveys to others the idea that no expert identity is being claimed; if no expertise is, in fact, shown, no claim needs to be defended. The phrase signals to hearers that they should treat factually faulty statements or deeds that have the wrong effects as the normal prerogative of people who are not and do not claim to be expert in what they are doing.

At the same time, variability in feared seriousness of response makes for variability within the category of hedging. At one extreme, a person may fear his words or deeds will drastically recast him in the eyes of others, and thus make attainment of his ends difficult. Persons who *are* expert, therefore, will often appeal to faulty memory, possible misunderstanding or over-specialization if they fear an impending act will lead to their re-typification as incompetent. Persons who occupy central, leadership positions in administrative organizations often adopt the practice of playing devil's advocate of positions they genuinely support, since they fear open and committed advocacy of position might erode their power and authority. At the other extreme, where people feel they have little to fear in the way of drastic re-typification, hedging is more like insurance, and often more like ritual; a way of reminding people that no great emphasis should be put on their success or failure, accuracy or error, in what they are about to say or do.

Credentialing.   Expressions of a different sort are employed when the individual *knows* the outcome of his act will be discrediting, but is nevertheless strongly committed to the act. Credentialing encompasses a group of expressions of this kind exemplified by the following: "I know what I'm going to say seems anthropomorphic, but . . ."; "I'm not prejudiced—some of my best friends are Jews, but . . ."; "Don't get me wrong, I like your work, but. . . .

In credentialing individuals seek to avoid an undesired typification they are certain will follow from an intended act. The expressions of credentialing try to accomplish this by establishing for the actor special qualifications or credentials that, he implies, permit him to engage in the act without having it treated in the usual way as a cue for typification. In the classic "some of my best friends" example, the speaker acknowledges that someone who says what he is about to say might be typified as a prejudiced person, but implies his friendships put him in a protected category of people who cannot be so typified. The man who sees human qualities in his dogs knows that speaking of them in an anthropomorphic way will make him seem foolish, and so seeks to avoid the typification by announcing he knows it could be made.

In this second example, knowledge of the negative aspects of an act is central to the establishment of a right to engage in the act anyway. Knowledge is a credential because it establishes the actor as one who may have *purpose* in what he is doing, so that others cannot easily regard him as an unknowing representative of a particular negative type. One who has purpose may have good purpose, whereas one who acts in blind ignorance of the implications of his act is presumed not to.

Sin Licenses.   Another category of expressions is employed when the actor is committted to a line of conduct and is certain of a negative response, but does not fear some specific undesired typification. In some instances of social interaction, actors anticipate that their acts will be treated as rule violations. Instead of a specific typification (e.g., racist, fool), the actor fears destruction of his identity as a "responsible member" of the encounter and the substitution of a "rule breaker" or "irresponsible member" typification of him. The focus of his talk and his concern is upon the rule which he fears will be invoked as a rebuke to his action. Hence the following examples: "I realize you might think this is the wrong thing to do, but . . ."; "I know this is against the rules, but . . ."; "What I'm going to do is contrary to the letter of the law but not its spirit. . . ."

Invoking the sin licensing disclaimer is equivalent to stipulating in advance that an act to follow might ordinarily be deemed a violation of a rule, and thus disruptive of the interaction that is taking place. The disclaimer is an effort to invoke in a specific situation the more general and commonly recognized principle that there are occasions on which rules may legitimately be violated without questioning the status of those who violate them. Just as accounts are invoked retrospectively as a way of placing rule violations in such a category, sin licensing disclaimers are invoked prospectively as a way of defining the conduct in advance. (But clearly there is less flexibility in the disclaimer—some excuses are good retrospectively but not prospectively.)

In many instances the sin licensing disclaimer is invoked seriously; that is, its user genuinely fears typification as a rule breaker. In other cases, however, where rules are routinely broken and participants aware of this fact, licenses to sin are requested and granted on a *pro forma* basis. In either case, the license to sin pays due respect to the rules even while establishing the conditions under which they may be broken.

Cognitive Disclaimers.   In routine social interaction, participants seldom have occasion to question one another's empirical grasp of the situation in which they are present. Participants generally assume substantive congruency between their own and others' grasp of the situation. Yet underlying any situation is the possibility that the words or deeds of one participant will be construed by others as lacking sense, as out of touch with empirical reality, as somehow indicating the individual's failure to perceive the situation adequately and correctly. While individuals generally assume that others will assume their acts make empirical sense, they know that some acts may be misconstrued, and that this misconstrual may lead to their own re-typification as lacking sense, as out of touch, as disengaged when they should be engaged, as irrational. Under conditions where they think their acts may be so questioned, individuals use cognitive disclaimers such as the following: "This may seem strange to you . . ."; "Don't react right away to what I'm going to do." "I know this sounds crazy, but I think I saw. . . ."

Cognitive disclaimers anticipate doubts that may be expressed concerning the speaker's capacity to recognize adequately the empirical facts of the situation in which he finds himself. By anticipating doubt, the disclaimer seeks to reassure others that there is no loss of cognitive capacity, that there is still agreement on the facts of the situation. In this form of disclaiming, as in the others, knowledge is a key element: by demonstrating in advance knowledge of a possible basis for re-typification, the individual establishes purpose for acts that might otherwise be taken as having no purpose, as reflecting a loss of cognitive control.

Appeals for the Suspension of Judgment. If much social interaction is pursued in situations in which people have common ends and work to achieve consensus on them and the means of attaining them, still in such interaction individuals recognize that on occasion their acts may offend even their friends. That is, people are aware that what they say and do may be offensive, angering or dismaying to those with whom they interact, unless and until they can place the act in a proper context, give it the "correct" meaning so far as the exchange is concerned. Under such circumstances, individuals appeal to their fellows to sus-

pend judgment until the full meaning of the act can be made known. "I don't want to make you angry by saying this, but . . ."; "Don't get me wrong, but . . ."; "Hear me out before you explode." are illustrative of appeals individuals make for the suspension of judgment.

Frequently such appeals take the form of appeals for the suspension of affect, in effect asking the other to hold back on what the actor fears will be a powerful affective response until full meaning can be transmitted. In other cases (e.g., "Don't react until I get this all out") the appeal is not to suspend specific affect, but merely to await full meaning. In either case, the disclaiming individual realizes that what he is about to do may disrupt the social situation, partly because the assumption of common purpose may be questioned, partly because it may promote his own re-typification as an "enemy" or "turncoat" and not a comrade, friend or colleague.

Responses to Disclaimers

The discussion has so far emphasized users' perspectives, grounding its classification in the intentions and expectations of those who disclaim. But the picture is incomplete until we grasp how it is that others respond to disclaimers and how their responses affect the course of social interaction.

From the user's standpoint, the disclaimer is an effort to dissociate his identity from the specific content of his words or deeds. Take, for example, the following use of credentialing: "I'm no racist, because I have a lot of black friends and associates, but I think black people want too much, too soon." In this and similar instances, two fundamental claims are made: first, there is an identity claim—specifically, a negative typification as a racist is disclaimed, and so the opposite, valued identity is claimed; second, there is a substantive claim—specifically, an expressed belief that blacks want improvements more quickly than they can or should be provided. People use disclaimers in order to secure the success of substantive claims, but without the possible negative implications for their identity claims.

By the phrase substantive claim we refer to

the fact that every word or deed has implications for the emerging definition of a situation and the joint action it contains. In the above illustration the substantive claim is a factual claim, that is, a statement that certain conditions are true of blacks. In other instances, substantive claims have to do with morality (e.g., "It is right to do what I am urging we do."), technical efficiency (e.g., "This is an appropriate way of doing things.") and the like. Every word or deed operates, in effect, as a claim that the situation should be defined in a certain way, or that it can be best defined in that way or that for all practical purposes that is the way to define it. While claims are not always (nor, perhaps, often) expressed in so many words, they operate to the same effect.

This distinction is crucial to our discussion of responses, for both uses of and responses to disclaimers proceed on these parallel levels of identity and substance. On one hand, others may either accept or reject the identity portion of the disclaimer, either attributing to the user the identity he seeks to avoid or supporting his existing identity in the situation. On the other hand (and somewhat independently of their response on the issue of identity), others may accept or reject the user's substantive claims, agreeing or disagreeing with his statements, regarding his actions as useful or dangerous, morally acceptable or prohibited.

From the user's point of view, a disclaimer is fully successful if it allows both types of claim to be accepted; the other concedes the substantive import of the user's actions or expressions and makes no undesired re-typification of him. In the example cited above, factual claims about blacks would be granted and no re-typification as a racist would take place. Under such a condition of "full success," we may assume, interaction proceeds on its course—a potential disturbance has been successfully skirted.

Less desirable, but still to be counted a partial success, is the condition where a substantive claim is rejected, but where a possible re-typification is not made. Following the same example, a result such as the following illustrates partial success: "I think you're wrong about the pace of black progress but, of course, I know you are not a racist." In this condition, while the user has failed to define the situation in the hoped-for manner,

he has at least succeeded in preserving his identity in the situation and avoiding re-typification.

In either of the above conditions, we can speak of the acceptance of a disclaimer in the sense that the user's identity is preserved intact. A disclaimer is said to be rejected when its user is typified by another in a negative way, whatever his response to the substantive claim. On one hand, it seems likely that most rejected disclaimers involve a rejection of both claims: the use of credentialing, as in the above example, would lead both to a denial of the factual claim being made *and* to the re-typification of the user as a racist. On the other hand, there is at least the logical possibility that a substantive claim will be granted, but that simultaneously the user will be re-typified. "Being right for the wrong reasons" is an illustration of a condition where factual claims are granted in the very process of altering a user's identity.

The acceptance or rejection of disclaimers is, however, a more complex and uncertain process than our elliptical discussion indicates. We have glossed over, thus far, the process of inference and signaling that is crucial to the outcome of a given disclaimer. The appropriate questions are the following: How is it that users infer acceptance or rejection of their claims? How is it that others signal acceptance or rejection of users' claims?

The questions of inference and signaling are, in the course of real social interaction, bound closely together; indeed, there is much reflexivity between the two. Whether a signal is, in fact, a signal is not concretely a matter of fact, but depends upon the interplay between the user's inference and the other's intent. What is intended to be a signal may be falsely construed or not construed at all, and what is not intended as a signal may be so construed, either favorably or unfavorably to the user's hopes. And part of the making of an inference involves its being made known to the other that an inference has been made, a linkage that is always subject to possible slippage.

For analytical purposes, however, we must separate inference and signaling. The former can be discussed by paying attention to the rules or procedures invoked by the user, whether inwardly or overtly, in an effort to determine the success of his disclaimer.

In the most elementary sense *prima facie* evidence of a disclaimer's success is to be sought in the other's overt response: if the response the user hoped to avoid is not forthcoming, he has evidence that his tactic has succeeded. If an interactant credentials his prejudicial statement, he may infer the success of his credentialing if no charge of prejudice is forthcoming. This will be so at the level of his identity claim, whatever the response given the substance of his action.

The possibility always exists, of course, that others will withhold cues that would enable the interactant to judge the success of his disclaimer. While much of our imagery of role playing and role taking suggests that actors are always forthcoming about their true judgments, there is no reason to assume that awareness contexts are typically open. Closed, pretense or suspicion awareness contexts may characterize the use and response to disclaimers as much as any other form of interaction. Thus, we must observe, inferences about success based on *prima facie* evidence must always be, for the actors who make them, somewhat tentative. Every use of a disclaimer risks the possibility that a user's identity may be damaged without his immediately discovering the damage.

More positively, users may infer acceptance or rejection from cues provided by others. Such cues, insofar as they are meant to signal acceptance, may take a variety of forms. The other may, for example, address himself explicitly to the issue raised by the disclaimer: "I realize you are no expert."; "I know you aren't prejudiced."; "I understand what you mean." These examples suggest responses that more or less explicitly signal the legitimacy of the disclaimer in the situation at hand. Sometimes the positive response may include the sharing of the disclaimer, which entails the other using an expression that indicates that he, also, shares the point of view of the user, that he too might, in similar circumstances, use the same disclaimer. We may assume that when others provide users with positive cues, inferences are made with more confidence and interaction continues on its course. Even here, however, there is slippage between intent and inference,

and a nod of the head that signifies to the user the acceptance of his viewpoint may be to the other a means of giving the user more rope with which to hang himself.

The question of inference and signaling also turns on the degree to which those who use disclaimers provide an opportunity for response. Social interaction is not always conducted with full attention to the etiquette of turn-taking; indeed, users of disclaimers may intentionally "rush" their interaction sequences in such a way that others are "left behind" and, having had no opportunity to object, are in the position of having agreed by default. An interaction sequence may be rushed by a refusal to yield the floor to another for a response or a refusal to "see" that the floor is wanted by another. A sequence may also be rushed where deeds follow so quickly upon words that commitments are made that cannot subsequently be escaped.

Opportunities for negative responses to disclaimers may also be limited if users are able to "finesse" interaction sequences. On the one hand, actors can "get away with" words and deeds that are gross threats to their identities if they undertake them in small steps, invoking seemingly minor disclaimers along the way. That is, small disclaimers are honored more readily, we may suggest, than large ones, but a series of small disclaimers may result in a major behavioral cue being treated as irrelevant to the actor's identity. On the other hand, it is not unreasonable to suppose that actors may on occasion make a disclaimer of far greater magnitude than their impending act calls for, knowing the other may thus be more likely to accept it. On any occasion where a disclaimer might be used, the user has some discretion in terms of associating his impending act with a possible negative typification of him. By exaggerating the possibly negative typification, and then proceeding with his word or deed, he hopes to secure acceptance by virtue of contrast.

The net outcome of successful disclaimers, whether the acceptance is voluntary or reflects the user's successful rushing or finessing of the interaction sequence, is that the user's identity in the situation is at least temporarily sustained. No re-typification in negative terms takes place, no disruption in the emergence of meaning occurs. Not only this, acceptance of a disclaimer, and particularly the acceptance of a series of disclaimers, commits both participants to the reciprocal identities being built up. As a situation proceeds and as disclaimers are employed successfully, we can hypothesize that it becomes more difficult for participants to reject subsequent disclaimers—the progressive solidification of identities lays the groundwork for easier disclaiming and, at some stage, makes it possible for actors to assume disclaimers and acceptances of one another rather than having to make each one explicitly.

How, then, are disclaimers rejected? What cues are sought or provided? What procedures are used to make inferences about acceptance? Again, in the simplest sense, *prima facie* evidence of rejection is to be found if the other explicitly avows what the disclaimer had sought to avoid. Rejection is certain if the other affirms that the very re-typification that the user feared is, in fact, to be made of him. "You should be an expert in this area!" "You've had plenty of time to work on a proposal." "If you know it's anthropomorphic, why are you saying it?" Expressions such as these are used as counters to disclaimers, indicating to the user in direct terms that his tactic has not worked, that he will be re-typified unless he can adduce evidence to show why he should not be.

The failure of a disclaimer makes its user subject to re-typification in the very terms his disclaimer provided to the other. This fact is both a weakness and a strength. It is a weakness, of course, because the use of a given disclaimer provides other interactants with a ready-made issue in terms of which the now-disrupted meaning of the context can be managed. Where hedging has been used, the issue is the identity of the user: thus, for example, a disclaimer of devil's advocacy may be met with a denial that only devil's advocacy is meant, that, in fact, the user is concealing his true purpose or goals, i.e., his true identity. Where credentialing has been employed, the issue becomes one of purpose or intent, specifically of good or bad intent, since the use of credentialing rests largely upon the implication that since the user knows the possibly evil connotations of

what he is about to do or say, he may have other than evil intent. Thus charges of evil purpose and identity concealment may also be made. Where sin licensing has been invoked, the issue turns on the applicability of a given rule to the act in question. Where cognitive disclaimers are used, the issue becomes one of fact and its interpretation. Where the appeal is to suspend judgment, the issue is whether, in the end, meaning was in fact clarified during the suspension.

To say that "the issue" turns upon this or that point is to say that the focus of interaction itself turns upon the disclaimer, its user's identity and the associated act. Since the user has, via his disclaimer, announced the problematic quality of his words or deeds, he has placed ready-made weapons at the disposal of the other. The question that arises at this point, therefore, is how interaction progresses when it focuses upon the disclaimer.

It is worth noting that up to this point, the user has sought to manage his own identity in the eyes of the other, whatever the outcome with respect to substantive claims. Now the issue is, basically, his identity, and what is important to the user is how that identity may be sustained. While the tactics of identity maintenance in such circumstances is a matter of empirical discovery, it seems likely that altercasting will play an important role in the proceedings.

Altercasting (Weinstein and Deutschberger, 1963) is a process in which actors endeavor to regulate the identities of others: going on the offensive in an argument, treating a particular child as the "baby of the family," creating a "straw man" and identifying an opponent with it are illustrations of the technique of altercasting. In each case, another's identity is governed, or an effort is made to have it be governed, by an actor's actions. (Altercasting is to be understood in contrast with identity as a phenomenon an actor manages for himself.)

The significance of altercasting in the disclaiming process lies in the fact that an identity established for another has implications for the identity of the altercaster. Identities are reciprocal, which is to say that participants in social interaction establish identities for themselves and each other in a mutually related texture where the position of one has implications for the position of another. In the disclaiming process, altercasting would appear to be significant because it offers the user a "last chance" to salvage his own identity by trying to establish for the rejecting other an identity that will reflect favorably on the rejected user. Having failed to disclaim an identity implied in his actions and utterances, the user may attempt to salvage his identity by more or less forcibly working on the identity of the other, seeking to portray the other in a light that makes his own discredit less serious, or even makes it disappear. Thus, to illustrate, the user may act towards the other as if the latter, too, shared in the discredit: following our example of the credentialing racist, the user may seek to apply the label racist to the other, perhaps by citing or alleging more serious violations on the part of the latter.

In addition to altercasting, the user may turn to various accounts (Scott and Lyman, 1968) as a way of extracting himself from his predicament. As a disclaimer is used and meets a negative response, it passes into the immediate past, and so becomes a proper object of an account. The user may excuse his conduct, thus defusing its relevance to his identity by accepting its undesirable nature by denying responsibility. Or he may attempt a justification, accepting responsibility but arguing for the irrelevance of his act to his identity.

The possible outcomes of rejected disclaimers, in terms of the course of the interaction and the identities of participants, are many, and difficult to summarize or generalize. Underlying all outcomes, however, is the basic fact that issues of substance have become transformed into issues of participants' identities. In effect, when disclaimers are rejected, a situation is transformed, with possibly unpleasant short and long-term consequences for the actor whose identity claims have been destroyed.

That a rejected disclaimer does not inevitably imply the loss of a desirable situated identity, and may in fact be a strength to the user, turns on the fact that a user may under some conditions *seek* to have his disclaimer rejected. If some actors are genuinely concerned with their identities in the eyes of others, others may be cynical in the use of disclaimers. Just as an individual may use

a disclaimer that is far out of proportion to the "real" implications of his conduct in the hopes that it will be more easily accepted, he may look ahead, construct alternative scenarios of the conversation on which he is embarked and choose disclaimers in such a way that discussion turns on issues he can best argue. If his disclaimer is accepted, he is able to pursue the line of conduct he had in mind. If it is rejected, he is in a relatively strong position to argue his case, to portray his partner's characterization of him as a "straw man," even though he is himself the source of the characterization.

CONCLUSION: THE DISCLAIMER AND SOCIAL THEORY

The disclaimer and the broader current of thought of which it is a part have significance for a long-standing problem in social theory. This is the question of how culture enters individual action or, more broadly, how social order and continuity are maintained. Culture, in most formulations, is the root of continuity. Parsons, (1966:5–7) for example, visualizes culture as akin to the genetic code of physical organisms. Just as the genetic pool of a species provides the parameters for individual phenotypes, so does culture provide the persisting identity for individual actions and interaction. Yet, the crucial question of how culture enters individual action has not been satisfactorily answered.

The most important link between culture and action is generally seen to be the socialization process. Following Mead's seminal account of the generalized other, and de-emphasizing his concern for emergence, heaviest stress has been placed on *internalization* as the means by which culture is transmitted and becomes influential upon action. From this perspective, internalization constitutes a functional equivalent to instinct in other animal species; the bee's dance is guided by a genetic template and man's by a deeply internalized normative structure. Although the origins of control are different, the consequences are the same. In both cases, the direction and substance of action are provided by a precognitive and involuntary hierarchy of preferences. In those (relatively rare) situations where deviance does occur, the reason is seen to be incomplete or faulty socialization and the link of culture to behavior is then maintained by mechanisms of external control in the form of sanctions.

The perspective sketched, or perhaps caricatured, above has been seriously questioned in recent years. The fundamental root of such questioning is empirical. While it is clear that certain cultural elements are deeply internalized, particularly language-based logical and inferential canons, primal esthetic preferences and so on, relatively little of routine social action appears to be guided by deeply internalized normative structures. Man does not act like a well-programmed social robot; indeed, in much of everyday social action, variation from normatively prescribed behavior is statistically "normal."

This point has been made from a number of different theoretical perspectives. Dennis Wrong (1961) has argued from a psychoanalytical perspective that sociologists typically err by viewing man as "over-socialized." Sociology, he claims, has historically failed to take account of residual and unsocialized libidinal energy, which continues to exert a dynamic and "unsocial" influence on individual action. David Riesman (1950) and Allen Wheelis (1958), while they don't dispute that traditional views of the link between action and culture may have fitted some earlier time, contend that such models are increasingly inappropriate for contemporary society. Modern man, they argue, is given by his socialization a diffuse capacity to read social cues and to make situationally appropriate responses, rather than any deeply internalized normative set.

A third important critique of internalization as the link between action and culture has emerged from the interactionist and neo-phenomenological traditions. In radical contrast to structural theorists who tend to view culture as given, interactionist and neo-phenomenological theorists are most concerned with the creative and problematic aspects of the relationship between action and culture. Erving Goffman's (1959) vision of the presentation of self as an often laborious and conscious "fitting" of one's line of conduct to cultural norms, Ralph Turner's (1962) substitution of "role-making" for "role-playing,"

and the ethnomethodological explications of the *et cetera* rule and similar subroutines (cf. Cicourel, 1970) all convey the same essential point: culture is largely exterior to the person and often problematic.

The foregoing questions and reconceptualizations have made the issue of cultural, and thus social, continuity particularly pressing. If indeed there is minimal deep internalization of culture, at least in contemporary society, how do we account for social order? How is it, faced with the ambiguities and contradictions of a complex society, that normative continuity and meaning are sustained in the actions of diverse and individualistic actors?

For a start, it would be well to view culture as learned, and only approximately so, instead of as internalized. Rather than being somehow akin to instinct, culture is best seen as a kind of shifting cognitive map of the social order and largely within the awareness of the actor. From this point of view, culture is environmental to action. It constitutes one of several sets of parameters within which action is framed. Although there is considerable openness to action, culture, meaning here situationally appropriate norms, meanings and judgmental standards, must be taken into account as the actor constructs his line of conduct. The disclaimer, along with accounts and vocabularies of motives, are among the means by which actors "take account" of culture. In the interests of preserving cathected identities, of making situations sensible, and of facilitating interaction, actors explicitly define the relation between their questionable conduct and prevailing norms. Collectively these might be called "aligning actions" in the sense that they are intended to serve as means of bringing problematic conduct into line with cultural constraints. The net consequence of aligning actions is to perpetuate normative order and meaning in the face of lines of conduct which are objectively at variance with situational norms and understandings.

REFERENCES

Cicourel, Aaron. "Basic and Normative Rules in the negotiation of Status and Role." *Recent Sociology: II.*

Edited by Hans Peter Dreitzel. New York: Macmillan, 1970, pp. 4–45.

Goffman, Erving. *The Presentation of Self in Everyday Life.* Garden City: Anchor, 1959.

Hall, Peter M., and John P. Hewitt. "The Quasi-theory of Communication and the Management of Dissent." *Social Problems* 18 (Summer 1970): 17–27.

Hewitt, John P. and Peter M. Hall. "Social Problems, Problematic Situations, and Quasi-Theories." *American Sociological Review* 38 (June 1973): 367–74.

McHugh, Peter. *Defining the Situation.* New York: Bobbs-Merrill, 1968.

Mills, C. Wright. "Situated Actions and Vocabularies of Motive." *American Sociological Review* 5 (October 1940):904–13.

Parsons, Talcott. *Societies: Evolutionary and Comparative Perspectives.* Englewood Cliffs, N.J.: Prentice-Hall, 1966.

Riesman, David. *The Lonely Crowd.* Garden City: Anchor, 1950.

Schutz, Alfred. *Collected Papers: II.* Edited by Maurice Natanson. The Hague: Nijhoff, 1964.

Scott, Marvin B. and Stanford M. Lyman. "Accounts." *American Sociological Review* 33 (February 1968): 46–62.

Turner, Ralph. "Role-taking: Process Versus Conformity." *Human Behavior and Social Process.* Edited by Arnold Rose. Boston: Houghton Mifflin, 1962.

Weinstein, Eugene and Paul Deutschberger. "Some Dimensions of Altercasting." *Sociometry* 26 (December 1963):454–66.

Wheelis, Allen. *The Quest for Identity.* New York: Norton, 1958.

Wrong, Dennis. "The Oversocialized Conception of Man in Modern Sociology." *American Sociological Review* 26 (April 1961):183–93.

SELECTED REFERENCES
PART FOUR

Berger, Peter L., and Thomas Luckman. *The Social Construction of Reality.* Garden City, N.Y.: Doubleday & Company, Inc., 1966. A valuable theoretical bridge between the sociology of knowledge and social psychology.

Blumer, Herbert. "Attitudes and the Social Act." *Social Problems,* vol. 3 (October 1955), pp. 59–65. A critique of "attitude," one of the most widely used concepts in social psychology.

Burke, Kenneth. *Permanence and Change.* New York: New Republic, 1936, pp. 30–53. An early statement on the relation between language and motives. Burke is also the author of the more recent *The Grammar of Motives* (New York: Prentice-hall, Inc., 1945) and *The Rhetoric of Motives* (New York: Prentice-Hall, Inc., 1950), which present this relationship in much greater detail.

Carroll, John B. (ed.). *Language, Thought, and Reality: Selected Writings of Benjamin Lee Whorf.* New York: John Wiley & Sons, Inc., and the Technology Press of Massachusetts Institute of Technology, 1956. Includes articles on the role of language in shaping perception and thought.

Cassirer, Ernst. *An Essay on Man.* New Haven: Yale University Press, 1944, pp. 27–56. Expounds the nature and function of symbols, which account for the evolution "from animal responses to human responses."

Foote, Nelson N. "Identification as the Basis for a Theory of Motivation." *American Sociological Review,* vol. 16 (February 1951), pp. 14–21. A useful companion piece to the selection in this part by Mills.

Langer, Suzanne. *Philosophy in a New Key.* New York: Penguin Books, Inc., 1942, pp. 42–63. On the logic of signs and symbols.

Levy, David M. "The Act as a Unit." *Psychiatry,* vol. 25 (November 1962), pp. 295–309. A psychiatrist adapts Mead's concept of the act to the analysis of mental disorder.

McCall, George J., and J. L. Simmons. *Identities and Interactions: An Examination of Associations in Everyday Life.* New York: The Free Press, 1966. A "refined version of symbolic interaction theory and the exchange theory of interaction."

Mead, George Herbert. *Mind, Self and Society.* Chicago: the University of Chicago Press, 1934, pp. 67–74 and 94–125. Descriptions of the development of significant symbols and the process of minded behavior.

Miyamoto, S. Frank. "The Social Act: Re-examination of a Concept." *Pacific Sociological Review,* vol. 2 (Fall 1959), p. 51–55. Emphasizes the need for research on "the organized character of the interactional process."

Perinbanayagam, R. S. "The Definition of the Situation: An Analysis of the Ethnomethodological and Dramaturgical Views." *Sociological Quarterly,* vol. 15

(Autumn 1974), pp. 521–541. A comparison of two viewpoints in definitions of situations.

Scott, Marvin B., and Stanford M. Lyman. "Accounts." *American Socological Review,* vol. 33 (December 1968), pp. 46–52. Concerned with the "acceptable utterances" people make in accounting for their untoward actions.

Stebbins, Robert H. "Putting People on: Deception of Our Fellowman in Everyday Life." *Sociology and Social Research,* 59 (April 1975), p. 189–200. Dramatistic interpretation.

Stewart, Kenneth L. "On 'Socializing' Attitudes: A Symbolic Interactionist View." *Sociological Focus,* 8 (January 1975), pp. 37–46. Attitudes as part of acts.

Strauss, Anselm L. *Mirrors and Masks.* Glencoe, Illinois: The Free Press, 1959. Examines some of the relationships between the definitions we apply to persons or other objects and our "plans of action" toward them.

Strong, Samuel W. "A Note on George H. Mead's 'The Philosophy of the Act.'" *American Journal of Sociology,* vol. 45 (July 1939), pp. 71–76. A good but difficult summary of the concept "the act."

Vigotsky, L. S. "Thought and Speech." *Psychiatry,* vol. 2 (February 1939), pp. 29–52. Argues for the indentity of thought and speech, as opposed to the conception of speech as merely the means for expressing thought.

White, Leslie T. "Mind Is Minding." *Scientific Monthly,* vol. 48 (1939), pp. 169–171. An eminent anthropologist views mind as behavior, paralleling the functionalist views of Dewey and Mead.

Williams, Robin M., Jr. "A Neglected Form of Symbolic Interactionism in Sociological Work: Book Talks Back to Author," *The American Sociologist,* vol. 11 (May 1976), pp. 94–103. An imaginative depiction of the "internal conversation" involved in writing a book.

PART five

Research
Implications and
Applications

At this point, we depart from the prior emphasis on an exposition of the basic principles of symbolic interactionism. While the preceding material analyzed the concepts and propositions of the perspective, in this section the readings present heuristic implications and illustrative analysis documenting the broad range of symbolic interactionist research. The topics include, among other things, family life, courtroom procedures, marihuana users, visible handicaps, mental patients, etc. Whether using qualitative or quantitative techniques of analysis, the researchers adhere to the basic methodological proposition: An understanding of human conduct requires study of the actors' covert behavior. Consequently, we find examinations of the meanings, definitions, images, and self-conceptions involved in both individual behavior and social interaction.

The article by Sheldon Stryker does much to refute the widely held view that symbolic interactionism does not generate researchable hypotheses. Not only does he indicate some of the questions on the family that emerge from the theory but also he suggests the kind of answers such research can provide. One of the important questions he raises is, Why are some fathers more committed to this role than others? A possible answer involves the relationship of significant others to differential self-identification.

The British courtroom is the focus of the article by Pat Carlen. Drawing upon the dramaturgic perspective, Carlen views the magistrates' court as a theater of the absurd. He shows how judicial personnel stage impressive, ritualistic performances aimed at convincing defendants, witnesses, and other observers of their credibility. In his view, the outcome is a senseless procedure of scant relevance to justice.

Although some critics of symbolic interactionism have argued that it is relevant only to understanding "normal" behavior, a substantial research literature is dispelling that notion. Symbolic interactionist research has contributed greatly to understanding the sociology and social psychology of deviance. The next four articles are cases in point. They deal with the specific ways deviant behavior is learned from others, including the various influences upon an individual's interpretations of personal experience and the effects of derogatory labels upon self-conceptions and social relationships.

Howard S. Becker's widely cited article describes how individuals learn to define the use of marihuana in terms favoring the continuation of such use. From fifty interviews with marihuana users, Becker derives a generalized sequence of stages culminating in the ability to enjoy marihuana use.

Interviews also supply the basic data of the selection by Teresa E. Levitin. Although many studies of the labeling process stress its negative effects upon the individual, she is concerned with the active efforts of the visibly handicapped to *resist* the deviant role and self-image. Levitin indicates that there are differing modes of resistance by the permanently handicapped from those used by the temporarily disabled. In both circumstances, however, her data reveal that their behaviors are not mechanical and inflexible responses to others, but are meaningful efforts to maintain personal identity and wholeness.

Clear support for the symbolic interactionist perspective, specifically in the study of deviant or disvalued behavior, is evident in the study by William R. Rosengren. His research, conducted over a period of six months, combines direct observation with several types of questionnaires. His data show that changes in self-conception tend to be associated with changes in the overt behavior of a small sample of emotionally disturbed boys.

Erving Goffman's earlier article (in Part III) is a useful preface to his study of the moral career of the mental patient. Although the concept of career is usually restricted to the professions, Goffman demonstrates its utility for explaining the changes in the self-conception of the patient in a mental institution. His article provides a detailed analysis of these changes as they take place during the pre-patient, in-patient, and ex-patient phases of this career.

Arlene K. Daniels, author of the concluding article in this Part, describes her article as "radical symbolic interactionism." Apparently influenced by the phenomenologists and ethnomethodologists, this paper examines the ways in which the label "mental illness" is assigned by military psychiatrists. The method and perspective of this paper attest to the viability and modifiability of symbolic interactionism.

A recurring criticism of symbolic interactionism has been its putative nonempirical character. Along with the selections in the preceding parts of this book, the articles in Part V may offset such criticism, although they represent only a small portion of the expanding body of symbolic interactionist research.

Symbolic Interaction
as an Approach to Family Research

Various commentators have stated that the ideas covered by the label symbolic interaction are part of the intellectual baggage of almost all who concern themselves with human behavior. On the other hand, persons identifying themselves as symbolic interactionists commonly hold that this theory suffers from general, albeit certainly undeserved, neglect. There is a good deal of validity in both views. Many social psychologists have made at least some of the ideas of symbolic interaction part of their theoretical equipment, whether or not they are aware of their debt. Yet the implications of this theoretical scheme are not always perceived and appreciated even by men calling themselves symbolic interactionists. The problem seems to be that at least some of the once-novel ideas of the theory have become, for many, simple commonplaces or platitudes, and like most platitudes, more likely to defeat thought than to stimulate it.

This paper is above all an attempt at a straightforward review of symbolic interaction theory. Its aim is to stimulate renewed interest in a simple, but relatively powerful, set of ideas which remains largely unexploited. It is perhaps particularly in the family field that these are open to exploitation.

Sheldon Stryker, "Symbolic Interaction as an Approach to Family Research," *Marriage and Family Living*, vol. 21 (May 1959), pp. 111–119. Copyright 1959 by National Council on Family Relations. Reprinted by permission.

A slightly amended version of a paper presented to the 21st Groves Conference on Marriage and the Family, Washington, D.C., April 15, 1958.

The theory being dealt with has a venerable tradition, beginning at least as far back as Hegel. Modern formulations have their roots in American pragmatism, in the writings of Peirce and James. Suggestions contained here were elaborated and systematized by James Mark Baldwin, John Dewey, Charles Horton Cooley and, most important of all, George Herbert Mead. Specifically in the family field, Waller, Burgess, Hill, and Foote represent persons whose work, to important degree, stems from this framework.

There is no single orthodoxy which is symbolic interaction theory. There is certainly a hard core of agreement, and there are certainly important differences, among representatives of the position. Some see it as no more than a set of concepts serving to sensitize one to aspects of social life, some as a general theory of human behavior. The present discussion proceeds on another view, which sees the theory as addressing itself to a relatively modest series of questions.

Theory can be taken to mean a set of assumptions or postulates with which one approaches some part of the empirical world, a set of concepts in terms of which this part of the world is described, and a set of propositions, emerging from the assumptions and relating the concepts, about the way this part of the world "works" which are checked against observations of that world. This presentation begins by noting briefly the general questions to which symbolic interaction theory is addressed, and turns successively to the assumptions underlying the theory, the concepts provided by the theory, and illustrative instances of the propositions which are the answers to its questions. It concludes by considering some of the implications of the theory for family research.

THE PROBLEMS TO WHICH THE THEORY IS ADDRESSED

As a social psychological theory, symbolic interaction addresses a set of interrelated questions, most of which take their place in the context of two major problems. The first is that of socialization: how the human organism acquires the ways of behaving, the values, norms and attitudes of the social units of which he is a part. The focus here is on development—that which happens over time to the human neophyte: the infant, the recruit entering the army, the student entering the university, the bride entering a new set of family relationships.

The twin of the problem of socialization is that of personality: the organization of persistent behavior patterns. Such organization cannot be assumed but must be demonstrated and accounted for. The task of a social psychology is to account for such organization insofar as it depends upon social relationships. It should be added that symbolic interaction addresses itself largely to the normal person—in the sense of the person without gross physical, physiological, or psychological defect.

To say that this position is oriented to the normal person is not to say that it is concerned only with personal organization, for the theory seeks to explore personal disorganization as well. As a matter of fact, one of the strengths of this position is that it treats personal organization and personal disorganization as facets of the same problem, rather than different problems, and that it can provide answers to both without invoking principles lying outside its theoretical scheme.

These are the major problems which symbolic interaction theory seeks to resolve. They have been stated in general form, for more specific formulation depends on the assumptions and concepts with which the theory approaches the parts of the world in which it has interest.

ASSUMPTIONS

The initial assumption is that, insofar as interests are social psychological, man must be studied on his own level. The position of symbolic interactionism is anti-reductionist; it argues that valid principles of human social psychological behavior cannot be derived from, or inferred from, the study of non-human forms. This assertion rests on the principle of emergence. Emergence suggests the existence of qualitative differences as well as quantitative continuities among the precipitates of the evolutionary process. If man is qualitatively different in some respects from other animal forms, it follows that principles derived from other forms cannot completely account for his behavior. The task of at least some social psychologists is to focus on that which is different in man.

A second assumption is that the most fruitful approach to man's social behavior is through an analysis of society. This assumption involves no assertion of some metaphysical priority of society over the individual. Social psychologists of one stripe have argued that society is *the* ultimate reality; social psychologists of another variety give ontological precedence to the individual, denying the reality of society. Either position leads to confusion and contradiction. Symbolic interaction has not resolved the argument; but it has bypassed it. It has done so by beginning its analyses with the social act. Its basic unit of observation is interaction, and from interaction both society and individual derive. It is worth noting that this formulation permits an articulation between sociology and social psychology which alternative frameworks can forge, if at all, only with great difficulty. Both begin with the same "building bricks": social actions. Sociology builds in one direction to the behavior of collectivities. Social psychology builds in another direction to the behavior of individuals. Those whose problems bridge the two fields, as is true of many students of the family, are provided with a framework facilitating movement from one level to the other, allowing systematic transactions between the two levels.

A third assumption concerns the equipment with which the newborn enters life. The human infant is, from this point of view, neither social nor antisocial, but rather asocial. It has the potentialities for social development. It is an active organism, it has "impulses," but these impulses are not channelized or directed toward any specific ends. Original nature is amorphous and plastic; it lacks organization.

A last assumption is that the human being is actor as well as reactor. The human being does not simply respond to stimuli occurring outside himself, In fact, what is a stimulus depends on the activity in which the organism is engaged: objects become stimuli when they serve to link impulses with satisfactions. The environment of the organism is a selected segment of the "real" world, the selection occurring in the interests of behavior which the human being himself has initiated. It is the assumption which leads to the fundamental methodological principle of symbolic interactions the demand that the investigator see the world from the point of view of the subject of his investigation.

These seem to be the assumptions underlying symbolic interaction theory. Not an assumption, but closely related to those discussed, is a predilection on the part of adherents of this theory to stay close to the world of everyday experience. The viewpoint develops out of such experience, and it is with such experience that it seeks to deal.

MAJOR CONCEPTS

An assumption of this theory, again, is emergence. The principle emergent on the human level is language behavior. The initial concern in this review of concepts thus must be with language and its correlatives.

The starting point is with the *act:* behavior by an organism stemming from an impulse requiring some adjustment to appropriate objects in the external world. A *social act* is one in which the appropriate object is another individual. But another individual does not "stand still"; he, too, acts with reference to the first actor. Thus every social act implicates at least two individuals, each of whom takes the other into account in the processes of satisfying impulses. Since such acts occur

over time, they have a history. This makes possible the appearance of *gestures,* defined as any part of the act which stands for, or comes to be a sign of, those parts of the act yet to occur. Thus, in responding to one another, individuals may be involved in what Mead called a "conversation of gestures": they may come to use early stages of one anothers' acts as indicators of later stages. Such gestures have meaning. Vocal sounds can serve as gestures, and they too may have meaning. The meaning of a gesture (an early stage of an act) is the behavior which follows it (the later stages of the act): meaning is, by definition, behavior. Some gestures have an additional property. They may mean the same thing, imply the same set of subsequent behaviors, to the organism which produces the gesture and that which perceives it. When this occurs, the gesture becomes a *significant symbol*. To illustrate: the cry of the infant may serve as a sign of hunger to the mother, and she responds by feeding the infant. The cry is a gesture whose meaning lies in the parental response. At a later stage, the child may call out "milk!" and, unless the appropriate parental response is made, protest vigorously. The word "milk" is here a significant symbol. Language, basically, is a system of significant symbols. This is equivalent to asserting that language is a system of shared meanings, and this in turn implies that language is a system of shared behavior. Communication between human beings presupposes these characteristics of language symbols.

Retreat is necessary before going forward. Symbols arise in the context of social acts, and they function in completing acts: they reflect the interests from which the acts stem. We respond to symbols as predicters of further behavior, our own as well as that of others. Since these symbols predict later behavior, they provide a basis for adjusting our activity before that later behavior has occurred. Thus symbols may be said to function in the context of the act in place of that which they symbolize, and may further be said to organize behavior with reference to that which is symbolized. Symbols entail a plan of action. To illustrate and summarize:

Thus if one hunter shouts to another, "A duck!" the second hunter immediately looks into the air and makes appropriate preparations for shooting at a bird on the wing. If the first hunter shouts, "Rabbit!" his partner responds in a different manner. Language symbols do not merely stand for something else. They also indicate the significance of things for human behavior, and they organize behavior toward the thing symbolized.[1]

Some symbols represent generalizations of behavior toward objects; these are *categories*. To categorize is to apply a class term to a number of objects, to signify that a number of different things are, for certain purposes, to be treated as the same kind of thing. Classification or categorization is essential to activity, for life would be impossible if one were forced to respond to every object in the world as unique. Class terms, or categories, are of course symbols, and as such they share the characteristics of symbols. They have meaning, they are cues to behavior, and they organize behavior.

Humans respond to a classified world, one whose salient features are named and placed into categories indicating their significance for behavior. In short, humans do not respond to the environment as physically given, but to an environment as it is mediated through symbols— to a *symbolic environment*. Persons frequently enter situations in which their behavior is problematic. Before they can act, they must define the situation, that is, represent it to themselves in symbolic terms. The products of this defining behavior are termed "definitions of the situations."

A particularly important kind of category is that called "position."[2] Positions are socially recognized categories of actors, any general category serving to classify persons: father, sergeant, teacher are positions by this usage, as are playboy, intellectual, blacksheep.

The significance of such categories is that they serve to organize behavior toward persons so categorized. An equivalent assertion is that in attaching one of these position designations to a person we are led to expect certain behaviors from him and we behave toward him on the basis of these expectancies. To the expectations with regard to behavior attached to a position the term "role" is given. These expectations are social in the same sense symbolic behavior is always social: the ultimate meaning of the positions to which these expectations apply is shared behavior. They are social in another and most important sense, namely, that it is impossible to talk about *a* position without reference to some context of *other* positions: one cannot talk about the behavior of father except with reference to the positions of mother, child, and so on. Thus every position assumes some counter-position, and every role presumes some counter-role. To use the term "role" is necessarily to refer to an interpersonal relation.

The discussion of categories has been couched in terms of an actor responding to objects in the external world, including people, by classifying them in functionally relevant ways. Under certain circumstances, an actor may apply such categories to himself: he may respond to himself as he responds to other people, by naming, defining, classifying himself. To engage in this kind of behavior is to have a *self*. Self can be defined in various ways, each calling attention to slightly different aspects of the same activity. Mead defined the self as that which is an object to itself. Others have discussed the self as a set of responses of an organism serving to organize other responses of the same organism. It is useful in the present context to define the self in terms of categories one applies to himself, as a set of self-identifications.

However defined, self refers to activity, to reflexive activity, and not to an object, thing, or essence. It is a necessary concept, from the standpoint of the symbolic interactionist, but it is one fraught with the dangers of reification. As Robert W. White notes:[3]

The necessity of using the concept of self does not confer the privilege of misusing it. As we use concepts in our thinking, they tend to get firmer and harder. Thought about fluid events tends to curdle

---

[1] Alfred R. Lindesmith and Anselm L. Strauss, *Social Psychology*, New York: Dryden Press, 1956, p. 63.

[2] Others have used the term "status" here. I prefer "position" in order to avoid the hierarchical implications of status. Positions may certainly be hierarchized, but hierarchy and position are conceptually distinct and it is important to distinguish between them.

[3] Robert W. White, *The Abnormal Personality*, New York: Ronald Press, 1948, p. 140.

and form solid clots. Before long we begin to think of the self as if it were a lump in the personality. It becomes a region, an institution, an entity. . . . In the end the self is standing like a solid boulder of granite in the midst of personality, and one's thinking about it is as flexible as granite.

The self is defined in terms of socially recognized categories and their corresponding roles. Since these roles necessarily imply relationships to others, the self necessarily implies such relations. One's self is the way one describes to himself his relationships to others in a social process.

The discussion thus far has presumed but not made explicit the concept of "role-taking," or alternatively, "taking the role of the other." Role-taking refers to anticipating the responses of others implicated with one in some social act. The meaning of the concept can best be elucidated through illustration. Consider the classroom instructor who presents to his students an especially difficult conception. He perhaps finds that the words ordinarily used to cover the topic do not allow the discussion to proceed beyond the immediate issue. He then casts about for words which will allow him to clarify the conception, and so allow him to move beyond it to further materials. How shall he select such words? Presumably he will do so in terms of what he knows or guesses about the backgrounds or experiences of the students before him. He will, in other words, attempt to put himself in the place of the students; he will attempt to anticipate their responses to the words he will use. He takes the role of the other.

Role-taking may involve the anticipation of responses of some particular other. More frequently, it involves the anticipation of responses of what Mead called the "generalized other." To revert to the classroom illustration, the instructor must deal with the class not as discrete individuals but as an organized unit, the members of which can be expected to behave in differentiated yet related ways. To take the role of the generalized other is to see one's behavior as taking place in the context of a defined system of related roles. The concept of reference group, as it is currently used, represents partially a restatement and partially an extension of the generalized other concept.

In comparatively recent work, the concept of "significant other" has come into use. This concept represents the recognition that, in a fragmented and differentiated world, not all the persons with whom one interacts have identical or even compatible perspectives; and that, therefore, in order for action to proceed, the individual must give greater weight or priority to the perspectives of certain others. To speak, then, of significant others is to say that given others occupy high rank on an "importance" continuum for a given individual.

One last set of concepts must be mentioned. Symbolic interaction makes unashamed use of "mental" concepts such as thinking, volition, and self-consciousness. The case can be put in stronger fashion; its judgment is that any scheme which rules out such concepts distorts the facts of human experience. However, its usage of these terms is not traditional. Where frequently these concepts are defined in such way as to place them outside the bounds of scientific discourse, symbolic interaction defines these terms behavioristically and, in so doing, permits their treatment within the conventions of scientific procedure. Thus, thinking is defined as the internalized manipulation of language symbols. Volition becomes the process of selecting among alternatives symbolically present in the experience of the individual. And self-consciousness is the activity of viewing oneself from the standpoint of others.

THE ANSWERS PROVIDED BY THE THEORY: ILLUSTRATIVE CASES

It will be impossible, given limitations of space, to do full justice to the complexities of the problems raised or the explanations provided by symbolic interaction theory; all that can be done is to review these in barest outline.

The problem of socialization has a number of interrelated facets, among them questions of how meanings are obtained by the human infant, how the self develops and is structured, and how thinking and objectivity arises in the course of experience.

The human infant, active but unorganized, is born into an ongoing set of social relationships. Such relationships are premised upon a set of shared meanings. The infant acts, but randomly: he thrashes his arms, he exercises his vocal cords. The adult responds to these actions, say the crying of the infant, by doing something to the infant— he feeds it, or changes it, or turns it over on its stomach. He will eventually find that response which will complete the act in a desired way, that is, stop the crying. There is in this situation an "impulsive" act which is, incipiently, a gesture, and there is incipient meaning as well. The incipient meaning is that part of the act supplied by the adult. In time, both the cry of the infant and the response of the adult become specialized; when this occurs, the cry is a gesture in the previously-defined sense. The significant point is that, since it is the adult who completes the act, it is he who supplies the meaning of the gesture. What kinds of completions will he supply? He is, of course, limited by the repertory of meanings available in the social unit of which he is a part. Further, the adult will have defined the situation, including his positional relationship to the infant, for example, that of father to son, and this definition will invoke the set of expected behaviors we call the role of the father. If the father is a middle class American, and if he takes the cry of the infant to mean that the infant is thirsty, his response will be to supply milk or water—but not wine or whiskey. The meanings attached to the gestures of the infant are social meanings, and they are supplied through his relationships with already socialized participants in an ongoing society.

The early activity of the child will include random vocalization. Eventually, too, he will imitate sounds others make. Others respond to the initially random vocalization by selecting out particular sounds and responding to these. They respond to the imitated sounds as well by acts which contain the adult meanings of these sounds. For the child, the correspondence between sound and meaning will be initially vague, but in the process of interaction over time the correspondence will become more pronounced. So, for example, the child may use the sound "ba" to refer to any approximately round object and, having played this game with daddy, may be led to roll any such object—ball, orange, egg—around the floor. The response of parent to the rolling of an egg—especially an uncooked one—will soon make clear that an egg is not a "ba" and thus is not to be rolled on the floor. In the course of time, child and parent will come to agree on what is and is not a ball, and thus a significant symbol will have come into existence. A sound, initially meaningless to the child, comes to mean for the child what it already means for the adult.

The "self" comes into existence in the same way. Just as the sound "ba" took on meaning through the responses of others, so too the human organism as an object takes on meaning through the behavior of those who respond to that organism. We come to know what we are through others' responses to us. Others supply us with a name, and they provide the meaning attached to that symbol. They categorize us in particular ways—as an infant, as a boy, et cetera. On the basis of such categorization, they expect particular behaviors from us; on the basis of these expectations, they act toward us. The manner in which they act towards us defines our "self," we come to categorize ourselves as they categorize us, and we act in ways appropriate to their expectations.

The evolution of the self is, of course, gradual; moreover, it is continual. This development is one of increasing complexity, in a sense, for as the child moves into the social world he comes into contact with a variety of persons in a variety of self-relevant situations. He comes, or may come, into contact with differing expectations concerning his behavior, and differing identities on which these expectations are based. Thus he has, through the role-taking process, a variety of perspectives from which to view and evaluate his own behavior, and he can act with reference to self as well as with reference to others. In short, the socialization process as described makes possible the appearance of objectivity. Furthermore, since these processes may be internalized through the use of language symbols, it also makes possible the appearance of self-control.

The individual, at the same time and through time as well, occupies a variety of positions in sets of social relationships. If he responded in each of these in terms of unique sets of role-expectations and self-definitions, his behavior would be discontinuous. Usually, however, there is a continuity and organization among the behaviors of a given individual. The question is how such personal organization can be accounted for. The basic answer provided by symbolic interaction theory uses the concepts of self, role, and definition of the situation. On entering an ongoing social situation, one responds to that situation by defining it. This definition includes the assignment of positions to others, and thus the setting up of expectations concerning their behavior. It, further, includes an assessment of self, that is, the assignment of positional identities to oneself. Others in the situation are, of course, engaged in the same kind of activity. The behavior that ensues is a function of such definitions. A crucial question thus becomes one of the congruence of definitions, situation, role and self, of the interacting persons. Congruence permits efficient, organized behavior. Expanding this, again noting that the individual moves through a variety of interpersonal situations, the congruence of definitions, and so the behavioral expectations these imply, is fundamental to continuity of behavior. Personal organization is thus seen as a function, not simply of that which the individual carries around with him, but of the relationship between that which he carries with him—in the form of self-concepts—and the situations in which he interacts with others as these are mediated symbolically.

When one asks what kinds of social conditions foster or permit such congruence, the generalized answer is that when meanings are widely shared in a society, or among those persons within a society with whom one actually interacts, congruence is likely.

What happens when meanings are diverse among the others with whom one interacts? Reversing the above process, but maintaining the same explanatory principle, it may be said that incongruities in definition and so incongruities in expectations will result, and that personal disorganization is the outcome. A number of possible types of incongruity may be suggested: conflicts or lack of coordination between self concepts and the expectations of others; conflicts among aspects of self called into play in the same situation; the temporal succession of expectations which do not articulate, and so on.

It may be worthwhile to take one type of incongruity, say lack of coordination between self

concepts and expectations of others, and note more closely its relevance to personal disorganization. At the same time, the question can be raised: under what circumstances do identities change? Suppose one enters a situation with a set of self identifications which include the name "professor," and suppose he defines the situation—for example, as a classroom—in such a way that this identity is appropriate. He will then presumably conduct himself in ways indicated by that identity. He speaks in judicious, measured tones, he adopts a knowledgeable air, and so on. He can behave this way only so long as his audience accepts this definition of himself and so responds in such ways as validate his behavior, by taking notes, by concentrating attention upon him, by directing questions at him. Suppose, however, the audience fails to accept this definition; they think him a fool rather than a professor (although perhaps the two are not completely incompatible). They disregard what he is saying, they challenge his competency, they pay more attention to friends in class than they do to him. In short, they fail to validate his self identification. How will he behave? It is highly probable that behaviors ordinarily inappropriate to the classroom will ensue. He will likely lose his judicious tones and become emotional. He is likely to act confused, uncertain, embarrassed, ambivalent. At the same time, since persons typically have considerable investment in identities, he very probably will attempt to defend himself. He may do so by redoubling his efforts to act the complete professor, by dismissing the incident as a joke, by regarding the audience as consisting of morons. But if, persistently, his identity as professor fails to be validated by others, he cannot retain that identity. Others validate identities by behaving in appropriate ways, ways which provide cues on the basis of which further performance in terms of the identity is possible. If these cues are not provided, then such performance is no longer possible, and the identity will fade.

IMPLICATIONS FOR FAMILY RESEARCH

Rather than attempt to detail implications of symbolic interaction for family research, a few brief indications of researchable questions stimulated by this theory will be presented.

One question, or set of questions, has to do with differential commitment to family identities. It is obvious, for example, that not all persons who are objectively fathers are equally committed to such an identity. What accounts for such differentials, for the fact that for one man identity as father supersedes all other ways in which he sees himself, while for another the father identity is relatively low on the self totem pole? The theory suggests that this will be a function of the extent to which one is defined by significant others as a father. It also suggests that the degree of congruence of definitions by significant others will be of import. Borrowing a phrase from studies of political behavior, could the presence or absence of "cross-pressures" deriving from others with whom one interacts account for this differential commitment, at least in some degree?

Perhaps of greater significance to students of the family is the question of the consequences of differential commitment to familial identities. Foote[4] has contended that differences in motivation of role performances may fruitfully be seen in these terms. Political apathy seems to be in good part a consequence of lack of commitment to a clear-cut political identity; it seems reasonable to suspect that apathetic familial behavior has a similar source. It is also quite possible that, for example, the prediction of divorce would be on sounder ground when questions dealing with commitment to family identities are included in batteries of predictive items.

Closely related to these questions is another set. Are there extra-familial identities which are in varying degree compatible with familial identities? What are the effects of identities deriving from diverse spheres of activity on one another, and on behavior in these diverse spheres? Someone has suggested that the deviant behavior of a man in a work situation which appears to be idiosyncratic when viewed in this limited context, may rather be a consequence of his position and role within his family. That is, for example, the rate-buster on the job may not be acting "self-

ishly," but may simply be acting in accord with his conception of self as family breadwinner. It is certain that one's extra-familial identities operate within the family situation. Which identities so operate, their specific mode of articulation with family identities, and their consequences for family relationships are questions of obvious importance.

Another set of questions can be phrased around the relationship of crises to identity. Crises will always threaten identifications, for the latter depend on stable activities of others with reference to oneself; and crises are likely to be important in the process by which identities change. It may be that adaptation in crisis situations is a function of the ease with which identities alter; adaptation to the death of a spouse, for example, might profitably be approached in these terms. Yet that ease with which identities are altered is not always functional is suggested by Hill's[5] research on war separation and return; in such multi-phased crises it may be that, at least for some, easy alteration of identity at one point creates problems at still another point. Such questions, too, are worth the research energies of students of the family.

A different kind of question suggested by the theory may be prefaced by relating an overheard conversation. A young lady was speaking of her relationships with her boy friend. The two were, apparently, sufficiently involved to talk about marriage and their future. But, it seems, they argued when they engaged in such talk. The basis for the argument was this: she labelled such talks "plans," he called them "dreams," and each bridled at the other's conception of their conversations. Nonsense? Arguing over mere words? Not when one has in mind the significance of defining behavior and the consequences of classification. Plan implies a greater stake in a projected course of action than does dream. Dreams suggest freedom of action, plans a commitment. Suggested here is the potential fertility of studying the courtship process, marital role relationships, parent-child relationships, and so on, in terms of role-linked symbolic behavior: for example, the investigation of possible sex-linked differences in

---

[4] Nelson N. Foote, "Identification as the Basis for a Theory of Motivation," *American Sociological Review*, 16 (Feburary, 1951), pp. 14–21.

[5] Reuben Hill, *Families Under Stress*, New York: Harpers, 1949.

defining family situations, and the consequences of such differential definitions as may exist.

Finally, the theory suggests that studies focusing on the role-taking process may be rewarding. Role-taking is a variable; anticipation of the responses of others is not always correct. Foote[6] and his associates have conducted an impressive series of studies designed to uncover means by which role-taking ability can be improved, on the assumption that role-taking ability, or empathy in their language, is one aspect of interpersonal competence. While this may well be justified, some research[7] indicates that if one expects that interpersonal adjustment will always result from accurate role-taking, he is likely to be disappointed. But this still leaves open questions of

the specific consequences, under varying conditions, of role-taking accuracy. Are the consequences the same, for example, when husband and wife share the same value framework and when they do not? Might it not be that accurate role-taking differs in its consequences as role relationships change, when a couple moves through the sequential stages of courtship, early marital experience, and later family experience? These, too, are questions worth raising and answering.

One final remark: symbolic interaction is not a general theory of human behavior. That is, it does not incorporate all the variables presumably important in accounting for human behavior, but rather selects from these a few for concentrated attention. Thus it would not do to deny the contributions of alternative theoretical views from which human behavior can be approached. It is contended, however, that alternative views can be enriched by taking into account the set of ideas which have been developed.

[6] Nelson N. Foote, Editor, *Developing Interpersonal Competence: A Manual of Procedures for Family Life Educators,* unpublished manuscript.

[7] See for example, Sheldon Stryker, "Role-Taking Accuracy and Adjustment," *Sociometry,* 20 (December, 1957), pp. 286–296.

Pat Carlen   36

The Staging of Magistrates' Justice

Metaphoric critiques of judicial proceedings have been done by mainly American writers: Garfinkel (1956), Emerson (1967) and Blumberg (1967), for instance, have all used dramaturgical or game imagery in analyses of courtroom interaction. In England, on the other hand the concern

has been different, and largely reformative. Analyses of sentencing patterns (Hood, 1962; King, 1972), surveys of the availability of legal aid (Patterson, 1971) and assessment of bailing procedures (Bottomley, 1970; Dell, 1970)—all have contributed to the current concern with improving, mainly by increasing the availability of legal aid, the quality of justice in general and the quality of magistrates' justice in particular.

Difficult though it would be to deny the im-

Pat Carlen, University of Keele, England, "The Staging of Magistrates Justice," *British Journal of Criminology,* vol. 16 (January 1976), pp. 48–55. Reprinted by permission.

mense contributions of the aforementioned studies, both the American theorists and the English investigators have tended either to ignore or to take for granted other, equally consequential, dimensions of socio-legal control: the coercive structures of dread, awe and uncertainty depicted by Camus and Kafka; the coercive structures of resentment, frustration and absurdity depicted by Lewis Carroll and N. F. Simpson. That the masterly descriptions of a Kafka or a Camus are unlikely to be bettered by sociologists is obvious. The idea, however, that such surrealism and psychic coercion properly belong to the world of the French novel, rather than to the local magistrates' court in the High Street, is erroneous. In this paper, based on two years' observation of the Metropolitan magistrates' courts, I shall argue that the staging of magistrates' justice in itself infuses the proceedings with a surrealism which atrophies defendants' ability to participate in them.

THE MAGISTRATES' COURT AS A THEATRE OF THE ABSURD

Traditionally and situationally, judicial proceedings are dramatic. Aristotle noted the importance of forensic oratory as a special device of legal rhetoric; playwrights as diverse as Shakespeare and Shaw appreciated the dramatic value of a trial scene; lawyers have always been cognisant of rhetorical presentations.

In 1950, nine years before Goffman's *The Presentation of Self in Everyday Life*, a lawyer, Jerome Frank, discussed the conventional ascription of character which occurs in law courts and which is dependent upon the tacit dimensions of interpersonal knowledge. Such analyses are nowadays the familiar stuff of the dramaturgical perspectives in sociology. Yet people do not only ascribe character to each other. Furniture, stage-props, scenic devices, tacit scheduling programmes, etiquettes of ritual address and reference—in short, all the paraphernalia of social occasions—are, both immediately and documentarily, indexed with consequential social meanings (Mannheim, 1952; Schutz, 1970). These meanings

can be set up as being either mundane (*i.e.* constitutive of and reflecting everyday realities) or puzzling (*i.e.* constitutive of and reflecting alternative everyday realities) or, less often, as being both mundane and puzzling (*i.e.* surrealistic). In hierarchically organised social institutions, however, certain people can monopolise and manipulate the scenic and scheduling arrangements of the most important public settings so that a coercive control, often spurious to the professed aims of the institution, can be maintained.

Within the courtrooms of the magistrates' courts tacit control of their spatial and temporal properties is the monopoly of the police and the judicial personnel. In practice both the staging and the prosecution of the criminal business becomes the responsibility of the police. This renders absurd the judicial rhetoric of an adversary justice, where, so the story goes, both prosecution and defence stand as equals before the law. Indeed, within the courtrooms of the magistrates' courts the ideal of adversary justice is subjugated to an organisational efficiency in whose service body-movement and body-presentation are carefully circumscribed and regulated, bewilderment and embarrassment are openly fostered and aggravated, and uncertainty is callously observed and manipulated. Human creativity is there, certainly, but it is celebrated as much in the covert deployment of tacit control techniques as it is in the innovative judicial action. Whereas, therefore, Goffman's dramaturgical analyses have focused on the everyday realities of the *cinéma vérité*, these notes on the staging of magistrates' justice will focus on the surrealist dimensions of the theatre of the absurd.

STAGING THE ABSURD

Though structurally opposed, the theatre of the absurd and the court of law have several phenomenological features in common. Their central divergence inheres in their opposed structural functions. Thus, whereas dramatists of the absurd intentionally and overtly utilise the plausible and the mundane to construct the overtly senseless and absurd, the mandarins of justice intentionally and covertly utilise the plausible and mundane to construct the covertly senseless and absurd.

In magistrates' courts, as in the theatre of the absurd, mundane and conventional ways of organising and communicating the operative meanings of social occasions are simultaneously exploited and denied. Yet their outcomes are situationally authenticated and the intermeshed structures of surrealism and psychic coercion are difficult to locate. This is because police and judicial personnel systematically present their coercive devices as being nothing more than the traditional, conventional and commonsensical ways of organising and synchronising judicial proceedings.

Space

The spacing and placing of people on public occasions is strategic to their ability to participate effectively in them. Even upon informal social occasions temporary spacing arrangements will at least decide which conversations can be heard by whom. On the most formal social occasions spacing arrangements, being more rigid, will, in addition to determining the mode and range of verbal interaction, emphasise the relative status of the people present. On ritual occasions, the rules of spacing and placing will, additionally, define the specific territorial rights and duties of those designated as occupiers of particular social space.

A magistrates' court is a very formal and ritualistic social setting; in it social space is preformed and distributed by the fixtures and fittings which comprise its definitive physical dimensions. The conditional essence of formality is the maintenance of existing social forms; the *raison d'être* of the criminal law is an assumption of the vulnerability of existing social forms. It is not surprising, therefore, to find that, in the courts, not even the usually implicit rules of spacing and placing are left to chance interpretation. Instead, judicial violation of the mundane expectations which usually enable fully adult people to cope with unfamiliar situations, judicial tolerance of flawed communication systems, and a judicial perversion of the accepted modes of conversational practice,

realise a structure of tacit coercion which makes nonsense of recent claims that judicial proceedings are loaded in favour of the defendant (CLRC, 1972; Mark, 1973).

In the courtroom spatial dominance is achieved by structural elevation and the magistrate sits raised up from the rest of the court. The defendant is also raised up to public view but the dock is set lower than the magisterial seat, whilst the rails surrounding it are symbolic of the defendant's captive state. Of all the main protagonists the defendant is the one who is placed farthest away from the magistrate. Between the defendant and the magistrate sit clerk, solicitors, probation officers, social workers, press reporters, police, and any others deemed to be assisting the court in the discharge of its duties. Spatial arrangements, however, which might signify to the onlooker a guarantee of an orderly display of justice, are too often experienced by participants as being generative of a kind of theatrical autism with all the actors talking past each other.

Difficulties of hearing are endemic to magistrates' courts. At one court where microphones are used they distort voices so badly that most people in the courtroom laughingly wince when they are turned on, and visibly sympathise with the lady magistrate who always has them turned off because "they make us sound like Donald Duck." At other courts they have microphones but do not use them. Magistrates and clerks can go to elaborate lengths to explain the meaning of legal phraseology to defendants who either do not hear them and say "Pardon, sir?" or who nod in the "dazed" or "blank" way noted by so many policemen and probation officers. Acoustics, however, cannot bear total responsibility for the chronic breakdown of communication in magistrates' courts. The placing and spacing of people within the courtroom is a further cause of the series of "pardons" and "blank stares" which characterise and punctuate judicial proceedings.

It has already been stressed that, in the courtroom, defendants and magistrates are set well apart from each other. Distances between bench and dock vary from court to court but in all courts such distances are certainly greater than those usually, and voluntarily, chosen for the disclosure of intimate details of sexual habits, personal relationships and financial affairs. Certain communications, as Edward Hall has stressed, are conventionally presented as intimate communications, and both their timing and situating are delicately arranged. Indeed, "there are certain things which are difficult to talk about unless one is within the proper conversational zone" (Hall, 1959).

In magistrates' courts, where the vast majority of defendants do not have a solicitor as a "mouthpiece," defendants are set up in a guarded dock and then, at a distance artificially stretched beyond the familiar boundaries of face-to-face communication, are asked to describe or comment on intimate details of their lives; details which do not in themselves constitute infractions of any law but which are open to public investigation once a person has been accused of breaking the law.

Further, during such sequences of interrogation, defendants' embarrassed stuttering is often aggravated by judicial violation of another taken-for-granted conversational practice. For in conventional social practice the chain-rule of question-answer sequence (Sacks, 1967; Schegloff, 1972) is also accompanied by the assumption that it is the interrogator who demands an answer. In magistrates' courts, however, defendants often find that they are continually rebuked, either for not addressing their answers to the magistrate, or for directing their answers to their interrogators in such a way that the magistrate cannot hear them. As a result, defendants are often in the position of having to synchronise their answers and stances in a way quite divorced from the conventions of everyday life outside the courtroom.

For defendants who often do not immediately distinguish between magistrate and clerk, for defendants who do not comprehend the separate symbolic functions of dock and witness-box, for defendants who may have already spent up to three hours waiting around the squalid environs of the courtroom—the surrealistic dimensions of meaning, emanating from judicial exploitation of courtroom placing and spacing, can have a paralysing effect. A senior probation officer summed up the present situation in the Metropolitan magistrates' courts very well when she commented: "Many of them don't even go into the witness-box because they can't face walking round there. They're too nervous."

Time

Though it is unlikely that absolute control of the situation can be obtained in a cramped courtroom which may have 30 to 40 people in its main area, and over that number in its public gallery, officials, as I have already argued, appear to be well aware of how to facilitate control through exploitation of the courtroom's physical dimensions. Courtroom ceremony is maintained partly to facilitate physical control of defendants and any others who may step out of place, and partly to refurbish the historically sacred meanings attached to law. Yet, because of the volume of criminal business dealt with by magistrates' courts, control of the proceedings is often precarious. Continuous inroads on the putative sanctity of the courtroom are made by the daily wear and tear of judicial proceedings which may involve the consecutive appearances of 20 or 30 defendants at one court session. A series of brief but complex scenes have to be welded into a fast-moving but judicially satisfying documentary. Lines of spatial demarcation provide the baselines for the overall performance; once the action starts the movement of documents and persons from the various regions of the court has to be synchronised by the mainly backstage activities of the police.

In the management of social occasions, time, like place, always belongs to somebody or some group. During formal social occasions certain persons are appointed to oversee the timing of events, to ensure both the continuity and punctuation of performances. During judicial proceedings in magistrates' courts the timing of events is monopolised by the police. They are the ones who set up the proceedings; it is their responsibility to see that all defendants arrive at court; it is their job to draw up the charge sheets; it is their job to ensure that all relevant documents are in the hands of the clerk of court. And policemen are very jealous of their competence in programming the criminal business. Like other occupational groups doing a complex job publicly and under constant criticism they have developed plausible accounts to "demonstrate the rationality" (Moore, 1974) of the court's timetable. For instance, when I talked with him, a court inspector appealed to commonsense when he insisted that it was "only sensible" to hear contested cases last: "Think of it from your own point of view: if you'd pleaded guilty you wouldn't want to hang around all afternoon for something that was going to take two minutes." Yet, for the majority of defendants, the court experience is characterised by long periods of waiting unpunctuated by any official explanations about the cause of the delays. Worse, because cases can be arbitrarily switched from courtroom to courtroom, a defendant can have his case heard in one courtroom while his friends (among them, potential witnesses) sit unsuspectingly in the public gallery of an adjacent courtroom. During the long hours of waiting, many defendants become more and more nervous, harbouring fears (usually unfounded) that they will be sent to prison and, in the majority of courts, unable to get either refreshments or the privacy in which to talk to their solicitors or probation officers.

So, defendants, told to arrive at court at 10 A.M., may wait one, two or even three hours before their cases are "called on," but the police do the court lists according to a rationality which is rooted in two strands of situational logic. First, they calculate the time a case will take from their experience of the past performing times of the presiding magistrate and clerk. Secondly, they treat as an organisational norm their assumption that quicker business should take precedence over longer business. What the policemen successfully present as commonsense, however, also has a symbolic pay-off. If, early on in the proceedings, it is established that the court dispenses a swift and sure justice, untarnished by the ambiguity which characterises the later contested cases, then the contested case can, structurally, be presented as the deviant case, the one which needs special justification and management. Successful assertion by the police of their claim to present these cases in their "own time" displays a basic feature of their control over the courtroom situation.

PRESENTATIONS

Agencies which routinely handle large numbers of people usually develop strategies for promoting their disciplined movement between and within regions. Conventionally, organisational traffic is facilitated by sign-posting, information desks, printed rubrics and organisational maps. In magistrates' courts, however, such information is almost non-existent. Arrows indicate courtroom, gaoler's office and various other offices, but inquiring of first-time defendants are predominantly dependent upon the oral and tactile directions of the police.

Defendants are escorted into the courtroom by the policeman calling the cases. Once the defendant is in the dock the escort acts as a kind of personal choreographer to him. He tells him when to stand up and when to sit down (often in contradiction of the magistrates' directions!), when to speak and when to be quiet, when to leave the dock at the end of the hearing. During the hearing the policeman can tell the defendant to take his hands out of his pockets, chewing-gum out of his mouth, his hat off his head and the smile off his face. Thus, even at the outset, a series of physical checks, aligned with a battery of commands and counter-commands, inhibits the defendant's presentational style. Once he is in the distraught state of mind where he just "wants to get it over," judicial fears that the defendant might slow down the proceedings by being "awkward" are diminished.

In contrast to their unceremonious and coercive presentation of defendants, magistrates, policemen, solicitors and other court personnel all project visual images of themselves, and verbally embellished images of each other which are designed to personify the absolute propriety of their situated (judicial) actions.

Most court-workers are concerned with maintaining credibility with the magistrate, but magistrates themselves argue that their own authority is invested in the *place* rather than in their trans-situational status as magistrates. They, nonetheless, see the degrees of respect shown for the court as reflections of, and on, the image of the bench, and many of the organisational and ceremonial strategies of stage-management centre around the presentation of the magistrate. His entrance to the courtroom is both staged and heralded. The opening of the court is signalled by the usher calling "All stand" and "Silence in court." Once everybody in the courtroom is standing in silence, the magistrate enters, his appearance being staged *via* the door of which he has the exclusive use, and which appears to seal off those innermost areas of the court to which the public never has access. Throughout the court hearing the usher ensures that the magistrate is granted deference, interposing himself between those who, without further intermediary, would try to hand documents or letters directly into the magistrate's hands. Each magisterial entrance and exit is marked by the same ceremony.

Inter-professionally and collusively a concerted portrayal of authority and wisdom is maintained by the ceremonial courtesies of complimentary addresses and reference. Frozen in the rhetoric of their own self-justificatory vocabulary the magistrate becomes "Your Worship" and "Your Honour"; the clerk of the court becomes the "learned clerk"; policemen become "public servants"; probation officers and social workers become "these experts who can help you." What in vulgar parlance might be called the "scratch my back" syndrome becomes in court the rhetorical embroidery on the judicial backcloth. By contrast, the defendant too often becomes just "this man," unentitled, "Smith."

DISCUSSION

People who work in a place usually have more control over its particular rules of placing, spacing and ritual etiquettes than do those who pass through it; magistrates' courts are not unusual in these respects. Most defendants do not find it odd or disturbing that the court has its own routine. What they do find frustrating is that, at the very times when they are both subject to and object of its rules, a fog of mystification permeates the court (Grigg, 1965). To speak plainly, the major existential attribute of court proceedings is that they *do* proceed, regardless of the structural inability of many of those present to *hear* what is going on, and despite the structural

inability of many of those present to *participate* in what is going on (Dell, 1970).

Given the coercion immanent in the very staging of magistrates' justice, what is one to make of the current arguments that increased legal aid will substantially protect defendants' interests? What is one to make of the suggestion that the advice of a duty solicitor should be available to every defendant?

A most interesting feature of "reformist" socio-legal analyses is that all proposed changes in judicial organisation centre on the defendant. *He* will be assisted, guided, spoken for, represented more often; *he* will be helped to present a more plausible case. If, however, such reforms are truly meant to elevate the defendant from marionette to co-star status, it is arguable, from the analyses presented here, that they must either be accompanied or be preceded by radical changes in the staging of magistrates' justice.

REFERENCES

Bottomley, A. K. (1970). *Prison Before Trial.* London: Bell.

Blumberg, Abraham (1967). "The Practice of Law as a Confidence Game." *Law and Society Review,* Vol. I.

Camus, Albert (1969). *The Outsider.* Harmondsworth, Middlesex: Penguin.

Carroll, Lewis (1971). *Alice in Wonderland.* London: Oxford University Press.

Criminal Law Revision Committee (1972). *Eleventh Report.* London: H.M.S.O.

Dell, S. (1970). *Silent in Court.* London: Bell.

Emerson, R. M. (1967). *Judging Delinquents.* Chicago: Aldine.

Frank, Jerome (1950). *Courts on Trial.* Princeton: Princeton University Press.

Garfinkel, H. (1956). "Conditions of Successful Degradation Ceremonies." *American Journal of Sociology LXI.*

Goffman, E. (1959). *The Presentation of Self in Everyday Life.* Garden City, N.Y.: Doubleday.

Hall, E. T. (1959). *The Silent Language.* Garden City, N.Y.: Doubleday.

Hood, Roger (1962). *Sentencing in Magistrates' Courts.* London: Stevens and Sons.

Kafka, Franz (1972). *The Trial*. Harmondsworth, Middlesex: Penguin.

King, M. (1972). *Bail or Custody*. London: The Cobden Trust.

Mannheim, K. (1952). *Essays in the Sociology of Knowledge*. London: Routledge and Kegan Paul.

Mark, Robert (1973). *Richard Dimbleby Lecture*. London: B.B.C. Publications.

Moore, Michael (1974). "Demonstrating the Rationality of an Occupation." *Sociology*, **8**, 1, January.

Patterson, A. (1971) *Legal Aid as a Social Service*. London: Cobden Trust.

Sacks, H. (1967). *Transcribed Lectures*. Mimeo.

Schegloff, E. A. (1972). Notes on a Conversational Practice Formulating Place, in D. Sudnow, *Studies in Social Interaction*. New York: Free Press.

Schutz, A. (1970). *Reflection on the Problems of Relevance*. New Haven: Yale University Press.

Simpson, N. (1960). *One Way Pendulum*. London: Faber.

Howard S. Becker   **37**

Becoming a Marihuana User

The use of marihuana is and has been the focus of a good deal of attention on the part of both scientists and laymen. One of the major problems students of the practice have addressed themselves to has been the identification of those individual psychological traits which differentiate marihuana users from nonusers and which are assumed to account for the use of the drug. That approach, common in the study of behavior categorized as deviant, is based on the premise that the presence of a given kind of behavior in an individual can best be explained as the result of some trait which predisposes or motivates him to engage in the behavior.[1]

This study is likewise concerned with accounting for the presence or absence of marihuana use in an individual's behavior. It starts, however, from a different premise: that the presence of a given kind of behavior is the result of a sequence of social experiences during which the person acquires a conception of the meaning of the behavior, and perceptions and judgments of objects and situations, all of which make the activity possible and desirable. Thus, the motivation or disposition to engage in the activity is built up in the course of learning to engage in it and does not antedate this learning process. For such

Howard S. Becker, "Becoming a Marihuana User." Reprinted from *The American Journal of Sociology*, vol. 59 (November 1953), pp. 235–242, by permission of The University of Chicago Press. Copyright 1953 by the University of Chicago.

Paper read at the meetings of the Midwest Sociological Society in Omaha, Nebraska, April 25, 1953. The research on which this paper is based was done while I was a member of the staff of the Chicago Narcotics Survey, a study done by the Chicago Area Project, Inc., under a grant from the National Mental Health Institute. My thanks to Solomon Kobrin, Harold Finestone, Henry McKay, and Anselm Strauss, who read and discussed with me earlier versions of this paper.

[1] See, as examples of this approach, the following: Eli Marcovitz and Henry J. Meyers, "The Marihuana Addict in the Army," *War Medicine*, VI (December, 1944), 382–91; Herbert S. Gaskill, "Marihuana, an Intoxicant," *American Journal of Psychiatry*, CII (September, 1945), 202–4; Sol Charen and Luis Perelman, "Personality Studies of Marihuana Addicts," *American Journal of Psychiatry*, CII (March, 1946), 674–82.

a view it is not necessary to identify those "traits" which "cause" the behavior. Instead, the problem becomes one of describing the set of changes in the person's conception of the activity and of the experience it provides for him.[2]

This paper seeks to describe the sequence of changes in attitude and experience which lead to *the use of marihuana for pleasure.* Marihuana does not produce addiction, as do alcohol and the opiate drugs; there is no withdrawal sickness and no ineradicable craving for the drug.[3] The most frequent pattern of use might be termed "recreational." The drug is used occasionally for the pleasure the user finds in it, a relatively casual kind of behavior in comparison with that connected with the use of addicting drugs. The term "use for pleasure" is meant to emphasize the non-compulsive and casual character of the behavior. It is also meant to eliminate from consideration here those few cases in which marihuana is used for its prestige value only, as a symbol that one is a certain kind of person, with no pleasure at all being derived from its use.

The analysis presented here is conceived of as demonstrating the greater explanatory usefulness of the kind of theory outlined above as opposed to the predispositional theories now current. This may be seen in two ways: (1) predispositional theories cannot account for that group of users (whose existence is admitted)[4] who do not exhibit the trait or traits considered to cause the behavior and (2) such theories cannot account for the great variability over time of a given individual's behavior reference to the drug. The same person will at one stage be unable to use the drug for pleasure, at a later stage be able and willing to do so, and still later, again be unable to use it in this way. These changes, difficult to explain from a predispositional or motivational theory, are readily understandable in terms of changes

in the individual's conception of the drug as is the existence of "normal" users.

The study attempted to arrive at a general statement of the sequence of changes in individual attitude and experience which have always occurred when the individual has become willing and able to use marihuana for pleasure and which have not occurred or not been permanently maintained when this is not the case. This generalization is stated in universal terms in order that negative cases may be discovered and used to revise the explanatory hypothesis.[5]

Fifty interviews with marihuana users from a variety of social backgrounds and present positions in society constitute the data from which the generalization was constructed and against which it was tested.[6] The interviews focused on the history of the person's experience with the drug, seeking major changes in his attitude toward it and in his actual use of it, and the reasons for these changes. The final generalization is a statement of that sequence of changes in attitude which occurred in every case known to me in which the person came to use marihuana for pleasure. Until a negative case is found, it may be considered as an explanation of all cases of marihuana use for pleasure. In addition, changes from use to nonuse are shown to be related to similar changes in conception, and in each case it is possible to explain variations in the individual's behavior in these terms.

This paper covers only a portion of the natural history of an individual's use of marihuana,[7] starting with the person having arrived at the point of willingness to try marihuana. He knows that others use it to "get high," but he does not know what this means in concrete terms. He is curious about the experience, ignorant of what it may turn out to be, and afraid that it may be more than he has bargained for. The steps out-

---

[2] This approach stems from George Herbert Mead's discussion of objects in *Mind, Self, and Society* (Chicago: University of Chicago Press, 1934), pp. 277–80.

[3] Cf. Roger Adams, "Marihuana," *Bulletin of the New York Academy of Medicine,* XVIII (November 1942), 705–30.

[4] Cf. Lawrence Kolb, "Marihuana," *Federal Probation,* II (July 1938), 22:25; and Walter Bromberg, "Marihuana: A Psychiatric Study," *Journal of the American Medical Association,* CXIII (July 1, 1939), 11.

[5] The method used is that described by Alfred R. Lindesmith in his *Opiate Addiction* (Bloomington: Principia Press, 1947), chap. i. I would like also to acknowledge the important role Lindesmith's work played in shaping my thinking about the genesis of marihuana use.

[6] Most of the interviews were done by the author. I am grateful to Solomon Kobrin and Harold Finestone for allowing me to make use of interviews done by them.

[7] I hope to discuss elsewhere other stages in this natural history.

lined below, if he undergoes them all and maintains the attitudes developed in them, leave him willing and able to use the drug for pleasure when the opportunity presents itself.

I

The novice does not ordinarily get high the first time he smokes marihuana, and several attempts are usually necessary to induce this state. One explanation of this may be that the drug is not smoked "properly," that is, in a way that insures sufficient dosage to produce real symptoms of intoxication. Most users agree that it cannot be smoked like tobacco if one is to get high:

Take in a lot of air, you know, and . . . I don't know how to describe it, you don't smoke it like a cigarette, you draw in a lot of air and get it deep down in your system and then keep it there. Keep it there as long as you can.

Without the use of some such technique[8] the drug will produce no effects, and the user will be unable to get high:

The trouble with people like that [who are not able to get high] is that they're just not smoking it right, that's all there is to it. Either they're not holding it down long enough, or they're getting too much air and not enough smoke, or the other way around or something like that. A lot of people just don't smoke it right, so naturally nothing's gonna happen.

If nothing happens, it is manifestly impossible for the user to develop a conception of the drug as an object which can be used for pleasure, and use will therefore not continue. The first step in the sequence of events that must occur if the person is to become a user is that he must learn to use the proper smoking technique in order that his use of the drug will produce some effects in terms of which his conception of it can change.

Such a change is, as might be expected, a result of the individual's participation in groups in which marihuana is used. In them the individ-

ual learns the proper way to smoke the drug. This may occur through direct teaching:

I was smoking like I did an ordinary cigarette. He said, "No, don't do it like that." He said, "Suck it, you know, draw in and hold it in your lungs till you . . . for a period of time."
I said, "Is there any limit of time to hold it?"
He said, "No, just till you feel that you want to let it out, let it out." So I did that three or four times.

Many new users are ashamed to admit ignorance and, pretending to know already, must learn through the more indirect means of observation and imitation:

I came on like I had turned on [smoked marihuana] many times before you know. I didn't want to seem like a punk to this cat. See, like I didn't know the first thing about it—how to smoke it, or what was going to happen, or what. I just watched him like a hawk—I didn't take my eyes off him for a second, because I wanted to do everything just as he did it. I watched how he held it, how he smoked it, and everything. Then when he gave it to me I just came on cool, as though I knew exactly what the score was. I held it like he did and took a poke just the way he did.

No person continued marihuana use for pleasure without learning a technique that supplied sufficient dosage for the effects of the drug to appear. Only when this was learned was it possible for a conception of the drug as an object which could be used for pleasure to emerge. Without such a conception marihuana use was considered meaningless and did not continue.

II

Even after he learns the proper smoking technique, the new user may not get high and thus not form a conception of the drug as something which can be used for pleasure. A remark made by a user suggested the reason for this difficulty in getting high and pointed to the next necessary step on the road to being a user:

I was told during an interview, "As a matter of fact, I've seen a guy who was high out of his mind and didn't know it."

[8] A pharmacologist notes that this ritual is in fact an extremely efficient way of getting the drug into the blood stream (R. P. Walton, *Marihuana: America's New Drug Problem* [Philadelphia: J. B. Lippincott, 1938], p. 48).

I expressed disbelief: "How can that be, man?"

The interviewee said, "Well, it's pretty strange, I'll grant you that, but I've seen it. This guy got on with me, claiming that he'd never got high, one of those guys, and he got completely stoned. And he kept insisting that he wasn't high. So I had to prove to him that he was."

What does this mean? It suggests that being high consists of two elements: the presence of symptoms caused by marihuana use and the recognition of these symptoms and their connection by the user with his use of the drug. It is not enough, that is, that the effects be present; they alone do not automatically provide the experience of being high. The user must be able to point them out to himself and consciously connect them with his having smoked marihuana before he can have this experience. Otherwise, regardless of the actual effects produced, he considers that the drug has had no effect on him: "I figured it either had no effect on me or other people were exaggerating its effect on them, you know. I thought it was probably psychological, see." Such persons believe that the whole thing is an illusion and that the wish to be high leads the user to deceive himself into believing that something is happening when, in fact, nothing is. They do not continue marihuana use, feeling that "it does nothing" for them.

Typically, however, the novice has faith (developed from his observation of users who do get high) that the drug actually will produce some new experience and continues to experiment with it until it does. His failure to get high worries him, and he is likely to ask more experienced users or provoke comments from them about it. In such conversations he is made aware of specific details of his experience which he may not have noticed or may have noticed but failed to identify as symptoms of being high:

I didn't get high the first time . . . I don't think I held it in long enough. I probably let it out, you know, you're a little afraid. The second time I wasn't sure, and he [smoking companion] told me, like I asked him for some of the symptoms or something, how would I know, you know. . . . So he told me to sit on a stool. I sat on—I think I sat on a bar

stool—and he said, "Let your feet hang," and then when I got down my feet were real cold, you know.

And I started feeling it, you know. That was the first time. And then about a week after that, sometime pretty close to it, I really got on. That was the first time I got on a big laughing kick, you know. Then I really knew I was on.

One symptom of being high is an intense hunger. In the next case the novice becomes aware of this and gets high for the first time:

They were just laughing the hell out of me because like I was eating so much. I just scoffed [ate] so much food, and they were just laughing at me, you know. Sometimes I'd be looking at them, you know, wondering why they're laughing, you know, not knowing what I was doing. [Well, did they tell you why they were laughing eventually?] Yeah, yeah, I come back, "Hey, man, what's happening?" Like, you know, like I'd ask, "What's happening?" and all of a sudden I feel weird, you know. "Man, you're on you know. You're on pot [high on marihuana]." I said, "No, am I?" Like I don't know what's happening.

The learning may occur in more indirect ways:

I heard little remarks that were made by other people. Somebody said, "My legs are rubber," and I can't remember all the remarks that were made because I was very attentively listening for all these cues for what I was supposed to feel like.

The novice, then, eager to have this feeling, picks up from other users some concrete referents of the term "high" and applies these notions to his own experience. The new concepts make it possible for him to locate these symptoms among his own sensations and to point out to himself a "something different" in his experience that he connects with drug use. It is only when he can do this that he is high. In the next case, the contrast between two successive experiences of a user makes clear the crucial importance of the awareness of the symptoms in being high and re-emphasizes the important role of interaction with other users in acquiring the concepts that make this awareness possible:

[Did you get high the first time you turned on?] Yea, sure. Although, come to think of it, I guess I really didn't. I mean, like that first time it was more or less of a mild drunk. I was happy, I guess, you know what I mean. But I didn't really know I was high, you know what I mean. It was only after the second time I got high that I realized I was high the first time. Then I knew that something different was happening.

[How did you know that?] How did I know? If what happened to me that night would of happened to you, you would've known, believe me. We played the first tune for almost two hours—one tune! Imagine, man! We got on the stand and played this one tune, we started at nine o'clock. When we got finished I looked at my watch, it's a quarter to eleven. Almost two hours on one tune. And it didn't seem like anything. I mean, you know, it does that to you. It's like you have much more time or something. Anyway, when I saw that, man, it was too much. I knew I must really be high or something if anything like that could happen. See, and then they explained to me that that's what it did to you, you had a different sense of time and everything. So I realized that that's what it was. I knew then. Like the first time, I probably felt that way, you know, but I didn't know what's happening.

It is only when the novice becomes able to get high in this sense that he will continue to use marihuana for pleasure. In every case in which use continued, the user had acquired the necessary concepts with which to express to himself the fact that he was experiencing new sensations caused by the drug. That is, for use to continue, it is necessary not only to use the drug so as to produce effects but also to learn to perceive these effects when they occur. In this way marihuana acquires meaning for the user as an object which can be used for pleasure.

With increasing experience the user develops a greater appreciation of the drug's effects; he continues to learn to get high. He examines succeeding experiences closely, looking for new effects, making sure the old ones are still there. Out of these there grows a stable set of categories for experiencing the drug's effects whose presence enables the user to get high with ease.

The ability to perceive the drug's effects must be maintained if use is to continue; if it is lost, marihuana use ceases. Two kinds of evidence support this statement. First, people who become heavy users of alcohol, barbiturates, or opiates do not continue to smoke marihuana, largely because

they lose the ability to distinguish between its effects and those of the other drugs.[9] They no longer know whether the marihuana gets them high. Second, in those few cases in which an individual uses marihuana in such quantities that he is always high, he is apt to get this same feeling that the drug has no effect on him, since the essential element of a noticeable difference between feeling high and feeling normal is missing. In such a situation, use is likely to be given up completely, but temporarily, in order that the user may once again be able to perceive the difference.

III

One more step is necessary if the user who has now learned to get high is to continue use. He must learn to enjoy the effects he has just learned to experience. Marihuana-produced sensations are not automatically or necessarily pleasurable. The taste for such experience is a socially acquired one, not different in kind from acquired tastes for oysters or dry martinis. The user feels dizzy, thirsty; his scalp tingles; he misjudges time and distances; and so on. Are these things pleasurable? He isn't sure. If he is to continue marihuana use, he must decide that they are. Otherwise, getting high, while a real enough experience, will be an unpleasant one he would rather avoid.

The effects of the drug, when first perceived, may be physically unpleasant or at least ambiguous:

It started taking effect, and I didn't know what was happening, you know, what it was, and I was very sick. I walked around the room, walking around the room trying to get off, you know; it just scared me at first, you know. I wasn't used to that kind of feeling.

In addition, the novice's naive interpretation of what is happening to him may further confuse

[9] "Smokers have repeatedly stated that the consumption of whiskey while smoking negates the potency of the drug. They find it very difficult to get 'high' while drinking whiskey and because of that smokers will not drink while using the 'weed' " (cf. New York City Mayor's Committee on Marihuana, *The Marihuana Problem in the City of New York* [Lancaster, Pa.: Jacques Cattel Press, 1944], p. 13.)

and frighten him, particularly if he decides, as many do, that he is going insane:

> I felt I was insane, you know. Everything people done to me just wigged me. I couldn't hold a conversation, and my mind would be wandering, and I was always thinking, oh, I don't know, weird things, like hearing music different. . . . I get the feeling that I can't talk to anyone. I'll goof completely.

Given these typically frightening and unpleasant first experiences, the beginner will not continue use unless he learns to redefine the sensations as pleasurable:

> It was offered to me, and I tried it. I'll tell you one thing. I never did enjoy it at all. I mean it was just nothing that I could enjoy. [Well, did you get high when you turned on?] Oh, yeah, I got definite feelings from it. But I didn't enjoy them. I mean I got plenty of reactions, but they were mostly reactions of fear. [You were frightened?] Yes, I didn't enjoy it. I couldn't seem to relax with it, you know. If you can't relax with a thing, you can't enjoy it, I don't think.

In other cases the first experiences were also definitely unpleasant, but the person did become a marihuana user. This occurred, however, only after a later experience enabled him to redefine the sensations as pleasurable:

> [This man's first experience was extremely unpleasant, involving distortion of spatial relationships and sounds, violent thirst, and panic produced by these symptoms.] After the first time I didn't turn on for about, I'd say, ten months to a year. . . . It wasn't a moral thing; it was because I'd gotten so frightened, bein' so high. An' I didn't want to go through that again, I mean, my reaction was, "Well, if this is what they call bein' high, I don't dig [like] it.". . . So I didn't turn on for a year almost, accounta that. . . .
>
> Well, my friends started, an' consequently I started again. But I didn't have any more, I didn't have that same initial reaction, after I started turning on again.
>
> [In interaction with his friends he became able to find pleasure in the effects of the drug and eventually became a regular user.]

In no case will use continue without such a redefinition of the effects as enjoyable.

This redefinition occurs, typically, in interaction with more experienced users who, in a num-

ber of ways, teach the novice to find pleasure in this experience which is at first so frightening.[10] They may reassure him as to the temporary character of the unpleasant sensations and minimize their seriousness, at the same time calling attention to the more enjoyable aspects. An experienced user describes how he handles newcomers to marihuana use:

> Well, they get pretty high sometimes. The average person isn't ready for that, and it is a little frightening to them sometimes. I mean, they've been high on lush [alcohol], and they get higher that way than they've ever been before, and they don't know what's happening to them. Because they think they're going to keep going up, up, up till they lose their minds or begin doing weird things or something. You have to like reassure them, explain to them that they're not really flipping or anything, that they're gonna be all right. You have to just talk them out of being afraid. Keep talking to them, reassuring, telling them it's all right. And come on with your own story, you know: "The same thing happened to me. You'll get to like that after awhile." Keep coming on like that; pretty soon you talk them out of being scared. And besides they see you doing it and nothing horrible is happening to you, so that gives them more confidence.

The more experienced user may also teach the novice to regulate the amount he smokes more carefully, so as to avoid any severely uncomfortable symptoms while retaining the pleasant ones. Finally, he teaches the new user that he can "get to like it after awhile." He teaches him to regard those ambiguous experiences formerly defined as unpleasant as enjoyable. The older user in the following incident is a person whose tastes have shifted in this way, and his remarks have the effects of helping others to make a similar redefinition:

> A new user had her first experience of the effects of marihuana and became frightened and hysterical. She "felt like she was half in and half out of the room" and experienced a number of alarming physical symptoms. One of the more experienced users present said, "She's dragged because she's high like that. I'd give anything to get that high myself. I haven't been that high in years."

[10] Charen and Perelman, *op. cit.*, p. 679.

In short, what was once frightening and distasteful becomes, after a taste for it is built up, pleasant, desired, and sought after. Enjoyment is introduced by the favorable definition of the experience that one acquires from others. Without this, use will not continue, for marihuana will not be for the user an object he can use for pleasure.

In addition to being a necessary step in becoming a user, the pleasure represents an important condition for continued use. It is quite common for experienced users suddenly to have an unpleasant or frightening experience, which they cannot define as pleasurable, either because they have used a larger amount of marihuana than usual or because it turns out to be a higher-quality marihuana than they expected. The user has sensations which go beyond any conception he has of what being high is and is in much the same situation as the novice, uncomfortable and frightened. He may blame it on an overdose and simply be more careful in the future. But he may make this the occasion for a rethinking of his attitude toward the drug and decide that it no longer can give him pleasure. When this occurs and is not followed by a redefinition of the drug as capable of producing pleasure, use will cease.

The likelihood of such a redefinition occurring depends on the degree of the individual's participation with other users. Where this participation is intensive, the individual is quickly talked out of his feeling against marihuana use. In the next case, on the other hand, the experience was very disturbing, and the aftermath of the incident cut the person's participation with other users to almost zero. Use stopped for three years and began again only when a combination of circumstances, important among which was a resumption of ties with users, made possible a redefinition of the nature of the drug:

It was too much, like I only made about four pokes, and I couldn't even get it out of my mouth, I was so high, and I got real flipped. In the basement, you know, I just couldn't stay in there anymore. My heart was pounding real hard, you know, and I was going out of my mind; I thought I was losing my mind completely. So I cut out of this basement, and this other guy, he's out of his mind, told me, "Don't, don't leave me, man. Stay here." And I couldn't.

I walked outside, and it was five below zero, and I thought I was dying, and I had my coat open; I was sweating. I was perspiring. My whole insides were all . . . , and I walked about two blocks away, and I fainted behind a bush. I don't know how long I laid there. I woke up, and I was feeling the worst, I can't describe it at all, so I made it to a bowling alley, man, and I was trying to act normal, I was trying to shoot pool, you know, trying to act real normal, and I couldn't lay and I couldn't stand up and I couldn't sit down, and I went up and laid down where some guys that spot pins lay down, and that didn't help me, and I went down to a doctor's office. I was going to go in there and tell the doctor to put me out of my misery . . . because my heart was pounding so hard, you know. . . . So then all weekend I started flipping, seeing things there and going through hell, you know, all kinds of abnormal things. . . . I just quit for a long time then.

[He went to a doctor who defined the symptoms for him as those of a nervous breakdown caused by "nerves" and "worries." Although he was no longer using marihuana, he had some recurrences of the symptoms which led him to suspect that "it was all his nerves."] So I just stopped worrying, you know; so it was about thirty-six months later I started making it again. I'd just take a few pokes, you know. [He first resumed use in the company of the same user-friend with whom he had been involved in the original incident.]

A person, then, cannot begin to use marihuana for pleasure, or continue its use for pleasure, unless he learns to define its effects as enjoyable, unless it becomes and remains an object which he conceived of as capable of producing pleasure.

IV

In summary, an individual will be able to use marihuana for pleasure only when he goes through a process of learning to conceive of it as an object which can be used in this way. No one becomes a user without (1) learning to smoke the drug in a way which will produce real effects; (2) learning to recognize the effects and connect them with drug use (learning, in other words, to get high); and (3) learning to enjoy the sensations he perceives. In the course of this process he develops a disposition or motivation to use marihuana which was not and could not have been present when he began use, for it involves and depends on conceptions of the drug which could only grow out of the kind of actual experience detailed above. On completion of this process he is willing and able to use marihuana for pleasure.

He has learned, in short, to answer "Yes" to the question: "Is it fun?" The direction his further use of the drug takes depends on his being able to continue to answer "Yes" to this question and, in addition, on his being able to answer "Yes" to other questions which arise as he becomes aware of the implications of the fact that the society as a whole disapproves of the practice: "Is it expedient?" "Is it moral?" Once he has acquired the ability to get enjoyment out of the drug, use will continue to be possible for him. Considerations of morality and expediency, occasioned by the reactions of society, may interfere and inhibit use, but use continues to be a possibility in terms of his conception of the drug. The act becomes impossible only when the ability to enjoy the experience of being high is lost, through a change in the user's conception of the drug occasioned by certain kinds of experience with it.

In comparing this theory with those which ascribe marihuana use to motives or predispositions rooted deep in individual behavior, the evidence makes it clear that marihuana use for pleasure can occur only when the process described above is undergone and cannot occur without it. This is apparently so without reference to the nature of the individual's personal makeup, or psychic problems. Such theories assume that people have stable modes of response which predetermine the way they will act in relation to any particular situation or object and that, when they come in contact with the given object or situation, they act in the way in which their makeup predisposes them.

The analysis of the genesis of marihuana use shows that the individuals who come in contact with a given object may respond to it at first in a great variety of ways. If a stable form of new behavior toward the object is to emerge, a transformation of meanings must occur, in which the person develops a new conception of the nature of the object.[11] This happens in a series of communicative acts in which others point out new aspects of his experience to him, present him with new interpretations of events, and help him achieve a new conceptual organization of his world, without which the new behavior is not possible. Persons who do not achieve the proper kind of conceptualization are unable to engage in the given behavior and turn off in the direction of some other relationship to the object or activity.

This suggests that behavior of any kind might fruitfully be studied developmentally, in terms of changes in meanings and concepts, their organization and reorganization, and the way they channel behavior, making some acts possible while excluding others.

---

[11] Cf. Anselm Strauss, "The Development and Transformation of Monetary Meanings in the Child," *American Sociological Review,* XVII (June 1952), 275–86.

Deviants as Active Participants in the Labeling Process: The Visibly Handicapped

What is a handicap in social terms? It is an imputation of difference from others; more particularly, imputation of an *undesirable* difference. By definition, then a person said to be handicapped is so defined because he deviates from what he himself or others believe to be normal or appropriate.

(Freidson, 1965:72)

Much of the literature of the last 15 years on social deviance has been written from a labeling perspective (Becker, 1963; Cicourel, 1968; Erikson, 1962; Gibbs, 1966; Kitsuse, 1962, 1972; Kitsuse and Cicourel, 1963; Lemert, 1951; Scheff, 1966; Schur, 1965). This perspective emphasizes the process by which actors become defined and treated as deviant. Since social norms are seen as problematic and no behavior is assumed to be inherently deviant, definitions of deviance vary with the actors who are observing and defining the activities. Indeed, the unique contribution of this perspective had been to assume that reactions to behavior, rather than any behavior itself, identify and define that which is deviant.

The conceptualization of deviance as a process by which members of a group, community, or society 1) interpret certain behaviors as deviant, 2) label persons who so behave as a certain kind of deviant, and 3) accord them the treatment considered appropriate to such deviants has clarified the active role of conventional and conforming actors (Kitsuse, 1962). However, the role of the deviant in this process has often been understated or ignored entirely: those engaged in the deviant behavior tend to be presented as passive or reactive, rather than as active agents in the labeling process. (See Filstead, 1972; or Rubington and Weinberg, 1968 for comprehensive collections of readings.)[1] Thus, when a leading exponent of the labeling perspective critically assesses it, he only suggests that "the self-conceptions of the deviating individual should be considered a crucial dependent variable, to which we should pay more attention than to the deviating behavior itself" (Schur, 1969:311). Might not the self-conceptions of the deviating individual also be considered a crucial *independent* variable?

The purpose here is to demonstrate that, indeed, those labeled deviant because of a physical handicap often take an active part in the labeling process: they initiate self-definitions; they insist that others define them in preferred ways, and the strategies they choose to negotiate and settle labeling issues vary with the social context in which such labeling occurs.[2]

---

[1] Exceptions to this tendency may be found in the work of Davis, 1961; Goffman, 1963; Lorber, 1967; Matza, 1969; Sykes and Matza, 1957; and Williams and Weinberg, 1970.

[2] As Turner (1972) has suggested, deviant labels refer to roles, not isolated acts. The label "heroin addicts," for example, has

Teresa E. Levitin, "Deviants as Active Participants in the Labeling Process: The Visibly Handicapped," *Social Problems* 22:4 (April 1975), pp. 548–557. Reprinted by permission.

Unstructured interviews with adults who had recently become physically handicapped through accident or illness were conducted over a several month period in the physical therapy waiting room of a large hospital. All respondents were outpatients who regularly came to the hospital for physical therapy; their handicaps ranged from the evident (loss of a limb) to the publicly invisible (mastectomy), from the permanent (paralysis) to the more temporary (whiplash). This paper focuses on those with evident or visible handicaps only. Since the author was undergoing physical therapy, problems in gaining cooperation were minimal.[3]

PHYSICAL HANDICAPS AS A TYPE OF DEVIANCE

The label "deviant" and the associated devaluation of an actor thus labeled are applicable to the physically handicapped. In a society that values physical health and attractiveness, the handicapped are less than fully acceptable. From a labeling perspective what is problematic is not whether a handicap will, in general, be defined as a type of deviance, but, rather, how specific attempts to apply that deviant label and role are initiated either by the disabled or by the normal and are negotiated in interaction.

The terms physical handicap and disability are often interchangeably used (Meyers, 1965; Wright, 1960). In this study, both terms will refer to someone who perceives himself/herself and is perceived by others as unable to meet the demands or expectations of a particular situation because of some physical impairment—i.e., an anatomical and/or a physiological abnormality. This definition is consonant with a labeling perspective: the concept handicapped has meaning only within a social context, when the expectations and demands of others are taken into account. The

bound feet of a Chinese noblewoman were a physical impairment that prevented her from walking easily, but she was not, by this definition, physically handicapped.[4]

Many different ways of classifying physical handicaps have been utilized (Barker, et al., 1953; Dembo, Leviton, and Wright, 1956; Freidson, 1965; Goffman, 1963; Lorber, 1967). Since a deviant role cannot be attributed until the act or state that violates social expectations is perceived, how evident the handicap is to others is a crucial classificatory dimension.[5]

Physiological impairments are not always immediately evident. Although hemophiliacs cannot participate in contact sports, they can carefully structure their social lives so that these impairments do not become widely known social facts. Other types of deviance may also be selectively hidden: no one at work may know that an employee is a homosexual, although it is known to friends. In short, those to whom the deviancy is evident may represent only a small segment of the deviant's social world. One limitation of the labeling perspective is that too little attention has been given to those arenas of life and to those subgroups where labeling as deviant does not occur because the deviant states or behaviors are not evident. In the case of the physically handicapped interviewed for this paper, however, the stigma was evident to friends, family, medical personnel, and the deviants themselves. For some, the permanently disabled, the impairment was irrevocable, in that prior social roles would never be filled as before. For others, the more temporarily disabled, there would be an eventual return to prior role expectations and obligations.

---

[4] A physically handicapped person is not conceptually identical to a person with a physical handicap. The former phrase connotes an actor who cannot meet *any* expectations or demands (a most unlikely circumstance), while the latter suggests an actor with any number of characteristics, one of which is a physical handicap. The shorter phrase is easier to use and therefore will be employed here; but it is important to remember that even severe impairments, depending on the situation, may not be handicaps.

[5] The labeling perspective has been criticized (Gibbs, 1966; Lorber, 1967) for the concept of "secret deviants" (Becker, 1963), those whose deviance has not been discovered. This conceptualization is a logical contradiction. Becker (1971) subsequently used the term "potentially deviant" to describe those engaged in activities likely to be defined as deviant by others.

---

an elaborate set of roles ranging from, for many, thief to, for some, musician, associated with it. The label is a summary statement about a number of expected behaviors or roles, and will be used as such in this paper.

[3] This paper does not deal with the profound pain—both psychological and physical—many respondents experienced and described. Of concern here is the more social fate of the handicapped.

TWO DIFFERENT TYPES OF SOCIAL SITUATIONS AND INTERACTION GOALS

Both the permanently and the more temporarily physically handicapped share a common concern. They do not want their deviance to become the keystone for definitions of themselves. They do not want others to believe and to act as though the deviant part of self is the entire self, obscuring other more positive, socially valued aspects of that self, no matter how evident or permanent the handicap may be. Yet, as a psychologist describing the physically handicapped notes, there is a tendency for judgments of "inferiority on one scale to spread to total inferiority of the person" (Wright, 1960:8). Similarly, a sociologist points out that "when deviant roles are compared with other roles, the most striking difference lies in the extent to which the role is identified with the *person* rather than the *actor* (Turner, 1972:312). Or in the more poignant words of an amputee: "I'm not just 'that person without legs'; I'm a whole person. I didn't lose my whole personality when I lost my legs; I just lost my legs." Goffman (1963:132–133) has noted that "the painfulness, then, of sudden stigmatization can come not from the individual's confusion about his identity, but from his knowing too well what he has become."

What one becomes is determined not only by others but also by the self. Denial that any change has occurred is folly; the handicap is too evident for persistent claims that one has not changed to be believed by anyone. Given the ineluctable imputation of some deviant identity and role, the challenge to the disabled is to establish a social identity that is more favorable than the identity of a totally devalued person and to obtain the most positive social statuses or outcomes possible. However, the temporarily and the permanently disabled differ in the kind of definition and elaboration they insist be given to their evident handicap. The definition of self that the temporarily handicapped actively promote is one that states "this deviance will *not always* be me." In contrast, the definition of self actively presented by the permanently handicapped is one that states "this deviance is *not all* of me."

Two different types of situations in which deviants asserted their preferred social labels and roles in interaction with normals were observed: sociable encounters and encounters with agents of social control, physical therapists.

Sociable encounters are those face-to-face contacts vividly described by Goffman (1959) in which actors who are relatively unknown to each other project definitions of themselves, and in which a "working consensus" about those definitions of self and the situation may or may not emerge. Davis (1961) has described face-to-face encounters that are somewhat but not too prolonged, friendly but not intimate, ritualized but not completely predictable as sociable encounters. P.T.A. meetings, business lunches, classrooms, professional conventions, parties, weddings, and airplane lounges are a few settings where sociable interaction occurs. The opportunities for informal, sociable contact between the physically handicapped and the normal are legion.

A second, and more limited, class of situations in which deviant and normal interact occurs because of the deviance itself. Since the purpose of these encounters is to treat or to reform or to punish the deviant, often regardless of the deviant's wishes, the normals can be seen as agents of social control. Different types of agents, often represented by different occupations, are involved in the detection, evaluation, and response to different types of deviance (Stoll, 1968). Doctors, vocational therapists, nurses, social workers, and physical therapists are all agents of social control routinely encountered by the physically handicapped. Both as members of a larger society that values physical health and attractiveness and as professionals in a particular occupational role, such agents try to return the deviant as much as possible to former, valued social roles.

SOCIABLE ENCOUNTERS WITH THE PERMANENTLY AND THE TEMPORARILY DISABLED

The social consequences of a physical handicap have been described in detail by Davis (1961), Goffman (1963), and Wright (1960). All agree that sociable encounters between the disabled and the normal are strained, inhibited, and uncomfortable for both parties because of uncertainty about how, if at all, the stigma ought to be acknowledged.

Davis (1961) postulates the mechanism of deviance disavowal as a way the handicapped can manage strained interaction with normals. If successful, this process permits the normal and the deviant to engage in open and spontaneous sociable interaction, for the obvious disability is recognized rather than denied, but not made central or disruptive to the encounter.

Davis' examples are primarily drawn from those who were visibly disabled by polio; and his concept of deviance disavowal is central to understanding how the permanently disabled handle social encounters. The more temporarily disabled, however, behave differently. Their visible stigma sets the stage for the same sort of strained and superficial interaction the permanently disabled face. Paradoxically, the temporarily handicapped tend to manage this interaction tension and project the definition of self they want accepted by *avowing* their deviance. Since their disability is evident but the prognosis is not, the temporarily handicapped are active, often aggressive, in making certain they are not given a label and role that has social consequences far more serious than those of a temporary stigma. It is not simply a matter of disavowing the label "permanently handicapped," but, rather, of trying to see that the normal has no opportunity even to contemplate such a label.

Even within a moment or two of meeting someone in a sociable encounter, the temporarily handicapped may avow their deviance. They may describe their accident or injury in great detail, provide unsolicited facts about their therapy, and note their prognosis.

Both politeness and curiosity usually keep the normal from trying to stop these avowal revelations. Thus, the deviant is able to continue to draw attention to his or her handicap, and it remains a central theme until the normal indicates acceptance of the identity the deviant is presenting and acknowledges the temporariness of the disability. A statement such as "Well, I'm glad you'll be OK again soon" is evidence that the desired message has been conveyed. Once the normal indicates

belief in the temporariness of the evident physical handicap, the breaking through stage analogous to that in the deviance disavowal process has occurred.

The final stage of Davis' disavowal process, that of establishing a normalized relationship, also occurs in the avowal process; but the content of the normalized definition of self is different. Those who have successfully *disavowed* their deviance have communicated a definition of self that says this handicap is only a *small part* of who I am. Those who have successfully avowed their deviance have communicated a definition of self that say this handicap is only a *temporary part* of who I am.

There are many ways the evidently handicapped provide information about preferred definitions. The permanently disabled begin to use props to introduce an unblemished aspect of self. A book, a political button, a religious symbol are newly acquired cues to their other, more socially valued labels and roles. One patient said "I bring along my knitting. Someone's bound to ask what I'm making or I'll say 'I'm knitting a scarf' or whatever and then I'll talk about all my other hobbies too." In contrast, the temporarily handicapped begin to use props to call attention to their stigma. One patient painted "Houdini" on his wheelchair, a clever way of setting the stage for his explanation that it would soon disappear.

Several of the permanently disabled noted that they were now much more apt to ask normals about their interests and activities than before they were handicapped. Such probing sometimes seemed motivated less by a genuine interest in that other's life than by the deviant's own desire to find shared concerns that would say, in effect: since I can do a lot of the things you do, I am obviously more than this stigma.

Several of the temporarily disabled noted that they were now much more apt to ask normals about their past illnesses and injuries than before they were handicapped. Reminding normals either of their own temporary deviance or that of their friends and family would permit the handicapped to say, in effect: like you or others you have known, I am only temporarily handicapped. One respondent was shocked at discovering himself insisting on a discussion of such events at a formal dinner.

Deviants other than the physically handicapped also find that their deviant aspects or roles often become the central social facts used in defining and evaluating them. Someone labeled an alcoholic may find that many other accomplishments are evaluated with the preface, "for an alcoholic" or "despite his (her) alcoholism," even though these accomplishments might have been exactly the same if the person were not an alcoholic. An outstanding, positively evaluated quality may also be taken as the focal point for labeling and evaluating the entire person. The very beautiful and the very brilliant may be heard to lament the fact that no one attends to their "true selves." In terms of social evaluation the beauty is very different from the beast, but in terms of how those social labels dehumanize each, they are, indeed, similar.

In sum, it is usually the case that spontaneous and comfortable sociable interaction between normal and deviant will not occur unless and until labeling issues have been settled in ways palatable to the handicapped, unless and until the permanently handicapped have successfully disavowed and the temporarily handicapped have successfully avowed the meaning and content of their deviant label and role.

ENCOUNTERS WITH AGENTS OF SOCIAL CONTROL

In contrast, a handicap is not a potential threat to interaction in physical therapy; rather, it is the reason for that encounter. Physical therapy, therefore, provides another type of social setting in which the handicapped actively shape the content and centrality of a deviant label and role.

In physical therapy situations, just as in sociable encounters, the handicapped do not want to be defined and evaluated only in terms of their deviance. Yet, both the avowal and disavowal strategies of sociable encounters are inappropriate to and incongruent with the demands and expectations of therapy: therapists need information about how their patients are responding to treatment; they expect patients to be willing to

describe themselves fully in terms of their disabilities and to cooperate in making those disabilities the continuing focus of the encounter; the handicapped need the skillful ministrations of their therapists and must provide the information about their disabilities that is needed for the exercise of those therapeutic skills. Given both the inevitable symbiotic relationship and the different goals for the interaction, interesting patterns of accommodation between physical therapists and their temporarily and permanently disabled patients evolve.

Those defined as permanently handicapped by themselves and their therapists try to present a definition of self like the definition presented in sociable interactions, one that says this handicap is *not all* of who I am. To accomplish this interaction goal in therapy, the permanently disabled find ways of introducing information about untainted parts of themselves.

Those defined as temporarily handicapped by themselves and their therapists try to present a definition of self like the definition presented in sociable interaction, one that says this handicap will *not always* be who I am. To emphasize the temporary nature of that deviance, they often act as though they have already recovered. They try to change the encounter to one of interaction between two normals by encouraging their therapists to behave in a self-disclosing and non-professional manner, by altercasting them into the role of friend (Weinstein and Deutschberger, 1963, 1964).

In effect, the permanently handicapped communicate that they will be "good patients" for their therapists only if they also can be "whole human beings" to them. A few were quite explicit about their demands: one said that if he were treated like a piece of damaged meat, he would be goat's (i.e. tough) meat. Since the therapists themselves tend to speak in very general terms about dealing with patients in warm and compassionate ways and about treating the person, not just the disability, there is usually a receptivity or willingness to relate to patients as multifaceted people. But it is the permanently disabled themselves who tend to initiate the introduction of and to provide the content for these other nontainted or normal roles. The mechanisms are very similar to those used by the permanently handicapped in sociable situations: props begin to be used, conversations are initiated, and topics are doggedly pursued until recognition and legitimation from the therapist of these valued identities and roles are forthcoming.

Some patients arrange to have their family and friends pick them up, not in the hospital waiting room, but right in the physical therapy area itself, even though the waiting room is the designated area. Patients will engage their therapists and friends or family in conversation, often prolonging the encounter until the therapist has indicated adequate interest in and agreement with the patient's activities with family and friends. One patient brought in her photo album to show her therapist. Later that week, another patient brought in her album to share with her therapist, and others soon followed suit. Another patient brought in samples of products he merchandized, but he made his sales pitch only to his therapist, not to other patients or therapists who were also potential customers.

Occasionally the demands to be labeled as more valuable than one's presence in therapy might suggest were blatantly manipulative: a patient changed her therapist's tepid interest in hearing about her (the patient's) son's wedding by saying something about her previous therapist not being interested and not being a very good therapist either. The duration of that therapy session was devoted to a discussion of the wedding, and of examples of what a good mother the patient both was and continued to be despite her permanent handicap.

It is with the temporarily handicapped, however, that serious problems in negotiating an identity acceptable to both therapist and patient are apt to occur, for the temporarily handicapped tend to insist on definitions unacceptable to the therapist. To emphasize that they will soon be well, and in anticipation of that time, they try to altercast the therapist into the role of friend, almost suggesting that they have already recovered, and are only in therapy because they enjoy sociable visits with their therapists. One patient even said that since he would not need to practice his exercises much longer, he would practice being a friend.

In order to induce their therapists to step out of their professional roles and disclose personal aspects of themselves, the temporarily handicapped may ask personal questions, inquiring about their therapists' families, asking how other patients are progressing, or generally presuming the kind of easy intimacy that occurs between people who are personally involved with each other. The therapists strongly resist these attempts at intimacy, believing that they cannot do their work properly if they become too involved with their patients. They insist that their patients must face their handicaps and deal with them realistically, however temporary those handicaps might be, and that therapy is the place where patients, however many other valued labels and roles they may have, are, ultimately, patients, not intimates. Thus, altercasting attempts are usually squelched: patients who invite their therapists to parties or to dinner find that their therapists neither accept these invitations nor ask them to their own homes. One respondent was "gravely wounded" when she found that she had not been invited to a shower her therapist had given for another therapist because, as she insisted, they should be "good friends." A patient who was told that the staff coffee room was off limits to him was perplexed, chagrined, and felt rejected.

Clearly there is more room for negotiation between patient and therapist than the formal structure of the hospital, norms, or roles suggest. Since the therapist's own successful performance depends, to some extent, on the co-operation of the patient, patients are able to negotiate from a position of some strength. Participation in therapy is voluntary, and the patient can, as a last resort, terminate contact with a therapist who is not adequately sympathetic. Indeed several patients mentioned that there had been a therapist so cold and unsympathetic to their needs that patients refused to deal with her. Her tenure at the hospital was brief.

It is primarily in the early stages of physical therapy that patients are most active in trying to define themselves in relation to their therapists. When the therapy is of long duration, the *modus vivendi* established usually seems to be the cordial but distant relationship preferred by the therapists, who are more experienced and more skilled than their patients in structuring the encounter in preferred ways. Since many of the temporarily handicapped need only a short period of therapy, tension and conflict rather than stable patterns of interaction and accommodation are more often observed.

SUMMARY

The evidently disabled adults interviewed in this study recognized the devalued statuses their recent illness or injury had brought them, but they vigorously and systematically tried to influence the content of their deviant label and role in ways most favorable to themselves. A major social problem for the handicapped is that normals tend to organize their perceptions and evaluations around the disability and to ignore the handicapped's many valued aspects and identities. These handicapped actively resisted such a social fate, but their preferred definitions and strategies varied with the duration of the disability (temporary or more permanent) and the type of encounter (sociable encounters and encounters with agents of social control).

Trying to negotiate a preferred definition of self is limited neither to the handicapped nor to other types of deviants, though examples of their behaviors are the basis of this paper. To the contrary, the active bargaining for preferred definitions, the attempts to negotiate a situation to one's own advantage, the subtle, and not so subtle, processes through which people agree to become who they are to each other are among the most basic elements of social life (see for example Carson, 1969; Emerson, 1969; Garfinkel, 1967; Goffman, 1959, 1963; McCall and Simmons, 1966; Shibutani, 1970). It is, however, instructive to examine how those apt to be labeled deviant initiate and direct these processes. In some sense, they have the most to lose. To be labeled as a particular kind of deviant may mean to incur a number of adverse consequences, such as punishment or isolation. Therefore, deviants in encounters with normals may be more active than normals encountering normals in trying to legitimate preferred definitions.

The physically handicapped, as one class of deviants, are particularly interesting. Since there is general agreement about the devalued status of a handicap, attention can be focused on the active ways in which such deviants assert themselves, even within the rather narrow range of choices or identities and roles that their handicap has left them. Attention to the active participation of the disabled in the labeling process provides a needed addition to the labeling perspective.

REFERENCES

Barker, R., Wright, B., Myerson, L. and Gonick, M. *Adjustment to Physical Handicap and Illness: A Survey of the Social Psychology of Physique and Disability.* New York: Social Science Research Council, 1953.

Becker, H. S. *Outsiders. Studies in the Sociology of Deviance.* New York: The Free Press of Glencoe, 1963.

———. "Labeling Theory Reconsidered." Proceedings of the British Sociological Association, 1971.

Carson, R. C. *Interaction Concepts of Personality.* Chicago: Aldine Publishing Company, 1969.

Cicourel, A. *The Social Organization of Juvenile Justice.* New York: Wiley, 1968.

Davis, F. "Deviance Disavowal: The Management of Strained Interaction by the Visibly Handicapped." *Social Problems* 9 (1961):120–132.

Dembo, T., Leviton, G. and Wright, B. "Adjustment for Misfortune—a Problem of Social-Psychological Rehabilitation." *Artificial Limbs* 3 (1956):4–62.

Emerson, J. "Negotiating the Serious Import of Humor." *Sociometry* 32 (1969):169–181.

Erikson, K. "Notes on the Sociology of Deviance." *Social Problems* 9 (1962):307–314.

Filstead, W. (ed.). *An Introduction to Deviance.* Chicago: Markham Publishing Company, 1972.

Freidson, E. "Disability as Social Deviance." *Sociology and Rehabilitation.* Edited by M. Sussman. Washington, D.C.: American Sociological Association, 1965, pp. 71–99.

Garfinkel, H. *Studies in Ethnomethodology.* Englewood Cliffs, New Jersey: Prentice-Hall, Inc., 1967.

Gibbs, J. "Conceptions of Deviant Behavior: The Old and the New." *Pacific Sociological Review* 9 (1966):9–14.

Goffman, E. *The Presentation of Self in Everyday Life.* New York: Doubleday Anchor Books, 1959.

———. *Stigma.* Englewood Cliffs, New Jersey: Prentice-Hall, Inc., 1963.

Kitsuse, J. I. "Societal Reaction to Deviant Behavior: Problems of Theory and Method." *Social Problems* 9 (1962):247–256.

———. "Deviance, Deviant Behavior, and Deviants: Some Conceptual Problems." *An Introduction to Deviance.* Edited by W. Filstead. Chicago: Markham Publishing Company, 1972, pp. 233–243.

Kitsuse, J. I. and Cicourel, A. "A Note on the Uses of Official Statistics." *Social Problems* 12 (1963):131–139.

Lemert, E. *Social Pathology.* New York: McGraw-Hill, 1951.

Lorber, J. "Deviance as Performance: The Case of Illness." *Social Problems* 14 (1967):302–310.

McCall, G. J. and Simmons, J. L. *Identities and Interactions.* New York: The Free Press, 1966.

Matza, D. *Becoming Deviant.* Englewood Cliffs, New Jersey: Prentice Hall, 1969.

Meyers, J. "Consequences and Prognoses of Disability." *Sociology and Rehabilitation.* Edited by M. Sussman. Washington, D.C.: American Sociological Association, 1965, pp. 35–51.

Rubington, E. and Weinberg, M. (eds.). *Deviance—the Interactionist Perspective* New York: The Macmillan Company, 1968.

Scheff, T. *Being Mentally Ill.* Chicago: Aldine, 1966.

Schur, E. *Crimes Without Victims.* Englewood Cliffs, New Jersey: Prentice-Hall, 1965.

———. "Reactions to Deviance: A Critical Assessment." *American Journal of Sociology* 75: (1969):309–322.

Shibutani, T. *Human Nature and Collective Behavior.* Englewood Cliffs, New Jersey: Prentice-Hall, Inc., 1970.

Stoll, C. "Images of Man and Social Control." *Social Forces* 47 (1968):119–127.

Sykes, G. and Matza, D. "Techniques of Neutralization." *American Sociological Review* 22 (1957):664–670.

Turner, R. "Deviance Avowal as Neutralization of Commitment." *Social Problems* 19 (1972):308–321.

Weinstein, E. and Deutschberger, P. "Some Dimensions of Altercasting." *Sociometry* 26 (1963):454–466.

———. "Tasks, Bargains, and Identities in Social Interaction." *Social Forces* 42 (1964):451–455.

Williams, C. and Weinberg, M. "Being Discovered: A Study of Homosexuals in the Military." *Social Problems* 18 (1970):217–227.

Wright, B. *Physical Disability—a Psychological Approach.* New York: Harper and Brothers, Publishers, 1960.

The Self in the Emotionally Disturbed[1]

As George H. Mead has pointed out, human beings tend to act on the basis of their inferences about the probable behavior of others toward them.[2] Moreover, our feelings about ourselves are mediated by how we think others feel about us. This is to say that much of our behavior is guided by what we think others are thinking and by our confidence in what we judge to be the readiness of others to act upon what we think they impute to us. In brief, it is axiomatic in Mead's psychology that there are functional relationships between how we see ourselves, how we see others, and how we think others see us. Similarly, basic to Mead's theory is the idea that such relationships have important consequences in overt behavior and are also phenomena of interpersonal perception.

While it may be logically reasonable to set forth such principles, the occasion to validate them by means of operational procedures is less frequently at hand. For it seems implicit in Mead's theory that it is necessary to take temporal changes into account in order to demonstrate empirically functional relationships among the self processes. Ideally, changes in the self would occur over a relatively long period of time during which the individual moves sequentially through the stages of the play, the game, and the generalized other. Moreover, once having developed to that stage of socialization, most persons maintain a rather stable and continuing set of relationships among the functions of the self. In terms of the consequences in overt behavior, Sullivan has referred to such stability as "the repeated situations which characterize a human life."[3] Whatever the terminology, however, the behavior of persons becomes relatively stable and predictable insofar as there is some convergence between how they see themselves, how they see others, and how they think others see them.

In the case of persons undergoing intensive psychiatric treatment, however, basic changes in interpersonal behavior frequently occur very rapidly. Therefore, the study of emotionally disturbed persons may offer opportunities to put to the test some aspects of Mead's theory which, under normal circumstances, would require either many years to do or could be done only by clinical or retrospective analysis.

With the exception of clinical descriptions of distorted self-concepts of individual psychiatric patients, little empirical evidence is available

William R. Rosengren, "The Self in the Emotionally Disturbed." Reprinted from *The American Journal of Sociology,* vol. 66 (March 1961), pp. 454–462, by permission of The University of Chicago Press. Copyright 1961 by The University of Chicago.

[1] Part of a four-year project in social psychiatry under Grant OM-21 from the National Institute of Mental Health, United States Public Health Service.

[2] George Herbert Mead, *Mind, Self, and Society* (Chicago: University of Chicago Press, 1934).

[3] Harry Stack Sullivan, *Conceptions of Modern Psychiatry* (Washington, D.C.: William Alanson White Psychiatric Foundation, 1947), p. vi.

TABLE 39.1.   Interpersonal qualities

Friendly-accepting	Hostile-rejecting
Generous	Selfish
Good	Bad
Nice	Mean
Smart	Dumb
Kind	Cruel
Brave	Afraid
Clean	Dirty
Well-liked	Ugly
Honest	
Strong	
Neat	

about the processes of self-definition, inference, and imputation among persons who have been institutionalized for emotional disturbance.[4] The purpose of this paper is to report the findings of a study of interpersonal inference and imputation among a group of institutionalized emotionally disturbed children whose chief reason for hospitalization was inadequate reciprocity with others. A major aim is to demonstrate empirically changes in the functional relationships of the processes of the self, before and after long-term residential treatment, and to report their relationships to other indexes of changed behavior.

The subjects were ten boys, ranging in age from ten to twelve years, who were receiving long-term residential treatment in a private psychiatric hospital for children. The total patient population numbered fifty-six, of which the subjects constituted one of six units. They had all received clinical diagnoses of "Passive-Aggressive Personality—Aggressive Type" and were the only patients in the institution who were homogeneously grouped on the basis of diagnosis and symptomatology. Such patients are more commonly referred to as "acting-out"; their overt behavior is generally typified by spontaneous verbal

and physical aggression, short attention span, and inability to delay gratifications, and they tend to have histories of interpersonal difficulties with both adults and peers. At the time of the first testing, all of the boys had lived together twenty-four hours a day for at least one year, and some for as long as two years.

PROCEDURES

Interpersonal Perceptions

In September, 1958, an "inference-imputation" test was administered to the subjects along with tests of several other criteria. This "Self-definition Test" involved nineteen interpersonal qualities which were dichotomized into those which are "friendly-accepting" and those which are "hostile-rejecting" in nature; these are shown in Table 39.1.

Two days prior to the individual testing sessions, each boy was asked the following "near-sociometric" questions: (1) "Which of the boys (in the unit) do you like best of all?" (2) "Which do you dislike the most?" (3) "Which do you think likes you the most?" and (4) "Which do you think dislikes you the most?"

For ease in administration, each quality was printed in India ink on a 5 × 7-inch card. Each boy then sorted the cards at least five times: (1) a description of himself *(self-definition)*, (2) a description of the boy he had chosen as the one he liked best *(imputation)*, (3) a description of the boy he had chosen as the most disliked *(imputation)*, (4) a description of himself from the point of view of the boy whom he thought liked him *(inference)*, and (5) a description of himself from the point of view of the boy whom he thought disliked him *(inference)*. Those boys who had been chosen by others as either "I think he likes me" or "I think he dislikes me" were then asked to describe the individuals who had chosen them in those ways.

One year later, in September, 1959, the boys underwent the identical sociometric and inference-imputation procedures.

---

[4] The most recent published attempt to put to test operational aspects of the social psychology of Mead is, perhaps, Carl J. Couch's "Self-attitudes and Degree of Agreement with Immediate Others," *American Journal of Sociology*, LXIII (1958), 491–96.

TABLE 39.2. Scale for behavior of rating "acting-out" patients

Symptomatic Behaviors	Non-symptomatic Behaviors
Irrelevant: Diffuse and random activity	*Relevant:* Goal-directed activity
Active: Mobile, labile, expressive behavior	*Passive:* Restrained, inexpressive, inactive behavior
Rejecting: Disassociates from others; rejects interactions	*Affiliative:* Associates with others; responds to and initiates interactions
Narcissistic: "Exclusive" interest in self	*Other-oriented:* Shows interest in others, positively or negatively
Dominant: Attempts to dominate, control, and direct	*Submissive:* Submits to domination, control, and direction by others
Succorant: Seeks help, assistance, support, and affection	*Nurturant:* Gives help, assistance, support, and affection
Aggressive: Attempts to destroy, humiliate, and degrade	*Blame avoidance:* Withdraws from or otherwise avoids aggression-eliciting situations
Immediacy: Seeks for immediate gratification	*Endurance:* Foregoes immediate satisfactions for future gratifications
Impulsive: Spontaneous and unreflectful behavior	*Deliberation:* Hesitant, cautious, and reflectful behavior
Non-verbal: Little talking of affiliative or rejecting type	*Verbal:* Much talking either of affiliative or rejecting type

Observation

Over a six-month period—from October, 1958, to March, 1959—the subjects were observed by a non-participant observer in a variety of situations for a total of sixty hours of direct observation. The overt behavior of the ten boys was rated on a "moreness-lessness" basis using the qualities of interaction listed in Table 39.2. Those on the left of the rating scale are symptomatic forms of behavior, while those on the right are non-symptomatic for this diagnostic category of patients. The methods, procedures, and findings of this part of the study are reported elsewhere.[5]

Control-eliciting Behavior

The behavior of patients of this type occasionally becomes so dangerous either to themselves or to others that, if some means of restraint were

not used, severe physical harm would result. In such instances the acting-out patient is placed alone in a locked room until his behavior becomes physically tolerable. Accurate records are maintained of the use of this means of restraint in the institution. These data were accumulated for each of the ten subjects at the end of one year.

Institutional Expectations

In both 1958 and 1959 the subjects responded to a test of "institutional expectations."[6] This consisted of ten story completions in which a boy was depicted as engaging in some moderately acting-out form of behavior in an institutional setting. The boys responded to each story by describing events which they expected would follow the incident which was presented. One, for example, read as follows: "Bob is supposed to take pills in the morning and in the afternoon. But he doesn't swallow them—he throws them

[5] See William R. Rosengren, "The Social Field in Relation to the Behavior of Emotionally Disturbed Children," *Sociometry* (in press).

[6] This was an adaption of a similar set of story completions reported in W. and J. McCord, *Psychopathy and Delinquency* (New York: Grune & Stratton, Inc., 1957).

out the window. One day the nurse found out about it and then . . ." The subjects' responses were classified as involving either hostile or benign institutional responses. An example of a hostile expectation is, "She (the nurse) drags him to the room and gives him needles and he gets sicker." An example of a benign expectation is, "She tells him that the pills help him so he takes them." Typically, the more severely disturbed the patient, the more hostile are his expectations and, presumably, his anticipatory responses to them.

TREATMENT OF DATA

Interpersonal Perceptions

Sums of "friendly-accepting" and "hostile-rejecting" choices were computed on the first (1958) and second (1959) series of self-definition tests on each of the dimensions—inference-imputation, definition-inference, and definition-imputation. The study was chiefly concerned with changes in the similarity and dissimilarity in choices of qualities in the one year. Because the total number of choices was not the same for all the subjects on either the first or the second series, changes were measured in terms of proportions rather than raw choice scores. Comparing, for example, the similarity of self-definitions and inferences, a "similar" choice was regarded as one in which the subject defined himself as generous and expected (inferred) that others (either the liked or disliked person) would also define him as generous. There were two possibilities for "dissimilar" choices; (1) the subject defined himself as generous but felt that the referent person would not so define him; or (2) the subject did not ascribe the quality of generosity to himself but felt that the referent person would define him as generous. Proportions of each similar inference-imputation, definition-inference, and definition-imputation dimension were computed in that fashion for each subject on the first and then on the second testing.

The significance of proportional change was computed through the use of the Wilcoxon Matched-Pairs Signed-Ranks Test, with probability levels derived directly from the value of T.[7] In all cases the one-tailed test was used because the direction of change was predicted.

The following classification was used for comparing the boys' patterns of interpersonal definition with the other indexes of change: Frequency distributions were made for the total quantity of proportional change under each perceptual relationship for each subject. Those whose total proportion of change in self functions was one standard deviation or more above the mean for the ten subjects were classified as "high self-changers." Those whose extent of change was one standard deviation or more below the mean are referred to as "low self-changers." In these terms there were three high and three low self-changers.

Other Indexes of Change

At the end of the six-month period of observation, frequency distributions were made of the extent of change in overt behavior as indicated by the rating scale (Table 39.2). The extent of change was determined by the difference between the sums of scores on the left side of the scale during the first three months and the sum of scores on the left side during the second three months. Three of the boys had undergone significant changes from symptomatic to non-symptomatic behavior (one standard deviation or more above the mean), and three had experienced comparatively little change in behavior (one standard deviation or more below the mean).

Similar frequency distributions were made of the number of "isolations" which each boy had elicited by his physically intolerable behavior during the first six months as compared with the second. Finally, computations were made on both the first and second testings of the number of "benign" [and] the [number of] "hostile" expectations of the institution which each boy had expressed.

[7] This statistic is described and probability tables presented in S. Siegel, *Nonparametric Statistics for the Behavioral Sciences* (New York: McGraw-Hill Book Co., 1956).

SOME EXPECTATIONS FROM MEAD'S THEORY

Clinical knowledge concerning the disturbance syndrome of the patients as well as participant observation for a year and a half formed the chief basis of the general hypotheses; Mead's principles of the interrelatedness of self-definition, inferences of others, and imputations by others underlay each expectation.

It was expected that on the first test the boys would define themselves quite differently from the ways in which they thought others would define them, as compared with the second test. Moreover, it was anticipated that the inferences they made of others on the first test would be different from others' actual imputations, as compared with the second test. More specifically in Mead's terms, it was expected that after one year the subjects would tend to "call out in themselves the responses which they think they call out in others" and that they would "call out in others responses similar to those which they think they call out in others."

Furthermore, it was anticipated that inferences of others would be less contingent upon the "liked-disliked" distinction on the second test as compared with the first. More specifically, it was expected that the boys would infer *more* friendly-accepting qualities of disliked persons and *less* friendly-accepting qualities of liked persons on the second test as compared with the first. Both of these related hypotheses were intended to serve as a means of empirically demonstrating whether the boys would make inferences concerning the ways in which they thought others viewed them with regard to a generalized conception of others' points of view—what might be referred to as the "generalized others"—or would persist in making inferences with reference to specific others in the environment.

Third, it was expected that the boys would tend to make different inferences concerning liked and disliked persons on the first test and more similar inferences on the second. Specifically, it was anticipated that inferences concerning disliked persons' imputations would be less accurate on the first test as compared with the second. Moreover, it was expected that inferences

concerning liked persons' imputations would also be less accurate on the first test than on the second, that is, that the boys would tend to "take the role of specific others" in regard to themselves in an inaccurate fashion on the first test and the "role of the generalized other" in a more accurate fashion on the second test.

Last, it was expected that the boys would tend to define themselves more similarly to the ways in which they thought others defined them on the second test as compared with the first. Specifically, the subjects would define themselves significantly more as they thought the disliked persons defined them. It was also anticipated that a similar change would take place with regard to the liked persons. These two propositions were designed to test the expectation that the subjects would tend to define themselves more in terms of a conception of a generalized other than in terms of a consideration of specific individuals about whom they had contrasting attitudes themselves.

In general, therefore, the data were analyzed with a view to determining the extent of convergence with some basic principles of Mead's social psychology.

First, it was expected that on the first test the subjects would tend to define themselves differently from the ways in which they thought others defined them, while on the second test self-definitions and inferences of others' imputations would be more similar. This expectation was borne out with respect to disliked as well as liked persons (Table 39.3). There was significantly more similarity between how the boys defined themselves and how they thought both liked and disliked persons would define them on the second test as compared with the first.

Second, it was expected that a comparison of the responses on the first and second tests would reveal an increased tendency for the boys to define themselves more as others actually defined them. This expectation was also borne out with regard both to liked and disliked persons, although with somewhat greater confidence in relation to the liked persons (Table 39.4). In general, the data suggested that on the second test the subjects defined themselves more like the ways in which they thought others would define

TABLE 39.3.   Similar self-definitions and inferences of others' imputations: signed-ranks proportions for first and second tests

Inference	N*	T	Less Frequent Sign	p (One-tailed Test)
Liked and disliked persons	10	3	—	>.005
Disliked persons only	10	9	—	>.025
Liked persons only	10	8	—	>.025

* Refers to the elimination of tied proportions between pairs. Levels of significance for N's less than 25 are determined directly from the magnitude of T.

TABLE 39.4.   Similar inferences of others and imputations by others: signed-ranks proportions for first and second tests

Person Making Imputation by	N*	T	Less Frequent Sign	p (One-tailed Test)
Liked and disliked	10	2	—	>.01
Disliked only	10	8	—	>.025
Liked only	10	0	—	>.005

* See n. to Table 3.

TABLE 39.5.   "Friendly-accepting" qualities inferred of specific others: signed-ranks proportions for first and second tests

Referent	N*	T	Less Frequent Sign	p (One-tailed Test)
Disliked person	10	1	—	>.005
Liked person	10	0	+	>.005

* See n. to Table 3.

them. Moreover, there was a tendency for the "others" actually to impute those qualities which the boys thought would be imputed to them.

Furthermore, it was predicted that the subjects would be less likely to infer hostile-rejecting qualities of the disliked persons and friendly-accepting qualities of the liked persons on the second test than they did a year earlier (Table 39.5). There was, in fact, a tendency for the boys to infer, proportionately, more friendly-accepting qualities of the persons whom they disliked and

less hostile-rejecting qualities on the second test. Moreover, they also tended to expect proportionately less friendly-accepting imputations by liked persons on the second test. These findings may indicate that on the second test the subjects made inferences on the basis of a somewhat more generalized view of themselves rather than of a conception of specific persons' probable views of them.

The fourth general expectation was related to the issue of the subjects' accuracy in making

TABLE 39.6. Similar inferences and implications: signed-ranks proportions for first and second tests

Referent and Inference-Imputation	N*	T	Less Frequent Sign	p (One-tailed Test)
All persons, all qualities	10	2	—	$> .01$
All persons, "friendly"	10	1	—	$> .005$
All persons, "hostile"	10	1	—	$> .005$
Liked persons, all qualities	10	0	—	$> .005$
Liked persons, "friendly"	10	6	—	$> .025$
Disliked persons, all qualities	10	8	—	$> .025$
Disliked persons, "friendly"	9	1	—	$> .005$
Disliked persons, "hostile"	9	0	—	$> .005$
Liked persons, "hostile"	6	3	—	$< .025$

* See n. to Table 3.

inferences about other persons' imputations to them. Was there, in other words, a tendency for the boys increasingly to "call out from others the responses which they thought they called out in others?" The findings with regard to person referent—liked and disliked—and type of qualities inferred—friendly or hostile—are reported in Table 39.6.

As Table 39.6 indicates, the most discriminating differentiation was that in which the referent person involved as well as the distinction between friendly and hostile qualities were controlled. The most significant change between the first and second test was with respect to the disliked rather than the liked persons. Specifically, the subjects tended to infer qualities of disliked persons more similar to those which were actually imputed to them by disliked persons on the second test, as compared with the first. Furthermore, while there was increased similarity concerning inferences of friendly imputations by liked persons which was not statistically significant, the changes which did appear were in the predicted direction. With this qualification, the data do suggest two tentative conclusions. First, the boys were more accurate in inferring those qualities which others actually imputed to them. Second, this might indicate that on the first test the boys attempted to define themselves from the point of view of specific others, and to do this in a comparatively inaccurate way. On the second test, however, they

seemed to define themselves from the point of view of a more generalized frame of reference which resulted, in fact, in considerably greater accuracy in inferring imputations by specific others.

Finally, it was anticipated that on the second test the boys would be more likely to define themselves in the same terms as they thought both the liked and disliked persons would define them. That is, greater similarity between self-definitions and inferences was expected. As can be seen in Table 39.7, significant changes could best be identified when the referent person and the type of interpersonal quality were controlled. Specifically, the boys did tend to define themselves somewhat more as they thought the disliked persons would define them, but only with regard to the hostile-rejecting qualities. Moreover, while the increased similarity in this regard relative to the liked persons was not beyond what could have been expected by chance alone, it was in the predicted direction. It might be concluded, therefore, that on the first test the boys defined themselves as they thought both liked and disliked persons would do, but only with regard to friendly-accepting qualities. On the second test, however, they showed an increased inclination to include hostile-rejecting qualities in the similarities between how they defined themselves and how they thought significant others would define them.

TABLE 39.7.   Similar self-definitions and inferences: signed-ranks proportions for first and second tests

Referent and Self-definition-Inference	N*	T	Less Frequent Sign	p (One-tailed Test)
All persons, "hostile"	9	0	—	>.005
Disliked persons, all qualities	10	5	—	>.01
Disliked persons, "hostile"	10	0	—	>.005
All persons, all qualities	9	10	—	<.025
All persons, "friendly"	10	22	+ = —	<.025
Liked persons, all qualities	10	14	—	<.025
Liked persons, "friendly"	10	10	—	<.025
Liked persons, "hostile"	9	8	—	<.025
Disliked persons, "friendly"	9	11	—	<.025

* See n. to Table 3.

When one contrasts the responses of the subjects on the first test with those on the second, several distinct patterns appear. On the *first* test they tended to define themselves dissimilar to the ways in which they thought others defined them. Second, both liked and disliked persons tended to impute to the subjects qualities dissimilar to those which the subjects expected would be imputed to them. Furthermore, the subjects tended to expect that liked persons would impute significantly more friendly-accepting qualities and that disliked persons would impute significantly more hostile-rejecting qualities. This is to say that their inferences about themselves appeared to be made with reference to particular persons in their immediate experience. Fourth, they were comparatively inaccurate in inferring what qualities others—both liked and disliked persons—would actually impute to them. Last, they tended to define themselves differently from the ways in which they thought both liked and disliked persons would define them with an accompanying tendency for them to be somewhat more sensitized to friendly-accepting than to hostile-rejecting attributes.

On the *second* test, on the other hand, they tended to define themselves more as they thought others defined them. Second, both the liked and the disliked persons tended to impute those qualities which the inferring subjects thought the others would. Third, the boys tended to expect that liked persons would impute significantly more hostile-rejecting qualities and that the disliked persons would impute more friendly-accepting qualities. Fourth, they were somewhat more accurate in inferring those qualities others actually imputed to them. Last, they tended to define themselves somewhat more as they thought both the liked and disliked persons would define them and were increasingly accurate in regard to hostile-rejecting qualities.

In terms of Mead's theory of the self, it would appear that on the first test the boys tended to (1) call out in themselves responses unlike those which they thought they called out in others, (2) call out in others responses unlike those which they thought they called out in others, (3) make inferences from the point of view of specific others rather than of a generalized other, and (4) define themselves in terms of specific other persons.

On the second test, on the other hand, they tended to (1) call out in themselves responses more like those which they thought they called out in others, (2) call out in others responses more like those which they thought they called out in others, (3) make inferences from the point of view of a generalized other rather than of specific others, and (4) define themselves in terms of a generalized other rather than of specific others.

RELATIONSHIP TO OTHER INDEXES OF CHANGE

Although these findings may well suggest that both the functions and the content of the self changed significantly in the one year, it is of further interest to know to what extent and in what ways such patterns might be associated with other indexes of change.

First, the three "high self-changers" were also the three boys whose overt behavior changed most significantly from symptomatic to non-symptomatic during the six months in which observational ratings of behavior were made: the boys whose self functions more nearly approximated Mead's ideal were those who experienced increasingly fewer difficulties with both their peers and the adults working with them. Conversely, those whose self processes changed the least along lines of Mead's expectations were those who continued both to initiate symptomatic interactions and reacted to others in a significantly symptomatic fashion.

Second, with regard to highly disruptive behavior which necessitated isolation of the patient, the three high self-changers were also those who were significantly less often isolated in the one year than formerly. On the other hand, those boys whose self processes changed the least were also the ones who were isolated either significantly *more* often, or as often, in the one year.

Last, with regard to expectations of the institution, the three high self-changers were also the boys whose expectations of the institution's actions toward them changed most significantly from "hostile" at the beginning of the year to "benign" at the end. Conversely, the "low self-changers" continued comparatively often to expect hostile action and seldom to expect benign action in the one year.

On the basis of these findings it is concluded that, in the boys studied, changes in the functions and content of the self were associated with overt changes in behavior as well as with changes in a somewhat more basic orientation toward their immediate social environment.

CONCLUSIONS

This paper has reported an attempt to relate data from a test of interpersonal inferences, imputations, and self-definitions to some of the chief assertions of Mead's social psychology. The findings are tentative, and the conclusions and interpretations which have been made are best regarded as only suggestive. Because of the small number of subjects involved and the difficulties characteristic of studies of interpersonal perception,[8] both the findings and the conclusions are best regarded as a preliminary effort.

The concept of the self as used in the social psychology of Mead is one that continues to be an intriguing basis for much speculation and interpretation. It also continues, however, to present many difficulties for empirical investigation and validation. The limited field study reported in this paper is an attempt to put the concept of the self to empirical test with a view to further elaborating its importance in human behavior.

[8] See, e.g., L. J. Cronbach, "Proposal Leading to Analytic Treatment of Social Perception Scores," in R. Tagiuri and L. Petrullo (eds.), *Person, Perception and Interpersonal Behavior* (Stanford, Calif.: Stanford University Press, 1958), pp. 353–78.

The Moral Career of the
Mental Patient

Traditionally the term *career* has been reserved for those who expect to enjoy the rises laid out within a respectable profession. The term is coming to be used, however, in a broadened sense to refer to any social strand of any person's course through life. The perspective of natural history is taken: unique outcomes are neglected in favor of such changes over time as are basic and common to the members of a social category, although occurring independently to each of them. Such a career is not a thing that can be brilliant or disappointing; it can no more be a success than a failure. In this light, I want to consider the mental patient, drawing mainly upon data collected during a year's participant observation of patient social life in a public mental hospital,[1] wherein an attempt was made to take the patient's point of view.

Erving Goffman, "The Moral Career of the Mental Patient," *Psychiatry: Journal for the Study of Interpersonal Processes,* vol. 22 (May 1959), pp. 123–142. Copyright © 1959 by The William Alanson White Psychiatric Foundation, Inc. Reprinted by special permission of The William Alanson White Psychiatric Foundation, Inc.

[1] The study was conducted during 1955–56 under the auspices of the Laboratory of Socio-environmental Studies of the National Institute of Mental Health. I am grateful to the Laboratory Chief, John A. Clausen, and to Dr. Winfred Overholser, Superintendent, and the late Dr. Jay Hoffman, then First Assistant Physician of Saint Elizabeth's Hospital, Washington, D.C., for the ideal cooperation they freely provided. A preliminary report is contained in Goffman, "Interpersonal Persuasion," pp. 117–193; in *Group Processes: Transactions of the Third Conference,* edited by Bertram Schaffner; New York, Josiah Macy, Jr. Foundation, 1957. A shorter version of this paper was presented at the Annual Meeting of the American Sociological Society, Washington, D.C., August, 1957.

One value of the concept of career is its two-sidedness. One side is linked to internal matters held dearly and closely, such as image of self and felt identity; the other side concerns official position, jural relations, and style of life, and is part of a publicly accessible institutional complex. The concept of career, then, allows one to move back and forth between the personal and the public, between the self and its significant society, without having overly to rely for data upon what the person says he thinks he imagines himself to be.

This paper, then, is an exercise in the institutional approach to the study of self. The main concern will be with the *moral* aspects of career—that is, the regular sequence of changes that career entails in the person's self and in his framework of imagery for judging himself and others.[2]

The category "mental patient" itself will be understood in one strictly sociological sense. In this perspective, the psychiatric view of a person becomes significant only in so far as this view itself alters his social fate—an alteration which seems to become fundamental in our society when, and only when, the person is put through the process of hospitalization.[3] I therefore exclude certain

[2] Material on moral career can be found in early social anthropological work on ceremonies of status transition, and in classic social psychological descriptions of those spectacular changes in one's view of self that can accompany participation in social movements and sects. Recently new kinds of relevant data have been suggested by psychiatric interest in the problem of "identity" and sociological studies of work careers and "adult socialization."

[3] This point has recently been made by Elaine and John Cumming, *Closed Ranks;* Cambridge, Commonwealth Fund, Har-

neighboring categories: the undiscovered candidates who would be judged "sick" by psychiatric standards but who never come to be viewed as such by themselves or others, although they may cause everyone a great deal of trouble;[4] the office patient whom a psychiatrist feels he can handle with drugs or shock on the outside; the mental client who engages in psychotherapeutic relationships. And I include anyone, however robust in temperament, who somehow gets caught up in the heavy machinery of mental hospital servicing. In this way the effects of being treated as a mental patient can be kept quite distinct from the effects upon a person's life of traits a clinician would view as psychopathological.[5] Persons who become mental hospital patients vary widely in the kind and degree of illness that a psychiatrist would impute to them, and in the attributes by which laymen would describe them. But once started on the way, they are confronted by some importantly similar circumstances and respond to these in some importantly similar ways. Since these similarities do not come from mental illness, they would seem to occur in spite of it. It is thus a tribute to the power of social forces that the uniform status of mental patient can not only assure an aggregate of persons a common fate and eventually, because of this, a common character, but

that this social reworking can be done upon what is perhaps the most obstinate diversity of human materials that can be brought together by society. Here there lacks only the frequent forming of a protective group-life by ex-patients to illustrate in full the classic cycle of response by which deviant subgroupings are psychodynamically formed in society.

This general sociological perspective is heavily reinforced by one key finding of sociologically oriented students in mental hospital research. As has been repeatedly shown in the study of nonliterate societies, the awesomeness, distastefulness, and barbarity of a foreign culture can decrease in the degree that the student becomes familiar with the point of view to life that is taken by his subjects. Similarly, the student of mental hospitals can discover that the craziness or "sick behavior" claimed for the mental patient is by and large a product of the claimant's social distance from the situation that the patient is in, and is not primarily a product of mental illness. Whatever the refinements of the various patients' psychiatric diagnoses, and whatever the special ways in which social life on the "inside" is unique, the researcher can find that he is participating in a community not significantly different from any other he has studied.[6] Of course, while restricting himself to the off-ward grounds community of paroled patients, he may feel, as some patients do, that life in the locked wards is bizarre; and while on a locked admissions or convalescent ward, he may feel that chronic "back" wards are socially crazy places. But he need only move his sphere of sympathetic participation to the "worst" ward in the hospital, and this too can come into social focus as a place with a livable and continuously meaningful social world. This in no way denies that he will find a minority in any ward or patient group that continues to seem quite beyond the capacity to follow rules of social organization, or that the orderly fulfilment of normative expectations in patient society is partly made possible by strategic measures that have somehow come to be institutionalized in mental hospitals.

vard Univ. Press, 1957; pp. 101–102. "Clinical experience supports the impression that many people define mental illness as 'That condition for which a person is treated in a mental hospital.'. . . Mental illness, it seems, is a condition which afflicts people who must go to a mental institution, but until they do almost anything they do is normal." Leila Deasy has pointed out to me the correspondence here with the situation in white collar crime. Of those who are detected in this activity, only the ones who do not manage to avoid going to prison find themselves accorded the social role of the criminal.

[4] Case records in mental hospitals are just now coming to be exploited to show the incredible amount of trouble a person may cause for himself and others before anyone begins to think about him psychiatrically, let alone take psychiatric action against him. See John A. Clausen and Marian Radke Yarrow, "Paths to the Mental Hospital," *J. Social Issues* (1955) 11:25–32; August B. Hollingshead and Fredrick C. Redlich, *Social Class and Mental Illness;* New York, Wiley, 1958; pp. 173–174.

[5] An illustration of how this perspective may be taken to all forms of deviancy may be found in Edwin Lemert, *Social Pathology;* New York, McGraw-Hill, 1951; see especially pp. 74–76. A specific application to mental defectives may be found in Stewart E. Perry, "Some Theoretic Problems of Mental Deficiency and Their Action Implications," *Psychiatry* (1954) 17:45–73; see especially p. 68.

[6] Conscientious objectors who voluntarily went to jail sometimes arrived at the same conclusion regarding criminal inmates. See, for example, Alfred Hassler, *Diary of a Self-made Convict;* Chicago, Regnery, 1954; p. 74.

The career of the mental patient falls popularly and naturalistically into three main phases: the period prior to entering the hospital, which I shall call the *prepatient phase;* the period in the hospital, the *inpatient phase;* the period after discharge from the hospital, should this occur, namely, the *ex-patient phase.*[7] This paper will deal only with the first two phases.

THE PREPATIENT PHASE

A relatively small group of prepatients come into the mental hospital willingly, because of their own idea of what will be good for them, or because of wholehearted agreement with the relevant members of their family. Presumably these recruits have found themselves acting in a way which is evidence to them that they are losing their minds or losing control of themselves. This view of oneself would seem to be one of the most pervasively threatening things that can happen to the self in our society, especially since it is likely to occur at a time when the person is in any case sufficiently troubled to exhibit the kind of symptom which he himself can see. As Sullivan described it,

> What we discover in the self-system of a person undergoing schizophrenic changes or schizophrenic processes, is then, in its simplest form, an extremely fear-marked puzzlement, consisting of the use of rather generalized and anything but exquisitely refined referential processes in an attempt to cope with what is essentially a failure at being human—a failure at being anything that one could respect as worth being.[8]

Coupled with the person's disintegrative re-evaluation of himself will be the new, almost equally pervasive circumstance of attempting to conceal from others what he takes to be the new fundamental facts about himself, and attempting

to discover whether others too have discovered them.[9] Here I want to stress that perception of losing one's mind is based on culturally derived and socially engrained stereotypes as to the significance of symptoms such as hearing voices, losing temporal and spatial orientation, and sensing that one is being followed, and that many of the most spectacular and convincing of these symptoms in some instances psychiatrically signify merely a temporary emotional upset in a stressful situation, however terrifying to the person at the time. Similarly, the anxiety consequent upon this perception of oneself, and the strategies devised to reduce this anxiety, are not a product of abnormal psychology, but would be exhibited by any person socialized into our culture who came to conceive of himself as someone losing his mind. Interestingly, subcultures in American society apparently differ in the amount of ready imagery and encouragement they supply for such self-views, leading to differential rates of *self*-referral; the capacity to take this distintegrative view of oneself without psychiatric prompting seems to be one of the questionable cultural privileges of the upper classes.[10]

For the person who has come to see himself—with whatever justification—as mentally unbalanced, entrance to the mental hospital can sometimes bring relief, perhaps in part because of the sudden transformation in the structure of his basic social situations; instead of being to himself a questionable person trying to maintain a role as a full one, he can become an officially questioned person known to himself to be not so questionable as that. In other cases, hospitalization can make matters worse for the willing patient, confirming by the objective situation what has theretofore been a matter of the private experience of self.

Once the willing prepatient enters the hospital, he may go through the same routine of experiences as do those who enter unwillingly. In any

---

[7] This simple picture is complicated by the somewhat special experience of roughly a third of ex-patients—namely, readmission to the hospital, this being the recidivist or "repatient" phase.

[8] Harry Stack Sullivan, *Clinical Studies in Psychiatry;* edited by Helen Swick Perry, Mary Ladd Gawel, and Martha Gibbon; New York, Norton, 1956; pp. 184–185.

[9] This moral experience can be contrasted with that of a person learning to become a marihuana addict, whose discovery that he can be 'high' and still 'op' effectively without being detected apparently leads to a new level of use. See Howard S. Becker, "Marihuana Use and Social Control," *Social Problems* (1955) 3:35–44; see especially pp. 40–41.

[10] See footnote 2; Hollingshead and Redlich, p. 187, Table 6, where relative frequency is given of self-referral by social class grouping.

case, it is the latter that I mainly want to consider, since in America at present these are by far the more numerous kind.[11] Their approach to the institution takes one of three classic forms: they come because they have been implored by their family or threatened with the abrogation of family ties unless they go "willingly"; they come by force under police escort; they come under misapprehension purposely induced by others, this last restricted mainly to youthful prepatients.

The prepatient's career may be seen in terms of an extrusory model; he starts out with relationships and rights, and ends up, at the beginning of his hospital stay, with hardly any of either. The moral aspects of this career, then, typically begin with the experience of abandonment, disloyalty, and embitterment. This is the case even though to others it may be obvious that he was in need of treatment, and even though in the hospital he may soon come to agree.

The case histories of most mental patients document offense against some arrangement for face-to-face living—a domestic establishment, a work place, a semipublic organization such as a church or store, a public region such as a street or park. Often there is also a record of some *complainant,* some figure who takes that action against the offender which eventually leads to his hospitalization. This may not be the person who makes the first move, but it is the person who makes what turns out to be the first effective move. Here is the *social* beginning of the patient's career, regardless of where one might locate the psychological beginning of his mental illness.

The kinds of offenses which lead to hospitalization are felt to differ in nature from those which lead to other extrusory consequences—to imprisonment, divorce, loss of job, disownment, regional exile, noninstitutional psychiatric treatment, and so forth. But little seems known about these differentiating factors; and when one studies actual commitments, alternate outcomes frequently appear to have been possible. It seems true, moreover, that for every offense that leads to an effective complaint, there are many psychiatrically similar ones that never do. No action is taken; or action is taken which leads to other extrusory outcomes; or ineffective action is taken, leading to the mere pacifying or putting off of the person who complains. Thus, as Clausen and Yarrow have nicely shown, even offenders who are eventually hospitalized are likely to have had a long series of ineffective actions taken against them.[12]

Separating those offenses which could have been used as grounds for hospitalizing the offender from those that are so used, one finds a vast number of what students of occupation call career contingencies.[13] Some of these contingencies in the mental patient's career have been suggested, if not explored, such as socio-economic status, visibility of the offense, proximity to a mental hospital, amount of treatment facilities available, community regard for the type of treatment given in available hospitals, and so on.[14] For information about other contingencies one must rely on atrocity tales: a psychotic man is tolerated by his wife until she finds herself a boy friend, or by his adult children until they move from a house to an apartment; an alcoholic is sent to a mental hospital because the jail is full, and a drug addict because he declines to avail himself of psychiatric treatment on the outside; a rebellious adolescent daughter can no longer be managed at home because she now threatens to have an open affair with an unsuitable companion; and so on. Correspondingly there is an equally important set of contingencies causing the person to by-pass this fate. And should the person enter the hospital, still another set of contingencies will help determine when he is to obtain a discharge—such as the desire of his family for his return, the availability of a "manageable" job, and so on. The society's

---

[11] The distinction employed here between willing and unwilling patients cuts across the legal one, of voluntary and committed, since some persons who are glad to come to the mental hospital may be legally committed, and of those who come only because of strong familial pressure, some may sign themselves in as voluntary patients.

[12] Clausen and Yarrow; see footnote 4.

[13] An explicit application of this notion to the field of mental health may be found in Edwin M. Lemert, "Legal Commitment and Social Control," *Sociology and Social Research* (1946) 30:370–378.

[14] For example, Jerome K. Meyers and Leslie Schaffer, "Social Stratification and Psychiatric Practice: A Study of an Outpatient Clinic," *Amer. Sociological Rev.* (1954) 19:307–310. Lemert, see footnote 5, pp. 402–403. *Patients in Mental Institutions,* 1941; Washington, D.C., Department of Commerce, Bureau of the Census, 1941; p. 2.

official view is that inmates of mental hospitals are there primarily because they are suffering from mental illness. However, in the degree that the "mentally ill" outside hospitals numerically approach or surpass those inside hospitals, one could say that mental patients *distinctively* suffer not from mental illness, but from contingencies.

Career contingencies occur in conjunction with a second feature of the prepatient's career— the *circuit of agents*—and agencies—that participate fatefully in his passage from civilian to patient status.[15] Here is an instance of that increasingly important class of social system whose elements are agents and agencies, which are brought into systemic connection through having to take up and send on the same persons. Some of these agent-roles will be cited now, with the understanding that in any concrete circuit a role may be filled more than once, and a single person may fill more than one of them.

First is the *next-of-relation*—the person whom the prepatient sees as the most available of those upon whom he should be able to most depend in times of trouble; in this instance the last to doubt his sanity and the first to have done everything to save him from the fate which, it transpires, he has been approaching. The patient's next-of-relation is usually his next of kin; the special term is introduced because he need not be. Second is the *complainant,* the person who retrospectively appears to have started the person on his way to the hospital. Third are the *mediators*—the sequence of agents and agencies to which the prepatient is referred and through which he is relayed and processed on his way to the hospital. Here are included police, clergy, general medical practitioners, office psychiatrists, personnel in public clinics, lawyers, social service workers, school teachers, and so on. One of these agents will have the legal mandate to sanction commitment and will exercise it, and so those agents who precede him in the process will be involved in something whose outcome is not yet settled. When the mediators retire from the scene, the prepatient has become an inpatient,

and the significant agent has become the hospital administrator.

While the complainant usually takes action in a lay capacity as a citizen, an employer, a neighbor, or a kinsman, mediators tend to be specialists and differ from those they serve in significant ways. They have experience in handling trouble, and some professional distance from what they handle. Except in the case of policemen, and perhaps some clergy, they tend to be more psychiatrically oriented than the lay public, and will see the need for treatment at times when the public does not.[16]

An interesting feature of these roles is the functional effects of their interdigitation. For example, the feelings of the patient will be influenced by whether or not the person who fills the role of complainant also has the role of next-of-relation—an embarrassing combination more prevalent, apparently, in the higher classes than in the lower.[17] Some of the emergent effects will be considered now.[18]

In the prepatient's progress from home to the hospital he may participate as a third person in what he may come to experience as a kind of *alienative coalition.* His next-of-relation presses him into coming to "talk things over" with a medical practitioner, an office psychiatrist, or some other counselor. Disinclination on his part may be met by threatening him with desertion, disownment, or other legal action, or by stressing the joint and explorative nature of the interview. But typically the next-of-relation will have set the interview up, in the sense of selecting the professional, arranging for time, telling the professional something about the case, and so on. This move effectively tends to establish the next-of-relation as the responsible person to whom pertinent findings can be divulged, while effectively establish-

---

[15] For one circuit of agents and its bearing on career contingencies, see Oswald Hall, "The Stages of a Medical Career," *Amer. J. Sociology* (1948) 53:227–336.

[16] See Cumming, footnote 3; p. 92.

[17] Hollingshead and Redlich, footnote 4; p. 187.

[18] For an analysis of some of these circuit implications for the inpatient, see Leila C. Deasy and Olive W. Quinn, "The Wife of the Mental Patient and the Hospital Psychiatrist," *J. Social Issues* (1955) 11:49–60. An interesting illustration of this kind of analysis may also be found in Alan G. Gowman, "Blindness and the Role of Companion," *Social Problems* (1956) 4:68–75. A general statement may be found in Robert Merton, "The Role Set: Problems in Sociological Theory," *British J. Sociology* (1957) 8:106–120.

ing the other as the patient. The prepatient often goes to the interview with the understanding that he is going as an equal of someone who is so bound together with him that a third person could not come between them in fundamental matters; this, after all, is one way in which close relationships are defined in our society. Upon arrival at the office the prepatient suddenly finds that he and his next-of-relation have not been accorded the same roles, and apparently that a prior understanding between the professional and the next-of-relation has been put in operation against him. In the extreme but common case the professional first sees the prepatient alone, in the role of examiner and diagnostician, and then sees the next-of-relation alone, in the role of advisor, while carefully avoiding talking things over seriously with them both together.[19] And even in those nonconsultative cases where public officials must forcibly extract a person from a family that wants to tolerate him, the next-of-relation is likely to be induced to "go along" with the official action, so that even here the prepatient may feel that an alienative coalition has been formed against him.

The moral experience of being third man in such a coalition is likely to embitter the prepatient, especially since his troubles have already probably led to some estrangement from his next-of-relation. After he enters the hospital, continued visits by his next-of-relation can give the patient the "insight" that his own best interests were being served. But the initial visits may temporarily strengthen his feeling of abandonment; he is likely to beg his visitor to get him out or at least to get him more privileges and to sympathize with the monstrousness of his plight—to which the visitor ordinarily can respond only by trying to maintain a hopeful note, by not "hearing" the requests, or by assuring the patient that the medical authorities know about these things and are doing what is medically best. The visitor then nonchalantly goes back into a world that the patient has learned is incredibly thick with freedom and privileges, causing the patient to feel that his next-of-relation is merely adding a pious gloss to a clear case of traitorous desertion.

The depth to which the patient may feel betrayed by his next-of-relation seems to be increased by the fact that another witnesses his betrayal—a factor which is apparently significant in many three-party situations. An offended person may well act forbearantly and accommodatively toward an offender when the two are alone, choosing peace ahead of justice. The presence of a witness, however, seems to add something to the implications of the offense. For then it is beyond the power of the offended and offender to forget about, erase, or suppress what has happened; the offense has become a public social fact.[20] When the witness is a mental health commission, as is sometimes the case, the witnessed betrayal can verge on a "degradation ceremony."[21] In such circumstances, the offended patient may feel that some kind of extensive reparative action is required before witnesses, if his honor and social weight are to be restored.

Two other aspects of sensed betrayal should be mentioned. First, those who suggest the possibility of another's entering a mental hospital are not likely to provide a realistic picture of how in fact it may strike him when he arrives. Often he is told that he will get required medical treatment and a rest, and may be out in a few months or so. In some cases they may thus be concealing what they know, but I think, in general, they will be telling what they see as the truth. For here there is a quite relevant difference between patients and mediating professionals; mediators, more so than the public at large, may conceive of mental hospitals as short-term medical establishments where required rest and attention can be voluntarily obtained, and not as places of coerced exile. When the prepatient finally arrives he is likely to learn quite quickly, quite differently. He then finds that the information given him about life in the hospital has had the effect of his having put up less resistance to entering than he now sees he would have put up had he known the facts. Whatever the intentions of those who participated in his transition from person to patient, he may sense they have in ef-

[19] I have one case record of a man who claims he thought *he* was taking his wife to see the psychiatrist, not realizing until too late that his wife had made the arrangements.

[20] A paraphrase from Kurt Riezler, "The Social Psychology of Shame," *Amer. J. Sociology* (1943) 48:458.

[21] See Harold Garfinkel, "Conditions of Successful Degradation Ceremonies," *Amer. J. Sociology* (1956) 61:420–424.

fect "conned" him into his present predicament.

I am suggesting that the prepatient starts out with at least a portion of the rights, liberties, and satisfactions of the civilian and ends up on a psychiatric ward stripped of almost everything. The question here is *how* this stripping is managed. This is the second aspect of betrayal I want to consider.

As the prepatient may see it, the circuit of significant figures can function as a kind of *betrayal funnel*. Passage from person to patient may be effected through a series of linked stages, each managed by a different agent. While each stage tends to bring a sharp decrease in adult free status, each agent may try to maintain the fiction that no further decrease will occur. He may even manage to turn the prepatient over to the next agent while sustaining this note. Further, through words, cues, and gestures, the prepatient is implicitly asked by the current agent to join with him in sustaining a running line of polite small talk that tactfully avoids the administrative facts of the situation, becoming, with each stage, progressively more at odds with these facts. The spouse would rather not have to cry to get the prepatient to visit a psychiatrist; psychiatrists would rather not have a scene when the prepatient learns that he and his spouse are being seen separately and in different ways; the police infrequently bring a prepatient to the hospital in a strait jacket, finding it much easier all around to give him a cigarette, some kindly words, and freedom to relax in the back seat of the patrol car; and finally, the admitting psychiatrist finds he can do his work better in the relative quiet and luxury of the "admission suite" where, as an incidental consequence, the notion can survive that a mental hospital is indeed a comforting place. If the prepatient heeds all of these implied requests and is reasonably decent about the whole thing, he can travel the whole circuit from home to hospital without forcing anyone to look directly at what is happening or to deal with the raw emotion that his situation might well cause him to express. His showing consideration for those who are moving him toward the hospital allows them to show consideration for him, with the joint result that these interactions can be sustained with some of the protective harmony characteristic of ordinary

face-to-face dealings. But should the new patient cast his mind back over the sequence of steps leading to hospitalization, he may feel that everyone's *current* comfort was being busily sustained while his long-range welfare was being undermined. This realization may constitute a moral experience that further separates him for the time from the people on the outside.[22]

I would now like to look at the circuit of career agents from the point of view of the agents themselves. Mediators in the person's transition from civil to patient status—as well as his keepers, once he is in the hospital—have an interest in establishing a responsible next-of-relation as the patient's deputy or *guardian;* should there be no obvious candidate for the role, someone may be sought out and pressed into it. Thus while a person is gradually being transformed into a patient, a next-of-relation is gradually being transformed into a guardian. With a guardian on the scene, the whole transition process can be kept tidy. He is likely to be familiar with the prepatient's civil involvements and business, and can tie up loose ends that might otherwise be left to entangle the hospital. Some of the prepatient's abrogated civil rights can be transferred to him, thus helping to sustain the legal fiction that while the prepatient does not actually have his rights he somehow actually has not lost them.

Inpatients commonly sense, at least for a time, that hospitalization is a massive unjust deprivation, and sometimes succeed in convincing a few persons on the outside that this is the case. It often turns out to be useful, then, for those identified with inflicting these deprivations, however justifiably, to be able to point to the cooperation and agreement of someone whose relation-

---

[22] Concentration camp practices provide a good example of the function of the betrayal funnel in inducing cooperation and reducing struggle and fuss, although here the mediators could not be said to be acting in the best interests of the inmates. Police picking up persons from their homes would sometimes joke good-naturedly and offer to wait while coffee was being served. Gas chambers were fitted out like delousing rooms, and victims taking off their clothes were told to note where they were leaving them. The sick, aged, weak, or insane who were selected for extermination were sometimes driven away in Red Cross ambulances to camps referred to by terms such as "observation hospital." See David Boder, *I Did Not Interview the Dead;* Urbana, Univ. of Illinois Press, 1949; p. 81; and Elie A. Cohen, *Human Behavior in the Concentration Camp;* London, Cape, 1954; pp. 32, 37, 107.

ship to the patient places him above suspicion, firmly defining him as the person most likely to have the patient's personal interest at heart. If the guardian is satisfied with what is happening to the new inpatient, the world ought to be.[23]

Now it would seem that the greater the legitimate personal stake one party has in another, the better he can take the role of guardian to the other. But the structural arrangements in society which lead to the acknowledged merging of two persons' interests lead to additional consequences. For the person to whom the patient turns for help—for protection against such threats as involuntary commitment—is just the person to whom the mediators and hospital administrators logically turn for authorization. It is understandable, then, that some patients will come to sense, at least for a time, that the closeness of a relationship tells nothing of its trustworthiness.

There are still other functional effects emerging from this complement of roles. If and when the next-of-relation appeals to mediators for help in the trouble he is having with the prepatient, hospitalization may not, in fact, be in his mind. He may not even perceive the prepatient as mentally sick, or, if he does, he may not consistently hold to this view.[24] It is the circuit of mediators, with their greater psychiatric sophistication and their belief in the medical character of mental hospitals, that will often define the situation for the next-of-relation, assuring him that hospitalization is a possible solution and a good one, that it involves no betrayal, but is rather a medical action taken in the best interests of the prepatient. Here the next-of-relation may learn that doing his duty to the prepatient may cause the prepatient to distrust and even hate him for the time. But the fact that this course of action may have had to be pointed out and prescribed by

professionals, and be defined by them as a moral duty, relieves the next-of-relation of some of the guilt he may feel.[25] It is a poignant fact that an adult son or daughter may be pressed into the role of mediator, so that the hostility that might otherwise be directed against the spouse is passed on to the child.[26]

Once the prepatient is in the hospital, the same guilt-carrying function may become a significant part of the staff's job in regard to the next-of-relation.[27] These reasons for feeling that he himself has not betrayed the patient, even though the patient may then think so, can later provide the next-of-relation with a defensible line to take when visiting the patient in the hospital and a basis for hoping that the relationship can be re-established after its hospital moratorium. And of course this position, when sensed by the patient, can provide him with excuses for the next-of-relation, when and if he comes to look for them.[28]

Thus while the next-of-relation can perform important functions for the mediators and hospital administrators, they in turn can perform important functions for him. One finds, then, an emergent unintended exchange or reciprocation of functions, these functions themselves being often unintended.

The final point I want to consider about the prepatient's moral career is its peculiarly *retroactive* character. Until a person actually arrives at the hospital there usually seems no way of knowing for sure that he is destined to do so,

---

[23] Interviews collected by the Clausen group at NIMH suggest that when a wife comes to be a guardian, the responsibility may disrupt previous distance from in-laws, leading either to a new supportive coalition with them or to a marked withdrawal from them.

[24] For an analysis of these nonpsychiatric kinds of perception, see Marian Radke Yarrow, Charlotte Green Schwartz, Harriet S. Murphy, and Leila Calhoun Deasy, "The Psychological Meaning of Mental Illness in the Family," *J. Social Issues* (1955) 11:12–24; Charlotte Green Schwartz, "Perspectives on Deviance: Wives' Definitions of their Husbands' Mental Illness," *Psychiatry* (1957) 20:275–291.

[25] This guilt-carrying function is found, of course, in other role-complexes. Thus, when a middle-class couple engages in the process of legal separation or divorce, each of their lawyers usually takes the position that his job is to acquaint his client with all of the potential claims and rights, pressing his client into demanding these, in spite of any nicety of feelings about the rights and honorableness of the ex-partner. The client, in all good faith, can then say to self and to the ex-partner that the demands are being made only because the lawyer insists it is best to do so.

[26] Recorded in the Clausen data.

[27] This point is made by Cumming, see footnote 3; p. 129.

[28] There is an interesting contrast here with the moral career of the tuberculosis patient. I am told by Julius Roth that tuberculous patients are likely to come to the hospital willingly, agreeing with their next-of-relation about treatment. Later in their hospital career, when they learn how long they yet have to stay and how depriving and irrational some of the hospital rulings are, they may seek to leave, be advised against this by the staff and by relatives, and only then begin to feel betrayed.

given the determinative role of career contingencies. And until the point of hospitalization is reached, he or others may not conceive of him as a person who is becoming a mental patient. However, since he will be held against his will in the hospital, his next-of-relation and the hospital staff will be in great need of a rationale for the hardships they are sponsoring. The medical elements of the staff will also need evidence that they are still in the trade they were trained for. These problems are eased, no doubt unintentionally, but the case-history construction that is placed on the patient's past life, this having the effect of demonstrating that all along he had been becoming sick, that he finally became very sick, and that if he had not been hospitalized much worse things would have happened to him—all of which, of course, may be true. Incidentally, if the patient wants to make sense out of his stay in the hospital, and, as already suggested, keep alive the possibility of once again conceiving of his next-of-relation as a decent, well-meaning person, then he too will have reason to believe some of this psychiatric work-up of his past.

Here is a very ticklish point for the sociology of careers. An important aspect of every career is the view the person constructs when he looks backward over his progress; in a sense, however, the whole of the prepatient career derives from this reconstruction. The fact of having had a prepatient career, starting with an effective complaint, becomes an important part of the mental patient's orientation, but this part can begin to be played only after hospitalization proves that what he had been having, but no longer has, is a career as a prepatient.

THE INPATIENT PHASE

The last step in the prepatient's career can involve his realization—justified or not—that he has been deserted by society and turned out of relationships by those closest to him. Interestingly enough, the patient, especially a first admission, may manage to keep himself from coming to the end of this trail, even though in fact he is now in a locked mental hospital ward. On entering the hospital, he may very strongly feel the desire

not to be known to anyone as a person who could possibly be reduced to these present circumstances, or as a person who conducted himself in the way he did prior to commitment. Consequently, he may avoid talking to anyone, may stay by himself when possible, and may even be "out of contact" or "manic" so as to avoid ratifying any interaction that presses a politely reciprocal role upon him and opens him up to what he has become in the eyes of others. When the next-of-relation makes an effort to visit, he may be rejected by mutism, or by the patient's refusal to enter the visiting room, these strategies sometimes suggesting that the patient still clings to a remnant of relatedness to those who made up his past, and is protecting this remnant from the final destructiveness of dealing with the new people that they have become.[29]

Usually the patient comes to give up this taxing effort at anonymity, at not-hereness, and begins to present himself for conventional social interaction to the hospital community. Thereafter he withdraws only in special ways—by always using his nickname, by signing his contribution to the patient weekly with his initial only, or by using the innocuous "cover" address tactfully provided by some hospitals; or he withdraws only at special times, when, say, a flock of nursing students makes a passing tour of the ward, or when, paroled to the hospital grounds, he suddenly sees he is about to cross the path of a civilian he happens to know from home. Sometimes this making of oneself available is called "settling down" by the attendants. It marks a new stand openly taken and supported by the patient, and resembles the "coming out" process that occurs in other groupings.[30]

[29] The inmate's initial strategy of holding himself aloof from ratifying contact may partly account for the relative lack of group-formation among inmates in public mental hospitals, a connection that has been suggested to me by William R. Smith. The desire to avoid personal bonds that would give license to the asking of biographical questions could also be a factor. In mental hospitals, of course, as in prisoner camps, the staff may consciously break up incipient group-formation in order to avoid collective rebellious action and other ward disturbances.

[30] A comparable coming out occurs in the homosexual world, when a person finally comes frankly to present himself to a "gay" gathering not as a tourist but as someone who is "available." See Evelyn Hooker, "A Preliminary Examination of Group Behavior of Homosexuals," *J. Psychology* (1956) 42:217–225; especially p. 221. A good fictionalized treatment may be

Once the prepatient begins to settle down, the main outlines of his fate tend to follow those of a whole class of segregated establishments—jails, concentration camps, monasteries, work camps, and so on—in which the inmate spends the whole round of life on the grounds, and marches through his regimented day in the immediate company of a group of persons of his own institutional status.[31]

Like the neophyte in many of these "total institutions," the new inpatient finds himself cleanly stripped of many of his accustomed affirmations, satisfactions, and defenses, and is subjected to a rather full set of mortifying experiences: restriction of free movement; communal living; diffuse authority of a whole echelon of people; and so on. Here one begins to learn about the limited extent to which a conception of oneself can be sustained when the usual setting of supports for it are suddenly removed.

While undergoing these humbling moral experiences, the inpatient learns to orient himself in terms of the "ward system."[32] In public mental hospitals this usually consists of a series of graded living arrangements built around wards, administrative units called services, and parole statuses. The "worst" level involves often nothing but wooden benches to sit on, some quite indifferent food, and a small piece of room to sleep in. The "best" level may involve a room of one's own, ground and town privileges, contacts with staff that are relatively undamaging, and what is seen as good food and ample recreational facilities. For disobeying the pervasive house rules, the inmate will receive stringent punishments expressed in terms of loss of privileges; for obedience he will eventually be allowed to reacquire some of the minor satisfactions he took for granted on the outside.

The institutionalization of these radically different levels of living throws light on the implications for self of social settings. And this in turn affirms that the self arises not merely out of its possessor's interactions with significant others, but also out of the arrangements that are evolved in an organization for its members.

There are some settings which the person easily discounts as an expression or extension of him. When a tourist goes slumming, he may take pleasure in the situation not because it is a reflection of him but because it so assuredly is not. There are other settings, such as living rooms, which the person manages on his own and employs to influence in a favorable direction other persons' views of him. And there are still other settings, such as a work place, which express the employee's occupational status, but over which he has no final control, this being exerted, however tactfully, by his employer. Mental hospitals provide an extreme instance of this latter possibility. And this is due not merely to their uniquely degraded living levels, but also to the unique way in which significance for self is made explicit to the patient, piercingly, persistently, and thoroughly. Once lodged on a given ward, the patient is firmly instructed that the restrictions and deprivations he encounters are not due to such things as tradition or economy—and hence dissociable from self—but are intentional parts of his treatment, part of his need at the time, and therefore an expression of the state that his self has fallen to. Having every reason to initiate requests for better conditions, he is told that when the staff feels he is "able to manage" or will be "comfortable with" a higher ward level, then appropriate action will be taken. In short, assignment to a given ward is presented not as a reward or punishment, but as an expression of his general level of social functioning, his status as a person. Given the fact that the worst ward levels provide a round of life that inpatients with organic brain damage can easily manage, and that these quite limited human beings are present to prove it, one

found in James Baldwin's *Giovanni's Room;* New York, Dial, 1956; pp. 41–63. A familiar instance of the coming out process is no doubt to be found among prepubertal children at the moment one of these actors sidles *back* into a room that had been left in an angered huff and injured *amour-propre.* The phrase itself presumably derives from a *rite-de-passage* ceremony once arranged by upper-class mothers for their daughters. Interestingly enough, in large mental hospitals the patient sometimes symbolizes a complete coming out by his first active participation in the hospital-wide patient dance.

[31] See Goffman, "Characteristics of Total Institutions," pp. 43–84; in *Proceedings of the Symposium of Preventive and Social Psychiatry;* Washington, D.C., Walter Reed Army Institute of Research, 1959.

[32] A good description of the ward system may be found in Ivan Belknap, *Human Problems of a State Mental Hospital;* New York, McGraw-Hill, 1956; see especially p. 164.

can appreciate some of the mirroring effects of the hospital.[33]

The ward system, then, is an extreme instance of how the physical facts of an establishment can be explicitly employed to frame the conception a person takes of himself. In addition, the official psychiatric mandate of mental hospitals gives rise to even more direct, even more blatant, attacks upon the inmate's view of himself. The more "medical" and the more progressive a mental hospital is—the more it attempts to be therapeutic and not merely custodial—the more he may be confronted by high-ranking staff arguing that his past has been a failure, that the cause of this has been within himself, that his attitude to life is wrong, and that if he wants to be a person he will have to change his way of dealing with people and his conceptions of himself. Often the moral value of these verbal assaults will be brought home to him by requiring him to practice taking this psychiatric view of himself in arranged confessional periods, whether in private sessions or group psychotherapy.

Now a general point may be made about the moral career of inpatients which has bearing on many moral careers. Given the stage that any person has reached in a career, one typically finds that he constructs an image of his life course—past, present, and future—which selects, abstracts, and distorts in such a way as to provide him with a view of himself that he can usefully expound in current situations. Quite generally, the person's line concerning self defensively brings him into appropriate alignment with the basic values of his society, and so may be called an *apologia*. If the person can manage to present a view of his current situation which shows the operation of favorable personal qualities in the past and a favorable destiny awaiting him, it may be called a *success story*. If the facts of a person's past and present are extremely dismal, then about the best he can do is to show that he is not responsible for what has become of him, and the term

sad tale is appropriate. Interestingly enough, the more the person's past forces him out of apparent alignment with central moral values, the more often he seems compelled to tell his sad tale in any company in which he finds himself. Perhaps he partly responds to the need he feels in others of not having their sense of proper life courses affronted. In any case, it is among convicts, 'wino's,' and prostitutes that one seems to obtain sad tales the most readily.[34] It is the vicissitudes of the mental patient's sad tale that I want to consider now.

In the mental hospital, the setting and house rules press home to patient that he is, after all, a mental case who has suffered some kind of social collapse on the outside, having failed in some over-all way, and that here he is of little social weight, being hardly capable of acting like a full-fledged person at all. These humiliations are likely to be most keenly felt by middle-class patients, since their previous condition of life little immunizes them against such affronts; but all patients feel some downgrading. Just as any normal member of his outside subculture would do, the patient often responds to this situation by attempting to assert a sad tale proving that he is not "sick," that the "little trouble" he did get into was really somebody else's fault, that his past life course had some honor and rectitude, and that the hospital is therefore unjust in forcing the status of mental

---

[33] Here is one way in which mental hospitals can be worse than concentration camps and prisons as places in which to "do" time; in the latter, self-insulation from the symbolic implications of the settings may be easier. In fact, self-insulation from hospital settings may be so difficult that patients have to employ devices for this which staff interpret as psychotic symptoms.

[34] In regard to convicts, see Anthony Heckstall-Smith, *Eighteen Months;* London, Wingate, 1954; pp. 52–53. For 'wino's' see the discussion in Howard G. Bain, "A Sociological Analysis of the Chicago Skid-Row Lifeway;" unpublished M.A. thesis, Dept. of Sociology, Univ. of Chicago, Sept., 1950; especially "The Rationale of the Skid-Row Drinking Group," pp. 141–146. Bain's neglected thesis is a useful source of material on moral careers.

Apparently one of the occupational hazards of prostitution is that clients and other professional contacts sometimes persist in expressing sympathy by asking for a defensible dramatic explanation for the fall from grace. In having to bother to have a sad tale ready, perhaps the prostitute is more to be pitied than damned. Good examples of prostitute sad tales may be found in Sir Henry Mayhew, "Those that Will Not Work," pp. 210–272; in his *London Labour and the London Poor*, Vol. 4; London, Griffin, Bohn, and Cox, 1862. For a contemporary source, see *Women of the Streets*, edited by C. H. Rolph; London, Zecker and Warburg, 1955; especially p. 6. "Almost always, however, after a few comments on the police, the girl would begin to explain how it was that she was in the life, usually in terms of self-justification." Lately, of course, the psychological expert has helped out the profession in the construction of wholly remarkable sad tales. See, for example, Harold Greenwald, *Call Girl;* New York, Ballantine, 1958.

patient upon him. This self-respecting tendency is heavily institutionalized within the patient society where opening social contacts typically involve the participants' volunteering information about their current ward location and length of stay so far, but not the reasons for their stay—such interaction being conducted in the manner of small talk on the outside.[35] With greater familiarity, each patient usually volunteers relatively acceptable reasons for his hospitalization, at the same time accepting without open immediate question the lines offered by other patients. Such stories as the following are given and overtly accepted.

> I was going to night school to get a M.A. degree, and holding down a job in addition, and the load got too much for me.

> The others here are sick mentally but I'm suffering from a bad nervous system and that is what is giving me these phobias.

> I got here by mistake because of a diabetes diagnosis, and I'll leave in a couple of days. [The patient had been in seven weeks.]

> I failed as a child, and later with my wife I reached out for dependency.

> My trouble is that I can't work. That's what I'm in for. I had two jobs with a good home and all the money I wanted.[36]

The patient sometimes reinforces these stories by an optimistic definition of his occupational status: A man who managed to obtain an audition as a radio announcer styles himself a radio announcer; another who worked for some months as a copy boy and was then given a job as a reporter on a large trade journal, but fired after three weeks, defines himself as a reporter.

A whole social role in the patient community may be constructed on the basis of these recipro-

cally sustained fictions. For these face-to-face niceties tend to be qualified by behind-the-back gossip that comes only a degree closer to the "objective" facts. Here, of course, one can see a classic social function of informal networks of equals: they serve as one another's audience for self-supporting tales—tales that are somewhat more solid than pure fantasy and somewhat thinner than the facts.

But the patient's *apologia* is called forth in a unique setting, for few settings could be be destructive of self-stories except, of course, those stories already constructed along psychiatric lines. And this destructiveness rests on more than the official sheet of paper which attests that the patient is of unsound mind, a danger to himself and others—an attestation, incidentally, which seems to cut deeply into the patient's pride, and into the possibility of his having any.

Certainly the degrading conditions of the hospital setting belie many of the self-stories that are presented by patients; and the very fact of being in the mental hospital is evidence against these tales. And of course, there is not always sufficient patient solidarity to prevent patient discrediting patient, just as there is not always a sufficient number of "professionalized" attendants to prevent attendant discrediting patient. As one patient informant repeatedly suggested to a fellow patient:

> If you're so smart, how come you got your ass in here?

The mental hospital setting, however, is more treacherous still. Staff has much to gain through discreditings of the patient's story—whatever the felt reason for such discreditings. If the custodial faction in the hospital is to succeed in managing his daily round without complaint or trouble from him, then it will prove useful to be able to point out to him that the claims about himself upon which he rationalizes his demands are false, that he is not what he is claiming to be, and that in fact he is a failure as a person. If the psychiatric faction is to impress upon him its views about his personal make-up, then they must be able to show in detail how their version of his past and their version of his character hold up much better

---

[35] A similar self-protecting rule has been observed in prisons. Thus, Hassler, see footnote 6, in describing a conversation with a fellow-prisoner; "He didn't say much about why he was sentenced, and I didn't ask him, that being the accepted behavior in prison" (p. 76). A novelistic version for the mental hospital may be found in J. Kerkhoff, *How Thin the Veil: A Newspaperman's Story of His Own Mental Crack-up and Recovery;* New York, Greenberg, 1952; p. 27.

[36] From the writer's field notes of informal interaction with patients, transcribed as near verbatim as he was able.

than his own.[37] If both the custodial and psychiatric factions are to get him to cooperate in the various psychiatric treatments, then it will prove useful to disabuse him of *his* view of their purposes, and cause him to appreciate that they know what they are doing, and are doing what is best for him. In brief, the difficulties caused by a patient are closely tied to his version of what has been happening to him, and if cooperation is to be secured, it helps if this version is discredited. The patient must "insightfully" come to take, or affect to take, the hospital's view of himself.

The staff also has ideal means—in addition to the mirroring effect of the setting—for denying the inmate's rationalizations. Current psychiatric doctrine defines mental disorder as something that can have its roots in the patient's earliest years, show its signs throughout the course of his life, and invade almost every sector of his current activity. No segment of his past or present need to be defined, then, as beyond the jurisdiction and mandate of psychiatric assessment. Mental hospitals bureaucratically institutionalize this extremely wide mandate by formally basing their treatment of the patient upon his diagnosis and hence upon the psychiatric view of his past.

The case record is an important expression of this mandate. This dossier is apparently not regularly used, however, to record occasions when the patient showed capacity to cope honorably and effectively with difficult life situations. Nor is the case record typically used to provide a rough average or sampling of his past conduct. One of its purposes is to show the ways in which the patient is "sick" and the reasons why it was right to commit him and is right currently to keep him committed; and this done by extracting from his whole life course a list of those incidents that have or might have had "symptomatic" significance.[38] The misadventures of his parents or siblings that might suggest a "taint" may be cited. Early acts in which the patient appeared to have shown bad judgment or emotional disturbance will be recorded. Occasions when he acted in a way which the layman would consider immoral, sexually perverted, weak-willed, childish, ill-considered, impulsive, and crazy may be described. Misbehaviors which someone saw as the last straw, as cause for immediate action, are likely to be reported in detail. In addition, the record will describe his state on arrival at the hospital— and this is not likely to be a time of tranquility and ease for him. The record may also report the false line taken by the patient in answering embarrassing questions, showing him as someone who makes claims that are obviously contrary to the facts:

> Claims she lives with oldest daughter or with sisters only when sick and in need of care; otherwise with husband, he himself says not for 12 years.
>
> Contrary to the reports from the personnel, he says he no longer bangs on the floor or cries in the morning.
>
> . . . conceals fact that she had her organs removed, claims she is still menstruating.
>
> At first she denied having had premarital sexual experience, but when asked about Jim she said she had forgotten about it 'cause it had been unpleasant.[39]

Where contrary facts are not known by the recorder, their presence is often left scrupulously an open question:

> The patient denied any heterosexual experiences nor could one trick her into admitting that she had

---

[37] The process of examining a person psychiatrically and then altering or reducing his status in consequence is known in hospital and prison parlance as *bugging*, the assumption being that once you come to the attention of the testers you either will automatically be labeled crazy or the process of testing itself will make you crazy. Thus psychiatric staff are sometimes seen not as *discovering* whether you are sick, but as *making* you sick; and "Don't bug me, man," can mean, "Don't pester me to the point where I'll get upset." Sheldon Messenger has suggested to me that this meaning of bugging is related to the other colloquial meaning, of wiring a room with a secret microphone to collect information usable for discrediting the speaker.

[38] While many kinds of organizations maintain records of their members, in almost all of these some socially significant attributes can only be included indirectly, being officially irrelevant. But since mental hospitals have a legitimate claim to deal with the 'whole' person, they need *officially* recognize no limits to what they consider relevant, a sociologically interesting license. It is an odd historical fact that persons concerned with promoting civil liberties in other areas of life tend to favor giving the psychiatrist complete discretionary power over the patient. Apparently it is felt that the more power possessed by medically qualified administrators and therapists, the better the interests of the patients will be served. Patients, to my knowledge, have not been polled on this matter.

[39] Verbatim transcriptions of hospital case record material.

ever been pregnant or into any kind of sexual indulgence, denying masturbation as well.

Even with considerable pressure she was unwilling to engage in any projection of paranoid mechanisms.

No psychotic content could be elicited at this time.[40]

And if in no more factual way, discrediting statements often appear in descriptions given of the patient's general social manner in the hospital:

When interviewed, he was bland, apparently self-assured, and sprinkles high-sounding generalizations freely throughout his verbal productions.

Armed with a rather neat appearance and natty little Hitlerian mustache, this 45 year old man, who has spent the last five or more years of his life in the hospital, is making a very successful hospital adjustment living within the role of a rather gay liver and jim-dandy type of fellow who is not only quite superior to his fellow patients in intellectual respects but who is also quite a man with women. His speech is sprayed with many multi-syllabled words which he generally uses in good context, but if he talks long enough on any subject it soon becomes apparent that he is so completely lost in this verbal diarrhea as to make what he says almost completely worthless.[41]

The events recorded in the case history are, then, just the sort that a layman would consider scandalous, defamatory, and discrediting. I think it is fair to say that all levels of mental hospital staff fail, in general, to deal with this material with the moral neutrality claimed for medical statements and psychiatric diagnosis, but instead participate, by intonation and gesture if by no other means, in the lay reaction to these acts. This will occur in staff-patient encounters as well as in staff encounters at which no patient is present.

In some mental hospitals, access to the case record is technically restricted to medical and higher nursing levels, but even here informal access or relayed information is often available to lower staff levels.[42] In addition, ward personnel

are felt to have a right to know those aspects of the patient's past conduct which, embedded in the reputation he develops, purportedly make it possible to manage him with greater benefit to himself and less risk to others. Further, all staff levels typically have access to the nursing notes kept on the ward, which chart the daily course of each patient's disease, and hence his conduct, providing for the near-present the sort of information the case record supplies for his past.

I think that most of the information gathered in case records is quite true, although it might seem also to be true that almost anyone's life course could yield up enough denigrating facts to provide grounds for the record's justification of commitment. In any case, I am not concerned here with questioning the desirability of maintaining case records, or the motives of staff in keeping them. The point is that these facts about him being true, the patient is certainly not relieved from the normal cultural pressure to conceal them, and is perhaps all the more threatened by knowing that they are neatly available, and that he has no control over who gets to learn them.[43] A manly

---

[40] Verbatim transcriptions of hospital case record material.

[41] Verbatim transcriptions of hospital case record material.

[42] However, some mental hospitals do have a "hot file" of selected records which can be taken out only by special permission. These may be records of patients who work as administration-office messengers and might otherwise snatch glances at

their own files; of inmates who had elite status in the environing community; and of inmates who may take legal action against the hospital and hence have a special reason to maneuver access to their records. Some hospitals even have a "hot-hot file," kept in the superintendent's office. In addition, the patient's professional title, especially if it is a medical one, is sometimes purposely omitted from his file card. All of these exceptions to the general rule for handling information show, of course, the institution's realization of some of the implications of keeping mental hospital records. For a further example, see Harold Taxel, "Authority Structure in a Mental Hospital Ward," unpublished M.A. thesis, Dept of Sociology, Univ. of Chicago, 1953; pp. 11–12.

[43] This is the problem of "information control" that many groups suffer from to varying degrees. See Goffman, "Discrepant Roles," Ch. 4, pp. 86–106; in *Presentation of Self in Everyday Life*; Monograph No. 2, Univ. of Edinburgh, Social Science Research Centre, 1956. A suggestion of this problem in relation to case records in prisons is given by James Peck in his story, "The Ship that Never Hit Port," in *Prison Etiquette*, edited by Holley Cantine and Dachine Rainer; Bearsville, N.Y., The Retort Press, 1950.

"The hacks of course hold all the aces in dealing with any prisoner because they can always write him up for inevitable punishment. Every infraction of the rules is noted in the prisoner's jacket, a folder which records all the details of the man's life before and during imprisonment. There are general reports written by the work detail screw, the cell block screw, or some other screw who may have overheard a conversation. Tales pumped from stool pigeons are also included.

"Any letter which interests the authorities goes into the jacket. The mail censor may make a photostatic copy of a prison-looking youth who responds to military induction by running away from the barracks and hiding himself in a hotel room clothes closet, to be found there, crying, by his mother; a woman who travels from Utah to Washington to warn the President of impending doom; a man who disrobes before three young girls; a boy who locks his sister out of the house, striking out two of her teeth when she tries to come back in through the window—each of these persons has done something he will have very obvious reason to conceal from others, and very good reason to tell lies about.

The formal and informal patterns of communication linking staff members tend to amplify the disclosive work done by the case record. A discreditable act that the patient performs during one part of the day's routine in one part of the hospital community is likely to be reported back to those who supervise other areas of his life, where he implicitly takes the stand that he is not the sort of person who could act that way.

Of significance here, as in some other social establishments, is the increasingly common practice of all-level staff conferences, where staff air their views of patients and develop collective agreement concerning the line that the patient is trying to take and the line that should be taken to him. A patient who develops a "personal" relation with an attendant, or manages to make an attendant anxious by eloquent and persistent accusations of malpractice can be put back into his place by means of the staff meeting, where the attendant is given warning or assurance that the patient is "sick." Since the differential image of himself that a person usually meets from those of various levels around him comes here to be unified behind the scenes into a common approach, the patient may find himself faced with a kind of collusion against him—albeit one sincerely thought to be for his own ultimate welfare.

In addition, the formal transfer of the patient

from one ward or service to another is likely to be accompanied by an informal description of his characteristics, this being felt to facilitate the work of the employee who is newly responsible for him.

Finally, at the most informal of levels, the lunchtime and coffee-break small talk of staff often turns upon the latest doing of the patient, the gossip level of any social establishment being here intensified by the assumption that everything about him is in some way the proper business of the hospital employee. Theoretically there seems to be no reason why such gossip should not build up the subject instead of tear him down, unless one claims that talk about those not present will always tend to be critical in order to maintain the integrity and prestige of the circle in which the talking occurs. And so, even when the impulse of the speakers seems kindly and generous, the implication of their talk is typically that the patient is not a complete person. For example, a conscientious group therapist, sympathetic with patients, once admitted to his coffee companions:

> I've had about three group disrupters, one man in particular—a lawyer [sotto voce] James Wilson—very bright—who just made things miserable for me, but I would always tell him to get on the stage and do something. Well, I was getting desperate and then I bumped into his therapist, who said that right now behind the man's bluff and front he needed the group very much and that it probably meant more to him than anything else he was getting out of the hospital—he just needed the support. Well, that made me feel altogether different about him. He's out now.

In general, then, mental hospitals systematically provide for circulation about each patient the kind of information that the patient is likely to try to hide. And in various degrees of detail this information is used daily to puncture his claims. At the admission and diagnostic conferences, he will be asked questions to which he must give wrong answers in order to maintain his self-respect, and then the true answer may be shot back at him. An attendant whom he tells a version of his past and his reason for being in the hospital may smile disbelievingly, or say, "That's not the way I heard it," in line with the practical psychia-

---

er's entire letter, or merely copy a passage. Or he may pass the letter on to the warden. Often an inmate called out by the warden or parole officer is confronted with something he wrote so long ago he had forgotten all about it. It might be about his personal life or his political views—a fragment of thought that the prison authorities felt was dangerous and filed for later use" (p. 66).

try of bringing the patient down to reality. When he accosts a physician or nurse on the ward and presents his claims for more privileges or for discharge, this may be countered by a question which he cannot answer truthfully without calling up a time in his past when he acted disgracefully. When he gives his view of his situation during group psychotherapy, the therapist, taking the role of interrogator, may attempt to disabuse him of his face-saving interpretations and encourage an interpretation suggesting that it is he himself who is to blame and who must change. When he claims to staff or fellow patients that he is well and has never been really sick, someone may give him graphic details of how, only one month ago, he was prancing around like a girl, or claiming that he was God, or declining to talk or eat, or putting gum in his hair.

Each time the staff deflates the patient's claims, his sense of what a person ought to be and the rules of peer-group social intercourse press him to reconstruct his stories; and each time he does this, the custodial and psychiatric interests of the staff may lead them to discredit these tales again.

Behind these verbally instigated ups and downs of the self, is an institutional base that rocks just as precariously. Contrary to popular opinion, the "ward system" insures a great amount of internal social mobility in mental hospitals, especially during the inmate's first year. During that time he is likely to have altered his service once, his ward three or four times, and his parole status several times; and he is likely to have experienced moves in bad as well as good directions. Each of these moves involves a very drastic alteration in level of living and in available materials out of which to build a self-confirming round of activities, an alteration equivalent in scope, say, to a move up or down a class in the wider class system. Moreover, fellow inmates with whom he has partially identified himself will similarly be moving, but in different directions and at different rates, thus reflecting feelings of social change to the person even when he does not experience them directly. As previously implied, the doctrines of psychiatry can reinforce the social fluctuations of the ward system. Thus there is a current psychiatric

view that the ward system is a kind of social hothouse in which patients start as social infants and end up, within the year, on convalescent wards as resocialized adults. This view adds considerably to the weight and pride that staff can attach to their work, and necessitates a certain amount of blindness, especially at higher staff levels, to other ways of viewing the ward system, such as a method for disciplining unruly persons through punishment and reward. In any case, this resocialization perspective tends to overstress the extent to which those on the worst wards are incapable of socialized conduct and the extent to which those on the best wards are ready and willing to play the social game. Because the ward system is something more than a resocialization chamber, inmates find many reasons for "messing up" or getting into trouble, and many occasions, then, for demotion to less privileged ward positions. These demotions may be officially interpreted as psychiatric relapses or moral backsliding, thus protecting the resocialization view of the hospital, and these interpretations, by implication, translate a mere infraction of rules and consequent demotion into a fundamental expression of the status of the culprit's self. Correspondingly, promotions, which may come about because of ward population pressure, the need for a "working patient," or for other psychiatrically irrelevant reasons, may be built up into something claimed to be profoundly expressive of the patient's whole self. The patient himself may be expected by staff to make a personal effort to "get well," in something less than a year, and hence may be constantly reminded to think in terms of the self's success and failure.[44]

In such contexts inmates can discover that deflations in moral status are not so bad as they had imagined. After all, infractions which lead to these demotions cannot be accompanied by legal sanctions or by reduction to the status of mental patient, since these conditions already prevail. Further, no past or current delict seems to be horrendous enough in itself to excommunicate a patient from the patient community, and

[44] For this and other suggestions, I am indebted to Charlotte Green Schwartz.

hence failures at right living lose some of their stigmatizing meaning.[45] And finally, in accepting the hospital's version of his fall from grace, the patient can set himself up in the business of "straightening up," and make claims of sympathy, privileges, and indulgence from the staff in order to foster this.

Learning to live under conditions of imminent exposure and wide fluctuation in regard, with little control over the granting or withholding of this regard, is an important step in the socialization of the patient, a step that tells something important about what it is like to be an inmate in a mental hospital. Having one's past mistakes and present progress under constant moral review seems to make for a special adaptation consisting of a less-than-moral attitude to ego-ideals. One's shortcomings and successes become too central and fluctuating an issue in life to allow the usual commitment of concern for other persons' views of them. It is not very practicable to try to sustain solid claims about oneself. The inmate tends to learn that degradations and reconstructions of the self need not be given too much weight, at the same time learning that staff and inmates are ready to view an inflation or deflation of a self with some indifference. He learns that a defensible picture of self can be seen as something outside oneself that can be constructed, lost, and rebuilt, all with great speed and some equanimity. He learns about the viability of taking up a standpoint—and hence a self—that is outside the one which the hospital can give and take away from him.

The setting, then, seems to engender a kind of cosmopolitan sophistication, a kind of civic apathy. In this unserious yet oddly exaggerated moral context, building up a self or having it destroyed becomes something of a shameless game, and learning to view this process as a game seems to make for some demoralization, the game being such a fundamental one. In the hospital, then, the inmate can learn that the self is not a fortress, but rather a small open city; he can become weary of having to show pleasure when held by troops of his own, and weary of having to show displeasure when held by the enemy. Once he learns what it is like to be defined by society as not having a viable self, this threatening definition—the threat that helps attach people to the self society accords them—is weakened. The patient seems to gain a new plateau when he learns that he can survive while acting in a way that society sees as destructive of him.

A few illustrations of this moral looseness and moral fatigue might be given. In state mental hospitals currently a kind of "marriage moratorium" appears to be accepted by patients and more or less condoned by staff. Some informal peer-group pressure may be brought against a patient who "plays around" with more than one hospital partner at a time, but little negative sanction seems to be attached to taking up, in a temporarily steady way, with a member of the opposite sex, even though both partners are known to be married, to have children, and even to be regularly visited by these outsiders. In short, there is license in mental hospitals to begin courting all over again, with the understanding, however, that nothing very permanent or serious can come of this. Like shipboard or vacation romances, these entanglements attest to the way in which the hospital is cut off from the outside community, becoming a world of its own, operated for the benefit of its own citizens. And certainly this moratorium is an expression of the alienation and hostility that patients feel for those on the outside to whom they were closely related. But in addition, one has evidence of the loosening effects of living in a world within a world, under conditions which make it difficult to give full seriousness to either of them.

The second illustration concerns the ward system. On the worst ward level, discreditings seem to occur the most frequently, in part because of lack of facilities, in part through the mockery and sarcasm that seem to be the occupational norm of social control for the attendants and nurses who administer these places. At the same time, the paucity of equipment and rights means that not much self can be built up. The patient finds himself constantly toppled, therefore, but with very little distance to fall. A kind

---

[45] In the hospital I studied there did not seem to be a kangaroo court, and so, for example, an engaging alcoholic, who managed to get two very well-liked student nurses sent home for drinking with him, did not apparently suffer much for his betrayal of the desires of the peer group.

of jaunty gallows humor seems to develop in some of these wards, with considerable freedom to stand up to the staff and return insult for insult. While these patients can be punished, they cannot, for example, be easily slighted, for they are accorded as a matter of course few of the niceties that people must enjoy before they can suffer subtle abuse. Like prostitutes in connection with sex, inmates on these wards have very little reputation or rights to lose and can therefore take certain liberties. As the person moves up the ward system, he can manage more and more to avoid incidents which discredit his claim to be a human being, and acquire more and more of the varied ingredients of self-respect; yet when eventually he does get toppled—and he does—there is a much further distance to fall. For instance, the privileged patient lives in a world wider than the ward, made up of recreation workers who, on request, can dole out cake, cards, table-tennis balls, tickets to the movies, and writing materials. But in absence of the social control of payment which is typically exerted by a recipient on the outside, the patient runs the risk that even a warm-hearted functionary may, on occasion, tell him to wait until she has finished an informal chat, or teasingly ask why he wants what he has asked for, or respond with a dead pause and a cold look of appraisal.

Moving up and down the ward system means, then, not only a shift in self-constructive equipment, a shift in reflected status, but also a change in the calculus of risks. Appreciation of risks to his self-conception is part of everyone's moral experience, but an appreciation that a given risk level is itself merely a social arrangement is a rarer kind of experience, and one that seems to help to disenchant the person who has it.

A third instance of moral loosening has to do with the conditions that are often associated with the release of the inpatient. Often he leaves under the supervision and jurisdiction of his next-of-relation or of a specially watchful employer. If he misbehaves while under their auspices, they can quickly obtain his readmission. He therefore finds himself under the special power of persons who ordinarily would not have this kind of power over him, and about whom, moreover, he may have had prior cause to feel quite bitter. In order

to get out of the hospital, however, he may conceal his displeasure in this arrangement, and, at least until safely off the hospital rolls act out a willingness to accept this kind of custody. These discharge procedures, then, provide a built-in lesson in overtly taking a role without the usual covert commitments, and seem further to separate the person from the worlds that others take seriously.

The moral career of a person of a given social category involves a standard sequence of changes in his way of conceiving of selves, including, importantly, his own. These half-buried lines of development can be followed by studying his moral experiences—that is, happenings which mark a turning point in the way in which the person views the world—although the particularities of this view may be difficult to establish. And note can be taken of overt tacks or strategies—that is, stands that he effectively takes before specifiable others, whatever the hidden and variable nature of his inward attachment to these presentations. By taking note of moral experiences and overt personal stands, one can obtain a relatively objective tracing of relatively subjective matters.

Each moral career, and behind this, each self, occurs within the confines of an institutional system, whether a social establishment such as a mental hospital or a complex of personal and professional relationships. The self, then, can be seen as something that resides in the arrangements prevailing in a social system for its members. The self in this sense is not a property of the person to whom it is attributed, but dwells rather in the pattern of social control that is exerted in connection with the person by himself and those around him. This special kind of institutional arrangement does not so much support the self as constitute it.

In this paper, two of these institutional arrangements have been considered, by pointing to what happens to the person when these rulings are weakened. The first concerns the felt loyalty of his next-of-relation. The prepatient's self is described as a function of the way in which three roles are related, arising and declining in the kinds of affiliation that occur between the next-of-relation and the mediators. The second concerns the protection required by the person for the version of himself which he presents to others, and the way in which the withdrawal of this protection can form a systematic, if unintended, aspect of the working of an establishment. I want to stress that these are only two kinds of institutional rulings from which a self emerges for the participant; others, not considered in this paper, are equally important.

In the usual cycle of adult socialization one expects to find alienation and mortification followed by a new set of beliefs about the world and a new way of conceiving of selves. In the case of the mental hospital patient, this rebirth does sometimes occur, taking the form of a strong belief in the psychiatric perspective, or, briefly at least, a devotion to the social cause of better treatment for mental patients. The moral career of the mental patient has unique interest, however; it can illustrate the possibility that in casting off the raiments of the old self—or in having this cover torn away—the person need not seek a new robe and a new audience before which to cower. Instead he can learn, at least for a time, to practice before all groups the amoral arts of shamelessness.

Arlene Kaplan Daniels   41

The Social Construction of Military Psychiatric Diagnoses[1]

INTRODUCTION

This paper analyzes the process of constructing psychiatric diagnoses in the military setting. The purpose of this case study is to examine the process of diagnosis in order to see how it contributes to the management of deviants. The particular method of deviance management is dependent upon the meaning of specific diagnostic categories in a variety of special contexts. The focus of this presentation is upon how restrictions in a specific setting affect the use of these diagnostic categories. In studying the process by which these categories become useful we may learn about both the application of deviant labels and the social construction of meanings.

This approach rests upon the theoretical perspective that Thomas P. Wilson has termed "the interpretive view of social interaction" or "radical symbolic interactionism." In this view definitions of situations and actions are never assumed to be settled once and for all by some lateral application of traditional or previously established standards. Instead one always expects that the meanings of situations and actions are dependent upon particular interpretations that are influenced by both the context of particular occasions and the participants involved in that interaction. Accord-

From "The Social Construction of Military Psychiatric Diagnoses" by Arlene Kaplan Daniels, pp. 181–205 in *Recent Sociology No. 2*, edited by Hans Peter Dreitzel, copyright 1970. Reprinted by permission of the author.

[1] I would like to thank Rachel Kahn-Hut for help in editing this paper.

ingly meanings are always subject to reformulation on subsequent occasions.[2] Using this theoretical approach, then, it is not surprising that psychiatric diagnoses will not "hold still" but waver, change, and adjust to circumstances.

The diagnosis of mental illness is dependent not only upon the symptoms of the patient; but also upon the doctor's awareness of the consequences that a specific diagnostic label may have for the career of the patient. The doctor's use of this knowledge in his application of specific labels is what is meant when we speak of "the social construction of psychiatric diagnoses." Through an examination of the process of diagnosis in one context, we can discover some of the crucial social factors influencing or determining the nature of any psychiatric diagnoses.

METHOD

The data gathered for this study come from informants practicing military psychiatry. (All quotations in this paper are from verbatim transcripts of interviews that I personally conducted. Biophrasing, where used, is indicated by brackets.) Most of the informants were practicing in large military hospitals and had in-patient responsibilities. But many were also in what is called Mental Hygiene or Command Consultation at regular posts and bases. Generally the process of military psychiatric diagnosis begins here in the psychiatric dispensaries or field units. Routinely, Mental Hygiene will screen all potential psychiatric cases coming to official attention in an area of military jurisdiction. Those cases that are seen as serious or problematic are then sent to the major military medical centers for more specialized consideration.[3] Over two hundred interviews have been collected since 1964.[4] While most of

them were conducted in Army settings, a few come from Air Force and Navy psychiatric services to ensure applicability of the analysis to any military psychiatry setting.

In the course of the interviews, information concerning diagnostic procedures in the military was obtained. Questions about these matters were couched in the military psychiatric language. Some examples of questions[5] specifically directed to residents in the military psychiatry training programs are:

1. What do you think of the diagnostic competency of the referral agencies?
2. Since all referrals are in-patients for relatively serious problems, how do you determine who returns to duty and who does not?
3. What percentage of the cases referred to you do you feel are simply referred for the purpose of administratively getting someone out of the way?
4. How often do you make direct contacts with unit commanders to help you in deciding final disposition?

These questions refer to some of the crucial decisions which military psychiatrists are asked to make in the services. Men whose future careers in the military are in any way problematic are ultimately reviewed or examined by the psychiatrist. His decision may be a major factor in the military decision to release or retain a man, to allow him special consideration or to withhold it. The psychiatrist is expected to use his professional judgment in evaluating each particular case. However the parameters of the psychiatric world—or the definition of where such professional judgments are appropriate—are set by the military regulations. They define what is to be considered mental illness and what is not; and then they indicate how the psychiatrist is to apply these interpretations. Military regulations also define the consequences which may befall any per-

[2] T. P. Wilson, "Conceptions of Interaction and Forms of Sociological Explanation," presented at the American Sociological Association Annual Meeting, San Francisco, September, 1969.
[3] A. K. Daniels, "Military Psychiatry: The Emergence of a Subspecialty," in E. Freidson and J. Lorber (eds.), *Reader in Medical Sociology* (New York: Atherton Press, 1970).
[4] The research of which this study is a part has been conducted under various auspices: The U.S. Army Research and Development Command (No. DA-MD-49-193-66-G9209 & 2212), the National Institute of Child Health and Human Development

(No. RO1 HD02776-10 BS), and an NIMH post-doctoral fellowship to study the relationship between military psychiatry and military legal procedures, 1F3-8885-01.
[5] I would like to thank Colonel Roy E. Clausen, Jr., M.C. for his assistance in constructing the interview schedule.

son who is certified as fitting within one or the other of these categories.

The military regulations about psychiatric diagnoses also provide a relatively neutral or middle ground for cases that are difficult to classify. And the consequences that may follow from this classification are similarly open for negotiation. So when the psychiatrist labels a man as: 1) mentally ill; 2) looking mentally ill at least for the moment; or 3) clearly not ill—even if showing bizarre or disturbing behavior, he becomes an important decision-maker in determining the fate of the patient at the hands of the military system. Thus, the psychiatrist has three major alternatives from which to choose in any specific diagnosis. The alternatives provide the labels and indicate the consequences that follow from their application.

The following three sections present the distinctions between mental illness and the other main diagnostic alternatives as they are understood within the military context. The remaining sections present a discussion of the application of these distinctions. The psychiatrist takes the consequences of each label into account when constructing a diagnosis. He has to consider what he hopes to accomplish for the patient—and then he applies the appropriate label which is likely to gain that end.

1. Who Is Mentally Ill?

Military regulations use a very restrictive definition of mental illness. This definition includes only the psychoses (paranoia, schizophrenia, and chronic depression are examples within that category). Restrictive definitions of illness are common in the military for two reasons. First, the Armed Forces have the mission to "preserve the fighting strength." This usually means: retain men in the field. The psychiatrist, as other medical examiners, should try to select those men in service who can recover sufficiently to serve again.[6] Therefore one of the important functions of the psychiatrist is to *not* diagnose, for the mental illness diagnosis is likely to result in limited duty assignment or discharge from the service. A sec-

[6] A. K. Daniels, *op. cit.*

ond reason for not diagnosing mental illness stems from the particular nature of the military organization's responsibility to its members. First, those mental illnesses that are recognized as diseases are considered medical disabilities equivalent to physical disabilities. Accordingly, the military offers compensation, particularly if disability occurred during, or was aggravated by, service activities "in the line of duty" (LOD, yes). In addition, the finding of illness usually outweighs other considerations for any soldier who is in disciplinary difficulties that may otherwise lead to legal action in the military court martial system: demotion, fines, or imprisonment. So while the mental-illness label does carry some stigma, it can offer advantages which may outweigh that disadvantage. From the standpoint of the military organization, the use of the disease label also offers benefits and liabilities. The organization benefits through removal of a problem; it demonstrates to the society at large that appropriate restitution has occurred. However it is expensive to offer such compensation. Thus it may be said that the mental-illness label offers both benefits and liabilities to all parties concerned.

There is an additional feature about mental-illness disability that makes application of this label even more restrictive than that for physical disability. Where accidents or illnesses have been clearly and physically disabling, the rationale for the whole procedure is much easier to grasp and more acceptable to everyone in the military than where the illness is "mental." Thus questions are not as likely to arise over these contractual responsibilities accepted by the military organization. Consequently, military psychiatrists must carefully consider the merits of the case to be made for illness, and the merits of the man to receive the mental-illness label. It is harder for a psychiatrist to convince a physical evaluation board (PEB) to accept an expensive decision than it is for other MD's to do so.

2. Who Appears to Be Mentally Ill But Is Not

A second category of patients appearing before the psychiatrist are those who exhibit bizarre or symptomatic behavior that might look like mental illness but that does not fit the restrictive definitions of mental illness applicable in military settings. Such behavior is considered within two residual or borderline categories. One borderline diagnosis is meant to suggest that a particular behavior is interpreted as a reaction to a unique stress situation rather than a stable personality pattern. (These diagnoses include such categories as "situational stress" and variants like "a stress reaction," "adult situational reaction.") The other borderline category suggests that a behavior *looks* like mental illness (*e.g.*, schizoid-affective type) but is not *really* mental illness (*e.g.*, schizophrenia). They are not *officially* mental illness but they suggest it. They carry overtones of the mental illness categories without necessarily providing their range of benefits.[7] These diagnoses may be used with greater freedom than those designating mental illness since they make no clear diagnosis of mental illness and carry no attendant obligations upon the military organization for disability benefits. These diagnoses are useful because they provide the psychiatrist with the greatest leeway in that they are the least consequential in the initiation of further administrative action for or against the patient. The value of the diagnosis is that it shares with mental illness diagnoses the potential for excuse or mitigation. That is, it may be argued that the serviceman is not responsible for his behavior and so the military organization should not punish him for any misdeeds. However, this is not an automatic interpretation of the meaning of the diagnosis. When he makes this diagnosis, the psychiatrist is not determining the consequences for the man's service career. Higher administrative boards eventually decide this question—taking into account the particular manifestations of behavior and the outcome that is seen as most advantageous for the service and the man. Depending upon the decision of these boards, the man may leave without heavy penalty or remain in the service.

[7] Of course, it must be understood that no psychiatric label or diagnosis is totally without consequences in the military organization, and any statement from a psychiatrist can ultimately be used by some official as a basis for requesting that a referral receive some kind of administrative action.

3. Who Is Definitely Not Mentally Ill?

This category is the one most often used by military psychiatrists. It is applied to a variety of disruptive behaviors within the military context (constant quarreling, many absences without leave, minor but chronic disobedience are examples). It also includes such "social" problems as alcoholism and homosexuality. The label usually given is the "character and behavior" diagnosis, or rather quasidiagnosis, which carries no implication of mental illness within official military regulations. It also offers absolutely no exonerative connotations for those caught up in disciplinary proceedings. The benefit for the serviceman is that no stigma of psychosis attaches to the label. The liability is that the diagnosis does not provide any excuse that the man so identified should not be considered responsible for his action.

Thus far we have considered the delimitations placed upon the psychiatrist's world by military definitions. Now let us consider how the psychiatrist comes to terms with these delimitations. When placing a label on an actual patient, the psychiatrist takes into account both the recognized consequences of the label within the military and the particular outcome he thinks most desirable and possible within the value system of the military. Given his understanding of how the label will be translated into legal and administrative terms, the psychiatrist evaluates each case that he sees. He has to decide what he wants to do and what he may do. What he may do depends upon social considerations not directly related to the diagnosis. Such considerations include the military view of the presenting symptom, the context in which it occurred, the amount of time already served in the military by the patient, the previous pattern of his career, and the nature of his relations with his commanding officers. Any or all of these considerations may have to be weighed in addition to those criteria involved in the definition of the diagnosis.

SOCIAL CONDITIONS AND VALUES WHICH AFFECT DIAGNOSES

In order to built an argument for one or another diagnosis, the psychiatrist raises such considerations as presenting symptom, context, and prior history of the patient. He weighs such considerations as "evidence" which suggests the feasibility of one or the other of these labels. Here is how one informant viewed the process.

Phobic or conversion symptoms or genuine suicide attempt, the [service] is more tolerant of than the aggressor. If you see someone whose marriage is disrupted, and acts out—depending on how deviant, in a social sense—he can be labeled as "character and behavior" disorder, situational reaction, a neurotic [depressive] or schizophrenic [psychotic]. These are the labels. Then you worry about the manifestations. If depressed, suicidal, delusional and drinking—the crucial thing is: In what context? In what setting did he engage in the symptoms? Now we can . . . taking these into account . . . call him psychotic, and show we are worried about him [because this *is* a mental illness category]. We can say he is a situational reaction. In this case, we say the problem doesn't exist.

In making such distinctions, then, the psychiatrist places an evaluation upon the case in military terms and offers a method of dealing with the problem it presents. Within this context he understands that the amount of leeway available to him in using the disease diagnosis is most clearly affected by the military merit of the man and the length of his service. These limitations reflect the values of the military system. They also reflect understandings about rules for retention of employees applicable in the larger society. One psychiatrist explained the rationale under which he worked in this way.

. . . The military psychiatrist has to serve two masters, in a way—the service and the patient. . . . You want to [retain] a guy . . . who can (1) function adequately, and (2) probably not get into trouble again, who will not be a burden. . . . You also want to keep in mind that you may make a big difference to the individual in sending him back. . . . Suppose he had some kind of an associative reaction. A very brief kind of upset. . . . He was in a bar and suddenly he went crazy and started hitting people, and somebody said he was psychotic and sent him to you. You can help this person make a good adjustment if you feel that he has a good chance . . . if he has a good character structure underneath what problems there may be. . . . The ones we chose to send back to duty were those who were in for several years . . . made good progression in rank, and had done a good job.

If the man returns to duty, he loses the discharge benefit possibilities; but he also avoids the label of one who is seriously mentally ill. And he receives a second chance to "make good" in his military job.

. . . How do we decide if the real psychotic patients stay or get out? If they have a long period of service, I consider them for going back to duty; if they don't, I think they ought to go out. . . . And this is sort of the directive we have had. If a person has a long period of service, and a year or two might make the difference for him; it might make all the difference to his pride and his self-image if he can complete twenty-year service and get out with an honorable discharge rather than a medical discharge with just as much disability—actually more—when you consider it is tax free. . . . He really wants to go back, then I go ahead and give him a chance. If you get these in-between people, they are under fifteen years and they are more than five, I think they ought to go out on a medical discharge.

Thus the doctor considers the problem of an employer's responsibility for his employees in addition to an absolute evaluation of the symptom. Military organizations thus shoulder some of the welfare responsibilities which most employing organizations today are expected to take. And, as is true for most employing organizations, the military responsibility for employees is less where the length of time in service is less. The psychiatrist provides the diagnosis which supports this generally valued position.

. . . Psychotic (diagnoses) . . . a legitimate illness in our setting. But also a means of disposing. You could take someone with a full-blown psychotic picture and by soft pedaling or omission could bring in a diagnosis of "situational reaction" or neurosis—if time in service or value to service warrants. Or play it the other way—if [we] felt [the condition existed prior to service] and so [we] could get rid of him easily [without paper work and expense connected with the medical discharge].

These considerations affect the recommendation the psychiatrist makes for the disposition (*i.e.,* separation from the service or return to duty) of anyone found to be mentally ill.

Thus, the seriousness of a psychiatric illness label—in terms of the responsibility of the military organization to the labeled—is considerably mitigated when the mentally ill person has been in the service a very short time. The illness label can be given; but social conditions suggest that the situation can be reasonably allowed to have occurred prior to service (EPTS [existed prior to service], LOD [line of duty], no) and therefore the types and amounts of disability benefits may be sharply curtailed. If the problem is seen by the psychiatrist as service-aggravated, *i.e.*, occurring during the line of duty (EPTS, LOD, yes), then he must build a strong case for this view in his diagnoses and explanation. The organizational tendency is to "expect" the psychiatrist to find the opposite (EPTS, LOD, no). Therefore, a somewhat stronger case must be built by the psychiatrist if he sees the former occurring rather than the latter. The psychiatrist has to build this argument in military terms using arguments that are valid within that value system.

> I had one rather severe paranoid schizophrenic in the clinic. . . . This was a kind of . . . unusual situation because he was in intelligence. . . . The job he had when he had his psychotic break entailed sitting long, long hours in the dark room, bugging another room—hearing and seeing everything that went on in the room while he himself was sitting in the dark. And, it is a kind of psychotic existence; and we kind of pushed this point . . . to justify our "line of duty" estimation that the problem was service aggravated [even though the medical board decision was that the problem Existed Prior to Service].

In general, then, the problem for the psychiatrist may be to decide whether, in any particular situation, the medical discharge or return to duty is the most humane and reasonable alternative. Then he must decide how to present his evaluation in the most persuasive manner possible.

Another social condition delimiting the leeway of the military psychiatrist is the particular policy set by each post or hospital commander. The psychiatrist will then have to take these "guidelines" set by his commander into account as well. Some commanders are very lenient in their acceptance of psychiatric use of the mental illness diagnosis (*e.g.*, offer medical discharges easily and recommend partial disability even for short terms of service). Other commanders are less lenient about the matter of mental disability

and suggest alternatives that are not likely to offer benefits (*e.g.*, use the medical discharge sparingly, but freely recommend the administrative discharge). Still other commanders demand a very strict interpretation of mental illness and are not at all lenient or permissive about those leaving service (*e.g.*, use neither type of discharge readily, leaving discharge decisions, if they arise, to other more punitive types of authorities). The military psychiatrist thus faces a number of varying and changing constraints, peculiar to this type of institutional setting, when searching for and diagnosing mental illness. And so he argues his cases with these contingencies in mind.[8]

Such diagnoses as "stress" and "schizoid reaction" or "borderline schizoid personality" can afford the psychiatrist some leeway in what exactly is meant. And they permit him to engage in evasive tactics. He may transfer a man from one jurisdiction to another by sending a patient to a distant hospital for further observation.

> A [psychiatrist] has been seeing a soldier who is going AWOL. He goes to the commander [and says, "this man is an] immature kid, impulse ridden, he acts out. I think you should administratively separate him." The C.O. says, "No . . . I'm not going to allow anybody to get away with that business" . . . and put[s] him in the stockade for court martial (proceedings as a prelude to a somewhat more punitive separation than that suggested by the psychiatrist). The patient then chooses another route of impulse . . . suicide gesture or threat. The [psychiatrist] is made very anxious by this, as are the (stockade authorities). They [informally indicate to the psychiatrist] if you want to call him sick and deal with him that way, you can have him. Otherwise, we are going to go ahead and court martial him. [The psychiatrist returns to the patient's] commander saying . . . "This commander is adamant. The [psychiatrist] feels that it is best for the whole situation to diagnose (the patient) . . . as a depressive reaction or something like that . . . and send him to the hospital.

The psychiatrist may intervene in these ways, in order to aid the proper functioning of the military organization as he sees it. He may also intervene, quite simply, for mercy. Labels of the situational

[8] A. K. Daniels, "The Captive Professional: Bureaucratic Limitations in the Practice of Military Psychiatry," *Journal of Health and Social Behavior*, Vol. 10, No. 4, December 1969.

or stress variety, and labels that suggest the possibility of psychosis but do not take full consequences for that type of label may be used by the psychiatrist when he feels that he ought to protect a man from punishment.

> We see a borderline schizoid personality kid who had gone AWOL. He had been gone for months . . . went back to the farm. He liked to talk to the cows. . . . He finally turned himself in because he began to feel guilty about [the absence]. The company wanted to boot him, and make an example of him because he had been gone for so long. I'm sure he's a better candidate than most to have a schizoid break. I really went to bat to get this man out. "A lot of other people you can make examples of. Let this poor boy go home." Spoke to a Colonel of Special Troops about it.

In the psychiatrist's view, his professional understanding of the patient's motivation is crucial in diagnosis. And therefore he may pit his own understanding of the motivation and capability of an individual against the view of some other military officer. By so doing, he exceeds his technical authority. But he does so with the techniques that he has been given by the organization (*e.g.*, diagnosis—transfer to hospital at a distant post). And so it may be said that this area of judgment is implicitly delegated to the psychiatrist by military authorities.

VALUE JUDGMENTS INVOLVED IN FINDING NO DIAGNOSIS OF MENTAL ILLNESS

When the psychiatrist cannot find any reason for diagnosing mental illness or something like mental illness, he is in effect withholding his ability to negotiate on behalf of the patient. Within the military system, this often means that the initiation of some disciplinary action or some other action that the patient does not wish to occur, has no further impediment. The psychiatrist may simply report that no psychiatric disease or mental illness is present. (A notation of "NPD" [no psychiatric diagnosis] or "NMI" [no mental illness] will then be all that he will write about the case when he signs his name.) But he may also describe the patient—or diagnose him—in terms

of the character and behavior disorder, or "c and b" as it is often called. This diagnosis is generally elicited when behavior by the person examined has been so disturbing, aggravating, or bizarre as to cause comment or trouble within the military system. Some justification that this person really is not mentally ill seems to be required. And so this diagnostic category is offered as a sort of explanation or rationale for why considerations surrounding mental illness diagnosis need not arise. In effect, the psychiatrist refuses to intervene on behalf of the patient; he may even implicitly or explicitly support the military organization's claim against the patient.

Thus the world which the psychiatrist constructs through his diagnoses bears many resemblances to the world of everyday life with its common-sense value judgments. The psychiatrist examines individual cases and assesses responsibility for behavior. In this activity he may see himself as a simple administrator or personnel manager making considered judgments about employment risks. If he takes this view, his diagnostic work merely expedites organizational procedures whereby men may be dismissed or "separated" from their jobs. Such men should be dismissed because, within the general "c and b" category, they are diagnosed as "emotionally unstable." "Instability" and "immaturity reactions" are also likely labels.

> His past history was one of running away, delinquent behavior, distaste with the Army. His diagnosis was emotionally unstable personality, aggressive type, chronic moderate. Oh, he was one of these guys who was offered the Army or jail. . . . His history of running away, delinquent behavior and enuresis indicate a personality which is chronically unstable. He is not motivated to serve. It is very likely that retention on active duty will result in further immature and aggressive acts. And [so] I recommend that he be separated under [an administrative regulation].

In general, the diagnosis reflects the psychiatric acceptance of the idea that the military organization has "thrown up its hands," so to speak, and is ready to reject the man.

> This category tends to encompass the group that rocks the system. [The certificate recommending an administrative separation says] "No impairment," [so

it is a] law enforcement rather than [a] psychiatric problem. [This type of separation allows for nice distinctions in the allotment of responsibility. The patient is either] unsuitable for our system [or] unfit for military service. . . . These people make waves, either [the] stormy AWOL way, or withdrawn or passive way. All of this behavior is kind of manipulative and disruptive. Military [authority] is less willing to keep these people than some of the sicker [in psychiatric terms, but who are not disruptive to the military system].

The implication is that, as far as psychiatry is concerned, punishment for such behavior may be just and deserved; however, it is not within the psychiatric province to consider the matter. Because the disorder is considered unappealing and untreatable, military psychiatrists are willing to diagnose but unwilling to give much attention to the "c and b."

My rationalization for [facilitating] discharges through character and behavior (diagnoses) is: I can't be of help. [The] line [commanders] can't hold them or they wouldn't get here.

And so an added implication suggested here is that the psychiatrist has no control in such matters, but he does possess evidence that such cases probably deserve the fate that befalls them. It is sometimes assumed that the whole referral and hospitalization system for the mentally ill really should not be put at the disposal of "c and b" cases who may really belong, quite simply, in jail.

I feel that [Fort X] should keep its own character disorders, and take care of them down there. And a guy who is tearing up the place, and you think he is a character disorder, then you call the MP and have him thrown in the stockade. A person who is felt to be a character disorder, who is not . . . sick and has been seen by a competent psychiatrist, does not have to be sent to another hospital to control his behavior. There are plenty of jails where people who behave miserably are controlled.

A final assumption implicit within the use of this category is that sometimes psychiatrists will fully accept their part in judging such symptomatic behavior pejoratively and consider it right and proper to do so.

But often psychiatrists tend to feel harassed and disgruntled when forced to spend much time with such cases. They feel burdened when pressed by exigencies of military life to go beyond simple diagnosis.

I regard a lot of the character and behavior disorders as a waste of time because, although they may be sick, I don't have the slightest idea what to do for them. And they're just making paper work for me. And they make lots of it. I've got a court martial coming up Monday that I have to testify at. . . . We sent him over to Medicine to have another disease worked up. He thought maybe they were using him for a guinea pig, so he got drunk, threatened suicide, and got back in our ward. After a couple of weeks, he bled all over me and I let him go out on pass. And he came back from pass drunk, a day late, pulled a gun on a nurse, demanded some Seconal—and from there on, the paper work really started to pile up. . . . And to me, it was just a total waste of time 'cause whatever his disorder is, it's not amenable to the type of psychiatry we're practicing right now.

Perhaps the implication here is that the psychiatrist really does not wish to enter into any extended negotiations about these cases once he has indicated his initial disinterest in them. However, the exigencies of military life sometimes restrict his leeway in these matters. And the reality that the psychiatrist constructs merely takes account of this restriction without much further comment.

To summarize, the use of the "c and b" label is applied by the psychiatrist to persons the psychiatrist accepts as disagreeable, aggravating, or otherwise unattractive to the military system. They have been given their chance for an evaluation to uncover some mental illness that might explain or excuse their behavior. If they had had a mental illness, an honorable "out" would have been provided. However, if a psychiatrist attests that they have no mental illness (but only a "quirk" or a "streak" of meanness, cowardice, depravity, hostility, or some other character flaw, as such are conceived in common-sense, lay evaluations) then they may take the consequences, as laid down in regulations, for whatever wrath they have incurred. The psychiatrist certifies that no moral, medical, or generally humanitarian considerations need mitigate the course of justice when he diagnoses "c and b."

In this area, then, there are many similarities

between the psychiatric, the military, and the common-sense construction of judgments and the attribution of motives. But this general category of character and behavior disorder also includes some problems where these three perspectives are not so clearly parallel.

Such problems as alcoholism and homosexuality are usually categorized as "c and b." But there are a variety of special understandings to consider on behalf of such sufferers (or culprits—depending upon point of view). The exigencies which spur these considerations are peculiar to military settings and clearly illustrate the social pressures affecting a diagnosis. Accordingly, each of these problems is examined separately below.

Alcoholism

Alcoholism is specifically exempted from the mental illness categories in the military psychiatric nosology. Thus alcoholics should be dismissed or "separated" from service. But in this case, the tendency informally encouraged by the military organization is to protect and excuse alcoholics rather than to use the full array of sanctions technically available. The view is embodied in the following expressions: "Give them another chance; try to rehabilitate them; suggest AA and other therapeutic devices to control the problem while the man remains on duty." Where these contradictions between regulation and informal policy exist, the negotiations over diagnoses can be seen most clearly. To facilitate opportunities for second chances, alcoholics or their intermediaries often request that the psychiatrist withhold the diagnosis of alcoholism in order to protect the offender from the formal requirement of prompt administrative separation. The argument for this exemption is usually made in terms of number of years the offender has already served. As in other types of diagnosis, length of service is an important consideration when formulating a diagnosis. But alcoholism may also be excused or ignored throughout the entire period of service.

> People don't want to get down and write "alcoholic" [on a man's record]. . . . The man's usually had 18

years experience. It is written all over his [medical] chart, but . . . in black and white. It's inferred. They write all around and give you a diagnosis of [something else]. They don't what to ruin his career. Actually, they would probably do him a favor by saying it.

Sometimes the alcoholics or their intermediaries who come to argue this point are high-ranking and powerful officers. Even when there are no such pressures, the possible injustice or hardship involved in "firing" a man, and so depriving him of an expected retirement pension, may weigh heavily with the psychiatrist.

> A major was hospitalized as a depressive. And the guy was a chronic alcoholic. . . . For ten years, on and off, he would get hospitalized every two or three years. . . . Once [he] got evacuated from Europe to Walter Reed. . . . All the time [for] depression, [and] the guy is an alcoholic—without question. He's also a very decorated soldier. . . . When sober, a very effective guy; when drunk, inadequate and couldn't stop. . . . And wouldn't show up for work. And people would cover up for him.
>   . . . On the post . . . it became very obvious that the problem was alcohol and nothing else, (even though) alcohol never, never came up . . . on his records. And he denied it. The only reason I wondered about it was that he showed up, the first time I saw him, . . . an hour late and drunk—and it was 9 or 10 o'clock in the morning. . . . I asked his commanding officer, "does this guy have a drinking problem?" [The colonel told me] "He drinks beer occasionally, but I've never seen him drunk." Nobody said he was an alcoholic. Well, the guy obviously was.
>   I don't think they knew, or they weren't willing to go that far in facing [the] alcoholic [question]. He admitted it himself. It got to the point. I hospitalized him twice: once for a short term, and saw him as an outpatient (afterward); put him on Antabuse, and I said, well this is a compromise. . . . The third hospitalization . . . I got him in AA.
>   But this time it came to post attention. The senior major and the colonel. . . . This was too much . . . too . . . many repeated instances of . . . not showing up for work. . . . I evacuated him to [a large military hospital], and I called [the hospital] and said, "Keep him and reassign him" . . . to save him from [the action that was beginning to start rolling on him]. I hospitalized him [with a diagnosis of] depression.

These considerations that the psychiatrist must weigh suggest that alcoholism may be associated with more "honorable" disabilities. And the alcoholic is more easily "managed" within the system than other deviants more abhorrent within the military framework (as the homosexual). The view that drinking is an important and manly pastime for a soldier is part of military culture. Thus, though the formal rules are similar in regard to both homosexuality and alcoholism, informal understandings require differing decisions or evaluations from the psychiatric practitioner.

Homosexuality

A far greater bone of contention for many psychiatrists is created by the requirement that they diagnose homosexuality. Homosexuality is also specifically exempted from the mental illness or disease categories in the military regulations. If the psychiatrist makes this diagnosis, it is likely to result in a special punitive administrative separation (the Army regulations number is AR 635–89) which may then result in an undesirable discharge. Officially, then, the evaluation of homosexuality in the military is a pejorative judgment even though a medical doctor diagnoses it. Psychiatrists may refuse to use the diagnosis—or even to see the patient—until the CID (Criminal Investigation Department) men do their homework. In effect, they become the diagnostic agents. When finally diagnosed by the psychiatrist, the problem is to get the patient quickly out of the service. Separation rather than treatment is the military expectation whatever the personal or professional view of the psychiatrist who expedites this process.

A guy comes in here and says, "I'm queer." So I send in a report that says this guy tells me that he is queer. CID are the ones that do all this. They . . . get all the statements and take all the pictures. I personally think that, except the obvious security risk involved, I don't see any reason why a homosexual can't be in the (service). Most of them . . . soldier fairly well.

However, less punitive types of administrative separations than the "89" may be arranged. In these situations, where the psychiatrist feels the military expectations contradict his own views of what is professionally appropriate, there are ways

of managing cases so that diagnosis and disposition are more palatable to both doctor and patient. An often-mentioned technique in negotiating to escape the diagnosis of homosexuality is simply to withhold information. The CID may find itself in difficulty about producing evidence where homosexuality cannot be proven. The psychiatrist may refuse to keep notes so there is nothing to subpoena; or he may destroy any notes that have incriminating evidence. Another alternative is that he may keep records in such vague and ambiguous language that no evidence is provided by them. Particularly when evaluating referrals who have fears about potential homosexuality, the psychiatrist has the greatest leeway to influence disposition through his diagnosis. Here he is only limited in his discretion by the discretion of the referral. Here are examples of policy in this matter from an Army and then a Navy psychiatrist.

. . . we specifically recommend [one of the other administrative discharges] and fought for no "89" [separations] unless a guy confessed [homosexuality] and [put it] in black and white, and there was no choice. . . . If a company commander has it in for a guy, and has a guy cold [on grounds of homosexuality], you don't go down the line for someone who has been nailed cold. Don't try to change reality, but use it [your discretion to be less punitive] when you have a chance of succeeding.

A young sailor comes in and says—I think with a tremendous amount of pain—that he's a homosexual. You have got to decide whether he's homosexual and in a panic, or manipulating the decision [i.e., trying to get out of the service on that pretext]. One way [to decide] is to indicate the dangers of this diagnosis and what's going to happen to him. Maybe a BCD [Bad Conduct Discharge] or DD [Dishonorable Discharge] if you confess, or if you dispute [the charge] they find you guilty. I never said homosexual [made the diagnosis] unless he had already told someone. My first question always was: "Who else have you told?" When I went to my chief officer, his first question was: "Who else have you told?" [If the homosexual suspect had not told anyone] we would put him on the hospital ward for some length of time, and write up some sort of character disorder, EPTS [Existing Prior to Service] to get him out.

The power of the psychiatrist to effect the outcome through diagnosis is also enhanced by his own judgment about how to "stretch" an evaluation in cases which come to trial. By judicious commission of his speculations to the record, a psychiatrist can influence the outcome in the direction he desires. An ex-Air Force psychiatrist described his tactics in the following manner.

A man in delivering cargo overseas got drunk and made a definite homosexual advance toward a member of his crew. I was called to give expert testimony. They wanted to know whether or not he was a homosexual. In my heart, I thought he was; but didn't take that position . . . what I did say was impossible to attack. I pointed out the vast quantity of alcohol the man had consumed. Enough to knock a man flat. I pointed out that a man coming out of anesthesia behaves in a way not regular [or usual]. [And I managed to get him off.]

Sometimes, to attain what he considers the appropriate end, the psychiatrist will enter in direct private negotiation with the patient. Keeping a wary eye on what incriminating evidence may already have been collected, what antagonisms have already been provoked, and what chances yet remain for the man to "make it" in the service, the psychiatrist offers the best "deal" that he can.

I haven't given anybody an "89." I have had two candidates for it, and I have talked to both of them and told them: "You have trouble. If you get caught, they will anchor you with this for life. You can get out on an administrative separation right now. Why don't you take it?" They always jump at it.

CONCLUSIONS

The preceding discussions of the management of specific types of deviance suggest how deviant categories are socially constructed. Special social contexts, like that provided by the military setting, show very clearly that the psychiatrist keeps well in mind a variety of contingencies that must be taken into account in formulating a diagnosis. The diagnosis may become the tangible representation of the way in which the psychiatrist negotiates with or for the patient. The psychiatrist may use his diagnostic power to negotiate *for* the patient with the system—buying time, opening the way for leniency in the management of a case, suggesting a way out of some difficulty. On the

other hand, it cannot be forgotten that the psychiatrist is also negotiating on behalf of the system, taking into account its coercive and regulatory powers over both the patient and himself. The powers of that system, the margins or boundaries to its regulations which cannot be transgressed, the rulings that must be supported—these are all realities that the psychiatrist translates into concrete, practical suggestions or recommendations when he signs certificates and presents diagnoses.

In this system, problems of diagnosis are inextricably mixed with questions about appropriate disposition. This confusion of area arises because psychiatry has always faced problems of circular reasoning in its explanations of human behavior.[9] In situations where diagnostic procedures carry clear consequences for disposition of cases, the principle seems to be: Tell me what is feasible or reasonable to do with this person and I will give you a diagnosis which can explain, justify, or in some cases, modify that disposition.

These principles are by no means limited to the military setting. Circumscriptions also exist in courts of law where psychiatrists for the defense and the prosecution each have a vested interest in a type of diagnosis that either does or does not permit further legal action against an accused. And diagnoses have just such meaning in these settings. Such problems also exist in prison psychiatry where the amount of leniency that can be introduced by psychiatrists through the range of diagnoses is quite curtailed.[10] (Powelson and Bendix, 1955.) In these settings the predominance of punitive and custodial values makes it difficult to present diagnoses which suggest lenient dispositions. This pattern is found in military prisons as well. The effect of the prison or custodial establishment is to encourage the psychiatrist to diagnose in certain directions only. As one psychiatrist serving in a military prison explained the situation, the psychiatrist can only diagnose punitively.

[9] See T. S. Szasz, *The Myth of Mental Illness* (New York: Hoeber-Harper, 1961), and N. Zinberg, "Psychiatry: A Professional Dilemma" in K. Lynn (ed.), *The Professions in America* (Cambridge: Houghton Mifflin Company, 1965), pp. 154–169.

[10] See H. Powelson and R. Bendix, "Psychiatry in Prisons" in A Rose (ed.) *Mental Health and Mental Disease* (New York: W. W. Norton, 1955), pp. 459–481.

They [command authorities] give us the kiss of death for negative recommendations [to their policies]. . . . They use the psychiatrist for their own purpose—so he gets blamed [if the decision should later come up for unfavorable review on an appeal]. To hell with the psychiatrist when he goes against their wishes. . . .

The categories that the psychiatrist uses do not exist in a vacuum. They are not independent of the circumstances in which they arise. And the more circumscribed the system in which he operates, the more influenced he is in the direction taken by his evaluations of the behavior he examines. Thus one can anticipate that the bureaucratic expectations of prison or prisonlike total institutions will be reflected in certain tendencies or trends of psychiatric diagnoses and dispositions. These comparisons in settings for practice suggest, of course, that psychiatry may be adaptable, that new methods and theories may be developed out of adversity. However, they also suggest that the construction of psychiatric reality may be almost entirely social. The actual disease base or the actual significance of the presentation of symptoms may be of such slight importance in the formulation of diagnoses as to warrant our rephrasing of Marx's dicta once again. Being determines consciousness, and social pressures determine psychiatric nosology.

SELECTED REFERENCES
PART FIVE

Becker, Howard S. *Outsiders.* Glencoe, Illinois: The Free Press, 1963, pp. 1–18. Shows how responses to deviation shape deviant behavior. This reference should be compared with the one by Lemert, below.

Brooks, Richard S. "The Self and Political Role: A Symbolic Interactionist Approach to Political Ideology," *The Sociological Quarterly,* vol. 10 (Winter 1969), pp. 22–31. Uses the TST to analyze left-wing and right-wing political roles.

Cohen, Albert K. "The Sociology of the Deviant Act." *American Sociological Review,* vol. 30 (February 1965), pp. 5–14. An effort to integrate anomie theory with Mead's role theory.

Denzin, Norman K. "The Methodological Implications of Symbolic Interactionism for the Study of Deviance," *British Journal of Sociology,* 25 (September 1974), pp. 269–282. An application of the "labeling encounter."

Deutscher, Irwin. "Words and Deeds: Social Science and Social Policy." *Social Problems,* vol. 13 (Winter 1966), pp. 235–254. A careful consideration of the implications of research findings on inconsistencies between verbalized attitudes and overt behavior. Applies the perspective of symbolic interactionism in explaining the findings.

Elkin, Frederick. *The Child and Society.* New York: Random House, 1960, pp. 25–30. Describes the role of significant others in early socialization.

Faris, Ellsworth. "The Retrospective Act and Education." *Journal of Educational Sociology,* vol. 14 (October 1940), pp. 79–91. A contemporary of Mead's at the University of Chicago analyzes some educational implications of a common form of human behavior: viewing one's own past behavior.

Gecas, Viktor, and Roger Libby. "Sexual Behavior as Symbolic Interaction." *The Journal of Sex Research,* vol. 12 (February 1976), pp. 33–49. An effort to organize research findings on sexual behavior in terms of the symbolic interactionist frame of reference.

Glaser, Barney G., and Anselm L. Strauss. "Awareness Contexts and Social Interaction," *American Sociological Review,* vol. 29 (October 1964), pp. 669–679. Considers the identities actors assign themselves and their co-actors among terminally ill patients in hospitals.

Goffman, Erving. *Stigma: Notes on the Management of Spoiled Identity.* Englewood Cliffs, New Jersey: Prentice-Hall, Inc., 1963. Analyzes feelings toward self and others of such "discredited and discreditable" persons as the physically deformed, the ex-mental patient, the drug addict, the prostitute, and the ugly.

Hall, Peter. "A Symbolic Interactionist Analysis of Politics," *Sociological Inquiry,* vol. 42 (no. 3–4, 1972), pp. 35–75. Argues against the view that symbolic interactionism is inherently apolitical.

Haskell, Martin R. "Toward a Reference Group Theory of Juvenile Delinquency." *Social Problems,* vol. 8 (Winter 1960–1961), pp. 220–230. Exemplifies a growing tendency to incorporate symbolic interactionism into theories of delinquent and criminal behavior.

Lemert, Edwin M. *Social Pathology.* New York: McGraw-Hill Book Company, 1951, pp. 75–78. Introduces the concept "secondary deviation" to describe how the reactions of others reinforce the individual's deviance.

Lindesmith, Alfred R. "Problems in the Social Psychology of Addiction." In D. M. Wilner and G. C. Kassebaum (ed.) *Narcotics.* New York: McGraw-Hill Book Company, 1965. The author is a prominent student of drug addiction, which he views from the perspective of symbolic interactionism.

Lofland, John. *Deviance and Identity.* Englewood Cliffs, New Jersey: Prentice-Hall, Inc., 1969. A symbolic interactionist approach to the subject.

Marshall, Victor W. "Socialization for Impending Death in a Retirement Village." *American Journal of Sociology,* 80 (March 1975), pp. 1124–1145. Participant observation and interviewing used to explore legitimations of dying.

Martin, Wilfred B. W. *The Negotiated Order of the School.* Canada: Macmillan, 1976. Application of the "negotiation framework" to teacher-pupil and teacher-teacher interaction.

Petras, John W. *Sexuality in Society.* Boston: Allyn and Bacon, 1973. Sex, gender, and sexuality viewed by a symbolic interactionist.

Plummer, Kenneth. *Sexual Stigma: An Intractionist Account.* London: Routledge and Kegan Paul, 1975. A consideration of sex as deviance.

Schwartz, Michael, Gordon F. N. Fearn, and Sheldon Stryker. "Note on Self Conception and the Emotionally Disturbed Role," *Sociometry,* vol. 29 (September 1966), pp. 300–305. A study of the deviant as role-maker.

Spitzer, Stephan P., and Norman K. Denzin (eds.). *The Mental Patient: Studies in the Sociology of Deviance.* New York: McGraw-Hill Book Company, 1968. Emphasizes the symbolic interactionist tradition.

Stebbins, Robert A. *Teachers and Meaning: Definitions of Classroom Situations.* Leiden: E. J. Brill, 1975. How teachers in two schools deal with the meaning of disorderly behavior, academic performance, and tardiness.

Stryker, Sheldon. "Role-Taking Accuracy and Adjustment," *Sociometry,* vol. 20 (December 1957), pp. 286–296. Hypothesizes that "the adjustment of the individual is a function of the accuracy with which he can take the role of the other(s) implicated with him in some social situation."

Turner, Ralph H. "Self and Other in Moral Judgment." *American Sociological Review,* vol. 19 (June 1954, pp. 249–259. Responses of 88 individuals and their friends toward the respondent's hypothetical involvement in a theft.

Turner, Ronny E., and Charles Edgley. "Death as Theatre: A Dramaturgical Analysis of the American Funeral." *Sociology and Social Research,* vol. 60 (July 1976), pp. 377–392. A useful complement to the article by Carlen (Selection 36).

Vercors (Jean Bruller). *You Shall Know Them.* New York: Pocket Books, Inc., 1955. A novel that raises the question: What are the attributes which most clearly distinguish humans from other living forms?

PART six

Appraisals of Symbolic Interactionism

The basic concepts and principles of symbolic interactionism focus attention upon the ongoing, constructed activities constituting human society and conduct. The utility of the perspective has been evidenced by its power to explain a broad range of conduct in a variety of contexts. Symbolic interactionists should not need to be reminded, however, that their ideas are, themselves, social constructions open to evaluation both from their own perspective and from the perspectives of other social psychologies. Some of our earlier readings (e.g., Selections 1, 3, 15, 20, 25) include a few such evaluations.

Appraisals of symbolic interactionism are neither new nor uninfluential. Decades ago, Herbert Blumer and Manford H. Kuhn placed the imprint of their own ideas and assessments upon the viewpoints of their predecessors. To many outside the perspective, however, symbolic interactionism has appeared to be a somewhat monolithic embodiment of sectarian truths. Cavalier disregard by many symbolic interactionists for the theories and data of various psychological schools of social psychology lends some support to this position. However, such insulation appears to be mutual, for psychologically oriented social psychologists have tended to ignore symbolic interactionism.

The spread of symbolic interactionism from its source at the University of Chicago has helped to diminish its insularity. A large and growing number of scholars, located throughout and beyond the United States, have assessed and modified older viewpoints. Increments to this knowledge produced by the dramaturgical and ethnomethodological approaches have also encouraged this development. It has seemed appropriate in this revised edition, therefore, to give special attention to the major points of the critics. The readings in this Part, along with others cited in the Selected References, can enrich and advance our understanding of both symbolic interactionism and the human condition.

A brief excerpt from a recent book by Randall Collins deals with symbolic interactionism and related perspectives as examples of an "aesthetic orientation." Such an orientation, he holds, aims at producing "intellectual work the experience of which is a value in itself," akin to art and literature. While emphasizing the necessity of insight, this orientation slights the quest for causal generalizations that are required by an explanatory sociology.

Jonathan H. Turner opens with a summary of symbolic interactionism's advantages over other theoretical perspectives. Still, his main concern is its neglect of social structure and organizations. While small groups and interindividual relationships are important, he points out, symbolic interactionists have not come to terms with the major collective units of the modern social world.

John Lofland's article attacks the "conceptually impoverished symbolic interactionist tradition at the University of Chicago in the late forties and early fifties" for generating some of the present weaknesses of the perspective. These weaknesses tend to center around a frequent failure to carry out systematic, cumulative analyses of interesting research findings. Symbolic interactionists have tended to interrupt their analyses short of formulating articulate and orderly generalizations that transcend the specific data.

The article by Joan Huber questions the pragmatic criteria of knowledge underlying symbolic interactionism, contending that they introduce certain ideological and epistemological biases which distort its image of collective social life. She contends that by failing to spell out clearly the nature of its theoretical postulates and methodology, the adherents of the perspective rely too heavily upon the emergence of truth from the views of the interactants under study. Thus, she claims that the researches of symbolic interactionism are too concerned with discovering the perspectives of people and not sufficiently concerned with formulating and applying its own theoretical and methodological perspective. Contrary views are available in rebuttals to her article by Blumer, Schmitt, and Stone *et al.*, which are cited in the Selected References of this Part.

The selection by Herbert Blumer is a review of a book by Erving Goffman, a leading exponent of the dramaturgical perspective. While agreeing with many of Goffman's procedures and interpretations, Blumer challenges Goffman's preoccupation excusively with face-to-face interaction. Also, he challenges Goffman's restriction of his work to the expressive *forms* of encounters, to the exclusion of the substantive *content* of the encounters. And, finally, Blumer questions the apparent assumption that human interaction is always organized and stable, which overlooks the dynamic, unstructured, and problematic character of many interpersonal situations.

Comparing and contrasting Harold Garfinkel's ethnomethodological perspective with the perspectives of Goffman, on the one hand, and Talcott Parsons, on the other, Alvin W. Gouldner attacks all three. His acerbic criticisms of Garfinkel's work cover substantive, methodological, and ideological matters. Illustrative of Gouldner's strictures are his assertions that ethnomethodology is ahistorical (ignoring the question of how definitions of social reality become established) and astructural (scanting the importance of conflicting interest groups in society).

As George Herbert Mead is the dominant figure in symbolic interactionism, and as the first selection in this book deals with his contributions to it, it is perhaps fitting to conclude with an appraisal of his efforts. Edwin H. Lemert, a founder of the societal reaction approach to deviance, offers criticisms of Mead's position and some positive suggestions for moving "beyond Mead." Although the concept of societal reactions has helped to clarify the sources and nature of deviant behavior, its ties to symbolic interactionism, the dramatistic metaphor, and ethnomethodology have fostered an excessive emphasis upon the labeling process. Lemert suggests that renewed attention to group structures would help in the study of deviance.

Interpretive Social Psychology

Another sociological approach which falls into the category of romanticist social science is the analysis of the flow of individual experience. There are various types of such analysis: symbolic interactionism, social phenomenology and ethnomethodology, and sociological existentialism; all of them go back ultimately to the German idealist tradition. Some of these—e.g., Lyman and Scott's (1970) *Sociology of the Absurd*—explicitly set an aesthetic aim: to capture the pathos or drama of human existence, especially the existential tragedy of man imposing fragile meanings on a meaningless world. Others, such as ethnomethodology, are far from overtly humanistic in style or content. Ethnomethodology and phenomenology tend to exist in symbiosis with a counterimage of positivistic science which is a constant target of attack. A hidden rivalry to science comes to the surface in the ethnomethodologist's more positive aim, which is to purify research procedures. In this respect, ethnomethodology is reminiscent of a hypercritical positivist methodology taken as an end in itself. Some of the same rivalry is found in symbolic interactionism, which, although extremely critical of positivist formulations, often puts itself forward as the basis for a truer scientific explanation of social behavior.

Nevertheless, all of the interpretive sociologies seem to be basically organized around an aesthetic approach to their subject matter. The emphasis on the subjectivity of the human actor, the time-bound processes of behavior and experi-

Randall Collins, *Conflict Sociology*. (New York: Academic Press, Inc., 1975), pp. 30–34. Reprinted by permission.

ence, and the denial of external structure and of the scientific ideal of explanation—all of these leave the interpretive sociologist in the position of needing some criterion for organizing what he is going to say. The scientific ideal of progressively more powerful causal explanation is explicitly denied as a valid goal, although the ideal of "truly" scientific knowledge is sometimes smuggled back in to defend the critics against the charge that they are purely negativistic. The interpretive sociologists can also find an exterior purpose through their utility in attacking the political premises assumed in positivist treatments of "deviance" and "social problems" generally.

But the core of the appeal of Cooley and George Herbert Mead, Schutz and Merleau-Ponty, Garfinkel, Lyman and Scott, and others is the experience of insight that they give into social reality. The interpretive sociologies are truer to life than structuralist models. They attempt to capture the flow of our own experience just as it is and to demonstrate that all else is a myth built up from individual performances. Since science must be about reality, interpretive sociologists claim to be the real basis for any scientific sociology, in contrast to theories derived from reified ideals about structures, attitudes, norms, and values. But this promise (or threat) is never really lived up to, for the interpretive sociologists do not develop and expand a body of testable generalizations. The scope of application may expand, as symbolic interactionist interpretations have been given of various kinds of deviance, career mobility, ethnic relations and so on. But this is a matter of repeating the insight so that one sees how each of these is a processual phenomenon built up by the individual actors. This has been the case with the symbolic interactionism; ethnomethodology—insofar as it moves beyond purely philosophical discussions—often seems to tread the same path, with its own peculiar sophistication but substantively similar results.

This emphasis on an insight experience is the hallmark of an aesthetic orientation. Negatively, it is set off against the cold, uninsightful, and hence unreal constructions of positivist science which interpretive sociology constantly criticizes. Positively, its own claim to value is the experience it gives of showing how things really are, not through the cumulative results of explanatory research, but all at once with a vision of the universal processes of human experience. Like great literature (especially in the romanticist version), it captures the particularity of individual human existence, the pathos of its boundedness in time, the subjectivity that gives man his freedom but also cuts him off from fully encountering others. At the same time, it approaches the classical literary ideal in demonstrating the universality of these phenomena, giving the experience of recognizing the universal in the particular. It is the constant potential for recreating these experiences in the reader that keeps interpretive sociology alive through endless repetitions, much as a Shakespearian play can return for an infinite number of engagements.

The ambiguity of this position must be faced. On the one hand, interpretive sociologists are quite right that a science must be true to the basic empirical reality it is trying to explain. A scientific sociology will have to be built on an understanding of the enacted, subjectivistic, interpretive nature of human experience. "Organizations," "societies," and so on must be seen through and through as the ephemeral creations of real men in the flux of constructing agreed-upon realities, which often are not really agreed-upon but inalterably plural. But having performed both a critical and a potentially reconstructive service for scientific sociology, the interpretive sociologists stop dead in their tracks. The aesthetic orientation—which provided from the wealth of the romanticist–idealist tradition both the critique of positivist social science and an alternative image of man—becomes an obstacle to moving any further.

Even where it proposes to reorient the foundations of scientific sociology, ethnomethodology has jealously guarded its boundaries, refusing to allow generalizations from outside its own precincts even in tentative status. It has maintained an absolutist, nonpragmatist ideal of truth as a stick that only itself escapes being beaten with—and this only because it usually fails to attempt serious generalizations. Symbolic interactionism, on the other hand, has lived in proximity with American positivism for half a century now, and has accommodated by pretending more directly to underpin a science of its own. Yet this has not come about, even with several decades of empirical research informed by the symbolic interactionist tradition. It has described occupations, careers, and deviance (and has contributed to the downfall of positivist theories in the latter area based on projections of political values), but it has built no generalized explanatory theory beyond a repetition of the same fundamentals. The generalizing efforts of Hugh Dalziel Duncan (1962) and Anselm Strauss (1971) point up the failures: a great deal of material is subsumed under the model, but formulation never moves to testable generalizations about the causes of variations in behavior.

It is the aesthetic orientation that brings them up short. For to state causal generalizations in this context would be to introduce the cold, unambiguous, and "external" qualities into human experience which the subjective, interpretist approach tries to overcome. Despite its occasional pretensions to develop a new science, interpretive sociology is bent on protecting a romantic version of human experience from science. Ambiguity is of the essence in romantic literature, for it is in the reader's responses to a complex of suggestions that its experience of drama is found. The processual quality of our lives, in the same way, derives its drama from the ambiguity of our future at any given time. To limit that ambiguity with causal principles is to circumscribe our sense of freedom and to risk losing the dramatic experience that symbolic interactionists mean to convey.[1]

What kind of sociology one wishes to do, of course, is a value choice that everyone makes for himself. Explanatory, practical, ideological, aesthetic—there is no one type that can arbitrarily be called right and the others wrong, but they are different modes of discourse and there is no excuse for confusing them. My concern at this moment is for a successful scientific sociology. To build this, I have argued, we must free ourselves from practical and ideological orientations and their aftereffects, and from aesthetic concerns as well. In the last case, however, there are important things to be borrowed for scientific sociology. The aesthetic critique has been crucial in freeing ourselves from the practical and ideological projections that have propped up a pretended, an unsuccessful, positivist science. The interpretive sociologists give us a firmer basis on which to build.

But we cannot linger forever admiring the insight. In order to build explanatory sociology, we must work at building, recognizing all the tentativeness and pragmatics of our formulations but not using these as an excuse for abandoning the enterprise. Ironically, even the fate of the insight experience favored by an aesthetic orientation may depend on such advances, for the insights of interpretive sociology have a way of palling. The flash of recognition, which hopeful sociology teachers have sought for decades to make their students experience when they are brought to see the very world they live in as enacted and interpreted, has been all too ephemeral. The general idea of the social nature of our world has crept into the public world view. Symbolic interactionists, for all their self-image as proponents of freshness and life in sociology, are themselves largely responsible for the feeling that sociologists give other names to what everybody already knows. Ethnomethodology left to itself seems likely to suffer the same fate. It is only by producing explanations that give the conditions for why one thing happens rather than another that sociology can recover some of its magic. Though there are dangers here of turning sociology into a drab determinism, any scientific sociology built up from an interpetive perspective will have built into it its own foil. It is the combination of determinism and freedom, after all, that constitutes the greatest art; advances in scientific sociology can move its aesthetics beyond a tired romanticism, hopefully into something greater.[2]

---

[1] To take just one example: the compelling arguments of David Matza (1969) for the importance of consciousness, drift, and the ongoing self-shaping of experience come up against a limit of their own making; consciousness is invoked as an arbitrary realm beyond causality, without considering what kind of determinants might be located at this very level. An approach to causal explanation of the ongoing process of negotiating cognitive realities is presented in Chapter 3 in this volume.

[2] Richard Brown has pointed out to me that there are nonromanticist aesthetics, especially in contemporary Continental literary criticism, that do not fit the foregoing characterization. Whether they can maintain a link to a truly scientific sociology remains to be seen; so far, French structuralism connects all too readily with the noncausal systems models from which scientific sociology has been trying to disentangle itself.

Symbolic Interactionism and Social Organization

SOME SUBSTANTIVE IMPLICATIONS

The assumptions, causal imagery, and even the research and theory-building strategies of Blumer and others point to the fact that the basic social process from which personality and social structures are constructed is symbolic interaction. Whether attention is drawn to the structure of personality or society, symbolic interaction among actors is the formative process that creates, sustains, and changes these emergent structures. Although the patterned aspects of personality or of social structure can enter into the course of interaction as "objects" of the situation which shape the interpretative, evaluational, definitional, and mapping processes of actors, symbolic interaction appears to be concerned primarily with the *process of interaction,* per se. The products of such interaction—personality and social structure—have received varying degrees of substantive concern in the literature, where the structuring of different types of personality[1] has

been given more substantive attention than the structuring of various patterns of social organization.

The substantive concern with the process of interaction offers a number of advantages over other theoretical perspectives. First, it would appear to correct for the imputed inattention of perspectives such as functionalism and conflict theory to the symbolic processes that underlie the construction and maintenance of patterns of social organization. Second, the concepts of symbolic interaction "theory" are probably more generic than the specific types of interaction advocated by other perspectives, with the result that concepts—such as exchange, communication, and information—can be subsumed by the concepts of symbolic interaction. Third, symbolic interactionist concepts can be used to embrace the full range of human relationships—such as conflict, cooperation, and domination—so that, in principle at least, symbolic interactionism would make unnecessary the construction of separate "theories" of each type of human relationship.

However, as promising as these facts would make the symbolic interactionist perspective appear, several substantive deficiencies remain. Much of symbolic interaction consists of gallant assertions that "society is symbolic interaction," without indicating what types of emergent structures are created, sustained, and changed by what types of interaction in what types of contexts. Much like the critics' allegations about Parsons's "social system" or Dahrendorf's "imperatively coordinated associations," social structural phenom-

Reprinted with permission from *The Structure of Sociological Theory* by J. H. Turner (Homewood, Ill.: The Dorsey Press, 1974), pp. 189–192.

[1] The long tradition of speculation and research on the process of socialization in the symbolic interactionist literature documents this contention. The comparatively sparse concern with how groups, organizations, and other forms of collective organization emerge and are sustained should document the lack of concern with patterns of social organization. However, in the area of collective behavior—crowds, mobs, riots, and so forth—symbolic interactionists have made a number of important contributions. And yet, this literature on such transitory collective phenomena makes the lack of attention on more stable patterns of social organization even more evident.

ena emerge somewhat mysteriously and are then sustained or changed by vague references to interactive processes. The vagueness of the links between the interaction process and its social structural products[2] leaves symbolic interactionism with a legacy of assertions, but little in the way of carefully documented statements about how, when, where, and with what probability interaction processes operate to create, sustain, and change varying patterns of social organization.

Accordingly, symbolic interactionism represents a vision of the social world which underemphasizes social structures, except as "objects" of actors' orientations or as "things" that somehow just emerge from interaction. Without linking, except by assertion, social processes and social structure, symbolic interaction offers a picture of a constantly flowing and fluctuating world, with actors symbolically interpreting, evaluating, defining, and mapping respective lines of action. While this vision certainly captures crucial social features, it would appear to do so at the expense of ignoring the structures that channel the symbolic processes of actors.

Another related problem with the symbolic interactionist perspective is its current inability to provide a useful set of concepts that can describe the interaction among collective organizations. While Blumer has been insistent that the same processes of interpretation, evaluation, definition, and mapping which characterize the interactions among individuals also pertain to interactions among collective units, he and other interactionists have yet to document just how this is so. At a very general level, it is quite likely that emergent social units do "size up" a situation and "then map" a line of action; however, it can be questioned whether this says very much about the way collective units interact and articulate with one another to form complex patterns of social organization. It seems likely that it will be necessary to develop additional concepts to account for these more complex linkages among larger social units; to the extent that this is necessary, then the concepts of symbolic interaction

may be applicable to only those levels of analysis where individuals are the interacting units. If such is the case, the current inability of symbolic interaction to document just how interaction creates, sustains, and changes social structures may be due, in part at least, to the fact that its concepts denote only a limited range of micro phenomena.

Until these problems are resolved by other than confident assertions about the nature of reality and of the causal processes such reality reveals, symbolic interactionism will leave unanswered the important substantive question: Social reality is constructed through a process called symbolic interaction, but just how does such interaction create, maintain, and change different features of social reality?

SYMBOLIC INTERACTIONISM: SOME CONCLUDING REMARKS

Symbolic interactionism advocates a clear-cut strategy for building sociological theory. The emphasis on the interpretive, evaluative, definitional, and mapping processes of actors has come to dictate that it is only through induction from these processes that sociological theory can be built. Further, the ever-shifting nature of these symbolic processes necessitates that the concepts of sociological theory be "sensitizing" rather than "definitive," with the result that deductive theorizing should be replaced by an inductive approach. Thus, whether as a preferred strategy or as a logical "necessity," the symbolic interactionist strategy is to induce generic statements, employing sensitizing concepts, from the ongoing symbolic processes of individuals in concrete interaction situations.

Such a strategy is likely to keep theorizing attuned to the processual nature of the social world. Currently, however, this approach has not been able to link conceptually the processes of symbolic interaction to the formation of different patterns of social organization. Furthermore, the utility of induction from the symbolic exchanges among individuals for the analysis of interaction among more macro, collective social units has yet to be demonstrated. Unless these problems can be resolved, it does not seem wise to follow exclu-

---

[2] With respect to the structuring of personality, symbolic interactionism has done a much better job of indicating how and in what ways symbolic interaction leads to the emergence of certain types of personality.

sively the strategy of Blumer and others of his persuasion. Until symbolic interactionists demonstrate in a more compelling manner than is currently the case that the inductive approach, utilizing sensitizing concepts, can account for more complex forms of social organization, pursuit of its strategy will preclude theorizing about much of the social world.

Symbolic interactionism does call attention to some important substantive and theoretical issues that are often ignored. First, it is necessary that sociological theorizing be more willing to undertake the difficult task of linking conceptually structural categories to classes of social processes that underlie these categories. To this task, symbolic interactionism has provided a wealth of suggestive concepts. Second, macro sociological theorizing has traditionally remained detached from the processes of the social world it attempts to describe. Much of the detachment stems from a failure to define concepts clearly and provide operational clues about what processes in the empir-

ical world they denote. To the extent that symbolic interactionist concepts can supplement such theorizing, they will potentially provide a bridge to actual empirical processes and thereby help attach sociological theory to the events it purports to explain.

As should be obvious, it is one thing to note that symbolic interactionism has great potential for correcting the past inadequacies of sociological theory and another thing to demonstrate exactly *how* this corrective influence is to be exerted. It may be well advised for symbolic interactionists to cease defining away the bulk of sociological theory and begin the difficult task of demonstrating in specific theoretical context (other than in socialization and personality theory) the utility of their perspective for supplementing (or replacing) other theoretical perspectives. In particular, symbolic interactionism needs to demonstrate with empirical evidence the utility of its tenets, especially in predicting variation in macro structural phenomena.

John Lofland **44**

Interactionist Imagery
and Analytic Interruptus

What I want to say may first be said in summary. I am going to suggest that in many instances we interactionists have been too "hung up" on our general imagery and have not seriously gotten

John Lofland, "Interactionist Imagery and Analytic Interruptus." From *Human Nature and Collective Behavior: Papers in Honor of Herbert Blumer*, edited by Tamotsu Shibutani (Englewood Cliffs, N.J.: Prentice-Hall, Inc., 1970), pp. 35–45. Reprinted by permission.

on to the main work that we have set for ourselves. As a result, at least one variety of interactionism is conceptually impoverished. One way in which this impoverishment might be corrected is for those of us who use an implicit paradigm of *strategic analysis* to stop engaging in what I shall call "analytic interruptus" and get on with the hard work.

Let me be clear that the friendly flagellation

to follow is also self-flagellation. I feel free to throw stones because I live in an identical glass house.

INTERACTIONIST IMAGERY AND WORK

One orientation within the interactionist perspective is particularly enamored of what is seen as the moving, ever changing, processual, constructive character of social life. Herbert Blumer has perhaps been foremost in championing this imagery of ordered flux. Again and again, in a variety of contexts and on a variety of topics, he has pounded home the image and the vision.

Action is built up in coping with the world instead of merely being released from a preexisting psychological structure by factors playing upon that structure. By making indications to himself and by interpreting what he indicates, the human being has to forge or piece together a line of action.[1]

Under the perspective of symbolic interaction, social action is lodged in acting individuals who fit their respective lines of action to one another through a process of interpretation; group action is the collective action of such individuals. . . . Human society is to be seen as consisting of acting people, and the life of the society is to be seen as consisting of their actions.[2]

A consciously directed and organized movement cannot be explained merely in terms of the psychological disposition or motivation of people, or in terms of the diffusion of an ideology. Explanations of this sort have a deceptive plausibility, but overlook the fact that *a movement has to be constructed* and has to carve out a career in what is practically always an opposed, resistant, or at least indifferent world.[3]

And there have been large numbers of scholars who believe that he and others were correct in this emphasis. Inspired by the abstract and charismatic imagery sponsored by figures such as Blumer—along with his predecessors such as George Herbert Mead, William I. Thomas and Robert E. Park and his contemporaries such as Everett C. Hughes—the descendants have wanted to translate such imagery into more concrete accomplishments.

Such a mission of translation has moved in at least three directions that are of interest here. First, some descendants have been overwhelmed by the task and have taken to a doctrinaire reiteration of the masters' teachings, writing very little beyond a doctoral dissertation. Although rarely mentioned in print, the research and writing "hang-ups" of many imbued with the interactionist vision are well known in the oral tradition of sociology. Second, the mission of translation has resulted in a body of general books and essays which attempt to make slightly more specific the general imagery and to apply it loosely to more specific substantive topics. Contributors to this line of work have included, aside from Blumer and Hughes themselves, Anselm Strauss, Howard S. Becker, Alfred Lindesmith, Tamotsu Shibutani, Gregory Stone and even C. Wright Mills in his early social psychological phase.[4] In remaining quite general, such books and essays function to "put one on top" of a topic, but they have fallen short in the task of detailed translation. Third, there has emerged an affinity between descriptive case studies and interactionism. Indeed, the qualitative case study has become identified as *the* research method of that variety of interactionism that here concerns us. However, because the interactionist perspective has remained so abstract, the empirical case studies flowing out of it have often seemed little better than the kind of descriptions that can be produced by conscientious journalists or literate laymen.

CONCEPTUAL POVERTY

In viewing this accumulated material, a peculiar feature begins to stand out, at least for me. That feature is the degree to which this material

[1] Herbert Blumer, "Sociological Implications of the Thought of George Herbert Mead," *American Journal of Sociology*, LXXI (1966), 536.

[2] Herbert Blumer, "Society as Symbolic Interaction," in *Human Behavior and Social Process: An Interactionist Approach*, ed. Arnold Rose (Boston: Houghton Mifflin Company, 1962), p. 186.

[3] Herbert Blumer, "Collective Behavior," in *Review of Sociology*, ed. Joseph B. Gittler (New York: John Wiley & Sons, Inc., 1957), 147. Italics in the original.

[4] Cf. the interactionist anthologies by Arnold Rose, *op. cit.*; and Jerome G. Manis and Bernard N. Meltzer, eds., *Symbolic Interaction: A Reader in Social Psychology* (Boston: Allyn and Bacon, Inc., 1967).

seems conceptually impoverished. It is characterized by (1) a general stance toward social life and (2) detailed descriptive information about this or that social location. But it seems sadly lacking in what one might call "mini-concepts" which are developed and treated with some care. There occur, certainly, encompassing conceptions such as "perspective," "negotiated social order," "impression management," and classic conceptions of the "act," the "self," "interaction," and the like, but there is very little attempt to develop limited and precise notions of microscopic social processes. It is instructive, indeed, to peruse what are currently perhaps the two leading texts of the tradition—Lindesmith and Strauss, and Shibutani—in terms of the proportion of sensitizing rhetoric they contain in relation to the number of carefully explicated and articulated concepts of social process that are conveyed.[5] (It is also instructive to contemplate how few distinctively interactionist textbooks have even been produced.) Recent anthologies of interactionist writings seem to display a similar problem of surplus sensitizing rhetoric as distinct from clear conceptual construction.

It is against this background of conceptual impoverishment that I think we can best understand two recent developments within interactionism. The first is the occurrence of, and attention to, the phenomenon that is Erving Goffman. I think that it is of more than casual interest to know that at least part of his intellectual development occurred in the context of the conceptually impoverished social psychological tradition at the University of Chicago in the late forties and early fifties. Goffman's subsequent emergence as the champion inventor of the mini-concept seems, at least in part, explicable as a response to the barrenness of the conceptual landscape of interactionist sociology. There is a sense in which Goffman has been to Chicago interactionism what Robert K. Merton was to Harvard functionalism. The latter made a loud call for "middle-range theory" in a similarly impoverished context, and pro-

pounded a few such theories. The former made hardly any call at all and propounded many "middle-range" concepts. Indeed, as one scholar has half-humorously commented, Goffman has more concepts than there are referents. On the consumer side, the attentiveness of interactionists to Goffman has, in part, to do with their lack of very much else to which to attend. Rather than having to make his way in the midst of intense competition among an outpouring of mini-concepts of an interactionist cast, Goffman has filled a virtual void.

A second development within interactionism that seems symptomatic of conceptual poverty is the occurrence of, and attention given to, the volume called *The Discovery of Grounded Theory* by Barney Glaser and Strauss.[6] Non-interactionists have tended to read this book as a license for subjectivism and a relinquishing of proper scientific procedure. Such a view seems to me not only to be erroneous but to miss what I take to be the more general and underlying thrust: a plea for the development of mini-concepts. The book is about procedures by means of which such concepts can be invented, or, as the authors put it, discovered. The procedure, called "constant comparative analysis," is the means by which they apparently hope the conceptual landscape of interactionism (and sociology more generally) can be made more lush. They attempt to provide us with something like a manual for the germination and care of concepts in our intellectual garden. They are, in a sense, agricultural extension agents bringing help to us interactionist farmers. The important point is that agricultural extension services—literal or metaphorical—get invented only because a need for them is felt. The need felt by Glaser and Strauss apparently arose in the context of a specific research project on dying. The *Discovery* volume is, rather incongruously, one of a four volume series, the other three of which deal with social aspects of dying.

This allegation of conceptual poverty might be taken as grounds for despair—as past defectors have so construed it—but I think there remain ample grounds for hope. It is not my intention

[5] Alfred R. Lindesmith and Anselm L. Strauss, *Social Psychology* (New York: Holt, Rinehart & Winston, Inc., 1968); Tamotsu Shibutani, *Society and Personality: An Interactionist Approach to Social Psychology* (Englewood Cliffs, N.J.: Prentice-Hall, Inc., 1961).

[6] Barney Glaser and Anselm Strauss, *The Discovery of Grounded Theory* (Chicago: Aldine Publishing Company, 1967).

here, however, to explore these in a general explication. I want now, rather, to narrow the focus
quite drastically and to make some suggestions
for the improvement of a single line of hopeful
endeavor within the interactionist tradition.[7]

STRATEGIC ANALYSIS

In many interactionist case studies a simple
but powerful paradigm of sorts has begun to crys-
tallize. With varying degrees of explicitness, interactionists use an operating orientation toward
their materials that seems to offer at least one
way in which social life can be analyzed while
(1) still being faithful to the general imagery we
seek to sponsor and (2) also being more articulate
in analysis by means of explicitly developed mini-
concepts.

Attuned as interactionists are to social life as
a *constructed* product of *active* humans, a number
of similar terms and styles that refer to a single
stance have begun to creep into their studies and
essays. Terms that denote this stance have included the following: management, strategies,
tactics, devices, mechanisms, maneuvers, strate-
gems, practices. These terms are used vis à vis
those aspects of social locations, more or less
amenable to control, that are acted upon or toward by persons so as to effect some desired outcome. In other words, there is here a stripped
down and modest version of game theory. However, it is a game theory that is not carried away
by its internal logic into the mystic regions of
hypothetical possibilities, but one that is attentive
to the *in situ* details of social life. Following Schelling, such a modest and substantively oriented version might be called simply "strategic analysis."[8]

At least from the heyday of Park, there appears in interactionist case studies a persistent
concern with ways in which people *qua*
interactants actually put together their lives. In
the early twenties, observers such as Nels Anderson were already orienting themselves to an anal-

ysis of means of coping with social locations. Thus,
in *The Hobo*, Anderson is partly concerned with
"How the Hobo Meets His Problem" and " 'Getting by' in Hobohemia," the latter being a classification and description of "the various devices that
are employed in accomplishing" more than a
"coffee-and" level of living.[9] In the flowering of
occupational case studies among Chicago interactionists in the fifties, there appears a repeated
concern with ways in which that which is
phenomenologically problematic is managed. So,
for example, we find the janitor written about
partly in terms of "the various means by which
he 'trains' tenants . . ." and four ". . . method[s]
of overt cutthroating" among janitors.[10]

More recently, such an orientation to ongoing strategic adaptation to, or management of,
problematic circumstances has become a virtually
rampant paradigm in interactionist case studies.
Almost regardless of the overt and central
themes, at the section and paragraph levels, a
more or less explicit strategic analysis is the operating principle of organization. Here are a few
examples.

Simmons, "On Maintaining Deviant Belief Systems":
Five "processes or 'mechanisms' facilitate the maintenance of divergent beliefs: 1. Selective attention. . . . 2. Active structuring. . . . 3. [Confirming]
interpretation. . . . 4. Differential association. . . .
5. Ambivalence of the divergent larger
culture. . . ."[11]

Scott, *The Racing Game:* "Whatever the order, the
jockey must at least *appear* to be riding energetically
and cleanly. To bring off these appearances the
jockey has developed certain communication strategies—*dramatic accentuation* and *concealment* or a
combination of both."[12]

Dalton, *Men Who Manage:* "Staff Counter Tactics."
"Actual or probable rejection of their ideas provokes
staff groups to (1) strengthen ties with top line; (2)
adhere to the staff role, but 'lean over backward'

---

[7] Among many hopeful lines of endeavor I will not here discuss,
particular mention should be made of interactionist analyses
of becoming, careers, and phase models of interaction.

[8] Thomas C. Schelling, "Strategic Analysis and Social Problems,"
Social Problems, XII (1965), 367–79.

[9] Nels Anderson, *The Hobo* (Chicago: The University of Chicago
Press, 1923), Part IV and Chap. iv.

[10] Raymond L. Gold, "In the Basement—The Apartment-Build-
ing Janitor," in *The Human Shape of Work,* ed. Peter L. Berger
(New York: The Macmillan Company, Publishers, 1964), pp.
20–26, 34–36.

[11] J. L. Simmons, "On Maintaining Deviant Belief Systems,"
Social Problems, XI (1964), pp. 250–56.

[12] Marvin B. Scott, *The Racing Game* (Chicago: Aldine Publishing Company, 1968), p. 43.

to avoid troubles down the line that can reverberate to the top; and (3) compromise with the line below the top levels."[13]

Bittner, "Police Discretion in Emergency Apprehension of Mentally Ill Persons": "In this paper we have tried to describe briefly certain practices of dealing with mentally ill persons." These include a set of "nonofficial ways of dealing with mentally ill persons" under the headings "restitution of control," "psychiatric first aid," and "continuing care."[14]

Roth, *Timetables:* Strategies used by patients to "move along faster through the hospital": have pressures applied by influentials outside the hospital; threaten to leave the hospital; threaten or undertake a "medication strike."[15]

Sudnow, *Passing On:* The morgue attendant's ". . . chief and daily problem was going about the hospital without, wherever he went, appearing to others to be working." His problem ". . . generally, [was] how to enter into any form of ordinary discourse without his affiliation with dead bodies intruding as a prominent way others attended to him." In response, "he attempted to convey a sense of not being at work by developing clear styles. . . ." ". . . one way. . . ." "A general strategy. . . ."[16]

Glaser and Strauss, *Awareness of Dying:* In order to sustain a closed awareness context, ". . . the staff members . . . use tactics intended to encourage the patient to make his own interpretations inaccurately optimistic."[17]

Becker, Geer and Hughes, *Making the Grade:* "In this chapter [number 6], we observe students as they go about the task of finding out what the rules are and where they stand with respect to them." "If the problems [of students] are similar . . . , students can develop a generalized set of actions . . . to which their own particular actions can be referred. It is this sort of individual action based on group perspectives that we discuss in the first section of this chapter [number 7]."[18]

[13] Melville Dalton, *Men Who Manage* (New York: John Wiley & Sons, Inc., 1959), p. 101.

[14] Egon Bittner, "Police Discretion in Emergency Apprehension of Mentally Ill Persons," *Social Problems,* XIV (1967), 292, 285–90.

[15] Julius A. Roth, *Timetables: Structuring the Passage of Time in Hospital Treatment and Other Careers* (Indianapolis: The Bobbs-Merrill Company, Inc., 1963), pp. 48–54.

[16] David Sudnow, *Passing On: The Social Organization of Dying* (Englewood Cliffs, N.J.: Prentice-Hall, Inc., 1967), pp. 54ff.

[17] Barney G. Glaser and Anselm L. Strauss, *Awareness of Dying* (Chicago: Aldine Company, 1964), pp. 36ff.

[18] Howard S. Becker, Blanche Geer, and Everett C. Hughes, *Making the Grade: The Academic Side of College Life* (New York: John Wiley & Sons, Inc., 1968), pp. 80, 93.

Aside from case study efforts, the general frameworks spawned by interaction theorists such as Goffman have rested heavily upon a strategic imagery. *Presentation of Self in Everyday Life* is thus largely oriented to specifying the sources of discredited impressions and "common techniques that persons employ to sustain . . . impressions." His essay "On Cooling the Mark Out" seeks to specify six strategies for "cooling out" people who have failed, combined with four strategic responses possibly available to "marks" who refuse to be cooled. And *Stigma* is even subtitled "Notes on the Management of Spoiled Identity."[19] Other more or less general frameworks have likewise been so attuned, as in Glaser and Strauss' awareness paradigm where "the tactics of various interactants as they attempt to manage changes of awareness context" ranks as one of six major elements.[20] Weinstein's important essay is explicitly entitled, "Toward a Theory of Interpersonal Tactics."[21]

This kind of orientation appears to me to make a promising start toward the work of translating interactionist imagery, such as that promoted by Blumer, into an actuality in depicting and understanding the social order. An important source of conceptual impoverishment has resided, however, in the fact that although there are many studies with a strategic orientation, not many have proceeded to truly strategic analysis.

ANALYTIC INTERRUPTUS

Interactionists of a strategic bent have been prone, rather, to what might be called "analytic interruptus." This label is intended to denote the practice of starting out to perform a certain task but failing to follow through to the implied, logi-

[19] Erving Goffman, *The Presentation of Self in Everyday Life* (Garden City, New York: Doubleday & Company, Inc., 1959), p. 15; "On Cooling the Mark Out: Some Aspects of Adaptation to Failure," *Psychiatry,* XV (1952), 451–63; and *Stigma* (Englewood Cliffs, N.J.: Prentice-Hall, Inc., 1963).

[20] Barney G. Glaser and Anselm L. Strauss, "Awareness Contexts and Social Interaction," *American Sociological Review,* XXIX (1964), 671.

[21] Eugene A. Weinstein, "Toward a Theory of Interpersonal Tactics," in *Problems in Social Psychology,* eds. Carl W. Backman and Paul F. Secord (New York: McGraw-Hill Book Company, 1966), pp. 394–98.

cal, or entailed conclusion. The label connotes the failure to reach an initially implied climax. Many of the studies cited above, and many others, suffer from analytic interruptus because they imply an analysis of mechanisms, devices, strategies, and the like but they neglect actually to do it. The presentations remain unsystematic, elusive, and simply suggestive of what given sets of such mechanisms, etc. might be as they have evolved in some concrete social location. In short, there is too frequently a failure to follow through. By actually following through I mean more specifically that the investigator goes to the time and trouble (1) to assemble self-consciously all his materials on how a given phenomenologically problematic topic is dealt with by the persons under study, (2) to tease out the variations among his assembled range of instance of strategies, (3) to classify them into an articulate set of what appear to him to be generic or phenomenological types of strategies, and (4) to present them to the reader in some orderly and preferably named and numbered manner. The result of such careful work can be a set of mini-concepts relating to the construction of social life and social order. Such exercises would be, at minimum, articulate depictions of little rivulets of constancy in the flux of social life.

For a concrete sense of varying degrees of analytic interruptus, the reader may review the little capsule pieces of the eight studies given above, which are ranked, roughly, in terms of the degree to which analytic interruptus is present. (Let me be clear. This ranking is in terms of the degree of analytic interruptus indicated in the capsule only. No judgment of any study in its entirety or of the substantive merit or empirical viability of the content is intended.) Among them, the one by Becker, Geer and Hughes is of particular note. The emerging but implicit paradigm of strategic analysis is apparently reaching the point where at least footnote reference must be made of the fact that investigators are not fully engaging in it.

It would be possible to study the kinds of actions students devise in response to particular problems of academic work, in the same way that one might, as we have already suggested, study the kind of information-seeking students devise in response to particular faculty practices, using the model of a game of strategy. We have not undertaken such a detailed analysis and confine ourselves to the generalized set of actions, developed in response to the generalized problems the college creates for all students, of which the particular actions developed for particular circumstances are special cases.[22]

As I said at the outset, I too live in a glass house and the same kinds of rocks can and should be thrown in my direction. Thus, in a work on a religious group, I blithely oriented the reader to a strategic analysis but throughout engaged merely a vague strategic orientation, constantly drawing back from the implications of the task set. Indeed, at one point I announced the intention to analyze "the devices adopted [by members] to manage [the] misinvolvement" of outsiders with the group, but then ignored the task altogether.[23]

Out of this discussion there arises, of course, the question of why there is a relatively high frequency of analytic interruptus. My own surmise about myself and others is a simple one. It is easier and takes less time to be vague than to be articulate. Strategic *analysis* prolongs the gap between research and publication. If it is possible to achieve a reasonable sense of completion and to put the material in print without going very far, then there is a propensity to do so. Detailed analysis of qualitative material is tedious and difficult, and promises no sure result. Little patches of articulate statements of strategy and management may appear in studies, but a thoroughgoing pursuit of them throughout can appear a less than inviting task. And, too, the unsystematic materials assembled in qualitative studies may reveal, at the time of analysis, enormous gaps. It is easier to slough over such gaps by means of a random assortment of examples than to go back into the field with an eye to intensive observation on a topic that may constitute but a few pages in the published report.

Moreover, given the virtual lack of codified concepts to draw upon, strategic analysis requires from the analyst considerable effort at creative discernment. It requires that he pore over his

[22] Becker, Geer and Hughes, *op. cit.*, p. 93, footnote 1.
[23] John Lofland, *Doomsday Cult* (Englewood Cliffs, N.J.: Prentice-Hall, Inc., 1966), Chap. i and p. 143.

materials with great intensity, very much on the model of procedure outlined by Glaser and Strauss. And it requires that he take the risk of inventing names for strategies, etc., opening himself to the charge of "needless jargon." Unfortunately, analytic interruptus is faster and easier.

In terms of the view taken here, however, it is also considerably less informative. Case studies of an analytic interruptus sort give us a "feel" for some sector of social life and they provide us with a "sense" of "what it is like." But we surely want more than feelings and senses, even though these qualities are not in themselves to be disparaged. We want in addition explicit—named, codified, documented—rendering of the little practices that make up that diffuse thing we call social life or interaction. It is to this task that we slovenly interactionists have barely begun to address ourselves, even though many of us have flirted with the possibility.

THE LARGER VISION

The admonition that interactionist case studies follow through on what they are already doing in a halfhearted way is, in effect, a request for a multitude of little lists of named strategies growing out of and attached to a likewise large number of case studies of particular social locations and situations. What can conceivably be accomplished through the creation of such a body of mini-concepts and empirical documentation? In longest and broadest terms one looks forward to a time when we will have carefully built back up to the large, abstract and magnificent imageries provided by people such as Blumer. The "building back up" can begin to occur when it is possible to engage in comparative analysis of interaction strategies as they evolve in various settings, being attuned to how the construction of superficially quite different social worlds can be, in terms of strategic constitution, quite similar. Thus, when we begin to see the possibility that strategies employed by Army Reserve enlisted men to avoid and decline the assignment of tasks by superiors

have a resemblance to those used by children in avoiding or declining the assignment of tasks by parents, we begin to get on the track of generic features of social locations in terms of similarities and differences in their strategic constitution. We begin to get on the track of locating and codifying translocational interaction strategies and enter upon the task of discerning various *sets* of strategies vis à vis generically delineated features of types of social locations.

The strain toward such generic and comparative theories of strategic constitution is already manifest in works which proceed directly to construct such frameworks. The most conspicuous instance of this is, again, the work of Erving Goffman. He and others have proceeded, however, in the absence of a solid body of studies and concepts of the kind I here counsel. They have made up the conceptual substance as they have gone along, rather than being able to collate and carefully build upon a wide range of delimited analyses. In having to short circuit the process of theory building they create magnificent structures that lack solid foundations, deal with a narrow range of possible concerns, and likely strike very wide of the long term target. It is ironic and a bit sad that the same theorist who at one point tweaks other theorists for failure to treat sociological concepts "with affection," comes himself to participate in the same fate:

> I think that at present, if sociological concepts are to be treated with affection, each must be traced back to where it best applies, followed from there wherever it seems to lead, and pressed to disclose the rest of its family. Better, perhaps, different coats to clothe the children well than a single splendid tent in which they all shiver.[24]

By proceeding carefully and in small ways with affectionate concern for the development of mini-concepts in strategic analysis, it will hopefully become possible to have *both* splendid tents and well-clothed children.

[24] Erving Goffman, *Asylums: Essays on the Social Situation of Mental Patients and Other Inmates* (New York: Doubleday & Company, Inc., 1961), p. xiv.

Symbolic Interaction as a Pragmatic Perspective: The Bias of Emergent Theory

As a socially-based approach to the relation of the individual and society, symbolic interaction (SI) has always been an important perspective in American sociology. Kuhn (1970:83) suggested that, unlike psychoanalysis, field theory, and learning theory, SI is logically consistent with basic social science propositions. As a research tradition, SI has produced insightful accounts of human interaction in natural settings. Yet even its adherents are doubtful about its methodology and the status of its findings. Blumer (1969:1) pointed out that the position of SI had never been clearly formulated and no reasoned statement of the methodological approach existed.

The SI tradition is related to a number of other approaches and techniques such as labelling theory, sociological phenomenology and existentialism, participant observation, qualitative sociology, and naturalism. No attempt to deal with the differences and similarities of these approaches to the SI tradition will be made in this paper, which is concerned, rather, with the overall historical drift. Yet their relationship to SI is important because even if, as Ehrlich (1972) asserts, what was scientifically most useful in the SI approach has already been absorbed into the mainstream of social psychology, many of the problems of SI methods still plague these other approaches.[1]

Events in the last decade have thrown the problems of SI methods into even greater relief. Many young sociologists are unhappy with the direction of the discipline, particularly with what they see as an overemphasis on quantification. They feel that social science has failed to come to grips with the real world (Blumer, 1966: vii).[2] Such concern has led to increasing criticism of standard methodology; the procedures which methodologists found so intriguing have not had the desired impact on research because the methodologists failed to communicate the substantive relevance of the tools they admired so much (Hill, 1970:18, 19). Apparently the SI tradition and similar approaches answer a need in the discipline; and, whatever their inadequacies, they will probably be around for some time.

Joan Huber, "Symbolic Interaction as a Pragmatic Perspective: The Bias of Emergent Theory," *American Sociological Review,* vol. 38, April 1973, pp. 274–284. Reprinted by permission.

An earlier draft of this paper was presented at the ASA meetings, August 1972. I am deeply grateful to J. David Lewis, Clark McPhail, and an anonymous reader, but especially to William Form for their comments on one or more successive drafts. All errors are my own.

[1] For example, Becker (1958:653) points out that the observational researcher faces the problem of convincing others of the validity of his findings; Bruyn (1966:174) says that there is currently no method to do this. Lofland (1971:vii) notes that, strangely, few instructions are available to show how qualitative observation and analysis is done.

[2] Filstead (1970:1, 8) cites Blumer, Clinard, Bruyn, Deutscher, Becker, Gouldner, and Horowitz as showing a concern with the current direction of the field.

The main thesis of this paper is that the SI tradition shares with the philosophy of pragmatism,[3] from which it originates, an epistemology which makes it reflect the social biases of the researcher and of the people whose behavior is observed. In a benignly liberal climate of opinion this outcome tends to go unnoticed; but in the long run, this kind of methodology is sensitive to the forces of social control. So far as I have been able to discover, SI methods have not been criticized from this point of view. The explication of this thesis begins by showing the relationship of SI and pragmatism.

The progenitors of the SI tradition include Dewey, Cooley, Baldwin, and Znaniecki, among others; but the chief architect was George Herbert Mead (Manis and Meltzer, 1967:1; Kuhn, 1970:71). Most of the published materials on which knowledge of his position is based were not originally intended for publication (Meltzer, 1959:27). His books, based on student notes, were published posthumously (Stevens, 1967:553). His articles were scattered in journals and out-of-print books until Reck's (1964:v) selection appeared. Mead was not a systematic writer. He found extemporaneous speaking to be his best medium and felt that men do their best thinking in conversation (Lee, 1945:v). Dewey (1932:xl) observed that at about the time of his death Mead was beginning to get a command of his ideas which made communication to others easier and more effective. SI thus began with an oral tradition which tended to persist. By the early sixties neither Faris, Thomas, nor Blumer had presented a rounded theoretical conception; hence much time was devoted to casuistical debating over questions of orthodoxy (Kuhn, 1970:71–2).

Mead was one of the leading figures of pragmatism (Shibutani, 1968:83; Gallie, 1966:31). Dewey, its main expositor, became a close friend of Mead's at the University of Michigan and their intellectual exchange continued at the University of Chicago where Mead taught from 1893–1931. Dewey provided the range and vision, Mead, the analytical depth and precision (Morris, 1934:xi). Dewey's daughter reported that the influence of Mead on Dewey, from the nineties on, ranked with that of James (Mills, 1966:296). Yet Dewey is usually ignored as a major influence on American sociology (Petras, 1968:18). Likewise, Mead tends to be ignored by philosophers (Mills, 1966:464). Possibly one reason for their neglect is that Mead's ideas were not readily accessible in his lifetime (Shibutani, 1968:83). However, American sociologists typically take little interest in philosophy and philosophers show little interest in the output of sociologists.[4]

Pragmatism, as Durkheim (1960:386) observed, was a reaction to the ideas of traditional rationalism.[5] Dewey and Mead, like Marx before them, thought that traditional philosophy was arid, formal, and useless. Moreover, the dominant social view held that customs derived from a fixed human nature which was, in turn, derived from an immutable god. Such ideas supported a rigid legal system which shored up a privileged social order. To use material and social factors to explain human arrangements unveiled the conservative bias of traditional ideas. Ironically, pragmatism had a similar bias, although Dewey and Mead and their followers were not aware of it. Nevertheless, all sociologists owe a debt to the pragmatists (and to Marx) for what now appears to be common sense: men make their own social world.

But pragmatism went far beyond this general assumption. According to Kaplan (1964:36, 42), pragmatism is a variant of semantic empiricism which, in turn, was a development of epistemic empiricism. From Locke through Kant, epistemic empiricism was the doctrine which held that ex-

---

[3] The paper refers mainly to Dewey's version of pragmatic philosophy. Pierce's conception is different (Lewis, forthcoming.) He thought that other pragmatists misunderstood his theories and his dominant attitude toward them was one of contempt. From Kant's *pragmatisch* Peirce adopted the name pragmatism, which became popular. This so irritated Peirce that he referred to his own formulation as "pragmaticism," a name which he thought was so ugly that no one would use it (Wennerberg, 1962:14–15). In this opinion he was correct.

[4] Mill's (1966) doctoral dissertation, a rare exception, is a sociological analysis of pragmatism rather than an assessment of the impact of pragmatic philosophy on sociology. Such an analysis is yet to be made. Mills (1966:464) omitted a detailed consideration of Mead's work but felt that the omission was intellectually unwarranted.

[5] Durkheim lectured on pragmatism at the Sorbonne, 1913–14. He wanted to find a formula that would preserve the essentials of rationalism but at the same time answer the valid criticisms that pragmatism had made. Stone and Farberman (1970:100–12) see Durkheim as more sympathetic to pragmatism than I do.

perience was a necessary condition of knowledge. Semantic empiricism, developed in the last hundred years, holds that not only knowledge but also meaning must necessarily include an experiential component. Two of the three major variants of semantic empiricism, logical positivism and operationism, ask the same question of any scientific assertion: Can its meaning be established and, if so, how? That is, can sense data be used for verification and, if so, what kind of rules govern such use? Pragmatism asks what difference it would make if a statement were true. The meaning of objects is the effect they produce (Dewey, 1916:309). That is, whether a belief is good or bad depends upon whether the activities which it inspires in the organism entertaining the belief have consequences which are satisfactory or unsatisfactory to it (Russell, 1945:825). What counts is not the origin of a proposition but its outcome, not the connections with experience antecedently given but with those to be instituted. Truth is thus dependent on human action. Those who feel that human beings are not always rational see pragmatism as a step on the road to madness, an intoxication with power (Russell, 1945:828) or as an all-out assault on human reason (Durkheim, 1960:363). SI shares this stress on the outcome of human action as a criterion of scientific truth.

Why should the stress on the outcome of an event as a criterion of truth render knowledge susceptible to social control? Briefly, because the future, unlike the past, is subject to manipulation by those who currently have power. "The past cannot be affected by what we do, and therefore, if truth is determined by what has happened, it is independent of present or future volitions; it represents, in logical form, the limitations on human power. But if truth, or rather "warranted assertibility," depends upon the future, then, in so far as it is in our power to alter the future, it is in our power to alter what should be asserted" (Russell, 1945:826).

In order to clarify the line of argument, I shall outline it here. In the SI approach, as in the pragmatic, formal logic has an ambiguous status. The place of the rational (logico-theoretic) component in validation is never spelled out clearly. When the place of theory is unclear, when

the theoretical expectations are not explicated, then the social givens of the present serve as an implicit theoretical formulation. In pragmatic doctrine, scientific truth is defined as whatever works best in a given situation, as judged by the investigator who observes the emergent outcome. A belief is judged by its effects; if the effects are good, then the belief is true, or has warranted assertibility. Later formulations held that truth is the emerging consensus of the participants in an interactive situation. All of these formulations have a status quo bias for, when no theoretical expectations are specified, and when truth is expected to emerge from interaction, then what is taken to be true tends to reflect the distribution of social power among the participants.[6] This assertion is supported by theory and research in group ranking and conformity (Zajonc, 1968:253-60). Dewey and Mead avoided confronting the power implications of the pragmatic model because they thought that the world was evolving from worse to better. Therefore, whatever worked was bound to be right, at least in the long run. However, the views of the latterday adherents of SI and related approaches are not explicitly evolutionary, nor is the implication of defining truth as an emergent social consensus of participants systematically confronted. I shall now discuss the main threads of this argument in detail, first, the relevant views of Dewey and Mead.

THE PRAGMATISM OF DEWEY AND MEAD

An aspect of pragmatism and SI basic to their sensitivity to social control is the ambiguous status of formal logic (Huber and Loomis, 1970). Philosophers of science distinguish between the logically necessary and the logically contingent, i.e., between mathematics-theory-logic and empirical

---

[6] The claim that SI methods have a status quo bias does not imply that scholars in this tradition are more conservative than other sociologists. I am arguing only that the model is especially susceptible to influence. Whether scholars in this tradition have a distinctive political viewpoint is a question I have not examined. I have no reason to suppose that they are anything but humanitarian liberals. Dewey was a kindly and admirable man. But this fact has no bearing whatsoever on the susceptibility of these methods to social bias.

observations; both are necessary for scientific knowledge (Braithwaite, 1963). A commonsense translation of this statement says that facts do not speak for themselves. But the status of the logico-theoretic component is not clear in SI and pragmatism. The difficulty derives from the influence of Hegel's dialectic.

Hegel claimed that the dialectic was a new logic, but this claim is false if one uses the usual definition of the word 'logic' (Mills, 1962:130). Hegel wanted to know if history had any meaning and posited the dialectic as a formal device to enable him to explain social change. In dialectical form, knowledge moves in stages from thesis, to antithesis, to synthesis; history obligingly repeats these stages empirically. "Process" and "emergent" are key words. To understand the result, one must understand the entire process because each stage contains the earlier stages in solution, so to speak; all have their place in the final whole. Because only the Whole is Reality, nothing partial can be quite true. Hence truth and falsehood are not sharply defined opposites. In Aristotelian logic, an entity can be defined as A or non-A. That is, entities can be analytically and empirically distinguished from one another. In the dialectic, entities simply merge into one another. Reality is one great Whole. One ought not study the eye of John Jones for Jones is an organic whole and to study his eye alone is pointless. Described in this fashion, the dialectic may strike some observers as nonsense. Most of the writers who use the word today leave it undefined, which is probably just as well.

In his early days Dewey was a Hegelian (Mead, 1936:151) and Hegel remained the chief source of Dewey's logic (Mills, 1966:357). The contradictions between thesis and antithesis became conflicting elements in a problematic situation (White, 1943:152). Dewey confused logic and empiricism; logic was thought to be both empirical and normative (Dewey, 1920:137), and ultimately derived from the acts performed (Dewey, 1929:163). But Dewey's view of what was good differed from that of William James in a way that was important for sociology. James had equated truth with what was good for the individual. Dewey saw the difficulties with this idea and declared that truth was public. A belief was to be judged by the consequences it had for many persons, not for just one person. This aspect of pragmatism may be what led Stone and Farberman (1970:15) to comment that pragmatism carried social psychology away from the psychologistic fallacy. From the standpoint of the present critique, it matters little whether the warranted assertibility of a proposition is based on the way it works out for one person or many.

Unlike Dewey, Mead was well aware of contemporary developments in symbolic logic (1943:202; 1936:Ch. 15; 1964:199 ff). Although he once claimed that the theory of the intelligent act fell within the realm of Hegel's logic (1964:8), and passages in his later work still indicate a strong dialectical aroma (1964:189), he finally concluded that the dialectic was a scientifically useless device that could be used to prove anything (1936:143). Yet his thought shows the influence of Hegel in a number of ways. His idea of sociality is basically holistic:

> The principle of sociality is that in the present within which emergent change takes place, the emergent object belongs to different systems in its passage from the old to the new because of its systematic relationship with other structures, and possesses the characters it has because of its membership in these different systems (Mead, 1932:65).

With this concept Mead attempts to avoid some of the difficulties of Aristotelian logic. Perhaps a clearer statement of the concept is the assertion that sociality is the capacity of being several things at once. "The animal traverses the ground in pursuit of his prey and is at once a part of the system of distribution of energies which makes his locomotion possible and a part of the jungle system which is a part of the life system on the surface of the inanimate globe" (Mead, 1932:49).

In addition to glossing over the distinctions between entities which characterize Aristotelian logic, Mead tended to ignore the logico-theoretic component in his notion of scientific methodology. His prescriptions for the practice of science sound very like the methods that Willer (1970:19) has described as empirical or magical thinking; when events A and B are connected only at the observational level. Mead's example of science indicates that he is discussing empirical thinking:

A child's explanation of the conduct of others and the savage's appeal to magic are uncritical uses of a method which requires only analysis and recognition of the implications of its technique to become scientific (Mead, 1938:91).

The basic difficulty is that Mead fails to make a sufficient distinction between a hypothesis and a theory, with the result that his work fails to describe the theoretical component adequately. Facts define themselves in scientific problems (Mead, 1964:260). Like Dewey, Mead sees science as beginning with an immediate problem, with an exception that conflicts with a law and leads to the appearance in the mind of the scientist of a hypothesis that will solve his problem (Mead, 1936:136). The test of an hypothesis is that the conduct that was going on can be continued. "It is the same sort of test which the animal finds. If it finds itself in a difficult situation and sees escape, it rushes off in that direction and gets away. This is a fair test of what we call a hypothesis" (Mead, 1936:349). An animal and a scientist do the same thing when they face a problem. They select some element in the situation to carry the act through to its completion. "The only test the animal can bring to such a reconstruction of its habits is the ongoing of its activity. This is the experimental test; can it continue in action? And that is exactly the situation found in science" (Mead, 1936:346). The test of truth is the ability to continue a process which has been inhibited (1936:350; 1964:328). If an hypothesis works, it becomes an accepted theory (Mead, 1936:353). The test of truth is ongoing conduct and truth is synonymous with the solution of a problem (Mead, 1964:328).

His view of the relationship of a scientific law to an hypothesis is much the same:

> You are undertaking to set up another law in place of the one which has been overthrown. The new law is tentatively set up as a hypothesis. You test it. When you have tested it, it becomes a working hypothesis. And if others test it and it works, it be- · comes an accepted theory (Mead, 1936:825).

To illustrate the scientific method, almost all of Mead's examples refer to the natural or physical sciences where consensus on goals is high and the solutions are technological. In a rare discus-

sion of a social problem, Mead (1964:261-2) says that various cult values—which are incommensurable—will prevent a solution; hence the scientist must learn to state, as far as possible, our social customs in terms of their functions. What the scientist is supposed to do when this much is accomplished Mead does not say. Because his works are cast in phylogenetic frame of reference (Petras, forthcoming) and because, like Dewey, Mead assumes that evolutionary processes will make the world better, the problem is minimized. Indeed, Mead often expressed the view that history was on the side of progress; inevitably the brotherhood of men on earth would emerge (Lee, 1945:75; Shibutani, 1968:87). If this assumption were true, then consensus on goals would trouble neither scientist nor citizen alike.

The scientific method, Mead thought, was only the evolutionary process grown self-conscious; scientific technique is simply doing "consciouslessly" what takes place naturally in the evolution of forms (Mead, 1936:371). As an example, Mead mentions the food problem, by which he means digesting materials that have cellulose coverings. Humans had to work out a means to get rid of the covering, i.e., milling. But Mead never mentions the problem of distribution. His position tends to be a purely analytical scheme which lacks content (Meltzer, 1959:29).

In addition to assuming that evolution was progressive, Mead and Dewey both assumed that men were naturally rational. In making inquiries, men "naturally" test and improve the operations in the course of what they are doing (Dewey, 1929:124). Mead (1934:379) thought that men were rational, capable of logical thinking, because they were social. Ethical judgments can be universal because the voice of all is the universal voice; that is, everyone who can rationally appreciate the situation will agree. Social reconstruction would presuppose a basis of common social interests, by all of those whose minds bring about the reconstruction:

> And the way in which any such social reconstruction is actually effected by the minds of the individuals involved is by a more or less abstract intellectual extension of the boundaries of the given society to which these individuals all belong, and which is undergoing the reconstruction—the exten-

sion resulting in a larger social whole in terms of which the social conflicts that necessitate the reconstruction of the given society are harmonized or reconciled, and by reference to which accordingly, these conflicts can be solved or eliminated (Mead, 1934:308–9).

The Hegelian influence appears in this passage. The conflicts are somehow going to dissolve in the larger social whole that is created. Mead simply did not allow for irreconcilable conflict. He felt that every interest involved would be considered, but added that "you cannot lay down in advance fixed rules as to just what should be done" (Mead, 1934:388). Indeed, were all men rational and evolution progressive, rules would not be very important. As Dewey put it, the educative process is all one with the moral process, since the latter is a continuous passage of experience from worse to better (Dewey, 1920:183). Science, reason, and progress were isomorphic and inevitable.

The problems of the pragmatic model would be less obvious in a small community with a high level of education and homogeneity of the values that people often squabble over. If people can agree on the way things are supposed to work, it is not so difficult for them to agree on whether things really do work out that way. On technological matters the degree of agreement is often high. It is on social matters that fights occur.

LATER FORMULATIONS[7]

Of the subsequent attempts to provide a methodological basis for SI, Blumer's (1969) is the most sophisticated. But he shows a Meadian ambiguity when he describes the theoretic component. He generally uses the words from the vocabulary of the hard-science methodologist, such as "theory" and "concept," but he gives them different meanings. Blumer (1969:24) says that a "prior picture" of the empirical world is an unavoidable prerequisite for its study. The four customary means for empirical validation (proper research design, replication, hypothesis testing, and operational procedures) are claimed to be inadequate because they can give no assurance that premises, problems, data relations, and so forth are empirically valid.[8] Since these four usual means will not do, Blumer concludes that the only way to get this assurance is to go directly to the empirical social world (Blumer, 1969:35). Blumer does not mean that the investigator should consult census data or surveys but rather that he or she should directly inspect group life. Direct familiarity is necessary, he says, because most sociologists hold their theoretical positions tenaciously; and they gratuitously accept concepts and beliefs as inherently true. These images shape inquiry and become a substitute for direct experience. But Blumer does not explain how scientists can approach reality with blank minds nor does he offer evidence to show that persons who follow the SI tradition hold to their concepts and positions any less tenaciously than those who do not. Nor is his conclusion at this point consistent with his earlier statement that a prior picture is necessary in order to study the world.

What the investigator should do, Blumer says, is to conduct an exploratory study, seeking acute, well-informed observers. The investigator should also aim to cast the problem in a theoretic form for analysis. But the usual theoretical procedures used in sociology will not do. What is needed is "inspection," an intensive focused examination of the empirical content of whatever elements are used for analysis, and the same kind of examination of the empirical nature of the relations between such elements (Blumer, 1969:43). The prototype of inspection is represented by the handling of a strange physical object. "We may pick it up, look at it closely, and test it in one way or another. Inspection is not preset, routinized; it is free and flexible, the antithesis of inquiry as outlined in current methodology" (Blumer, 1969:44).

The crucial deficiency of social theory, Blumer (1954:5) says, is the ambiguous nature of its concepts.[9] There are two ways to solve the prob-

[7] In recent years the two foremost exponents of the SI point of view have been Herbert Blumer and the late Manford Kuhn (Manis and Meltzer, 1967:vi), and four major varieties of the tradition have been identified (Petras and Meltzer, forthcoming).

[8] Blumer's criticism of the discipline is extraordinarily persuasive. As a critic, he is without peer.

[9] Willer and Webster (1970) also conclude that the amount of theory in sociology is small because sociologists conceptualize incorrectly. Their prescription is unlike Blumer's. Rather than

lem. First, to develop precise procedures that will yield a definitive empirical content, relying on standardized techniques and mathematical categories. This way will not establish genuine concepts related to the natural world. The other way is to accept sociological concepts as sensitizing rather than definitive. This approach is spared the logical problems confronting the first, but it forfeits the achievement of definitive concepts with specific objective bench marks. It depends on faithful reportorial depiction and analytical probing; and it remains in close and continuous relation with the natural social world (Blumer, 1954:9–10).

Thus theory is seen to emerge from direct observation, with little specification of the rules of logic or procedure to be used. The investigator is urged to use well-informed observers. But if the observers fail to agree among themselves, on what grounds does the investigator choose one view rather than another? Do the observers ultimately shape the theory that emerges? What ensures the objectivity or reliability of the investigator? Many scholars currently involved in SI and related research styles ignore some of these questions and disagree on others. Let us examine some responses to these questions.

The Meadian tradition requires the researcher to maintain both his own and the actor's perspective. Unless he addresses this problem, he cannot warrant his findings on scientific grounds and will be open to the charge that they are no different from those of a lay actor (Cicourel: 1964:52). But those who do sociology in this style do not always confront this issue clearly. For example, researchers are advised to cultivate close relationships with those they study because such persons can check on the emerging theory (Denzin, 1971:168). Equal weight cannot be given to informants because their motives for aiding the observer shape the character of their information. But the reader is not told how the researcher knows which informants to drop. Becker (1970) avoids the problem of separating his views from those of the participants by opting for the side of the underdog. Because values are said to be

using the concepts of everyday experience, observables, or descriptive terms, sociologists should define constructs expressing abstract properties of entities for use in theories.

an implicit part of any scientific enterprise, nothing is gained by not frankly taking sides. This solution fails to distinguish the findings of sociologists from the findings of anyone else, and hence is unsatisfactory to those who hold that sociologists can claim special competence. Gouldner (1968: 105) notes, that the problem of identifying an underdog is ignored, as well as the problem of knowing which dog to side with in a hierarchy of stratified dogs.

The phenomenologists encourage a complete merging of the views of the researcher and the interactive situation, for fear that a scientific hypothesis will create the very reality that the scientist defines in his design. As Bruyn (1966:271, 273) notes, the traditional empiricist sets up preconceived realities which he seeks to verify; the phenomenologist wants to keep his preconceptions to a minimum and avoid anticipating causal relationships. Research interests are to be guided by the subject as given. The ambiguous view of theory which characterized the Meadian tradition is thus made consistent by eliminating the need for theory.

The objectivity of the scientist is also a source of difficulty. Dewey's (1939:775) criterion of truth was a method, to be used by intelligent men who would have a sympathetic regard for persons of differing views. The guarantee of objectivity was the social sensitivity of the observer to the needs of others (Dewey, 1920:147). To judge the credibility of grounded theory, Glaser and Strauss (1967:230) use a criterion based on the feelings of empathy aroused in the observer; if the reader is so caught up in the description that he feels as if he were in the field, he is more likely to be convinced of the accuracy of an account than if the description were flat and unconvincing. The judgment is also based on the assessment of how the researcher came to his conclusions, whom he interviewed, and how he might have appeared to those he studied. Douglas (1970:13 ff) advised that a "review" of the experience taken for granted by the natural, or everyday-life stance, will enable the researcher to understand what is going on. What the review should consist of and how the researcher knows that he has done it properly is not explained.

Summarizing earlier efforts, Denzin (1970: 26) concluded that no single method will ever meet the requirements for the validation of inter-action theory and therefore recommended multi-ple methods. The proper strategy cannot be de-rived solely from principles in research manuals because it is an "emergent" process, contingent on the investigator, the research setting, and his theoretical perspective (Denzin, 1970:310). The formulation appears to be a mixture of standard methods added to a derivative of the research prescription advanced by Dewey and Mead.

DISCUSSION

A major legacy of pragmatism to the Meadian tradition is the ambiguity toward the logico-theo-retic component in scientific research. When the theoretical formulation is primitive, when it "emerges" from the research, or when it is absent, then investigators will tend to use implicitly their own social givens as a theory. When the subjects studied by the sociologist participate in the formu-lation of emerging theory, then their own givens are added to the emerging theory. The subjects studied by sociologists in the SI tradition have made such problems less obvious. Much of the research has focused on people who have little social power or influence: little children, skid row bums, drug addicts, mental patients, immigrants, delinquents, and assorted deviants.[10] The investi-gators are typically persons who are deeply sym-pathetic to and understanding of the underdogs they study, but the fact remains that any lack of consensus among the participants in such situa-tions can be settled by the researcher with little backtalk from the participants.

The problem of scientific objectivity raised by lack of a prior theoretical formulation, by the absence of clear-cut criteria for selecting credible informants would be highlighted were the re-searcher to inspect a group of topdogs, say, the

executives of a major corporation. In this situa-tion, the researcher's colleagues might be uneasy if the researcher could not distinguish between theoretical concepts and observed behavior, if the hierarchy of credibility of the informants were arbitrary, and if other such judgmental proce-dures could hardly be replicated. Which of the participants in an interactive setting is to have most influence in determining the shape of an "emerging" theory is a question that the SI model has not confronted.

The most important way to improve the prac-tice of SI sociology would be for its adherents to confront the problems raised by their ambigu-ity toward the logico-theoretic component in their work. Their use of the customary vocabulary of methodology illustrates the ambiguity. Often such words as theory, hypothesis, concept are given meanings which are quite different from those they have when used by conventional meth-odologists. In this situation, the rational discussion of important issues in the discipline is difficult. Every group, of course, has a right to define words any way it chooses; but when words already have a consensual definition, to give them a different one obfuscates communication.

Furthermore, nothing prevents a detailed ob-servational account from being informed with no-tions from a stratification theory or any other the-ory. For the researcher to spell out in advance and in detail what is expected and why it is ex-pected is more work than transcribing events with the atheoretical simplicity of a blank mind. But such preliminary spadework would help to integrate the findings into a larger body of work, hence make them more meaningful. To be sure, the production of theory in sociology is beset with many unsolved problems. Nevertheless, the prior construction of logically-related propositions is important in science because it gives the re-searcher a chance to lose the game. A theoretical formulation forces researchers to bet on a particu-lar outcome and to explain why they bet the way they do. In the absence of such a formulation, the researcher always wins, for any outcome is permissible.

The paper has criticized the SI tradition, one of the most important approaches in the discipline of sociology. Along with ethnomethodology and

[10] Meadian sociology has been accused of ignoring the reality of social stratification. The labelling theory of deviance, a deriva-tive of the SI approach, is an apparent exception. Deviance occurs because some powerful groups can impose their rules on subordinates (Becker, 1963:17). The focus of research shifts from types of deviance to the processes by which people become deviant (Kitsuse, 1964:87). This development shows great prom-ise but thus far a detailed analysis of the institutional arrange-ments which enforce definitions has not been made. That is, the theoretical approach has not been well developed.

other styles in the holistic tradition, however, SI has retained a freshness in its approach to data which is often lost when aggregate data emerge from the bowels of the computer. Blumer's injunction to look at real people makes good sense. The detailed accounts of the way people behave make good reading. Some of these rich reports may well survive studies awash with mathematical formulations.[11] But the practitioners of SI remain nervous lest their reports be confused with mere journalism. Their fear is justified. What is needed is a frank confrontation with a major legacy of pragmatism. In the absence of theory, the social givens of the researcher and the participants serve as a theoretical framework, giving the research a bias which reflects the unstated assumptions of the researcher, the climate of opinion in the discipline, and the distribution of power in the interactive setting. Much SI research reflects a kindly concern for the people who are studied because SI methods attract those who delight in observing the nuances of human behavior. Nevertheless, when the criterion for truth is what people do, when theory emerges from practice, then the biases of those who do and act are embedded in the theory.

REFERENCES

Becker, Howard S. "Problems of Inference and Proof in Participant Observation." *American Sociological Review* 23 (December 1958):625–60.

———. *Outsiders: Studies in the Sociology of Deviance.* New York: Free Press, 1963.

———. "Whose Side Are We On?" *Qualitative Methodology: First Hand Involvement with the Social World.* Edited by William H. Filstead. Chicago: Markham, 1970, pp. 15–25.

Blumer, Herbert. "What Is Wrong with Social Theory." *American Sociological Review* 19 (February 1954):3–10.

———. "Foreword." *The Human Perspective in Sociology.* Edited by Severyn T. Bruyn. Englewood Cliffs, N.J.: Prentice-Hall, 1956, pp. iii–vii.

———. *Symbolic Interactionism: Perspective and Method.* Englewood Cliffs, N.J.: Prentice-Hall, 1969.

Braithwaite, R. B. *Scientific Explanation.* New York: Cambridge University, 1963.

Bruyn, Severyn T. *The Human Perspective in Sociology.* Englewood Cliffs, N.J.: Prentice-Hall, 1966.

Cicourel, Aaron V. *Method and Measurement in Sociology.* New York: Free Press of Glencoe, 1964.

Curtis, James E. and John W. Petras. *The Sociology of Knowledge: A Reader.* New York: Praeger, 1970.

Denzin, Norman K. *The Research Act: A Theoretical Introduction to Sociological Methods.* Chicago: Aldine, 1970.

———. "The Logic of Naturalistic Inquiry." *Social Forces* 50 (December 1971):166–82.

Denzin, Norman K. (ed.). *Sociological Methods: A Sourcebook.* Chicago: Aldine, 1970.

Dewey, John. *Essays in Experimental Logic.* Chicago: University of Chicago, 1916.

———. *Reconstruction in Philosophy.* New York: Henry Holt, 1920.

———. *The Quest for Certainty.* New York: Minton, Balch, 1929.

———. "Prefatory Remarks." *The Philosophy of the Present.* Edited by George Herbert Mead. Chicago: Open Court, 1932, pp. xxxvi–xl.

———. "Experimentation in Moral Theory." *Intelligence in the Modern World: John Dewey's Philosophy.* Edited by Joseph Ratner. New York: Modern Library, 1939, pp. 775–778.

Dewey, John, A. M. Moore, H. C. Brown, G. H. Mead et al. *Creative Intelligence.* New York: Henry Holt, 1917.

Douglas, Jack D. (ed.). *Understanding Everyday Life: Toward the Reconstruction of Sociological Knowledge.* Chicago: Aldine, 1970.

Durkheim, Emile. "Pragmatism and Sociology." *Emile Durkheim, 1858–1917: A Collection of Essays with Translations and Bibliography.* Edited by Kurt H. Wolff. Columbus: Ohio State University, 1960, pp. 386–436.

Ehrlich, Howard. *Personal Communication,* 1972.

Filstead, William J. (ed.). *Qualitative Methodology: Firsthand Involvement with the Social World.* Chicago: Markham, 1970.

Gallie, W. B. *Peirce and Pragmatism.* New York: Dover, 1966.

Glaser, Barney G. and Anselm L. Strauss. *The Discovery of Grounded Theory: Strategies for Qualitative Research.* Chicago: Aldine, 1967.

Gouldner, Alvin W. "The Sociologist as Partisan: Sociol-

[11] Many of the studies using the latest techniques of quantification are also examples of empirical thinking (Willer, 1970), and are relatively atheoretical.

ogy and the Welfare State." *The American Sociologist* 3 (May 1968):103–16.

Hill, Richard J. "On the Relevance of Methodology." *Sociological Methods: A Sourcebook.* Edited by Norman K. Denzin. Chicago: Aldine, 1970, pp. 12–19.

Huber (Rytina), Joan and Charles Loomis. "Marxist Dialectic and Pragmatism: Power as Knowledge." *American Sociological Review* 35 (April 1970): 308–18.

Kaplan, Abraham. *The Conduct of Inquiry: Methodology for Behavioral Science.* San Francisco: Chandler, 1964.

Kitsuse, John I. "Societal Reactions to Deviant Behavior: Problems of Theory and Method." *The Other Side: Perspectives on Deviance.* Edited by Howard S. Becker. New York: Free Press, 1964, pp. 87–102.

Kuhn, Manford. "Major Trends in Symbolic Interaction Theory in the Past Twenty-five Years." *Social Psychology Through Symbolic Interaction.* Edited by Gregory P. Stone and Harvey A. Farberman. Waltham, Mass.: Xerox, 1970, pp. 70–87.

Lee, Grace Chin. *George Herbert Mead: Philosopher of the Social Individual.* New York: King's Crown, 1945.

Lewis, J. David. "Peirce, Mead, and the Objectivity of Meaning." *Kansas Journal of Sociology.*

Lofland, John. *Analyzing Social Settings: A Guide to Qualitative Observation and Analysis.* Belmont, Cal.: Wadsworth, 1971.

Manis, Jerome G. and Bernard M. Meltzer. *Symbolic Interaction: A Reader in Social Psychology.* Boston: Allyn and Bacon, 1967.

Mead, George Herbert. *The Philosophy of the Present.* Edited by Arthur E. Murphy with prefatory remarks by John Dewey. Chicago: Open Court, 1932.

———. *Mind, Self & Society.* Edited, with introduction, by Charles W. Morris. Chicago: University of Chicago, 1934.

———. *Movements of Thought in the Nineteenth Century.* Edited by Merritt H. Moore. Chicago: University of Chicago, 1936.

———. *The Philosophy of the Act.* Edited, with introduction by Charles W. Morris in collaboration with John M. Brewster, Albert M. Dunham, and David L. Miller. Chicago: University of Chicago, 1938.

———. *Selected Writings.* Edited, with introduction, by Andrew J. Reck. Indianapolis: Bobbs-Merrill, 1964.

Meltzer, Bernard N. *The Social Psychology of George Herbert Mead.* Kalamazoo, Mich.: Western Michigan University, 1959.

Mills, C. Wright. *The Marxists.* New York: Dell, 1962.

———. *Sociology and Pragmatism: The Higher Learning in America.* New York: Oxford University, 1966.

Morris, Charles W. "Introduction." *Mind, Self & Society.* Edited by George H. Mead. Chicago: University of Chicago, 1934, pp. ix–xxxv.

Petras, John W. "John Dewey and the Rise of Interactionism in American Social Theory." *Journal of the History of the Behavioral Sciences* 4 (January 1968):18–27.

———. "George Herbert Mead's Theory of Self: A Study in the Origin and Convergence of Ideas." *The Canadian Review of Sociology and Anthropology.*

Petras, John W. and Bernard N. Meltzer. "Theoretical and Ideological Variations in Contemporary Interactionism." *Catalyst.*

Reck, Andrew J. "Preface" and "Editor's Introduction." *Selected Writings.* Edited by George Herbert Mead with introduction by Andrew J. Reck. Indianapolis: Bobbs-Merrill, 1964, pp. v–lxxii.

Russell, Bertrand. *A History of Western Philosophy.* New York: Simon and Schuster, 1945.

Shibutani, Tamotsu. "Mead, George Herbert." *International Encyclopedia of the Social Sciences 10.* Edited by David L. Sills. New York: Macmillan and Free Press, 1968, pp. 83–87.

Stevens, Edward. "Biographical Note: G. H. Mead," *American Journal of Sociology* 72 (March 1967): 551–7.

Stone, Gregory P. and Harvey A. Farberman (eds.). *Social Psychology Through Symbolic Interaction.* Waltham, Mass.: Xerox, 1970.

Wennerberg, Hjalmar. *The Pragmatism of C. S. Peirce: An Analytical Study.* Lund, Sweden: CWK Gleerup, 1962.

White, Morton C. *The Origin of Dewey's Instrumentalism.* New York: Columbia, 1943.

Willer, David and Murray Webster, Jr. "Theoretical Constructs and Observables." *American Sociological Review* 35 (August 1970):748–57.

Willer, David and Judith Willer. *Systematic Empiricism: Critique of a Pseudo-Science.* Englewood Cliffs, N.J.: Prentice-Hall, 1972.

Willer, Judith. *The Social Determination of Knowledge.* Englewood Cliffs, N.J.: Prentice-Hall, 1970.

Zajonc, Robert B. "Conformity." *International Encyclopedia of the Social Sciences 3.* Edited by David L. Sills. New York: Macmillan and Free Press, 1968, pp. 253–260.

Action vs. Interaction

Erving Goffman has gained well-deserved recognition as an innovative scholar of high order. Through a series of noteworthy publications he has shown himself to be the dissector par excellence of the close interplay between human beings in face-to-face association. His forte is the minute analysis of the social positioning of participants as they take heed of each other, inspect each other, address each other, move toward or away from each other, parade before each other, lay claims on each other, insulate themselves against each other and make a range of varied adjustments to each other. With his gifts of sensitive perception, creative imagination and adroit conceptualization he can take an area of intimate human interplay which appears to us as flat and humdrum and show it to be intricate, dynamic and dramatic. Further, he forces us to see order in such areas of complex interplay—an order that is seemingly rooted in the generic requirements of human association. His analyses are made from the perspective of sociology and social psychology and must be recognized as contributions to these disciplines.

The general characterization of Goffman's scholarly work applies to the present volume, *Relations in Public*. This volume carrying the subtitle *Microstudies of the Public Order* consists of six interrelated articles with an illuminating preface and a lengthy appended essay. The common area of the studies is the "field of public life" which Goffman identifies as the "realm of activity that is generated by face-to-face interaction and organized by norms of co-mingling—a domain containing weddings, family meals, chaired meetings, forced marches, service encounters, queues, crowds and couples." Goffman's special concern is with the ground rules (the "norms of co-mingling") that regulate face-to-face contact in this field of public life. The ground rules establish "public order." Public order consists of the "patterned adaptations" to such rules, "including conformances, by-passings, secret deviations, excusable infractions, flagrant violations, and the like." At the cost of omitting a great deal of the insightful observations made in this book by Goffman, the gist of his analysis can be summarized in the following points.

1) In their face-to-face relations in the public arena human beings are engaged in scanning or reading each other and, in turn, presenting themselves through externalization so that they are read in appropriate ways by others who are scanning them. The interplay that takes place in public situations occurs through such externalization and scanning.

2) Human beings bring a series of territorial claims into their public relations. These territorial claims or "preserves" are represented by such forms as "personal space," "the turn" (as in forming a queue at a ticket window) and the "stall" (a well-bounded space such as a chair or a beach mat). In their association in public situations human beings are engaged in staking out their preserves, in meeting the encroachments of others on their respective preserves and in avoiding intrusion into the preserves of others. The interplay

of territorial claims constitutes a very important dimension of the public order.

3) In their face-to-face encounters and contacts human beings employ interpersonal rituals (such as gestures of recognition, greeting ceremonies and inquiries as to one's health) which serve to open access to each other, establish the degree of such access, link persons to each other in given ways, maintain or reestablish contact with one another, and place people in proper position to each other. Goffman calls these interpersonal rituals, "supportive interchanges." They permeate public life, introducing a highly important dimension of order.

4) The maintenance of public order (as defined above) is not, as it would seem, a mere matter of obedience to social norms but involves an employment of "remedial interchanges" which allow for the reestablishment of relations that have been breached by the infraction of norms. These remedial interchanges take the form chiefly of "accounts" (explanations which strip the infraction of its offensive character), "apologies" and "requests" (solicitations for permission to perform the infraction). The use of accounts, apologies and requests define the infraction in such a way as to leave intact the integrity of the social norm that has been violated. Remedial interchange is a constant feature of interaction in public life, providing an organizational means of sustaining the public order in the face of its violation.

5) Of great importance in the arena of public life are "anchored relations"—those between individuals who know each other and know that they know each other. Such individuals in each other's presence in a public gathering reveal the nature of their relationship by the use of posture, gesture and vocal expression. Goffman calls these indications of anchored relationship "tie-signs." Tie-signs represent both the existence and the functioning of an important part of the social order; they enable observers to classify one another, and they provide self-assurance to those who recognize that they are tied together.

6) The conditions of living for human beings, as for animals, require individuals to be constantly on the alert for happenings that seem unnatural, dangerous or wrong. Thus, the activity of humans falls into two modes: going about their business and being at the same time on the watch for alarms, threats and dangers. This latter mode of activity constitutes an important dimension of human conduct in face-to-face association, with participants having to be ready to detect the unusual and the abnormal in the appearance or acts of others. The interplay of participants thus embodies a recurring scanning of the actions of others for signs of threats and alarms and a concealing of signs of one's own actions that might lead others to suspect something unusual or abnormal. Goffman borrows the term "Umwelt" from animal ethology to stand for the area of potential alarm, and then he classifies the sources of alarm as they exist in the Umwelts of human beings. The public order consists of a process of participants forming and maintaining their respective Umwelts. As mutual trust and the sense of normal presentation become shaky in face-to-face association the public order deteriorates.

The foregoing bare-boned six-point digest necessarily ignores the rich panoply of treatment contained in the work under review. But the digest is sufficient to allow us to make a critical assessment of the approach to sociology and social psychology which the book reflects. Such an assessment is definitely in order in the light of Goffman's prominence in these disciplines and of his growing influence on sets of disciples.

The assessment should begin with the reminder that Goffman is dealing with the area of human group life that is constituted by face-to-face meetings and association. He regards this area as having a distinctive makeup, with its own structure of relations, its own forms of interaction, its own sets of norms and its own array of investments by the human "self." It thus constitutes in its own right a domain for study. This preoccupation with the area of face-to-face relations provides both the strength and the weakness of Goffman's analyses.

We need not dwell on the positive side of Goffman's work. It is sufficient to note that his penchant for probing into face-to-face relations has led him to dig out and treat seriously what social scientists, pretty much across the board, never see or at the best regard as trivia. Who among them, for example, would be likely to take such a commonplace matter as the utterance of greetings and show its important role in social interaction? Or who would seek to analyze the social role of hand-holding in American society— a matter which Goffman has done in a most discerning and illuminating manner? In showing, through his perceptive analyses, the important role which these kinds of matters have in human group life Goffman forces social scientists to include what they have been notoriously prone to neglect. Alfred North Whitehead has written somewhere words to the effect that genius in scientific scholarship consists of subjecting to minute inspection objects which are taken for granted just because they are under our noses. In terms of this criterion Goffman's work ranks high.

In the opinion of this reviewer an additional word of commendation is in order—in this instance with regard to Goffman's research procedure. In the true spirit of a scientific pioneer he is ever ready to probe around in fresh directions in place of forcing his investigation into the fixed protocol so frequently demanded in contemporary social science research. Fortunately, his interests are in untangling the empirical world rather than in paying obeisance to some sanctified scheme for doing so. Through the use of choice accounts of human experience he cuts through to important observations that are not yielded by hosts of stylized findings.

Now for the weaknesses. The weaknesses in Goffman's approach stem from the narrowly constricted area of human group life that he has staked out for study. He has limited the area to face-to-face association with a corresponding exclusion of the vast mass of human activity falling outside of such association. Further, he has confined his study of face-to-face association to the interplay of personal positioning, at the cost of ignoring what the participants are doing. Valid questions are set by each of these two lines of restriction. Let me explain.

In the case of the first restriction one may ask how realistic it is to treat face-to-face association as a distinctive domain, with a makeup independent of the group activities in which the face-to-face interaction takes place. Despite a theoretical position which stakes out face-to-face association as such a conceivable separate domain,

Goffman wavers on this matter in his actual treatment—as in confining several of his face-to-face analyses in the present book to American society. The issue here, however, is more than the old question of the relation between culture and face-to-face association; it is rather a matter of ascertaining how concrete ongoing group activities affect the face-to-face interaction involved in them and how, contrariwise, the face-to-face interaction influences the ongoing activities. Goffman's scheme deters him, indeed theoretically excludes him, from addressing this vital question. Thus, the framework of the present book rules out a consideration of how the public order, which he narrowly conceives in terms of the ground rules of face-to-face association, interacts (if at all) with the wider public order conceived of in terms of the interplay of organized groups and institutions. Unless Goffman and his followers address empirically the question of the relation between face-to-face association and the wider context of group activity in which such association is lodged, his type of study will remain on a question-begging premise.

The deficiencies set by the second line of restriction are more decisive and profound. Goffman does not treat the content of face-to-face association in its natural breadth but picks out, instead, a narrow portion of it as his domain of study. This portion is restricted to the personal positioning of the participants to one another as they observe each and thus ignores, essentially, their acts or what they are doing. Goffman recognizes that the participants in face-to-face interaction are engaged in doing something; he refers repeatedly to this something as "their business in hand." This business in hand must be seen, in the opinion of this reviewer, as the activity which initiates and sustains face-to-face association. Yet it is precisely this central strand of activity in face-to-face association that Goffman casts aside. Goffman states his position nicely in two sentences, "The individual does not go about merely going about his business. He goes about constrained to sustain a viable image of himself in the eyes of others." Goffman is concerned with the area represented by the second sentence and is unconcerned with the area represented by the first sentence. This restriction of concern has highly important implications that should be specified and discussed briefly.

First, it follows that Goffman covers only a part of the social interaction that takes place between human beings in their face-to-face association. Indeed, he leaves out what is most central in social interaction, namely, the fitting together of the respective acts of the participants as they endeavor to do what is called for in their group or joint action. To restrict interaction to the niceties of personal interadjustment is to swerve far from the process which George Herbert Mead has made the keystone of his profound analysis of social interaction. What Goffman elects to reject—the interaction of people as they go about their business, as they fit their lines of action to one another—is precisely what Mead sees as the prime stuff of human association, whether it be face-to-face or more remote association. Human interaction, as Mead emphasized, consists fundamentally of efforts of the participants to grasp what each other is doing or plans to do and then to direct one's own act in the light of this knowledge. Instead, to treat face-to-face interaction as though it consists of efforts to create and sustain personal impressions is to misrepresent its true nature.

The interdependency of the interaction with others and the interaction with oneself is inescapable in the case of human beings—that is what a "self" means. Consequently, the severe constriction that Goffman has imposed on social interaction necessarily distorts, in turn, the extent and the manner in which he sees the human being as handling himself in face-to-face association. There can be no doubt that beginning with his early notable book, *The Presentation of the Self in Everyday Life,* Goffman sees the human being as preoccupied with the kinds of impressions he is making on others. This theme runs through his works, including the book under review. Without minimizing the fact that human beings in one another's presence are sensitive to how they are being regarded, it is farfetched to assume that this form of self-awareness constitutes the major concern of the human being in handling himself. People in association just do not go around with their attention constantly focused on how they

are being regarded and on how they can influence the way in which they are regarded. At various times they do this, and some people do it more than others. But this does not constitute the central content of what the person does in interacting with himself. Instead, self-interaction is concerned primarily in guiding oneself in what one does. The scanning of others and the externalization of oneself, to which Goffman gives such a conspicuous place in face-to-face association, are much more than ascertaining or controlling how one is being regarded by one's associates; such scanning and externalization are primarily a matter of ascertaining what one's associates are intending to do and of indicating to them what one intends to do. In his treatment Goffman has shifted self-interaction away from the construction of action by the actor to meet the actions of others; instead, he has put in its place the much narrower form of self-interaction concerned with self-regard. This leads to a one-sided treatment of the "self" and gives an inadequate and inaccurate picture of how the human being handles himself in face-to-face interaction.

Let me turn from the deficiencies that stem from the failure of Goffman's perspective to cover certain vital dimensions of the empirical world he is addressing. In the final words of this review I would like to note an additional weakness that lies strictly within the domain to which he has limited himself in the present book. This domain, as he states, consists of the *"patterned* adaptations" (my emphasis) to the "norms of co-mingling" in face-to-face association. Even the infractions of these norms come in the form of patterned adaptations. This view of the domain of co-mingling as already organized sets up a static world; theoretically, it shuts out consideration of how norms and the patterned adaptations to them either come into being or deteriorate and pass away. Yet, the norms and the patterned adaptations to them must obviously have a history and be subject to transformation in the course of their careers. This aspect of his domain is left untouched by Goffman.

One would hope that Goffman would bring his fertile mind to bear on the weaknesses that have been outlined.

Ethnomethodology

Among other emerging theoretical standpoints based upon infrastructures fundamentally at variance with the Parsonsian is that advanced in Harold Garfinkel's Ethnomethodology. Like Parsons, Garfinkel is deeply interested in the requisites of social order. Unlike Parsons, however, he assigns no special importance either to the role of a mutuality of gratifications or to that of shared moral values. Instead, and in a more Durkheimian manner, Garfinkel is concerned with the cultural level and, in particular, with a kind of *secularized* "collective conscience." Influenced by Alfred Schutz's phenomenology, his attention is focused largely on the structure of the shared and *tacit—* that is, ordinarily unutterable—rules and knowledge that make stable social interaction possible. For Garfinkel, then, the social world is held together not by a morality tinged with the sacred, but by a dense collective structure of tacit understandings (what men know and know others know) concerning the most mundane and "trivial" matters, understandings to which no special importance, let alone sacred significance, is normally attributed if, indeed, they are noticed at all.

Like Goffman, Garfinkel focuses on everyday life and on routine activities, rather than on critical events or dramatic public incidents. He regards all people as being "practical theorists," collaboratively creating meanings and understandings of one another's activities. His methodology has a strongly monistic vector, there

From *The Coming Crisis of Western Sociology*, by Alvin W. Gouldner, © 1970 by Alvin W. Gouldner, Basic Books, Inc., Publishers, New York.

being no radical difference between sociologists and other men. At the same time, however, Garfinkel criticizes all normal sociology for failing to understand this properly. In other words, while he sees the continuity between professional and practical theorists, he also wants professional social theorists to behave in a more selfconscious manner than practical theorists, by becoming aware of their own involvement in the common sense world. Seeing social reality as created and sustained in the mundane activities of ordinary men, Garfinkel seeks to understand social situations from the "inside" as it were, as it appears to the men who live it; he seeks to communicate *their* sense of things, with an almost Nietzschean hostility to conceptualization and abstraction, and particularly by avoiding the conceptualizations conventional to normal sociology. Thus he erects few or none of the conceptual towers that both Parsons and Goffman like to build.

Even though he stresses the significance of time as intrinsic to meaning, Garfinkel's, like Goffman's, social world is a world outside of time. He is ahistorical and does not limit his generalizations to a given era or a specific culture. While deeply concerned with how definitions of social reality become established, he is not interested in why one definition of social reality becomes prevalent in one time, or place, or group, and another elsewhere. The process by which social reality becomes defined and established is not viewed by Garfinkel as entailing a process of struggle among competing groups' definitions of reality; and the outcome, the common sense conception of the world, is not seen as having been shaped by institutionally protected power differences. There is a way in which Garfinkel's concern with the anchoring character of shared meanings expresses a sense of a world not in conflict so much as in dissolution, of a diffuse multiformity of values rather than a clearly structured conflict of political and ideological groups. He seems to be responding to a social world in which sex, drugs, religion, family, school, all are uncertain, and in which the threat is more of an entropic winding-down rather than of taut conflict.

In an old conceptual distinction, Garfinkel is the ethnographer of the folkways rather than of the mores. Quite unlike Parsons, Garfinkel apparently does not believe that social stability requires that the rules or values be deeply internalized within persons or their character structure. In fact, the tacit implication of his ingenious and upsetting "experiments" is that men (most particularly college students) may rather easily be made to act at variance with them. In this, Garfinkel seems to operate with much the same assumption that Goffman does: that is, both seem to premise a social world resting on tacit understandings that, however important as a foundation for all else, are still fragile and rather readily eluded. The cultural foundation, in short, is precarious, and its security apparently rests, in some part, on its sheer invisibility or taken-for-grantedness. Once made visible, however, it rather readily loses its hold. Unlike Parsons, Garfinkel communicates no sense of the unshakable stability of social foundations.

The concrete differences in the specific character of these varying tacit rules is not examined by Garfinkel. His attention, rather, is largely focused, first, on demonstrating their sheer existence, and, second, on demonstrating their role in providing a secure background for social interaction. As a result, there is a strong tendency for each rule thus exposed to appear somewhat arbitrary, for each is assigned no distinct function or differential importance and is, in effect, interchangeable with a variety of others, all making some contribution to a stabilizing framework for interaction. To perform this stabilizing function, some other rule might conceivably do just as well. His emphasis, then, leads to a conception of these rules as conventions, and thus to a view of society

as dependent on the merely conventional—that is, on what are, in effect, rules of the game. Garfinkel normally exposes these rules through game-like "demonstrations" of what happens when some men, without informing others of their intent, deliberately proceed to violate these tacit understandings. And all parts of society, including science (with its rigorous method), are seen to depend on these common sense, arbitrary rules and procedures.

Unlike Goffman, Garfinkel takes no sensuous delight in the world of appearances. Rather, he conceives of the truly important part in the social world as practically invisible, as so familiar that it is a world taken-for-granted and unnoticed. The task Garfinkel sets himself is to destroy this taken-for-grantedness and to strip the cultural foundation of its cloak of invisibility. He is not engaged in locating the familiar commonplaces within the framework of some theory thereby to endow it with deeper meaning and enrich experience with it, which is one of the most deeply Romantic of Goffman's tactics. Garfinkel aims, primarily, at baring and unmasking the invisible commonplace by violating it in some manner until it betrays its presence.

It would be a mistake, however, to conclude that Garfinkel is engaged only in an archaeological excavation of hidden cultural foundations, for his excavations proceed largely through the demolition of small-scale worlds. If Goffman's work may be conceived of as an attack upon certain forms of lower-middle-class smugness, or morality, Garfinkel's is an attack upon the common sense of *reality*. Thus students are instructed to engage friends or acquaintances in ordinary conversation and, without indicating that anything special is afoot, to pretend ignorance of everyday expressions: "What do you mean, she had a 'flat tire'?" "What do you mean, 'how is she feeling'?" Undergraduates are assigned the task of spending time with their families, all the while acting as if they were boarders in their own homes. Again, students are instructed to engage someone in conversation and, while doing so, to assume that the other person is trying to trick or mislead them; or they are instructed to talk with people while bringing their noses almost to the touching point.

At first blush, these demonstrations seem to have a prankish collegiate quality, but this view of them as "harmless fun" wears thin as one reads the reactions of the "victims," as Garfinkel sometimes correctly calls them: "She became nervous and jittery, her face and hand movements . . . uncontrolled." "Quarreling, bickering, and hostile motivations become discomfitingly visible." There was "irritation and exasperated anger," "nasty developments frequently occurred." "I actually came to feel somewhat hated and by the time I left the table I was quite angry." "Attempted avoidance, bewilderment, acute embarrassment, furtiveness, and above all uncertainties of these as well as uncertainties of fear, hope, and anger were characteristic."

These, then, are the pained responses normal to persons whose conceptions of social reality have been violated, and, indeed, quite deliberately assaulted. It must be understood, however, that painful though they are, these responses are not unanticipated but expected by Garfinkel. As he says in one connection, the responses *should be* those of bewilderment, uncertainty, internal conflict, psycho-sexual isolation, acute, and nameless anxiety along with various symptoms of acute depersonalization."

The cry of pain, then, is Garfinkel's triumphal moment; it is dramatic confirmation of the existence of certain tacit rules governing social interaction and of their importance to the persons involved. That he feels free to inflict these costs on others, on his students, their families, friends, or passersby—and to encourage others to do so— is not, I would suggest, evidence of a dispassionate and detached attitude toward the social world, but of a readiness to use it in cruel ways. Here, objectivity and sadism become delicately intertwined. The demonstration is the message, and the message seems to be that anomic normlessness is no longer merely something that the sociologist studies in the social world, but is now something that *he inflicts upon it* and is the basis of his method of investigation.

There is nothing that is quite so reminiscent of Garfinkel's demonstrational methodology as the "happening," which, however, usually lacks the unblinking hurtfulness of Garfinkel's techniques, and may also have a larger social purpose.

In the "happening," something like this occurs: shortly before noon, say, in Amsterdam, a group of youths gathers in one of the busier squares and, just as luncheon traffic begins to mount, they release into the streets one hundred chickens. These, of course, distract and amaze the drivers; accidents may happen; traffic halts; crowds gather, further tying up traffic; routines come to a stop as everyone gathers around to watch and laugh as the police attempt to catch the chickens. Garfinkel might say that the community has now learned the importance of one hitherto unnoticed rule at the basis of everyday life: chickens must not be dropped in the streets in the midst of the lunch hour rush.

Behind both the "happening" and the ethnomethodological demonstration there is a common impulse: to bring routines to a halt, to make the world and time stop. Both rest on a similar perception of the conventional character of the underlying rules, on a view of them as lacking in intrinsic value, as arbitrary albeit essential to the conduct of routine. And both are forms of hostility to the "way things are," although the ethnomethodologist's is a veiled hostility, aimed at less dangerous targets. Both communicate at least one lesson: the vulnerability of the everyday world to disruption by violation of tacitly held assumptions. Underneath the ethnomethodological demonstration, then, there is a kind of anarchical impulse, a genteel anarchism, at least when compared with the "happening." It is an anarchism that will, to some extent, appeal to youth and others alienated from the status quo, and that may also congenially resonate the sentiments of some on the New Left. It is a way in which the alienated young may, with relative safety, defy the established order and experience their own potency. The ethnomethodological "demonstration" is, in effect, a kind of microconfrontation with and nonviolent resistance to the status quo. It is a substitute and symbolic rebellion against a larger structure which the youth cannot, and often does not wish to, change. It substitutes the available rebellion for the inaccessible revolution.

In any event, it seems quite evident that, while nominally centered on the *analysis* of social order, Garfinkel's ethonomethodology is infused with a structure of sentiments directly at variance with the Parsonian. The very frequency with which its often dense and elephantine formulations are attractive to the young is indicative of its congeniality to the new structure of sentiments held by some of them, as well as of their readiness to seize upon almost anything that promises an alternative to Parsonsianism. If Goffman's social theory was a "cool" or "hip" sociology congenial to the politically passive 1950's, Garfinkel's is a sociology more congenial the the activistic 1960's, and particularly to the more politically rebellious campuses of the present period.

Edwin M. Lemert   48

Beyond Mead: The Societal Reaction to Deviance

What I prefer to call the sociology of deviance now appears to be under attack from so many quarters, both for what it is and what it is not, that a sense of embattlement is inescapable. The diverse, perverse, and tangential nature of the criticisms makes it difficult to tell friend from foe. Sensitive to this state of affairs, Peter Manning (1973) in a review essay of surpassing excellence asserts that a grey fog has settled over the field. This I can discount as the natural fog of good men's minds; but his further allegations that the theoretical impetus of deviance sociology is spent and that a state of exhaustion and conceptual decay prevails, I found painful and much harder to reconcile with my proprietary interests.

I should say parenthetically that reading the essay left me spelled by the beauty of its words and niceties of expression, as well as overwhelmed by its sense of prophecy. It recalled me to an old auctorial ideal espoused by James Branch Cabell, namely that we should write beautifully of things as they are. But having had time to cast off Manning's spell, I conclude that sociologists sometimes write beautifully of things as they are not and that in striving for rhetorical symmetry their conclusions may go beyond what facts will support. In this case I must object that the allegations of its sadness and senility ignore the theoretical potential of deviance sociology, its continuing research output, its influence on the diversion movement in criminal justice, and its striking impact on younger, highly articulate sociologists in Britain. Granting the slow stain and constant erosion of all ideas, it seems to me that even with age deviance sociology still is "majestic in decay."

But without further pause on the decadence issue, I would like to deal with what may cause some of the faithful to cry sacrilege, namely the deficiencies of G. H. Mead's conception of symbolic interaction and their implications for the study of deviance. My purpose is not to add to the theoretical confusion but to clear some of it away, and hopefully free up sociological energies

Edwin M. Lemert, "Beyond Mead: The Societal Reaction to Deviance," *Social Problems* 21:4 (April 1974), pp. 457–468. Reprinted by permission.

Presidential address, Society for the Study of Social Problems, annual meeting, August, 1973.

to exploit in the measure it deserves its least worked area, namely the societal reaction. In order to maximize the clarity of my discussion I will recap what the term has meant to me.

Some years ago in my early work on deviance I used the term societal reaction to comprehend a number of processes by which societies respond to deviants either informally or through their officially delegated agencies (Lemert, 1951). While communication of invidious definitions of persons or groups and the public expression of disapproval were included as part of the societal reaction, the important point was made that these had to be validated in order to be sociologically meaningful. Validation was conceived as effective social control taking form as isolation, segregation, penalties, supervision, or some kind of organized "treatment." In effect, this was a kind of middle range conceptual orientation to a body of data.

Societal reaction theory distinguished objective as well as subjective aspects of deviance, recognizing a relationship between the nature, degree, extent, and visibility of deviance and corresponding form and intensity of the societal reaction. It also allowed that attributes of deviants and the form of their deviance affected the way in which societal definitions were internalized, most easily seen in biological anomalies and physical handicaps. Among the objective influences on the societal reaction were noted technology, procedures, and limitation of agency personnel and resources. However, these did not get much elaboration or application, save in the discussion of changing tolerances for crime.

Then, as in my later work on deviance (Lemert, 1973), I emphasized the need to begin the analysis with the societal reaction, more particularly social control, rather than with etiology. Herein lay the distinctiveness of the societal reaction approach, which sought to show how deviance was shaped and stabilized by efforts to eliminate or ameliorate it. In retrospect, the break with structural conceptions of deviance and the traditional concern of sociology with causes was by no means complete. This I now believe to have been less a matter of theoretical asymmetry than an encounter with a perennial problem of sociological theory, namely how to establish a connection between symbolic systems, social systems, and physical systems, without denying the obvious fact that human beings make choices that affect as well as are affected by the system. According to J. F. Scott's (1963) informed analysis, even the grand theorist of our age, Talcott Parsons, failed to reach an ultimate solution of this problem.

This question was pretty well obscured during the 1950's and 1960's, probably because of the tremendous growth in our national production and the belief that affluence was easily procurable for all, abetted by Keynesian economic theory aimed at little more than preventive maintenance of the marvelous machine making it all possible. But recently the avalanche of population growth, swift exhaustion of resources, environmental destruction, plus an "energy crisis" have made an awareness that human choices can either sustain or destroy the physical and technological basis on which they are made. Physical environments formerly taken as constants and merely limiting now can be seen changing in foreseeable time spans, and it becomes possible to speak of responses and feedback from the physical world. Even the vulgarization and deserved criticism of the ecology movement cannot quiet the deepening appreciation that man is inescapably part of a larger bio-physical system.

SYMBOLIC INTERACTION

Over the decades of the present century sociology moved steadily away from early social science, which had sought standing ground on biology, geography, and economics. Within sociology, social psychologists pushed farthest along this path, retaining only some nominal allegiance to organic and natural history analogies. And within social psychology, it has been those sociologists concerned with deviance who have laid the greatest and most exclusive emphasis on the sociopsychological process as the determining element in social life. It has been asserted that the one theme uniting the otherwise diverse views of labeling theorists, Neo-Chicagoans, or West Coast school, as they are variously called, is their fealty to the symbolic interactionism of G. H. Mead (Schur, 1969).

Nevertheless, it may be asked whether the prevailing definition of deviance as a group creation through labeling and the adoption of an "underdog" view of the symbolic process do not do a disservice to Mead. Labeling unfortunately conveys an impression of interaction that is both sociologistic and unilateral; in the process deviants who are "successfully labeled" lose their individuality; they appear, as Bordua (1967) says, like "empty organisms" or, as Gouldner (1968) puts it, "like men on their backs" (Walton 1973). The extreme subjectivism made explicit by the underdog perspective, reflecting sympathy for the victim and antipathy towards the establishment, also distorts by magnifying the exploitative and arbitrary features of the societal reaction. But more important, it leaves little or no place for human choice at either level of interaction.

Actually the difficulties may lie in the ambiguities and uncertainties of Mead's ideas themselves. While Mead reconciled the objective and the subjective in general terms by making self and other dual aspects of a common behavioral process, the specifics of the process with respect to choice making were far from clear. Other strictures inhere in Mead's conception of the societal other; his unformed ideas about society, primarily that of one generalized other; are a poor source for a modern theory of the societal reaction (Meltzer 1967; Kolb 1967). This is amply demonstrated in the dramatistic descriptions of the societal reaction which revolve around the idea of symbolic interaction.

THE DRAMATISTIC METAPHOR

Most of the currently held representations of the societal reaction are metaphors having in common a curious primitive quality. In his one article on the subject, Mead (1928) spoke of the "modern organization of taboo"; later Tannenbaum (1937) called the process the dramatization of evil, equatable with ancient Hebraic scapegoating; Garfinkel (1956) depicted it as ceremonial degradation based on suprapersonal values of the tribe; others have termed the process stigmatization, victimization, exclusion, and conferral of an invidious property. Becker (1963) drew on a re-

constructed incident of clan reaction to incest in the far off Melanesian islands to epitomize the contingency of the labeling process. The anachronistic overtones in these figures are unmistakable.

While fabrication of a pristine state of affairs, and the use of analogies and metaphors for purposes of analysis are inviting, it is also true that they may become the ties that bind; in this case the dramatistic metaphors, or life-as-a-theatre analysis, traceable from Mead's comparison of social interaction to dramatic play and games, carry reductionistic implications hard to evade. The inescapable concomitants of the play are a scenario, actors who play prescribed parts, striking conjunction of actions, outward expression of inner conceptions, and denouement to an unequivocal end. The significant implication is that the societal reaction rests upon a kind of programmed consensus, a point made explicit by the concepts employed in many studies of agencies of social control. When "others" are agents of groups their decisions and actions are seen as the expression of rules, "routine practices," "common typifications," "proverbial characterizations," or racialclass bias, all strongly reminiscent of Durkheimian collective representations. Reification of one locus of power, insistence on group sustaining functions of deviance and uncritical acceptance of custodial treatment institutions as "total" give a further cast of Durkheimian solidarity to groups against which deviants are said to stand as outsiders (for criticism of dramaturgic analysis, see Messinger, 1962, Zicklin, 1968, Garfinkel, 1967, 145 ff.).

One consequence of the use of the abovementioned analogies to describe the societal reaction is to restrict conflict to that between the group and the person it seeks to label. No questions rise about possible effects of dissensus within the dominant group nor that generated by the intrusive claims of other groups. Becker's rules which create deviance appear as agreed upon, if not derived from an overarching establishment, at least from the subculture or occupational culture of the labelers; this despite knowledge that the salient problem for agents of social control such as police and court people is how to choose from among a plethora of rules at hand and how to find a basis for choice itself. There is little that

I can find in labeling theory which deals with this kind of conflict and choice making in the context of a pluralism of groups so conspicuous in modern society.

ETHNOMETHODOLOGY—THE METHODOLOGY OF CULTURE

To say that revolutions in thought come to devour their own may overstate the case but there now comes a younger generation of ethnomethodologists, existentialists, or phenomenologists in sociology who attack labeling theory as insufficient explication of the societal reaction process. Sensitive to the fragmentation, divisiveness, and pluralism of the contemporary social world, these writers stress the fluidity and provisional nature of the dynamics by which good and evil, and conformity and deviance emerge. While these thinkers are still allied with symbolic interactionism, they reject the Meadian concept of social role, and insist that "reality" lies under, beyond, or apart from institutional structures. Rules are replaced by concepts of "deeper rules," "relational rules," or preconceptions of social interaction (Douglas, 1970). In starkest form the ethnomethodologists assert that confrontations or collective action generating deviance are little more than negotiated understandings contrived in a world without meaning or which is "absurd" (Lyman and Scott, 1970).

The concomitant process has been called "work" or the "social construction of reality," situated in nature. Apart from this, however, clarification is meager, suggesting the difficulties which ethnomethodologists have in rising above a kind of raw "here and now" empiricism in the research application of their ideas. The low level of characterization of the stigmatization of clients at the hands of a welfare organization as a process of "muddling through." He concludes (Scott 1970):

This, in turn, implies that one can only speak of constructed meanings of stigma in the sense that they are genuinely manmade.

As the term denotes, ethnomethodology contends that cultures or subcultures set fundamental rules for determining what is perceived as real.

In arguing for this position its partisans deepen the entanglement of deviance study in reductionism and subjectivism. The denial of any objective reality is made explicit in a statement by Erich Goode (1969):

The only reality available to individual consciousness is a subjective reality . . . meaning is read into every situation, event, object and phenomenon.

FURTHER DILEMMAS

Insofar as ethnomethodologists hold that constructions of deviance rest on perceptions or "grounds" which are determined by cultural or subcultural screens, their ideas turn into solipsisms, recapitulating the difficulty from which Mead tried to rescue Watsonian behaviorism. In a narrow sense it is true that culture sets up an apperceptive base from which those enculturated respond selectively to define good and evil independently of other aspects of the actions they perceive. Culture may provide people with meanings that keep them acting for long periods in ways that appear to be irrational, meaningless, or even fantastic. The pure culturologist or ethnomethodologist looking at such behavior concludes that culture or social construction of reality can make anything good or bad, denying that there is any standard common to mankind that affects his efforts.

This kind of generalization can be made true only by denying that man learns or responds on any other basis than what is symbolically transmitted. Actually it is only in cases where a cultural definition of what happens is reinforced by anticipated results that men are free to selectively define reality in this circular manner. In effect they may react as if only part of what happened actually happened, thus identifying a whole pattern of action as a cultural or perceptual phenomenon.

But as W. F. Cottrell (1972) convincingly demonstrates, while some of our responses depend on symbolically acquired meanings, others require for their validation direct feedback from our bodies or the physical world; and still other responses can be made or learned only through direct experience of the doing of them. From this point of view any pattern of human reaction to others, individual or collective, is a mixture or product of prior symbolically transmitted knowledge, past knowledge acquired from experience with the objective world and newly invented meanings derived from immediate experience with the social and physical worlds.

CHANGE IN THE SOCIETAL REACTION

It is primarily by treating the societal reaction as a residue after all factors operating to produce it have occurred that the impression of its subjective symbolic character can be maintained. While granting that the residues of social action are symbolically transmitted, looking at the action from the perspective of change directs attention to its non-symbolic antecedents. This is made clear in Cottrell's (1972) words:

> If culture be treated as a residue . . . then of course what is found there includes all the norms, the results of all strivings, as well as all knowledge that will be symbolically transmitted. But how much of what was there yesterday is still there . . . How much of what is there now is new, now to be symbolically transmitted but not learned that way? . . . if . . . our model permits us to look elsewhere we may see that culture change was preceded by technological invention, or that certain kinds of deleterious social relationships were selected out of that culture when new knowledge made it possible to discover their influence . . . It is only in the comparative short run that culture can make anything good. . . .

A great many of the studies of agencies controlling deviance have been synchronous in nature, describing and analyzing portions and pieces of a social process. Many have been timeless and without provenience. Consequently when attention is turned to the rise and fall of moral ideas and the transformation of definitions of deviance, labeling theory and ethnomethodology do little to enlighten the process. This is especially true as it pertains to the interaction of groups. A sociopsychological model focused on symbolic interaction in the Mead tradition either leaves groups vague entities or psychologizes their action. This can be seen in the proposition that new moral and legal categories are the work of moral entrepreneurs or crusaders with a sense of mission to impose their morality on others (Becker 1963). One version of this idea has it that such crusaders seize on a single moral issue as a symbol for reform in an effort to preserve a common way of life threatened by social change. Motivation presumably is purely symbolic, monolithic, and divorced from distributive material or means considerations (Gusfield, 1966).

Looking beyond symbolic politics for pertinent theory on the societal reaction is scarcely more rewarding. Radical critics and those who write on the politicization of deviance properly have noted the superficiality of the moral crusader formulation, as well as faulting labeling theory generally for its neglect of conflict and power. But the alternative theory of so-called radical sociology I find very generalized, as well as doctrinaire. Neither the Marxian concept of class, the power elites of Mills, nor the new left "urban alliance" of blacks and students have much immediate or practical use for research into the dynamics of the societal reaction. At best they substitute ideologies for things like group rules and define power as outcome of action or an attribute rather than as a process, e.g., "power is the ability to enforce one's moral claims."

In sum, radical critics reify power only slightly less than those they criticize; and in order to dramatize their criticisms they sometimes get caught up in the subjective, phenomenological perspective they seek to reject. Indeed some recent radical critiques seem bent on restoring machismo to the deviant and distinguishing the stout hearted and red blooded deviants who defy the system from those who live in its chinks and crannies. But even those on the sinistral side who call for sociologists to stigmatize the oppressor instead of their victims compound contradictions of power by insisting that high ranking persons are deviants even though they admittedly hold the power indispensable to defining deviance (Liazos, 1972).

Empirical materials to aid in formulation of theory on the evolution of morals and law unfortunately are sparse, for history seldom has recorded the kinds of events relevant to the task. Yet that which is available: J. Hall's (1935) studies of the evolution of the law of theft, research on the growth of vagrancy laws (Chambliss, 1964), commission reports on the poor laws, recent English articles on the politics of deviance (Taylors, 1973), my own work on change in the California Juvenile Court Law (1970), along with investigations into the origins and working of the Probation Subsidy Program in California, make it doubtful that the emergence of new morality and procedures for defining deviance can be laid to the creations of any one group, class, or elite. Rather they are the products of the interaction of groups. The workings of legislatures reveal the multifaceted interaction they have with such groups as well as the complexities of their own internal interaction through committees, majorities, and minorities. Judges, court workers, administrators, and police further interact to qualify the effective reach of new substantive law by jurisdictional and procedural adaptations. To understand the interplay of many groups out of which materialize new categories of moral and legal control requires a model of interaction quite different than those fathered by the psychologically oriented thought of Mead or from those of the class conflict theorists.

GROUP INTERACTION

Group interaction is best understood as a process resting on evaluation in which individuals sort out their purposes or values in terms of their dependence on groups necessary for their satisfaction. In so doing they give up some values in order to satisfy others, at the least possible sacrifice. The pattern of group action which results will reflect the claims and power of all those involved in the interaction; and the priorities it follows often are at considerable variance from the value hierarchies of individual participants. When a chain of interaction occurs between groups, the disparity between values dominate in final action, and the values of any one group member may be enormous. Police may acquiesce in positions of legislation taken by their representative association which deeply offend their sense of morality and justice because other values which have been given precedence are at stake in concurrent legislation. Legislators, too, may be captured by their

group commitments so that they must pass bills which are grossly contrary to values they personally espouse.

The order in which interests, claims, or values get satisfied reflects not only group allegiance but also the availability of means for their satisfaction and the costs of such means, measurable by time, energy, and other values expended. Laws and rules made by this kind of process often express the values and norms of no group or person but rather their dilemmas, compromises, expeditious adherence to procedures, and strictures of time and budgets. For this reason it becomes difficult or impossible to predict the emergence of new definitions and controls of deviance by introspecting or "taking the role of the other" to discover what it is the minds of those making the change. Nor can predictions be made successfully by imputing cultures, subcultures, or life styles to the agents of change.

What has been said is well illustrated by reference to the interaction of a variety of professional associations which took part in revising the Juvenile Court law in California in 1961, a change which narrowed the jurisdiction of the court and effectively modified definitions of delinquency (Lemert, 1970). Each association sorted out the proposed changes in terms of its own values, supporting or resisting according to whether the changes were seen as a means of achieving their existing values or called for sacrifices deemed intolerable. In the change, probation officers gave up their accustomed right to employ a number of informal procedures but got more power *vis-à-vis* the police in decisions to detain juveniles. Police lost this power but got badly needed clarification of arrest powers. Judges lost their considerable freedom to handle the court informally, but they along with interested attorneys gained by the introduction of guarantees of certain rights to minors. All three professional groups had splits for and against the changes, and their conflicting positions were arrived at for different reasons and in different ways. Ultimately resistance among probation officers disappeared because the resisters had to choose between continued opposition and preservation of their association, which it threatened to destroy. Opposition among judges centered around one of their members who remained against the changes throughout but ultimately chose not to risk loss of reputation among his other colleagues by protracted resistance. Police resistance, primarily among Juvenile Officers from the south state, got stymied by the structure of their lobbying committee, which was dominated by chiefs who were more concerned with evidentiary bills and a death penalty bill than they were with juvenile justice.

STRUCTURES AND THE SOCIETAL REACTION

It is clear from what has been said that social structures influenced the outcome of the legislation in question. This happened in several ways, such as limiting the access of some groups to the legislature, allocating power in a manner so that the decision of one committee was crucial, and the special autonomy to act given to the group which initiated the changes. However, here I wish to emphasize for theoretical reasons how structures become instrumentally important as vehicles or channels by which feedback from direct experience with the objective world modifies choice—in this instance how new structures affect dissemination of new knowledge which selects out old patterns or paradigms.

The movement to change the juvenile court law, although it had outside leadership, was something less than a moral crusade, nor could it be described realistically as a popular movement shaped by public opinion. Leaders were a few attorneys, some probation officers, correctional administrators, and college professors, from among whom was organized a commission within the California Youth Authority and the Department of Corrections. Joint sponsorship by the two organizations and later loss of interest by the CYA top people in the movement made it much like an autonomous staff operation. Several of the attorneys were attracted to the movement in its early stages mainly from frustrating encounters with highhanded judges in juvenile courts, but the focus and articulation of the movement owed much to organizational features introduced with creation of the CYA.

In essence, the movement was a challenge to the traditional *parens patriae* conception of the juvenile court, although it was not so represented. Social action grew out of an accumulation of new facts and information that raised serious doubts about the efficacy of the basic philosophy of the court. The main source of such information was input at the Board created for a different purpose, to hear and dispose all cases referred to CYA. This, together with reports from its field consultant division, allowed staff and Board members for the first time, circa 1944, to develop a statewide impression of what the juvenile courts were like in fact and to begin to appreciate the discrepancies between their ideology and their performance. A number of Board members after repeatedly listening to stories of youth coming before them grew convinced that injustices were being done.

The problem of the Commission became one of convincing persons with power to change the law that this was true. Given this general stance, the Commission did in a sense try to reconstruct the symbolic reality of the juvenile court, chiefly by means of a statewide survey, hearings, and presentations before legislative committees. But their report was late in appearing and was not very good at that; and the Commission's presentations before the powerful Senate Judiciary Committee, a majority of whose members were opposed to any change, fell short.

The event which did more than any other to undercut and select out the existing *parens patriae* conception of the juvenile court came from the unsolicited testimony of a single upstate judge who had come to defend the old style court and fight the changes sought by the Commission. A somewhat quaint, anachronistic figure in a black suit and a furled umbrella, he told in fine detail how he ran what was in effect an inquisitorial system of juvenile justice, ordering arrested youths into detention until by confessing their misdeeds they showed the remorse he considered necessary for their rehabilitation. The impact on a committee composed entirely of lawyers, former district attorneys, and a former judge was like that of a bomb in an echo chamber.

This strongly indicates that when a radical change is contemplated on the basis of new ideas about reality, it most likely occurs when there is a validation of the ideas in direct sensory experience—in this case a living breathing judge of the type the commissioners ineptly tried to fix as an image. The situation was dramatic because it was so real and because it was not staged.

Legislators—at least those in California—are well accustomed to staged presentations and highly sophisticated efforts to create realities favorable to the causes of lobbyists. As a matter of fact, they have committee techniques of their own designed to cope with these, that which might be called counter staging, set up to give the impression of responding to the voices of the public. Underneath, legislators tend to be toughminded; and the prevalence of lawyers among them sets rigorous standards for what will be accepted as facts or evidence. That they have problems of obtaining objective measures of the harmful effects of deviance and of consequences of proposed programs for its control none will deny. The problems face social scientists as well as legislators, but they do not seem sufficient reason to believe that legislators have no way of getting feedback from the objective world.

It remains to comment on the effects of direct experience with physical or ecological consequences of patterns of social control as influences on change. From these flow costs, by which is meant the time, energy, and money costs of means to implement various methods of control. In a context of change this refers to anticipated as well as experienced costs. An important principle is that changes in the definition and control of deviance may be due not to any alteration in value systems but to changes in their costs of satisfaction. An increase in costs, such as the time needed to deliver a youth to detention, may change the disposition of cases by police or probation officers even though their preferences are to follow an old pattern.

Anticipated changes in the costs of means to ends affected both the support for and opposition to the 1961 Juvenile Court Law revision. Los Angeles county sheriff people favored the change because the new arrest procedures simplified and helped the efficiency of their delinquency control operations. Police, on the other hand, both north and south, were concerned that the 48-hour limit imposed in the new law for investigations prior to detention hearings would make their jobs impossible. And indeed this was the case so far as their old procedures were concerned, especially in counties like Los Angeles, which had set up a detention control unit within its probation department. As a result, it became harder to use the juvenile court as an adjunct for extra-legal police methods. "Weekenders," youth swept up by police and detained in order to break up or curb local disorders, tended to disappear as a category.

Judges, probation officers, supervisors, and county executives in many instances were painfully aware that the proposed law revision would cost a great deal more money in order to provide counsel for minors, engage court reporters, and prepare records for court hearings. How to raise such funds was a critical issue in a number of counties. The requirement of two and possibly three court hearings could only increase the workload of the court and probation department, which meant either more tax funds or greater expenditures of time and effort by court personnel from judges on down.

The strong opposition to the law change by police and probation officers in the southern part of the state came from recognition of the hard fact that it would end the use of jail for detention, which was an intrinsic feature of the delinquency control system there. This eventuality was felt keenly in Long Beach, where a new wing of the jail had been constructed for such a purpose.

Higher standards of proof mandated by the law change and the new power of probation officers to dismiss at intake meant that more time had to go into police investigations and reports. This was more fully appreciated after some experience with the new law, and it fostered a changed categorical attitude that "either you have a case, or you don't." An organizational reflection of this change was the decision of the Los Angeles Police to eliminate its juvenile bureau and turn its work over to the detective bureau.

Herein may lie one of the main outcomes of the 1961 law change, namely a growing tendency to redefine delinquency more exclusively as law violations, and to differentiate such cases from so-called delinquent tendencies cases, many of which began to be handled by other means.

Comments now are heard from probation officers that "601's (the code term for such cases) are on their way out."

CONCLUSION

It has been my contention that existing theories of deviance are ill suited to account for the complexities of the societal reaction in modern society. In place of a sociopsychological model I have proposed a group interaction model and tried to show how it clarifies the shifting significance of ends and means and their costs in the emergence of new patterns of social control. The chief gain is a method for specifying the way in which human choices affect the societal reaction without generalizing the claims of others or reducing them to reified ideas of culture, class, or power. It also shows how costs of changes in social control feed back into decisions to make changes, without the necessity of relying on older deterministic conceptions of the effects of the physical world on the social.

The possibility exists that the special subject matter of procedural law change within a bureaucratic context of correctional agencies puts the group interaction model in a more favorable light than if it were applied to substantive legislation of a more obviously "moral" nature, such as marihuana laws, temperance laws, and anti-pornography statutes. Yet I note a recent study of the evolution of our marihuana laws which advisedly chooses an organizational perspective emphasizing bureaucratic utilitarian values in its explanation (Dickson, 1968). I am also reminded of A. M. Lee's (1944) older pluralistic analysis of the temperance movement, which still stands unreconciled with the symbolic crusade theory of the same phenomenon.

A study of social control in Cuba, touching on censorship and sex behavior, not only has challenged the validity of the notion of moral entrepreneurs but also accentuates the need to fit concepts of social control to the differentiation of interests and groups in particular societies (Looney, 1973). All of which tells me that deviance sociologists can do better with working tool concepts than with ambitious theory. They obviously

"can't go home again" to old style structural, positivist sociology any more than conservative sociologists can stomach the extremes of labeling theory. But there may be a less pretentious midground on which to meet—if not they, then a less committed generation of sociologists yet to come.

REFERENCES

Becker, Howard. *Outsiders.* Glencoe, Illinois: Free Press, 1963.

Bordua, David. "Recent Trends: Deviant Behavior and Social Control." *Amer. Acad. Polit. Soc. Science* 57: (1967)149–163.

Chambliss, William. "A Sociological Analysis of the Law of Vagrancy." *Social Problems* 12 (1964): 67–77.

Cottrell, W. F. *Technology, Man and Progress.* Columbus: Charles Merrill Pubs, 1972.

Dickson, Donald. "Bureaucracy and Morality: An Organizational Perspective on a Moral Crusade." *Social Problems* 16 (1968):143–156.

Douglas, Jack. *Deviance and Respectability.* New York, London: Basic Books, 1970.

Garfinkel, Harold. "Conditions of Successful Degradation Ceremonies." *Amer. Jr. Sociol.* 61 (1956): 420–24.

Goode, Erich. "Marihuana and the Politics of Reality." *Jr. Health and Social Behavior.* 10 (1969):84.

Gouldner, Alvin. "The Sociologist as Partisan: Sociology and the Welfare State." *American Sociologist* (May 1968): 103–116.

Gusfield, Joseph. *Symbolic Crusade.* Urbana, London: Univ. Illinois Press, 1966.

Hall, Jerome. *Theft, Law and Society.* Indianapolis: Bobbs Merrill, 1935.

Kolb, William. "A Critical Evaluation of Mead's 'I' and 'Me' Concepts." *Symbolic Interaction* (Manis and Meltzer).

Lee, A. M. "Techniques of Reform: An Analysis of the New Prohibition Drive." *Amer. Sociol. Rev.* 9 (1944):60–69.

Lemert, Edwin. *Social Pathology.* New York: McGraw-Hill, 1951.

———. *Legal Action and Social Change.* Chicago: Aldine Pub. Co., 1970.

———. *Human Deviance, Social Problems and Social Control.* Englewood Cliffs, New Jersey: Prentice-Hall Inc., 1973.

Liazos, Alexander. "The Poverty of the Sociology of Deviance: Nuts, Sluts and Perverts." *Social Problems* 20 (1972):103–120.

Looney, Martin. "Social Control in Cuba." *Politics and Deviance*. Edited by Ian and Laurie Taylor. London: Penguin, 1973, pp. 42–60.

Lyman, Standford, and Marvin Scott. *A Sociology of the Absurd*. New York: Appleton-Century-Crofts, 1970.

Manning, Peter. "Survey Essay on Deviance." *Contemporary Sociology* 2 (1973):123–128.

Mead, G. H. "The Psychology of Primitive Justice," 1928.

Meltzer, Bernard N. "Mead's Social Psychology." *Symbolic Interaction*. Edited by Jerome Manis and Bernard Meltzer. Boston: Allyn and Bacon, 1967.

Scott, John. "Changing Foundations of a Parsonian Scheme of Action." *Amer. Soc. Rev.* 28 (1963):716–734.

Scott, Robert A. "Construction of Conceptions of Stigma by Professional Experts." In Douglas, 1970.

Schur, Edwin. "Reaction to Deviance: A Critical Assessment." *Amer. Jr. Sociol.* 75 (1969):309–322.

Tannenbaum, Frank. *Crime and the Community*. New York: Col. Univ. Press, 1937.

Taylor, Ian, and Laurie Taylor. *Politics and Deviance*. London: Penguin, 1973.

Walton, Paul. "The Case of the Weathermen: Social Reaction and Radical Commitment." *Politics and Deviance*. Edited by Ian and Laurie Taylor. London: Penguin, 1973.

SELECTED REFERENCES
PART SIX

Bales, Robert F. "Comment on Herbert Blumer's Paper," *American Journal of Sociology*, Vol. LXXI (March 1966), pp. 545–547. A critique of Blumer's rendition of the Meadian perspective.

Blumer, Herbert. "Comment on 'Symbolic Interaction as a Pragmatic Perspective: The Bias of Emergent Theory.'" *American Sociological Review*, 38 (December 1973), pp. 797–798. Response to the selection by Huber.

Brittan, Arthur. *Meanings and Situations*. London: Routledge and Kegan Paul, 1973, pp. 189–204. A symbolic interactionist's reservations about the perspective.

Collins, Randall, and Michael Makowsky. *The Discovery of Society*. New York: Random House, 1972, pp.

202–214. Favorable evaluations of dramaturgical sociology and ethnomethodology.

Coser, Lewis A. "Two Methods in Search of a Substance," *American Sociological Review*, vol. 40 (December 1975), pp. 691–700. An unfavorable appraisal of ethnomethodology (and of path analysis).

Cuzzort, R. P. *Humanity and Modern Sociological Thought*. New York: Holt, Rinehart and Winston, Inc., 1969, pp. 173–192. A balanced appraisal of Goffman's work.

Gouldner, Alvin F. *The Coming Crisis of Western Sociology*. New York: Basic Books, Inc., 1970, pp. 378–395. An appraisal of Goffman's and Garfinkel's perspectives by a distinguished critic of sociological theorizing.

Huber, Joan. "Reply to Blumer: But Who Will Scrutinize the Scrutinizers?" *American Sociological Review*, 38 (December 1973), pp. 798–800. Pertains to her selection in this part.

Kanter, R. M. "Symbolic Interactionism and Politics in Systematic Perspective." *Sociological Inquiry*, 42 (1972), pp. 77–92. A critical appraisal of the relevance of symbolic interactionism.

Lichtman, Richard. "Symbolic Interactionism and Social Reality: Some Marxist Queries." *Berkeley Journal of Sociology*, 15 (1970), pp. 75–94. The author contends that symbolic interactionism ignores objective conditions.

McNall, Scott G. and James C. M. Johnson. "The New Conservatives: Ethnomethodologists, Phenomenologists, and Symbolic Interactionists." *The Insurgent Sociologist*, vol. V (Summer 1975), pp. 49–65. Attacks the assumptions and political implications of major theoretical perspectives.

Petras, J. W. and B. N. Meltzer. "Theoretical and Ideological Variations in Contemporary Interactionism." *Catalyst*, 7 (Winter 1973), pp. 1–8. Discusses various forms of bias among symbolic interactionists.

Reynolds, Janice and Larry Reynolds. "Interactionism, Complicity and the Astructural Bias." *Catalyst*, 7 (Winter 1973), pp. 76–85. Supports criticisms of ideological bias of symbolic interactionism with survey data.

Schmitt, Raymond L. "SI and Emergent Theory: A Reexamination." *American Sociological Review*, 39 (June 1974), pp. 453–456. Another reply to the Huber selection.

Stevens, Edward. "Sociality and Act in George Herbert Mead." *Social Research*, vol. 34 (Winter 1967), pp. 613–631. A critical analysis of some of Mead's ideas.

Stone, Gregory P., David R. Maines, Harvey A. Farberman, and Norman K. Denzin. "On Methodology and Craftsmanship in the Criticism of Sociological Perspectives." *American Sociological Review,* 39 (June 1974), pp. 456–463. Still another rebuttal of the Huber article.

Wilson, Thomas R. "Conceptions of Interaction and Forms of Sociological Explanation." *American Sociological Review,* 35 (August 1970), pp. 697–710. A useful analysis of normative and interpretation perspectives.

Zeitlin, Irving M. *Rethinking Sociology: A Critique of Contemporary Theory.* New York: Appleton-Century-Crofts, 1973, pp. 183–256. Discusses purported shortcomings of dramaturgical sociology, ethnomethodology, and symbolic interactionism.

Conclusion

Having presented the major ideas and criticisms of symbolic interactionism, we shall conclude this book by repeating its basic propositions and assessing the more common and significant adverse criticisms leveled against it. Listed below are the basic theoretical and methodological propositions:

1. The meaning component in human conduct: Distinctively human behavior and interaction are carried on through the medium of symbols and their meanings.
2. The social sources of humanness: The individual becomes humanized through interaction with other persons.
3. Society as process: Human society is most usefully conceived as consisting of people in interaction.
4. The voluntaristic component in human conduct: Human beings are active in shaping their own behavior.
5. A dialectical conception of mind: Consciousness, or thinking, involves interaction with oneself.
6. The constructive, emergent nature of human conduct: Human beings construct their behavior in the course of its execution.
7. The necessity of sympathetic introspection: An understanding of human conduct requires study of the actors' covert behavior.

The major adverse criticisms of symbolic interactionism have focused on: (1) the indeterminism adopted by many of its exponents; (2) its presumed inapplicability to the study of social organization; (3) related to the preceding criticism, its unconcern with the power aspect in human relationships; (4) its neglect of the emotional dimension in human conduct; (5) its failure to come to grips with the unconscious; and (6) the limited researchability of some of its concepts. In the following paragraphs, we shall review and evaluate these negative allegations.

1. Viewing behavior in terms of the interplay between the "I" and the "Me" aspects of self, Mead's closest followers built into such behavior an unpredictable, indeterminate dimension. For some, this interplay is the fundamental source of innovation in society. Exponents of the Iowa School, however, reject the concept of the "I" (the chief source of indeterminism)

and the explanation of social innovation on the basis of the emergent, creative element in "I"–"Me" interaction. However, a probabilistic approach to explaining and predicting behavior may provide a middle ground between the Meadian view and its critics.

2. In the continuing debate between advocates of symbolic interactionism and those of both structural-functionalism and Marxist sociology, each side refers to the putative shortcomings of the other relative to level or scope of analysis. The former perspective is held to be limited to such microsociological phenomena as intra- and interpersonal relations, while the latter is presumed to apply only to such macrosociological phenomena as institutional and societal patterns. At the same time, adherents of each theory reject the restrictions in scope placed upon their theory by their critics. That symbolic interactionists have failed to give adequate attention to macroscopic social phenomena cannot be denied; but that this failure is intrinsic to the perspective is debatable. For, among numerous possible examples, Tamotsu Shibutani and Kian M. Kiwan[1] and Niels Winther Braroe[2] have dealt with ethnic stratification; Ralph H. Turner and Lewis M. Killian[3] with collective behavior; Melville Dalton[4] with formal organization in industry; C. Addison Hickman and Manford H. Kuhn[5] with economic phenomena; and Harvey A. Farberman with the automobile industry.[6] And, finally, a recent monograph by Randall Collins[7] clearly demonstrates the feasibility of integrating at least one variant of symbolic interactionism, Goffman's dramaturgical approach, with the macro level of analysis.

3. One feature of social structure that has been singled out by critics as particularly intractable to treatment by symbolic interactionism is that of power. It is alleged that the perspective appears to treat human relationships as though all actors have equal influence in the negotiation of shared realities.[8] While this allegation is frequently a valid one, the cited studies of ethnic relations certainly recognize the existence of differential power and its effects upon mutual perceptions and interaction. Even more evident consideration of power is found in interactionist theories of deviance (e.g., labeling theory), which attend to power differentials in the defining and handling of deviant behavior.

4. Present-day symbolic interactionists have followed Mead in overlook-

---

[1] *Ethnic Stratification* (New York: Macmillan, 1965).

[2] *Indian and White* (Stanford: Stanford University Press, 1974).

[3] *Collective Behavior* (Englewood Cliffs, N.J.: Prentice-Hall, 1957).

[4] *Men Who Manage* (New York: Wiley, 1959).

[5] *Individuals, Groups, and Economic Behavior* (New York: Dryden, 1956).

[6] "A Criminogenic Market Structure: The Automobile Industry," *Sociological Quarterly*, vol. 16 (Autumn 1975), pp. 438–457.

[7] *Conflict Sociology: Toward An Explanatory Science* (New York: Academic Press, 1975), especially chapter 3, "Microsociology and Stratification."

[8] See, for example, L. Shaskolsky, "The Development of Sociological Theory in America—A Sociology of Knowledge Interpretation," in L. T. and J. M. Reynolds (eds). *The Sociology of Sociology* (New York: McKay, 1970).

ing the role of the emotional component in human behavior and interaction. The affective aspects of the self, personal relationships, and large-scale social phenomena are so thoroughly ignored, except in considerations of "emotional contagion," in the area of collective behavior, as to suggest an unacceptable image of human beings as purely rational. In partial extenuation of this oversight, however, has been an occasional concern with the sentiments, those emotions which Cooley characterized as entailing sympathy, or role-taking. Thus, Erving Goffman[9] and Edward Gross and Gregory P. Stone[10] have analyzed embarrassment, Kurt Riezler[11] has written on shame, and Cooley's concern with self centered upon self-feeling. It is nonetheless true of symbolic interactionists, as of most other social psychologists, that they have given scant attention to such emotions as love, hate, anger, joy, and sorrow.

5. Closely related to the preceding stricture is another that concerns scanting of the irrational aspect in human behavior. It is difficult to find a considered discussion of the unconscious in the writings of symbolic interactionists. The few references tend to renounce the concept without substituting adequate explanations. There is no reason to assume that the perspective cannot accommodate unconscious phenomena, obdurate though they may be. Just as different *levels* of awareness are recognized for symbolic interaction and nonsymbolic interaction, so can they be recognized for conscious and unconscious (as well as subliminal) processes of behavior.

6. It is with regard to its heuristic value that most critics of symbolic interactionism believe themselves to be on firmest ground. The paucity of significant research generated by the perspective is especially reflected in the parts of this book on society and on mind. Contributing to this deficiency is the vague, intuitive character of various concepts formulated by Mead, some of which have not yet been revised or discarded. "Impulse," "meaning," the "I," "objects," "images," and other ambiguous and inconsistently used concepts persist in substantially the same nonoperationalized form in which Mead used them. It remains to be seen whether Norman K. Denzin's[12] fairly recent textbook and collection of readings, which emphasize the methodology of symbolic interactionism, will help to facilitate an increase in the research output of the perspective's users.

The considerable number of empirical studies in this book, and the many more listed in the Selected References, attest to the researchability of this perspective. Yet it continues to be true that such researches are still comparatively sparse—and difficult. This fact may be accounted for, in part, by some of the shortcomings described above. Also influential in

---

[9] *Interaction Ritual* (Garden City: Doubleday, 1967), pp. 97–112.

[10] "Embarrassment and the Analysis of Role Requirements," *American Journal of Sociology*, vol. 60 (July 1964), pp. 1–15.

[11] "Comment on the Social Psychology of Shame," *American Journal of Sociology*, vol. 48 (January 1943), pp. 457–465.

[12] *The Research Act: A Theoretical Introduction to Sociological Research Methods* (Chicago: Aldine Publishing Company, 1970); and *Sociological Methods: A Sourcebook* (Chicago: Aldine Publishing Company, 1970).

this regard is the symbolic interactionist injunction to "respect the nature of the empirical world and organize a methodological stance to reflect that respect."[13] The view of humans as constructing their own behavior, and of human society as a *process* of interaction, has appeared to be beyond the research capabilities of most social psychologists.

Given the adverse criticisms of symbolic interactionism, why has this frame of reference commended itself to most sociologically oriented social psychologists? The answer probably lies in the fact that symbolic interactionism clearly constitutes the most sociological of social psychologies. Adopting a distinctly sociological perspective, it directs attention to the social derivation of the human being's unique attributes; it describes mind and self as society in microcosm; it describes how the members of any group develop and form a common world; it illuminates the character of human interaction by showing that humans share the meaning of one another's behavior instead of merely responding to each other's overt behavior; and, in numerous other ways, it implicates the individual with society and society with the individual.

As we have suggested more than once in the foregoing material, the perspective of symbolic interactionism is not a finished product. Each succeeding edition of this volume has demonstrated modifications, both substantive and methodological. Moreover, symbolic interactionists have been increasing their reflexive awareness, as much of the material in Part VI demonstrates. The perspective of symbolic interactionism affords us an understanding of its own development. Like other perspectives, it undergoes continual construction, rather than perennially expounding a set of received truths, and it can be expected to undergo periodic criticism and modification. As with our past editions, our hope is that the present volume will facilitate its testing and revision. That hope is sustained by the previously mentioned growing reflexiveness of symbolic interactionists.

[13] Herbert Blumer, *Symbolic Interactionism: Perspective and Method* (Englewood Cliffs, New Jersey: Prentice-Hall, Inc., 1969), p. 60.

Index